THE NATIONAL TRIBUNE CIVIL WAR INDEX

A Guide to the Weekly Newspaper Dedicated to Civil War Veterans, 1877-1943

Volume 1: 1877-1903

Compiled by

Richard A. Sauers

SB

Savas Beatie

California

Library of Congress Cataloging-in-Publication Data

Names: Sauers, Richard Allen, compiler.
Title: *The National Tribune Civil War Index: A Guide to the Weekly Newspaper Dedicated to Civil War Veterans, 1877-1943* / compiled by Dr. Richard A. Sauers.
Description: First edition. | El Dorado Hills, California: Savas Beatie, 2017. | Decades in the making, Dr. Rick Sauers' unique multi-volume reference work *The National Tribune Civil War Index: A Guide to the Weekly Newspaper Dedicated to Civil War Veterans, 1877-1943* lists every article (1877-1943). The first two volumes are organized by author, his unit, title, and page/column location. The third volume—the main index—includes a subject, author, and unit guide, as well as a "Unit as Sources" index that lists articles that mention specific commands but are written by soldiers who were not members of that unit. As an added bonus, this reference guide includes the contents of both *Tthe National Tribune Scrapbook* and *The National Tribune Repository*, two short-lived publications that included articles by veterans, and a listing of the major libraries that have *National Tribune* holdings. Dr. Sauers' work provides Civil War researchers and writers access to the valuable contents of *The National Tribune*, the premier Union veterans' newspaper of the post-Civil War era, primary source material. | Includes bibliographical references and index.
Identifiers: LCCN 2017043010 (print) | LCCN 2017044839 (ebook) |
ISBN 9781940669748 (volume 1, ebk) | ISBN 9781940669755 (volume 2, ebk) |
ISBN 9781940669762 (volume 3, ebk) | ISBN 9781611213645 (volume 1: alk. paper) |
ISBN 9781611213652 (volume 2: alk. paper) | ISBN 9781611213669 (volume 3: alk. paper)
Subjects: LCSH: United States—History—Civil War, 1861-1865—Sources—Indexes. | United States—History—Civil War, 1861-1865—Personal narratives—Indexes. | United States—History—Civil War, 1861-1865—Veterans—Periodicals—Indexes. | United States—History—Civil War, 1861-1865—Anecdotes—Periodicals—Indexes. | National tribune (Washington, D.C.)—Indexes. | National guardsman and American standard—Indexes. | National tribune, incorporating the national guardsman and the American standard—Indexes. | National tribune, the stars and stripes, the national guardsman, the American standard—Indexes. | National tribune scrap book—Indexes.
Classification: LCC Z1242 (ebook) | LCC Z1242 .S28 2017 (print) | DDC 016.9737—dc23
LC record available at https://lccn.loc.gov/2017043010

First Edition, First Printing (standard edition)

SB
Savas Beatie LLC
989 Governor Drive, Suite 102
El Dorado Hills, CA 95762

Phone: 916-941-6896
E-mail: sales@savasbeatie.com
Web: www.savasbeatie.com

For John McElroy,
whose tireless work with *The National Tribune*
contributed so much to our study of the Civil War

EXPERIENCES OF A PRISONER IN DIXIELAND

Cheering of the Prisoners at Andersonville Foretold a Removal. Anxious Moments—Wilson's Cavalry Forced Abandonment Of Prisoners Sent to Florida, Where They Reached the Union Lines and Were Sent North.

By STEPHEN FRENCH, Co. D, 111th Ill., 3121 Thorn St., San Diego, Calif.

(Continued from last week.)

We expected pretty harsh treatment upon getting back to prison; but upon being taken into Capt. Wirz's office that old Austrian never turned his head from his desk to look at us. He received the order from the Provost Marshal at Albany turning us over to him, called our names therefrom, called a Sergeant from an adjoining room and said, "Take these men to the stockade." From his broken English we thought he said, "Take those men to the [illegible]." We were expecting him to say [illegible].

Our friends were glad and sorry to see us [illegible]. We had been away from them about a week, had had enough to eat for several days past, and had come in with a plentiful supply to last several days longer. The day was cold for that country. The wind was blowing from the northwest. We got a place on the hillside south of the stream that ran thru the stockade and next the deadline on the west side of the prison.

The prisoners, about 3,000, were all that city. Soon we saw Capt. Wirz coming alongside of the train. We had not seen him before on this move. He appeared to be in a better humor than usual and tried to speak pleasantly. He informed us that he had just received orders from Gen. Pillow, Commandant of Southern prisons, to take us to Jacksonville, Fla., and turn us loose, if our men would not receive us.

"By tam," said he (he always tried to swear), "You-uns going to your own home now; goin' sure this time. "By tam."

The boys did not manifest any great enthusiasm at his statements. They had no confidence in him, but replied pleasantly, "Bully for you, Captain; bully for you."

Without unloading us the engine was attached to the other end of the train and started back toward Andersonville. Passing other trains loaded with prisoners on the way, we arrived there first. Our suspense was now agonizing. The train stopped, but no order was given to unload. Soon we saw them putting provisions on the train instead of taking

camp. Guards were all withdraw[n ex]cept a small camp patrol. With [...] comrades, I went about a mile and [...] from camp on a foraging expediti[on on] our own hook and got some fresh [but]termilk and corn bread. Here w[e saw] our first orange grove—a small o[ne, by] moonlight, but were not much [inter]ested in orange culture then.

From Live Oak to Lake City we [were] taken on another wreck of a ra[ilroad,] where rolls of the prisoners were [made] out. We were required to sign [the] rolls. What the rolls were for, I [never] learned. They could not have bee[n pa]roles, for no oath or agreement w[as at]tached. The papers contained our [names,] description, and place and time o[f cap]ture, opposite which, in a colum[n for] the purpose, we affixed our signatu[res.]

As we filed past the table, eac[h man] personally signing his name to t[he pa]per, the Johnny soldiers looking [on in] astonishment. "Why, they can all [write!] Just look there—every man can w[rite!"] were the exclamations we heard.

They stared at us in perfect a[stonish]ment. Such a body of men who [could] all write was something unusua[l and] wonderful to them. I think tho[se] surprise and exclamations enable[d sev]eral of the boys to write who [would] otherwise have asked a comrade [to af]fix their signatures for them. B[ut we] wanted them to think that we cou[ld not] only write, but cipher too. That [, I] imagine, exhibited both writing [and] ciphering.

Here we were informed by so[me of] them that Lincoln had been assass[inated.]

UNDER THE OLD FLAG—HOMEWARD BOUND

Table of Contents

Introduction
vii

Where to Find *The National Tribune*
xiv

Abbreviations
xvi

Volume 1: 1877 - 1903
1

Compiler's Biography
354

National

ONE DOLLAR A YEAR

WASHINGTON, D.

Introduction

The *National Tribune* was the premier newspaper published for Union veterans of the Civil War and their families. George E. Lemon, a wounded veteran of the 125th New York Volunteer Infantry, was the brains behind the genesis of this paper. Lemon, a pension lawyer by trade, started the *Tribune* in October 1877 as an eight-page monthly sheet, listing the following reasons for publishing the paper:

1. To help influence Congress to pass a law equalizing the bounties paid to Civil War veterans;

2. To lobby for the passage of a law to mandate that pensions for wounded, disabled, injured, or families of deceased soldiers would begin from the time of death or discharge from service on account of disability;

3. To obtain pensions for Mexican War veterans;

4. To include on the pension rolls all survivors of the War of 1812 and all widows of deceased veterans; and

5. To lobby Congress to remedy defects in the existing pension laws, especially Section 4717 of the Revised Statutes.

Lemon chose a phrase from Abraham Lincoln's Second Inaugural Address to describe the *Tribune's* mission: "To care for him who has borne the battle, and for his widow and orphans."

In March 1879, the paper changed publishers when The National Tribune Company of Washington, D.C. assumed printing responsibilities. George E. Lemon & Company remained as advisors. The paper continued as a monthly issue until June 1881, and after a month's hiatus, became a weekly newspaper on August 20, 1881, when volume 1 #1 of the new series began. By this time, the *Tribune* had become a driving force in the pension battle and was attracting a wider reading audience, especially among members of the Grand Army of the Republic, the major organization of Union veterans.

In the August 20 edition, Lemon included the following editorial: "We shall be glad at all times to hear from any of our soldier or sailor friends who have matters of historical interest, incidents, or amusing anecdotes of the war to relate." At first, readers were slow to respond and Lemon, following the tradition of period newspapers, excerpted or copied Civil War articles from other papers such as the *Philadelphia Weekly Times.*

By mid-1882, articles from veterans were beginning to pour into the *Tribune's* office. Men of all ranks from privates to generals contributed to paper's rising success. Although it continued to cover issues of vital interest to pensioners, the increasing number of historical articles and letters greatly added to the overall appeal of the paper. Lemon also began including weekly pages devoted to GAR news, primarily individual post information and reunion notices and events. The Sons of Union Veterans and Women's Relief Corps also received space in the paper.

In 1884, Lemon brought John McElroy to the paper as managing editor. McElroy, who was the editor of the *Toledo Blade*, was born in Greenup County, Kentucky in 1846. His father died when he was young, and he moved to St. Louis, Missouri, where in his young teens he worked as an apprentice in the printing trade. He served with local Union troops around St. Louis before enlisting with the Union Army at the age of 16 in 1863 as a private in Company L, 16th Illinois Cavalry. McElroy was one of a few dozen men captured in a skirmish near Jonesville, Virginia, in January 1864. He was initially sent to Richmond, and then on to Andersonville prison that February. McElroy suffered through all the horrors of that prison during the terrible summer of 1864. That October, he was moved to Savannah, Georgia, and a few weeks later to a new prison in Millen, Georgia called Camp Lawton. McElroy would be moved to several other camps during the final months of the war. Once the Civil War ended, McElroy was released and eventually settled in Chicago, where he resumed work in the printing industry. Fourteen years later he published his famous memoir *Andersonville: A Story of Rebel Military Prisons, Fifteen Months a Guest of the So-Called Southern Confederacy* (Toledo: D. R. Locke, 1879).

It was under McElroy's firm guidance that the *National Tribune* became the premier veterans' newspaper. He remained its editor until his death on October 12, 1929. After George Lemon died in December 1896, McElroy also became the *Tribune's* publisher when the firm of McElroy, Shoppell & Andrews purchased the paper.

McElroy enticed prominent officers to contribute their recollections. Notables such as John Pope, William P. Carlin, Robert H. G. Minty, August V. Kautz, Green B. Raum, Abner Doubleday, and Oliver O. Howard penned major articles or series for the *Tribune.* And, of course, their former comrades scrutinized such recollections very closely and did not hesitate to praise or condemn.

The subjects of the thousands of Civil War articles in the *National Tribune* ranged from the major battles of Gettysburg, Antietam, Chickamauga, Franklin, and Atlanta, to scores of obscure skirmishes and actions, some of which went unreported in the official records. Veterans also used the pages of the *Tribune* to argue among themselves dozens of questions. Who fired the opening shots at Gettysburg? Who recaptured DeGress's battery at Atlanta? Where did the phrase "grab a root" originate? Which brigade was actually the first Iron Brigade? Where was the last battle of the war? Who raised the first flag in Atlanta? Who was the youngest veteran? The oldest? Which battery fired the shot that killed General Leonidas Polk? How was Stonewall Jackson shot? And by whom? Such topics might seem petty with the passage of time, but to proud Union veterans, these arguments were important, and the editors of the *Tribune* gladly allowed their paper to be used by the men in blue to recall the glory years of 1861-1865.

As time went on, Confederate soldiers also contributed to the paper, although not in great numbers. In addition to the serializations of such notables as J. P. Cannon of the 27th Alabama and George D. Mosgrove's recollections of service with John Hunt Morgan, Southern veterans occasionally wrote articles in reply to bombastic criticisms of their former enemies. Southern cavalrymen, for example, tried to help set the record straight when they wrote about the decimation of the 6th United States Cavalry at Fairfield, Pennsylvania, while others wrote about the death of General John F. Reynolds at Gettysburg.

During the *National Tribune's* heyday (1880s-1900s), a number of regular columns appeared in the newspaper. These included:

The Question Squad
Loyal Woman's Work
For the Ladies
Sunday Meditation
Washington Gossip
Our Correspondents
Our Rural Topics
Recent Literature
News of the Week
Humor
Congress
Personal
Mustered Out
Sons of Veterans
Relief Corps News
The Grand Army

Under McElroy's direction, the *Tribune* published a number of serializations over the years. Many of these runs were later extracted and published as separate paper-bound books. Such titles included Augustus Buell's *The Cannoneer* and a number of McElroy's own writings on the war as well as his fictional series about the adventures of Si Klegg, a bumbling Union private. The paper also published three volumes of *The National Tribune* Scrapbook, a series of accounts not published in the paper, and *The National Tribune* Repository (1907-1908), another series of original articles. In the late 1890s the company also issued a set of paper-bound books under the series name "Great War Books" at the cost of only a quarter each, including:

J. O. Kerbey, *The Boy Spy In Dixie*
J. O. Kerbey, *Further Adventures of the Boy Spy*
Lafayette C. Baker, *Secret Service*
Augustus Buell, *The Cannoneer*
William Pittenger, *Capturing a Locomotive*
Alf Wilson, *Adventures of Alf Wilson*
Albert D. Richardson, *The Field, Dungeon, and Escape*
Albert D. Richardson, *A Personal History of U. S. Grant*
Horace Greeley, *The American Conflict* (2 volumes)
J. T. Headley, *The Great Rebellion* (2 volumes)
National Tribune Soldier's Handbook
Further Mishaps to Si Klegg and Shorty: The Second Year of Their Service

These paperback books were published with a uniform brown cover and measured 8.5 x 5.5 inches. The paper was produced from cheap wood pulp, so it is rare to find one today in good condition. *The Tribune's* hardcover books used better paper and can be found in better condition, as can the Repository and Scrapbook series.

In the late 1890s, newspaper also published a series of books called "The National Tribune Library." In 1897, this series included the following volumes:

1. *Statistics of the War*
2. *Lincoln's Words*
3. John McElroy, *Miscellaneous Memoranda*
4. *Pension Statistics*
5. John McElroy, *History of Slavery in the United States*
6. Byron Andrews, *President Monroe and His Doctrine*
7-8. John McElroy, *Commanders of the United States Army*, 2 volumes
9. Byron Andrews, *The Story of Cuba*
10. John McElroy, *The Life of Major General George H. Thomas*
11. John McElroy, *The Life of Major William McKinley*
12. John McElroy, *The Life of Major General Philip H. Sheridan*
13. H. E. Weaver, *Chronological Record of Battles, etc.*
14. John McElroy, *The Life of Admiral David G. Farragut*
15. John McElroy, *Some of the War Fun*

16. John McElroy, *Fair Ohio* [songs and music]
17. John McElroy, *Glorious Pennsylvania* [songs and music]
18. John McElroy, *Some Poetry of the War*
19. John McElroy, *The Life of General U. S. Grant*
20. H. E. Weaver, *Memorial Day Poetry and Oratory*
21. John W. Fisher, *The Hawaiian Islands*

These "books" were more like long articles, and usually around 32 pages for the biographies. In its issue of July 1, 1897, McElroy recorded that the company had sold 100,000 copies during the prior year.

Over the course of time, newspaper underwent some modifications. In late 1906, most Civil War articles disappeared from the front page as the paper began publishing material from other veterans. By the time World War I began, Civil War material had been reduced to one page as few veterans were left to contribute to the paper. In 1911, McElroy wrote in an editorial entitled "Our New Dress" that the paper was changing a bit in order to entice enough new subscribers to reach one million subscriptions. New columns included Farm and Garden, News from Our Colonies in Lynn Haven, Woman and the Home, and Humor of the War. Fighting Them Over became Sketches and Echoes.

During this decade, the paper's office moved to a slim four-story building at 44 G Street Northeast, only one block from Union Station, the Washington city post office, and the Government Printing Office. Originally built as the Terminal Hotel, the building was heavily remodeled and remained the office of the paper until the early 1980s. By that time, the building was badly in need of expensive repairs, so the paper sold it to the government and moved elsewhere.

In its edition of July 19, 1917, the paper's title changed to *The National Tribune, incorporating the National Guardsman and the American Standard.* The change reflected the paper's broadening scope to include the push for pension benefits for veterans of the Spanish-American War, the Peking Expedition, and the recent border troubles with Mexico. By including these veterans, McElroy ensured that the paper would continue to exist even as the number of Civil War veterans continued to decline with each passing month. After McElroy died, W. L. Mattocks took over as editor. Mattocks, born in 1875, was a Spanish-American War veteran and former editor of the American Standard. Former senator and Spanish-American War veteran Rice W. Means was president of the corporation from 1927-1937.

On January 7, 1926, the paper became the *National Tribune, Stars and Stripes. The Stars and Stripes* had been the official newspaper of the American Expeditionary Force during World War I and had been discontinued overseas in 1919. *The Stars and Stripes* had continued publication in Washington to help espouse the pension and relief causes of recent veterans. Both papers formed a united front in the continuing struggle to care for America's veterans. The paper remained with this title until January 7, 1963, when the title became *The Stars and Stripes, National Tribune.* In 1999, the paper was sold to iServed.com, an internet multimedia military content and solutions provider based in Pittsburgh, Pennsylvania. Soon thereafter, in May 2000, iServed changed its name to Stars and Stripes Omnimedia and continued publishing a print version of the *Stars and Stripes* (the old subtitle *National Tribune* was dropped completely from the masthead), as well as an on-line version at www.stripes.com. The conern became financially insolvent and Stars and Stripes Omnimedia went out of business in 2002. The paper's assets were acquired by *Stars and Stripes*, a military paper that began publication during World War II.

National Tribune highlights include:

1877: Begins publication as a monthly pension newspaper;
1881: August 20–becomes a weekly newspaper;
1883: February 22: expands to seven columns;
March 15: "Fighting Them Over" column begins
1884: February 7: lists 77,159 subscribers;
September 4: "Condensed Letters" column starts;
1885: April 30: Obituaries begins as a regular feature;
November 19: Si Klegg stories begin serialization;
1886: February 25: Colonel Milo B. Stevens' Soldiers Bulletin merged with the *Tribune*
1887: January 27: "Picket Shots" replaces "Condensed Letters";
1893: June 8; "Their Records" series begins;
1897: April 29: "Their Records" series ends, replaced for a few issues by "Making a Record" column;
July 8: The first photograph ("Sherman and His Generals") appears in the paper;
1904: April 5: The "Fighting Them Over" column becomes "Recitals and Reminiscences";
1911: April 20: last issue published with Civil War articles on the front page;
1931: January 15: "Veterans of the Civil War" page premiers;

The Scope of this Guide

I first discovered the *National Tribune* at the United States Army Military History Institute, Carlisle Barracks, Pennsylvania, in the early 1980s. At the time I was a graduate student at The Pennsylvania State University searching for new sources of information for my dissertation. In the same institution was a typescript listing the highlights of the Civil War material in the *Tribune*, compiled by Helen H. Ellis of the Detroit Public Library in the late 1960s.

Dr. Richard J. Sommers, who was then the Archivist of the Institute, suggested the need for a better index to the *Tribune*. I embarked on this ambitious undertaking in late 1983. During the next several years I worked through all forty reels of microfilm, visited the former headquarters of the National Tribune Corporation on the outskirts of Washington, and compiled several notebooks of articles in chronological order, from 1877 to 1943.

Included in this guide are all the major Civil War articles as well as the vast majority of letters appearing in the "Fighting Them Over" column that featured rebuttals and arguments over previous articles. I have included all biographical material relating to Civil War veterans as well as notices of battlefield monument dedications.

The paper also published a "Condensed Letters" section later re-titled "Picket Shots." This column printed highlights from letters that were not deemed important enough to print in their entirety. I have noted the major letters in this series but have not included them in the indices. From 1893 to 1897, the paper included a series called "Their Records," which provided capsule unit histories to readers. I decided to omit this series because the summaries are very brief and much better unit summaries are readily available, including in publications such as Frederick Dyer's *A Compendium of the War of the Rebellion.* I have also omitted the majority of the ever-increasing obituary notices that appeared in most issues. (The current guide merely notes page and column numbers of obituary notices.) Vast amounts of fiction were published in the pages of the *Tribune*, especially the Si Klegg series. I omitted these as well. The copious amount of GAR material needs an indexer of its own and several years to complete such a guide.

Occasionally I noticed typographical errors in names and have corrected these when known. I consulted the Soldiers and Sailors system on the National Park Service website to identify the names of authors, especially very similar names or to add first names when only last names were available. I would appreciate hearing from researchers who can document any additional errors so they can be corrected in future editions.

There are two parts or volumes to this guide-index. The first two comprise the guide to the *National Tribune*, a chronological presentation of the Civil War contents of each issue from 1877 to 1903 in Volume 1, and from 1904 to 1943 in Volume 2. Each entry includes the page and column numbers, the author's name, his unit (when known), the title of the article, and a brief note on the article's subject if the title does not suggest it. Obituary sections include nominal listings. The longer columns with more names only have page and column noted. Thereafter are the listings for both the *National Tribune* Repository and the *National Tribune* Scrapbook.

Volume 3 consists of an Author Index, a Subject Index, a Unit Index (which consists of articles written by members of these units), and a Units as Sources Index (which includes articles about certain units not necessarily written by members of those units, as well as biographies of members of the unit). All four are alphabetical and are referenced by issue date (1877 to 1943). The major subject headings are broken down into subheadings in order to allow readers seeking finite information on a subject to locate the desired information as quickly as possible. Many of the larger battles and campaigns have the entries broken down into the Union corps and divisions that participated. I felt this approach would be easier than trying to divide the entries by topic. Cross references are used when needed.

Of course, it is also highly entertaining to simply read through the contents of issue after issue just to see what the veterans were writing about and when they were doing so.

The National Tribune is a goldmine of information for anyone studying and/writing about the Civil War. I hope users find it useful.

Where to Find *The National Tribune*

The National Tribune can be found in a variety of libraries across the United States. A few institutions have complete files of the paper, but most repositories seem to have incomplete runs.

The Chronicling America section of the Library of Congress's website (http://chroniclingamerica.loc.gov) offers a fairly complete list of repositories. The name changes of the paper each have one entry in the Chronicling America section, so be sure to check each one to follow the newspaper's long history. The Library of Congress microfilm set of 40 reels (1877-1940) was copied for Antietam and Gettysburg, among other places. A gap from October 6, 1904 through September 28, 1905, exists in the Library of Congress' own holdings. The Ohio Historical Society has a microfilm copy covering this gap.

The following list includes only the major libraries that have extended runs of *The National Tribune*:

Antietam National Battlefield Park, Sharpsburg, MD. 1877-1917.

Center for Research Libraries, Chicago, IL. 1932-1938, 1942-1946.

Detroit Public Library, Detroit, MI. 1896-1940.

Gettysburg National Military Park, Gettysburg, PA. 1877-1940.

Library of Congress, Washington, DC. 1877-1940. In addition to the 40 reels of microfilm, the LOC also has available the years 1877-1917 as a digitized version that is located on the

"Chronicling America" section of their website, www.loc.gov. Click on Newspapers and then find "Chronicling America." Perform a search for *The National Tribune.*

Massachusetts Historical Society, Boston, MA. 1882-1887, 1889-1895, 1915.

New York Public Library, New York, NY. 1884-1894.

Stars and Stripes Museum/Library, Bloomfield, MO. 1903-1905, 1908, 1910-1995, 1997-1999.

United States Army Heritage & Education Center, Carlisle, PA. 1877-1940.

University of Texas, Austin, TX. 1929-1946.

University of Toledo, Toledo, OH. 1877-1921.

Western Kentucky University, Bowling Green, KY. 1889-1894, 1897, 1903-1917 (lots of missing issues).

Western Reserve Historical Society, Cleveland, OH. 1883-1916.

www.newspapers.com. Sponsored by Ancestry.com, this subscription website includes digitized issues of The National Tribune from 1877-1911.

Wisconsin Historical Society, Madison, WI. 1882-1917.

Abbreviations

AADC: Acting Aide de Camp
AAG: Assistant Adjutant General
AAQM: Acting Assistant Quartermaster General
ADC: Aide de Camp
AIG: Assistant Inspector General
Art: Artillery
Bg: Brigade
Biog: Biography
Btn: Battalion
Bty: Battery
Btys: Batteries
CSA: Confederate States of America
Cav: Cavalry
Cmpn: Campaign
Co: Company
Dept: Department
Div: Division
ES: Eastern Shore
Eng: Engineer
Enr Mil: Enrolled Militia
Gen: General
HQ: Headquarters

Hvy: Heavy
Inf: Infantry
Jct: Junction
LtCol: Lieutenant Colonel
Mtd: Mounted
Obit: Obituary
Off: Officer
Ord: Ordnance
PA Res: Pennsylvania Reserves
PHB: Potomac Home Brigade
POW: Prisoner of War
Prov: Provisional
RR: Railroad
Res: Reserve
SS: Sharpshooters
SM: State Militia
US: United States
USC: United States Colored
USCT: United States Colored Troops
USMC: United States Marine Corps
USN: United States Navy
USS: United States Ship
VRC: Veteran Reserve Corps
Vet: Veteran
( ): Denotes unit of author
[ ]: Clarifies or identifies subject of article

Tribune.

PRESIDENT AND PANAMA CANAL.

...ys Not to Control Interior Traffic—Trade Between Oceans Already Thriving—Democrats May Make Trouble.

"I won't play in your y

TWO-PARTY AMITY IMPOSSIBLE.

Taft and Cannon Not Playing Together—But Former Speaker May Lead Minority.

Volume 1: 1877 - 1903

1877

October

No Related Articles

November

11:3. "President Lincoln a Duelist."

December

No Related Articles

1878

January

30:1-3. Porter Farley (140th NY), "Reminiscences of Gettysburg." [*Rochester Democrat & Chronicle*]

February

33:1-3. "Andersonville."

34:1-3, 35:1-3, 39:1-2. "Extracts of the Report on the Treatment of Prisoners of War by the Rebel Authorities."

March

41:1-3, 42:1-3, 43:1-3. "Libby Prison, Richmond, Va."

April

54:1-2. "The Truth of History." [*Harrisburg Telegraph*, W. H. H. Davis vs. Simon Cameron on the enlistments of troops in 1861]

May

No Related Articles

June-December

Missing from Microfilm

1879

January

No Related Articles

February

No Related Articles

March

19:1. G. N. Bachelor, "Soldiers' Anecdotes." [Rosseau at Perryville]

19:2. "An Incident of Gettysburg." [*Boston Transcript*, Barlow-Gordon Affair]

April

32:1. "An Iowa Mother Who had 11 Sons in the U.S. Army—Their Record." [Elizabeth Uprigh, Butler County]

32:1. "Another Lincoln Anecdote."

May

35:3. E. H. Ropes (3rd NJ Art), "A Reminiscence of Gettysburg—Gen. Webb's Brigade."

June

42:1-3, 43:1. "Decoration Day." [speech of William McCandless at Gettysburg on May 30]

44:3. Obit: James Shields.

48:1. "Foraging for Chickens." [Pvt. Justice of an IN regiment in May 1864]

48:2. "A Memory of the War. The Amputation of Gen. [A. V.] Rice's Limb." [Kennesaw Mt]

July

56:1. Godfrey Hardy (31st NJ), "A War Incident."

August

64:1. John Duncan (15th KY), "An Anecdote of Gen. Rosseau."

September

66:3. George C. Morgan (98th OH), "A Reminiscence of Chickamauga—Gen. Steedman's Division."

67:3. "The Secret Intelligence Among Southern Negroes During the War." [*Toledo Blade*]

October

74:2. J. T. Wolverton, "An East Tennessee Anecdote."

74:3, 75:1. "Johnny Clem, 'The Drummer Boy of Chickamauga.'"

November

85:3. JM (48th PA), "A Soldier's Beautiful Letter." [written 6/25/64]

88:1. "The Angel of Castle Thunder."

December

No Related Articles

1880

January

2:3. John Duncan (15th KY), Letter about Perryville.

February

10:1-2. Reuben P. Reed (55th IL), "The Battle of Shiloh from My Own Standpoint."

March

22:2-3. "The Death of John Wilkes Booth." [interview with Capt Edwin P. Doherty in the *New Orleans Picayune*]

April

No Related Articles

May

39:1. "How Lincoln Squelched a Marquis." [of Hartington]

39:2. "His Conscience was Relieved." [Anecdote on John B. Bachelder's lecture at Buffalo]

June

43:3. W. H. Riland (93rd PA). His Service.

July

49:1-3, 50:1-2. "Close Quarters." [CSA soldier's escape from train to Fort Delaware on 2/2/6?]

55:1-3. "Sentenced and Shot."

August

No Related Articles

September

66:1-3. "The Battle of Groveton or Second Bull Run." [Fifth Corps soldier]

October

73:1-3. "Antietam. One of the Great Battles of the War."

November

No Related Articles

December

No Related Articles

1881

January

No Related Articles

February

11:3. "How Sickles Saved His Life." [Gettysburg]

March

No Related Articles

April

25:1-3, 26:1-2. "An American Andre. How a Great-Grandson of Martha Washington was Hanged During the Civil War as a Spy." [William O. Williams & Walter G. Peter on 6/9/63]

May

32:1-3. Henry T. Owen, "The Turning of the Tide. Gen. Pickett's Grand Charge at Gettysburg." [*Philadelphia Times*]

35:2. John B. Gordon, "On the Picket Line."

35:3. "The First Bull Run Fight." [Postmaster King in the *New York Times and Messenger*]

38:1-2. "The Youngest Soldier."

38:3. "Queer Happenings in War." [*Detroit Free Press*; covers Franklin, Fort Wagner, and White River]

June

43:2. "Andersonville." [current view]

44:1. A. R. Mullen (PA), William Dyas (117th NY), J. T. Suter (IL), "Young Soldiers."

July

Not on Microfilm

August 20

1:1-2. "Three November Days. What Benjamin F. Taylor Saw in 1863. Bragg's Defeat. Mr. Taylor's Account of the Battles Before Chattanooga . . ."

1:3-4. "Bull Run to Washington. The Great Skedaddle by a Survivor." [*National Republican*]

1:5. Obit: Robert Patterson.

2:1-2. "The Ghost of a Lantern." [signal corps in January 1862]

3:1-3. "In Front of Yorktown." [Porter's Division]

3:3. "Fighting for Posterity." [Anecdote about J. A. Early]

5:2-4. Biog: William W. Dudley (19th IN).

August 27

1:1-2. "In Front of Yorktown," Part 2.

1:3-4. "At Chancellorsville." [*Philadelphia Times*]

3:1-3. "Three November Days," Part 2.

3:3. "The Old Man Wants Them Guns." [anecdote about G. H. Thomas at Nashville]

September 3

1:1-2. "In Front of Yorktown," Part 3.

1:3-4. "Harrison's Landing, 1862. The Rebel Shelling of the Union Army." [7/31/62]

3:1-5, 5:3-4. "Three November Days," Part 3.

7:3. "A Daring Expedition." [William B. Cushing and gunboat *Monticello*, *San Francisco Chronicle*]

7:4. (4th MI Cav), "A Close Shave." [*Philadelphia Press*, about Dick McCann's Confederate cavalry]

September 10

1:1-2. PDH, "The Attack on Lee's Mills." [4/16/62]

1:3-4. "Petersburg Revisited. An Irishman's Idea of the Crater." [*Philadelphia Times*]

2:5. "Historical Drumsticks." [*Niles Mirror*, concerning sticks carried by the 24th MI]

3:1-4. J. S. Slater (13th NY), "Malvern. The End of the Seven Days."

September 17

1:3-4. "Appomattox Court House. The Place Where Lee Surrendered." [*Philadelphia Times*]

1:5. Obit: Ambrose E. Burnside.

3:1-5. J. S. Slater (13th NY), "At Gaines's Mill. Scenes and Incidents of the Battle." [*National Republican*]

5:2. Obit: James Starr (6th PA Cav, Meade ADC), John G. Parr (139th PA), K. R. Breese (USN), William M. Gregg (23rd, 179th NY).

5:4. Biog: Silas M. Bailey (8th PA Res).

September 24

3:1-4. J. S. Slater (13th NY), "The Grand Review. A Never-to-be-forgotten Scene."

3:1. Henry H. Brownell, "Marching Home." [poem]

October 1

1:1-2. George Reynolds (15th IA), "Gen. McPherson's Death."

1:2. "Suit Against Gen. Banks." [versus William R. Hodges of New Orleans]

1:3-4. J. S. Slater (13th NY), "Yellow Jackets." [bees at Malvern Hill]

3:1-3. "Torn Battle Flags. Wrecks and Relics of the War."

October 8

1:1-2. "Gen. Sherman's Letter. What General Rosecrans Says of It." [*San Francisco Chronicle*, regarding Chickamauga]

3:1-5, 7:3-4. St. Clair A. Mulholland (116th PA), "At Fredericksburg, December 13, 1862." [*Philadelphia Times*]

October 15

3:1-4. E. P. Alexander, "The Battle of Gettysburg. An Account of the Last Day's Fighting." [*Louisville Courier Journal*]

3:4. Thomas Reynolds, "An Incident of Shiloh."

5:5. Obit: Daniel C. Rodman (7th CT).

October 22

1:1-2. One of Hancock's Brigade, "The Gatling Gun. At Garnett's, June 27th and 28th, 1862."

3:1. George P. Lathrop, "Keenan's Charge." [poem about 8th PA Cavalry at Chancellorsville]

3:1-3. J. S. Slater (13th NY), "Chased by Guerrillas, A Personal Reminiscence." [1863, near Alexandria, VA]

4:3. William H. Bentz (8th PA Cav), "From One of Keenan's Men."

4:4. H. D. O'Brien (1st MN), "The Flag of the Yallabusha Rifles." [1/19/62, 15th MS vs. 2nd MN]

8:2. "Big Hush Money." [March to the Sea anecdote]

October 29

1:2, 5:2-4. "An Incident of Libby Prison."

3:1-4. G. N. Galloway (95th PA), "In the Wilderness." [*Philadelphia Times*]

4:4. Obit: John Edwards, Jr. (3rd US Art).

5:1. "More About Captured Flags." [Yallabusha Rifles]

5:1. Obit: George E. Wentworth (30th MA, 76th, 82nd USCT]

5:2-4. "Libby Prison."

November 5

1:2. Obit: John Mix (3rd NY Cav, 2nd US Cav).

3:1-4. J. S. Slater (13th NY), "Mechanicsville. Beginning of the Seven Days."

November 12

1:1-2. "A Great Battlefield. In and About the Shenandoah Valley." [*Boston Sunday Herald*]

3:1-3. "Sixteen Years After. The Battle of Sharpsburg." [M Quad in the *Detroit Free Press*]

3:4. "Stood By His Gun." [*New York News*, concerning Price's retreat from Little Rock in September 1863]

November 19

3:1-4. "Crocker's Iowa Brigade. From an Address by Gen. W. W. Belknap."

November 26

1:1-2. J. S. Slater (13th NY), "Some Historic Places Where Our Soldier Boys Suffered." [hospitals in Washington area]

3:1-3. Cecil Clay (58th PA), "Capture of Fort Harrison. How the Rebels Failed to Retake It." [*Philadelphia Times*]

4:4. Lyman R. Ingraham, "A Correction." [Gatling guns]

December 3

1:1-2. "Sketches of Hospital Life."

3:1-4. Herbert E. Hill, "Sheridan's Ride."

3:4. F. Jordan, "An Episode of the Blockade." [*Philadelphia Times*, regarding Charleston in early 1863]

3:5. "An Incident of the Late War." [*Hoosac Valley News* about Andersonville]

4:4. Obit: James Gillette (3rd MD, Geary's staff).

8:1. "The Eccentricities of Bullets."

December 10

1:1-2. "Some Familiar Places in and About the Capital." [Old Capitol Prison, Camp Convalescent]

3:1-2. "The Bucktail Rifles. Where the Rebel General Ashby Fell." [*Philadelphia Times*]

3:3-5. "Was It a Dream?" [Second Manassas]

3:5. Allston W. Whitney, "A War Reminiscence." [Fitzhugh Lee exchange for US officer in Libby Prison]

8:1.Obit: Hugh J. Kilpatrick.

December 17

1:4. Obit: Henry S. Banning (87th, 121st, 125th, 195th OH).

3:1-3. Charles L. Martin, "The Treason of Twiggs. An Ex-Rebel Tells the Shameful Story." [*Philadelphia Times*]

3:3-4. "Saved by a Corpse." [Port Hudson]

3:5. Seaman Sterling (*Brooklyn*), "Incidents of the Late War."

December 24

1:1-2. "Pacific Coast. Some Interesting Reminiscences."

3:1-5. Frank E. Moran (73rd NY), "The Bright Side of Libby." [*Philadelphia Times*]

December 31

1:1-5, 3:3-5. G. C. Kniffin, "Army of the Cumberland and the Battle of Stone River."

3:1-2. William S. Rosecrans, "Battle of Ball's Bluff."

6:1-3. Harry M. Kieffer (150th PA), "Recollections of a Drummer Boy. The First Day at Gettysburg." [from *St. Nicholas*]

1882

January 7

1:1-5, 3:2-5. Kniffin, Part 2.

3:1. "The Battle of Gettysburg. What Gen. Ewell Wanted to Do." [from General Meade's letter]

3:1. "Where is He Now?" [Orion P. Howe, 55th IL, at Vicksburg, 5/19/63]

4:4-5. Biog: Thomas M. Browne (7th IN Cav), Charles H. Joyce (2nd VT), R. R. Dawes (6th WI), A. H. Pettibone (20th WI), John B. Rice (10th, 72nd OH), James W. Wadsworth (general's son), C. C. Matson (16th IN), John W. Caldwell (9th KY), Charles B. Simonton (CSA), George C. Cabell (18th VA CSA), L. C. Latham (1st NC CSA), W. P. Hepburn (2nd IA Cav), T. M. Rice (OH), E. F. Stone (48th MA), George W. Steele (12th, 101st IN), W. R. Cox (2nd NC CSA).

5:1-2. Biog: Thomas B. Hood (76th OH).

January 14

1:1-5, 3:2-4. Kniffin, Part 3.

3:4-5. "Harrison's Landing, 1862. Rebel Account of the Night Attack." [reports of S. G. French and W. N. Pendleton]

4:5. "Grant and Fitz-John Porter."

January 21

1:1-5. Kniffin, Part 4.

3:1-3. "Grif," "Stranger Than Fiction. A Reminiscence of the War."

3:5. "He Brought the Flag." [IN regiment in MS]

8:1. John C. Kensil (150th PA), "Gettysburg Coincidence."

January 28

1:1-5. Kniffin, Part 5.

3:1-2. W. M. Boroughs (24th AL), "What Regiment was It? Capture of Missionary Ridge." [*Philadelphia Times*]

3:2. Benjamin M. Prentiss, "Reminiscences of Shiloh." [*Boston Herald*]

5:4. Obit: Silas Casey.

February 4

1:2. Obit: R. B. Mitchell.

1:5, 5:3-5. "Memories of Burnside."

3:1-3. J. H. Simpson (120th IN), "Battle of Kernstown. How Jackson was Beaten." [*Philadelphia Times*]

3:4. "It Held the Flag." [being wounded in battle]

February 11

1:3-4. "Gun-shot Wounds. A Few Remarkable Cases Cited."

3:1-5. "Cole the Pirate. His Attempt to Capture the *Michigan*." [*Philadelphia Press*]

February 18

1:1-4. G. C. Kniffin, "Morgan's Rough Riders. His Kentucky Raid, December 1862."

3:1-3. "Cole the Pirate," Part 2.

3:4. "Anecdotes of General Buford."

February 25

1:1-5. G. C. Kniffin, "Col. Coburn's Brigade. How It was Captured by Van Dorn." [Thompson's Station]

3:1-3. Thomas H. Cross (16th VA), "Battle of the Crater." [*Philadelphia Times*]

3:3-4. "Hold the Fort." [*Iowa State Register*]

3:4. "The Spectre of Vicksburg Siege. Gen. Burbridge's Orderly in a Nightshirt."

5:5. Obit: J. B. G. Baxter (3rd WI).

March 4

1:1-5. G. C. Kniffin, "Streight's Georgia Raid."

3:1-3. C. B. Brockway (Bty F, 1st PA), "Across the Rapidan." [*Philadelphia Times*]

3:4-5. Obit: Robert Timpany (7th US).

5:4. Obit: Lorenzo Lorain (Bty L, 1st US).

March 11

1:1-4. W. S. Rosecrans, "Tullahoma Campaign."

3:6. Edward E. Bryant, "Fighting for the Right to Surrender." [Col. Joyce of Arkansas, in 1865]

3:6. G. P. Eberhart (25th IL), "The First Regiment on Mission Ridge."

5:1. "Garfield and Rosecrans."

March 18

1:1-4. G. C. Kniffin, "A Perilous Enterprise." [Carter's December 1862 Tennessee raid]

1:5-6, 6:1-5. "Garfield-Rosecrans. Extraordinary Interest Aroused Throughout the Country."

1:4. "A Confederate Soldier's Opinion." [Appomattox]

3:4-6. J. A. Watrous (2nd WI), "A Strange Story." [*Milwaukee Republican*, about A. D. Bennett, 2nd WI]

4:2-4. "Let Us Have Peace." [Rosecrans-Garfield]

5:6. M. P. Hanson,"First to Prepare for War." [*Milwaukee Sunday Telegraph* regarding Company B, 1st WI]

6:6. Biog: George S. Merrill (4th MA).

March 25

1:1-6, 3:5-6. W. S. Rosecrans, "Chattanooga Campaign." [includes Chickamauga]

3:1-3. Loring G. Emerson (USS *Passaic*), "Life on an Iron-clad."

April 1

1:1-6. G. C. Kniffin, "A Race for Life. John Morgan's Raid Through Kentucky, Indiana, and Ohio."

3:1-2. Emerson, Part 2.

3:3. Carolus, "The 32nd Indiana at Rowlett Station."

3:3-4. "How a Methodist Preacher was Imprisoned for Stealing Chickens."

3:5. "An Interesting 'War Relic'." [Marlin Schwein has been wandering 17 years with his equipment & tent]

April 8

1:1-6. Kniffin, "Race for Life," Part 2.

3:1-3. Samuel D. Sturgis, "The Battle of Guntown."

3:3-5. "A Blockade Runner's Story." [John P. Smith and CSS *Alice*]

3:5. "Bloody Repulse at Corinth."

5:5. Obit: Stephen D. Hurlbut.

April 15

1:1-4. G. C. Kniffin, "Cumberland Gap."

3:2-3. "An Incident at Hatcher's Run." [10/64, from *St. Nicholas*]

3:3-4. T. S. Potter (8th OH), "Reminiscences of Spottsylvania."

3:5. "Hell is Better Than This." [march to Chickamauga of 21st Corps]

April 22

1:1-5. Kniffin, Part 2.

1:6, 2:1-3. "A Noble Woman's Work. Important Campaigns that were Planned by Miss [Anna Ella] Carroll."

2:4-5. "Photographing the Dead on the Battlefield." [Antietam]

3:5. "Youngest Soldier."

April 29

1:1-5. Kniffin, Part 3.

1:6, 2:1-3. "Stephen A. Hurlbut."

2:4-5. John Frith (113th IL), "The Guntown Affair. The Other Side."

2:5. "That 'Bloody Repulse' at Corinth."

3:3-4. W. J. Whitney (57th PA), "Origin of the Army Badge."

3:5. Obit: E. F. Fachtz (5th, 8th MD).

May 6

1:1-5. G. C. Kniffin, "Gen. Wm. P. Sanders."

1:6, 2:1-2. "Tullahoma Campaign. March of Mitchell's Cavalry from Triune to Decherd." [from "Mitchell's Cavalier" 7/25/63]

2:3. S. J. Lindsay (58th IN), "Chickamauga. A Ballad."

2:4. J. William Jones, "Lee and the Chaplains."

2:4. "An Old Eagle at the Mast-head." [Port Royal]

2:4-5. "An Absurd Fiasco of the War." [*Philadelphia Times*, Richmond scare on 4/21/61]

3:3. "Youngest Soldier."

3:5-6. "Incident of the Port Hudson Siege."

7:1-2. "Honors to the Brave. Remains of the Late Gen. Hurlbut Quietly Laid to Rest."

May 13

1:1-5. G. C. Kniffin, "Siege of Chattanooga."

1:6, 2:1. "Our Army at Vicksburg. Sinking of the Gunboat *Cincinnati*. A Sailor's Brave Act."

2:1. "A Foraging Chaplain." [Moran of the 12th WI]

May 20

1:1-5. Kniffin, Part 2.

1:6, 2:1. "Dash for Liberty. March of Union Refugees from North Carolina to Kentucky."

2:1. "Capt. John L. Clem, the Drummer Boy of Chickamauga."

8:2. J. W. Kirkley, "To Whom Does Honor Belong?" [Gettysburg, reference to Bty H, 3rd PA]

May 27

1:1-4. "Tullahoma Campaign. Occupation of Middle Tennessee. Wilder's Brigade at Hoover's Gap."

1:5-6, 2:1. George F. Steahlin (7th PA Cav), "Stanley's Cavalry. Col. Minty's Sabre Brigade at Guy's Gap."

2:1-2. J. E. Hatchitt, "How Gen. Sanders Died."

2:3. "Youngest Soldier."

June 3

1:1-5. "Maryland in the War." [1861]

1:5. Joseph H. Carter, "East Tennessee Refugees."

June 10

1:1-5. "Maryland in the War," Part 2.

1:6, 2:1-2. "Holly Springs."

8:4. "Fitz-John Porter. Senator Sewell's Bill to Restore Him to the Army."

June 17

1:1-3. "Siege of Chattanooga. Wheeler's Raid in Middle Tennessee—Pursuit by Union Cavalry.

1:4-6. "The Story of a Scout. Thrilling Adventures of Levi H. Naron."

8:3. "Face to Face at Gettysburg. A Pleasant Reunion of Federals and Confederates on the Old Historic Battleground."

June 24

1:1-5, 6:5-6. "Raising the Siege. Storming Lookout Mountain."

July 1

1:1-5. "Burnside in Tennessee. Jones in Western Virginia."

3:4-5. "A Family of Soldiers." [Wenk Family, NY]

6:1. Sara Mathews, "Battle of Mission Ridge." [poem]

July 8

1:1-4. "Burnside in East Tennessee. Battle of Blue Springs."

1:6, 2:1-3. "Freelance," "Southern Prison Life." [Andersonville]

2:5. Obit: Robert M. A. Hawk.

July 15

1:1-5. "The Army of the Ohio. Two Confederate Cavalry Raids and What They Accomplished." [Cluke and Pegram]

1:6, 2:1-2. "Southern Prison Life," Part 2.

2:3. A. B. Smith (97th OH), "Reminiscences of the War. Some Interesting Incidents of the Army of the Cumberland.

July 22

1:1-5. "The Army of the Ohio. The Union Cavalry Assume the Offensive in Lively Engagements."

1:6, 2:1-3. Charles E. Troutman (12th NJ), "The Blue Trefoil in the Chapparal at Chancellorsville."

2:4-6. "Southern Prison Life," Part 3. [7/31-8/2/64]

3:1. "The Coming Reunion at Gettysburg." [Zook monument]

5:6. Obit: Mary Todd Lincoln.

July 29

1:1-5. "Missionary Ridge."

1:6, 2:1-2. "Southern Prison Life," Part 4. [8/3-12/64]

3:1-5. "The Pennsylvania Veterans' Grand Reunion at Gettysburg."

August 5

1:1-5. "Missionary Ridge," Part 2.

1:6, 2:1-4. "Southern Prison Life," Part 5. [8/13-31/64]

2:5-6. T. S. Potter (8th OH), "The Battle of Gettysburg."

August 12

1:1-5. "Missionary Ridge," Part 3.

1:6, 2:1-2. "Southern Prison Life," Part 6. [9/1-10/64]

2:3-4. A. J. Eidson (148th IL), "The Girl Soldier."

August 19

1:1-5. "Missionary Ridge," Part 4.

1:6, 2:1-2. "Southern Prison Life," Part 7. [9/11-20/64]

2:5-6. A. Newton (46th IL), "An Incident of Shiloh."

8:2. E. E. Phillips, "Our Southern Prison Sketches." [Libby]

8:3. WDG (6th Corps HQ), "Checked by Effective Artillery." [Saylor's Creek]

August 26

1:1-5. "Missionary Ridge," Part 5.

1:6, 2:1-2. "Southern Prison Life," Part 8. [9/21-10/4/64]

8:1. E. A. Teed (51st NY), "Graphic Sketch of a Battle." [Antietam]

September 2

1:1-3. A. E. Burnside, "Burnside's Expedition. Capture and Occupation of Roanoke Island." [from paper read in Rhode Island]

1:4. George H. Chase (2nd NY Cav), "A Scrap of History. General Kilpatrick's Desperate Encounter with a Rebel Major." [Brandy Station]

1:4. "Took the General's Advice." [140th PA and Hancock, winter 1862/3]

1:6, 2:1-3. "Southern Prison Life," Part 9. [10/5-18/64]

8:1. John W. Manning (22nd PA Cav), "Brutal Murders at Belle Isle."

September 9

1:1-5. "Battle of Kernstown."

1:6, 2:1-2. "Southern Prison Life," Part 10. [10/19-11/7/64]

1:5. "A Famous Regiment. The 7th Pa. Vol. Cav.—Its Organization and Record."

2:4-6. George Morgan, "Western Battlefields. How Franklin, Tenn., Looks After the Lapse of 18 Years." [*Philadelphia Times*]

5:4-5. "The 51st Penna. Battle-Flags." [Spotsylvania flags returned to regiment]

8:1-2. William H. Wood (2nd NY Cav), "Where Raw Dog was a Luxury." [Belle Isle]

September 16

1:1-2. Ransom T. Powell, "Brave Little Red Cap. The Young Orderly of Monster Wirz at Andersonville."

1:3-4. Abner Doubleday, "Chancellorsville. Gen. Stonewall Jackson's Rout of the Eleventh Corps." [from his book]

1:5-6, 2:1-2. "By Field and Flood. The Story of Lieut. Newlin's Escape from Danville." [73rd IL]

2:2. J. Scott, "Lee as a Humorist." [*Philadelphia Times*]

2:3-4. "Southern Prison Life," Part 11. [11/8-16/64]

5:4. Kennedy Marshall, "A Famous Flight. How the First News of Bull Run was Brought to Washington."

7:2. Henry Argetsinger, "Andersonville."

7:3. Silas W. Crocker (6th PA Res), "The Horrors of Salisbury."

7:4. A. S. McDowell (84th IL),"'Push Them, Colonel, Push Them'." [Rossville Gap]

September 23

1:1-3. Powell, Part 2.

1:4-6. Newlin, Part 2.

3:3-4. "Dlorah (13th NYSM), "An Anecdote of General Butler."

6:5-6. "Southern Prison Life," Part 12. [11/17-24/64]

7:3-4. "George Morgan, "Lookout Mountain. The Old Battle-field as It Looks Today." [*Philadelphia Times*]

7:5-6. Doubleday, Part 2.

September 30

1:1-3. Powell, Part 3.

1:4-6, 2:1. Newlin, Part 3.

2:2-3. "Southern Prison Life," Part 13. [11/25-12/2/64]

3:2-3. "Antietam. Laying the Corner-stone of a Soldiers' Monument—Oration by Gen. H. A. Barnum."

4:4-5. H. B. Vanneman (84th IN), "The Battle of Franklin."

7:3-4. "Battle of Franklin."

7:5-6. Doubleday, Part 3.

October 5

1:1-3. Powell, Part 4.

1:4-6. Theodore Gerrish (20th ME), "The Field of Antietam."

1:6. D. R. Hundley (31st AL), "Jackson, of Tennessee." [*Philadelphia Times*]

2:1-3. "Southern Prison Life," Part 14. [12/3-8/64]

7:4-6. S. Woodson Price (21st KY), "Some Famous Fighters Interesting Anecdotes Concerning the Great Generals of the War."

October 12

1:1-4. "Siege of Knoxville."

1:5-6. Powell, Part 5.

6:5-6. "Southern Prison Life," Part 15. [12/9/64-1/9/65]

7:3-4. A. W. Ellis, "Shiloh. Nelson's Division on that Bloody Field—Interesting Reminiscences."

7:5-6. Price, Part 2.

October 19

1:1-4. "Siege of Knoxville," Part 2.

1:5-6, 2:1. William Pittinger, "A Deed of Daring. The True Story of the Capture of a Rebel Railway Train."

2:2-3. "Southern Prison Life," Part 16. [1/10-30/65]

7:1. James A. McGinley (5th NY Cav), "That Andersonville Hanging."

7:1-2. Morris Eldred (45th PA), "The Siege of Knoxville."

7:3-4. Powell, Part 6.

7:5-6. Gerrish, Part 2.

October 26

1:1-4. "Siege of Knoxville," Part 3.

1:5-6, 2:1. Pittinger, Part 2.

2:2-3. "Southern Prison Life, " Part 17. [1/31-2/21/65]

7:4-5. Powell, Part 7.

7:5-6. "Another Gettysburg Monument." [14th CT]

7:6. "Official Records of the War."

November 2

1:1-4. "Siege of Knoxville," Part 4.

1:5-6. Pittinger, Part 3.

2:1-3. "Southern Prison Life," Part 18. [3/17-6/8/65]

7:3-4. Powell, Part 8.

7:5-6. "Old John Brown." [*Philadelphia Press*]

November 9

1:1-4. "Siege of Knoxville," Part 5.

1:5-6. Pittinger, Part 4.

2:1-2. J. B. Kilbourne, "The March to the Sea."

4:5. T. J. Bryant (14th IL), "Buell's Laurels. The Situation at Shiloh Reviewed—Who Won the Day?"

7:3-4. Powell, Part 9.

7:6. "Resaca After 18 Years." [*Philadelphia Times*]

November 16

1:1-4. "Siege of Knoxville," Part 6.

1:4. "The Brave Corporal at Chancellorsville."

1:5-6. Edwin H. Miner, "Prisoners of War." [Andersonville]

2:1-3. "By Field and Flood. An Interesting Postscript to Lieut. Newlin's Story."

2:3. "A Plea for the Battle-Flags." [*Kansas City Journal*]

2:3. L. B. Smith (4th MI Cav), "A Letter from Another Survivor."

7:3-4. Powell, Part 10.

7:5-6. H. T. Talbott (10th WI), "Trying to Escape." [Salisbury]

November 23

1:1-5. Theodore Gerrish (20th ME), "Battle of Gettysburg."

1:6, 2:1-3. Horace Capron (14th IL Cav), "Stoneman's Raid. The Cavalry Expedition to the Rear of Atlanta."

2:3. W. W. Jellison (96th IL), "Andersonville."

5:4-5. J. D. Vautier (88th PA), "Ex-Prisoner of War."

7:3-4. Powell, Part 11.

November 30

1:1-4. Gerrish, Part 2.

1:5-6. Capron, Part 2.

3:4-5. "Prison Experiences. Little Red Cap Continues His Description of Andersonville."

3:6. A. N. Fritchey (1st MD PHB Cav), "Andersonville Hanging."

7:3. Untitled article about donation of CSN naval flag to GAR Post 37 in New Jersey

December 7

1:1-4. Gerrish, Part 3.

1:5-6. Capron, Part 3.

6:5-6. "Prison Experiences," Part 2.

7:6. William Fulks (7th WI), "Where Gen. Dudley Lost His Leg." [Gettysburg]

December 14

1:1-4. Gerrish, Part 4.

1:5-6. Capron, Part 4.

3:5-6. "Prison Experiences," Part 3.

7:2. Charles Campbell (81st OH), "Another Account of the Andersonville Hanging."

December 21

1:1-4. Gerrish, Part 5.

1:5-6. "Truth of History. Gross Perversion of Facts by a Northern Newspaper. Burning of Marietta. . . . Sherman's March to the Sea." [reply to M Quad in the *Detroit Free Press*]

2:3. Thomas W. Cocker (7th NJ), "Another Reminiscence of Andersonville."

2:5. "Prison Experiences," Part 4.

2:6. How a Hero Fell. General Sherman's Description of the Death of General McPherson."

December 28

1:1-4. Gerrish, Part 6.

1:5-6. S. L. Coulter, (64th OH), "Battle of Franklin."

3:5-6. "Prison Experiences," Part 5.

1883

January 4

1:1-4. Gerrish, Part 7.

1:5-6. "Chickamauga."

1:4. B. F. Stelley (20th OH), "The Death of McPherson."

2:5. John C. Tressel (96th OH), "Tyler Prison."

3:5-6. "Prison Experiences," Part 6.

January 11

1:1-4. Gerrish, Part 8.

1:5-6. "Chickamauga," Part 2.

2:5-6. Joshua L. Chamberlain (20th ME), "Lee's Surrender." [*Brunswick Telegraph*]

2:6. Bret Harte, "John Burns of Gettysburg." [poem]

3:5-6. "Prison Experiences," Part 7.

3:6. "The First Gun of the Rebellion." [1861 Mississippi River firing on steamer]

January 18

1:1-4. Gerrish, Part 9.

1:5-6. "Chickamauga," Part 3.

2:6. J. L. Dunn, "Woman in the War." [Clara Barton]

3:5-6. "Prison Experiences," Part 8.

3:6. Robert P. McRae, "The Six Raiders." [Andersonville]

3:6. T. H. Grove (72nd OH), "From Another Eye-Witness." [Andersonville raiders]

January 25

1:1-4. Gerrish, Part 10.

1:5-6. Theodore Gerrish (20th ME), "Round Top. Mr. Gerrish Replies to a Criticism of His Book." [letter in *Post and Camp*, Phila]

1:6. "Story of a Sword Returned to Its Owner by a Va. Lady After Many Years." Capt. J. L. S. Kinner, 27th MA, reported *Sacramento Record-Union*]

2:5. S. M. Childs (VRC), "A Narrow Escape. The Experience of One of Pap Thomas' Boys at Chickamauga."

2:6. F. H. Coppernoll, "A Regiment in Rags." [Andersonville]

February 1

1:1-5. Alvin P. Hovey, "Pittsburgh Landing."

1:5. Henry Guekert (39th OH), "Further Facts as to the Death of Gen. J. B. McPherson."

1:6. Allen Buckner (79th IL), "Battle of Franklin."

1:6. Horace Capron (14 IL Cav), "A Strange Story—Wonderful Vitality of a Wounded Officer." [Herbert Mayo, 14th IL Cav]

February 8

1:1-3. "Mossy Creek."

1:4-6. "My Maryland. The Part Borne By Her Troops in the Gettysburg Campaign."

1:6. Thomas Riseman (AAG, 2nd Div, 14th Corps), "More About the Death of McPherson."

2:6. George S. Kimball, "Andersonville."

2:6. R. P. Black (103rd PA), "The Mysterious Spring. An Andersonville Prisoner Relates the Story of Its Origin."

2:6. Thomas J. Libby, "Salisbury. A Leaf Experience of a Survivor of that Pen."

February 15

1:1-3. "Dandridge. The Occupation and Sudden Evacuation."

1:3. M. E. Boysell (58th OH), "Pittsburgh Landing."

1:4-6. "My Maryland," Part 2.

1:6. Don Carlos Buell, "A Tribute to Gen. Nelson."

2:5. Henry Devilliz, "Where Famine Stalked. The Struggle for Existence in Southern Prison Pens."

2:5. James M. Burk, "The Price of Liberty at Andersonville."

2:5. Thomas Charberau, "The Soldier's Rainbow of Promise."

2:5. W. J. Byerby, "Life at Cahawba Prison."

2:5-6. Isaiah Steigelman, "Tough Times at Salisbury."

2:6. Charles D. Gibson, "A Reminiscence of Tyler Prison."

2:6. R. L. B. Hill, "How We Treated Rebel Prisoners." [Camp Douglas]

February 22

1:1-4. William S. Rosecrans, "Rich Mountain."

1:4. William H. Ray (80th IN), "Burning of Marietta."

1:5. Biog: Charles F. Manderson (19th OH).

1:6. "The Battle of Corinth." [from CSA diary]

1:7. "Capture of Cumberland." [Gettysburg Campaign]

3:6. A. C. Jones, "The 2nd Colorado. Some Further Reminiscences of a Famous Cavalry Regiment." [encloses letter from George West, 3rd WI Cav]

6:3. Biog: E. S. Osborne (8th, 149th PA).

7:1-4. "Fate of a Monster. Arrest, Trial, and Execution of Commandant Wirz, of Andersonville."

March 1

1:1-3. "The War in the West. View of the Political Situation in Kentucky. Camp Dick Robinson. . . ."

1:4-6. C. H. Fish, "The Signal Corps."

1:6-7, "My Maryland," Part 3.

1:7. Leland J. Webb (16th WI), "Was There a Surprise?" [Shiloh]

7:1-2. "Scenes at Camp Ford."

7:2. E. W. Bagshaw, "How Rebel Prisoners Fared." [Camp Morton]

March 8

1:1-5. Horace Capron (14th IL Cav), "Capron's Cavalry. Operations on the Tennessee

River Below Pulaski." [1864 Nashville Campaign]

1:5. Washington L. Elliott, "Mossy Creek."

1:6-7. "War in the West," Part 2.

7:5. Thomas C. Davis (38th IL), Letter about Andersonville.

March 15

1:1-5. James C. Veatch, "The Battle of Shiloh."

1:6-7. "War in the West," Part 3.

3:7. FCH (12th CT), "Port Hudson."

3:7. CHS (45th OH), "A Brave Confederate Colonel." [Monticello, KY]

3:7. James A. Waltman (7th IL), "Battle of Pittsburgh Landing."

3:7. W. W. Sutliff (2nd IA), "Battle of Pittsburgh Landing."

3:7. "Mrs. Charles Williams, "The 2nd Colorado Again."

7:2. Charles Winters, "That Treacherous Tug Once More." [NC 1861]

7:2. W. W. Hensley, "What a Soldier Never Forgets." [being a POW]

7:4. George Scott (123rd NY), "That Andersonville Spring Once More."

7:4. Ichabod Preston (WI), "How Wirz's Bloodhound was Poisoned."

7:4. H. R. Andrews (12th IA), "Dark Days in Dixie. Experiences in Southern Prisons. A Sketch of Cahawba."

March 22

1:1-3. C. W. Putnam (25th MA), "Burnside Expedition. The Voyage from Annapolis to Hatteras Inlet . . ."

1:4-5, "Fish, Part 2.

1:6-7, 5:7. James Beale (12th MA), "A Slashing Criticism. The Eleventh Corps on the Field of Gettysburg."

2:3-4. Silas W. Crocker (6th PA Res), "A Dash for Freedom. How a Party of Salisbury Prisoners Effected Their Escape."

2:5-7. C. H. Ray, "John Brown of Old, and the Last of His Work."

3:7. "Songs of the Camp."

7:6. A. S. Clyne (63rd NY), "The Andersonville Spring Once More."

7:6. N. Lanpheor (85th NY), "The Andersonville Spring. . ."

7:6. Ezra W. Corse (16th WI), "That 'Surprise' at Shiloh."

7:6. Henry C. Kendall, "A Curious Relic of the Rebellion." [CSA provost Marshal's sign from Petersburg]

March 29

1:1-4. Horace Capron (14th IL Cav), "Defense of the Crossing of the Duck River Against Hood's Advance."

1:5-7. Fish, Part 3.

2:4. "Twenty Years After. How Andersonville Now Looks to Travelers North." [*Cincinnati Journal*]

2:5-7. John F. Hill (89th OH), "Good-Bye to Dixie. An Ohio Soldier's Story of His Escape from Danville."

3:7. "Price's Raid. How Major Smith of the Independent Colorado Met His Death." [*Sedan Times* (KS)]

7:5. R. W. Surry (7th IL Cav), "Letter About Shiloh."

7:5. F. A. Niles (49th IL), "Several Surprises at Shiloh."

7:5-6. B. Smith (17th IL). "What Another Soldier Thinks About It." [Shiloh]

7:6. Joel Wright (65th OH), "The Dandridge Fiasco."

7:6. S. G. Parker (53rd IL), "Recollections of 'Old Abe'." [8th WI eagle]

7:6-7. Charles H. Barlow, "Custer's Last Order."

7:6-7. Charles H. Barlow, "A Mighty Good Story–And True." [Gaines' Mill]

7:7. "General Upton's Last Order." [6/10/65]

8:3. William E. Otter (71st PA), "The Story of a Soldier's Watch."

April 5

1:1-3. Alvin P. Hovey, "Surprise at Shiloh."

1:3. "Nelson at Shiloh." [*Louisville Commercial*]

1:4-7. Fish, Part 4.

2:3-4. Hill, Part 2.

2:6. J. E. Greene (15th MA), "The Story of a Sword." [*Worcester Spy*, regarding Ball's Bluff]

2:7. "Songs of the Camp."

5:3-4. "The Truth at Last. Discovery of General Grant's Order Removing General Thomas."

7:5-6. R. P. Black (103rd PA); George Weber (11th PA Res); Thomas H. Mann (18th MA); J. F. Wheeler (149th NY); S. G. Burdick (85th NY); William W. Fuch; T. C. Davis (38th IL); J. N. Sweeny; C. B. Forster (16th IL Cav); "About Andersonville Spring."

April 12

1:1-4. C. W. Putnam (25th MA), "Burnside's Expedition. Roanoke Roanoke Island, Its Defenses and Defenders."

1:5-7. Fish, Part 5.

2:3-4. Hill, Part 3.

2:5-7. D. H. Baker (25th MO); William Easlick (15th MI); D. C. Anderson (43rd IL); T. J. Bryant (14th IL); F. C. Cromwell (12th IA); William French (21st MO); William M. Orr(21st MO), "Shiloh. How the Battle Began."

April 19

1:1-4. "The War in the West. The Kentucky State Guard and the Home Guard . . . ."

1:5-7. Fish, Part 6.

2:5-6. Hill, Part 4.

2:6. "Songs of the Camp."

2:7. "A Famous Exploit. How the Rebel Signal Flag was Shot Away at Lookout Mountain." [*Dayton Journal*]

7:2. M. G. Reeves (11th IA); O. S. Smith (8th OH); Henry Reinoch (55th IL); R. M. Kelly, "Echoes of Shiloh."

7:5. Robert W. Wood, "From an Engineer of the Andersonville Tunnel."

April 26

1:1-3. "The War in the West. Uprising of the Unionists in East Tennessee. . . ."

1:4-7. Fish, Part 7.

2:4-5. Hill, Part 5.

2:6. Edward A. Garden (57th OH), "A Graphic Picture of the Battle of Shiloh."

2:6-7. (10th WV), "Two Drummer Boys' Exploit."

2:7. "Harker's Brigade at Chickamauga."

2:7. Charles A. Long (111th PA), "A Good Word for the Twentieth Corps." [Peach Tree Creek]

7:4. A. H. Hutchinson, "The Experience of Four Tyler Prisoners."

7:4. E. R. Stillman (85th NY), "Was Gen. Casey Surprised?" [Fair Oaks]

7:5-7.. W. L. Goss, Thomas C. Davis (38th IL), Theodore Wiseman, "Andersonville Spring."

May 3

1:1-5. Porter Farley (140th NY), "Bloody Round Top."

1:5. William C. Rawalle (2nd US Cav), "Sturgis at Mossy Creek."

1:6-7. C. A. Kuhl (14th IL), "Pittsburgh Landing. The Historic Battle-ground of Shiloh Revisited."

1:7. W. B. Roby (ADC, 1st Div, 14th Corps), "Peach Tree Creek."

2:4. Songs of the Camp."

2:5-7. Hill, Part 6.

3:6-7. E. H. Gregg (10th KS), "Just Before the War. John Brown in Iowa—An Exciting Journey to the Front."

5:7. "Merrill's Farewell Order." [2nd MO Cav]

7:3. Henry H. Wright (6th IA), "An Iowa Soldier's Story of Shiloh."

7:3. Jacob Fink, John P. Wheeler (55th IL), "The 55th Illinois at Shiloh."

7:3-4. A. J. Lowder, "The Battle Before Atlanta."

7:4. George C. Ketchum (7th OH), "The 7th Ohio at Summerville."

7:4. C. T. Cousins (2nd MO), "Recaptured by Rebel Bloodhounds." [Tyler]

7:6. H. B. Vanneman (84th IN); John Hays (18th OH Bty), "That Gunner's Exploit. The Destruction of the Rebel Signal Station at Lookout Mountain."

7:6. H. D. Winship (33rd IL), S. G. Parker (63rd IL), W. B. Britton (8th WI), Charles H. Lee (8th WI), "Old Abe Letters."

May 10

1:1-3. J. B. Kilbourne, "The March to the Sea."

1:4-7. John C. Ropes, "Cedar Mountain."

2:2. Henry H. Searl (35th IL), "That Famous Shot at Lookout Mountain."

2:3-4. Hill, Part 7.

2:7. J. W. Arten, "Another Survivor of a Terrible Wound." [Henry D. O'Brien, 1st MN]

7:4. T. J. Bryant (14th IL), "The Story of Shiloh."

7:4. James Oates (9th IL), "The 9th Illinois at Shiloh."

7:4-5. J. F. Ferguson (31st IN), "The Army Surprised or the Commanders Careless." [Shiloh]

7:5. A. S. McCormick, "Andersonville as It is."

7:5. H. S. Beaman, "Another Comrade's Visit to Andersonville."

7:5. Stephen Hammond, "One of Andersonville's Living Skeletons."

7:5. S. F. Alliger (80th NY), "A Defense of the New York State Militia."

7:6. Charles H. Fish (signal corps), "Comrade Fish and His Critics."

7:6. S. C. Hutchinson (52nd OH), "The Fourteenth Corps at Lovejoy Station."

7:6-7. C. A. B. Fox (86th IL), "The Fight on September 1st."

7:7. Joseph Engomar (46th PA), "The Achievements of the Twentieth Corps."

7:7. J. F. Hill (89th OH), "Who was He?" [11/62 WV—found body of a Union soldier from 1861]

7:7. George E. York (3rd IA Cav), "The Military Record of 5 Brothers." [had brothers in 21st MO and 13th IA]

May 17

1:1-4, 7:7. "Army of the Potomac."

1:5-7. Kilbourne, Part 2.

2:1-2. "Dear Old Uncle John, The Famous Commander of the Sixth Army Corps." [Philadelphia Times]

2:2. "The *Manassas*." [*New York World*]

2:3-4. "Some Old War Songs."

2:5-7. Hill, Part 8.

2:6. "Gen. Early on the Burning of Chambersburg."

7:1-2. William A. Simonds (127th IL), "The Siege and Capture of Vicksburg."

7:2. P. M. Radford (Eng), "Gen. Schofield at Pulaski."

7:2. Benjamin F. Mattern (38th OH), "Baird's Charge at Jonesboro."

7:2-3. E. E. Russell, "Where Hood Gathered No Acorns." [Peach Tree Creek]

7:3. SML (9th NJ), "The 9th New Jersey at Roanoke Island."

7:3. J. C. Wheeler (149th NY), "Speaking Up for the Twentieth Corps." [Peach Tree Creek]

7:3. Smith W. Higgins (USS *Highlander*), "The First Flag Planted on Roanoke Island."

7:5-6. L. B. Moore (36th IN), "His First Battle. An Indiana Boy's Experience in the Second Day's Fight at Shiloh."

May 24

1:5-7. Kilbourne, Part 3.

2:6-7. "The Reynolds Monument." [Gettysburg]

3:6-7. Hill, Part 9.

7:1-3. C. H. Fish (52nd IL), "A Very Daring Raid. About Streight's Expedition and the Fight at the Bridge."

7:4. J. L. Martyn (38th IN), "A Just Tribute to the Valor of the Twentieth Corps." [Peach Tree Creek]

7:4. Frederick Banta (44th IN), "The Twenty-first Corps at Chickamauga."

7:4-5. A. Scott (78th IL), G (38th OH), "The Battle of Jonesboro."

7:5. Lyman H. Essex (8th NY Cav), "The Exploits of a Yankee Mare."

7:5. (NJ), "Rivals of Crocker's Brigade." [6th Corps NJ Brigade]

May 31

1:1-4. "The War in the West. Confederate Occupation of Kentucky. Sherman's Moves."

1:5-6. Kilbourne, Part 4.

1:6-7. "After His Critical Review. Theodore Gerrish in Reply to Comrade Beale." [Gettysburg]

1:7. W. L. Elliott, "The Battle of Moss Creek."

3:3-4. Hill, Part 10.

7:1. Henry E. Clarke (29th OH), "The Fight for the Battery at Peach Tree Creek."

7:1-2. J. W. Hogue (102nd IL), James H. Gaff (129th IL), "Disputed Actions of the Twentieth Corps."

7:2. Oscar F. Avery (11th MI), "The Chickamauga Campaign a Success."

7:2. J. W. Kinnear (29th OH), "The Surrender of Atlanta."

7:2-3. Thomas J. Parker (18th IN), "The Question of a Surprise at Cedar Creek."

7:3. L. W. J. Gilson (15th MI), William F. Montgomery (103rd IL), "Walcutt's Charge at Little Kennesaw."

7:3. Thomas Litchfield (14th OH), "Baird's Division at Jonesboro."

7:3. Addison Tarquary (86th IL), "The Fourteenth Corps at Lovejoy Station."

7:3. James Reid (10th CT), "No One in Front But the Enemy." [Roanoke Island]

7:4. (30th OH), "A Capital Story About the Fifteenth Corps Badge."

7:5-6. George W. Dolsen (8th IA Cav), "Left on the Field. The Exciting Adventures of a Wounded Ex-Andersonville Prisoner."

7:6. Eli J. Wamsley (65th IN), "An Interesting Story of Andersonville."

7:6. Charles W. Carter (4th MA), "Did They Make Good Their Escape?"

7:6. Peter H. Kipp (1st US Ss), "Five Brave Brothers."

June 7

1:5-7. Joseph W. Kirkley, "Gen. Lee's Retreat. Leisurely Pursuit by the Army of the Potomac . . . ."

7:1-3. Hill, Part 11.

7:4. J. Huntington (5th CT), "A High Private on the Battle of Chancellorsville."

7:4-5. Michael P. Cohn (9th CT), "Who Began the Famous Vicksburg Canal?"

7:5-6. W. H. Wells (79th OH), "A Western Man's Account of Peach Tree Creek."

7:6. R. N. Ashmore (15th US), "The Regulars at Jonesboro."

7:6. Nelson F. Kimball (125th IL), "Morgan's Division at Jonesboro."

7:6. Joseph E. Vantine (USS *Richmond*), "The Rebel Ram *Manassas*."

7:6-7. Sumner L. Clark (22nd MI), "The Signal Flag on Lookout Mountain."

June 14

1:1-4. "The War in the West. Thomas at Dick Robinson. Zollicoffer in East Tennessee."

1:5-7. Comte de Paris, "Grant at Vicksburg." [5/22/63]

7:1. M. B. McNitt (19th MI), Thomas M. Bell (102nd IL), "The Charge at Resaca."

7:1-2. W. F. Bain (16th IL), John D. Cosgrove (78th IL), "More About the Battle of Jonesboro."

7:2. W. G. Bradford (81st OH), J. M. Sherwood (66th IN), W. G. Power (39th IA), "Streight's Raid."

7:2. L. Smadley (30th IA), A. Barney (66th IL), "Who Recaptured the DeGress Battery?"

7:2. ABC (30th OH), "That Charge of Harrow's Division."

7:2-3. W. M. Barns, "What Became of the 89th Ohio's Colors?" [Chickamauga]

7:3. L. U. Humphrey, "The Fifteenth Corps at Peach Tree Creek."

7:3. "The Capture of Candle's Brigade." [Gladesville, VA, 7/7/63]

7:3-4. George C. Clouds (5th OH), "A Reminiscence of Cross Keys."

7:4. Alonzo R. Stewart (11th ME), "A Succession of Surprises." [Fair Oaks]

7:4. (43rd IN), "Recollections of Tyler Prison."

7:4. John Gerard (6th VT), "'Potomac Jack's' Prison Experiences."

June 21

1:1-4. Phil Sheridan, "Appomattox." [*North American Review*]

1:5-6. R. C. Brown, "Battle of Spring Hill. The 64th Ohio Vol. Inf. in the Tennessee Campaign."

1:7. T. F. Shuey. "From a Boy's Diary. How the Battle of Gettysburg Impressed a College Student There."

3:4. Obit: John C. Parks (22nd IL).

5:3-4. Biog: Judge Foraker (89th OH).

5:5. Daniel White (31st ME), "Charging the Crater."

7:1. J. F. Iliff, "Lookout Mountain. A Brilliant Account of the Exploits of Osterhaus' Division."

7:1-2. T. P. McReynolds (4th IA), "An Iowa Comrade's Account."

7:2. G. W. Sutherland (13th IL), E. A. Wood (26th IL), "What Illinois Soldiers Say." [Lkt Mt]

7:3. Thomas D. Goundrey (141st NY), "The Twentieth Corps. Some Further Criticisms Concerning Its Disputed Actions and Achievements." [Peach Tree Creek]

7:3. D. G. Blodgett (10th IN Bty),"Wagner's Brigade at Stone River."

7:3. J. T. Hunt (40th IL), D. S. Logan (26th IL), "The Affair on the Left at Little Kennesaw."

7:4. W. H. Peterson (Bty H, 1st NY), "The 1st New York Light Artillery at Peeble's Run." [3/1/65]

7:5. "The Story of a Prison Escape that Resembles Comrade Hill's." [One of Newlin's party]

7:5. W. H. McGuire (12th KS), "The Story of a Boy's Escape from Dixie." [Tyler]

7:5-6. Elijah Kepner (7th IL Cav), "Eighteen Months a Prisoner." [Libby]

7:6. George W. Healey, "A 5th Iowa Cavalryman at Andersonville."

7:6. H. B. Vanneman (84th IN), "How the Rebel Flag at Lookout Mountain was Shot Down."

7:6. George C. McClelland (5th PA Cav), "The Burning of William and Mary College."

7:6. E. Smith (NY), "A Fighting Family."

7:6. Aaron Longenfelter (55th IL), "No Nom de Plumes for Him." [Atlanta battle]

June 28

1:1-5. George E. Pond, "Cedar Creek."

1:6-7. F. W. Perry (10th WI), "Chickamauga."

3:5. (62nd OH), "One Who was There. Some Entertaining Reminiscences of the Siege of Morris Island."

3:6. DHH, "Seen in Dreams. A Gallant Captain of the 3rd Ohio—An Incident of Streight's Raid."

3:6. "Ready to Die. The Touching Appeal of Warren's Men at Mine Run." [from Swinton and an address by Captain Field of Battery L, 4th US]

3:6. J. W. Ridge, "A Precious Relic of Cahawba Prison."

3:7. Henry H. Preston (6th NY Cav), "A Very Close Shave. How a Rebel Shell Came Near Defeating the Purpose of Sheridan's Ride."

5:4. W. S. Rosecrans, "Rosy on Little Phil. Some Interesting Incidents Concerning Sheridan's Early Career."

5:5. "Where Bones Crashed. What General [Morton C.] Hunter had to Say About the Battle of Chickamauga."

7:1-2. J. B. Haldeman (66th IL), J. M. Naylor (81st OH), "Who Recaptured the DeGres [sic] Battery in the Battle Before Atlanta?"

7:3. Samuel Scott (58th IL), "The 16th Corps, and Something About the Hard Marching It Did in the South."

7:3. S. C. Hutchinson (52nd OH), "Last Words About Jonesboro."

7:4. Isaac M. Burton (5th VT), "Vermont Veterans, and the Hot Fight They had at Savage's Station."

7:4. Henry E. Sellers (1st ME Hvy Art), "A Charge that Rivaled the Light Brigade's."

7:4-5. W. A. Simmons (127th IL), "The Vicksburg Canal—Some Sensible Observations."

7:5. (1st MD Cav), "An Incident of Second Bull Run."

7:5. J. L. Millikan, "Reminiscences of the First Battle of the War." [6/2/61]

July 5

1:1-4. "The Wild Cat Fight. Zollicoffer Defeated in His Attempt to Invade Kentucky."

1:4. "Beecher in London." [*New York Herald*]

1:5-7. General William H. Lytle. A Biographical Sketch of One of Ohio's Illustrious Sons."

3:4. William Wallick (51st IN), "Told by Survivors." [Andersonville]

3:4-5. Charles H. DePuy (1st MI Ss), "Union and Rebel Prisons Compared."

3:5. H. T. Talbott (10th WI), "Scenes at Salisbury."

3:5. J. N. Sweeny, "Loyalty to the Last." [exchange at Florence, SC]

3:5. X. C. Reed (4th KY), "Captured on the Stoneman Raid."

3:7. "Some Very Young Soldiers."

3:7. Frederick Heller (10th MO), "The Long-Horned Toad of Monroe." [Monroe City bombardment]

5:3. "The Lee Statue. Unveiling Ceremonies at Lexington, Va.—A Boastful Oration."

7:1. E. J. Foster (10th VT), I. Burk (47th PA), "Union Opinions About Cedar Creek."

7:1. D. Weaver (18th US), William King (16th US), "Recollections of Chickamauga."

7:1-2. W. H. Wood, "An Incident of the Battlefield." [Fredericksburg]

7:2. (3rd NY), "That Keg of Beer, and the Trouble It Caused—An Incident of the Siege of Suffolk."

7:2-3. T. Cotton (129th IL), "'M Quad's' Nonsense About Shiloh."

7:3. A. S. Clyne (63rd NY), "Comrade Clyne's Recollections of Andersonville."

7:3. Mrs. Dr. Buck, "Reminiscences of Fighting Joe." [funeral]

7:3-4. William A. Fulk (59th IN), "The 15th Corps at Tunnell Hill."

7:4. Joseph Whitcomb (USN), "The First Volunteer-Another Claimant."

7:4. H. J. Brademeyer (10th IN Cav), "Whipped by an Old Woman." [Huntsville, AL]

7:5-6. "Fighting Families, and How They Responded to the Call for Volunteers."

7:6-7. C. R. Pomeroy (45th IL), "The Medon Station Affair."

July 12

1:1-4. Andrew A. Humphreys, "The Pursuit of Lee." [from book]

1:5-7. R. W. Surby (7th IL Cav), "The Grierson Raid."

1:7. Albert S. Cole, "Ben, The Signal Officer."

2:6. "The Flag Comes Home." [VMI returned 164th NY colors]

2:7. John Super (10th WI), "Twice a Prisoner."

3:5-7. M. R. Johnson (15th MA), H. S. Stevens (14th CT), Joel S. Stevens (16th ME), "Those Slips of Paper. How Warren's Men Came to Pin Them on Their Blouses, at Mine Run."

7:1. Martin V. Hargrove (23rd NJ), "Chancellorsville—Sedgwick's Movement."

7:1-2. Henry C. Hickerson (11th NJ), "Another New Jersey Soldier's Experience."

7:2. Frank Doster (IN Home Gd), "A Fatal Panic. One Bloody Incident of the Famous Morgan Raid in Indiana."

7:2. J. A. Mather (67th OH), "The D——d Western Brigade at Morris Island."

7:2-3. B. F. Stevenson (22nd KY), "The Fall of Arkansas Post."

7:3. G. W. McKinsey (9th IN Bty), "The Affair of Yellow Bayou."

7:3. Patrick Ballard (10th MO Cav), "The Battle of Brice's Crossroads."

7:4. "Assault of Allatoona."

7:4-5. J. S. Randall (66th IL), "An Old Controversy and a New One." [DeGress's Battery]

7:5. CAK (14th IL), "Corporal Jones. How a Pass from Grant Opened the Road to Temporary Fortune."

7:5. S. E. Farrington (12th NJ), "The Battle of Reams's Station."

7:5. James Fenton (19th IL), A. Lane (35th OH), Samuel F. C. Garrison (40th IA), "Who Shot Away that Signal Flag?" [Lookout Mt]

7:6. TFS, "The First Amputation of the War." [by Surgeon New, 7th IN]

July 19

1:1-3. "The Bridge Burners. An Expedition to Burn Railroad Bridges in East Tennessee. Fight at Ivy Mountain. Nelson's Fight with Williams in East Kentucky."

1:4-6. Surby, Part 2.

1:6. "Bombardments. Their Effect at Charleston and Vicksburg—Insignificant Loss of Life."

1:7. "Battle of Gettysburg. Did General Meade Desire to Retreat on the Second of July?"

1:7. "Lee's Surrender. The Story of the Capitulation as Told by Grant Himself."

3:5-7. R. P. Black (103rd PA), W. J. Klose (184th PA), Will Colton, "Dark Days in Dixie. Reminiscences of Southern Prison Pens Related by Former Inmates." [stories are about Florence, Andersonville, and comparison between Andersonville and Camp Morton]

3:7. John C. Taylor (89th IL), "Going Home Blind."

7:1. JLM (38th IN), "A Gallant Charge." [Jonesboro]

7:1. Hiram A. Harrington (2nd MN), "Gen. Robt. L. McCook's Commission."

7:1-2. (81st OH), J. R. Baird (81st OH), Dick Thayer (9th IA), "Capture of the DeGres [sic] Battery—The Question Settled."

7:2. D. S. Brittin (35th NJ), "Who Saved the Trains at Decatur?"

7:2. George Barkhamer (19th OH), "Riding Morgan's Mule."

7:2-3. C. Disbrow (21st IL), Nathan Edison (16th IL), "The Affair at Monroe Station, Mo."

7:3. JGT, "Incidents of the Virginia Campaign." [mine operation]

7:3. S. S. Baldwin, "After the Battle of Richmond, Ky."

7:4-5. Joel J. Finney (57th IN), "Bloody Battle. A Soldier's Description of the Field of Franklin."

7:5. Joseph C. Freeman (24th OH), "The 24th Ohio Vol. Inf. at Stone River."

7:5. Charles Chandler (6th IA), "The First Troops to Enter Savannah."

7:5. William L. Johnson (116th IL), "The Assault of Fort McAllister."

7:6. J. W. Massie (77th IL), "Another Reminiscence of Arkansas Post."

7:6. George Armstrong (3rd MA Cav), "'Lie Down, Cavalry!'." [Fisher's Hill]

7:6. C. J. Madden (102nd OH), "Appearances are Deceptive." [Perryville]

July 26

1:1-5. George H. Gordon, "Bloody Ball's Bluff."

1:5. A. H. Wood (6th NY Cav), "How Reno Fell."

1:6-7. Surby, Part 3.

2:7. "A Northern Prison. How Rebel Captives Fared at the Elmira Stockade."

3:4-5. "Fighting Families. . ."

3:6. TG (48th USCT), "Coleman's Crossroads."

3:6-7. Robert E. Bigbee (4th OH), J. J. Waley (152nd NY), G. R. Buckman (1st MN), "More About Mine Run."

3:7. "Jeff Davis' Capture. The Official Report of General Thomas in Regard to It."

3:7. John Bracken, "The *Cumberland's* Flag."

4:7. "Last Battle of the War." [*Albuquerque Journal*, regarding Palmetto Ranch]

5:7. Obit: Edward O. C. Ord.

7:1. George Barkhamer (19th OH), "On Picket Before Chattanooga—A Wild Cavalry Charge."

7:1-2. W. G. Hamrich (39th OH), "Incidents of the Battle Before Atlanta."

7:2. J. Hollywood (10th NY), "Capture of Norfolk-President Lincoln's Strategy."

7:2-3. W. W. Gardner (13th US), "How the 13th USA Saved Sherman from Capture."

7:3. J. W. Ansell (62nd OH), "Some Further Reminiscences of Morris Island."

7:3. John L. Richland (111th OH), "A Sad Roll Call at Andersonville."

7:4-5. Ira Miller, "The 17th Indiana, and the Part It Took in the Famous Wilson Raid."

7:5. David Ross (7th MA), "The Assault on Marye's Heights."

7:5. S. C. Van Tassel (USS *Mahopac*), "The First Gun Navy."

7:5. W. H. Austin (16th IL), "The Affair at Tiptonville."

7:5-6. Samuel Plumer (41st OH), "Another Survivor of the First Battle of the War."

7:6. J. M. Emery (3rd PA Hvy Art), "The Mortality at Salisbury Prison."

August 2

1:1-6. "Wilson's Creek Fight."

4:6. "Gordon on Sheridan." [*New York Tribune*]

4:6. J. M. Richardson (16th OH), "The First Amputation of the War."

7:1-2. Surby, Part 4.

7:2-3. H. A. Tripp (29th ME), "Pleasant Hill."

7:3-4. A. J. Ricks, "Ricks' Ride. Carrying the News of Lee's Surrender to Sherman's Army."

7:4. W. A. Simmons (127th IL), "Arkansas Post."

7:5. Lindsay Steele (30th IL), "The Fight at Britton's Lane."

7:5. B. F. Stivers (9th WV), "The Action at Winchester, July 20, 1864."

7:5. George W. Butt (10th MO Cav), "The Affair at Brice's Crossroads."

7:5. Edward I. Ramsay (43rd IN), "When the Camp Ford Prisoners were Exchanged."

7:6. H. C. Cruger (34th IN), "Gen. Hooker's Visit to Rock Island Prison."

7:6. John Rayburn (36th WI), "The Coldwater Skirmish."

8:1. "An Old War Song, and How It was Originally Introduced Into the Army." [When This Cruel War is Over; *Brainerd Tribune* (MN)]

August 9

1:1-3. JLM, "Spring Hill."

1:3-4. F. W. Hall, "Burnt Hickory. How Harden Led the Gallant Charge of the 1st Wisconsin."

1:5-6. J. G. Graham (3rd NH), "Morris Island."

1:6. Robert West (51st NY), Henry Little (1st ME Cav), "Reno's Death."

1:7. W. G. Bradford, "Charleston Under Fire."

1:7. "How Gen. Devens was Saved at Ball's Bluff."

2:1-7. "Old Army Ballads."

3:5-7. Surby, Part 5.

7:1. D. G. Blodgett, "The 10th Indiana Battery at Moccasin Point."

7:1-2. John L. McGuire (51st IL), "Bradley's Brigade at Franklin, Tenn."

7:2. B. F. Magee, "The Cavalry Fight at Decatur, Ga."

7:2-3. G. D. Gray (10th MO), "The Fight at Champion Hills, Miss."

7:3. M. M. Clothter (6th MA Cav), "Yellow Bayou, A Correction."

7:3-4. H. S. Lowry (14th IL), "Affair of Monroe Station—Allatoona."

7:4. A. Brandley (23rd KY), "As to Where Forrest Got His First Whipping." [8/28/62, Round Mountain, TN]

7:4-5. WEM (16th OH), G. W. Baum (2nd IN Cav), J. L. Millikan (16th OH), "The First Amputation of the War." [Philippi]

7:5. W. R. Johnson (15th MA), "Where the Flag was a Welcome Sight." [Chancellorsville]

7:5. James N. Taylor (145th IL), "Treatment of Rebel Prisoners in Northern Prisons." [Alton, IL]

7:6. H. H. Van Camp (27th OH), "A Good Joke on Gen. Nelson."

August 16

1:1-4. "Battle of Belmont."

1:5-6. Washington L. Elliott, "The War in Missouri."

2:4-7. Surby, Part 6.

2:7. George S. Canfield, "Battlefields and Relics. Chickamauga and Stone River Fields After Twenty Years." [*Brainerd Times*]

2:7. E. C. Stedman, "Kearny at Seven Pines." [poem]

7:1. Phillip Dines (41st OH), "Stone River, Some Disputed Points."

7:1. A. S. McDowell, "The 84th Illinois Speaks." [Stones River]

7:1. Robert Townsend, "The 23rd Kentucky Speaks." [Ibid]

7:1-2. L. J. Pentecost, "The 36th Indiana Speaks." [Ibid]

7:2. Edward T. Lincoln, "Flanigan's Heroism. A Brave Deed that Saved the Life of a Helpless Man." [Resaca, 1st KY]

7:2. W. W. Angelo (10th IL), "Not Only Last, But Almost 'Left'." [Atlanta—Jonesboro movement]

7:2-3. E. W. Metcalfe (129th IN), "A Reminiscence of Rocky Face."

7:3. E. W. Metcalfe, "Guerrilla Gurley. How the Murderer of General McCook was Never Executed."

7:3. LL (16th MA), "The Capture of Norfolk."

7:3-4. J. D. Rumnell (18th MO), "General McPherson's Death."

7:4. E. R. Sherman (22nd NY), "They Drank Same Canteen." [Second Manassas]

7:4. Thomas J. Parker (18th IN), "The Capture of Fort Esperanza, Texas."

7:4. WEM (120th OH), "The First Union Colors at Arkansas Post."

August 23

1:1-2. J. E. Hanger, "The First Amputation as Described by the Survivor."

1:2-3. E. W. Metcalf, "Baker at Ball's Bluff."

1:3-4. A. B. Crummel (30th OH), E. V. Richards (51st PA), Matthew Campbell (20th MI), "Reno's Death."

1:4. S. Van Tassel (USS *Mahopac*), "Siege of Charleston."

1:4-5. E. R. Phillips (48th OH), "Imprisonment of a Flag." [Tyler, TX]

1:5-6. L. Emery (7th NH), J. J. King (62nd OH), "Morris Island."

1:6-7. H. J. Walker (12th WI), "The Coldwater Skirmish."

1:7. JOK (5th IN Cav), "Among the Tombs. The Hot Fight in the Graveyard at Blountsville, East Tenn."

2:4-5. Surby, Part 7.

2:6. R. P. Black (103rd PA), "The Florence Fiend. Something About Barlett's Cruelties to Prisoners."

2:6-7. David H. Smith (20th PA Cav), "Mortality at Florence and Salisbury."

7:1. Henry J. Walker (12th WI), "The 17th Corps at Atlanta."

7:1. J. V. Mason (16th IL), "Another Account of the Monroe Station Affair."

7:1. F. E. Coffee, "The 1st Kentucky at Stone River."

7:1. T. M. Young (4th MN), "Brave Deeds at Allatoona."

7:2. William C. Littlefield (14th IA), "Smith's Guerrillas. How the Boys of the 16th Corps Came to be Called So."

7:2-3. W. S. Meek (Opdycke's Brigade), "Fun and Forage."

7:3. Jotham H. Orr (5th NY Hvy Art), "In the Valley."

7:3. J. C. Tressel (96th OH), "General Burbridge at Arkansas Post."

7:3-4. T. Cotton (129th IL), "The Nameless Graves in the Shiloh Cemetery."

7:4. Robert P. McRae (11th PA Cav), "The Fight at South Anna Bridge."

7:4. W. M. Barnes (89th OH), "A Touching Meeting. An Ohio Soldier's Recognition of an Old Enemy at Columbus." [Chickamauga incident]

7:5. Jacob Krissinger (15th OH), "The Fourth Corps."

August 30

1:1-2. P. Mitchell (16th OH Bty), "At Champion's Hill."

1:2-3. H. R. Cowan (1st ME Cav), "A Very Novel Capture Indeed." [4/4/65]

1:3. W. H. Records (72nd IN), "Wilder at Chickamauga."

1:3. William H. H. Benefiel (17th IN), "The Bridge at Mooresville, Ala."

1:4. Thompson, [George W.] (123rd IL), "Song of Wilder's Brigade."

1:4-5. John S. Bosworth (15th IA), "Before Atlanta. The Day that McPherson Fell and Belknap Won His Stars."

1:5-6. (52nd USCT), "Coleman's Crossroads."

1:6-7. H. A. Tripp (29th ME), "Red River Campaign."

2:4-6. Surby, Part 8.

2:6. George S. Canfield, "Ohio's 'Fighting Parson'." [*Brainerd Times*, about Rev. Granville Moody, 74th OH]

2:7. "General Morgan's Death. The Kentucky Belief that he was Murdered After the Surrender—The Facts." [*New York Tribune*]

2:7. "They Met by Chance. How Gordon, the Confederate Spy, was Saved by General [B. F.] Kelley." [*Grafton Sentinel* (IA)]

7:1. William N. Brown (65th IL), "Spring Hill."

7:1. EHC (112th IL), "An Illinois Soldier's Opinion." [Franklin]

7:1-2. Joel J. Finney (57th IN), "Schofield's Blunder at Franklin."

7:2. John Pennock (33rd IL), "No Use for Skirmishers."

7:2-3. Benjamin F. Heckert (16th IA), "At Cumberland Gap." [1862]

7:3. George Yuncker (51st IL), "Bradley's Brigade at Chickamauga."

7:3-4. N. B. Hood, "The 6th Wisconsin Battery at Corinth."

7:4. Perry I. Quick (8th MI Cav), "The Stoneman Raid."

7:4-5. Thomas Cox (USS *Yantic*), "A Lively Hail from a Jack Tar."

7:5. B. Cornell, "The Strange Exploit of the 1st New Jersey Cavalry." [6/62 captured CSA sloop on the Rappahannock River]

7:5. D. A. Lookhart (61st PA), "Where the Colors Never Looked Brighter." [Chancellorsville]

September 6

1:1-3. "Army of the Ohio. Its Organization under Major-General Don Carlos Buell. Rowlett Station Fighting. The 32nd Indiana in Its First Engagement. Fight at Sacramento. Forrest's Cavalry Led by a Beautiful Young Lady."

1:4-7. Washington L. Elliott, "St. Louis to Corinth. The 2nd Iowa Cavalry in Its First Engagement."

2:6-7. Surby, Part 9.

5:1-5. "A Week at Camp Geary. The Encampment of the Grand Army at Gettysburg. [monuments dedicated]

7:1. Benjamin F. Boring, "The 30th Illinois at Belmont."

7:1. William H. Dougherty, "The 5th Indiana Cavalry's Charge at Blountsville."

7:1. George H. Knott, "The Color Sergeant of the 127th Illinois." [Arkansas Post]

7:1. AH (100th IL), "Some of the Vicissitudes of War." [Dalton, GA]

7:1-2. Edmund Rutter (18th US), "The Regulars at Stone River."

7:3. W. H. Knox (76th PA), "Morris Island Again."

7:3. Warren S. Hecox, "The 3rd New York Artillery to the Front." [Morris Island]

7:4. Eli J. Wamsley (65th IN), "Prison Days." [Andersonville and Florence]

7:4. George W. R. Petibone (8th NY Hvy Art), "The Heavy Mortality at Salisbury."

September 13

1:1-4. "Shenandoah Valley."

1:4-7, 3:7. W. N. Morgan (123rd OH), S. J. Campbell (30th MA), William B. Stark (34th MA), S. S. Mathers (13th WV), Theodore W. Krauft (128th NY), John P. Beech (4th NJ), Samuel D. Shipley (30th MA), letters about Cedar Creek.

2:4-5. Surby, Part 10.

2:6. Justice Hall (5th IA Cav), "Florence."

2:6. T. P. Sayre (21st IL), "Castle Thunder."

2:6. S. Ank (14th PA Cav), "Held as a Hostage." [Libby]

2:6. George Banner (19th IN), "Red Headed Barrett." [Florence]

2:6-7. J. A. Sweeny (75th OH), "The Florence Fiend."

2:7. A. J. Willsey, "A Ghastly Death Roll." [Camp Ford]

2:7. William Walner (USS *Signal*), "The Thumb Screw at Tyler Prison."

2:7. George W. Copley (144th IL), "How Rebel Prisoners Fared."

3:4. Jacob Finck (55th IL), W. C. Staton (103rd IL), "Trying to Put Him on the Track Again." [Chattanooga]

3:5. A. P. Carr (34th IN), "The Last Fight. The True Story of the Affair Told by a Survivor." [Palmetto Ranch]

3:5. (51st PA), "How General Reno was Killed."

3:5-6. W. H. Rosevelt (165th NY), "The Siege of Port Hudson."

7:1. W. G. Hamrick (39th OH), M. D. Griffin (39th OH), "The 16th Corps at Atlanta."

7:1-2. Ira J. Bloomfield (26th IL), "Col. Bloomfield's Recollections." [Atlanta]

7:2-3. B. R. Wade, "The Signal Service. A Sequel to Lt. Fish's Story—How McPherson Fell."

7:3. T. H. Carney (5th NY), L. A. Price (3rd VT), A. H. Pickle (1st MN), J. S. Bosworth, C. M. Wood (40th IN), "Casualties of War."

7:4. Thomas M. Shields (6th IL Cav), "Sergeant Shields Corrects Comrade Surby." [Grierson's Raid]

7:5. Allison W. Cheney (30th IL), "The 12th Illinois Cavalry Not at Britton's Lane."

7:5. Walter Scott (47th IL), Letter about Abbeville, MS, 8/23/64.

7:5-6. George B. Morgan, "The 23rd New York at Chantilly."

7:6. Samuel Vanhorn (Bty B, 1st WV), "The Fight at Leetown." [7/3/64]

September 20

1:1-4. "Garfield in Kentucky. [Middle Creek, Gen. Humphrey Marshall]

1:4-5. J. A. Lumbard (147th PA), "The White Stars, and Their Splendid Defense of Culp's Hill, Gettysburg."

1:5-6. W. H. Record (72nd IN), "Hoover's Gap."

1:6-7. J. L. Bowen, "A Noble Life. The Chaplain of the 37th Mass. and His Work." [Frank C. Morse]

2:3-4. Surby, Part 11.

2:5-6. "After Many Years. Frank W. Smith's Visit to Andersonville—Interesting Relics."

6:2. Obit: Samuel M. Wolff (1st OH).

7:1. C. M. Wood (40th IN), "Wagner's Brigade at Stones' River."

7:1. C. F. Kimmel (66th IL), "Another Account of the Rome Crossroads Affair."

7:1-2. Oscar F. Avery (11th MI), "Smith of Brooklyn." [Johnsonville, TN during Nashville Cmpn]

7:2. W. A. Bartholomew (59th IN), "Another Defense of the 6th Wisconsin Battery." [Corinth]

7:2-3. William W. Scott (1st ME Hvy Art), "How Colonel Chaplin Fell."

7:3. W. B. Taliaferro, "Fort Wagner."

7:3-4. "The Costly Charge of the 81st N.Y." [Cold Harbor]

7:4. "Pretty Good for Low." [OH family]

7:4. William S. Webster (58th PA), "The Capture of Norfolk, Va."

7:4-5. W. H. Hutchinson, "It was Gen. Ullman."

7:5. G. W. New (7th IN), "The First Amputation." [*Madison Courier*]

7:5-6. Alexander L. Whitehall (9th IN), "Saved by an Axe. A Curious and Stirring Incident During the Battle of Nashville."

8:2. Charles Treichel, "Another Gettysburg Monument Projected."

September 27

1:1-7, 8:2. Carleton, "Veterans of the Valley. The Virginians Give Sheridan's Boys a Rousing Welcome."

2:4. Adam Dixon (104th NY), William W. Bush (28th NY), "Miss Van Lew and Young Ross." [Libby Prison]

2:7. J. S. Bosworth (15th IA), "McPherson's Death."

2:7. Horace B. Jones (QM Dept, WV), "Some Further Reminiscences of Cedar Creek."

5:3-4. H. C. Cartwell (Bty A, 1st MI), "As to the Dead-Line." [Andersonville]

7:1. C. E. Shank (7th WV Cav), "Gen. Averill's Salem Raid."

7:1. J. F. Starcher (3rd WV), "Captured on the Salem Raid."

7:1-2. Joshua Groft (14th PA Cav), "Averill's Queer Skirmish at Rockly Gap."

7:2. Isaac High (32nd IA), "The Strength of the Confederate Armies."

7:2. Samuel Houston, "How Sigel Lost His Guns at Wilson's Creek."

7:2-3. E. Marsh (33rd IL), "Probably a Slip of the Pen." [Franklin]

7:3-4. Andy Lany, "6th Ohio Cavalry and Their Brilliant Achievements—A Dash with Custer." [Aldie, Upperville]

7:4. Frank Holsinger (8th PA Res), "South Mountain."

7:4. H. A. Tripp (10th ME), "Banks in the Valley."

7:4-5. Eugene A. Cory (159th NY), "The Nineteenth Corps in the Valley."

7:5. Gilbert Eaton (7th CT), "Fort Wagner Again."

7:5. J. G. Graham (3rd NH), "Pocotaligo."

7:6. Royal A. Wheeler, "The 7th Minnesota's Farewell Orders."

October 4

1:1-4. "Shiloh's Scapegoats."

1:5-7, 5:3. J. S. Bosworth, "Crocker's Brigade." [reunion]

7:1. J. S. Chandler (5th VT), "The Vermont Brigade at Marye's Heights."

7:1. J. F. Starcher (3rd WV), "Milroy's Brigade at Cedar Mountain."

7:1-2. W. D. Thompson (97th OH), "Another Raid on Bosworth's Bakery." [Kennesaw Mt losses]

7:2. C. D. Heald (2nd MA), (1st MN), G. R. Buckman (1st MN), J. F. Iliff (13th IL), "A Sharp Contest for the Honor of being the First Three-Years' Regiment."

7:2-3. S. C. Corbett (2nd MA Cav), "When Mosby's Saddle was Emptied." [8/24/63 Centreville, VA]

7:3. F. W. Goodyear (7th CT), Andrew Winter (6th CT), "Fort Wagner."

7:3. John A. Eichar (8th IN Cav), "Some Dashing Cavalry Exploits."

7:3. Samuel Vanhorn (Bty B, 1st WV), "The Misfortune of a West Va. Battery." [12/24/62]

7:4. CG (140th PA), "One of the War's Humble Heroes." [Spotsylvania]

7:4. Henry K. Young (16th US), T. M. Adams (15th IN), "Stone River."

7:4-5. F. E. Coffee, "The 1st Kentucky at Stone River."

7:5. A. Doering (9th IN), "Hazen's Boys at Stone River."

7:6. A. A. Phillips (111th OH), "Col. Bond's Sagacious Conduct at Rocky Face Ridge."

8:2. Jasper N. Ohlwine (30th IN), "The Fourth Corps."

October 11

1:1-4. "The War in Kentucky. How the Battle of Mill Springs was Fought and Won."

1:5-7. Henry J. Walker (12th WI), "In Front of Atlanta."

3:5. "A Turtle Awaiting Its Soldier Owner." [shell inscribed by Henry Durl, 7th NY Hvy Art]

7:1. John L. Walker (50th OH), "Another Account of the Battle of Franklin."

7:1. Thomas C. Yates (4th Co OH Cav), "Something Further as to the Death of McPherson."

7:1-2. D. C. Cameron, "The 1st Wisconsin Battery at Tazewell."

7:2-3. L. R. Collins (50th IL), "It was a Battle. An Illinois Soldier's Opinion of the Fight at Allatoona."

7:3. J. D. Graham (50th IL), "Colonel Hanna's Gallantry." [Allatoona]

7:3. Daniel Goodwin (Bty K, 1st US), "Williamsport and Boonsboro."

7:4. Priestly Young (15th MA), "Somebody Blundered. Some Further Reminiscences of Baker and Ball's Bluff."

7:4-5. Henry D. O'Brien (1st MN), "Neither Baker Nor Stone to Blame."

October 18

1:1-4. "General O. O. Howard's Personal Reminiscences of the War of the Rebellion." [West Point in 1861]

1:4. N. H. Bostwick (52nd OH), "A Soldier's Gratitude." [*Nashville American*, regarding Kennesaw Mt]

1:5-7. "Fort Donelson."

2:4. Samuel S. Boggs (21st IL), "Florence."

2:4-5. J. R. Brown (6th WV Cav), "The Andersonville Spring."

2:5. George W. Benjamin (85th NY), "Give Us a Hand, Old Fellows." [Florence]

5:6-7. Carleton, "A Day at Bull Run, and How a Party of Federals and Confederates Spent It."

7:1. Tillford Dagger (116th IN), "How Gen. Samuel Jones Gobbled Up a Wagon Train." [Clinch Mt. 12/6/63]

7:1. Alfred N. Middleton (1st IN Hvy Art), "More About Spanish Fort and Blakely."

7:1. Jacob Fink (5th US Vet Vols), "A Good Joke on the 5th Conn. Vols."

7:2. "Mother of Co. B, 85th Pa. Vol. Inf."

7:3. FJP, "The 21st Iowa at Vicksburg."

7:3. William H. Wood (2nd NY Cav), "Thrilling Experience of the Harris Light Cavalry."

7:3. L. Steele (30th IL), "The Spiking Party at Island No. 10."

October 25

1:1-2. Howard, Part 2. [secession and war comes]

1:3-5. Carleton, "The Second Bull Run."

1:6-7, 8:2. "Fort Donelson," Part 2.

5:3-4. "Gen. Stedman Dead."

7:1. Ira E. Hicks (7th CT), "The Assault on Fort Wagner."

7:1. W. L. Williams, "The 6th Connecticut's Valor."

7:1-2. W. F. Smith (6th CT), "What Another Comrade Says."

7:2. T. W. Morgan, "The Position of the 76th Penna."

7:2-3. James T. Wolverton (6th TN), "The Lively Experience of Col. Hurst, 6th Tenn." [1863, Sumerville, TN]

7:3. Charles Winters, "Fort Fisher, and the Work of the *Monticello* Along the North Carolina Coast."

7:4. L. B. Bennett, "The 4th Wisconsin at Port Hudson."

November 1

1:1-3. Howard, Part 3.

1:4-5. P. M. Radford, "Where Heroes Rest. An Interesting Account of the National Cemeteries in Tennessee."

1:6-7. "Fort Donelson," Part 3.

5:4-5. "Gettysburg Revisited. Representatives of Mass. Regiments Locating the Memorial Tablets."

7:1. George D. Moore (8th TN), "Were Spears Used at Knoxville?"

7:1. (51st PA), "Did Not Use Spears."

7:1. W. W. Tyson (45th PA), "How Opinions Do Differ."

7:1-2. Austin Curtin (45th PA), "Another Comrade Who Never Saw the Spears."

7:2. S. F. Brown (1st East TN Cav), "A Comrade Who Saw the Spears."

7:2. M. C. White (8th MI Cav), "Who the Spy Was." [Knoxville—Ephraim Todd]

7:2-3. G. S. Killgore (3rd WI Cav), "Spirited Action Not in History." [Fort Gibson, 5/63]

7:3-4. J. S. Gray (21st IN), "The Battle of Baton Rouge."

7:4. N. D. Brown (12th WI), "Carrying the News of Savannah's Fall to the Fleet."

7:4. S. E. Parker, "Where the 30th Iowa Lost Its Colonel." [Vicksburg]

7:5. Henry A. Fistle, "From a Veteran of the 100th Ohio." [Utoy Creek]

7:5. W. F. Cox (63rd IL), "Britton's Lane—Wrong Again."

7:5. A. S. Thompson (2nd IA), "Which Corporal was It?" [Fort Donelson]

8:2. "Return of an Old Battleflag." [CT GAR Post to LA Guards]

November 8

1:1-3. Howard, Part 4. [going to the front]

1:1-5. Radford, Part 2.

1:6-7. "Fort Donelson," Part 4.

2:7. W. S. Sumner (3rd WV), W. A. Morris (3rd WV Cav), "Averill's Raid. More Reminiscences of that Dashing Expedition into Virginia."

3:1-3. "Philip H. Sheridan. He Assumes Command of the Army. An Epitome of His Services."

5:3-5. Speed S. Fry, "General Fry's Story of Mill Springs, and How Zollicoffer Fell By His Hand."

5:5-6. William C. Kise, "The 10th Indiana at Mill Springs."

5:6-7. G. W. Lewis (124th OH), "Missionary Ridge."

6:7. J. Edmonds (120th IL), "Some of the Amenities of Camp Life."

6:7. F. W. Thayer (169th NY), "Christmas at Fort Fisher."

7:1. Charles F. Kimmel (66th IL), "The Battle of Phillips' Creek, Miss."

7:1-2. W. H. Records (72nd IN), "Wilder's Brigade at Hoover's Gap."

7:2-3. M. Craven, "Fair Oaks, and the Part the 105th Penna. Took in the Battle."

7:3. O. F. Perkins, "The 4th Minnesota at Allatoona."

7:3. F. C. Luce, "The 23rd Mass. at Roanoke Island."

7:4. F. P. Candee, "Before Atlanta, and the Part the 11th Iowa Played There."

7:4. Jacob Feather (1st PA Cav), "The Sloop Captured by Cavalry."

7:4-5. Benjamin F. Berth (2nd MA Cav), "Where Mosby's Saddle was Emptied."

7:5. W. W. Thorpe (3rd NY), "Big Bethel."

November 15

1:1-3. Howard, Part 5.

1:3. S. C. Wright (29th MA), "The 29th Mass.' Valor." [Fort Saunders]

1:3. George M. Williams (5th IA Cav), "The Fight at Sugar Creek, Tenn."

1:3. Charles Ruff (56thPA), "Who Opened the Battle of Gettysburg?"

1:4-7. "Fort Donelson," Part 5.

1:7. Peter H. Kipp (1st US Ss), "A Thrilling Incident of Bull Run."

3:1-3. A. S. Fitch (107th NY), "Thick of the Fight. Some Tragic Scenes at the Battle of Dallas, Ga."

6:2-3. M. A. Abbott (7th MI), "A Michigan Soldier's First Fight." [Edwards' Ferry, VA]

7:1-2. E. S. Church (42nd IL), "The Spiking Party at Island No. 10."

7:2-3. J. H. Bradford (30th IL), "In Front of Atlanta."

7:3. James H. Harris (117th IN), "General Brady and General Jones."

7:3-4. Isaac N. Skillman (75th OH), "Where are They Now?" [Andersonville escape]

7:4. Charles D. McClure (72nd IN), George W. Butt (10th MO Cav), "Army Vicissitudes. The Mysterious Search to Which Wilson's Command was Subjected."

7:4-5. "An Unpublished Letter from Wirz."

7:5. J. B. Mattack (15th IN Bty), "A Lucky Indiana Battery."

9:1-2. Carleton, "A National Mecca. The Field of Gettysburg and Its Memorials."

9:3-5. "Off with Grierson. A Dashing Raid in the Rear of Hood's Army and Its Results." [12/64]

9:6-7. Radford, Part 3.

12:1. J. W. Foreman, "The 13th Regulars Battleflags."

12:2. Thomas Hynes, "Where Lyon Fell."

12:3-4. Edward Roberts (7th IL), "Sick and in Prison." [Charleston]

12:4. William H. Clark (92nd NY), "Where Libby Prisoners Served as Army Nurses."

November 22

1:1-4. Howard, Part 6. [DC mobilization]

1:4. George W. Hubbard (3rd ME), "From a Member of Gen. Howard's Regiment."

1:5-7, 8:2. "Fort Donelson," Part 6.

3:4-6. Radford, Part 4.

6:6. IR (65th IL), J. F. Bowen (95th OH), "The Battle of Nashville."

6:7. J. B. Kennedy (100th PA), "Fort Sanders."

7:1. E. R. Johnson (3rd US), "The Affair of Santa Rosa Island."

7:1-2. "The 20th Indiana at Hatteras."

7:2. J. A. Young (7th IN Cav), "Battle of Guntown."

7:3. MES, "Baton Rouge. A Loyal Lady's Description of the Battle—How Her House was Turned into a Hospital."

7:3-4. Elias P. Drake (4th US Cav), "From a Member of Minty's Brigade." [Smith's Crossroads 8/63]

7:4. "Chickamauga." [*Columbus Herald* 11/4]

7:4. E. H. Martin (115th IL), "Steedman at Chickamauga."

November 29

1:1-5. Howard, Part 7. [First Mansassas]

1:5. James G. Jeffries (46th IL), "Still Fighting for the Pastry." [heavy losses]

1:6-7. John A. Joyce (24th KY), "Kennesaw Mountain."

3:2-3. W. W. Boyd, "A Lively Skirmish. The Experiences of the 16th Ohio in the Tazewell Affair."

3:3-4. William F. Moyer, "Cedar Mountain and the Gallant Behavior of the 1st Pa. Reserve [Cavalry]."

5:5. "Old Jubal Early. Some Characteristic Anecdotes of the Irreconcilable Virginian."

6:4. "William J. Bolton." [story about col. of the 51st PA coughing up a bullet]

7:1. F. G. Hastings (1st NY Mtd Rifles), "The Affair at Charles City Crossroads."

7:1. H. P. Walker (47th IL), "The 8th Wisconsin Eagle."

7:1-2. Joseph Edmonds, "The Late Col. R. C. Kise." [120th IN at Wise's Forks, NC]

7:2. R. J. Cooper, "The 96th Illinois at Chickamauga."

7:2-3. J. A. Benedict (2nd VT), "Marye's Heights, and the Gallant Charge of the Old Vermont Brigade."

7:4. (6th IL Cav), "A Day with Grierson. The Ride from Pearl River to Garlandville—Some Interesting Incidents."

8:1-2. John K. Tyler (121st NY), "Glorious Cedar Creek."

8:2. B. M. Kerr (17th PA Cav), "What Regiment Opened the Battle of Gettysburg?"

8:2. L. B. Smith (4th MI Cav), "That Mysterious Search Again."

December 6

1:1-3, 8:2-3. Howard, Part 8. [McClellan, Ball's Bluff]

1:4-6, 3:5. Carleton [Charles C. Coffin], "Saving the Nation. The Story of the War Retold for Our Boys and Girls." [beginning]

7:1-2. "The 6th Corps at Cedar Creek."

7:2-3. Perry I. Quick (8th MI Cav), "Hard Lines! The Pitiful Experience of a Union Prisoner in Southern Pens."

7:3. Lindsay Steele, "The 30th Illinois at Belmont."

7:3-4. "Youngest Soldier."

7:4. R. W. Surby (7th IL Cav), "A Queer Gospel."

December 13

1:1-5. Howard, Part 9.

1:6-7, 8:2-3. Carleton, Part 2.

3:4. "The 12th Iowa at Fort Donelson."

7:1. J. Randall (6th NY), "The Affair of Santa Rosa Island."

7:1. S. D. Savage (2nd VT), "A Vermont Soldier on Gen. Howard's Articles." [First Manassas]

7:1. "The 1st Minnesota at Bull Run."

7:2. Mrs. C. H. Cook, "The Dead of Cahawba Prison."

December 20

1:1-6. Howard, Part 10. [movement to Peninsula]

1:6. A. W. Evans (82nd NY), "The Baltimore Passage in 1861."

1:7, 8:2-4. Carleton, Part 3. [6th MA, 7th NY]

1:6. Jesse Jeffery, "The 5th Maine at Bull Run."

7:1-2. 47th IL letter about the regiment through Iuka-Corinth]

December 27

1:1-3. Howard, Part 11. [Yorktown, Williamsburg]

1:4-6. Carleton, Part 4. [border states and VA]

1:7, 8:3. "Capture of Nashville. General Buell's Advance on Bowling Green, Ky. . . ."

3:4-5. Frank A. Burr, "Sheridan's Ride." [*Philadelphia Press*]

7:1. "The Mine Explosion."

7:1. J. H. Wolfe (8th MI), "Were the Guns Capped?" [Mine]

7:1. S. H. Reynolds, "The 73rd Indiana at Decatur." [AL, 10/64]

7:2. William Iliff, "The 11th Illinois at Fort Donelson."

7:2. E. H. Trick (5th VT), "The 26th New Jersey and Their Mutton."

1884

January 3

1:1-3. Howard, Part 12. [Williamsburg]

1:3. Cyrus S. Hecox (Bty F, 3rd NY), "Deveaux Neck."

1:4-6. Carleton, Part 5. [WV 1861]

1:6. "Battle of Kernstown. An Interview with the General Who Whipped Stonewall Jackson." [J. H. Stine in the *Fort Wayne Gazette*]

1:7, 8:1-2. "Island Number Ten."

3:1-2. E. E. Nutt (20th OH), "Fight at Atlanta. Work of the 78th and 20th Ohio that Day."

3:3-4. Thomas A. Jackson (18th WI), "Holding Allatoona."

3:5-6. "Attack on Corinth. How Price and Van Dorn were Routed There."

3:7. R. W. Surby (7th IL Cav), "Colliersville." [Fall 1863]

5:2. "A Dying Soldier's Will Made at Antietam, and Just Admitted to Probate." [Kingsbury case]

5:3. "The First Prisoner at Belle Isle and Andersonville." [*Pittsburgh Ledger*, about George M. Meadville, 76th PA]

5:4. Obit: Andrew A. Humphreys.

7:1. J. F. Warner (7th IA), "Smith's Division at Donelson."

7:1-2. William Kutz (55th IL), "Beat It Who Can." [heavy losses of his company]

7:2. FC (6th IL Cav), “An Incident of the War.”

7:2. William F. Haller (111th OH), “The 13th Kentucky Volunteers.”

7:2. James Flanagan (4th MA Cav), “Those Guidons Again.”

7:3-4. Michael Heiman (87th PA), “Christmas in Dixie. Adventures of Two Andersonville Prisoners Bound North.”

January 10

1:1-3, 8:1-2. Howard, Part 13. [Peninsula]

1:4-6. “Island Number Ten,” Part 2.

1:7, 2:1-2. Carleton, Part 5. [First Manassas]

3:4. D. P. K. Laven (11th PA Res), “The First Prisoner at Belle Isle.”

3:4-5. George Scott (123rd NY), “Prison Memories. The Bright and Dark Side of Andersonville Twenty Years Ago.”

7:1-2. Robert A. Friedrich (2nd KS), “Reminiscences of Wilson’s Creek.”

7:2. T. W. Lippincott (6th IL Cav), “Hatch’s Division at Nashville.”

7:2-3. J. L. Randle (2nd TN), “Fort Saunders as It is Today.”

7:3. Lewis Butler (67th OH), “A Memorable Charge. An Ohio Colonel’s Recollections of the Assault on Fort Wagner.”

7:4. William B. Thrall, “The 7th Vermont at Baton Rouge.”

7:4. H. A. Tripp (29th ME), “The Truth About Sheridan’s Ride.”

7:4. George W. Oby (6th US Cav), “The Evacuation of Yorktown.”

7:4-5. W. Joyce, “The Fighting 61st New York.” [3/25/65]

7:5. J. C. Smith (96th IL), “As Gen. Smith Saw It. The True Story of General Steedman’s Gallantry at Chickamauga.”

January 17

1:1-3, 8:1-2. Howard, Part 14. [Fair Oaks]

1:4-6. Carleton, Part 6. [aftermath of Manassas]

1:6. W. T. Shaver (32nd MO, 12th MO Cav), “‘Carleton” and Missouri Loyalty.”

1:7, 2:1-4. W. S. Rosecrans, “Friends and Foes. Our Statesmen as Viewed from a Soldier’s Standpoint.”

7:1-2. H. H. Bowles (6th ME), “The Storming of Marye’s Heights.”

7:2. (48th PA), “The Petersburg Mine.”

7:2-3. T. C. Garrigan (38th NY), “Kearney at Williamsburg.”

7:3. J. P. Ward, “One Night on Picket. The Experience of a New Jersey Veteran Before Petersburg.”

7:3-4. J. J. Sullivan, “The 43rd N.Y.V.I. at Williamsburg.”

7:4. “The 20th Indiana, and How Gen. Wise Didn’t Gobble It Up at Hatteras.”

7:4-5. W. S. Ayres, “The 78th Ohio at Bald Hill.” [Atlanta]

8:2. E. W. Smith, “The 5th New Hampshire at Fair Oaks.”

January 24

1:1-2, 8:1-3. Howard, Part 15. [Fair Oaks]

1:3-5. Carleton, Part 7. [Wilson’s Creek]

1:5. V. M. Hodgson (67th NY), “He Placed the Blanket Under Gen. Howard’s Head.” [Fair Oaks]

1:6-7, 2:1-2. “Battle of Pea Ridge.”

6:3-4. Kate B. Sherwood, “The Story of a Premonition. How the Drummer Boy of Mission Ridge Came to be Written.” [regarding John S. Kountz, 37th OH]

6:4. S. W. Huptonstall (Bty D, 5th US), “Griffin’s Battery at Hanover Court House.”

6:5. T. P. Bailey (3rd VT), “At Williamsburg.”

6:5. Frank C. Wasley (2nd NH), “Hooker’s Division at Williamsburg.”

6:5. Edward C. Euston, “The 93rd Pa. Vols. at Williamsburg.”

7:1-2. Thomas W. Pate (USS *New Era*), "Fort Pillow Massacre."

7:2-3. JSS, "Hanover Court-House, and the Hot Work of the 13th New York Volunteers."

7:3. Peter Robertson, "Monacacy, and the Gallant Stand of the 106th New York Against Early."

7:3-4. R. K. Shaw, "The 63rd Ohio—A Disputed Point."

7:4. John P. Beech (4th NJ), "Belle Isle in '62."

7:4. Eli J. Wamsley (65th IN), "A Methodist Minister's Visit to Andersonville."

January 31

1:1-2, 8:1-2. Howard, Part 16. [Peninsula]

1:3-4, 8:3. Carleton, Part 8. [Mill Springs]

1:5-6, 3:3-6. William T. Shaw, "Up the Red River."

2:2. "One of Pennsylvania's Boy Soldiers." [J. D. Golden, 9th, 78th PA]

7:1. Henry Garver, "The 5th Pa. Reserves."

7:1. L. H. Ripley, "The 1st Michigan's March Through Baltimore."

7:1-2. Henry O. Nickerson (3rd RI Hvy Art), "The 3rd Rhode Island Artillery at Deveaux Neck."

7:2. P. H. Taylor (1st MN), "Savage's Station. Nursing the Wounded—The Hospital in the Barn and Its Occupants."

7:2. H. B. Markland (72nd PA), "The Second Corps."

7:3. KBS, "Steedman's Generosity."

7:3. "Gen. Custer's Farewell Order."

7:3. M. L. Trotter (3rd IN Cav), "Opening the Ball at Gettysburg."

7:5. Story about 124th New York monument at Gettysburg.

February 7

1:1-2, 8:1. Howard, Part 17. [Allen's Farm, Savage's Station]

1:3-4, 8:2. Carleton, Part 9. [Fort Henry]

1:5-6, 8:3. Shaw, Part 2.

2:7. Harriet D. Emons, "Ministering Angels. The Touching Reminiscences of a Devoted Army Nurse." [Alexandria, VA]

7:1. D. H. Underhill, "The 2nd Iowa at Fort Donelson."

7:1-2. REL, "The 93rd Pennsylvania Again."

7:2. E. R. Stillman, "Fair Oaks, and the Behavior of the 85th New York in that Battle."

7:2-3. E. Coombe (116th IL), "The 28th of July Before Atlanta."

7:3. J. L. Randle (2nd TN), "Lookout Mountain as It is Today."

February 14

1:1-2, 8:1. Howard, Part 18. [Glendale, Malvern Hill]

1:3-4, 8:2-3. Carleton, Part 10. [Fort Donelson]

1:5-6, 3:5-7. Shaw, Part 3.

2:6-7. Emons, Part 2.

2:7. "The Legion of Honor Which General Rosecrans Undertook to Establish in the Army of the Cumberland."

3:2. George W. Kremer (11th PA Res), "One of the First Prisoners at Belle Isle."

7:1. V. M. Hodgson, "The 1st Long Island (or 67th New York) Vols. at Fair Oaks."

7:1-2. C. W. Green (12th NY), "Butterfield's Brigade at Gaines's Mill."

7:2-3. C. W. Gilman, "5th New Hampshire, and the Part It Took in the Battle of Fair Oaks."

7:3. S. D. Davis (1st VT Cav), "Experience of an Ex-Prisoner—One of Thousands." [Richmond area, Andersonville]

7:3. Carleton, "Carleton and His Critics."

7:4. W. G. McClellan (78th IL), "Chickamauga. The Story About Steedman and the Colors—Another Version."

February 21

1:1-2, 8:1. Howard, Part 19. [Cedar Mountain]

1:3-4, 8:3. Carleton, Part 11. [Island #10]

1:5-6, 3:4-5. Shaw, Part 4.

2:5-6. Emons, Part 3.

3:3. O. O. Howard, "Naglee's Brigade at Fair Oaks."

3:4. W. Simpson, "The Reminiscences of an Officer on Gen. Banks' Staff."

7:1. Lorenzo Durham, "Something About the 4th Illinois Cavalry." [Holly Springs]

7:1. W. H. Clark, "The 92nd New York at Fair Oaks."

7:1-2. J. L. Brown, "The 78th Ohio in Close Quarters." [Atlanta]

7:2. Benjamin Mepham, "The 33rd New York, and Its Gallant Behavior at the Battle of Williamsburg."

7:2-3. John J. Sherman (8th NY Hvy Art), "The Prisoner Who Sang at Belle Isle."

7:3. W. T. McDougle, "An Indiana Soldier at the Battle of Monocacy."

7:3. Matthew L. Kinksom (72nd NY), "Sickles' Brigade on the Peninsula."

7:3-4. J. Hinson (1st OH), "The Baltimore Passage."

7:4. O. R. McNary (103rd PA), "Casey's Division at Fair Oaks."

7:4. G. S. Smiley, "Sherman's Farewell Speech to the 6th Iowa."

7:4. "The 62nd Pennsylvania at Hanover Court House."

7:4. J. D. Jackson, "The 5th Wisconsin at Williamsburg."

7:5. "General Canby's Military Record."

February 28

1:1-2, 8:1. Howard, Part 20. [Second Manassas]

1:3-4, 8:2-3. Carleton, Part 12. [Shiloh]

1:5-6, 3:6-7. Shaw, Part 5.

2:6. Emons, Part 4.

3:6-7. G. S. Smith (48th OH), H. N. Fairbanks (30th ME), "Correspondence of Participants." [Red River]

7:1. Charles Schaffer (3rd US), "The Regulars at Santa Rosa Island."

7:1-2. Frank Gilliland (31st OH), "Hanged with a Hickory Withe." [1st GA Militia member at Chattahoochie River]

7:2. J. A. Abbott (13th IN), "Deserted Farm. An Indiana Veteran's Account of the Battle—The Siege of Suffolk."

7:3. George S. Scullin (Bty A, 1st NY), "Empire Battery at Fair Oaks—Col. Bailey's Death."

7:3. Edward Willis, "The 62nd New York at Fair Oaks."

7:3. N. A. Alexander (Bty A, 1st NY), "The Napoleon Guns at Fair Oaks."

7:3-4. A. P. McFarland, "The 4th Iowa at Pea Ridge."

7:4. "The 38th Wisconsin's Visitors at Petersburg."

8:1. Charles J. Walton (51st NY), "The First Soldiers' Paper of the War."

March 6

1:1-2. Howard, Part 21. [Harper's Ferry, McClellan]

1:3-4, 8:1. Carleton, Part 13. [New Orleans]

1:5. W. H. Clark (92nd NY), "A Hard Road to Travel." [ride to hospital after Fair Oaks]

1:5-6. Shaw, Part 6.

3:3-4. Emons, Part 5. [Gettysburg]

3:3-4. T. Cotton (129th IL), "Gen. O. O. Howard and His Sunday School."

4:5-6. "He Deserves It. How Senator Manderson Earned His Pension." [19th OH at Lovejoy Station, 9/2/64]

7:1. J. J. Jones (3rd WI Cav), "The Baxter Springs Massacre."

7:2-3. George Pressler (93rd OH), "Johnson's Division at Chickamauga."

7:3. F. P. Nichols (7th MI Cav), WHR (108th NY), S. D. Davis (1st VT Cav), "The Frederick Spy. His Name was Richardson, But was He Young or Old?"

7:3. Ira N. Dey (85th NY), "Gen. Casey's Daring at Williamsburg."

7:4. E. E. Williams (Bty A, 1st IL), "The First Soldiers' Paper."

8:2. H. L. Smith (7th IA), "Battle of Belmont."

March 13

1:1-2, 8:1. Howard, Part 22. [Harper's Ferry, South Mountain]

1:3-4, 8:2. Carleton, Part 14. [Memphis]

1:5-6, 8:3. C. H. Fish, "The Shiloh Campaign."

3:7. Emons, Part 6. [late 1863 transfer to Nashville and Murfreesboro]

4:5-6. "The Corps Badges. How and When They Originated and What They Symbolize."

7:1. Charles A. Fuller, "The 61st New York at Fair Oaks."

7:1-2. John M. Tobin (9th MA), "General Porter's Dispositions at Gaines' Mill."

7:2. W. J. Whiting, "The 57th Pa. at Fair Oaks."

7:2. A. H. Apted (16th MI), "No Cavalry at Gaines' Mill."

7:2. (12th CT), "Weitzel's Old Brigade." [Port Hudson]

7:3. J. W. Dove (115th IL), "Chickamauga. Another Account of General Steedman's Gallantry on that Bloody Field."

7:4-5. Albion P. Pease (AAG, Dept. MO), "The Blackest Page. Some Statistics as to Mortality in Rebel and Union Prisons."

March 20

1:1-2, 8:1. Howard, Part 23. [South Mountain]

1:3-4, 8:4. Carleton, Part 15. [*Monitor*]

1:5-6, 8:2-3. Fish, Part 2.

2:6-7. Emons, Part 7. [Chattanooga]

4:7. A. W. Morley (7th OH), Findley Brandon (100th PA), John Hayes (16th IA), C. A. Roy (McClellan Dragoons), William Striblen (27th OH), Henry Tape (27th OH), F. J. Walton (13th PA Res), "First Soldiers' Paper. The Candidates State Honor Continue to Multiply Rapidly."

4:7. "The Builder of the Red River Dam."

7:1. J. W. Hofmann, "The 56th Pa. at Gettysburg."

7:1. E. R. Reid, "The 2nd Wisconsin Sticks to Its Claim." [Gettysburg]

7:1-2. P. Robertson (106th NY), "A Reminiscence of Cold Harbor."

7:2-3. William F. Moyer (1st PA Cav), "Brandy Station."

7:3. F. F. Coggin (165th NY), "Camp Ford."

7:3-4. A. N. Shumard, "The Colors of the 48th Ohio at Tyler."

7:4. David W. Young (139th PA), "Three Shining Names. The Men Who Bore Off the Honors at Petersburg." [4/2/65]

7:4. Chauncey Fish (9th NY Hvy Art), "Wounded in the Back." [Winchester 9/19/64]

8:3. A. L. Morey, "The 98th New York at Fair Oaks."

March 27

1:1-2, 8:1. Howard, Part 24. [Antietam]

1:3-4, 8:2. Carleton, Part 16. [Yorktown, Vicksburg]

1:5-6, 8:3. Fish, Part 3.

2:7. W. H. Hutchinson (99th USCT), "Something More About the Red River Dam."

3:3-4. Emons, Part 8.

7:1. S. N. Stewart (34th IN), "The Last Battle of the War."

7:1. W. H. Hawkins, "The 25th Indiana at Fort Donelson."

7:1-2. P. H. Taylor (1st MN), "The Dead at Savage's Station."

7:2-3. George H. Johnston (AAG, Naglee), "Casey's Division. Still Another Account of Its Gallant Behavior at Fair Oaks."

7:3-4. Andrew Lany, "Principally Daisies. A Good Story of the Early Days of the 18th Ohio."

7:5-6. C. D. Nichols, "Cahawba Prison."

8:1. Amos Sniff, "The Capture of the 16th Iowa." [Atlanta]

7:4. J. V. Pierce (147th NY), "Gettysburg. Last Words as to What Regiment Opened the Battle."

7:4. Joel B. Swett, "The 8th New York Cavalry at Gettysburg."

7:4-5. S. H. Wright (75th NY), "The First Prisoners at Camp Ford."

8:1. C. C. Wilson, "The 13th Illinois and Its Old Missouri Camping Grounds."

April 3

1:1-2, 8:1. Howard, Part 25. [Antietam]

1:3-4, 8:2. Carleton, Part 17. [Peninsula]

1:5-6, 8:3. Fish, Part 4.

3:2. A. L. Brown (4th MN), L. B. Heald (59th IN), "Opinions Differ. Who Raised the Colors on the Jackson Court-House?"

3:2. E. M. Low (9th IL), "As to Being Wounded in the Back."

3:3-4. Emons, Part 9.

5:2. Mrs. Frances E. Hicks (35th MA), "The 25 Heroes of Antietam."

7:1. James H. Crandall (Bty A, 1st NY), "The 1st New York Artillery at Fair Oaks."

7:1. Mrs. F. W. Craine, "Another Account."

7:1-2. J. W. Lee (7th IN), "The Soldiers Who were Whipped at Hampstead." [TX, Custer order 9/65]

7:2. J. L. Eberhart (8th PA Res), "The Penna. Reserves. An Interesting Sketch of the Famous Crack Division."

7:2. S. C. Wright (29th MA), "How Lt. Morris of the *Cumberland* was Saved."

7:2-3. W. H. Dixon, "The 87th Ohio at Harper's Ferry."

7:3. S. A. Walker (15th OH), Augustus E. Zhitler (109th PA), "The Frederick Spy. Some More Interesting Letters Concerning the Hanging of Richardson."

7:3. Charles H. Fish, "Something More About the 57th Illinois Infantry."

7:3-4. George P. Spear, "The Lady Davis Gun." [Island #10]

April 10

1:1-2. Howard, Part 26. [post-Antietam]

1:3-4, 8:1. Carleton, Part 18. [Peninsula]

1:5-6, 8:2-3. Fish, Part 5.

3:3-4. Emons, Part 10.

3:4. C. M. Broadwell (Bty I, 1st US), "Ricketts' Battery at Fair Oaks."

3:4. C. F. Wood (4th ME), "A Hard Road to Travel." [Fair Oaks]

3:4. H. H. Bowles (6th ME), "Relieved by the Rebels." [Salem Church]

3:4. E. F. Shallenberger (85th PA), "Under the Fire of the Swamp Angel."

7:1. E. M. Beardsley (126th IL), "Gen. Grant's Trip Through Mississippi in '62." [Holly Springs]

7:1-2. Charles W. Sarchett, "The 9th Iowa at Pea Ridge."

7:2. Charles T. Reber (2nd MD), "Burnside's Men, and Something About Their Gallant Charge at Second Manassas."

7:2-3. Charles W. Watson (35th WI), "The Expedition Against Mobile."

7:3. William A. Simmons (127th IL), "After the Siege. An Illinois Soldier's Account of a Ramble Through Vicksburg."

7:3. Lawrence Ripley, "The 207th Pa. at Petersburg."

7:4. S. E. Parker (30th IA), R. D. Cramer (30th IA), "The Death of Col. Torrence." [Cherokee Station]

8:1. J. H. Gould, "The 72nd Illinois at Franklin."

April 17

1:1-2, 8:1. Howard, Part 27. [Chambersburg Raid, Burnside]

1:3-4, 8:2-3. Carleton, Part 19. [Peninsula]

1:5-6, 8:4. Fish, Part 6.

3:1-4. Charles W. Walton (51st NY), "Siege of Knoxville."

6:6-7. "Veterans at Shiloh. An Interesting Account of Their Recent Excursion to the Battlefield."

7:1. H. E. Phinney (13th CT), "With Weitzel in Louisiana."

7:1-2. John Thompson (51st IL), "General G. W. Roberts and Stone River."

7:2. J. J. Sherman, "The Song that was Sung at Belle Isle."

7:2-3. D. N. Steele, "Some Further Particulars of Zollicoffer's Death."

7:3. Henry Vessey (2nd MN), "Bob Custer. A Graphic Account of the Capture of the Noted Guerrilla."

7:3-4. Jesse Smith (3rd WI Cav), "Some Further Reminiscences of Baxter Springs."

8:3. James H. Jackman (7th IN Cav), William Williams (5th PA Res), "Soldiers' Papers of the Old War Days."

April 24

1:1-2, 8:1. Howard, Part 28. [Fredericksburg]

1:3-4, 8:2. Carleton, Part 20. [Cedar Mountain]

1:5-6, 8:3. Fish, Part 7.

3:3-4. Jasper N. Olwine (30th IN), "Too Many for Them. How Nine Quartermasters Saved a Whole Division." [Perryville Campaign]

7:3. Michael Heiman (87th PA), "That Charge at Cold Harbor."

7:3. E. M. Tinkham (148th NY), "The 24th and 25th Corps."

7:5-6. A. C. Ranard (22nd IN), "A Soldier Who Obeyed Orders."

7:6. Walter B. Norton (8th NY Cav), "The Last Word About the First Shot." [Gettysburg]

May 1

1:1-2, 8:1. Howard, Part 29. [Fredericksburg]

1:3-4, 8:2. Carleton, Part 21. [Pope]

1:5-6, 8:3. Fish, Part 8.

2:7. "The First Manassas. Gen. J. A. Early on 'What Might Have Been'." [*New Orleans Times-Democrat*]

3:3-4. Robert P. Black (103rd PA), "Plymouth Pilgrims, and How They Came to be Captured—A Survivor's Story."

5:5. Obit: Emerson Opdycke (41st, 125th OH).

7:1. J. P. Van Nest, "The 120th Ohio's Red River Experiences."

7:1-2. T. D. McGillicuddy, "The 50th Illinois at Fort Donelson."

7:2. John Garver (70th NY), "Sickles' Brigade, and the Part that It Played at the Battle of Williamsburg."

7:2-3. Charles H. Eager, "The 15th Mass. at Antietam."

7:3. Thomas Stephenson (25th OH), "Doesn't Want It Rubbed In." [Jackson in the Valley 1862]

7:3. Fred Sommers (19th OH), "How Senator Manderson was Wounded."

7:3. William Joyce (USS *Chillicothe*), "The Death of Lieut.-Commander Couthout." [Red River]

7:3. (9th NY Cav), "The Union Advance from Yorktown to Williamsburg."

7:4. Gilbert L. Eberhart (12th PA Res), "Something Further About the Bucktails."

7:4. W. A. Hall, "The 121st Ohio at Chickamauga."

7:4. E. Kirby, "The First Prisoners at Camp Ford."

7:4-5. L. A. Pierce (3rd VT), "At the Sight of the *Teaser*."

8:1. Thomas J. Smith, "Two Spies Instead of One." [Richardson]

8:1. James H. Burke, "The 95th Ohio at Jackson, Miss."

May 8

1:1-2, 8:1. Howard, Part 30. [Fredericksburg]

1:3-4, 8:2. Carleton, Part 22. [Second Manassas]

1:5-6, 8:3. Fish, Part 9.

3:4. James L. Ferris (USS *Kanawha*), Henry Yeatsch (5th MN), Mrs. Ellen Williams (2nd CO Cav), John B. Embick (5th PA), "Soldiers' Papers."

4:6. "A Chat With Sheridan. The Story of His Raid Around Richmond, as Told by Himself."

7:1. H. B. Kelly, "The 3rd Wisconsin at Frederick, Md."

7:1. W. H. Ward (7th VT), "The Capture of Mobile."

7:1-2. A. W. Stillwell (5th WI), "An Interesting Campaign Suddenly Interrupted." [9/18/64]

7:2-3. Daniel Meehan, "Fair Oaks Again, and the Part Taken by the 57th Pa. in the Battle."

7:3. A. C. Merrill, "Baton Rouge. A 6th Michigan Comrade's Recollections of the Fight."

7:3-4. W. H. Proctor, "Stonewall Jackson and Berdan's Sharpshooters." [Chancellorsville, 3rd GA]

7:4. John P. Beech, "Crampton Pass, and the Part Taken by the 4th New Jersey in the Engagement."

7:4. James Barr (65th IL), "The First Troops Across the Chattahoochie."

8:2. N. J. Marble, "The 38th Wisconsin's Colors." [1864 VA]

May 15

1:1-2, 8:1. Howard, Part 31. [Fredericksburg]

1:3-4, 8:2. Carleton, Part 23. [Maryland invasion]

1:5-6, 8:3. Fish, Part 10.

5:5. N. B. Hood, "The 6th Wisconsin Battery at Jackson, Miss."

7:1-2. Alexander McArthur (12th KS), "Gen. Steele's Expedition."

7:2-3. Phil Kearny, "Glendale. Kearney's Report of the Desperate Battle—General Robinson's Gallantry."

7:3. D. A. Bradley, "The 2nd Connecticut at Cold Harbor."

7:3-4. George W. Oby (6th US Cav), "The Cavalry Advance on Williamsburg."

7:4. "The Drummer Boy of the Rappahannock." [Dan Williams, 24th NJ]

7:4. Jeremiah H. Rickel, "It was the 59th Indiana." [Jackson, MS]

7:4. U. B. Kinsey (51st OH), "The Man Found Hanging at Vining's Station."

7:4. James A. Ralston, "Where the 61st Ohio Began Its Career."

7:5. W. A. Potter (21st MA), "The Siege of Knoxville."

May 22

1:1-2, 8:1-2. Howard, Part 32. [Chancellorsville]

1:3-4, 8:3. Carleton, Part 24. [Antietam]

1:5-6, 2:7. Fish, Part 11.

2:7. John W. Rogers (107th IL), "The Rebel Spy Hanged at Knoxville."

3:1-4. Carleton, "Old Battlefields. Veterans' Excursion to Fredericksburg, Chancellorsville and the Wilderness."

5:5. W. H. Records (72nd IN), "Wilder's Brigade. The Story of the Crossing of the Chattahoochie."

7:1. A. R. Walker, "The 2nd New Hampshire at Williamsburg."

7:1. George Nolan (69th NY), "One Soldier Who Did Not Drink or Smoke."

7:2-3. G. F. Bertine (146th NY), "A Prisoner's Pluck. Sick and Nearly Starved to Death, But Resolved Never to Give Up."

7:3. W. P. Brown (2nd US Cav), "What Interrupted the Music at Fredericksburg."

7:3. H. A. Tripp (10th ME), "How Gen. Mansfield was Killed."

7:3. H. A. Tripp (10th ME), "Knapp's Battery at Cedar Mountain."

7:3-4. F. Van Vleit (2nd MA Hvy Art), "The Capture of Plymouth, N.C."

7:4. M. F. Danford (25th OH), George C. Clouds (5th OH), W. C. Hendrickson (1st NJ Cav), "Fremont's Campaign Against Jackson."

8:2. Fred P. Calkins (16th IL Cav), "The Sumptuous Living at Belle Isle."

8:2. R. E. Looker (13th PA Res), "The Pay of the Bucktails."

May 29

1:1-2, 3:5-6. Howard, Part 33. [Chancellorsville]

1:3-4, 8:1-2. Carleton, Part 25. [Antietam]

1:5-6, 8:3. Fish, Part 12.

5:4. J. H. Mace (2nd NH), "Yankee Doodle—Or Some Other Doodle." [Williamsburg]

6:5. Obit: William McKenna (69th PA).

7:1. F. L. Phillips, "The 2nd Wisconsin at Gettysburg."

7:2-3. John W. Hamlin (26th IN), E. H. Thomas (19th IA), W. I. Bragg (19th IA), W. F. Patton (6th MO Cav), G. W. Salsman (6th MO Cav), J. P. Robens (176th NY), "First at Camp Ford."

7:3. Charles K. Erwin (45th IL), "The Owner Found for that Sutler's Check Picked Up on Shiloh's Bloody Field."

7:3-4. Crosby Johnson (76th OH), "The Cheraw Explosion." [3/65]

8:2. John M. Fry (42nd OH), "A Soldiers' Paper Edited by the Boys Themselves."

June 5

1:1-2, 8:1. Howard, Part 34. [Chancellorsville]

1:3-4, 8:3. Carleton, Part 26. [Bragg, Morgan's Raid]

1:5-6, 8:2. Fish, Part 13.

3:1-4. R. W. Surby (7th IL Cav), "A 64-Days' March. How Hatch Checkmated Hood in the Fall of 1864."

4:6. "The 61st Pa. Revisits Fair Oaks."

7:1. V. P. Twombly, "The 2nd Iowa Inf. at Fort Donelson."

7:1. U. B. Pearsall (48th WI), "Builder of the Red River Dam."

7:1-2. William H. Beal, "General Sherwood and the 111th Ohio Vol. Inf."

7:2-3. J. W. Hofmann, "Gettysburg Again. General Hofmann on the Action of the 147th New York at the Opening of the Battle."

7:3. S. H. Wright (75th NY), "Sabine Pass."

7:3-4. C. Pittman & editor. "Milroy's Brigade at the Second Bull Run."

7:4. George D. Adams (74th NY), "A Rebel Mail Route." [Port Tobacco, MD-Mathias Point, VA]

June 12

3:1-3. Howard, Part 35. [Brandy Station]

3:4-6. Fish, Part 14.

5:4. William J. Ramage, "The 19th Illinois Infantry as 'Printer Boys'."

5:5. William H. Hartwell (9th NH), "How the Music was Cut at Fredericksburg."

7:1-2. Carleton, Part 27. [Bragg in Kentucky]

7:2. William H. Golder, "The 8th Iowa at the Capture of Mobile."

7:3. William L. Diehl (30th IL), C. F. Green (50th IL), "Death to Foragers—Sherman's Retaliatory Order."

7:3. Thomas McAllister (1st MD Cav), "The Capture of Longstreet's Ammunition Train."

7:3. Frederick E. Bullis (106th NY), "The 6th New York Heavy Artillery at Cold Harbor."

7:4. D. M. Bingaman, "The 20th Indiana at Chancellorsville."

7:4. L. B. Morgan, "The 32nd New York Inf. at Crampton Pass."

7:4. H. C. Magoon, "The Dead at Salisbury Prison."

7:4. John G. Waldie (74th IL), "The Knoxville Spy Question Settled."

7:5. D. M. Jack (4th TN Cav), "The Unknown Soldier's Grave Near Corinth."

June 19

1:1-2, 8:1. Howard, Part 36. [Winchester]

1:3-4, 8:2-3. Fish, Part 15.

1:5-6, 5:5. Carleton, Part 28. [Perryville]

5:2. Obit: William McCandless (2nd PA Res).

7:1. W. H. Finch, "The 11th Missouri at Nashville."

7:1. (85th NY), "From One of the Plymouth Pilgrims."

7:1-2. J. D. Hagadorn, "A Drummer Boy at Eight." [John J. Falkenstein, 7th WV, 3rd MD PHB]

7:2-3. J. W. Hofmann (56th PA), "Gettysburg. General Hofmann Replies to the 2nd Wisconsin's Claim."

7:3. Warren Gibbs (1st VT Cav), "Was Fremont Driven Out of the Valley?"

7:3. L. Rossiter, "The 5th Wisconsin at Fredericksburg."

7:3. W. E. Webster (1st NY Bty), "Cowan's Battery at Antietam."

7:3-4. R. R. Sargent, "A 7th Vermont Boy Who was at Baton Rouge."

7:4. Seldon Page (11th MA), "Hooker's Boys. A Mass. Veteran's Reminiscences of the Williamsburg Battle."

7:4. John Morton, "The Colonel of the 37th Indiana." [George W. Hazzard]

7:4-5."General Logan at Resaca." [*New York Times*]

7:5. Obit: George H. Biddle (95th NY).

June 26

1:1-2, 8:1. Howard, Part 37. [cavalry fighting]

1:3-4, 8:2. Carleton, Part 29. [slavery issue & contrabands]

2:1. B. F. Gordon (36th IA), "Mark's Mills."

3:1-3. Fish, Part 16.

3:6. H. P. Walker (47th IL), "Cord-Wood, Not Rails. How Gen. Logan Enforced One of Gen. Grant's Orders." [Grand Junction area]

7:1. T. W. Lippincott (6th IL Cav), "A Reminiscence of Port Hudson."

7:1-2. Hiram Marsh, "The 8th United States Prisoners."

7:2. C. W. Greene (12th NY), "Blackburn's Ford."

7:2. "Talking of Drummer Boys." [Edward Deck, 14th KY]

7:2. M. A. Nott, "The 6th Kansas Boys at Camp Ford."

7:2-3. (21st IL), "A Paper Published by Grant's Old Regiment."

7:3. A. B. Straw plus one unidentified veteran of same regt), "Morgan's Raid, and the Experiences of the 9th Pa. Cavalry."

7:3-4. J. M. Baird, "The 112th Illinois at Knoxville."

7:4-5. Isaac Hall, "Iverson's Brigade, and the Part the 97th New York Played in Its Capture."

July 3

1:1-3. Howard, Part 38. [march to Gettysburg]

1:4-6. Carleton, Part 30. [Iuka]

1:7, 2:1-2. Fish, Part 17.

2:2. Curtis Buck (Bty B, 1st MI), E. McCarty (72nd OH), "Shiloh Echoes."

2:5. David Shively (114th PA), "A Blighted Career. The Work of Two Bullets at Gettysburg—A Sad Story,"

3:3-4. "Stories of Sheridan. His Personal Characteristics—Something About His War Horses."

3:4. J. M. Ferguson (3rd, 6th MO Sm Cav, 13th MO Cav), "Salisbury Prison—A Comrade's Memorial Day Visit to the Site—The Cemetery."

7:1. George A. Root (7th IL Cav), E. W. Coleis (11th IN Cav), S. S. Hite (6th IL Cav), "Some Letters About Hatch's Raid."

7:1. Frank Gilliland, "The 17th Ohio at Resaca."

7:1. W. S. Brown (18th OH), "Short Mountain Crossroads." [8/29/62, TN]

7:2. Thomas Bell (8th NY Cav), "Longstreet's Train. Another Account of How It was Captured by the Escaping Union Cavalry."

7:2-3. James Hane, "Can the 81st N.Y. Verify This Story?" [*Utica Observer*, about woman in the regiment]

7:3. T. C. Garrigan (38th NY), "A Wounded Colonel's Heroism." [Col. Strong at Williamsburg]

7:3. C. E. Smith, "Harper's Ferry, and the Part the 32nd Ohio Vols. Played There."

7:3-4. G. W. Tainter (USS *Choctaw*), "A Shot Navy." [Sabine Pass]

7:4. W. L. Wade (11th IA), "Bald Knob. The Part Taken in the Fight by Crocker's Iowa Brigade."

7:4. T. T. Daniels (2nd IL Cav), "Montgomery's Cavalry at Morganzia Bend."

7:4. Edwin F. Hamilton (13th NY), "A Call for the 5th Alabama." [Gaines' Mill question]

7:5. J. H. Pettigrew (38th IL), "Carlin's Brigade at Perryville."

July 10

1:1-3. "Gen. W. T. Sherman's Address on the Life and Services of Gen. T. E. G. Ransom."

1:4-6, 8:3. Carleton, Part 31. [Corinth]

1:7, 2:1. "Little Shell-Anna. A Touching Incident of the Atlanta Campaign. Born in Battle. How General Logan Became Godfather to the Fatherless."

2:5-6. Fish, Part 18.

3:7. "Fitz-John Porter. Full Text of the President's Veto of the Bill."

7:1. A. N. Reece (124th IL), "The 8th Iowa at the Capture of Mobile."

7:1. J. D. Remington (73rd IL), "Some Reminiscences of General Opdycke." [Franklin]

7:1-2. H. J. Walker (12th WI), "Another Soldiers' Paper."

7:2. D. E. Sweet (11th IA), J. N. Moulton (9th IA), William A. Hunter (13th IA), "Colors at Columbia. First Planted by the 13th Iowa, But Claimed by the 9th."

7:2-3. James Oren (87th PA), "Sixth Corps at Cold Harbor—Prison Reminiscences."

7:3. N. Sessions, Frank H. Cobb (1st US Ss), "The 23rd Georgia. What the 1st Regiment, Berdan's Sharpshooters, had to Do with Its Capture." [Chancellorsville]

7:3. J. W. Laybourn, "The 3rd Ohio at Perryville."

7:4. "Logan and McPherson. The Two Heroes of the Memorable Battle of Atlanta."

7:5. Theodore Eads (51st IL), "One of the Last to Leave Andersonville."

8:2. "Col. Jennison. Some Interesting Incidents of His Adventurous Career in the War." [7th KS Cav]

8:2. "Gettysburg. Celebrating the 21st Anniversary—Dedicating Monuments." [14th, 17th CT, 124th NY, 27th, 153rd PA]

July 17

2:1-2. Carleton, Part 32. [Hatteras, Port Royal]

2:3-4. Fish, Part 19.

2:5-6. "Chat with Sheridan. That Railroad Yarn-His Famous Ride—Lee's Last Ditch."

7:1. H. H. Bowles (6th ME), "The Artillery Duel at Antietam."

7:1. J. G. Faris, "The 86th Illinois at Perryville."

7:4. T. M. Beatty, "The Newspaper Published by the 19th Illinois."

July 24

3:1-2. Napoleon B. Washington, "Poor Mike Mahone. The Story of an Unknown and Unrewarded Hero." [Iuka, Vicksburg]

3:3-4. Carleton, Part 33. [Roanoke Island]

3:5-6. J. J. Grover (71st OH), AJ (41st IL), S. S. Price (14th IL), Eli B. Dawson (77th OH), R. B. Griggs (77th OH), A. S. Winchester (39th OH), F. R. French (2nd KY), John Yarnell (53rd IL), Nathan Nicholson (36th IN), J. W. Clemson (46th OH), George W. Kneipp (48th IL), T. G. Boss (16th WI), Fred S. Hutchinson (15th MI), J. Hinson (signal corps), S. C. Allen (8th IL), "Shiloh. Last Words from Our Contributors. Interesting Points Elucidated."

6:3. William J. Landram, "That Iowa Sergeant at Vicksburg."

6:6. Thomas Kennedy (12th IN), "An Indiana Soldier's Foraging Experience."

7:1-2. R. W. Surby, "A Cavalry Sketch. The 7th Illinois Cavalry at the Battle of Moscow, Tenn."

7:2. W. G. Malin (15th OH), "A Prisoner's Story." [Andersonville and Millen]

7:2-3. (63rd OH), "The Fight at Corinth."

7:3. A. S. Winchester. "The First Soldiers' Paper—the 39th Ohio at the Front."

July 31

3:1-3. Carleton, Part 34. [Beaufort, Fort Macon, blockade]

3:3. J. E. Funkhouser (36th IA), "The Site at Camp Ford." [present condition]

3:4-5. "Cavalry Raids. The Ill-Fated Expeditions to the Rear of Atlanta."

3:6. "A Famous Army Nurse." [*Buffalo Express*, about Mrs. Davis, 69th NY]

4:2-3. Biog: John S. Kountz (37th OH).

4:6. Obit: Walter Harriman (11th NH).

5:1-2. L. F. Gould, "A Joke on Sheridan. East Tennessee Pies and Plug Tobacco, Woman Soldiers, Scouts and Spies."

7:1. Hosea C. Aldrich, "Cahawba Prison, and the Horrible Treatment Which Our Veterans Received There."

7:1-2. William Miller (77th OH), "Two Brothers at Mark's Mills."

7:2. L. E. Tripp (5th MI Cav), "With Custer at Yellow Tavern and in the Raid Around Richmond."

7:2-3. B. F. Strong, "The 101st Ohio at Perryville."

7:3. F. J. Hall (70th NY), "Where Jackson Fell. A Veteran's Idea of Where the Spot Can be Located."

7:3. J. B. Harris (34th IN), "An Incident of Champion Hills."

7:3. E. F. Jones, "The 2nd Iowa Cavalry as Printers."

August 7

1:4-6. Carleton, Part 35. [Pea Ridge]

2:3-4. "Washington Forts. Encircling the National Capital with a Cordon of Earthworks."

3:1-4. Frank D. Mason & John W. Fry (42nd OH), "Chickasaw Bluffs."

3:4. A. S. Winchester (39th OH), "The Iuka Campaign."

3:4. (99th NY), "'Off for the War.' Funny Experiences of the First Volunteers of the War."

6:3. W. B. McPherson (8th WI), "'Old Abe,' The Eagle of the 8th Wisconsin." [Corinth]

7:1. E. M. Eckley (11th MO), William Reavis (56th IL), "Battle of Corinth."

7:1-2. J. S. Lemmon (5th IA Cav), "The Last to Leave Andersonville."

7:2. Stuart F. Hoskinson (73rd IL), "Franklin."

7:2. V. M. Hodgson (67th NY), "Storming Marye's Heights."

7:2-3. E. A. Wilson (1st US Ss), "Who Captured the 23rd Georgia?"

7:3. G. S. Robinson (115th IL), "Chickamauga. Two Glimpses of the Field by a Wounded Man."

7:3-4. W. F. Sutherland (QM), "Execution of Champ Ferguson."

7:4. C. M. Butt (25th WI), "Cheraw. Destruction of Ordnance Stores There."

7:4-5. J. S. Bosworth (15th IA), "July 22, 1864. Gallantry of Logan, Giles A. Smith and Others on that Terrible Day."

8:2. L. A. Rose (42nd IL), "From Chickamauga to Andersonville."

8:3. William P. Derby (27th MA), "Roanoke Island. Where the Credit Belongs."

8:3. "Col. Hatch. His Wounds at the Battle of Moscow—Who Commanded in the Fight?"

8:3. S. W. Crane, "The 9th New Jersey at Roanoke."

August 14

1:6-7. Carleton, Part 36. [abolition of slavery]

2:3-4. "Washington Forts," Part 2.

2;5. Benjamin Woodward (22nd IL), "Mother Bickerdike."

3:1. (63rd Ohio), "Corinth."

3:1-2. William White (5th MI Cav), "Death of Dahlgren."

3:2. (11th MI), "A Scout's Experience. Captured on the Stoneman Raid—Threatened as a Spy—Attempts to Escape."

3:2-3. D. F. Marshall (Bty H, 1st US), "The Deaths of Generals Berry and Stonewall Jackson."

3:3. George E. Davis (10th VT), "Captor or Prisoner. An Incident of Monocacy Battle, July, 1864."

3:3. WHG (78th IL), "A Chickamauga Incident."

3:3. T. E. Hunt (10th MO), "'Poor Mike Mahone'." [Iuka]

3:3. J. M. Drake "The 9th New Jersey at Roanoke Island."

3:4. Noah T. Frederick (22nd IA), "That Iowa Sergeant." [Vicksburg]

3:4. D. W. Wood, "The 20th Ohio at Atlanta."

3:4. Robert Duncan (29th IL), "The Expedition Against Spanish Fort."

3:4. Benjamin Urton (7th KY Cav), "Camps Dick Robinson and Nelson."

3:4. W. S. Stewart, "The 11th Missouri at Corinth."

3:4-5. William Marland, "The 2nd Mass. Battery at Baton Rouge."

3:6. T. Cotton (129th IL), "That Lonely Grave."

6:6. Cliff Warden, "Anna Ella Carroll."

7:3. W. H. Tallman, "The 2nd Michigan Cavalry and the Raid in the Rear of Atlanta."

August 21

1:1-3, 2:4-6. George E. Davis (10th VT), "Washington's Peril. Checking Jubal Early's Northern Raid."

1:4-6. Carleton, Part 37. [blacks in the war]

2:3. W. J. Landrum, "General T. E. G. Ransom."

3:1. Charles C. Wehrum (12th MA), "Iverson's Brigade. Its Capture at Gettysburg—The Regiments that Forced Its Surrender."

3:1. JCM, "The 16th Iowa at Iuka."

3:1-2. A. C. Menor (13th WI), "A Cahawba Prisoner."

3:2. John L. Taylor (2nd IA Cav), F. T. Gilmore (63rd OH), "Battle of Corinth. The Part Taken in It by the 63rd Ohio and the 11th Missouri."

3:2. W. H. Scorsby (115th NY), "Surrender of Harper's Ferry."

3:2-3. William H. Redhouse (99th NY), "Another of the Naval Brigade."

3:3. J. J. Bailey (9th IL Cav), "Moscow, Tenn."

3:3. (7th IL Cav), "Moscow Again."

3:4. Judson W. Currier (6th ME), "Marye's Heights. Composition of the Storming Column."

3:4. Charles Frye (6th ME), "Storming Marye's Heights."

3:4. G. W. Watson, "Execution of Champ Ferguson."

3:4. T. S. Young (2nd OH Bty), "Incidents of Champion Hills."

3:4-5. W. R. Nash, "The 25th Illinois at Pea Ridge."

3:5. Hans Powell, "Ulric Dahlgren. Was His Corpse Mutilated and Insulted—Call for More Information."

3:6. J. E. Saunders (2nd NH), "A Queer Dungeon."

August 28

1:1-3. Howard, Part 39. [Chattanooga relief]

1:4-6. Carleton, Part 38. [Stuart's raid, Burnside]

1:7, 2:1. Return I. Holcombe, "Massacred Soldiers. The Brutal Slaughter at Centralia, Mo."

2:2-4. Frank H. Mason and John W. Fry (42nd OH), "Arkansas Post."

2:5-6. R. Scott (37th IL), "An Amateur Spy. A Turn of Duty in Discovering Nests of Missouri Rebels."

3:1. L. W. Barnard (3rd NY Cav), "Before Petersburg. Diary of a New York Cavalryman. Stirring Experiences." [5/30-6/11/64]

3:1-2. J. S. Lemmon (5th IA Cav), "Cavalry Raids Near Atlanta."

3:2-3. J. J. Whitney (18th WI), "Allatoona."

3:3. Fred Reitz (21st WI), "Foraging. An Interesting Trip After Rations in the Heart of South Carolina."

3:3-4. B. F. Stevenson (22nd KY), "Chickasaw Bayou."

3:4-5. S. S. Cane, "The 7th Mo. Cavalry."

3:5. John H. Thurston (4th MN), "A Scene at Corinth."

3:5. William P. Gladson (8th IA Cav), "The McCook Raid."

3:5. N. D. Brown (12th WI), "Who Held Bald Hill?"

3:6. George C. Jenkins (Bty B, 2nd IL Art), "Corinth Again."

3:6. (9th IL Cav), "The Fight at Moscow."

3:6. O. B. Lawrence (24th IN), "Andrews's Division." [Mobile]

5:3. "More Claims to a Late Muster-Out."

5:3. Joel R. Swett, "They Scooped Up Forrest." [8/30/62]

6:4. D. M. Hays (15th OH), "That Lonely Grave."

September 4

1:1-3. Howard, Part 40. [Wauhatchie]

1:4-6. Carleton, Part 39. [Fredericksburg]

1:7, 2:1-3. Frank H. Mason & John W. Fry (42nd OH), "Vicksburg Campaign."

3:1. H. H. Van Camp, "Chickamauga. The Stubborn Fight Made by the 21st Ohio."

3:1. A. L. Brown (4th MN), "The Artillery at Iuka."

3:1. Orange S. Pratt, "The 7th Mass. at Marye's Heights."

3:2. (73rd IL), "Reminiscences by an Illinoisan of Generals Sheridan and Logan. Why He is Fond of Them."

3:2-3. James Van Houten (7th IL Cav), "The 7th Ill. at Somerville, Tenn."

3:3. Halsey Lathrop (6th PA Res), "Salisbury. The Outbreak of the Prisoners and Its Murderous Repercussion."

3:3. William J. Landram, "That Iowa Sergeant."

3:3-4. J. Cole (8th WI), "Evacuation of Iuka."

3:4. William Blyke, "A Slander Refuted. The Story False that the President's Brother was Shot by His Own Men." [Major William Arthur, 4th NY Hvy Art]

3:4. Charles D. Palmer (1st WI Cav), "A Wisconsin Soldier's Song Book."

3:4. Howard Barwis, "The 119th Pa." [Fredericksburg 1863]

3:5. "Gettysburg." [12th NJ monument]

September 11

1:1-3. Howard, Part 41. [Chattanooga preliminaries]

1:4-6. Carleton, Part 40. [Fredericksburg]

1:7, 2:1-2. C. A. Hobbs (99th IL), "Matagorda Bay. End of a Long Cruise on the Tempestuous Waters of the Gulf. A Chilly Norther. Capturing Fort Esperanza and Indianola . . . ."

2:3. "Texas Unionists. The Terrible Massacre of the Nueces. Slaughter of Wounded Men."

2:5. H. N. Dunlap (5th KS Cav), "Bushwhackers. Lively Experiences Along the 'Kansas Line'."

3:1. D. M. Conner (1st IN Cav), "Chancellorsville. General Devens's Response for the Humiliating Defeat."

3:1-2. (9th IL Cav), "In Re Moscow."

3:2-3. R. M. Dihel (30th IL), W. S. Ayers (78th OH), C. M. Fuller (78th OH), M. Loop (68th OH), "Champion's Hill."

3:3. T. G. Orr (5th IA), "The Battle of Iuka."

3:3-4. "Steele's Army."

3:4. W. Atkinson, "A Brave Boy. Story of the 'Champion' of the 3rd Va. Cavalry. A Sharpshooter Who did Deadly Work." [John L. McMurray]

3:4. J. A. Quigley (The 49th Pa. at Marye's Heights."

3:5. W. H. Bradford (110th USCT), "A Mock Execution."

3:5. William P. Derby (27th MA), "New Berne."

3:5-6. James S. Schermerhorn (127th IL), "The Capture of Arkansas Post."

3:6. "The 21st Ohio at Chickamauga."

4:7. Charles W. Parker (16th CT), "Who Stole the Pigs?"

4:7. E. W. McElroy (45th PA), "The Outbreak at Salisbury."

5:2. W. M. Stewart (21st MA), "Where the Credit Belongs." [Roanoke Island]

5:2. Hugh L. Thompson (3rd WI Cav), "Loyalty in Southwest Missouri."

5:2. G. Chalmers (12th IN), "The Explosion at Cheraw."

5:3. Charles A. Hale (5th NH), "Gettysburg, The Work Being Done by the Battlefield Memorial Association."

September 18

1:1-3. Howard, Part 42. [Lookout Mountain]

1:7, 2:1-2. Carleton, Part 41. [Fredericksburg]

3:1. Lorenzo Durham, "The Fight at Moscow, and the Part the 61st U.S.C.T. Took in the Action."

3:1-2. E. M. Robbins, "The 20th N.Y. Cavalry." [12/10/64]

3:2. L. E. Bicknell (Andrews Sharpshooters), "Marye's Heights. As to the Work Done by the Second Division of the Second Corps."

3:2. V. M. Hodgson (67th NY), "The 1st Long Island's Work."

3:2-3. W. H. Armstrong, "The 1st N.Y. Mounted Rifles to the Front." [Petersburg]

3:3-4. J. D. Remington, "Missouri in 1862. Saving the D. Vernon—Wetting the Bushwhacker's Caps."

3:4. A. E. Ripley (44th IL), "Pea Ridge."

3:4. L. B. Crocker (55th IL), "Chickasaw Bayou."

3:4-5. (1st WI), "That 'Masked Battery'." [Witz Adams, Liberty, MS]

3:5. M. C. Wilson (38th IN), "Chickamauga. The Third Brigade of the Third Division, Fourteenth Army Corps."

3:5. John W. Beaty (91st IL), "Prairie Grove."

3:6. Condensed Letters: L. G. Flenner (76th OH), Arkansas Post; Henry Colin (42nd IN), Youngest.

5:4. (7th CT), "A New Enemy. The Time When Gen. Joe R. Hawley Showed the White Feather."

5:4. J. S. Bosworth (15th IA), "A Warning that did Not Warn." [Shiloh]

7:5. John M. Ewing (15th OH), George A. Root (7th IL Cav), W. E. Hamilton (8th MI), "Premonitions."

8:3-4. WSB, "The *New Ironsides.* The Blockade of Charleston—Bombardment of the Forts."

September 25

1:1-3. Howard, Part 43. [Missionary Ridge]

1:4-6. Carleton, Part 42. [Rosecrans]

1:7, 2:1-3. Mason & Fry, Part 2.

3:1. D. W. Lindsay (Bty B, 1st NY), "'In Battery.' Fun at Fredericksburg—Silencing a Battery—Unhealthiness at Chancellorsville and Gettysburg."

3:1-2. Albert S. Ashmead, "Stuart's Raid."

3:2. J. E. Shepard, "Drewry's Bluff. The Gallant 9th N.J."

3:2-3. J. K. Mason (19th IA), "The Capture of Spanish Fort."

3:3. R. M. Hoskinson (73rd IL), "Chickamauga. A Father and Son Escape Rebels."

3:3. CS, "The 55th Ohio at Chancellorsville."

3:4. J. W. Morton (19th IA), "Prairie Grove."

3:4-5. A. R. Barlow (157th NY), "Ziba Cleyes. The Modest Tale of the Company Cook."

3:5. W. E. Baldwin (29th OH), F. A. Seymour (7th OH), W. H. Poor (7th OH) G. W. Holloway (29th OH), Sol R. Smith (12th OH), "Port Republic."

3:6. Phillip Jenkins (77th IL), "Arkansas Post Again."

3:6. Condensed Letters: H. C. Buffington (23rd WI), Red River; C. D. Maylor (11th VT), 6/23/64; George W. Culp (14th IA), Cahawba Prison.

5:3. F. W. Browne (23rd MA), "New Berne."

5:3. S. J. Henderson (4th IN Bty), "Lincoln's Tenderness." [Metcalfe-Gurley, 8/16/63]

5:3-4. E. A. Wilson (1st US Ss), "Presentiments."

7:5. "'Johnny.' Another Girl Who was Discovered Wearing the Blue." [6th US Cav]

October 2

1:1-3. Howard, Part 44. [Missionary Ridge]

1:4-6. Carleton, Part 43. [Stones' River]

1:7, 2:1-3. Mason & Fry, Part 3.

3:1. A. L. Brown (4th MN), Q. O. Russell (4th MN), William Campbell (26th MO), B. Knoepfelt (16th IA), "Iuka. The 48th Indiana's Conduct, and the 11th Ohio Battery's Losses."

3:1-2. (1st NY Mtd Rifles), "Foraging in Virginia."

3:2. David Ginther (61st PA), D. Bond (1st MN), "Marye's Heights."

3:2-3. James Beale (12th MA), "Chancellorsville."

3:3. C. D. Morris (33rd IL), "Bruinsburg. The First Regiment to Land—Running Into the Enemy at Port Gibson."

3:3. J. P. Van Nest (120th OH), "More About the Capture of Arkansas Post."

3:3-4. George E. Harrington (40th NY), "The Third Army Corps to the Front." [Fredericksburg]

3:4. J. H. White (12th WI Bty), "Allatoona."

3:4. F. M. Gee (32nd WI), "Capture of Gun at Cheraw, S.C."

3:4-5. D. O. Pickard (2nd US Ss), "Who Captured the 23rd Georgia?"

3:5. E. G. Wetmore, "The 21st Ohio at Chickamauga."

3:5. T. D. W. Manchester (22nd WI), "The Case of Col. [William L.] Utley." [contraband slave boy story]

3:5-6. Condensed Letters: Lewis Hutchins (40th MA), Cold Harbor.

5:2. Obit: Thomas C. Fillebrown (USN).

7:5. H. Clay Hartwell, "A Yankee Trick in a Rebel Prison." [Belle Isle]

October 9

1:1-3. Howard, Part 45. [Knoxville]

1:4-6. Carleton, Part 44. [Stones' River]

1:7, 2:1-2. Mason & Fry, Part 4.

3:1. John G. Reid, (1st WV), "Port Republic."

3:1-2. J. S. Chandler (5th VT), "The 49th Pa. at Marye's Heights."

3:2. A. W. Stillwell (5th WI), "Premonitions. Killed on the Rappahannock."

3:2. O. J. Ribble (14th WI), "Wounded at Vicksburg."

3:2. William H. Githens (78th IL), "Other Cases." [wounds]

3:2-3. Thomas M. McKelvey (76th PA), "The Wreck of the *Quinnebaug*." [7/20/65]

3:3. John M. Morris (46th OH), "A Chicken-Roost Raid."

3:3. Hugh L. Thompson (3rd WI Cav), "Southwest Missouri. The Terrible Cost of Loyalty in that Section."

3:4. A. R, Barlow (157th NY), "Union Treatment of Rebel Prisoners." [Morris Island]

3:4. George P. Hall (78th IL), "From a Prisoner's Diary." [Savannah, Millen]

3:5. S. S. Knapp (10th KS), "Prairie Grove."

3:5. S. S. Woohn (56th OH), "The Cairo Hospital."

3:5. F. E. Cheney (16th IA), "The Gun at Rock Island Arsenal."

3:6. Condensed Letters: William Burghart (54th NY), Chancellorsville; A. Z. Converse (40th OH), Lookout Mountain.

4:6-7. Wallace Foster (13th IN), "General Post Office, Army of the Potomac."

5:3. S. C. Cheney (12th WI), "Allatoona."

5:3. Balfour Cowan, "Passing the Batteries at Vicksburg."

5:4. (PA), "Chancellorsville."

8:3. T. G. Van Meter (37th IN), "An Amusing Incident."

October 16

1:1-3. Carleton, Part 45. [Stones' River]

1:4-6. "Loyal Mountaineers. Bushwhackers Harry the Unionists of Eastern Kentucky. Retaliating Schemes. Trapping Guerrilla McKenzie in Whitney County. Stough's Operations. The Successful Ambuscade at Horseshoe Bend."

2:4. "A Historic Sword. A Gift Purchased for Gen. Reynolds, But Which He Never Saw." [*Columbia Herald*]

3:1. R. H. Martin (46th IN), C. A. Hobbs (99th IL), Frank Swigart (46th IN), "Port Gibson."

3:2. William Wilson, "The 66th Illinois at Dallas."

3:2. J. J. Weiler (17th IN), "The Last Man Killed."

3:3. J. H. Osborn (55th OH), "Chancellorsville Again."

3:3. William Blasie (43rd NY), "Marye's Heights."

3:4. George S. Newman (38th IN), "Chickamauga."

3:4. (PA Res), "No Foraging Allowed." [Fredericksburg]

3:5-6. Condensed Letters: J. P. Wood (23rd WI), Pleasant Hill; George H. Welsh (94th IL), Prairie Grove; J. G. Gates (8th IN Cav), Rosseau's Raid; John J. Hawkins (39th IL), Drewry's Bluff; J. T. Stanhope (2nd MO Cav), Youngest; Martin Folder (78th PA), Oldest;

Daniel Youken (WV), Port Republic; William Jones (42nd OH), Bruinsburg; T. J. Lacey (19th IL), Chickamauga; J. W. Wickham (33rd IL), Gen. Mower; L. F. Parish (17th IA), Iuka; William E. Loring (141st PA), Gettysburg; H. L. Buchanan (30th MO), Vicksburg siege.

5:3. "End of Rebellion. Official Correspondence. Looking to the Cessation of Hostilities."

October 23

1:1-3. Carleton, Part 46. [Farragut, Baton Rouge]

1:4-6. M. McCoy (2nd OH), "First Bull Run."

3:1. J. S. Weaver, "Ready for a Raid. Some of the Exploits of the 11th Pa. Cav."

3:1. I. B. Kinkead (77th OH), "That Lonely Grave Again."

3:1-2. E. R. Kilpatrick (3rd IA Cav), "Who Captured Gen. Marmaduke?"

3:2. J. W. Rumple (55th OH), "Chancellorsville Again."

3:2. Jess S. Langston (110th OH), "He Buried the Wrong Man." [Spotsylvania]

3:2. S. A. Ranlett (36th MA), "Not that Lieut. Holmes." [Knoxville]

3:3. J. G. Harker (109th NY), William H. Thompson (38th WI), J. P. Fitch (38th WI), "Fort Mahone. What Regiment was First in the Fort, and Who First Planted the Colors?"

3:4. C. D. Morris (33rd IL), "Vicksburg. A Graphic Description of the Charge." [5/22/63]

3:4-5. Charles W. Black, "Harper's Ferry Cowards. A Comrade of the 32nd Ohio Vindicates His Regiment."

3:5. Robert H. Taylor (20th IN), "How the Rebel Rifle-pits were Captured." [Fort Hell 1864]

3:5. J. R. Lowe (55th OH), C. O. Holt (30th ME), F. N. Hamlin (161st NY), F. S. Brunn (78th OH), "Premonitions."

3:6. Condensed Letters: A. C. Sherman (18th IN), Port Gibson; James A. Brown (10th IL), Chickamauga Campaign

4:2-3. "Beauregard's 'Battle of Bull Run'." [editorial about *Century Magazine* article]

5:4. John H. Dickson (60th IN), G. D. Armstrong (97th IL), "Who Planted that Flag? Arkansas Post Again."

5:6. W. Gardner (115th NY), "The Oldest Man."

October 30

1:1-3. Carleton, Part 47. [Chickasaw Bayou, Arkansas Post]

1:4-6. Albert Green (9th IL), "Max Steiner. The Adventures of a German Boy During the War."

1:7, 2:1-2. McCoy, Part 2.

3:1. J. S. Covert (Bty H, 1st OH), "Port Republic."

3:1-2. C. H. Ulmer (41st IL), "The Charge at Jackson."

3:2. W. H. Armstrong (1st NY Mtd Rifles), "The Blackwater. Fight at the Ford—The Damage Done by Thirty Determined Rebels."

3:3. A. H. Worthern (7th MO Cav), "Prairie Grove."

3:3. John A. Van Doren (21st IN Bty), "Chickamauga."

3:3. J. H. Craven (96th OH), "Vicksburg. The Offer to Surrender."

3:3. J. C. Lindsey (7th OH), "The Man Who Opened the Atlanta Campaign." [L. O. Craig, Bty D, 1st OH]

3:4. Charles F. Kimmel (66th IL), "The Fight at Dallas. An Extract from an Illinois Soldier's Journal."

3:4. Charles Grant, "The Cracker Line Brings Up Rations for the Army of the Cumberland."

3:4-5. R. Miller (1st MI Cav), "Yellow Tavern. Who Took the Guns in the Great Cavalry Battle There?"

3:5. A. R. Kibble (12th WI Bty), (81st OH), "Allatoona."

3:6. William Howland (8th US), "Captured in Texas. How Gen. Twiggs Turned Traitor."

3:6. Condensed Letters: Simon T. Callahan (64th IL), Cheraw; Benjamin B. Edmands (36th MA), Campbell's Station.

5:4. C. D. Morris (33rd IL), "'Let Up.' Comrade Morris Thinks He Has Been Pounded Enough."

November 6

1:1-3. Carleton, Part 48. [Mud March, Hooker, Kelly's Ford]

1:3. C. C. Bowen (6th OH), "Stone's River."

1:4-6. Free S. Bowley (30th USCT), "The Crater."

1:7, 2:1. O. B. Ormsby, "Gen. T. E. G. Ransom. A Premature End of a Knightly Gentleman."

3:1. Simon Van Akin, Jr. (1st US Ss), "Who Captured the 23rd Georgia?" [Chancellorsville]

3:1. G. W. Gillis (6th OH Cav), "A Narrow Escape." [Dahlgren's Raid]

3:1. W. J. Landram, "Gen. Logan's Courage." [Vicksburg siege]

3:2. S. J. Bailey (9th IL Cav), "Moscow Again."

3:2. A. Beattie (4th NY Hvy Art), "In Front of Petersburg." [from diary entry of 11/17/64]

3:3. George F. Usry, "Horse Trading, and How Sherman's Bummers Conducted the Business."

3:3. Cyrus Sears, "The 11th Ohio Battery at Iuka."

3:4. Thomas H. Moore (19th IA), "Prairie Grove Again."

3:4. W. P. Pease (99th IL), "Port Gibson Again."

3:4. C. D. Hadley (14th IA), "Premonitions."

3:4-5. Michael P. Coen (9th CT), "Baton Rouge."

3:5. Charles W. Walton (51st NY), "A Hero of Roanoke." [LtCol. de Monteil, 53rd NY]

3:5. B. S. Batchelor (2nd MN), "Fun in Camp. Life at Chattanooga During the Siege."

3:5. JGR, "Shields at Kernstown."

3:6. Moritz Tschoepe (24th WI), "A Hot Day. Reminiscences of the Battle of Peach Tree Creek Before Atlanta."

3:6. H. S. Archer (28th ME), "Fort Butler. A Lively Little Battle in La. During the Siege of Port Hudson."

3:6. Condensed Letters: L. D. Butler (20th IN), Savage's Station & Phil Kearny.

November 13

1:1-3. William Pittenger, "Engine Thieves."

1:4-6. Howard, Part 46. [encampments at Chattanooga]

1:7, 2:1-2. Carleton, Part 49. [Chancellorsville]

3:1-2. D. D. Rose (11th MI), "Stone's River."

3:2. M. G. Aldrich (26th IA), "Resaca."

3:2. W. B. Roby (33rd OH), "From Gen. Carlin's Aid." [brigade composition during Chattanooga & Atlanta]

3:3. S. A. Ranlett (36th MA), "Jackson, Miss. Sufferings of the Ninth Corps."

3:3. Henry J. Lyda (USS *Essex*), "The *Essex* and the *Arkansas*."

3:3. James P. Byrne, "Pauline Cushman."

3:4. William Deacon (87th NY), "The Third Corps. Why Do Historians Seem to Agree in Ignoring It?"

6:3. George H. Uhler (93rd PA), "Honoring Their Dead." [Gettysburg monument]

6:4-5. "Anna Ella Carroll. History of the Movement For Her Relief."

November 20

1:1-3. Pittenger, Part 2.

1:4-6. Howard, Part 47. [march to Gettysburg]

1:7, 2:1-2. Carleton, Part 50. [Chancellorsville]

3:1. WIlliam A. G. Cobb (8th US), "Twiggs's Victims."

3:1-2. J. Cole (8th WI), "Col. Murphy and Holly Springs."

3:2. Charles W. Walton (51st NY), "Petersburg. The Battle of the Mine."

3:2. D. L. McKay (99th NY), "Roanoke and New Berne."

3:3. J. B. Shaw (10th IN), "The Fourteenth Corps. History of the Organization of the Third Division."

3:3. Henry G. W. Cronk, "The 120th Indiana." [NC 1865]

3:3. A. R. Proper (3rd VT), "Army of the Potomac Post-Office."

3:3. I. G. Miller (2nd US Ss), "How the Rebel Rifle-Pits were Captured." [9/9/64]

3:4. G. Norton, "*Gen. Thomas*. The Gunboat that did Great Service at Decatur."

3:4. James N. Nye (17th OH), "Chickamauga."

3:4. George B. Jenness (34th IL, 4th US Vet Vols, 18th KS Cav, 19th KS Cav), Who Served the Longest?"

3:5. S. C. Gallup (3rd VT), Oliver Edwards (10th MA), Henry Brunner (1st WV Cav), "Premonitions."

3:5-6. R. H. Martin (46th IN), "Won't Let Comrade Morris Rest."

3:6. A. P. Carr (34th IN), "The Last Man Killed."

5:3. Biog: O. P. G. Clarke (2nd RI).

5:3. Henry Guckert (39th OH), "The Men Who were Blown Up at New Madrid."

5:5. Timothy Miles (11th MI Cav), "The Fight at Saltville, Va."

6:3. "Company E, 'Round-Heads'." [*New Castle News*, about 100th PA]

6:3. J. P. McGahey (190th PA), "Was It Apple or Locust?" [Appomattox tree]

7:3. G. Chalmers, "The 12th Indiana. A Regiment that Marched 6,000 Miles in Its Four Years of Service."

November 27

1:1-4. Howard, Part 48. [Gettysburg]

1:5-7. Pittenger, Part 3.

2:1-3. Carleton, Part 51. [Chancellorsville]

3:1-2. H. H. Martin (20th IA), "Mobile Bay. A Graphic Account of the Operations by Land and Water."

3:2. Alex Bird (154th NY), "The Eleventh Corps at Chancellorsville."

3:2. William Marland (2nd MA Bty), "Baton Rouge."

3:2. T. Cotton (129th IL), "The Grave of Rogers." [Corinth]

3:3. Hugh L. Thompson (3rd WI Cav), "Missouri Rebels." [correction]

3:3. W. A. Bartholomew (59th IN), "The Charge at Vicksburg."

3:4. J. M. Johnson (21st MO), "The Longest Service."

3:4. William H. H. Stone (11th OH Cav), Thomas Legge (4th IA Cav), "The Capture of Marmaduke."

3:4. J. C. Tressel (96th OH), "Suggestions as to Correspondents—The Surrender at Vicksburg."

3:4. D. M. Conner (1st IN Cav), "Who was Responsible for the Surprise at Chancellorsville?"

3:5. William B. Witcraft, "The Brave 10th Illinois." [Chattanooga]

3:5. H. K. Young (16th US), "Stone's River."

3:6. Condensed Letters: James W. Huntzinger (21st IN), Baton Rouge; John A. Boyd (64th IL), Cheraw.

7:4. (1st WV), "Port Republic."

December 4

1:1-4. Pittenger, Part 4.

1:5-7. Carleton, Part 52. [Chancellorsville]

2:5-6. J. E. Stinzer (9th IL), "Corinth. A Rebel Officer's Account of His Experiences in the Fight." [from Lieut. Labruzan, 42nd AL]

3:1-2. William Charleton (11th WI), E. L. Hawk (114th OH), John R. Holbrook (11th IN), Port Gibson. Who Commenced the Fight?"

3:2. Warren C. Hursh, "The 1st N. J. Cav."

3:3. H. J. La Four (33rd MO), "Nat Leavitt."

3:3-4. J. C. Harris (83rd PA), S. C. Wright (29th MA), "Was It Apple or Locust?" [Appomattox tree]

3:4. William W. Watkins, "A Famous Cavalry Raid." [Kilpatrick's Atlanta Raid]

3:4. Silas Benham, "Gen. Benham at Carrick's Ford." [7/18/61]

3:5. "Did You Know Kidney? Evidence Wanted for the Man Who Killed a Famous Guerrilla." [John P. Kidney, 4th MI]

3:5. S. W. Taylor (52nd PA), "Casey's Division at Fair Oaks."

3:5. John W. Cornish (58th IL), "A Corinth Reminiscence." [10/2/62 raid by guerrillas]

3:5-6. Condensed Letters: H. H. McCulloch (7th IN), Youngest.

5:4. T. H. Capern (4th NJ), "Another Case of Premonition."

5:5. George Graham (13th IN), "Who Wrote that Bogus Order?"

December 11

1:1-3. Pittenger, Part 5.

1:4-6. E. C. Culp (25th OH), "The Eleventh Corps, and the Defeat It Met at Chancellorsville. Who was Reponsible?"

1:7, 2:1-2. Carleton, Part 53. [Chancellorsville]

3:1. Peter B. Ayars (99th PA), "Petersburg. The Capture of the Rebel Pickets in Front of Fort Hell."

3:1-2. Cyrus Spore (5th WI), "The 'Wind Up' at Petersburg."

3:2. "Logan's Gun Car. A Fort on Wheels Which Did Good Work." [Jackson TN 1862]

3:2. B. F. Jones (1st WV Cav), "Battle of Port Republic."

3:2. R. I. Patterson (19th IN), "The 'Iron Brigade' at Gettysburg."

3:3. Frank Swigart (46th IN), "Bruinsburg." [corrections]

3:3. C. D. Morris (33rd IL), "Comrade Morris Comes Back."

3:3. H. C. Denny (18th IN), "Who Captured the Guns at Magnolia Hills?" [Port Gibson]

3:4. JB (16th IL), "The 5th Wisconsin Battery at Resaca."

3:4. J. D. Remington (73rd IL), "The Fight at Franklin."

3:4. T. Cotton (129th IL), "That Lonely Grave Opened."

3:5. A. L. Brown, "The 4th Minnesota at Iuka."

3:5. C. H. Enos, "The Hospital in the Wilderness." [6th Corps]

3:5. C. T. Hilton (8th ME, 117th USCT), "The Longest Service."

3:5. Frank L. Benepe, "The Oldest Man." [Samuel Widock (41st IL)]

3:6. Joseph McCoy (10th PA Res), "A Rebel Deserter's Grave."

December 18

1:1-3. Pittenger, Part 6.

1:4-7. Howard, Part 49. [Gettysburg]

3:1-2. C. E. Goldsbaugh [sic] (5th MD), "Winchester."

3:2. R. Hannaford (2nd OH Cav), "Chancellorsville. A Survey of the Field Upon Which the Battle was Fought."

3:3. Charles S. Brooks (4th VT), "'Bose.' A Sheep that was Not Palatable."

3:3-4. Carl Schwigler (103rd NY), "'Whit.' The Only Mounted Man in the Battle of James Island—Where He Got His Horse."

3:4. Lorenzo Durham (61st USCT), "Moscow Again."

3:4. W. B. Keith, "The 35th Indiana."

3:5. S. C. Wright (29th MA), "A Sea Captain's Ruse. Fooling the Pirate Semmes, of *Alabama* Fame."

3:5. "The Pa. Reserves."

3:5. George C. Clouds (5th OH), "Port Republic."

3:6. L. D. Rarick (207th PA), "Premonitions."

5:2. L. B. Bennett (4th WI), "The Rebel Ram *Arkansas*."

5:2. P. M. Sharrot (56th NY), "Casey's Division at Fair Oaks."

December 25

1:1-4. Orlando B. Willcox, "Alexandria. Graphic Account of Its Capture and Occupation in 1861."

1:5-7. Pittenger, Part 7.

2:1-2. Carleton, Part 54. [blockade]

2:3-4. "Jeff Davis. Alexander H. Stephens's Very Frank Opinion of Him." [letter to Herschel V. Johnson, 4/5/64]

3:1. G. F. Warner (134th NY), "Chancellorsville."

3:1. James Beale (12th MA), "Chancellorsville. Col. Culp' Versus Comrade Conner's Recollections."

3:1-2. Joseph Marsh (USS *Winnebago*), "The *Tennessee*."

3:2. John M. Lovejoy (121st NY), "Rappahannock."

3:2. J. T. Abbott (5th ME), "The Second Brigade." [Rappahannock Station]

3:2. J. E. Leasure (16th OH), "Chickasaw Bluffs."

3:3-4. E. K. Barnhill (73rd IN), "Streight's Raid."

3:4. Edward Short, "The 87th Indiana is Heard From."

3:4-5. J. W. Hogue (102nd IL), D. S. Hunter (2nd MN), George A. Clarke (4th MN), A. Lawrence (102nd IL), "Those Chaplains Again."

3:5. R. H. Crist (21st IN), "The Rebel Ram *Arkansas*."

3:5. Edward S. Past (1st MN), "Apple versus Locust." [Appomattox]

3:5. Henry Infield (97th OH), "The Fight at Franklin."

3:5. George A. Clarke (4th MN), "Who Planted the Flag at Jackson?"

5:2. H. McKinsey (125th IL), "The Charge at Kennesaw."

8:2. J. H. Craven (96th OH), "Fort Morgan."

1885

January 1

1:1-3. Howard, Part 50. [Gettysburg]

1:4-7. William Rickards (29th PA), "'Above the Clouds.' The Brilliant Movement by Which Lookout Mountain was Captured."

2:1-4. Pittenger, Part 8.

3:1-2. A. R. Prescott (Bissell's Eng), "The Gun Car."

3:2. James Beale (12th MA), "Gettysburg. A Revision of General Howard's Account of the Battle."

3:2. Henry A. Tripp (10th ME), "Cedar Mountain."

3:3. JWA (3rd IN Cav), "Kilpatrick's Dash Around Atlanta."

3:4. J. S. Covert (Bty H, 1st OH), "Port Republic."

3:4. R. Dexter (100th NY), "Casey's Division at Fair Oaks."

3:5-6. S. M. Lanham, "A Fearful March from Matagorda Bay to San Antonio."

5:3-4. Theodore Austine (78th IL), "Andersonville."

5:4. William E. Loring (141st PA), "How Gen. Graham was Captured at Gettysburg."

8:3. H. M. Anderson (3rd ME), "Chancellorsville."

8:3. J. F. Bowen (95th OH), "The First Flag at Jackson, Miss."

8:3. R. B. Fielding (11th IN), "Who Captured the Guns at Magnolia Church?"

8:3. F. L.Squires (2nd VT), "Who Stole Those Pies?"

January 8

1:1-4. Frank H. Mason & J. H. Fry (42nd OH), "On the Teche. Soldiering Amid the Bayous of Louisiana."

1:5-6. Edward Hatch, "Moscow, Tenn."

1:7, 2:1-2. Carleton, Part 55. [Suffolk-Norfolk]

2:3-6. Pittenger, Part 9.

3:1. J. C. Harris (83rd PA, 5th Corps HQ), "Gettysburg. The Rebel Repulse at Round Top."

3:2. Charles A. Hale (5th NH), "Col. Cross. Did He Write Poetry?"

3:2. J. V. Pownall (29th IN), "Stone's River."

3:2. A. J. Sanger, "The 22nd Michigan Flag." [in possession of 54th VA]

3:3. John Shaw (7th MO Cav), "An Unlucky Scouting Party." [Spring 1864 near Pine Bluff, AR]

3:3. William A. Aspenwall (47th IN), "Hovey's Division at Port Gibson."

3:3. J. J. York (7th MO), "The First Union Flag at Vicksburg."

3:4. A. B. Hutchinson (49th PA), "Rappahannock."

3:4. William M. Davis (4th MN), "Iuka."

3:5-6. Lanham, Part 2.

7:6. (1st IA), "A Hard Rations Army Song." [MO 1861]

January 15

1:1-4. Howard, Part 51. [Gettysburg]

1:4. A. R. Barlow (157th NY), "A Defense of the Eleventh Corps."

1:5-7, 2:1-5. William T. Sherman, "Jefferson Davis. A Terrible Indictment of the Chief of the Southern Confederacy."

3:1-2. "The Big River Bridge, and the Fight Between Co. E, 33rd Ill., and Jeff Thompson's Men."

3:2. S. Grimshaw (52nd OH), "The Charge at Kennesaw."

3:3. "Why the Bridge at Port Republic was Not Burned."

3:3. Augustus Hansen (35th MA), "Who Planted the Flag at Jackson?"

3:3. D. W. Smith (120th IN), "Hovey's Division at Resaca."

3:4-6. Pittenger, Part 10.

6:6. A. J. Rowinsky (19th OH), "Spring Hill to Franklin."

7:3. D. M. Conner, "The 12th Indiana."

7:3. A. J. Manley, "The 14th Wisconsin at Corinth."

January 22

1:1-4. William P. Carlin, "Before the War. What the Regular Army Found to Do Thirty Years Ago."

1:5-7. Carleton, Part 56. [PA Campaign plans]

2:1-4. Pittenger, Part 11.

3:1-2. John G. Reid. "Gettysburg. Criticism on Gen. Howard's Monograph on the Battle. Documents Bearing on the Case. Letter of Gen. Gibbon. Howard's Letter of Thanks to Col. Carroll."

3:2. John L. Jacobs (184th PA), "Andersonville. How a Soldier Escaped by Personating a Dead Man."

3:2. Alexander Bird (154th NY), "Chancellorsville."

3:2. J. B. Round (121st NY), "Rappahannock."

3:3. (10th MO), "Jackson, Miss. Who Planted the Flag on the Court-house?"

3:3. John W. Cornish (Bty K, 1st MO), "July 4, 1863. The Way Prentiss's Command Celebrated It at Helena, Ark."

3:3. J. W. Mullery (5th NH), "Col. Cross."

3:4. W. H. Armstrong (1st NY Mtd Rifles), "Longstreet's Expedition." [Suffolk]

3:5. John N. Beach (40th OH), "Lookout Mountain."

January 29

1:1-3. Carlin, Part 2.

1:4-6. Howard, Part 51. [post-Gettysburg]

1:6-7. J. T. Chalfant (11th PA), "Libby Tunnel. Who is Entitled to the Honor of Manning and Digging It?"

1:7. Ira E. Hicks (7th CT), "Battery Strong. An Interesting Account of the Monster Gun that did Grand Work at Charleston."

2:1-4. Pittenger, Part 12.

3:1. W. Simpson (Banks' AADC), "The Teche Campaign."

3:1. F. C. Jones (64th NY), "The Last Fight of the Army of the Potomac."

3:2. Daniel M. Conner (1st IN Cav), "Chancellorsville."

3:2. D. Lostutter, Jr. (7th IN), "Port Republic."

3:3. Nelson P. Lord (18th CT), "Winchester."

3:3. L. H. Dewey (10th MI), "The Charge at Kennesaw."

3:3. George H. Clough (4th RI), "The Youngest Soldier."

3:3. James W. Louks (2nd NH Bty), "Premonition."

3:4. Obit: James Hammond (3rd OH).

3:4. A. C. Parliman (177th PA), "Suffolk."

3:4. W. L. Ayers (78th OH), "The First Troops to Enter Vicksburg."

3:5. V. True (10th ME), "Cedar Mountain."

3:5. W. S. Campbell, "An Exciting Chase." [St. Charles, AR, 1864/65, vs. Col. Logan's guerrillas]

3:5. Samuel Kelso (Bty D, 1st OH), "The Battle of Ivy Mountain."

3:6. Condensed Letters: George W. Hess (82nd OH), Chancellorsville.

February 5

1:1-3. "Pegram's Raid." [1863 KY]

1:4-6. Carleton, Part 57. [Gettysburg opening]

1:7, 2:1-2. William P. Carlin, "Military Memoirs."

2:3-4. Pittenger, Part 13.

3:1-3. John M. Baer (120th OH), "Snaggy Point Slaughter. Capture of City Belle, John Warner, and Three Gunboats."

3:3. M. M. Lacey (69th IN), "Charge at Vicksburg."

3:3. I. J. Heaps (27th IL), "A U. S. Senate Way Down in Dixie." [captured at Belmont, POW at Memphis]

3:4. "The Acorn. The Corps Formerly Commanded by Gen. Geo. H. Thomas."

3:4. Brewer Smith (65th OH), "Spring Hill to Franklin."

3:4. (8th OH), "Port Republic."

3:5. Alonzo Cowgill (10th IN), "First Division, Army of the Ohio."

3:5. Richard Oulahan (164th NY), "Suffolk. The Irish Legion—Circumstances of the Killing of Col. Kimball."

February 12

1:1-3. "Pegram's Raid," Part 2.

1:4-6. Carlin, Part 2. [pre-war]

2:2-4. Pittenger, Part 14.

2:4. "Death of a Brave Sailor. Charles B. Pyne's Experience in the Navy During the Late

Civil War." [*Boston Globe*; took part in Fort Sumter boat attack]

2:4. "A Hero of Millen Prison." [*Detroit Free Press*, about Louis Abear, MI Cav]

3:1-2. "Libby Prison. A Picture of Life There by an Ex-Inmate."

3:2. W. A. Bentley (signal corps), "Howard at Gettysburg."

3:3. J. A. Wright, "The 1st Minnesota. Its Part in the Battle of Gettysburg."

3:4. Evan H. Mitchell (54th IN), "The 'Yearlings.' A Comrade Defends Them and Tells of Chickasaw Bayou."

3:4. Joe Worthington (Bty B, 1st WV), "Port Republic Again."

3:5. R. E. McBride (13th PA Res), "The Bucktails. Some Notes in the History of that Gallant Band."

3:5. William W. Perry (82nd PA), "Young Enough."

3:6. Condensed Letters: John F. Huss (13th IL), Chickasaw Bluffs.

6:6. (92nd IL), "At Chattanooga."

February 19

1:4-6. Carlin, Part 3. [Shiloh, Corinth]

1:7, 2:1. "Pegram's Raid," Part 3.

2:2-4. Pittenger, Part 15.

3:1-2. James E. Stewart (2nd KY), "Shiloh."

3:3. JMR (1st IA Cav), "The Brave Feat of Two Young Ladies." [flag of 2nd NJ Cav at Mansfield]

3:3. Joseph J. Huston (80th OH), "Who Planted the Flag at Jackson, Miss.?"

3:3. James A. Hunter, "The 7th Kansas Cavalry."

3:4. Benjamin F. Cook (12th MA), "The Eleventh Corps at Gettysburg."

3:5. A. J. Hamilton (12th KY Cav), "The Libby Prison Tunnel."

3:5. "The First Union Flag at Richmond." [Gov. R. J. Oglesby to John A. Andrew, 5/23/65]

3:5. Adam Leake (29th PA), William E. Narregan (195th PA), Alexander Terrel (42nd OH, 5th US Cav), G. O. Culver (203rd PA), "The Youngest Volunteer."

February 26

1:1-4. Carlin, Part 4. [Louisville Campaign]

1:5-7. Carleton, Part 58. [cavalry fighting]

2:1-4. Pittenger, Part 16.

2:5. J. Willard Brown (signal corps), "The Siege of Corinth."

2:6. Jonathan Labrant (58th IL), "Who Stole the Tobacco?"

3:1. W. H. Armstrong, "A Good Record. Sketch of the Services of the 1st N.Y. Mounted Rifles."

3:2-3. David W. Lindsay (11th IL), "In the Beginning. The Experience, Spicily Told, of a Recruit in the Original 'Three Months' Service'."

3:3. S. W. Taylor (52nd PA), "Naglee's Old Brigade. Its Splendid Services in the Peninsula Campaign."

3:3. C. E. Goldsborough (5th MD), "Winchester."

3:4. Charles Emerson (7th ME Hvy Art), "A Pleasant Foraging Expedition."

3:4. C. J. Madden (102nd OH), "Relics of Three Wars."

3:5-6. Condensed Letters: W. C. Hotterb(45th PA), has Bible of W. W. Hutchinson (46th VA); John Newland (MO), Jackson; George W. Hitchcock (89th NY), Suffolk; A. P. Heminger (121st OH), Kennesaw Mountain; R. N. Ashmore (MS River Flotilla); John Wilson (8th KY), Lookout Mountain; J. H. Watson (57th IN), Franklin; N. B. Abbett (33rd IN), Atlanta; L. D. Shearer (138th PA), 4/6/65.

5:2. James Beale (12th MA), "Comrade Beale Heard From." [Gettysburg]

5:2. "Death of Gen. [T. E. G.] Ransom."

5:3. S. E. Jones (12th WI Bty), "Iuka."

5:3. George A. Clarke (4th MN), "Who Planted the Flag at Jackson?"

5:3-4. Alonzo Cowgill (10th IN), "The First at Chickamauga."

6:3. J. Bresnahan (27th IN), "Chancellorsville."

7:6. R. B. McCollum (110th OH), "Who Killed A. P. Hill?"

8:4. "An Amusing Episode." [Abercrombie's 3/62 advance toward Winchester]

March 5

1:1-3. Carlin, Part 5. [Perryville]

1:4-6. J. H. Wilson, "Freedom's Knight, Who Fought for Liberty in Many Lands. Maj. Ernst J. Hoffmann, Chief Engineer of the Eleventh Army Corps.

1:7, 2:1-2. Carleton, Part 59. [move north]

2:3-4. Pittenger, Part 17.

3:1-2. R. C. Huskey, "The Western Flotilla. Adventures of the Gunboats Taylor [sic] and Lexington."

3:2. C. H. Enos (122nd NY), "How the Sixth Corps Heard the News of Lee's Surrender."

3:2. H. E. Carpenter (21st CT), "Siege of Suffolk."

3:3. W. S. Brown (18th OH), "Capture of Huntsville. The Exploits of Mitchell's Division Along the Memphis and Charleston Railroad."

3:4. H. S. Melcher (20th ME), "Little Round Top."

3:4-5. F. E. Olney (40th OH), "'Above the Clouds'."

4:7. "General Grant His Disease Incurable." [*New York Sun*]

March 12

1:1-7, 2:1-2. H. V. Boynton, "Chickamauga. The Sanguinary Fight for the Possession of Chattanooga."

3:2. N. J. Marble (38th WI), "Fort Steadman."

3:2-3. P. Winsor (29th MA), "*Monitor* and *Merrimac*. Corrections by an Eye-witness of the Fight."

3:3. S. C. Bunstine (10th IL Cav), "That San Antonio Murder." [11/22/65]

3:5. J. M. Bute (12th IL Cav), Jacob Rebhun (3rd MI), R. H. Rawlins (53rd OH), S. T. Johnson (11th MO Cav), Samuel S. Statler (55th PA), George H. Clough (5th RI), D. L. Brewer (1st MI Cav), Will H. Widener (13th KS), J. Musgrove (31st NJ), "Youngest Volunteer."

5:1-4. Pittenger, Part 18.

8:1-2. E. B. Lufkin (13th ME), "The Perils of the Ocean. The Voyage of the Transport Mississippi from Boston to Ship Island."

8:2. H. H. Lyman (147th NY), "Gen. Howard Criticized." [Gettysburg]

8:2-3. George E. Harrington (40th NY), "The Midnight Charge at Chancellorsville."

8:3. Frank Burt (89th NY), "On the Nansemond."

8:3. D. Bates (121st NY), "Rappahannock Station."

8:3-4. "The 24th Michigan at Gettysburg."

8:4. W. S. Mitchell (31st NJ, Bty B, NJ Art), "The Last Fighting. Some Official Statements Respecting the Battle that Ended the War."

10:1-2. "General Grant's Illness."

11:5. L. K. Westcott (38th IL), "From One of Gen. Carlin's Boys." [5/62]

12:2. Obit: George H. Preble (USN).

March 19

1:1-3. J. C. Lee (55th OH), "Somebody's Blunder, Which Caused the Rout at Chancellorsville."

1:4-6. Carlin, Part 6. [advance to Stones' River]

1:6. H. V. Boynton, "Chickamauga. A Correction in Regard to Reynolds' Division."

2:4-5. Pittenger, Part 19.

3:1-2. E. C. Culp (25th OH), "Gettysburg. Recollections of the Great Fight by a Participant."

3:2-3. T. F. Allen (7th OH Cav), "Pegram's Raid. The Battle of Dutton Hill."

3:3. C. H. Hooper, "First Flag in Richmond."

3:3. (2nd NJ Cav), "A Fine Story Spoiled." [JMR 2/19]

3:3. William W. Watkins, "The 5th Iowa Cavalry."

3:4. T. H. Stevens (124th IN), "The March to Franklin."

3:4-6. Condensed Letters: J. F. Troutner (3rd IA), Jackson 7/63; G. L. Wheelock (37th MA), Saylor's Creek.

5:2. Obit: Thomas Plunkett (21st MA).

5:3. "Youngest Soldier. Several More Claims Put On File."

March 26

1:1-5. Carlin, Part 7. [Stones' River]

1:6-7, 2:1. Carleton, Part 60. [Gettysburg]

2:2. Charles C. Gilbert, "Gen. Gilbert. The Authority Under Which He Exercised Command in the Army of the Ohio."

2:3-6. Pittenger, Part 20.

3:1-2. "Libby Prison. 'Yankee' Writes Again. Capts. Flynn and Sawyer Drawn for Execution."

3:2. T. H. B. Lemley, "From a 1st West Va. Trooper." [Port Republic]

3:3. Henry C. Harrison (27th IN), "Sherman's Bummers."

3:4. John W. Fry (42nd OH), "Fry to the Front. He Replies Personally to His Comrades Who have Criticized Him."

3:4. W. B. Seaton (9th TN Cav), "Death of John Morgan."

3:5-6. Condensed Letters: D. F. Scott (45th IL), first flag in Vicksburg.

8:4. "General Grant's Condition."

April 2

1:1-4. Carlin, Part 8. [Chickamauga Campaign]

1:5-6. W. W. Carruth, "Lieut. John T. Greble. The First Regular Army Officer Killed in the War."

2:3-6. Pittenger, Part 21.

3:1. George S. Myers (101st OH), "Death of Gen. Polk."

3:1. H. H. Martin (20th IA), "'Land Lubbers' at Sea. Some Unpleasant Experiences While Crossing the Gulf of Mexico." [Texas 1865]

3:2. D. C. McCollum (87th IN), "Chickamauga."

3:2. W. A. Cannon, "Fort Donelson. Gallant Fight of the 83rd Ill. Against Overwhelming Odds."

3:3. "Perryville. Gen. C. C. Gilbert's Position During the Engagement."

3:3. George A. Manning, "The Libby Tunnel."

3:3-4. S. W. Crocker (191st PA), "The 190th and 191st Penna."

3:4. D. M. Wilcox (10th MA), "The *Monitor* and the *Merrimac*."

3:5. A. L. Brown (4th MN), "The Charge at Vicksburg."

3:5. "Youngest Soldiers."

4:7. Obit.

April 9

1:1-7, 2:1-6, 5:3-4. "U. S. Grant. Career of the Greatest Soldier of the Day."

3:1. Hugh L. Thompson (3rd WI Cav), "'Bushwhackers.' The Trials of Loyalty in Southwest Missouri."

3:2. Robert Williams (1st IA), "Death of Gen. Lyon."

3:2. Harvey T. Beazel (88th IN), "A Hoosier Boy's Story. Gen. Ransom's Death—The First Flag at Raleigh and Andersonville."

3:3. William R. Ramsey (150th PA), "The 'Bucktails.' An Interesting Sketch from a One-legged Comrade."

3:3. A. J. Moore (207th PA), "Fort Steadman."

3:3-4. C. H. Warren (8th NY Cav), "Congratulatory Order from Gen. Custer." [4/9/65]

3:4. Charles H. Morse (117th USCT), "Chickamauga."

3:4. J. B. Dodge (30th IN), "The Libby Tunnel."

3:5. R. J. Devore (66th OH), "A Reminiscence of Ringgold."

April 16

1:1-5. John W. Fuller, "A Terrible Day. The Fighting Before Atlanta, July 22, 1864."

1:6-7, 2:1-2. Carlin, Part 9. [Chickamauga]

2:3-5. Pittenger, Part 22.

3:1-2. C. A. Kuhl (14th IL), "Fort Donelson. Present Aspect of the Field of that Famous Fight."

3:2. Joseph W. Fisher (5th PA Res), "Round Top Again."

3:2. Enos Pierson, "The 54th Indiana at Chickasaw."

3:3. H. L. Thompson (3rd WI Cav), "Southwest Missouri." [addition]

3:4. C. D. Morris (33rd IL), "The Charge at Vicksburg."

3:4. "The Youngest Soldier."

3:4. John C. Lang (100th IL), "Spring Hill to Franklin."

3:4. (1st ME Hvy Art), "Those Baked Beans."

3:5. J. W. Pearman, "Did His Widow Get the Sword?" [Hatcher's Run, 2/65, AQM, Col. 20th MA killed]

4:5-6. "General Grant."

April 23

1:1-4. Carleton, Part 61. [Gettysburg]

1:5-7, 2:1. Carlin, Part 10. [Chattanooga]

2:2-6. Pittenger, Part 23.

3:1-2. George Q. Gardner (5th WI Bty), "Perryville. The Part Gen. Post's Brigade Took in the Fight."

3:2. Harvey Reid (22nd WI), "Libby Prison. A Comrade's Experience in the Hospital There."

3:2-3. E. A. Mass (88th PA), "Libby Tunnel Once More."

3:3. George Lounsberry (36th IL), "Spring Hill to Franklin."

3:3. James Packard (5th NY Cav), "Concerning Gen. Kilpatrick."

3:3. "The Youngest Soldier."

3:3. John Langton (15th OH Bty), "Who Killed Gen. Polk?"

3:3. G. W. Clark (4th MI Cav), "The Tullahoma Campaign."

3:4. A. R. Barlow, "Another Shot at Comrade Beale."

3:4. George C. Goodwin (1st ME Cav), "The Surrender of Lee."

3:4. Wayne Carpenter (67th OH), "The Wind Up."

3:4. George C. Goodwin (1st ME Cav), "The Surrender of Lee."

3:5. H. G. Lehmann (32nd OH), "Death of Gen. Ransom."

3:5. Henry M. Reed (4th KY), "Boynton's Chickamauga."

3:5. A. J. Adams (141st PA), "The Fight at the Peach Orchard."

3:5. D. C. McCollum (87th IN), "Gen. H. V. Boynton."

3:6. Charles D. Miller (76th OH), "DeGrasse's Battery."

April 30

1:6-7, 2:1. Frank Swigart (46th IN), "Up the Red River."

2:3-6. Pittenger, Part 24.

3:1. Joseph M. Leeper (140th NY), "Gettysburg. The Part Taken in the Battle by the Fifth Corps."

3:1. (62nd PA), "Col. McQuade."

3:1. J. S. Chandler (5th VT), "He Corrects Comrade Taylor." [Petersburg]

3:2. H. L. Thompson (3rd WI Cav), "Bushwhackers. A Spirited Campaign After Livingston and His Gang."

3:3. William W. Perry (82nd PA), "Sailor's Creek."

3:3. Philip Dines (41st OH), "The Cracker Line."

3:3. Joseph H. Young, "Capture of the 33rd Indiana." [3/4/63]

3:4. Return I. Holcombe (10th MO), "Who Cared for the Body of Gen. McPherson?"

3:4. W. H. Morse (22nd WI), "Capture of Fayetteville, N.C."

3:4. J. D. Remington (73rd IL), "From Spring Hill to Franklin."

3:5. F. M. Wheeler (141st NY), "The Blackberry Expedition."

3:5. Oscar Ludwig, "The 20th Illinois at Vicksburg."

3:5. J. A. Correll (51st OH), "Whose Cow was Killed?

4:7. Obit.

May 7

1:7, 2:1-3. Carleton, Part 62. [Gettysburg]

2:4-6. Pittenger, Part 25.

3:1. James Beale (12th MA), "Gettysburg."

3:1. J. S. Leomon, "The 5th Iowa Cavalry at Fort Donelson."

3:2. W. C. Clark, "Holly Springs."

3:2. "Who Stole that Goose?" [pet of 14th IN]

3:2. J. B. Nall, "A Life in Jeopardy. A Tennessean Who was Trapped Into Acting as Spy." [Chickamauga Campaign]

3:3. C. J. Lemon (25th IA), "Another Goose Thief. How a Hungry Soldier Captured the Succulent Bird."

3:6. "The Youngest Soldier."

3:6. Condensed Letters: R. A. Patterson (57th IL), 7/22/64; Fred T. Taylor (13th PA Res), Gettysburg.

4:5. Obit.

5:4. Biog: Henry A. Barnum (12th, 149th NY).

May 14

3:1. Graham Watts (67th PA), "Crutchfield's Watch. Who Took the Watch from His Body After the Fight at Saylor's Creek?"

3:2. Samuel Kelso (Bty D, 1st OH), "Sanders's Raid. Destruction of the East Tennessee and Georgia Railroad."

3:3-4. Thomas E. Rose (77th PA), "Libby Tunnel."

3:4. J. D. Schnaitman (1st MI), "The Tunnel at Columbia Prison."

3:4. A. D. Stine (33rd OH), "What Troops were the First to Enter Raleigh, N.C.?"

3:5. W. S. Kimball, "The 13th Mass. at Gettysburg."

3:5. James P. Sullivan (6th WI), "Gettysburg."

3:5. T. A. Gossett, "Andersonville."

3:6. E. L. Pattee, "A Plucky Man." [James P. Goff, Bty B, 1st WV]

8:1-4. "Gettysburg After Twenty Years. Visit of the First Corps to the Field."

May 21

1:1-4. Carlin, Part 11. [beginning of Atlanta Campaign]

1:5-7, 2:1. Carleton, Part 63. [Gettysburg]

2:2-3. Pittenger, Part 26.

3:1. N. D. Hinchell (Bty F, 1st NY), "Who Carried Off that Stone." [Yorktown stone marking spot where Cornwallis surrendered]

3:1. S. L. Coulter (111th IL), "DeGrasse's Battery."

3:1. O. R. Pomroy, "The 45th Ill. at Vicksburg." [5/22/63]

3:2. J. Pinnock (14th IN), "That Goose Again." [issue of 4/30]

3:2. J. S. Harrold (14th IN), "Did Anybody Else Eat the Goose?"

3:2. Thomas McFarland (175th OH), "From Spring Hill to Franklin."

3:3. Martin Steele (30th IL), "How Gen. McPherson Fell."

3:4-6. "Old Battlefields. Visit of the Sixth Corps to Their Virginia Camps."

4:7. Obit.

May 28

1:1-5. Carlin, Part 12. [end of Atlanta Campaign]

1:6-7. J. C. Black, "The Battle's Lesson. Gen. Black's Eloquent Address on the Field of Gettysburg."

2:3-5. Pittenger, Part 27.

3:1. A. Brandley (23rd KY), "The Cracker Line."

3:1. James E. Shellenberger (94th OH), "Capture of Raleigh, N.C."

3:2. E. D. Libbey, "The 6th Maine [Battery] in the Peach Orchard."

3:2. W. S. Coen, "The 5th Iowa Cavalry. Its Christmas Party in 1864."

3:2. W. M. Prouty (31st IA), "Columbia, S.C. The First Regiment to Enter the City."

3:3. Joseph B. Sansom (83rd IL), "Fort Donelson."

3:4. George Sperry, "The Waynesboro Fight, and the Part the 22nd New York Cavalry Took in the Affair."

3:4. W. H. Davis (10th MI), "The Capture of Fayetteville, N.C."

3:4. W. H. Harmon, "Kilpatrick and the 1st [NY] Mounted Rifles."

3:4. Earl M. Rogers (6th WI), "A Brave Deed at Gettysburg."

3:5. W. Bristow (24th KY), "The Confessional. Who Took His Meat?"

4:7. Obit: Albert F. Dow (39th MA), Joseph C. Batcheldore (25th MA, 4th RI), O. H. Marston (VT).

June 4

1:1-4. Carleton, Part 64. [Vicksburg]

1:5-7, 2:1. N. N. Hill (3rd MO Cav), "A Far-West Fight. A Graphic Sketch of a Campaign Beyond the Mississippi. Battle of Hartsville."

3:1-2. E. S. Coan, "Round Top. A Shot from the 20th Maine, Aimed at Comrade Fisher."

3:2. John N. Colsher (1st KY), "Belle Isle."

3:2. Porter Watson (105th OH), "The Death of Col. Creighton." [Ringgold]

3:3. E. C. Culp. "From the 25th Ohio. A Correction as to Gettysburg, and a Sketch of the Closing Days of the War."

3:4. William Beckler (8th ME), "Absolutely the "Last Fight'."

3:4. (1st MI Eng), "Mitchell's Alabama Campaign."

3:5. J. L. Rice (15th WI), "Death of Gen. Polk."

3:5. A. P. McFarland (4th IA), "DeGrasse's Battery."

3:5. John G. Springer (10th IL Cav), "Who Got There First?" [Little Rock capture]

3:5. A. Whittlesey (41st OH), "How James Dines was Killed." [7/3/64]

3:5. S. E. Chandler (24th NY Cav), "Did His Friends Get His Ring?"

3:5. J. B. Gable (122nd PA), "Gen. Whipple." [death]

June 11

1:1-4. Carlin, Part 13. [post Atlanta happenings]

1:5-7, 2:1. Carleton, Part 65. [Vicksburg]

3:1-2. H. M. Kellogg (55th OH), "Chancellorsville."

3:2. (62nd PA), "The Death of Col. Black at Gaines's Mill."

3:2. J. B. Rowe (2nd MO Cav), "What was the First Regiment to Cross the Arkansas River?" [Little Rock capture]

3:3. Jeff. J. Hibbets (32nd OH), "Fayetteville, N.C."

3:4. F. E. Hoover (64th OH), Joseph Edmonds (120th IN), "Spring Hill and Franklin."

3:4. Joseph S. Clarke (7th OH), "Where Col. Creighton Fell." [Ringgold]

3:5. Robert F. Bartlett (96th OH), "The Teche Campaign."

3:6. Condensed Letters: John Van Buren (107th IL), Spring Hill-Franklin.

4:7. Obit.

June 18

1:1-5. Carlin, Part 14. [March to the Sea]

1:6-7, 2:1-2. Carleton, Part 66. [Vicksburg]

3:1-2. H. C. Sergeant (12th IL Cav), "Up the Red River."

3:2. J. R. Tisdale (29th MO), "The Fifteenth Corps at Atlanta."

3:3. C. M. Fuller, "The 78th Ohio at Jackson, Tenn." [6/62]

3:3. Philip Assmus (8th NY Cav), "Maj. Compson at Waynesboro."

3:3. Joseph B. Sansom (83rd IL), "He Wants an Error Corrected." [in his article of May 28]

3:3. M. Schnepp (1st NY Mtd Rifles), "He Would Like to Find His Fellow Prisoners."

3:3. G. S. Keener (10th PA Res), "The Second Day at Gettysburg."

3:4. John J. Sewell (24th KY), "Who Stole Dave Lawson's Gun?"

3:4. J. B. Souder (52nd OH), "Death of Gen. McCook." [Kennesaw]

3:4. A. Brauneller, "The 39th Indiana at Pittsburgh Landing."

3:4. F. Canfield (13th IA), "The First Regiment to Enter Columbia, S.C."

3:4. A. N. Shumard (48th OH), "The Charge at Vicksburg."

3:5. Harry Van Houten, "The 13th Illinois at Little Rock."

3:5. "A Persecuted Soldier. An Attempt to Punish a Comrade for an Act Committed During the War." [MO 1864]

5:1-5. W. F. Hinman (65th OH), "The Army Pests."

June 25

3:1. J. S. Lemmon (5th IA Cav), "Fort Donelson Again."

3:1. S. E. Chandler (24th NY), "First Brigade, First Division, First Corps."

3:1-2. J. S. Harrold (14th IN), "Lost Sword and Belt." [Chancellorsville]

3:2. Webster Rogers (4th MA Cav), "Gen. Potter's Raid." [from Georgetown, SC]

3:2. Mrs. R. H. Sinnott, "A Hospital Nurse's Story."

3:3-6. "Grant's Memoirs."

3:6. C. F. Engle (82nd OH), "The Sumptuous Fare at Belle Isle."

4:6. Obit.

July 2

4:5. Obit.

5:3. James Kephart, "The Flag Not Captured. The 13th U.S. Infantry in the Charge at Vicksburg."

5:3. R. S. Murphy, "The Mississippi Marine Brigade."

5:3. P. B. Anthony (11th NC), "Where is the Owner of the Canteen?" [Gettysburg]

5:6. E. L. Faulkner (5th PA Res), "The Capture of Gen. Reynolds."

5:6. John Van Kirk, "The 36th Wisconsin at Cold Harbor."

6:6. J. C. Lee (55th OH), "Ohio at Gettysburg. An Important Meeting of Soldiers."

7:1. R. B. Scott (67th IN), "The Teche Campaign."

7:1-2. E. M. Stapleton (1st IA Cav), "Little Rock."

7:2. E. Bristow (8th MO Cav), "Fight at Ashley's Station, Ark."

7:2. HJL (33rd MO), "Chickens. A Nocturnal Raid on a Planter's Henroost."

7:2-3. F. P. Spencer (17th IA), D. A. Mulvane (80th OH), "Correcting Carlin. His Statement Denied as to Colored Troops Taken by Hood at Atlanta."

7:3. W. M. Prouty (31st IA), "Once More to the Breach. Whose Flag Floated Over the State House at Columbia, S.C.?"

July 9

1:1-4. Carlin, Part 15. [Carolinas]

1:5-7. Carleton, Part 67. [Jackson, Port Hudson]

3:1. (6th MO), "Atlanta. A Comrade's Personal Experience in the Battle of July 22."

3:1. D. H. Chandler (5th IN Bty), "Death of Gen. Polk."

3:2. W. T. Fisher (2nd MO Cav), "'Merrill's Horse the First Troops to Enter Little Rock."

3:2. W. C. Yard (4th PA Cav), "A Bee Hunting Expedition."

3:2. George E. Billington (USS *Lafayette*), "Running the Batteries." [Vicksburg]

3:3. Jacob Fink (55th IL), "DeGrasse's Battery."

3:3. George Tompkins (25th OH Bty), "The First to Cross the River at Little Rock."

3:4. Oscar M. Reece (5th IA Cav), "More 'Last Battles.' A Strong Claim Filed on Behalf of Wilson's Cavalry."

3:4. W. H. Bentley (77th IL), "The 22nd of May at Vicksburg."

3:4. Samuel L. Wells (22nd NY Cav), "A Mild Kick from a Cavalryman." [Waynesboro]

3:5. A. F. Bartlett (33rd MO), "Patriotism in the West. Recollections of the Battle of Springfield, Mo." [1/8/63]

3:5. W. Bristow (24th KY), "East Kentucky in 1861. The Conflict Between Loyal Men and Rebels."

3:6. J. C. Harper (56th OH), "The Teche Campaign Again."

3:6. Thomas Montgomery, "The 48th Ohio at Vicksburg."

4:7. Obit.

5:2. Gettysburg's Field. Three Additions to the Memorials of the Great Battle." [29th, 98th PA, 20th CT]

5:4-5. William E. Loring (141st PA), "Gettysburg."

7:3. "Mother Bickerdyke."

8:4. A. S. Coe (147th NY), "Chancellorsville."

8:4. G. L. Childress (66th IL), "DeGrasse's Battery."

8:4. J. E. L. Miller, "A Naval Reminiscence." [Harriet Lane]

July 16

3:1-2. George Q. Gardner (5th WI Bty), "The Artillery at Resaca."

3:2. Philip Dines (41st OH), "The Four Brave Brothers."

3:2. Charles W. Smith (2nd US Ss), "Gen. Whipple's Death."

3:3. W. L. Lacewell (7th TN), "Through the Lines. Adventures of a Party of Loyal Tennesseans."

3:3. J. Q. Symons, "The 39th Indiana at Shiloh."

3:3. Arthur McDonald (176th NY), "A Prisoner's Story of Salisbury."

3:3. E. T. Lee (41st IL), "The Columbia, S.C., Controversy."

3:4. George W. Toms (5th NY Cav), "The Wilson Raid." [6/64]

3:4. Gottfried Obhardt (7th NY), "Big Bethel."

3:4. G. W. Wilson, "The 13th Iowa at Columbia."

3:5. Daniel E. McLean (25th NY Cav), "The Fight at Fort Stevens."

3:5. George D. Lee (102nd NY), "The Second Day at Gettysburg."

3:5. H. C. Whitaker (2nd NY Cav), "It was Not Whiskey, But It was Something that Disgusted the Drinker." [Gettysburg Campaign]

3:6. "The Youngest Soldier."

4:7. Obit.

July 23

1:6-7, 2:1. Carlin, Part 16. [Carolinas]

3:1-3. (46th PA), "Chancellorsville."

3:3. A. G. Thompson, "McPherson's Death. The Sad Story of His Orderly, Who Saw Him Die."

3:4. E. T. Lee (41st IL), "The Long-lost Flag of the 53rd Illinois." [Jackson 7/12/63]

3:4. George C. Elliott (127th IL), "The Capture of Fayetteville, N.C."

3:4. Arthur S. Whitcomb, "A Kid Soldier."

3:4. R. M. McMaster (33rd IN), "The First to Enter Fayetteville, N.C."

3:4. "How a Flag was Saved." [Co. D, 23rd IL, at Lexington, MO]

3:4. Henry Lehmar (30th IA), W. H. Wiseman (76th OH), "DeGress's Battery."

3:5. James Brewster (33rd IL), "Neglected Graves." [Ship Island]

3:5. L. M. Penfield, "At Gettysburg. The 20th Conn. Unveils Its Monument, July 3."

3:6. E. R. Barnhill, "'On a Sour Apple Tree.' How the Famous Song had Its Origin." [*Winchester Argus*]

4:7. Obit.

6:2. "Ohio Veterans to Visit Gettysburg."

July 30

1:6-7, 2:1-3. Carlin, Part 17. [Carolinas]

3:1-2. G. Schleiter (74th PA), "The Eleventh Corps. Who was Responsible for Its Disaster at Chancellorsville?"

3:2. "27th Connecticut Monument at Gettysburg."

3:2. "Lieut. Kingsbury's Death." [11th CT 9/17/62]

3:2. S. E. Parker, "The Flag of the 13th Iowa." [Columbia]

3:2. F. A. Patterson (3rd IA Cav), "Little Rock Again."

3:3. (65th IL), "Spring Hill to Franklin."

3:3. S. Hathaway (3rd IA Cav), "The Little Rock Squabble Again."

3:3. Thomas Yost (21st IL), "The Captured Cannon at Stone River." [Nolinsville Gap]

3:4. (9th IA), "The DeGrasse [sic] Battery Again."

3:4. E. O. Kimberley (Band, 1st Bg, 3rd Div, 15th Corps), "Two Anecdotes of Logan." [South Carolina and Bentonville]

3:4. Frank Doster (11th IN Cav), "Another 'Last Battle'." Palmetto Ranch]

3:4. George E. Lowry (13th IN), "Lances in the Rebel Army." Peninsula 6-7/63]

3:5. J. F. McGinnis (81st OH), "An Irritable Colonel. An Anecdote About the Commander of the 9th Illinois." [August Mersy at Corinth]

3:5. R. H. Martin (46th IN), "He Corrects 'Carleton' and Comrade Bartlett." [Teche Campaign and Champion Hill]

3:6. Isaac Keith (12th IN), "The Death of Gen. Polk."

4:5. Obit.

5:1-5. Obit: Ulysses S. Grant.

August 6

1:1-3. Carlin, Part 18. [Bentonville to end of war]

3:1-2. J. S. Lemmon, "The 5th Iowa Cavalry, and Its Brilliant Charge at Sugar Creek, Tenn."

3:2. (65th IL), "Hovey's Division at Resaca."

3:2. C. W. Sarchett (9th IA), "He Settles It." [Columbia]

3:2. E. C. Woods (41st OH), "An Anecdote of Gen. Nelson."

3:3. G. B. Kenniston (5th ME), "A Noble Act. An Incident of Libby Prison."

3:3. C. M. Norton (1st MI Cav), "A Death List of Andersonville."

3:4. (18th PA Cav), "Sheridan and Custer at Cedar Creek."

3:4. J. S. Smith (122nd PA), "Gen. Whipple's Death."

3:4. J. W. Ragsdale (13th IA), "The First to Enter Columbia."

3:5. Jack L. Herbert (2nd IA Cav), "Col. Hatch. The Service He Rendered on the Grierson Raid."

3:5. W. H. Morse (22nd WI), "Fayetteville, N.C., Again."

3:6. W. M. Prouty, "The Flag of the 13th Iowa Again." [Columbia]

3:6. "Youngest Soldier."

4:7. Obit.

August 13

2:5. A. S. Sampson (33rd WI), "The Flag of the 53rd Illinois."

3:1. A. S. Coe (147th NY), "The 14th N.Y. Zouaves. A Free and Easy Regiment Which did Good Service."

3:2. William H. Conard, "Hartsville. How the 104th Illinois Squared Accounts with the Johnnies."

3:2. A. J. Underwood (1st MN), "A Brave Vermonter." [Antietam]

3:2. James A. Hall (2nd ME Bty), "Correcting the Records." [Cedar Mt]

3:3. P. M. Voorhis (32nd OH), "The Seventeenth Corps at Columbia, S.C."

3:3. A. R. Barlow (157th NY), "Gen. Schimmelpfennig. How He Escaped Capture at Gettysburg."

3:3. W. C. Yard (4th PA Cav), "How the Corn Left the Crib."

3:4. I. M. Adair (86th IN), "Columbia to Spring Hill."

3:4. R. B. Winn, "He Produces the Record in Favor of the 13th Iowa." [Columbia, SC]

3:4. "John D. Cohern (PA), "We'll Hang Jeff Davis on a Sour Apple Tree."

3:4. E. L. Mowers (15th IL), "Gen. Rogers. A Comrade's Memories of the Chairman of the Board of Pension Appeals."

3:5. Samuel Bloomer, "How the 1st Minnesota Lost Its Colors." [6/29/62]

8:3. "At Gettysburg. Encampment of the Dept. of Pa."

August 20

3:1-2. "Gettysburg. A Spirited Account of the Battle, and the Part Taken Therein by the 8th Ohio."

3:2. "The Youngest Soldier."

3:3. John W. Bannan, "Columbia, S.C. A Member of the 4th Iowa Consults His Diary."

3:3. William H. Seaman (98th OH), "The Battle of Bentonville, N.C."

3:4. H. E. Evans (20th WI), "Recollections of the Battle of Springfield, Mo."

3:4. J. W. Conard, "Death of Lieut. Greble." [Big Bethel]

3:4. R. K. Baird (2nd OH Cav), "Lances in the Rebel Army." [Valverde]

3:5. William Thompson, "Merrill's Horse. A Member Tells the Story of a Bloody Little Battle in Northeast Missouri." [7/18/62, Memphis, 2nd MO Cav]

3:5. D. H. Bishop (107th IL), "Judah's Division at Resaca."

3:5. A. J. Cropsey (129th IL), "How Grant Punished a Disobedient Railroad Conductor."

3:6. George A. Peeler (36th IL), "Spring Hill to Franklin."

4:7. Obit.

August 27

1:6-7, 2:1-3. Carleton, Part 68. [Chickamauga]

2:5. Charles S. Tripler (12th US), "Jeff Davis in Prison." [*San Francisco Alta*]

3:1. James B. Shadle (34th IN), "More Last Battles. A Long Delayed Reply."

3:1. O. O. Smith (4th OH Cav), "Another 'Last Battle'." [West Point, GA]

3:2. William Hutcheson (6th IN Cav), "Morgan's Raid in Indiana."

3:2. John G. Faris (86th IL), "Another Mule Story About Fayetteville, N.C."

3:2. Alexander E. Holland (25th OH), "Chancellorsville."

3:2. Henry Roback (152nd NY), "How a Flag was Saved." [Cold Harbor]

3:3. J. A. Stewart (101st OH), "Stone's River."

3:3. Gottfried Ebhardt, "The 7th New York Volunteers."

3:3. W. W. Allen (signal corps), "Gen. McPherson's Death."

3:4. Alexander Ralston (11th IL), "DeGrasse's [sic] Battery."

3:4. A. L. Morey (98th NY), "Rebel Lances." [Fair Oaks]

3:5. J. C. Harris (83rd PA, 5th Corps HQ), "Chancellorsville."

3:5-6. E. H. Smith (1st IA Cav), "Little Rock."

3:6. Frank Hoppin (13th MI), "Foraging Under Difficulties."

4:5. Obit: Samuel Bodle (30th IN), James K. Patterson (5th WI).

5:3. William Leonard (signal corps), "The Death of Gen. Polk."

5:5. Lemuel K. Morton (1st PA Res), "Moral Courage in Battle." [Second Manassas]

8:4. (18th PA Cav), "Two Instances. The Cowartdly Lieutenant and the Brave Boy." [Glendale, 3rd PA Res; Cedar Creek, 18th PA Cav]

September 3

1:7, 2:1-2. Carleton, Part 69. [Chickamauga]

3:1. S. J. Tinsman (9th NJ), "Attention, 3rd N. H. Speak Up Now, Like Little Men." [Drewry's Bluff]

3:1. "In Front of Petersburg. The 97th Pa. Boys Getting a Good Meal."

3:1-2. W. C. Yard (4th PA Cav), "Feeding the Army Under Difficulties."

3:2. "Knoxville. A Comrade Tells Some Interesting Anecdotes Connected with the Siege."

3:2. J. S. Stanley (31st WI), "He Mistook Our Motive." [Bentonville]

3:3. H. Emrich (13th IL Cav), "The Crossing at Little Rock Still Disputed."

3:3. E. O. Kimberley (1/3/15th band), "Burning of Columbia."

3:3. Wells H. Shearer (66th IL), "DeGrasse's [sic] Battery Once More."

3:4. J. H. Springer (1st IA Cav), "Silver Creek." [MO, 1/8/62]

3:4. George W. Oby (6th US Cav), "Who Threw the Brick at the Rebel Guard?" [Libby Prison]

3:4. B. F. Clough, "Burning of the Flagship Black Hawk."

3:5. John J. Bowen, "The Quartermaster Department."

3:6. John B. Mason (1st SC Rifles), "What Regiment? An Inquiry by a South Carolinian as to a Zouave Regiment." [Gaines' Mill]

4:4. E. R. Montfort (75th OH), "Ohio at Gettysburg."

4:7. Obit: Charles Freudenberg (52nd NY).

September 10

1:7, 2:1-3. Josiah P. Dry (123rd OH), "Up the Shenandoah. Operations of the Army of West Virginia."

3:1-2. Isaac Hall (97th NY), "Iverson's Brigade. An Old Controversy Regarding Its Capture Renewed." [Gettysburg]

3:3. "Gettysburg. What the 14th Indiana did in the Fight."

3:3. D. R. McClintock (205th PA), "Fort Steadman."

3:3. A. L. Wright (10th PA Res), "An Eastern Boy Puts in His Oar."

3:4. A. B. Crummel (30th OH), "DeGrasse's Battery."

3:4. Gottfried Ebhardt (7th NY), "Big Bethel."

3:5. R. H. Barton (1st OH Cav), "McPherson's Death."

3:5. Edward B. Meatyard (64th USCT), "Col. Mersy, of the 9th Illinois."

3:5. William Cogswell, "Bentonville. The Part Cogswell's Brigade Took in the Fight."

3:6. D. C. Krone, "The 41st Illinois at Columbia, S.C."

September 17

1:7, 2:1-4. Dry, Part 2.

3:1. John Haley (17th ME), "Chancellorsville. A Maine Comrade Thinks Gen. Howard is Not Treated Fairly."

3:1. J. R. Tisdale (29th MO), "Chickasaw Bayou."

3:2. W. G. Putney, "Battery I, 2nd Ill. Art. Some Interesting Anecdotes from the Bugler."

3:2. M. L. Adams (121st OH), "Averysboro and Bentonville, N.C."

3:3. George W. Toms (5th NY Cav), "Kilpatrick's Cavalry at the Battle of Gettysburg." [includes Hanover]

3:3. R. M. Marvin (31st IA), "The First Flag at Columbia, S.C."

3:4. C. L. Overley (16th KY), "Spring Hill to Franklin."

3:4. George S. Wible (100th OH), "Belle Isle."

3:4. George A. Welton (6th MI Cav), "An Unpleasant Steamboat Excursion." [Spring 1862]

3:4. H. Flandes (13th IN), "She Followed Her Lover." [female soldier in 37th IL]

3:5. A. A. Tofte (15th WI), "The Captured Cannon at Nolinsville Gap." [12/26/62]

3:5. Lewis Follett (76th OH), "DeGrasse's Battery."

3:5. Henry J. Walker (12th WI), "Lances in the Rebel Army."

3:6. W. George (139th PA), "A Very Young Soldier." [about woman giving birth in another regiment]

4:7. Obit.

September 24

1:7, 2:1. William S. Rosecrans, "What 'Old Rosy' Says. The Alleged Mistakes of the Chickamauga Campaign. 'Carleton' Criticized."

1:6. William P. Carlin, "Bentonville."

3:1-2. W. C. Beck (19th NY Bty), "Fort Steadman."

3:2. Leander Free (38th IN), "Captain Dilger's Battery." [Atlanta Campaign]

3:2. Sol R. Smith (8th OH Bty), "The Guns at Knob Gap."

3:2. J. Harvey Hanford (124th NY), "Gettysburg."

3:3. O. S. Barrett (4th MI), "They Didn't Mix Gunpowder in Their Whisky." [Gaines' Mill]

3:3. G. W. West, "The Flag of the 37th Massachusetts."

3:3. Will L. Welch (23rd MA), "'Carleton' Criticized. Why the Troops were Transferred from North Carolina to South Carolina."

3:3. "The Youngest Soldier."

3:4. W. G. Putney (Bty I, 2nd IL), "Chickamauga."

3:5. S. S. Carver (36th IL), "Spring Hill to Franklin."

3:5. James D. Forbes, "The 22nd N.Y. An Interesting Account of Its Doings by a Member."

3:6. Condensed Letters: Jacob Sennett (34th IL), W. A. Payton [12th IL], Bentonville; E. A. Crandall (23rd WI), 13th Corps badge; S. F> Moore (118th OH), DeGress' battery; A. G. Harriman (6th ME), John Brown's Body song; James Gregory (86th IN), first flag on Missionary Ridge; George Zinn (25th OH Bty), Little Rock.

4:5-6. Obit.

5:3. "The First Union Flag Captured by the Confederates Returned to Its Owner." [7/18/61 Peninsula]

8:3. "A Battle Flag Captured at the Battle of Franklin to be Returned After Many Years." [57th IN captured by 11th TN]

October 1

1:1-5, 3:2-5. J. Adams Smith (USN), "Sinking the Alabama."

4:4. George Kimball, "Iverson's Brigade. The 12th Mass. did Join in the 'Charge'."

4:5. W. C. Yard (4th PA Cav), "A Word for the East. One Who Thinks the West did Not Do All the Fighting."

4:5-6. Alfred Davenport (5th NY), Edward Boyle (6th US), "Duryea's Zouaves."

4:6. Henry C. Vaughn (24th KY), "An Open Confession."

5:1. B. Cornell, "The 1st N.J. Cavalry. Some Amusing Incidents of Their Initiation into the Art of War."

5:1. S. R. Nelson (2nd MO Cav), "Pikes as Well as Lances in the Rebel Army."

5:1-2. Charles W. Harrington (15th US), "This Settles the Lance Question."

5:2. "Chickamauga."

5:2. R. H. Martin, "Don't Like Dictionary. A Comrade's Raid Upon the Tribune's Learned Correspondents."

5:3. W. W. Allen (signal corps), "Who was Really Shot?" [3/2/65 Black Creek SC]

5:3. R. Hannaford (2nd OH Cav), "The Last Man Killed."

5:4. R. J. Heath (34th IL), "Bentonville."

5:4. J. C. Ambrose (120th OH), "An Ohio Man Talks." [Bentonville]

5:4. R. B. Winn (40th MO), "Spring Hill to Franklin."

8:1. "A Grand Letter from Gen. Sherman While in the Field Before Atlanta." [8/10/64 to Daniel J. Martin]

12:2. "Returning Southern Flags." [27th MA returning 7th NC colors taken at Newbern]

October 8

1:7, 2:1. John A. Logan, "A Worthy Tribute to the Dead Commander, Gen. U. S. Grant."

3:1. F. C. Jones (64th NY), "How the 140th Pa. Got Captured." [Chancellorsville]

3:1. Leroy Shelley (8th VT), "Let Us Have Peace." [Cedar Creek]

3:1. (18th OH), "Gen. John B. Turchin."

3:1. Hartwell Osborn (55th OH), "A Few Words About Bentonville."

3:2. Godfrey Bohrer (34th IN), "The Last Battle. The Fight at Palmetto Ranch."

3:2. Reinhard Straussing (17th IN), "Who Captured the Flag?" [Captain Terry's Texas Rangers]

3:3. (82nd IN), (65th IL), "At Rocky Face."

3:4. J. M. Glover (3rd MO Cav), "Little Rock."

3:5. S. B. Humbert (31st IA), L. S. Taylor (15th IA), "Columbia, S.C."

3:5. (81st OH), "Death of Col. Rodgers at Corinth."

3:5. W. H. Records (72nd IN), "Wilder's Brigade at Rome, Ga."

4:7. Obit.

October 15

1:6-7, 2:1. Carleton, Part 70. [Charleston]

3:2. DAL (61st PA), "In the Days of the Draft."

3:4. "Another Monument at Gettysburg." [13th MA]

3:5. John W. Fry (42nd OH), "Army of the Tennessee. Plain Words from a Comrade Criticizing Its Effectiveness."

4:1. J. M. Lovejoy (121st NY), "Rappahannock Station."

4:1-2. James F. Fitts (114th NY), "Shenandoah Campaign."

4:2. Basil Norris (surgeon), "Lancers in the Rebel Army."

4:2. James C. Stevenson (100th PA), "Fort Steadman."

4:2. George C. Jenkins (1st AL Cav), "Kilpatrick's Capture."

4:2. A. M. Bealy (4th PA Cav), "Scared by a Glass Eye."

4:2. H. E. Dickinson (24th NY), A. C. Tibbals (14th NY), "The Iron Brigade."

4:3. Silas W. Crocker (6th PA Res), "Gettysburg."

4:4. Thomas W. Baird, "The 5th Connecticut at Cedar Mountain."

4:4. George K. Swope (1st PA Res), "Pa. Reserves. What They Were, and Some of the Fighting They Did."

4:4. O. C. J. Shipnes (15th WI), "The Guns at Knob Gap."

4:5. Henry J. Lyda, "The Sultana Disaster."

4:5. Oliver Edwards, "The 37th Massachusetts Colors."

4:5. D. O. Pickard (US Ss), "Death of Col. Broadhead."

4:6. "The Youngest Soldier."

5:1. Henry Brunner (1st WV Cav), "Hunter's Raid."

5:1. Thomas Gilmore (107th NY), Henry A. Tripp (29th ME), "The 'Star' Badge."

5:1. J. R. Norris (16th OH), "Chickasaw Bayou."

5:2. Joshua Groft (14th PA Cav), "Random Shots."

5:2. P. S. Moore (40th IN), "Wagner's Brigade." [Chattanooga]

5:2. William H. Miller (83rd NY), "They All Helped to Do It." [Gettysburg]

5:2. (81st OH), "Col. Rodgers at Corinth."

5:3. Myron Failing (111th NY), "Gen. Alexander Hays at Gettysburg."

5:3. Theodore A. Worrall (97th PA), The Tenth and Eighteenth Corps at Cold Harbor."

5:3. A. Al. Abbott, "The 12th Michigan."

5:3. E. Price (118th OH), "Srgt. Ferguson's Account." [Knoxville]

5:4. E. O. Kimberly 1/3/15th band), "March to the Sea."

6:3-5. Biog: John C. Black (11th IN, 37th IL).

8:1-3. "Col. Ellsworth. His Death at Alexandria. Leaves from His Diary Before the War."

October 22

1:6-7, 2:1. Carleton, Part 71. [Charleston]

3:1-2. Alfred Davenport (5th NY), "Duryea's 'Red Legs.' The Reputation of the 5th N.Y. Ably Defended and Established."

3:2. H. S. Finkenbiner (107th OH), "The Eleventh Corps at Chancellorsville."

3:3. William E. Loring (141st PA), "A Rough Hospital."

3:3. A. W. Slayton (25th MI), "That Cavalryman's Feat." [Munfordville KY 12/62]

3:4. James P. L. Weems, "A Touch of Nature." [meeting of US and CS wounded soldiers after the war]

3:4. "How 'Uncle Jack' Smoked a Cigar with the Dead General." [Grant and John J. Glasscock, 29th IL]

3:4-5. "Recovering a Body at Midnight." [5th NJ at Manassas 1/63]

3:5. C. A. Kuhl (14th IL), "The Story of a Bell, Stolen and Brought Home as a Trophy from Texas."

3:5. "The 51st Pa. They Revisit the Crater at Petersburg, Va."

3:5. Alfred E. Rand (16th VT), "A Gallant Sergeant." [Gettysburg]

3:5. "The Youngest Soldier."

6:7. Obit.

8:3. "A Rebel Battleflag Returned." [13th CT returned flag of St. Mary's Cannoniers captured at Irish Bend, LA]

October 29

1:6-7, 2:1-2. John W. Fry (42nd OH), "Capture of Mobile."

4:1. B. F. Finley (5th NY), "Duryea's Zouaves. Their Courage at Gaines' Mill."

4:1. W. A. Wintermute (76th OH), "Bentonville."

4:2. C. E. Husted (3rd OH Cav), "The Fight at Rome, Ga."

4:2. Jonathan Thatcher (15th IA), "He was Certainly Shot." [Black Creek, SC]

4:2. S. H. Barnett (1st WV Cav), "Col. Broadhead's Letter to His Wife."

4:2. J. E. Chaffee (Geary's Div), "How the Johnnies Lost Their Hay."

4:3. H. N. Palmer, "Columbia, S.C., Once More."

4:3. R. K. Shaw, "The 63rd Ohio at Corinth."

5:1. "Bragg's Retreat from Murfreesboro in January 1863." [from Southern Bivouac]

5:1. F. W. Bashore, "Gen. Long's Order When He Left His Command at Macon, Ga."

5:2. J. H. Dawson (66th IL), "Spring Hill to Franklin."

6:6. Obit.

8:1-3. "Booth's Captors. Distribution of the Reward Money. Other Interesting Facts."

12:3. "Gettysburg Monuments. [27th CT]

12:3. W. H. Brown (127th USCT), "A Romantic Story of the War." [Fort Harrison]

November 5

1:6. Obit: John C. Lent (23rd OH).

1:6-7, 2:1. Carleton, Part 71. [Chattanooga]

3:1-2. E. S. Coan (signal corps), "The Army of the Potomac. Its Services Compared to Those of the Army of the Cumberland."

3:2. Jerome Reese (91st IN), "A Fight at Cumberland Gap." [2/22/64]

3:3. Sol Yewell (13th IN), "Mars and Venus." [music]

3:3. Theodore Wiseman (AAG, 2nd Div, 14th Corps), "Bentonville."

3:3. T. M. Beatty (19th IL), "They All Got There First," Missionary Ridge]

3:4. H. H. Burgess (27th OH), "Col. Frank Lynch, and the Desperate Wound He Received at Atlanta."

3:5. L. W. Murdock, "Cedar Creek."

4:6. "Indiana at Gettysburg."

4:6. Obit: John C. Lent (23rd OH).

5:4-5. "Gen. McClellan Dead."

8:4. "Indiana's Dead Heroes. Monuments Erected at Gettysburg to Six Hoosier Regiments."

November 12

1:7, 2:1-2. Free S. Bowley (31st USCT), "Life in Prison. Experiences of Union Officers at Columbia, S.C."

3:1. W. Bristow (24th KY), "In Kentucky During the Early Days of the War."

3:1. D. W. Page, "The Hanging of Serg't. Ferguson."

3:1. Jess S. Langston (110th OH), "Notes from a Musician's Bugle."

3:2. S. L. Coulter (64th OH), "Taking of Chattanooga."

3:2. Jacob Laux (27th OH), "They Thought He was a Spy." [5/64 Stevenson Jct AL]

3:3. Samuel Dunham (63rd PA), "Death of Gen. Hays. Where and How He Fell at the Battle of the Wilderness."

3:3. E. A. Perry (14th NY), "The Charge of Duryea's Zouaves at Gaines's Mills."

3:4. Charles H. Budd (2nd IA), "Col. Rodgers. His Death at Corinth."

3:4. T. H. Carney (5th NY), "It was a Black Horse." [Warren at Gaines' Mill]

3:4. P. H. Goodrich (20th CT), "An Eastern Man at Bentonville."

3:4. Edward Willis (62nd NY), "Why were They Short of Rations?" [6/62]

3:4. Samuel Keenan (124th OH), "Wagner's Brigade at Mission Ridge."

3:5. W. S. Brown (18th OH), "The Cracker Line."

4:7. Obit.

5:4-5. "Mrs. George H. Thomas. She Gives Some Interesting Reminiscences of 'Old Pap'."

November 19

3:1. (1st NY Dragoons), "Capehart's Brigade, and the Gallant Services It Rendered at the Close of the War."

3:1. A. Hougland (66th IL), "He Wants It Righted." [organization of 66th IL]

3:1. A. Houghland (66th IL), "He Wants to Write."

3:2. J. C. Harris (83rd PA, 5th Corps HQ), "The Battle of the Wilderness."

3:2. G. M. Butterfield (31st ME), "Two Maine Regiments."

3:2-3. A. G. Jacobs (6th OH Cav), "The Cavalry Charge at Aldie."

3:3. (4th IA Cav), "Some Rebel Relics."

3:3. I. F. Kelley (6tH WI), "The Iron Brigade."

3:3. W. W. Dougherty (5th IN Cav), "Crossing the Bridge Over Green River."

3:3. G. L. Lang (12th WI), "The First on Mission Ridge."

3:4. Charles M. Case (64th IL), "A Word about Bentonville."

3:4. C. W. Dey (126th NY), "Brigade Designations." [flags]

4:5. Obit.

5:4. "On the Battlefields. The Excursion of G. H. Thomas Post, Cincinnati, to Chattanooga and Atlanta."

November 26

10:3. "General Hancock on the Gettysburg Battlefield."

10:5. F. L. Braun, "Little Mac's Bodyguard."

December 3

1:1-5, 2:5-6. H. A. D. Merritt (5th NY Cav), "Dahlgren's Raid."

1:6-7, 2:1-2. Carleton, Part 72. [Chattanooga]

3:1-2. Arthur Hendricks (5th NY), "Duryea's Zouaves."

3:2. (28th IL), "The Charge at Jackson, Miss."

3:3-4. John H. Prather (91st OH), "The Lynchburg Raid."

3:4. J. W. French, "The 14th Connecticut at Gettysburg."

3:4. W. S. Goss (7th MA), "In Defense of the Army of the Potomac."

3:4. William F. Smith, "The 6th Connecticut Did Not Surrender." [Fort Wagner]

December 10

3:1. Charles F. Lewis, "Chancellorsville. An Able Defense of the Action of the Eleventh Corps on that Field."

3:2. Thomas J. West, "Parson Browlow. Interesting Sketch of How the Knoxville Whig was Escorted from Camp Nelson to Knoxville."

3:3-4. Charles J. Wehrum (12th MA), "Gettysburg."

3:4. J. T. Wood, "Lances in the Rebel Army."

3:4. J. J. Brown (USS *Ozark*), "The Result of Going to a Wedding Without an Invitation." [captured 10/15-16/64, Tunica Bend, LA]

4:7. Obit.

December 17

1:7, 2:1-3. Thomas P. McElrath, "St. Leger Grenfell, the Master Spirit of the Plot to Burn Chicago."

3:1. D. B. McCreary, "The 145th Pa. The True Story of that Affair at Chancellorsville."

3:1-2. Alfred Davenport, "The 5th New York."

3:2. J. P. Van Nest (120th OH), "The Thirteenth Corps' Badge."

3:2. J. S. Thompson (10th VT), "An Incident of the Wilderness."

3:3. J. E. Beckley (95th IL), "Capture of Mobile."

3:3. A. H. Vail (61st NY), "Brag is a Good Dog."

3:3. C. A. Potter (1st CT Hvy Art), "The First Monument to Grant." [Peabody, KS]

3:4. G. C. P. Cleveland (2nd ME Cav), "The Fight at Thibodeaux, La." [6/63]

3:4. J. B. Norris (51st OH), "The Sultana Disaster."

3:4. Mrs. R. H. Sinnott (nurse), "She Saved His Arm."

3:4. D. H. Bishop (107th IL), "Another Story of the Bridge." [Green River, TN]

3:5. "The Colonel Dodged." [103rd NY at Fredericksburg]

3:5. John R. Wilkins (5th VT), E. R. Zellar (36th IL), Charles W. Bayne (22nd PA Cav), Ernest Scott (13th OH Cav), Fred Cossum (75th NY), George H. Uhler (93rd PA), "Men of Many Wounds."

5:4. T. J. McBeath (13th MO), "The War in Missouri."

6:7. Obit.

7:4-5. Biog: William E. McLean (43rd IN).

December 24

1:1-5. W. W. Jackson, "The Battle of Shiloh. The Brilliant Services of the "Fighting Fourth Division'."

1:6-7. Earl M. Rogers (6th WI), "How Wadsworth Fell."

3:1-3. E. B. Lufkin (13th ME), "Life on Ship Island."

3:3. Nathaniel Gilpin, "The 118th Pa."

3:3. Charles Waterhouse (20th ME), "The Army of the Potomac at Malvern Hill."

3:4. C. W. Dey (126th NY), "Brigade and Division Flags."

3:4. Alfred K. Oates (74th NY), "A 'Wandering Jew'." [George Thatcher—oldest veteran]

3:4. W. H. Nunamaker (25th IL), "Gen. W. H. Gibson's Farewell Order."

3:4. Robert O. Link (14th Corps), "A Western Man Grows Ironical."

3:5. A. C. Byerly (MS Marine Brig), "More 'Loyal Rebels'."

3:5. P. P. McCune (65th OH), "Chattanooga and Franklin."

3:5. "Some More 'Kids'."

4:7. Obit.

December 31

1:1-3. Howard, Part 52. [Gettysburg]

1:4-6. A. L. Mabbett (24th CT), "At Port Hudson."

3:1. A. F. Sperry (33rd IA), "Last Siege of the War. Well-Told Incidents of the Capture of Mobile."

3:2. W. M. Prouty (31st IA), "What Gen. Sherman Says About It." [Columbia SC]

3:2. (WI), "The Iron Brigade."

3:2. V. V. Williams (18th IN), "A Reminiscence."

3:3. John H. Bohn (92nd IL), "Taking of Chattanooga."

3:3. C. E. Bassett (124th IL), "The Excelsior Banner." [drill competition]

3:3-4. J. A. Pettis (5th NJ), "The Jersey Brigade." [Chancellorsville]

3:4. J. E. Walton, "The 30th Ohio. Some Reminiscences of the Battle of Antietam."

3:4-5. "Kentucky Troops. Some Facts Concerning the Troops Furnished by that State."

3:5. Coburn D. Outten (45th KY), J. M. Adair (86th IN), "The First on Mission Ridge."

4:7. Obit.

1886

January 7

1:1-4, 2:5-7. Edward L. Barnes, "The 95th New York. Sketch of Its Services in the Campaigns of 1862."

1:5-6. Wallace W. Johnson, "About the Bucktails. . . . Up the Shenandoah. . . ."

3:1. "The Lynchburg Raid."

3:1. J. M. Garven (126th OH), "The Sixth Corps in the Wilderness."

3:2. (Bty L, 1st OH), "A Useful Prisoner. How an Arrested 'Suspect' Provided His Guards with Toothsome Viands."

3:2. (10th IL), "One Regiment that Slung No Gore."

3:2. Samuel Dunham (63rd PA), "Compliments to the West."

3:3. "A Snowball Battle." [1/63 Frankfort KY between 44th, 100th, 103rd, 104th OH]

3:3. Louis H. Breker (MO), "He was a Kid."

3:3. A. H. Taylor (1st IA Cav), "Bayonets and Sabers."

3:3. Joseph G. Eldred (1st MI), "The Fifth Corps at Antietam."

3:4. H. H. Martin (20th IA), "Lances in the Rebel Army." [Mobile]

3:4. A. H. Bocher (73rd IN), "Capt. Jack Warner." [Libby Prison]

3:4. T. B. Fouch (Loudoun Rangers), "Another Witness." [Capt. Warner]

3:4. W. H. Smith (7th IN Cav), "He Wonders Why They were Punished."

3:4. Samuel A. McNeil (31st OH), "Thomas' Corps at Mission Ridge."

4:5. Obit.

January 14

1:4-7. W. W. Jackson, "On the Hatchie." [Corinth Campaign]

2:3-4. "Burnside to Hooker. A Valuable Contribution to War History." [*Magazine of American History*]

3:1. C. W. Greene (12th NY), "The 118th Pa. The Bloody Fight at Shepherdstown Ford."

3:1-2. William C. Staples, "The Tuscarora."

3:2. J. Weidensall (84th PA), "The 'Bull Pen.' A Few Incidents of the Fight at Hatcher's Run." [10/27/64]

3:2. George W. Toms (5th NY Cav), "The Saber was Useful." [5/63 vs. Mosby at Warrenton Jct]

3:3. James P. Weems, "The 21st Illinois. How Gen. Grant Commenced His Career in the Late War."

3:3. John Weigel, "The 76th Pa. at Fort Wagner."

4:6. Obit.

January 21

1:1-3. William E. Curtis, "General Phil Sheridan."

1:4-6. John W. Fry (42nd OH), "James A. Garfield. His Character and Career as a Soldier."

1:7, 2:1. A. W. Tucker, "'Orange Blossoms.' Services of the 124th New York at Gettysburg."

3:1-2. Luis Emilio (54th MA), "Fort Wagner."

3:2. B. F. Gilman (32nd MA), "Regiments Losing the Most Men."

3:2. S.W. Aldrich (Bty A, 1st RI), "What Regiment was It?" [Antietam]

3:2. J. WWhite (2nd WI), "The Iron Brigade."

3:3. George Shatswell (15th IL), "He Liked the Account." [12/24/85 Jackson about Shiloh]

3:3. J. E. Carter, "A Soldier in Trouble. A Union Man Arrested for Killing a Murderous Rebel 21 Years Ago." [J. L. Sigman, 14th KY Cav]

3:3. John S. Mavity, "The 24th Kentucky."

3:3. Charles Matthews (8th KY), "Planting the Flag on Lookout Mountain."

3:4. S. L. Wilson (5th WI Bty), "He Knows Who Set the Rosin Pit on Fire." [Black River SC 2/65]

4:7. Obit.

5:4-5. Biog: George C. Rogers (15th IL).

January 28

1:1-5. A. E. Glanville (10th MN), "Gen. A. J. Smith's Raid, and the Meeting He had with Forest at Tupelo."

1:5. Mortimer D. Leggett, "The Excelsior Banner."

3:1. D. R. Sanders (81st IL), "Spanish Fort."

3:2. A. R. Bander (Bty C, 2nd USC Art), "A Lively Expedition." [6/64 from Vicksburg]

3:2. A.C. Merrill (6th MI), "A Reminiscence of Ship Island."

3:2. Andrew Ballweg (6th WI), "The Iron Brigade."

3:3. John L. Richard (111th OH), "Who was He?" [Lt. Sam Davis, CSA spy]

3:4. John B. Gandolfo (178th NY), "The Sixteenth Corps at Mobile."

4:5. Biog: W. P. Hepburn (2nd IA Cav).

4:5. Obit.

February 4

1:1-4. George A. Robertson, "The Great Captain. Gen. Dent Gives Some Personal Recollections of Grant."

1:5-7. Thomas W. Bradley (124th NY) and Peter B. Ayars (99th PA), "At Gettysburg. The Splendid Work Done by Smith's Battery. The Gallant Charge of the 124th N.Y. and 99th Pa."

3:1-2. David Ross (7th MA), "The Wilderness."

3:2. J. R. Tisdale (29th MO), "Around Chattanooga. Lookout Mountain, Mission Ridge, and Ringgold."

3:2. D. Leahy, "The 9th Connecticut."

3:3. A. J. Deming (13th PA Res), "Bucktails at Gettysburg."

3:3. B. T. Bevelle (23rd MO), "The Battle of Shiloh."

3:3. B. F. Finley (5th NY), "The 5th New York."

3:4. E. T. Lee (41st IL), "Col. Jackson's Shiloh Article."

3:5. "A Brave Army Nurse in Distress." [Mother Eleanor C. Ransom]

4:5. Biog: Thomas M. Browne (7th IN Cav).

4:6. Obit.

February 11

1:7, 2:1. John B. Turchin, "Bayonet and Saber. Their Value as Weapons in Modern Warfare. Successful Charges. Cold Steel at Chickamauga and Mission Ridge. Scaling the Malakoff. How a Bayonet Charge Ended the Crimean War."

3:1. (7th IN), "At Gettysburg. How a Proposed Night Attack by the Enemy was Foiled."

3:1. T. W. Gibson (47th IL), "Capture of Mobile."

3:2. William J. Shirley (11th PA Cav), "Kelley's Store."

3:2. Charles Van Wye (23rd MO), "The Battle of Jonesboro."

3:2. W. W. Bush (28th NY), "Another Tribute to the 'Merciful' Jack Warner."

3:2. J. Y. Lummis (25th IL), "Missionary Ridge."

3:3. A. L. Hathaway (8th MI Cav), "Lances in the Rebel Army."

3:4. William E. Loring (141st PA), "A Convalescent Camp."

4:5. Biog: Thomas J. Henderson (112th IL).

4:6-7. Obit.

5:5. Obit: Gen. David Hunter.

February 18

1:5-7, 2:1-4. Obit: Winfield S. Hancock.

3:1. W. C. Yard (4th PA Cav), "A Raid on the Sutlers."

3:2. Charles H. Snedecker (124th IL), "Spanish Fort."

3:2. Charles Smith (49th PA), "He was Not as Good as Comrade Duvall."

3:2. Frank Fritz (3rd MI), "How I was Introduced to Old Abe."

3:2. E. H. Gregg (10th KS), "Kansas Claims Twins, Triplets, and Jeff Davis's Son."

3:2. Walter B. Scates, "The Badge of the Thirteenth Corps."

3:3. N. D. Brown, "A Western Man Gets Mad."

3:3. O. V. Joslyn, "A Bullet Through the Head." [Lucien L. Sanborn, 6th VT]

3:3. T. S. Potter (8th OH), "A Sickening Sight. The Execution of Two Bounty-Jumpers."

3:4. O. C. Bowen (6th OH), Samuel W. Bird (35th IL), "Mission Ridge."

3:4. W. W. Perry (82nd PA), "The Sixth Corps at the Wilderness."

3:5. S. W. Taylor (52nd PA), "Are They Living?" [11/29/64 escapees from Charleston to Morris Island]

4:7. Obit.

February 25

1:5-7, 2:1. G. J. Trenaman (USN), "Striving for Liberty. The Story of Five Soldiers Who Escaped from Meridian Bull-Pen."

3:1. R. C. Howard (124th IL), "Capture of Mobile."

3:2. William Clark (2nd TN), "A Fatal Mistake. How a Flag of Truce was Fired On." [Fall 1862 Cumberland Gap]

3:2. W. H. Edsall (22nd IL), "The First on Mission Ridge."

3:2. John W. Wilson (57th IN), "The First to Enter Chattanooga."

3:2. E. Bassett (8th IL Cav), "Where Did He Go?" [5/63 smuggler]

3:3. Lindsay Steele (30th IL), "The Battle of Belmont."

3:3. T. W. Baird (21st MO), "Shiloh."

3:3. D. A. Luckhart, "The 61st Pa. at Fair Oaks."

3:4. John H. Prather (91st OH), "The Lynchburg Raid. Sufferings of the Army on that Disastrous Retreat."

3:4. "Florence. A Christmas in the Gloomy Prison Made Jovial with a Mess of Peas."

4:5. Biog: J. B. Weaver (2nd IA).

4:7. Obit.

5:3-4. "The Forty-ninth Congress. The Fitz-John Porter Bill Passed by the House."

March 4

1:6-7, 2:1-2. "How a Fort was Taken. The Investment and Bombardment of Fort Pulaski."

3:1. J. E. Smith (4th NY Bty), "The 'Devil's Den.' Its Defense at Gettysburg by Smith's Battery and Its Supports."

3:1. A. L. Brown, Mitchell S. Barney (31st IL), "That Prize Flag."

3:2. James P. Suter (13th PA Cav), "Hatcher's Run."

3:2. M. G. Yarnell (36th IL), "That Baking Soda. A Humerous Story of a Feast had by Some of the 36th Ill. Boys."

3:2. J. S. Lemmon (5th IA Cav), "A Christmas in Andersonville."

3:3. W. D. Spaulding, "The Stocks. How a Fawning Soldier was 'Hoist with His own Petard'."

3:3. F. H. Crago (22nd PA Cav), "Lincoln's Love for the Soldier."

3:3. W. W. Barnett, "Hatchie Bridge."

3:3. William L. Gilman, "The 15th Massachusetts."

3:4. Frank L. Osborn (Bty H, 3rd NY), "That Providence Regiment. The Mutual Mistake of Chaplain and Driver."

4:5. Biog: Albert C. Thompson (105th PA).

4:5. Obit: W. R. Rowley (45th IL, Grant's staff).

4:5-6. Obit.

March 11

1:7, 2:1. Z. T. Griffen (122nd NY), "In the Wilderness."

3:1. A. H. Fitch (33rd WI), "Tupelo."

3:2. (126th OH), "Monocacy."

3:2. George H. Allen (4th RI), "Hatcher's Run, as Told in a Comrade's Diary."

3:3. P. S. Moore (40th IN), "Warner's Brigade at Chattanooga."

3:3. (6th WI), "The Regiment that Rescued the Rhode Island Battery at Antietam."

3:3. William Knight (88th IN), "His Tongue was Alright."

3:4. E. C. Culp (25th OH), "A Note from a Prisoner's Diary." [7/22/62 shooting]

3:4. William A. Potter (21st MA), "South Mountain and Antietam."

3:4. James M. Russell (1st IA Cav), "Missouri Guerrillas. Their Horrible Work at Centralia, Mo."

4:5. Biog: William Warner (33rd WI).

4:6. Obit: E. C. Culp (25th OH).

March 18

1:6-7, 2:4-5. George B. Jenness, "Gen. A. D. McCook. A Soldier's Pen in Defense of a Gallant Officer."

3:1. J. N. Brown, "It Did Sling Gore. A Comrade Denies that the 10th Ill. was a Pacific Regiment."

3:1. W. T. Chapman (103rd OH), "They Did Not Succeed." [attempt to take Kentucky out of the Union, 1862-63]

3:1. William Bracken (88th USCT), "The Sultana Disaster."

3:1. P. C. Smith (119th IL), "Mobile."

3:2. T. Sprague (66th IL), "Inscription in an Old Cemetery Near Cheraw, S.C."

3:2. George W. Hufford, "Losses of the 19th Indiana."

3:2. C. E. Bassett (124th IL), "The Siege of Vicksburg."

3:2. John K. Shellenberger (64th OH), "Garfield at Chickamauga."

3:2. J. W. Smalley (16th IL Cav), "A Joke on Gen. Stoneman."

3:3. John C. Casey (7th WI), "That Cherry Tree." [Appomattox]

3:3. Lewis Blundin (28th PA), "The Regiment that Supported the 1st R.I. Artillery at Antietam."

3:3. Thomas . Davis (38th IL), "Knob Gap Once More."

3:4. Robert A. Walton (12th MI), "The Battle of Shiloh."

3:4. Joseph E. Miner (15th MA), "Spottsylvania."

3:4. "Youngest."

4:5. Biog: Charles A. Boutele (USN).

4:7. Obit.

March 25

1:6-7, 2:1. John S. Schenck (16th IL), "In the Carolinas."

3:1. Charles M. Castle (102nd IL), "Averysboro."

3:1. F. Vogl (KS), "Youngest."

3:2. George B. Halsted, "Treated as Felons. How Officers of Pope's Army were Treated by Proc. of Jeff Davis."

3:2. L. W. Richardson (68th OH), "On the Hatchie."

3:3-4. S. C. Thompson (100th NY), "He Lacked Sand. A Reminiscence of Morris Island."

3:4. James Poole (13th US), "Who Shaved the Horse's Tail?"

4:7. Obit.

April 1

1:1-6. John A. Logan, "Bull Run."

3:1. T. J. McBeath (50th IL), "Campaigning in 1861. The Adventure of Some Illinois Boys in Missouri."

3:1. J. C. Robinson (70th OH), "About a Sword."

3:1. J. C. Ambrose (113th OH), "Where is that Flag?" [CSA battery flag captured at Jonesboro]

3:2. D. C. Hagle (11th MO), "The Red River Campaign."

3:2. Charles Edinborough (67th NY), "The Sixth Corps at the Wilderness."

3:3. E. V. Smith (27th IA), "General A. J. Smith."

3:3. W. W. Angelo, "The 10th Illinois. A Comrade of that Regiment Claims It Did Some Good Fighting."

4:5. Biog: Oscar L. Jackson (63rd OH), James D. Brady (37th NY).

4:7. Obit.

5:5. Will L. Welch (23rd MA), "Roanoke Island, and the Part Hawkins's Zouaves Took in the Affair."

8:3. H. H. Hurst (30th IL), "Retaliation." [3/65 SC]

8:4. John Latta (1st AL Cav), "Kilpatrick's Surprise." [Monroe Crossroads]

8:4. R. B. Van Gardner (23rd NY), "The Iron Brigade Again."

8:4. E. T. Lee (41st IL), "The Prize Drill."

April 8

1:1-7, 2:1-2. Logan, Part 2.

3:6-7. Carleton, Part 74. [Knoxville]

4:1. John H. Mansur, "Knoxville. A Member of the Signal Corps Relates How the Siege Ended."

4:1. Elijah Walker, "The 4th Maine at Gettysburg."

4:1. George I. Mosher, "The 53rd Illinois at the Hatchie."

4:2. "The First Skirmish. How Some Loyal Boys Kept the Johnnies from Capturing the Boat." [McCoy's Ferry, Potomac River]

4:2. John A. Coleman (18th IL), "He Knows the Rebels had Lances."

4:3. E. Barber (112th NY), "Cold Harbor."

4:3. E. B. Lufkin (13th ME), "He Did Not Like Ship Island, Anyhow."

4:3. John Heintzelman (Bty K, 1st MO), "Who was the Old Captain?" [Shiloh]

4:4. Scott W. Jones (12th PA Cav), "A Rebel Stampede. How the Johnnies were Driven from Frederick, Md." [1864]

4:4. M. J. Clerihan, "He Says the 10th Illinois 'Did Sling Gore'."

4:4. J. E. Bishop (76th IL), "Fort Blakely, Ala."

4:4. Grove H. Dutton (147th NY), "Losses of the 24th Mich. at Gettysburg."

6:5-6. Biog: Joseph H. Potter (12th NH).

6:6. Biog: Truman A. Merriman (92nd NY).

6:7. Obit.

11:1-2. "A Beautiful Rebel. A Woman to Whose Charms Officers Yielded Their Loyalty." [Rose Greenhow]

11:2. "Hancock's Heroism at Gettysburg." [*Brooklyn Eagle*]

11:2-3. "Through the Rebel Lines in a Hand Car." [*Chicago Inter-Ocean*; Tennessee to Louisville]

12:2-3. Biog: B. F. Gott (57th, 174th NY), Thomas Bell (8th NY Cav), Edward A. Dubey (10th NY), James McLeer, Henry A. Phillips (47th NY), George S. Little (97th NY).

12:3. "C. F. Smith's Opinion of Other Officers." [*St. Louis Globe-Democrat*]

12:4. "He Doesn't Forget. Col. Hapgood's Lecture at Concord."

12:4. "Farragut in Mobile Bay."

12:4. "The Rebel Administration's Surrender." [*Washington Star*]

April 15

1:1-7, 2:1. Logan, Part 3.

2:5. Nathaniel Session (1st US Ss), "Gettysburg. A Skirmish Which had an Important Bearing on that Great Victory."

2:5. "The First Time He Saw Federal Cavalry." [*Cincinnati Commercial Gazette*, regarding J. S. Wise at Appomattox]

4:1. J. P. Van Nest, "The Thirteenth Army Corps Badge."

4:1. Samuel Dunham (63rd PA), "The Wilderness."

4:1. C. E. Bassett (124th IL), "The Siege of Vicksburg."

4:2. J. E. Walton (30th OH), "Antietam."

4:2. Milton Barnes (97th OH), "Taking of Chattanooga."

4:3. R. A. Clark (14th NJ), "Monocacy."

4:3. John E. Packard (8th KS), "Missionary Ridge Again."

4:4. V. D. Eddy (44th NY), "How the Boys Got the Heifer to the Stockade."

4:4. Max Forvilly (14th WI), "Gen. A. J. Smith's Raid on Tupelo."

4:4. Matthew McEnenny (86th IN), "Missionary Ridge Again."

4:5-6. Joel J. Finney (57th IN), "Franklin."

4:6. P. S. Galley (14th IL), "Protecting the Ballot Box in Tennessee."

4:6. W. B. Bailey)92nd IL), "The First to Enter Chattanooga."

5:2. Grove H. Dutton (147th NY), "Weldon Railroad. Its Capture by the Fifth Corps."

5:3-4. Sergt. Reyburn, "Tales of the Picket-Fire. The Story of a Scout in Tennessee."

5:4. B. F. Boring (30th IL), "Nightgown Brigade."

6:7. Obit.

11:1-2. Richmond Wolcott (10th IL), "A December March. The Scamper from Chattanooga for the Relief of Burnside."

11:2. "A Terrible Ordeal." [*St. Louis Republican*, about Union colonel at New Hope Church, 5/27/64]

12:1-2. John B. Turchin, "Bayonet and Saber."

12:3. P. C. Smith (119th IL), "Gen. A. J. Smith at Tupelo."

April 22

1:1-2. Carleton, Part 75. [1864 plans]

1:1-6. Logan, Part 4.

1:7. "At Nashville. Gallant Service of the 15th Indiana Battery."

4:1. I. K. Young (89th IL), "Chickamauga."

4:2. Charles M. Cone, "On the Hatchie. The 12th Michigan the First to Cross the Bridge."

4:2. L. G. Nelson (15th WI), "New Hope."

4:2. C. W. DeMotte (20th IN), "An Incident of Libby."

4:3. George Schloetzer (82nd IL), "A Prank of Cupid. How a Deserter was Saved."

4:3. W. H. Bolson (16tH WI), "He Corrects Comrade Baird." [Shiloh]

4:3. (81st OH), "Death of Col. Rogers."

4:3. Frederick Seeman, "The Services of the 25th Missouri at Shiloh."

4:4. C. E. Engle (82nd OH), "The Eleventh Corps at Chancellorsville."

4:5. C. H. Pease, "Jonesboro. The 17th N.Y. in the Fight."

4:5. H. C. Remlow (10th MI), "Jonesboro. Another Account."

5:3. F. Opperman (167th OH), "The Lynchburg Raid."

6:1. Biog: Francis A. Walker (15th MA).

6:6. Biog: Benjamin LeFevre (OH).

6:7. Obit.

11:1-2. Emily T. Charles, "Gen. Hancock. An Hour With Him in His Home."

12:1-2. H. A. Tripp (10th ME), "Cedar Mountain."

April 29

1:1-5, 2:6. Marcus A. Reno, "'Boots and Saddles.' The Cavalry of the Army of the Potomac. Corps Organization. Its Gallant Leaders, from Stoneman to Sheridan."

1:6-7, 2:1-2. Tripp, Part 2.

3:1-2. H. Emrich (13th IL Cav), "The Camden Trip. Six Weeks of Marching and Fighting. Jenkins's Ferry."

3:3. Andrew Fuchs (146th NY), "Two Incidents of Gettysburg."

3:3. W. W. Jackson (15th IL), "The First Muster for Three Years."

3:3. Jonathan L. Bruce (3rd KY Cav), "Lances in the Union Army."

3:3. Benjamin A. Spear (57th MA), "Youngest Generals."

3:5. Augustus Pomranke, "How the 3rd Wisconsin Got Soft Bread."

4:6. Biog: Wager Swayne (43rd OH).

4:7. Obit.

May 6

1:1-4. Mortimer D. Leggett, "Battle of Atlanta."

1:5-7. Tripp, Part 3.

3:1. Edward Bennett (44th NY), "Gettysburg."

3:2. E. T. Lee (41st IL), "Shiloh."

3:2. James Smith (21st MO), "It was Capt. Fulton." [Shiloh]

3:2. Lewis Filler (13th OH), "The 3,000 Prisoners Taken at Stone River."

3:3. Edward I. Ramsay (43rd IN), "New Madrid."

3:3. Hiram L. Finch (34th NY), "A Ball Through the Head." [W. Evans, 1st NY Dragoons]

3:3. O. H. Frink (124th IL), "Mobile and Spanish Fort."

3:4. John F. kennedy (78th OH), "The Excelsior Prize Drill."

3:4. George A. Smith (7th OH Cav), "They Cut Through the Bottom of the Car." [railroad to Andersonville]

3:4. Theodore Cook, "The 9th N.Y. at Roanoke."

3:5. J. E. Macklin (16th IN), "How Capt. C. T. Doxey Captured a Rebel Camp." [Red River Campaign]

4:6. Biog: John B. Weber (44th NY), Charles S. Baxter (27th NY).

4:7. Obit.

May 13

1:1-6. Leggett, Part 2.

2:6. "Gen. Whitaker and the Spent Ball." [*Chicago Inter-Ocean*, Chickamauga]

3:1. Isaac L. Burnes, "The 10th Mich. Cav. Its Long Marches—An Honest Sergeant."

3:2. "'Carleton' Criticized." [Knoxville]

3:2. Evelyn Kelsey (9th CT), "Ship Island."

3:2. G. C. Murphy (124th IL), "That Prize Banner Again."

3:3. William J. Shirley (11th PA Cav), "Siege of Suffolk, as Taken from a Comrade's Diary."

3:3. C. B. Shouse, "The 53rd Ill. at the Hatchie."

3:3. J. M. Lovejoy (121st NY), "Division Flags."

3:4. James S. France (17th NY), "Battle of Jonesboro."

3:4. J. C. Powell (2nd PA Cav), "Hatcher's Run."

3:4. John F. Iliff (13th IL), "Blair's Brigade at Chickasaw Bayou."

3:5. E. G. Waring (16th WI), "Shiloh."

3:5. P. D. Davis (6th MO), "A Woman Soldier." [Charles Johehous, 6th MO, killed at Resaca]

3:5. James Fisher (17th IN), "Wilder's Brigade at Chickamauga."

3:5. I. L. Smith (36th IN), "The Prisoners Captured at Stone River."

3:5. R. Collins [scout], "The First to Enter Fayetteville."

3:6. Lewis Blundin (28th PA), "Cedar Mountain."

4:5. Biog: M. D. Leggett.

4:6. Obit.

6:6. "Shot Through the Heart, and Yet They Keep Living Right Along."

8:2. "Monument of the 69th Pa. at Gettysburg."

May 20

1:1-6. C. E. Troutman (12th NJ), "The Second Corps. How Grandly It Met the Shock at Gettysburg."

3:1-2. John K. Shellenberger (64th OH), "Missionary Ridge."

3:3. A. H. Brown (96th OH), "Mobile."

3:3. H. Ramsey (3rd IA Cav), "Florence. How a Starving Comrade Traded His Boots for a Meal."

3:3. "Battle of Wise's Forks."

3:4. W. F. Bacon (13th IL Cav), "The 'Mule Whacker'."

3:4. Joseph Myers (120th OH), "The First to Land at Bruinsburg."

3:4. A. N. Jennings (121st NY), "Gen. Wadsworth's Death." [quoting from the diary of a CSA officer in his possession]

3:4. (4th RI), "Hawkins's Zouaves at Roanoke Island."

3:4. H.C. Neff (1st OH), "What Became of Dat Cullud Genman?"

3:5. T. L. Sullivan (13th MO Cav), "Missouri Butchery. Some of Quantrall's Bloody Work." [11/3/62 near Harrisonville]

3:5. Charles W. Scharff (115th NY), "The Battle of Cold Harbor."

4:4-5. Biog: John H. Ketcham (150th NY), Martin A. Haynes (2nd NH).

4:7. Obit.

6:2. Biog: A. L. Conger (115th OH).

6:7. George I. Miller (53rd IL), "The Battle of the Hatchie."

8:5. Obit: Albin Schoepf.

May 27

1:1-6. J. A. Bigelow (5th MI Cav), "'Draw Saber, Charge!' The Michigan Brigade at Gettysburg."

1:7, 2:1-2. J. A. Bering (48th OH), "Sunday at Shiloh."

2:3-4. "A Picture of War. A Glance at the Army Medical Museum in Washington."

3:1. W. J. Landrum, "Vicksburg. Gen. Landrum Tells About the Surrender of Vicksburg."

3:1. Arthur S. Fitch (107th NY), "New Hope Church. How Sherman was Held in Check Eleven Days."

3:2. A. W. Huber (7th PA Cav), "A Successful Forage."

3:2. Robert Trotter (10th NY Cav), "Comrade Trotter Criticizes Gen. Reno."

3:3. Edward B. Long (1st NJ), "The First Bull Run. The Retreat from that Disastrous Field."

3:3. "The 1st Connecticut Heavy Artillery."

3:3. Ole Steensland (15th WI), "Knob Gap Once More."

3:3. James Stephenson (14th WI), "Gen. Smith's Raid on Tupelo."

3:4. Owen K. Smith (50th PA), "A Doctor Who Did Grand Service as a Spy." [Dr. William Beall, Washington County, MD, 7/64]

3:4. John B. Burris (3rd MO Cav), "How Jeff Thompson was Captured."

3:4. N. Patterson (32nd OH), "The Flag of Truce at Vicksburg."

3:4. Joseph N. Barrett (25th IN), "The First to Cross the Bridge." [Hatchie]

3:5. S. A. McNeil (31st OH), "New Hope Church."

3:5. "Men of Many Wounds, Who Have Suffered for Their Country."

3:5. J. N. Stanford (18th US), "The Charge Up Mission Ridge."

3:5. G. L. Pearson (94th OH), "Did the Officers Eat the Dog?" [Cowan's Station TN]

3:5. J. W. Morgan (109th NY), "The 38th Wisconsin at Fort Mahone."

4:5. Biog: Edwin S. Osborne (149th PA).

4:5. Obit.

8:4. "After 24 Years. Revisiting the Battlefields of Antietam and South Mountain."

June 3

1:1-5. Frederick Ford, "'Stand to the Wheel!' Down the Kanawha Between Lines of Blazing Carbines. . . ." [3/29/63]

1:6-7, 2:1. Jacob Higgins (125th PA), "At Antietam."

3:1. O. D. Thatcher, "1st Minnesota at Bull Run."

3:2-3. H. S. Hunter (1st MN Bty), "Pittsburgh Landing."

3:3. Willard Elmore (143rd NY), "How He Saw Them. A Comrade of the 143rd N.Y. Tells of Bentonville and Averysboro."

3:3. C. A. Timpkins (137th NY), "The First to Enter Atlanta."

3:4. L. B. Waddington, "The 38th Wisconsin at Fort Mahone."

3:4. W. W. Cook (9th MI Cav), "Morgan's Defeat at Cynthiana."

3:4. J. H. Cook, "Saving the Bridge Over the Chattahoochie River."

3:4. R. H. Martin (46th IN), "The Badge of the Thirteenth Corps."

3:5. J. S. Myers (153rd PA), "The Eleventh Corps at Gettysburg."

3:5. "Comrade Tripp Defends Himself." [Cedar Mt]

4:3-4. "Monument to the Berdan Sharpshooters." [Gettysburg]

4:6. Obit.

4:7. "General Hiram Berdan."

8:3. "The 12th N.J. at Gettysburg." [monument]

June 10

1:1-4. Carleton, Part 76. [Wilderness]

2:2-4. Obit: George J. Stannard, George G. Benedict.

3:1. M. G. Reed (51st PA), "Antietam. How the 51st Pa. Took the Bridge."

3:1. A. M. Sample (1st WV Cav), "The Fight with Mosby at Warrenton Junction." [5/63]

3:2. Samuel Dunham (63rd PA), "Spottsylvania."

3:2. W. O. Hubbell (12th KS), "The Camden Trip, and the Fight at Jenkins's Ferry."

3:3. W. D. Hughes (146th NY), "Duryea's Zouaves."

3:3. W. W. Gardner (13th US), "The Man Who Clipped the Horse's Mane."

3:3. E. A. Wilson (1st US Ss), "An Incident of Gettysburg."

3:3. W. D. Meeker (28th IL), "Hurlbut's Division at the Hatchie."

3:4. Nathaniel Mullin (10th IL), "New Madrid."

3:4. F. Springer, "The 13th Pa. Cavalry at Hatcher's Run."

3:4. F. M. Work (1st WV Cav), "An Incident After the Battle of Cross Keys."

3:5. E. C. Lucas (8th KY), "Lookout Mountain."

4:6. Biog: Edmund N. Morrill (7th KS Cav).

4:7. Obit.

6:6. "On to Gettysburg. The Great Reunion of the Third Corps on July 2."

6:7. "Another Memorial at Gettysburg." [73rd PA]

8:3. "The 15th Mass. Visits Gettysburg, Antietam, and Ball's Bluff."

8:5-6. Crosby Johnson (76th OH), "The Battle of Atlanta."

8:6. C. F. Waldron (29th OH), "Cedar Mountain."

June 17

1:1-5. Carleton, Part 77. [Spotsylvania]

1:6-7, 2:1-3. H. Balling, "An Artist's Memories. Mr. Balling's Reminiscences of Lincoln, Grant and Sherman."

2:3. E. D. Tasker (4th ME), "The 'Devil's Den'."

2:3. R. M. Dihel (30th IL), "The Tuscumbia at Bruinsburg."

3:1-3. John Bresnahan (27th IN), "Cedar Mountain."

3:3. W. D. O'Brien (1st MN), "They Planted Shells." [Yorktown]

3:4. E. T. Lee, "A Sacred Relic. Return of the Blue Field Flag of the 41st Illinois." [captured 7/12/63]

3:5. Milton Ringland (11th IL Cav), "Gen. A. J. Smith. A Comrade Tells How He Took a Midnight Tramp with the General." [at Memphis with USCT]

3:5. J. W. Rumple (55th OH), "Cogswell's Brigade at Bentonville."

4:5. Biog: A. J. Holmes (24th, 37th WI), James T. Johnson (6th IN Cav, 8th TN Cav).

4:7. Obit.

8:3. "Delaware Monuments at Gettysburg."

June 24

1:1-4. Carleton, Part 78. [Spotsylvania]

1:5-6. "A Friend in Need. An Officer's Story of the Best Day's Work of His Life." [IA colonel 2/26/65 train from Florence to Goldsboro]

2:5-6. "Gen. Berdan Finds Himself Overwhelmed with Correspondence."

3:1-3. John T. Booth (36th OH), "Battle of Lewisburg."

3:3. E. M. Downing, "The 10th Ill. A Comrade Insists that It Slung Some Gore."

3:3. L. A. Patterson, "The 101st Illinois at Atlanta."

3:3. Charles M. Cone (12th MI), "On the Hatchie Once More."

3:4. J. P. Northrup (2nd NJ), "The Jersey Blues."

3:4. Benjamin C. Wilson (13th TN Cav), "Flintlocks in the Union Army."

3:4. John C. Tressel (96th OH), "That Flag of Truce Again." [Vicksburg]

3:4. E. B. Maxham (1st VT), "The First Regiment to Encamp in Virginia."

3:5. G. T. Kurtz (18th MO), "Sixteenth Army Corps at Atlanta."

3:5. J. L. Richard (111th OH), "A Happy Prisoner. He Thinks Bread, Beef, Pickled Pork, etc. Hard Prison Fare." [Camp Chase]

3:5. J. Q. A. Zombro (107th IL), "Both Eyes Shot Out."

3:5. H. Morgan (8th KY), "An Unpalatable Meal at Florence."

3:6. H. M. Riggs (92nd USCT), "The Plot Failed. How the Attempt to Seize the Steamer was Frustrated." [Red River]

4:6. Biog: William McKinley (23rd OH).

4:6. Obit.

6:6. "Gettysburg. Those Who are Going to the Great Reunion."

8:7. "Another Gettysburg Monument." [28th MA]

July 1

1:1-3. Carleton, Part 79. [North Anna]

3:1-2. Charles H. Myerhoff (14th IN), "Battle of Winchester." [Kernstown]

3:2. Frank L. Hicks, "The 7th West Virginia at Antietam."

3:3. Cy Crisman, "The First Flag in Chattanooga."

3:3. Joseph Ames, "38th Wisconsin at Fort Mahone."

3:3. C. W. Dey (126th NY), "Division and Brigade Flags."

3:3-4. C. A. B. Fox (86th IL), "Bentonville."

3:4. A. S. Thompson, "The 5th N.Y. Cavalry at Warrenton." [5/3/63]

3:4. Joseph M. McGuire, "The 38th Illinois in the Tullahoma Campaign."

3:4. J. B. Armentrout (47th IL), "Where is the Leaden Gun?" [Memphis 1864, homemade rifle]

3:5-6. A. S. Round (34th NY), "Antietam."

4:3. "The Cavalry at Gettysburg." [reunion in 1887]

4:5-6. Biog: Egbert J. Viele, J. C. Burrows (17th MI).

4:6. Obit.

5:3. Biog: John Taylor (2nd PA Res).

5:4-6. "Fitz-John Porter. The Bill Passed by the Senate to the President."

8:5. "Corporal Rhial Honored. The First Union Soldier Killed on Northern Soil Reinterred on the Spot Where He Fell." [6/22/63]

July 8

1:1-5. A. E. Glanville (10th MN), "Battle of Nashville."

1:6-7, 2:1-2. H. D. O'Brien (1st MN), "Battle of Oak Grove."

2:3-6. "At Gettysburg. Encampment of the GAR of Penna."

3:1. H. V. Van Vechten (1st NY Mtd Rifles), "Siege of Suffolk, as Related in a New York Cavalryman's Diary."

3:2-3. J. Hinson (33rd OH), "Bentonville."

3:3. Lewis Blundin (28th PA), "Comrade Blundin Wants Fair Play." [Cedar Mountain]

3:4. J. J. Billow, "The 208th Penna. A Brief Sketch of Its History."

3:5. J. C. Kittelman (69th IN), "Vicksburg. How Gen. Grant Obtained a Foothold in the Rear of the Rebel Stronghold."

3:5. George W. Toms, "The 5th N.Y. Cavalry at the Wilderness."

3:6. W. E. Seaman (89th IL), "Death of Col. [Duncan J.] Hall at Chickamauga."

3:6. Emil Graf (1st MN), "The First Three-Years' Muster."

3:6. Charles Banks (1st OH), "Who Clipped the Horse's Manes and Tails?" [of Col. Bowman, 93rd OH]

4:5. Biog: John M. Farquhar (89th IL), Joseph Lyman (4th IA Cav, 29th IA).

4:7. Obit.

6:6. Biog: Daniel Caldwell (13th PA Cav).

July 15

1:1-7, 2:1. "Gettysburg. Great Speech of Gen. Sickles on the Battlefield July 2."

2:3. "The Great Reunion. Officers of Both Armies Visit Gettysburg." [cavalry battlefield]

3:1. David Edwards (30th OH), "Antietam."

3:1. W. P. DeLand (1st OH), "The First on Missionary Ridge."

3:1. J. W. Chrisinger, "The Sultana Disaster."

3:2. John H. Prather (91st OH), "Stephenson's Depot."

3:3. W. W. Jackson, "Gen. Lauman. Comrade Jackson Strongly Defends that Brave Officer."

3:3. James M. Rogers (10th CT), "The Hawkins Zouaves' Charge at Roanoke Island."

3:3. Scott W. Jones (12th PA Cav), "They Drove the Rebels from the Blackberry Patch."

3:4. Henry A. Tripp (29th ME), "In Defense of the Nineteenth Corps."

3:4. E. S. Pitkin (13th VT), "Willcox's Brigade at Gettysburg."

3:4. John Robinson (2nd MI Cav), "Perryville."

3:4. J. E. Graham (43rd OH), "The Siege of New Madrid."

3:5. C. A. Partridge (96th IL), "Lookout Mountain."

3:5. James Wilson (9th IA), "Atlanta. The Fifteenth Corps in the Battle."

3:6. C. W. Smith (30th MO), "Vicksburg. How the Dispatches were Carried to Admiral Porter."

3:6. Frederick L. Brown (2nd WV), "The First Muster."

3:6. C. A. Hobbs (99th IL), "The Thirteenth Corps at Mobile."

4:4. "The Third Corps at Gettysburg." [editorial]

4:6. Biog: David B. Henderson (12th IA).

4:7. Obit.

8:4. "Sickles at Gettysburg. Gen. Howard Talks About the Commander of the Third Corps."

8:5. John L. Mathews (47th USCT), "Fort Hill."

July 22

1:1-7, 2:1-4. Sickles, Part 2.

2:5. Biog: Christian Klein (28th, 147th PA).

3:1. B. F. Magee, "Chickamauga."

3:1-2. C. W. Buvinger (39th OH), "Death of Col. Rogers." [Corinth]

3:2. E. R. Reed, "Bill Anderson. How the Brutal Guerrilla was Killed."

3:2. J. G. Savage (2nd WV), "Cedar Mountain."

3:2. M. S. O'Connor, "Duryea's Zouaves."

3:3. S. D. Morgan (10th IL), "New Madrid."

3:3. J. A. Capen (7th KS Cav), "Gen. A. J. Smith's Fight from Pontotoc to Tupelo."

3:4. J. E. Walton (30th OH), "Antietam."

3:4. A. C. Brown (2nd OH), "Dog Soup. How Col. Scribner and Staff Feasted on the Hindquarters of a Bull-Dog."

3:5. S. W. Bird (35th IL), "Stone River."

3:5. C. R. Glazier, "Michigan Cavalry Brigade. A Toot from One of Its Musicians." [Gettysburg]

3:6. J. B. Keyes, "The 16th Wisconsin at Shiloh."

4:6. Biog: Jacob M. Campbell (54th PA).

4:7. Obit.

5:4. "The Granite State. The New Hampshire Veterans at the Gettysburg Reunion."

July 29

1:1-6, 2:3-5. William McCarter (116th PA), "Fredericksburg."

3:1. Henry D. O'Brian (1st MN), "Gettysburg. Comrade O'Brian Takes Issue with Gen. Sickles and Says the Third Corps was Attacked."

3:1-2. H. A. Tripp (10th ME), "Cedar Mountain."

3:2. L. G. Allen, "Army of the Potomac. One of the Berdan Sharpshooters Takes Up the Cudgel." [Antietam]

3:2. T. C. Bailey (14th IN), "Who Got His Sword?" [Cold Harbor]

3:2. Samuel B. Hall (44th IL), "A Sacred Relic." [lost colors at Jackson]

3:2. William Flugga, "The Color Bearer of the 134th Pennsylvania."

3:3. A. H. Sanders (16th IA), "Shiloh."

3:4. G. W. Spahr (3rd MO Cav), "The Camden Trip."

3:4. J. H. Smith (6th MI), "The Colors of the 7th Vermont." [Port Hudson]

3:4. Daniel H. McAbee (76th PA), "Cold Harbor."

3:5. L. A. Howard (7th MI), "The 'Colonel.' A Brave Old Horse that Went Through 18 Battles." [Norman J. Hall's steed]

3:5. M. J. Clerihan (10th IL), "New Madrid."

4:3. "Berdan's Sharpshooters at Gettysburg."

4:5. Biog: Charles E. Brown (63rd OH).

4:7. Obit.

6:7. J. V. McNeely, "Vicksburg. How the Gunboats Ran the Blockade."

6:7. W. H. Weston (16th IN), "Munson's or Henderson's Hill?" [LA, 3/21/64]

August 5

3:1. H. J. Walter (30th IL), "Battle of Belmont."

3:1. Warner Mills, "The 32nd Ohio at Atlanta."

3:1. William H. Smith (5th NY), "Duryea's Zouaves."

3:2. George L. Childress (66th IL), "Atlanta. The Fifteenth Corps—DeGress's Battery."

3:2. John T. Yarnell, "The Flag of the 53rd Illinois." [Jackson 7/12/63]

3:2. C. J. Gardner (97th OH), "The First Union Soldier to Enter Chattanooga."

3:3. Frank D. Garretty (15th KY), "Perryville."

3:3. M. D. Lane (17th OH), "The 17th N.Y. and the 17th Ohio." [Jonesboro]

3:4. Jesse Warner, "Sherman's March."

3:4. John Goodmiller (45th IL), "He Wants More Fun and Less Gore."

3:4. S. C. Mendenhall (76th OH), "Battle of Atlanta."

3:4. G. B. Lamme (8th OH Cav), "The Retreat from Lynchburg."

3:5. J. E. Walton, "The 30th Ohio. March Through S.C.—At Columbia."

3:5. H. G. Lehmann (32nd OH), "That Flag of Truce." [Vicksburg]

4:6-7. Biog: G. G. Symes (2nd, 25th WI), Charles J. Brumm (5th, 76th PA).

4:7. Obit: David B. White (81st NY), Asa Morris (53rd IL), N. M. Harmer (82nd PA).

August 12

1:1-4. Carleton, Part 80. [Red River]

1:3. Joseph N. Schneider (14th IN), "Winchester."

1:4. John S. Mather (9th IA), "The Fifteenth Corps." [Atlanta]

3:1-2. N. N. Hill (3rd MO Cav), "Chasing Marmaduke."

3:2-3. "Trevillian Station. How Custer Saved the Flag and How His Brigade was Helped Out of a Tight Place."

3:3. Jonathan Harlan (34th OH), "Stevenson's Depot."

3:3. George B. Crawford, "A Gallant Family." [Smith brothers, Brilliant, OH]

3:3. Phil Bessor (208th PA), "He Delivered the Order to Col. Heintzelman." [Fort Stedman]

3:4. Isaac Drew (2nd TN), "Andersonville."

3:4. W. H. H. Kennedy (11th PA Res), "Who Got General Meade's Christmas Dinner?"

3:4. William M. Stewart (21st MA), "Antietam. The First to Cross the Bridge."

3:5-6. N. Sessions, L. Y. Allen (1st US Ss), "Berdan Sharpshooters. Two Interesting Letters Describing the Important Service They Rendered at Gettysburg."

3:6. J. L. Cameron, "The 12th Ohio Cavalry at Cynthiana."

4:2-3. Biog: Lucius Fairchild (2nd WI).

4:6. Biog: John Swinburne (NY surgeon).

4:7. Obit.

5:5. H. J. LaTour (33rd MO), "Henderson Hill."

6:7. George Van Houten, "Bill Anderson."

August 19

4:3. "John Burns at Gettysburg."

4:6-7. Obit.

5:3. "Gettysburg Memorial Church."

5:4. "Soldiers in Congress." [Biogs of Horace B. Strait (9th MN), A. H. Pettibone (20th WI)]

6:2. Moncena Dunn, "Fredericksburg. How the 19th Mass. Charged Across the River."

6:2-3. Lewis Blundin (28th PA), "Cedar Mountain."

6:3. George P. Nickolai (48th OH), "Shiloh."

6:3. Urban Homsburg (22nd IN), "The Battle of Perryville."

6:4. George E. Lowry (13th IN), "On the Blackwater. A Desperate Skirmish at the Ford."

6:5. S. W. Taylor, "The 52nd Pa. The First to Enter Charleston, S.C.—Graphic Account of the Evacuation."

6:5. Isaac P. Force, "The 26th Pennsylvania."

6:6. GGB, "Wilcox's Brigade at Gettysburg."

6:6. George H. Allen (4th RI), "Another Possum. How a Soldier Angled for His Discharge."

August 26

1:6-7, 2:1. "Gen. D. E. Sickles Defends the Course Pursued by Him at Gettysburg."

2:2-3. Biog: Benjamin F. Kelley.

2:4. Biog: Horatio B. Hackett (81st PA).

3:1. F. B. Nickerson (8th OH), "Gettysburg."

3:1. J. W. Bouldin (29th IA), "Jenkins's Ferry."

3:2. George Haskin (63rd OH), "Col. Rogers's Death." [Corinth]

3:2. W. D. Longwell (16th US), "Jonesboro."

3:3. J. P. Allum (1st WV Cav), "The Fight with Mosby at Warrenton Junction." [5/2/63]

3:3. Thomas A. Murphy (1st OH Bty), "He Corrects Comrades Edwards and Prather." [Antietam]

3:3. Theodore Herrling (1st WI), "The Battle of Perryville."

3:3. Warner Mills (32nd OH), "He Thinks One Capture in Four Years Enough."

3:3. O. B. Fuller (22nd IL), "The Battle of Belmont."

3:4. Robert J. Street (7th MD), "Explosive Musket Balls."

3:4. P. C. Wright (29th MA), "Seniority of Muster."

3:4. N. H. Karns (18th OH), "The Sultana Disaster."

3:4. O. W. Birmingham (10th MI Cav), "How They Helped the Escaped Prisoners."

3:5. M. D. Leggett, "Battle of Atlanta."

3:5. J. C. Munger, "The 16th Iowa at Atlanta."

3:5. W. M. Morris (3rd WV Cav), "Stevenson's Depot."

3:5-6. Charles Slemmer (125th NY), "The Third Corps at Gettysburg."

3:6. Thomas Everetts, "The 7th Vermont at Port Hudson."

4:5. Biog: B. W. Perkins (83rd IL, 16th USCT), B. M. Cutcheon (20th MI).

4:7. Obit.

September 2

1:1-4. Carleton, Part 81. [Red River]

1:5-7, 2:1. W. E. Parmelee (Bty H, 1st OH), "At Gettysburg."

2:4. "Ben and Spot. Interesting Sketch of Gen. Kilpatrick's Servant and His War Horse 'Spot'."

3:1. Wilbur A. Potter (21st MA), "Antietam. To Whom Does the Honor of Taking the Bridge Belong?"

3:1. D. L. Murdock (77th IL), "The 7th Vermont was Not Properly Officered."

3:1. George A. Welton (6th MI), "He Wants to Go For Both of Them." [Port Hudson]

3:2. T. D. Pollock (30th IA), "Columbia, S.C. Comrade Pollock Quotes from His Diary in Relation to Its Capture."

3:2. "The Burning of Columbia, S.C."

3:2. James M. Bell (1st MO Eng), "New Madrid. He Draws His Diary on Comrade Clerihan."

3:2-3. J. R. Tisdale (29th MO), "The Skirmish at Florence, S.C."

3:3. Guy T. Gould, "The Horizon. Graphic Account of How She Went Down While Running the Blockade at Vicksburg."

3:3. John T. Booth (36th OH), "The 2nd W.V. Cavalry at Lewisburg."

3:4. D. G. Hagle (11th MO), "Robinett."

3:5. F. R. Poole (2nd MO SM Cav), "The Marmaduke Raid. The Fight from Cape Girardeau to Chalk Bluff."

3:5. A. C. Stevens (116th IL), "Atlanta. The Fifteenth Corps in the Battle."

3:5-6. J. H. Myers (55th IL), "Atlanta."

3:6. Sanuel Dunham (63rd PA), "A Claim for the Foster Family."

3:6. W. H. Posson (45th IL), "How Gen. Leggett Helped the Boys to have a Merry Christmas."

4:2-3. "How They Would Make History Read." [John B. Bachelder and W. A. Morgan's accounts of the cavalry battle at Gettysburg]

4:6. Biog: Samuel S. Carroll (8th OH), Louis Fitzgerald (40th NY).

4:7. Obit.

5:5. Biog: S. R. Peters (73rd OH).

6:5. H. C. Farnsworth (29th OH), "The Fight at Dug Gap, Ga."

September 9

1:1-6. R. W. Surby (7th IL Cav), "Hatch's Hard Riders. The Brilliant Services of the Cavalry at Nashville."

1:7, 2:1-3. Carleton, Part 82. [Red River]

3:1. A. D. Basore (44th IL), "McCook's Corps at Perryville."

3:1. J. H. Smith (6th MI), "The 7th Vermont." [Port Hudson]

3:1. John V. Bishop (21st IN), "He Corrects Both G'men." [Port Hudson]

3:1. Lewis E. Leigh, "The 1st Connecticut Heavy Artillery."

3:1. "The 22nd Illinois at Belmont."

3:2. L. C. McClenthen, "The Muster of the 1st Minnesota."

3:2. R. Hannaford, "The 2nd Ohio Cavalry, and the Desperate Charge It Made March 31, 1865."

3:3. George E. Lowry (13th IN), "Deserted House."

3:3. E. F. Grow (1st MN), "Comrade Grove Answers the Conundrum."

3:4-5. L. J. Allen, "Kelly's Ford." [Autumn 1863]

3:5. Edwin W. Smith (54th OH), "Atlanta."

3:5. Theodore Botkin (44th OH), "The 2nd W.V. Cavalry at Lewisburg."

3:6. A. F. Medford (40th OH), "Lookout Mountain."

3:6. John Lynch, "Antietam. The 11th Conn. the First to Cross the Bridge."

3:6. S. D. Spear (77th OH), "The Surprise at Shiloh."

4:5-6. Biog: Edwin H. Conger (102nd IL), James Laird (MI).

4:7. Obit.

5:5. "Gen. Berdan and His Famous Sharpshooters at Gettysburg."

September 16

1:1-5. Fred E. Dennis, "The 8th New Jersey. How It Faced the Music at Williamsburg."

1:6-7, 2:1-2. Joseph Cracklin (2nd KS), "Fighting in the West. Battle of Wilson's Creek. Where the Gallant Lyon Fell."

2:3. Biog: J. S. Robinson (82nd OH).

2:5. "Lincoln's Substitute in the Field." [*Washington Critic*]

3:1. Fred E. Miller, "The 1st Minnesota. How that Gallant Regiment was Mustered and Sent to the Front."

3:1. Nelson Egbert (10th NY Cav), "On Picket. How a Porker Scared a N.Y. Cavalryman."

3:2. Peter Staffin (4th OH Cav), "Is It True?" [Burning of Rome Arsenal]

3:2. W. J. Landram, "Sabine Cross-Roads."

3:2. James R. Roberts, "The 40th Illinois at Shiloh."

3:2. S. J. Campbell (30th MA), "The 7th Vermont Again."

3:3. F. M. Thompson (8th KY), "Lookout Mountain."

3:3. Z. A. Baltzell (2nd MO SM Cav), "Chasing Marmaduke."

3:3. G. W. Gragg (6th MA), "The 13th Indiana at Joyner's Ford."

3:4. A. J. Grayson (6th IN), "A Lucky Signal. How Private Moore Got His Company Out of a Bad Fix." [1864 TN RR duty]

3:5. G. Koontz (142nd IN), "Graybacks versus Hog Lice."

3:5. J. R. McCoy (1st WV Cav), "Around Lynchburg."

3:6. John C. Aaron (116th IL), "The Battle of Atlanta."

4:5-6. Biog: William J. Bolton (51st PA).

4:7. Obit.

September 23

1:1-4. Theodore Wiseman (AAG, 2nd Div, 14th Corps), "Battle of Jonesboro."

1:5-7. George A. Robertson, "Out of Libby Prison. An Officer Captured at Chickamauga Tells His Adventures." [for Theodore S. West]

3:1. N. W. Reddick (30th IL), "Atlanta."

3:2. J. E. Walton (30th OH), "Antietam and Columbia."

3:3. W. T. Butcher (97th IN), "Entering Columbia."

3:3. E. S. Vernon (78th OH), "Who Burnt that Cotton Gin?" [3/63 MS]

3:3. J. K. P. Stephens (6th IN Cav), "He Speaks for the Crouse Family." [10 sons, Clay County, IN]

3:3. O. S. Barrett, "The 4th Michigan at Gettysburg."

3:4. H. Emrich (13th IL Cav), "Around Little Rock. Lively Skirmishing on the Arkansas Prairies." [8/63]

3:5. George W. Toms, "The 5th N.Y. Cavalry." [Wilderness]

3:6. J. N. Rose (Bty A, 1st OH), "McCook's Corps at Perryville."

4:5. Biog: James D. Morgan (10th IL).

4:7. Obit.

September 30

1:1-6. H. E. Warner, "Among the Philistines. Surrendering to the Enemy Without a Fight." [3/25/63 Brentwood, TN]

1:7, 2:1-2. Walter H. Parcels (50th NY Eng), "Five Days in the Field. A New York Engineer at the Battle of the Wilderness."

3:1-2. C. H. Fish (signal corps), "'Hold the Fort.' Credible Testimony Concerning the Famous Dispatch at Allatoona."

3:2. I. J. Lichtenberg (5th NY Cav), "The Wilderness."

3:2. William H. Cole, "The 126th N.Y. at Gettysburg."

3:3. C. R. Newman (5th RI Hvy Art), "The Evacuation of Charleston, S.C., and the First to Enter the City."

3:3. D. W. Jeffers (24th MA), "An Old Field Order." [11/2/64 from Col. H. M. Plaisted]

3:3. R. T. Henderson, "An Incident of the Wilderness." [About Col. Joseph Hays, 18th MA]

3:3. R. M. Peck (1st US Cav), "Sibley and His Tent."

3:4. A. E. Quaife (28th IA), "He Wants a Fair Shake." [Sabine Crossroads]

3:4. Charles A. Curtis (18th US), "Munfordville."

3:5. Henry Trauernicht (2nd MO), "McCook's Corps at Perryville."

4:5. Biog: Louis E. Atkinson (1st PA Cav, 188th PA).

4:7. Obit.

October 7

1:1-3. C. W. Wiles, "On Horseback. Incidents inthe History of the 10th N.Y. Cavalry." [Aldie, May 1864, Weldon RR]

1:4-7. H. Allspaugh (31st OH), "Chickamauga."

2:1-3. John C. Lang (100th IL), "Reminiscences. Some Breezy Recollections of an Illinois Infantryman."

2:3. J. A. Bering (48th OH), "Sunday at Shiloh."

2:4. J. C. McClelland, "Justice to the 1st Iowa. It Did Not Run at the Battle of Wilson's Creek."

4:1-2. George E. Lowry (13th IN), "The Siege of Suffolk."

4:2. Henry Gale (1st NY Dragoons), "From a N.Y. Dragoon."

4:2. (15th PA Cav), "Chasing Hood."

4:3. William W. Watkins, "The 5th Iowa Cavalry."

4:3. E. L. Allen (13th NJ), "Gen. Robinson at Resaca."

4:3. Henry Emrich (13th IL Cav), "The Marmaduke Raid."

4:4. F. E. Hoe (2nd MA Bty), "The 7th Vermont." [Baton Rouge]

4:4. John Woods (67th OH), "The Capture of Gen. Walker."

5:1. Ren Barker (66th IL), "DeGress's Battery."

5:1. W. B. Hibbs (17th IA), "Explosive Musket Balls." [Vicksburg]

5:1. M. McCormick (99th USCT), "Who Built the Dam?"

5:2. Henry Cordes (18th US), "The Regular Brigade at Jonesboro."

5:2. William S. Archer (7th OH Cav), "The Cavalry at Nashville."

5:2. G. W. Pepoon (96th IL), "An Incident of Chickamauga."

5:3. A. McKirahan (43rd OH), "A Good Family Record."

5:4-5. J. P. Smith, "Stonewall Jackson. The Manner in Which He Met His Death." [*Century Magazine*]

6:6. Biog: Charles H. Grosvenor (18th OH).

6:7. Obit.

7:3-4. Biog: Mrs. Elizabeth D'Arcy Kinne (President, Woman's Relief Corps).

8:3. Biog: Moses Veale (109th PA).

8:5. "New York at Gettysburg. Marking the Positions of the Monuments."

10:1. Biog: Samuel W. Backus (2nd MA Cav).

October 14

1:1-5. Francis A. Walker, "Sumner at Fair Oaks."

1:6-7, 2:1. Carleton, Part 83. [Atlanta Campaign]

2:2. Hiram Berdan, "The Sharpshooters. Who Commanded Them on the Reconnaissance at Gettysburg."

3:4-5. M. W. Lindsley (1st NY Dragoons), "Cavalrymen at Issue." [Wilderness]

3:5. Henry A. Tripp (29th ME), "Gen. Dick Taylor Prevaricated." [Sabine Crossroads]

4:1-2. C. E. Goldsborough, "Blue and Butternut. A Graphic Description of Lee's Occupation of Frederick, Md., in 1862."

4:2. John S. Brush (1st NY), "The Earliest Muster."

4:3. E. T. Lee (41st IL), "The Charge at Jackson."

4:3. W. D. Blackman, "The Sanders Raid." [6/63]

4:4. Charles H. Myerhoff (14th IN), "'Bricktop' Carroll. His Brigade at Antietam and the Wilderness."

4:4. A. F. Robinson, "The 1st N.Y. Dragoons." [Trevilian Station]

4:4. John H. Buhn (92nd IL), "Wilder's Brigade at Chickamauga."

4:5. E. L. H. Barry (89th IL), "All About a Cup."

4:5. R. M. Marvin (31st IA), "Columbia, S.C. How and By Whom the Surrender was Received."

4:5. Crosby Johnson (76th OH), "Battle of Atlanta."

5:1. John H. Prather (91st OH), "Army of West Virginia. Its Gallant Fight Against Early at Winchester."

5:2. Milton Reynolds (8th NY Cav), "A Cavalryman Who was Not Strapped to His Horse."

5:2. Austin Murphy (18th US), "The Regulars at Jonesboro."

5:2. S. A. McNeil (31st OH), "Mission Ridge Once More."

5:2. David Allen (155th PA), "An Incident of Chancellorsville."

5:6. W. P. Brown, "The Sibley Tent."

6:6. Biog: Lewis Hanback (27th IL).

6:7. Obit.

7:3-4. W. W. Jackson, "Southern Loyalists. What It Cost to be True to the Union."

10:6. "Veterans at Gettysburg." [139th PA, 7th, 10th, 37th MA]

October 21

1:1-4. Francis A. Walker, "Couch at Fair Oaks."

1:5-7, 2:1-2. Carleton, Part 84. [Resaca, Cassville]

2:3. Biog: G. J. R. Miller (106th PA).

3:4. Biog: Orlando B. Willcox.

4:1-2. W. W. King, "Pacific Coast Soldiers. Sketch of the Organization of the 1st California."

4:2. David G. Blodgett (10th IN Bty), "First in Chattanooga."

4:2. Lewis Blundin (28th PA), "'Above the Clouds.' What a Pennsylvanian Knows About Lookout Mountain."

4:2. J. V. Pownall (29th IN), "The Quaker Guns at Corinth."

4:3. Simon Neidhoff, "In Caves and Mountains. The Supreme Test of Loyalty in East Tennessee."

4:3. John F. Dearborn (2nd NH), "Explosive Bullets." [5/5/62]

4:4. M. J. Burns (3rd IA Cav), "Chasing Marmaduke."

4:4. C. A. Brasher (25th KY), "Gen. Lauman."

4:5. Charles O. Muser (29th IA), "Jenkins's Ferry."

5:1. N. Egbert (10th NY Cav), "Hatcher's Run."

5:1-2. "The 1st N.Y. Dragoons."

5:2. S. D. Fulmer (105th PA), "The Third Corps, and Its Gallant Leader, Gen. Sickles, at Gettysburg."

5:2. C. B. Dennis, "A Toy from Antietam."

5:2. Marion Overhiser (17th IN Bty), "A Hoosier at Cedar Creek."

6:7. Obit.

7:3-5. W. W. Jackson, "Southern Loyalists. Fierce and Deadly Conflict with a Band of Guerrillas."

8:3. "Chickamauga." [*Cincinnati Commercial Gazette*]

8:4-5. "The Late E. M. Stanton." [*Washington Evening Star*]

9:1-2. F. L. Brown (2nd WV), "On the Cheat River. A Regiment Demoralized by a Mis-chevous Ventriloquist."

October 28

1:1-4. Francis A. Walker, "Hancock at Gettysburg."

1:5-7, 2:1. Albert G. Brackett (3rd US Cav), "Battle of Ezra Church."

2:3. "A War Mystery. Romantic Incident of the Siege of Atlanta." [*Atlanta Constitution*]

4:1. S. W. Durant (127th IL), "The Fifteenth Corps. It was Neither Defeated Nor Driven in the Battle of Atlanta."

4:1-2. W. T. Butcher (97th IN), "Flanking Atlanta."

4:2. Andrew Geddes (1st IA), "At Wilson's Creek."

4:2. E. H. Gregg, "An Incident of the First Bull Run."

4:3. W. F. Smith, "Capture of Gen. Walker. The 6th Conn. Took Him."

4:3. E. B. Row, . . . "And So Did the 67th Ohio."

4:3. William H. Peck (1st CT Hvy Art), ""He 'Got There First' Once." [Fort Mahone]

4:4. R. N. Ashmore (15th US), Anthony Franckhauser (19th US), "Regulars at Jonesboro."

4:4. John Algoe (10th MI), "Capturing a Mill. A Gallant Exploit on Peach Tree Creek."

4:5. O. B. Hayden (9th IN Cav), "Disagreeing Troopers." [12/17/64 Franklin]

5:1. Peter Meagher, "The 17th N.Y. A Graphic Sketch of Its Service at Jonesboro."

5:1. A. R. Depew (188th PA), "The Capture of Fort Harrison."

5:1-2. J. R. King (1st MN), "Who Got in First?"

5:2. Calvin & Stephen Crouse, "The Crouse Family. A Grand Record of Patriotism and Sacrifice."

5:2. Peter Meagher (17th NY), "A Remarkable Record." [brothers in Co.A, 61st PA]

6:7. Obit.

7:4-5. "L. D. Simmonds, "On a Gunboat. The General Thomas Running the Batteries at Decatur, Ala."

8:1-2. Silas Adams, "The 19th Maine. A Sharp Criticism of Gen. Sickles from the Pine Tree State." [Gettysburg]

8:2. T. Cracklin (2nd KS), "The Battle of Belmont."

November 4

1:1-5. Francis A. Walker, "Warren at Bristoe."

1:6-7, 2:1. C. W. Wiles, "On Horseback. Leaves from the Record of the 10th N.Y. Cavalry." [Brandy Station, Trevilian]

2:2. "Perryville. Letter from Gen. Starkweather, and His Official Report."

3:1-2. A. R. Phillips (36th OH), "Battle of Lewisburg."

3:2. Thomas A. Mayes (25th IL), "Mission Ridge."

3:2. P. Winsor, "Col. Mersy's Brigade, and What It Did Under Col. Adams at Atlanta."

3:3. J. C. Harris (83rd PA, 5th Corps HQ), "Sickles at Gettysburg."

3:3-4. "The Fales Family." [Thomaston, ME]

3:4. C. R. Grant, "The 7th Vermont." [Baton Rouge]

3:4. "Explosive Musket Balls." Brief letters from Paul C. Morgan (2nd NH), E. L. Farechild (72nd IL), Charles H. Lynch (18th CT), B. F. Shearer (32nd OH), W. H. Weston (16th IN), Henry A. Langenberg (22nd IA), J. W. Delano (65th OH), J. H. Smith (6th MI), John C. Livezey (36th IN), J. R. King (4th WV), Frank S. Wells (45th IL), J. Q. A. Campbell (5th IA).

4:6. Biog: James O'Donnell (1st MI).

4:7. Obit.

November 11

1:1-4. Carleton, Part 85. [Dallas, New Hope Church]

1:5-7, 2:1-3. D. B. McConnell, "The 9th Indiana."

2:4. "The 89th Ohio. Gen. Turchin Tells How It was Captured at Chickamauga."

3:1. George R. Sutton (1st MO Cav), "Jeff Thompson's Capture."

3:2. Thomas Dodd (6th US Cav), "With Sheridan." [Todd's Tavern]

3:2. Charles L. Ballard, "An Assault on the 38th Wisconsin Repelled." [Fort Mahone]

3:2. S. G. Parker (63rd IL), "Guarding a Gunboat and Praying for a President." [Eastport at Mound City in 1862, Hurlbut's 1863 Memphis order]

3:2. John Savage (25th MI), "Brave Tennesseans and Their Gallant Leader." [3rd East TN at Nashville]

3:3. Joseph E. Nutter (1st MA), "Stonewall Jackson. A Comrade Says He was Wounded by the Fire from the 1st Mass."

3:3. E. W. Parker (7th WI), "The Iron Brigade."

3:3. N. S. Swett (2nd Co MA Ss), "He Thinks Gen. Sickles Claims Too Much." [Gettysburg]

3:4. Hiram Oldroyd (20th NY Cav), "The Union Colors at Petersburg."

4:5. Editorial supporting CSA monuments at Gettysburg.

4:6. Obit: Jesse S. Norton (21st OH).

5:3. Biog: John Wallace (1st PA Res, 157th, 191st PA).

5:4. Henry N. Fairbanks (3rd ME), "'Old Abe' and the Flag. A Soldier's Impressions of President Lincoln in 1861."

8:5. Warren C. Hursh (1st NJ Cav), "Battle of Hawes's Shop."

November 18

1:1-6. Charles E. Troutman (12th NJ), "Chancellorsville."

1:6. James D. Proudman (3rd NH), "On Morris Island."

1:6. John D. Frank (Bty G, 1st NY), "Hazzard's Battery."

1:7, 2:1-2. R. C. Rankin (7th OH Cav), "In The Saddle. Service of the Cavalry at Nashville."

3:1. George E. Lowry, "The 13th Indiana. Gallant Service Under Gen. Butler in the Army of the James."

3:1-2. Joseph Cracklin (2nd KS), "Capt. Cracklin Responds." [Wilson's Creek]

3:2. Charles Van Wye, "The 17th N.Y. at Jonesboro."

3:2. J. F. Fehrenbaker (Bty F, 2nd US), "Capture of the Regular Battery at Atlanta."

3:2. H. F. Standish (10th CT), "Gen. Walker's Capture."

3:2. H. D. O'Brien, "The 1st Minnesota at Gettysburg."

3:3. J. L. Newton (75th IL), "The Fight at Perryville."

3:3. John H. Bohn (92nd IL), "The Occupation of Chattanooga."

3:3. James B. Wilde (13th NJ), "A Tribute to a Noble Woman." [Mrs. Catherine Conover, nurse in Washington and Chester]

3:4. G. W. Spahr (3rd MO Cav), "Southeast Missouri. Operations of the Army Under Gen. Davidson."

4:7. Obit.

November 25

1:1-4. Carleton, Part 86. [Kennesaw Mountain]

1:5-7, 2:1. A. G. Bennett (21st USCT), "Taking Charleston. Occupation of the City in the Early Part of 1865."

2:4. Francis A. Walker, "Tribute to Hancock."

3:1. James McMahon (41st OH), "Pickett's Mills."

3:2. H. C. Hackett (1st MI Cav), "Had a Joke on the Colonel."

3:2. George E. Lowry (13th IN), "Cold Harbor."

3:3. William G. Parker (1st MD Cav), "Brandy Station."

3:3. E. C. Reed (2nd WI), "In Libby Prison. A Reminiscence of a N.Y. Boy Who Died There."

3:3. John S. Manning (100th NY), "Another Regiment that Captured Gen. Walker."

3:4. Ira Carr (2nd US Ss), "A Sharpshooter at Gettysburg."

4:6. Biog: Alvin P. Hovey.

4:7. Obit.

8:3. "A Confederate Monument." [2nd MD, Gettysburg]

December 2

1:1-4. Carleton, Part 87. [Peach Tree Creek]

1:4. Lewis Blundin (28th PA), "Lookout Mountain."

1:5-7, 2:1. A. L. Morey (98th NY), "At Chapin's Farm."

2:3-4. "Missent War in Cipher." [*Detroit Free Press*, regarding a message sent 9/1/62]

3:1-2. William W. Welch (53rd IL), "The Charge at Jackson."

3:2. J. Eugene Mathewson (Bty A, 1st NY), "A Strayed Artilleryman."

3:3. W. C. Hickman (5th OH), "That "Five Ohio" Sutler."

3:3. William H. Merritt, "The 1st Iowa. The Commanding Officer of that Regiment Takes the Floor." [Wilson's Creek]

3:3. Charles Allinger, "The 2nd Missouri at Perryville."

3:4. B. F. Gates (26th CT), "Army of the Gulf."

4:6. Biog: William Cogswell (2nd MA).

4:7. Obit.

December 9

1:1-5. Carleton, Part 88. [Atlanta]

1:6-7, 2:1-2. E. B. Lufkin (13th ME), "Life in a Fort. Thirteen Months of Garrison Duty in Fort St. Philip."

2:2. "Calm and Candid." [W. T. Sherman at Goldsboro, from the Detroit Free Press]

2:2. "Kilpatrick's Profanity." [*Philadelphia Record*]

3:1-2. William McCarter (116th PA), "A Picket Story." [11/62]

3:2. S. S. Hite (6th IL Cav), "A Family Gives Forty-seven Years of Service." [Hite brothers from Tazewell County, TN]

3:2. George H. Stowits (100th NY), "Col. L. S. Payne, the Water Scout."

3:2. Horace N. Williams (8th CT), "Rodman's Brigade at Antietam."

3:3. Ignatz Fanz, "The 6th Tenn. How It Took a Hand in the Battle of Nashville."

3:3. C. D. Rawson, "The Rawson Family." [Jamaica, VT]

3:3. John A. Joyce, "It was the 24th Kentucky that First Crossed Nose's Creek in the Advance on Atlanta."

3:4. A. G. Weissert (8th WI), "Col. Murphy at Iuka."

3:4. "An Incident of Gen. Sumner." [Antietam]

3:4. E. F. Gillen (2nd WV Cav), "The Fight at Lewisburg."

4:7. Obit.

December 16

1:1-4. Carleton, Part 89. [Ezra Church, Jonesboro]

1:5-7, 2:1-3. Wiley Britton (6th KS Cav), "On the Border. The Outbreak of Secession in Missouri in 1861."

3:1. John H. Prather (91st OH), "Army of West Virginia. Its Active Part in the Battle of Opequan."

3:1. A. G. Brackett (3rd US Cav), "Capture of Murray's Battery at Atlanta."

3:2. "At Resaca. The Capture of the Four-Gun Battery."

3:2. W. M. Stotts (1st AR), "A Word from an Arkansas Traveler." [Poison Springs]

3:2. S. A. McNeil (31st OH), "It Gives Some Light." [man found hanging near Chattahoochie River]

3:2-3. L. J. Allen (1st US Ss), "Berdan's Sharpshooters. The Reconnaissance at Gettysburg on the Morning of July 2."

3:3. O. S. Barrett, "The 4th Michigan. The Warm Place It was in at Chancellorsville."

3:3. James Hane, "'Rally Round the Flag.' How It was Sung by the 81st New York at Fort Harrison."

3:4. C. F. Branch (VT), "Concerning Pikes and Fort Harrison."

3:4. A. E. Glanville (10th MN), "McMillan's Brigade. A Proposition to Erect a Monument at Nashville."

3:4. "The Fall of Charleston. Testimony of Eye-Witnesses Twenty Years Ago." [3/8/65 letter and newspaper clippings]

4:7. Obit.

December 23

1:1-6. John W. Fry (42nd OH), "Cumberland Gap. Its Importance as a Strategic Point During the War."

1:7, 2:1-2. Frank Swigart (46th IN), "In Rear of Vicksburg."

3:1. A. A. McLauchlin, "The 115th N.Y. The Gallant But Unsuccessful Charge at Cold Harbor."

3:1-2. A. F. Robinson (1st NY Dragoons), "They Got the Bulge on the Officers."

3:2. Theodore F. Ramsey (15th PA Cav), "Hood's Pontoons and Wagons."

3:2. E. R. Sly (14th OH), "Going Foraging."

3:2. R. W. Smith (Stoneman's staff), "A New Version of Gen. Polk's Death."

3:3. Robert Callahan, "They Kept Going. A 29th Pa. Man Tells How the 'White Star' Shone on Lookout Mountain."

3:3. George C. Stewart (2nd CT Hvy Art), "Petersburg. A Claim for the First Entry Filed from the Nutmeg State."

3:3. George A. Beck (37th WI), "The Occupation of Petersburg."

3:3. Till Dagger (116th IN), "The Trouble at Walker's Ford." [12/2/63]

3:4. W. S. Hunt (2nd KS), "Where Lyon Fell."

3:4. C. L. Linton, "Saving the Guns. It was Part of the 140th Pa. that Saved the Battery at Chancellorsville."

4:7. Obit.

December 30

1:1-7, 2:1-4. "John A. Logan Dead."

3:1. G. F. Tillinghast (11th CT), "Antietam Bridge."

3:1-2. M. W. Houck, "The 77th Pa. A Sketch of Its Part in the Battle of Stones' River."

3:2. L. E. Pond (7th WI), "An Episode of Gainesville."

3:2. George W. Dixon (81st OH), "Was Gettysburg a 'Decisive' Battle?"

3:2. John Fisher (125th IL), "A Few Words About Kennesaw."

3:3. S. W. Durant (127th IL), "'Carleton' Corrected." [Atlanta]

3:3. J. H. Jewett (8th CT), "Concerning Two Flags. " [Fort Harrison]

3:3. R. Sharpe, "Gen. Meade. A Word to Those Who Criticized His Caution After Gettysburg."

3:3. E. H. Bowman (27th IL), "The Dead at Belmont."

3:4. Charles A. Tompkins (137th NY), "A Wholesome Suggestion."

3:4. D. A. Lockhart (61st PA), "The Sixth Corps. Brief Sketch of Its Brilliant Service in the Shenandoah Valley."

3:4. A. J. Buckles (19th IN), "A Kid's Good Record."

3:4. J. V. Albertson (25th NJ), "Jerseymen at Suffolk."

4:7. Obit.

8:3-4. A. D. Frankenberry (signal corps), "Hold the Fort. The Signal Messages Between Kennesaw and Allatoona."

1887

January 6

1:1-6. "His Last Review." [Story on Logan Funeral].

1:7, 2:1-3. John W. Fry (42nd OH), "Cumberland Gap. Fortified and Made Impregnable by Gen. G. W. Morgan. . . . Tazewell."

2:5. C. A. Lang (111th PA), "'Old Ben,' and How He Silenced the Guns of a Rebel Battery." [Lost Mountain, GA]

3:1. A. L. Morey, "The 98th N.Y." [Chapin's Farm]

3:1-2. J. M. McClintock (signal corps), "Very "Hard" Cash. Concerning Some Money that was Got and Some that Wasn't."

3:2. S. A. Clark (1st VT), "Big Bethel."

3:3. John K. Tyler (121st NY), "'Massa Linkum's' Men. How and By Whom was Made the First Entry into Petersburg."

3:3. Alexander Becher (2nd KS), "Wilson's Creek."

3:3. J. H. Trundy (6th ME), "Hancock at Williamsburg."

3:4. George H. Uhler (93rd PA), "With Sedgwick. At Fredericksburg During the Battle of Chancellorsville."

3:4. S. W. Bird (35th IL), "The Bugle was to Blame." [New Hope Church]

3:4. H. Dunn (25th IA), "A Friend in Need."

3:4. Louis P. Lienberger (76th PA), "What Became of the Dog Slayer?" [Belle Island]

4:7. Obit.

5:4. Charles W. Harrington (15th US), "New Hope Church."

5:5. "Maine at Gettysburg. Monuments to Commemorate the Service of Her Sons."

6:7. N. A. West, "He Flagged the Historic Message." [Allatoona]

8:3-4. Charles Robinson (8th USC Hvy Art), "About the Bayonet."

January 13

1:1-6, 2:5-6. August V. Kautz, "John Morgan's Raid Through Ohio's Fresh Fields and Pastures Green."

1:7, 2:1-4. John W. Fry (42nd OH), "Cumberland Gap. The Evacuation and Retreat to the Ohio River."

3:1. J. P. Allum (1st WV Cav), "Gathering Them In. With Sheridan and Custer in the Closing Campaign."

3:2. E. Howard (Bty F, 2nd US), "Murray's Battery. Concerning Its Capture in the Battle Before Atlanta."

3:2. Nelson V. Hutchinson (7th MA), "Gettysburg. A Comrade Gives His Reasons for Thinking It a Decisive Battle."

3:2. George H. Murdock (1st MI Ss), "The Michigan Men. The Early Birds that Caught the Worm at Petersburg."

4:7. Obit.

8:3-4. C. W. Wiles (10th NY Cav), "The 'Wind-Up.' The Last Campaign that Closed at Appomattox."

8:4. L. C. Oliver (13th NH), "Fort Harrison."

8:4. James P. Shaw (31st OH), "Those Skeletons by the Chattahoochie."

January 20

1:1-5. Frederick T. Grant, "Gen. U. S. Grant. His Son's Memories of Him in the Field."

1:6-7, 2:1-2. Rush C. Hawkins, "Hawkins's Zouaves. Charge of the 9th N.Y. at Roanoke Island."

3:1-2. E. Ware (13th NH), "Battery Harrison."

3:2. H. A. Bull (8th NY Cav), "Brandy Station."

3:2. J. D. Wilkinson (1st MO), "'Comrade, Shake!'"

3:3. D. M. Osburn (40th IN), "Gen. George D. Wagner, and How He 'Cussed' Because They Wouldn't Let Him Fight at Perryville."

4:7. Obit.

5:4-5. Obit: William B. Hazen.

8:2. John M. White (15th NJ), "He Got the Flag. The Desperate Courage of a Jerseyman at Spotsylvania."

8:3-4. H. L. Ambrose (3rd KY Cav), "Kentucky Troopers Who Saved Rosecrans's Ammunition Train at Stones' River."

January 27

1:1-6. Grant, Part 2. [Port Gibson, Raymond]

1:7, 2:1-2. James F. Fitts (114th NY), "With Sheridan. Graphic and Spirited Defense of the Nineteenth Corps."

2:2. Forsyth, "7th Ohio Sharpshooters." [Cedar Mountain]

3:1. Lewis Blundin (28th PA), "The White Star People." [Lookout Mountain]

3:1. J. W. Long (2nd IA), "They Wore Gray, But They were Well Clad and Fed and were Not Easily Scared." [Fort Donelson]

3:2. Michael Mueller (32nd IN), "Willich's Boys."

3:2. A. B. Hodge (Bty I, 2nd IL), "A Question Answered." [retreat from Chickamauga]

3:2. "Col. Ellsworth's Last Letter."

3:2. E. A. Jackson (63rd IL), "Death of Gov. Harvey, of Wisconsin."

3:3-4. Picket Shots: Eugene F. Hawley (5th CT), Joseph Borland (139th PA), Gettysburg; L. A. Labadie (19th MI), Resaca; S. D. Raeper (41st OH), George Pressler (93rd OH), New Hope Church; C. Reed (15th OH), death of Polk; F. W. Songer (111th OH), Atlanta; J. H. Bitting (55th OH), Peach Tree Creek; William Funk (116th IL), Chattanooga; C. B. Cozens (60th NYH), Z. Harp (35th IN), Lookout Mountain; F. M. Mead (114th NY), Elijah Beller (28th IA), Shenandoah Valley 1864.

4:6. (80th OH), "Mother Anna B. Kerr Not Forgotten." [Iuka, Corinth]

4:7. Obit.

5:4-5. Biog: James B. Coit (2nd, 14th CT).

8:1. S. L. Hart (10th WI), "Gen. Buell's Signal Corps at Shiloh."

8:2. (37th IL), "Pea Ridge."

8:2. Albert G. Brackett, "Another Patriotic Family." [his own]

8:2. Eli Stringer (93rd IN), "The Guntown Trip."

8:3-4. J. M. Rife (7th WV Cav), "A Brave Dash. An Incident of Campaigning on Cheat Mountain."

8:4. J. C. Jeffers (100th OH), "How He Got Left."

February 3

1:1-6. Grant, Part 3.

1:7, 2:1. J. H. Greene (8th WI), "Out of the Lines. How the Order Against Harboring Negroes was Evaded."

2:2-3. W. W. Jackson, "Southern Loyalists. An Interesting Sketch of the 1st Mississippi."

2:5. S. A. Clark (1st VT Cav), "Gen. Farnsworth, and How He Fell in a Cavalry Charge at Gettysburg."

3:1. W. G. Miller (61st PA), "At Fair Oaks."

3:1. Moses McFarland (8th VT), "Cedar Creek."

3:2. "The Morgan Raid. Some of the Good Work Done by the Indiana 'Home Guards'."

3:2. H. W. Phelps (95th OH), "A. J. Smith's Troops. How They Fought at Nashville and Chased Rebels in Missouri."

3:2. Michael Dougherty (17th WI), "Two Brave Boys." [March to the Sea, Oconee River crossing]

3:3. Picket Shots: WIlliamsburg.

4:7. Obit.

8:2. C. E. Adams, "Logan at Atlanta."

8:3. Ferdinand Connor (36th OH), "A Good Story. How Mrs. Gen. Hayes Put Another Pocket in a Recruit's Blouse."

8:3. Henry Tobey (75th IL), "They Wanted Water." [Jonesboro]

8:4. Biog: Joseph W. Kay (10th, 22nd NY).

February 10

1:1-5. Grant, Part 4.

1:6-7, 2:1. Cassius M. Clay, "Washington at the Outbreak of the Rebellion."

2:3. Anderson (PA), "What was the Object of It?" [1st NY Cav and Gen. McClellan after the retreat from Gaines' Mill]

2:3. J. L. Hummel (8th IN), "Lockhart Again. An Indiana Soldier Pays His Compliments to the Gallant Captain." [Cedar Creek]

2:3. W. W. Allen (signal corps), "Fiction Versus History." [McPherson at Atlanta]

3:1. George P. Hawkes (21st MA), "Roanoke Island. Mass. Replies to Gen. Hawkins, 9th N.Y. Zouaves."

3:2. E. C. Mount (4th IA), "Osterhaus's Division. It Had a Hand in the Battle of Lookout Mountain."

3:2. Henry Morrison, "The Rebel Capital. An 11th Conn. Comrade Describes the Occupation of Richmond."

3:3-4. Picket Shots: Atlanta Campaign, prison cells, Guntown, Petersburg.

4:5. Obit.

4:7. George R. Shaw (75th IL), "Lookout Mountain."

4:7. L. A. Pierce (3rd VT), "Williamsburg."

8:2. W. F. Smith (4th IA Cav), "Gen. Grant. How He Took a Smoke from a Soldier's Pipe."

8:2. Lemuel Jones, "The 130th Indiana. A Comrade Writes of Nashville, and Tells a Persimmon Story."

8:3-4. Joseph Davis (30th MA), "Cedar Creek."

8:4. Jonathan Harlan, "The Harlan Fighters." [Lotus, IN]

8:4. S. R. Evril (13th PA Cav), "Moses Waugh's Colic."

February 17

1:1-3. John Pope, "Missouri in 1861."

1:3. Charles Chandler (6th IA), "Griswoldville."

1:4-7, 2:1. "Soldier and Patriot." [tributes to Logan]

2:4. L. J. Dyke (111th PA), "The 'White Star' Still Shining Where It Did 23 Years Ago at Lookout."

3:1. F. M. Piles (14th WV), "The Eighth Corps Files Its Claim for Part of the Glory at Cedar Creek."

3:1. Franklin B. Case, Jr., "The 15th Michigan at Atlanta."

3:2. William W. Watkins, "The 5th Iowa Cavalry." [Franklin]

3:2. T. D. Walbach (16th OH), "The Tazewell Fight."

3:2. H. D. Pierce (2nd CT Hvy Art), "Who's Got My Haversack?"

3:3-6. Picket Shots: Nashville, Fort Harrison, Vicksburg, Perryville, Fort Mahone, Chickamauga, East Tennessee, Brandy Station, Mitchel's Division, Chancellorsville, Richmond.

4:7. Obit.

8:2. E. M. Tinkham (148th NY), "The Rebel Capital. A Dozen 'Schoolmarms' Could Have Entered Richmond."

8:3-4. Willard Musson (107th IL), "At Franklin."

February 24

1:1-3. Pope, Part 2.

1:4-7, 2:1. A. L. Morey (98th NY), "At Chapin's Farm."

2:2-3. Z. T. Griffin (122nd NY), "The Sixth Corps. [Cedar Creek]

3:1. John Strang (11th IA), "Crocker's Iowa Brigade. How It Fought in the Battle Before Atlanta."

3:2. "At Fair Oaks. Concerning the Magnificent Charge of the 'Forlorn Hope'."

3:2. Thomas J. Bradney (34th OH), "New Madrid."

3:3-6. Chattanooga, Williamsburg, Morgan Raid, Cumberland Gap, Hawkins' Zouaves, Shenandoah Valley, Antietam.

4:7. Obit.

8:3-4. Hugo Mulertt (10th NY Cav), "With the Led Horses. 'Number 4's' Adventures at Dinwiddie Court-House."

March 3

1:1-4. Pope, Part 3.

3:1. S. J. Campbell (30th MA), "In the Valley. The Shenandoah Campaign of the Nineteenth Corps."

3:1. J. G. Norton (23rd WI), "The Story of a Bake-Oven."

3:2. George H. McKinney (AAQM), "Up the Red River. The Wagon Train of the Fourth Division, Thirteenth Corps, was Not Captured at Mansfield."

3:2. "The Mistake They Made." [Morgan Raid]

3:3-6. Picket Shots: Chattanooga, Atlanta Campaign, Petersburg.

4:5. Obit.

6:2. B. A. Campbell (6th ME), "The Rebel Spy's Song."

8:2. S. C. Bunstine (10th IL Cav), "Chasing a Woman. A Novel Footrace After a Fugitive Vender of 'Duck Eggs'."

8:3-4. E. M. Downing (10th IL), "Bummer Warfare."

March 10

1:1-3. Pope, Part 4.

1:3. Alexander B. Pope (22nd WI), "Peach Tree Creek."

1:4-6. Walter H. Parcels (50th NY Eng), "Laying a Bridge. Recollections of an Army of the Potomac Pontonier. At North Anna."

1:7. James E. Catlin (45th PA), "White and Black. A Novel Review of Prisoners in the Streets of Petersburg."

1:7. C. J. Phillips (9th NY Cav), "Stuart's Cavalry, and How It was 'Reviewed' by the Union Troopers at Brandy Station."

3:1. Nelson A. Pinney (104th OH), "Fierce Work at Franklin."

3:1-2. J. W. McClanahan (53rd IL), "Gen. Lauman. Further Testimony Regarding the Charge at Jackson."

3:2. S. A. Clark (1st VT Cav), "Nothing to Hinder. A Gallant Charge and a Bloodless Victory." [7/12/62, Culpeper]

3:2. C. L. Benson (1st VT Hvy Art), "Cedar Creek."

3:2. W. H. Hornaday (63rd IN), "'With Charity to All'." [Nashville]

3:3-6. Picket Shots: Atlanta Campaign, Shiloh, Corinth, prisons, Franklin, Gettysburg, Wilson's Creek, Lower Mississippi, Carolinas, Shenandoah Valley.

4:7. Obit.

5:1. Biog: Julius D. Rhodes (5th NY Cav).

8:3-4. H. W. Day, "Gen. Ewell. A Staff Officer Tells the Story of His Capture."

8:4. J. R. Tisdale (29th MO), "Fishing Under Fire." [5/27/64]

March 17

1:1-3. Ben P. Poore, "In War Times. The National Capital Just Before the Outbreak."

1:4-6, 2:5. Wilbur H. Webber (6th MI), "Fall of New Orleans."

1:7, 2:1-3. C. W. Keifer (14th-15th IL Vet Btn), "A Prisoner of War. A Veteran Illinois Soldier in Andersonville."

3:1. Henry A. Warren (21st MA), "Roanoke Island. How the Works were Carried and Who Carried Them."

3:1. William J. Shirley (11th PA Cav), "Capture of the 'Rocket' Battery." [12/2/62]

3:1-2. James Max (7th IN), "Port Republic."

3:2. S. B. Jenkins (12th WV), "At Cedar Creek."

3:3-6. Picket Shots: Shenandoah Valley, Fort Harrison, Williamsburg, Richmond, Chattanooga, Guntown, Roanoke Island.

4:6. Obit.

8:2. A. M. Potter (74th IL), "A Brave Corporal Who Would Not Give Up the Flag to the Johnnies." [Kennesaw]

8:2. H. Emrich (13th IL Cav), "The Fortune Teller's Pig."

8:3. (66th IL), "A Sharpshooter."

8:3. Augustus Merrill (1st ME), "The Sixth Corps. A Maine Soldier in California Speaks For It."

8:4. E. Wilcox (8th WI), "Col. Murphy. A Comrade Thinks He Suffered Great Injustice at the Hand of Gen. Grant."

March 24

1:1-3, 2:6. Ben P. Poore, "Saving the Capital."

1:4-7. Keifer, Part 2.

3:1. George E. King, "Connecticut Cannoneers. A Sketch of the Long Service of the 1st Conn. Heavy Artillery."

3:2. W. H. Glass (49th PA), "The Picket-Guard. The Adventures of Two Soldiers Who were Caught Sleeping on Post."

3:2. W. H. H. Stone (11th OH Cav), "A Tough Story. [Morgan's Raid 1863]

3:2. S. W. Bird (35th IL), "Willich's Bugles Again." [New Hope Church]

3:3-6. Picket Shots: Vicksburg Campaign, Nashville, Atlanta Campaign.

4:6. Obit.

4:7. J. M. Lovejoy (121st NY), "Capture of Petersburg."

4:7. George A. Root (7th IL Cav), "Cavalry at Nashville."

5:2. Arial Howard, "'Nigger' Catchers. The Hard Time They had in the Camp of the 8th Vermont."

8:2. Valentine Zink (38th OH), "The 'Blue Acorn'." [Jonesboro]

8:2. Jerome Shoemaker (64th IL), "He Surrendered. How Some Illinois Soldiers Played It on a Comrade."

8:3-4. L. F. Gould (73rd IL), "Going Foraging." [post-Nashville]

March 31

1:1-3. Ben P. Poore, "On to Richmond."

1:4-7, 2:1. Keifer, Part 3.

2:5. "Sedgwick Monument. The Commission Visits Alsop's Farm."

3:1. A. D. Berry, "5th Michigan Badges."

3:1. E. M. Adams (20th MI), "Petersburg." [4/2/65]

3:1. John Wilson, "He Put It There. The Story of an 8th Kentucky Officer Who Says He Placed the Flag on Lookout."

3:2. John W. Dieley (84th IL), "On the Mountain." [Lookout]

3:2. Owen Hicks (7th OH), "Above the Clouds."

3:2. H. S. Hawthorne (121st NY), "Gen. Ewell and Custis Lee."

3:3-6. Picket Shots: Chattanooga.

4:3. "New York at Gettysburg."

4:7. Obit.

5:4. "The Late Gen. [George E.] Love. His Conspicuous Gallantry and Brilliant Services at Cedar Creek." [116th NY]

8:2. Joseph Jones (11th MO), "The 8th Wisconsin Eagle."

8:2. Ira Tinkham (83rd IL), "He Learned Something. A Joke was Not as Funny as He Thought It Would Be."

8:2-3. John B. Spaulding (18th MI), "'Little Devil.' How He Defended a Pile of Corn and Afterward Became a Preacher."

April 7

1:1-3. Ben P. Poore, "Girding for the War."

1:4-6, 4:7. A. G. Brackett (9th IL Cav), "Arkansas Travelers. Campaigning Under Curtis in the Southwest." [Stewart's Plantation]

1:7, 2:1-2. "The Soldier. Eloquent and Thrilling Speech of Gen. John Black at the Camp-fire, Col. Kit Carson Post."

2:3. C. B. Fairchild (27th NY), "Libby Prison. Reminiscences of a New York Boy Who Died There."

2:3. John Swyer (9th VT), "Reaching the Goal. How the 9th Vermont Double-quicked into Richmond."

2:3. William Conner (25th MA), "Roanoke Island."

2:6. M. Buchannan (118th IN), "Walker's Ford."

3:1. W. P. Brown (22nd NY Cav), "Why They were Shot. The Question Answered Concerning Capt. Summers and Sergeant Koontz." [Shenandoah Valley, 5/65]

3:1. James M. Lawrence (126th OH), "The Capture of Gen. Ewell."

3:2. (USS *Port Royal*), "In the Navy. Forcastle Yarns Spun by a Seaman."

3:2. Robert Doyle, "Chickamauga. The Battery that Defended the Gap in the Union Line."

3:2. C. H. Cowdin, "The 34th Ohio. Some Personal Notes of a 'Peculiar' Regiment."

3:3-6. Picket Shots: Shenandoah Valley, Chattanooga, New Madrid, Navy, March to the Sea, Antietam.

4:6. Allen (4th US Cav), "A Daybreak Dash into a Rebel Camp." [Shelbyville, TN]

4:6. Obit.

4:7. E. S. Russell (Bty I, 1st IL), "Waterhouse Battery. A Cavalryman Claims that Hatch's Troops Recaptured It." [Nashville]

4:7. Michael Regan (23rd IL), "'Lumber Jim.' The 'Black Sheep' in the Flock at Cahaba and Andersonville."

8:2. V. N. Kolb (3rd MD Cav), "About a 'Jack.' A Comrade's Adventures with the Long-eared Brute."

8:2. H. L. Frisbie (113th IL), "A Deadly Weapon that was Eloquently Presented to an Illinois Lieut."

8:2-3. John T. Frederick (10th OH Cav), "Capturing a Skillet. An Ohio Man's Adventure in the Camp of the 92nd Illinois."

April 14

1:1-3, 5:4-5. John C. Robinson, "The First Corps. Its Important Services at the Battle of Gettysburg."

1:4-6. S. A. McNeil (31st OH), "At Chickamauga. The Fighting and Maneuvering on the First Day."

1:6. J. S. Chandler (5th VT), "The Bayonet a Nuisance."

2:2. J. L. Blaisdell (USS *Mohican*), "From the Gun Deck. A Few Observations by One of the 'Jolly Tars'."

2:3-6. "The Army Corps. How Organized and Commanded, and the Badges They Wore."

2:6. R. H. Martin (46th IN), "At Port Gibson."

3:1. George B. McKenney (7th MA), "Williamsburg."

3:1. J. H. Masten, "The 1st N.Y. Lincoln Cavalry."

3:2. F. W. Gates (115th IL), "Chickamauga."

3:2. A. E. Matthews (1st MI Cav), "Burning a Camp. How the Members of the 104th N.Y. Lost Their Nice Things." [ca 5/25/62]

3:3-6. Picket Shots: Williamsburg, Atlanta, Vicksburg, Nashville, Richmond, Shenandoah Valley, Chattanooga.

4:5-6. Obit.

4:6-7. Levi Culver, "The 7th Indiana. A Brief Resume of Its Services During the War."

4:7. J. H. Greene, "The 8th Wisconsin Eagle."

4:7. J. W. Cushman, "The 92nd Illinois. How It Made the First Entry into Chattanooga."

5:3. John Algoe (10th MI), "A New Year in Dixie. Taking to the Front an Ammunition Train for Rosecrans at Stones' River."

8:2. W. F. Sharrer (22nd PA Cav), "Let Us Have Peace. The Controversy Over Cedar Creek and Fisher's Hill."

April 21

1:1-4. Robinson, Part 2.

1:5-7, 2:1. Noble D. Preston (10th NY Cav), "Hawes's Shop."

2:2. H. A. Tripp (29th ME), "The Late Gen. Love. Something Further About the Flag Captured at Cedar Creek."

3:1. Wilbur H. Webber (6th MI), "In the Far South. The Second Raid to Pontchatoula, La. An Infantry Dash on Camp Moore." [5/63]

3:2. W. P. DeLand (1st OH), "New Hope Church."

3:2. W. W. Williams (10th NY Cav), "The Last Fight." [4/9/65]

3:2. John R. King, "The 6th Maryland at Fort Mahone."

3:3. "'Opdycke's Tigers.' An Order Issued After the Battle of Chickamauga."

3:3. Henry Pott (75th IL), "An Illinois Boy's Experience." [Jonesboro]

3:3. Charles Soule (1st OH), "Ohio to the Front." [first company]

3:3. Henry Pott (75th IL), "An Illinois Boy's Experience." [Jonesboro]

3:4-6. Picket Shots: Vicksburg, Franklin, Atlanta, Shenandoah Valley.

4:6. Obit.

5:4. "A Sound of Revelry. A 'Light Fantastic' Reminiscence of the Second Corps." [2/22/64]

7:3. J. E. Lutts (192nd OH), "The Shooting of Summers and Koontz."

8:2. "Captain Andrews's Remains. The Remains of the Leader of the Mitchell Raiders Found After a Search of Ten Years."

April 28

1:1-5. James T. Haviland (127th NY), "Secession's Cradle. How Charleston Passed Again Under Federal Control."

1:6-7, 2:1-4. Frank Swigart (46th IN), "Champion Hills."

3:1. B. F. Jones (49th PA), "Sailor's Creek."

3:1. William Bakhaus (47th OH), "Logan at Atlanta."

3:2. Henry H. Mundy (14th NJ), "Gen. H. G. Wright."

3:2. Charles Van Gorder (39th IA), "Allatoona."

3:3. J. B. Shallenberger, "Gallant Charge. How 45 Cavalrymen of the 22nd Pa. Tried to Take a Battery." [Kernstown 7/64]

3:3. George H. Stowits (100th NY), "Gen. Walker. Something About His Capture, as Told by a Staff Officer."

3:3. J. C. Taylor (14th NJ), "How Gen. Sedgwick Fell."

3:4-6. Picket Shots: Shenandoah Valley, Vicksburg Campaign, Peninsula Campaign.

4:5-6. Obit.

4:6. George W. Cox (27th MI), "Fort Mahone."

4:7. H. A. Tripp (29th ME), "As Good As Any. A Maine Soldier Talks in Defense of the Nineteenth Corps."

5:4. Biog: Wesley Merritt.

6:6. Newt Stanford (18th US), "He Held the Haversack."

6:6-7. H. F. Chew, "The 9th N.J. at Roanoke Island."

6:7. E. V. Smith (27th IA), "A. J. Smith's 'Guerrillas.' What They did After the Battle of Nashville."

6:7. Robert E. Kenney (31st MO), "North and South. A Comparison Between the Treatment of Union and Confederate Prisoners."

8:3. Biog: T. J. Thorp (85th NY).

8:4. J. R. Kidd (5th IA Cav), "A Story of Grant. The Acts of Considerate Kindness that Endeared Him to His Soldiers."

May 5

1:1-5. John Pope, "Island Number Ten."

1:6-7, 2:1-2. J. S. Bosworth (15th IA), "Burning of Columbia."

2:2. James C. Foster (59th USCT), "The Colored Troops. How the 55th and 59th Behaved on the Guntown Trip."

2:4. I. A. Stringham (89th NY), "Roanoke Island."

3:1. W. McEvoy (3rd IL Cav), "Gen. Fremont in Missouri."

3:1. John K. Shellenberger (64th OH), "That Yelling at Chickamauga."

3:2. C. H. Burrows (124th IL), "Champion Hills."

3:2. Sheldon M. Moore, "The 111th Pa. A Comrade Tells How It, Too, had a Hand in the Fight on Lookout Mountain."

3:2. A. Lynch (192nd OH), "Why They were Shot." [Summers and Koontz]

3:3. J. S. Alexander (67th IN), "A Bake-oven, a Banner, and a Reunion."

3:3. H. M. Bayless (2nd MN), "Mill Springs."

3:3. (5th NY Cav), "He Wants to Know." [Second Manassas]

3:4-6. Picket Shots: Shenandoah Valley, Chattanooga.

4:5-6. Obit.

4:7. Joseph A. Porter (118th IN), "Walker's Ford."

4:7. A. Stinson, "The 19th Maine at Fredericksburg."

4:7. William S. Horton (5th MI Cav), "Who Can Tell?" [refusal of US authorities for Jacksonville exchange of POWs]

4:7. G. H. Weeks (103rd OH), "How They Crossed Noses Creek."

5:4. J. R. King, "Minnesota's Claim for the First Volunteer, First Company and First Regiment."

5:4. Silas W. Barnard (3rd NY Cav), "A Mystery Explained."

6:7. Walter M. Fulton (26th MA), "At New Orleans."

6:7. H. F. Chew (12th NJ), "First in Petersburg."

6:7. J. S. Drenan (11th VT), "Torn to Pieces by Blood Hounds." [Charleston prison]

6:7. WHC, "Massachusetts was There." [first company]

8:2. Dennis Mulligan (34th OH), "In the Shenandoah."

8:2. John F. Rector (29th IL), "Holly Springs."

8:3-4. Robert W. Miller (6th MO SM Cav), "Troopers in Trouble and How Yankee Ingenuity Got Them Out of It." [Springfield, MO, Winter 1863/64]

8:4. R. C. Rankin (7th OH Cav), "Cavalry at Nashville."

May 12

1:1-5. Pope, Part 2.

1:5. "The New Avenue at Gettysburg."

1:6-7, 2:1-3. Merlin C. Harris (96th NY), "Fort Harrison."

2:3. Robert Doyle, "Writing 'History.' A Comrade Spicily and Sharply Criticizes 'Carleton'." [Polk, Atlanta Cmpn]

2:5. N. B. Easton (20th IN), "The Treatment of Union Prisoners." [Andersonville]

2:5. S. A. Clark (1st VT Cav), "Orange Court-house." [8/62]

2:6. George A. Smith (7th OH Cav), "At Millen Prison."

3:1. T. H. Merry (2nd MA Cav), "A Cavalryman's Story of the Battle of Cedar Creek and the Gallantry of All the Troops Engaged."

3:1. F. Siebold (26th WI), "Wisconsin Got It, Anyway." [Peach Tree Creek]

3:2. Washington Christy (Bty E, PA Art), "Peach Tree Creek."

3:2. W. H. Church (2nd WI), "At Fredericksburg. The Crossing of Wadsworth's Division of the First Corps, April 20, 1863."

3:3. A. S. McDowell (84th IL), "Echoes from the Front. The Work of the Deadly Bullet on the Atlanta Campaign."

3:3. J. W. Hinkley (3rd WI), "Gov. Harris, of Tenn. Used a 'Pike'."

3:4-6. Picket Shots: Prisons, Chattanooga, fast travelers.

4:6. Obit.

4:7. H. M. Dihel (30th IL), "Champion Hills."

4:7. C. E. Blackwell (9th NJ), 'Roanoke Island."

4:7. William Riley (51st NY), "Roanoke Island."

4:7. (44th NY), Alexander Lydy (1st WV Cav), H. J. Leasure (1st WV Cav), H. R. Bard (1st VT Cav), "At Gettysburg."

4:7. George W. Bryant (122nd OH), Murry S. Cross (87th PA), "Gen. Sedgwick's Death."

4:7. Samuel Naylor (78th IL), E. Springer (129th IL), "The Atlanta Campaign."

5:2. G. W. Clark (MN), "The Falstaffs. The Southern Writers Who Glorify Their Valorous Deeds."

5:3. J. C. Bescher (62nd NY), "They had the General's Breakfast."

5:5. Wilbur Hale (120th NY), "Reminiscences."

8:2. S. Carver (36th IL), "Opdycke's Brigade. Its Gallant Rush to the Breach at the Battle of Franklin."

8:2. Charles E. Applebaugh (110th PA), "Concerning Shields's Division."

8:2-3. James A. Smith (200th PA), "Getting into Petersburg."

8:3. C. W. Harrington (15th US), "The Flag on Lookout."

8:3. L. J. Webb (Bty E, 1st IL), "Guntown."

May 19

1:1-5. Aquila Wiley (41st OH), "Gen. Hill Answered. An Able Reply to a Confederate Sketch of Chickamauga."

3:1. E. A. Carter (26th IL), "The Eagle Brigade."

3:1. W. L. Stork, "Lookout Mountain. A Plain Statement from One of Gen. Geary's Staff Officers."

3:1. R. W. Morris (90th PA), "The First Corps at Gettysburg."

3:2. James Burns (39th IN), "Chickamauga."

3:2. Milton Reynolds, "The 8th N.Y. Cavalry at Beverly Ford."

3:3. A. McFadden (13th OH Cav), "Dinwiddie."

3:3. R. C. Rankin, "Ohio Again to the Front."

3:4-6. Picket Shots: Richmond, Atlanta Campaign.

4:5-6. Obit.

5:3. "Gen. Sedgwick. Unvailing [sic] of the Memorial Tablet at Spottsylvania."

5:4. Obit: William B. Woods (76th OH).

8:2. Henry Calkins (21st WI), "The Pet Pig. How Some Hungry Soldiers Supplied Their Wants."

8:2. C. W. Cook, "The 76th N.Y. at Gettysburg."

May 26

1:1-4. Thomas J. Wood, "The Fourteenth Corps. Its Brilliant Operations at the Battle of Nashville."

1:5. John H. Prather (91st OH), "The Valley Campaign."

1:6-7, 2:1. William E. Curtis, "The Secret Service. Work of the Pinkerton Detectives During the War."

2:2-3. Thomas Moloney (8th MI), "Trip to Hilton Head."

2:5. L. B. Brainard, "The 124th Ohio. A Brief Sketch of Its Part in the Battle of Chickamauga."

3:1. George Hugunin (147th NY), "At the North Anna."

3:2. J. M. Lovejoy (121st NY), "Spottsylvania."

3:2. Stephen Quaife (13th KS), "Prairie Grove."

3:2-3. J. H. Penney (19th OH), "About the 'Ghosts.' Some Very Substantial Spooks at New Hope Church."

3:3. S. A. Clark (1st VT Cav), "Cedar Creek."

3:3. William J. Shirley, "'Draw Saber—Charge!' A St. Patrick's Day Dash of the 11th Pa. Cavalry at Franklin, Va." [3/63]

3:4-6. Picket Shots: Petersburg, last campaign, prisons, Navy, New Madrid, Peninsula Campaign.

4:5-6. Obit.

4:7. A. D. Frankenberry (15th PA Cav, signal corps), "'Hold the Fort!'."

5:3. Hosea D. Loftis (2nd NC MI), "Walker's Ford."

8:2-3. Obit: James L. Selfridge (46th PA).

8:3. John M. Moody (66th IL), "Moody's 'Misfit'."

8:4. Michael Coleman (2nd WI), "Bull Run."

8:4. W. H. Matchett, "The 40th Ohio. Wrested from the Rebels the Battery at the Craven House."

8:5. H. J. Hawkins (6th MD), "Stick to the 'Prodder.' A Comrade Makes a Good Defense of the Bayonet as a Weapon."

June 2

1:1-4, 2:5. Wood, Part 2.

1:6-7, 2:1. Thomas Bell (8th NY Cav), "At Harper's Ferry. How the Cavalry Escaped Out of the Toils."

2:2-3. H. Allspaugh (31st OH), "Mission Ridge."

2:6. Richard T. Jacobs, "Kentucky in 1861. The Courage and Wisdom of the Union Men in the Legislature."

3:1. "Gen. Custis Lee. How He was Captured by Two Men of the 37th Mass."

3:1. Warren C. Hursh (1st NJ Cav), "Hawes's Shop."

3:2. Robert P. McRae (11th PA Cav), "A Raider in Dixie. A Pa. Cavalryman's Adventures While a Prisoner of War."

3:2. James Barr (104th OH), "Franklin."

3:3. (32nd WI), "At Columbia."

3:3. W. J. Brown (1st WV Cav), "Winchester."

3:4-5. Picket Shots: Shenandoah Valley, Williamsburg, Carolinas.

4:4-5. Obit.

4:5. T. M. Robertson (6th IN Cav), "The Cavalry at Nashville."

4:7. N. R. Gruells, "Andersonville."

4:7. W. J. Wright (78th PA), "New Hope Church."

5:5. S. B. Barron (3rd TX Cav), "From the Other Side. A Confederate Cavalry Officer Tells of Hood's Rear Guard after Nashville."

5:5. J. D. Dillenback (Chicago Board of Trade Bty), "Gen. Turchin's Advice to the Boys."

5:5. W. E. Stevens (12th MI), "Grab a Root."

6:5. Joshua Dewees (97th OH), "Entering Chattanooga."

6:7. John W. Blake, "The 29th Wisconsin. How Bravely It Met the Shock of Battle at Port Gibson."

8:2. George M. Withers (104th OH), "More About 'Old Abe'."

8:2. H. V. Boynton (35th OH), "Gen. J. B. Steedman."

8:3-4. Hugo Mulertt (10th NY Cav), "At Sailor's Creek."

8:4. Charles Otis, "On a Gunboat. Frightful Casualty on the USS *Chillicothe* in the Yazoo Pass."

June 9

1:1-5. H. C. Whitaker (2nd NY Cav), "Carbine and Saber. Warm Work for the Troops Under Gen. Kilpatrick. The Fight at Aldie." [includes Brandy Station]

1:6-7, 2:1. Charles O. Musser (29th IA), "A Western Battle." Gallant Fighting on the Soil of Arkansas. Attack on Helena."

2:2-3. S. R. Norris (7th OH), "Ohio at Gettysburg."

2:3. E. K. Barnhill (73rd IN), "'Charge Bayonet.' A Comrade Thinks the Prodder was a Useful Factor in the War."

2:3. H. G. Newbert, "Gen. Steedman. An Instance of His Splendid Executive Ability."

2:3. S. J. Langdon (94th IL), "'Grab a Root." Another Explanation of Its Origin—Yelling It at Gen. Grant."

2:4-5. "Corporal Tanner. He Produces Some Interesting Evidence as to His Wounding." [James Tanner, 87th NY, at Second Manassas]

3:1. Warren L. Holbrook (1st PA Cav), "Davies's Brigade. The Services of These Gallant Troopers in the Last Campaign."

3:2. J. W. Barron (54th IL), "Ashley Station." [8/24/64]

3:2. Nelson A. Pinney (104th OH), "Reilly's Brigade at Franklin."

3:3. George F. Peaks (6th ME), "Williamsburg."

3:3. I. M. Adair (86th IN), "On to Atlanta. Something About the Battles of New Hope Church and Pickett's Mills."

3:4-6. Picket Shots: Franklin, Nashville, Atlanta, March to the Sea, Vicksburg, Wilson's Creek, prisons.

4:7. Obit.

5:2. Obit: Granville Moody (74th OH).

5:3. Biog: D. C. Putnam (25th MA), James E. Stewart (2nd KY, 167th OH), Ira W. Wallace (60th OH).

8:2. (23rd MI), "An Army Dentist."

8:2. Charles Porter (11th VT), "Cedar Creek."

8:2. William M. Berkshire (7th KY Cav), "Sergt. Smith and the Soap Trough."

8:3-4. E. B. Lufkin (13th ME), "Outpost Life. A 'Soft Job' on the Shore of Lake Ponchartrain."

8:4. Wilbur H. Webber (6th MI), "Fort St. Philip."

8:5. F. M. Riddle (3rd IN Bty), "The 'Last Battle.' How the Brave Union Soldiers Went Over Fort Blakely."

8:5. J. B. Kuykendall (31st IL), "The Battery at Champion Hills."

June 16

1:6-7, 2:1-2. John W. Lacock (93rd IN), "The Guntown Trip."

2:3-4. Amasa Johnson (9th IN), "Chickamauga."

3:1. Mary Bolen, "'Old Abe.' An Authentic Sketch of the Proud Bird of the 8th Wisconsin."

3:1. E. S. Norvell (6th MD), "Sedgwick's Death."

3:2. Hiram H. Ashmore (25th IL), "Stones' River."

3:2. A. L. Morey (98th NY), "The Rifle a 'Nuisance'."

3:2. Robert Kelley (13th MO Cav), "He Didn't Need a Bugle."

3:3. J. A. Stark (29th WI), "They Don't See Alike. How Some Things Appeared to a Wisconsin Veteran." [Port Gibson]

3:3. Silas Smith (6th ME), "The Battle of Williamsburg."

3:4-6. Picket Shots: Red River, Vicksburg, Shenandoah Valley, Grant, Petersburg, Chattanooga, General Walker, prisons.

4:7. Obit.

5:5. James E. Martin (7th IN), "At Fredericksburg."

5:5. E. C. Rodgers (5th VT), "Concerning Some Colors." [Cedar Creek]

8:2. M. V. Ashby (16th IL), "Good for the Soul. An Open Confession of the Stealing of a Major's Supper."

8:4. A. L. Brown (4th MN), "The Flag at Jackson."

8:4. A. L. Bailey (9th IN), "Gen. Walker. A Personal Sketch and His Own Statement Regarding His Capture." [William S. Walker]

June 23

pages 1-2. "A Loyal Blizzard." [proposed return of CSA flags]

2:4-5. A. E. Mathews (1st MI Cav), "Gen. Stuart's Death."

2:5-6. Adam Dixon, "Burning a Camp. The Wild Adventures of the 104th N.Y. at Thoroughfare Gap."

3:1. P. C. Mills, "Early War Times. How the 5th Mass. Made Its Way to the Front."

3:2. E. T. Lee (41st IL), "The Battle of Shiloh."

3:2. A. A. Jones (65th IL), "Burnt Hickory."

3:3. LeRoy Mason (121st OH), "The Gap at Chickamauga."

3:3. C. M. Castle (102nd IL), "'Dallas Woods.' The Days and Nights of Fierce Fighting at and Near New Hope Church."

3:4. James Barr, "The 'Milk of Human Kindness'." [Franklin & Col. Stevens of the 31st MS]

3:4. J. E. Ingraham (93rd IL), " They 'Held the Fort'."

3:5-6. Picket Shots: William Webble (76th NY), John W. Bruce (7th WI), Gettysburg.

4:7. Obit.

5:4. R. A. Tubbs (1st VT Hvy Art), "In the Valley."

7:7. F. Vogl (Reg Eng Btn), "Fredericksburg."

7:7. Michael Regan (23rd IL), "Fremont in Missouri."

7:7. W. J. Carson (15th US), "A Bugler Replies to Gen. Wiley." [Chickamauga]

8:2. T. S. Potter (8th OH), "A Scared Contraband." [1862 Shenandoah Valley]

June 30

1:6-7, 2:1-2. Lacock, Part 2.

2:3-5. J. W. Elliott (44th USCT), "By Fire and Flood. The Awful Disaster to the Steamer Sultana."

4:7. Obit.

5:3. "They Got the Flags. How Two of the Captured Banners were Taken." [John G. Merritt of 1st MN at Manassas and William B. Hincks of 14th CT at Gettysburg]

5:4. "Berdan Sharpshooters. Letter from Gen. Berdan in Regard to Their Movement." [Gettysburg]

8:4-5. H. H. Miller (77th IL, 81st USCT), "Good Stories."

July 7

1:1-5, 2:6. John A. Logan, "The Siege of Corinth." [from his The Volunteer Soldier]

3:1-2. D. E. Straight (100th USCT), "The Colored Troops in the Charge on Overton's Hill at Nashville."

3:3. Harrison Zentz, "The 98th Ohio. A Brief Sketch of What It Did Toward Putting Down the Rebellion."

3:3. W. S. Shields (Bty G, 1st PA), "A Brave Civilian." [7/4/64 near Point of Rocks, MD]

3:3. James Harmon (22nd IN), "Was He a Spy?" [Kennesaw Mountain]

3:4. A. H. Russell (19th WI), "On the Dome. Planting the Flag Over the Rebel Capitol in Richmond."

3:4. W. S. Coen (5th IA Cav), "Untwisting the Twist." [Nashville]

3:4. (48th PA), "Fort Mahone. Capt. Jack Crawford Has Something to Say About the 48th Pa."

3:5-6. Picket Shots: Chattanooga, Atlanta, Colonel Murphy, Williamsburg, Franklin.

4:7. Obit.

5:3-5. "At Gettysburg. Blue and Gray Clasp Hands in Fraternal Greetings."

5:5. "A Monument at Gettysburg." [13th NJ]

8:2. Herbert J. Tillapaugh, "A Woman's Ruse. How She Put to Flight a Company of Confederate Cavalry." [Missouri]

July 14

1:1-5. Henry Romeyn (14th USCT), "The Colored Troops. Origin and Service in the Army of the Cumberland."

3:1. Joseph L. Jackson (33rd NY), "Williamsburg."

3:1-2. Josiah T. Young (36th IA), "Fort Pemberton."

3:2. B. F. Johns (49th PA), "The 'Bloody Angle'."

3:2. Joseph Jones (11th MO), "Some Reminiscences of the Eagle Brigade and the 26th Illinois."

3:3. D. B. Baker (1st MO Eng), "After a Bee-Gum." [SC 1865]

3:3. T. Cotton (129th IL), "Shiloh Revisited."

3:3. John Seltzer (1st WV Cav), "The Death of Gen. Farnsworth."

3:4. A. Neat, "Gen. Schoepf. A Comrade Thinks He was the Real Hero of Mill Springs, or Logan's Crossroads."

3:5-6. Picket Shots: Shenandoah Valley, Atlanta.

4:7. Obit.

6:7. "Youngest Soldier." [Avery Brown, OH]

8:4. (Elgin Bty IL), "He Got Away. The Fugitive Slave Law Did Not Work Well in the Army."

July 21, 1887

1:1-5. Romeyn, Part 2.

2:4. (25th MI), "Butler at New Orleans."

2:5. L. C. Trotter (13th IN Cav), "He Does Not Understand It." [Nashville Campaign]

2:5. "They had Pluck. The Wonderful Courage and Patient Endurance of the Volunteer Soldiers."

2:5. W. W. Irish (10th NY Cav), "On Picket. The Varied Adventures of Some Cavalrymen Down by the James River."

3:1-2. F. T. Hawley (20th WI), "Prairie Grove."

3:2. George L. Warren (157th NY), "The Eleventh Corps. The First Day at Gettysburg."

3:2. H. W. Phelps (95th OH), "Random Shots. A Comrade Tells of Some Letters from the Boys." [A. J. Smith in MO and at Nashville]

3:3. I. N. Stanford (18th US), "The Regular Brigade of Baird's Division at the Battle of Chickamauga."

3:3. J. H. Dickson (60th IN), "'Carrion Crow.' A Sketch of a Lively Scrimmage in the Pelican State."

3:3. W. P. McClure (51st IN), "An Incident of the Charge on Overton's Hill." [Nashville]

3:3. Willaim T. Walker (4th DE), "Concerning Col. LaMotte."

3:4. George A. Manning (2nd MA Cav), "Who Set the Fire?" [Columbia]

3:4. J. W. Winter (19th ME), Clinton Bradshaw (71st NY), "Who Shot Off the Tree? The Oak that was Cut Down by Bullets at Spotsylvania."

3:5-6. Picket Shots: Moving on Richmond, Atlanta, Gettysburg, Grab a Root phrase.

4:4. "Monument at Hanover, Pa."

4:6. Obit.

5:1. E. R. Reed (2nd WI), "Fredericksburg." [4/63 crossing]

5:1-2. William S. Beebe (Ord Off, Army of the Gulf), "Cane River."

5:2. John Wilson (8th KY), "Lookout Mountain."

5:2-3. Josiah Missong, "The 55th Pa. What It Did and Suffered at Fort Harrison."

5:3. William Q. Huggins, "The First Volunteer."

5:3-4. Abram Beam, "The 211th Pa. Heard From."

5:4. Picket Shots: prisons, Chattanooga, Nashville.

6:2. Edwin Hedden (40th NJ), "First in Petersburg."

6:7. J.C. Harris (83rd PA), "Battles and Losses."

6:7. H. J. Conover (130th IL), "The Mobile Campaign."

6:7. Thomas Moloney (US Eng Btn), "The Crossing at Fredericksburg." [4/63]

8:1. J. M. Doubleday (20th IN), "Grant's Narrow Escape From Being Bucked and Gagged by an Indiana Colonel."

8:3. John T. Frederick (10th OH Cav), "Stampeded 'Yanks.' A Scurvy Trick that was Played by Some Ohio Troops." [Carolinas Campaign]

8:5. J. S. Robinson, "Ohio at Gettysburg."

8:5. Andrew P. Fox (5th NY), "Fredericksburg."

July 28

1:1-5. Romeyn, Part 3.

1:6-7, 2:1-3. Noble D. Preston (10th NY Cav), "Gregg's Division. Its Participation in the Stoneman Raid of 1863."

2:4-5. A. E. Matthews, "The 6th Maine. Its Superb Gallantry at Rappahannock Station."

3:1. E. T. Lee (41st IL), "Fort Donelson."

3:1. E. W. Hoyt (93rd NY), "Captain Hobart's Pluck."

3:2. William H. H. Small, "The 7th Maine. It had a Finger in the Pie at Williamsburg."

3:2. I. W. Hoskins (38th IN), "Scribner's Brigade. The Good Fighting It did at Pumpkin Vine Creek."

3:2. C. R. Cox (1st MD), "Purnell's Legion. Something About Its Organization and Services."

3:3. Lewis Blundin (28th PA), "A Farewell Shot." [Lookout Mountain]

3:3. S.C. Armstrong (22nd NY Cav), "A Blast from a Cavalryman's Bugle."

3:3. John McElhatten (103rd PA), "Duty in the Rear. Experiences of a Soldier on Provost Guard in Philadelphia." [Summer 1862]

3:4. H. A. Snyder (41st IL), "Spilled Honey. Two of Sherman's Bummers on Their Travels."

3:4. H. R. Carven, "The 55th Ohio at Peach Tree Creek."

3:4. Levi Huntley, "The 37th Mass. First in Petersburg."

3:5-6. Picket Shots: Moving on Richmond, Vicksburg, last fight.

4:6-7. Obit.

5:5. H. V. Boynton, "Battle Banners. An Hour with the Flags on Missionary Ridge." [*Cincinnati Commercial Gazette*]

6:3. T. H. Eaton, "An Incident at Gettysburg." [Pickett's Charge and Sgt. F. Smith, 14th VA]

6:3. S. A. Clark (1st VT Cav), "In the Beginning. The Tribulations of Some Green Vermont Cavalrymen."

6:3. J. Toldham (13th IA), "Don't Blame the Artist-He Wasn't There." [Columbia]

8:2. R. C. Crowell, "Canned Peaches. Something About Brave Men Who had Their Weak Points."

August 4

1:1-5. Romeyn, Part 4.

1:5. M. F. Ames, "The 7th Mass. Something About Its Service at Williamsburg and Elsewhere." [also includes Salem Church]

1:6-7, 2:1-2. H. D. O'Brien (1st MN), "Mechanicsville."

2:4. B. P. Entriken (8th WI), "A Clear Statement of the Regiments that Followed the Wisconsin Eagle."

2:4. W. H. Moore, "The 30th Iowa at Lookout Mountain."

2:4. L. H. Marshall, "A Badge for the Thirteenth Corps."

3:1-2. "After Sumter. On the Upper Potomac in the Early Days of the War."

3:2. J. L. Blaisdell (USS *Mohican*), "From the Gun-deck. A Jack Tar Writes of the Hilton Head Expedition."

3:2. Charles A. Clear, "The Fight at Gettysburg."

3:3. "Gen. Steedman. His Brilliant Services at Chickamauga."

3:4. A. J. Florey (8th IL), "Champion Hills."

3:4. J. C. Beresford (2nd OH), "Gen. Nelson's Death."

3:4. W. H. Barger (1st WI Cav), "The Last Battle." [Columbus, GA, 4/17/65]

3:6. J. W. Kenagy (34th IN), "No Doubt It was a Hard Fight." [Champion's Hill]

4:4. Obit: George H. Patch (19th MA).

4:5. (Bty D, 5th US). "On Little Round Top." [from Rittenhouse's MOLLUS paper]

4:7. Obit.

5:3. "Sheridan Veterans. Another Excursion to the Southern Battlefields."

5:3. "A Trip to Gettysburg." [8th IL Cav]

5:3. "Another Monument at Gettysburg." [95th PA]

8:2. John H. Johnson (Purnell Legion), "Another Misfit."

8:2. N. B. Fisher (37th OH), "The Western 'Diversionists'."

8:3. E. W. Smith (5th NH), "The Story of a Hen."

August 11

1:1-5, 2:6. John W. De Peyster, "The Third Corps. Its Service the Last Ten Days of the Closing Campaign."

1:6-7, 2:1-2. Romeyn, Part 5.

2:2. "After Many Years. Confederate Money Loaned in Prison Camp Repaid in Greenbacks." [*Bangor Commercial*]

3:1. E. S. Coan (signal corps), "The North Anna."

3:1. W. P. Wolf, "The 175th Ohio at Franklin."

3:2. L. F. Parrish (17th IA), "At Jackson. How the Rebels were Driven from the Capital of Mississippi."

3:2. (37th IL), "Burying a Quartermaster."

3:2. James E. Porter (2nd OH), "They Got Furloughs."

3:3. J. L. Grinnell, "The 34th Indiana. A Vindication of Its Record at Champion Hills."

3:3. E. W. Sprague, "A Relic of Camp Ford, Tyler, Texas."

3:3. V. F. Biddleman (83rd OH), "The Fight at Fort Blakely."

3:4. D. J. Vance (4th IA Cav), "'The Last Battle.' The Night Fight of Upton's Division of Wilson's Cavalry, at Columbus, Ga."

3:4. H. P. Walker (47th IL), "The Eagle Brigade Again."

3:4. C. E. Bassett (124th IL), "First in Vicksburg- About Some Honey."

3:4. John Watson (48th PA), "About Fort Mahone."

3:5-6. Picket Shots: Helena, Moving on Richmond.

4:5. Obit.

8:3. Wilbur H. Webber (6th MI), "Saved Their Bacon. Roasting a Pig Under Artillery Fire."

August 18

1:1-4. F. C. Robinson (1st WV Cav), "Sailor's Creek."

1:5-7, 2:1. A. Morris (2nd OH), "The Army Mail."

2:2-3. Aquila Wiley (41st OH), "Wood's Division. Its Gallant Assault Upon Missionary Ridge."

2:5. J. B. Lindsay (50th OH), "Franklin."

2:6. W. H. Bentley (77th IL), "Last Battle of the War."

3:1. C. N. Barrett (46th PA), "Stonewall Jackson. The Circumstances Under Which He Fell at Chancellorsville."

3:2. J. W. Lacock (93rd IN), "He Took Them Off. How a Sergt, Stripped an Ex-Confederate Officer of His Insignia of Rank." [Gainesville, AL, 6/65]

3:2. (IL), "Gen. Wood was Right." [Nashville]

3:2. Julius D. Rhodes (31st ME), "Fort Mahone."

3:3. H. A. Tripp (29th ME), "Up Red River."

3:3. William V. Allen (32nd IA), "The Eagle Brigade and Fort Blakely."

3:3. W. F. James (63rd OH), "Not a Repulse, But Only a Sacrifice of Life for a Purpose." [Salkahatchie River, SC]

3:3. G. L. Childress (66th IL), "Before Atlanta. The Recapture of DeGress's Battery and the Bursting of the Gun."

3:4. James J. Han (28th WI), "Helena."

3:4. (37th IL), "Fort Blakely."

3:5-6. Picket Shots: Shiloh, Gettysburg.

3:6. S. A. McNeil (31st OH), "Chickamauga."

4:7. Obit.

5:4. "Another Monument Dedicated." [Gettysburg, 5th CT]

5:4. W. F. Tart (89th IL), "Willich's Bugles." [New Hope Church]

5:5. J. T. Wiesman (Bty D, 1st IL), "An Artilleryman Makes a Correction." [Champion's Hill]

6:4. (71st NY SM), "Col. Ellsworth."

6:6. "Ohio at Gettysburg. Dedication of the State Monuments on the Battlefield."

8:2. O. S. Barrett (4th MI), "Fun in Camp."

August 25

1:1-4. Wilbur H. Webber (6th MI), "Baton Rouge."

1:5-7, 2:1. S. C. Fry (Bty D, 1st OH), "The Sanders Raid." [6/63]

3:1. J. A. Soliday (12th OH Cav), "The Saltville Raid."

3:2. James M. Whallon (11th MI), "Chickamauga. The Confederate Losses and Forces Engaged."

3:2. J. Cornelius Smith, "The 1st Kentucky Battery. How Its Guns were Lost and Recaptured at Franklin."

3:2. W. J. Brown (1st WV Cav), "Gen. Farnsworth. How He Fell in the Furious Charge at Gettysburg."

3:3. H. H. Lyman (147th NY), "Battle of Gettysburg."

3:3. A. M. Gurnsey (124th IL), "Champion Hills."

3:4. E. Garland (4th IA), "Capturing a Locomotive." [John Houck, 55th IL]

3:4. William Soden (23rd WI), "Up Red River. Concerning the Fight at Sabine Crossroads."

3:4. E. A. Crandall (23rd WI), "Sabine Crossroads."

3:4. John Shafer (143rd PA), "First in at Gettysburg."

3:5-6. Picket Shots: Atlanta, Red River, Grab a Root phrase.

6:4. William M. Saer (2nd PA Hvy Art), "The Flag of the 2nd Penna. Heavy Artillery." [Fort Harrison]

September 1

1:1-5, 2:5-6. E. R. Monfort (75th OH), "In West Virginia. One of the Important Early Campaigns of the War." [Grafton to McDowell]

1:6-7, 2:1. Samuel Roberts, "The 72nd Pennsylvania. The Trying March from Falmouth to Gettysburg."

2:1. "Gettysburg Memorial Commission." [PA]

2:4. R. P. Stone, "The Thirteenth Corps. The Question of a Badge to be Considered at St. Louis."

2:6. "Ohio Memorials at Gettysburg."

3:1. T. F. McCoy (107th PA), "In the Wilderness."

3:1. J. B. Jewett (98th OH), "Atlanta."

3:2. Thomas Gilmore (107th NY), "New Hope Church."

3:2. Almon Bradford (45th OH), "Mill Springs."

3:3. E. A. Carter (26th IL), "The Eagle Brigade."

3:3. A. P. Brown, "Peach Tree Creek. The Crossing of the Twentieth Corps, July 19, Led by the 149th New York."

3:3. "The 5th Mass. A Comrade Thinks It has been Neglected by Historians."

3:4. T. J. Wright (8th KY), "They had to have It. How the Needs of Some Starving Sufferers at Chattanooga were Relieved."

3:4. W. H. Hornaday (63rd IN), "The Cavalry in the Fight." [Nashville]

3:4. J. H. Fulton (64th OH, 2nd OH Hvy Art), "The Ohio Men did Not Object to Serving with the Colored Troops."

3:4. (Bty M, 1st IL), "Steedman at Chickamauga."

3:5-6. Picket Shots: Chattanooga, Atlanta, Fredericksburg, Mobile, prisons.

4:7. Obit.

5:2. "An Old War Horse." [*Concord Patriot*, about J. N. Patterson's steed]

8:3-4. Willard Musson (107th IL), "Soldiering. A Few Sketches and Anecdotes of Army Life."

September 8

1:1-6. J. M. Rife (7th WV Cav), "Averill's Raid." [12/63]

1:7, 2:1-6. J. C. Harris (83rd PA), "The Record of the Fighting Done by the Army of the Potomac. The Official List. Engagements Credited to All the Various Organizations."

3:1. S. A. Clark (1st VT Cav), "Brandy Station." [10/11/63]

3:1. Elliott V. Smith (27th IA), "Fort Blakely"

3:2. J. M. Bowman (4th IA), "Pea Ridge."

3:2. H. L. Robinson (8th NH), "Entering Richmond."

3:2. Philip Dines (41st OH), "About a Rainbow."

3:3. J. H. Taggart (50th OH), "Franklin."

3:3. R. H. Martin (46th IN), "Champion Hills."

3:3. P. Mitchell (66th OH), "Gen. Polk. Why a 66th Ohio Comrade Thinks Knapp's Battery Killed Him."

3:4. P. O. Avery (4th IL Cav), "Donelson and Henry."

3:4. F. M. Mead, "The 114th N.Y. at the Battles of Pleasant Hill and Sabine Crossroads."

3:4. Henry E. Phelps, "The 185th New York."

3:5-6. Picket Shots: Moving on Richmond, last fight, Mobile, Atlanta, prisons.

4:7. Obit.

8:3. "The 4th Ohio at Gettysburg." [monument]

September 15

3:1. C. Woodruff (64th OH), "The Havoc of War. The Losses of Some Ohio Regiments, Compiled from Official Sources."

3:1. Thomas J. Shelley (81st OH), "Atlanta."

3:2. George W. Toms (5th NY Cav), "Hanover, Pa."

3:2. Eli R. Westfall, "The 32nd Ohio. Its Claim to the Capture of the Battery at Champion Hills."

3:2. George V. Card (13th NH), "The Rebel Capital."

3:3. W. P. Harman (12th IN Cav), "Murfreesboro."

3:3. W. Warner (1st VT Cav), "Gen. Farnsworth. How He Fell in the Cavalry Charge at Gettysburg."

3:3-4. Butler Fitch (8th NY Bty), P. C. Regan (7th NY), George H. Jourdan, AAG to Naglee), "The 55th New York. Its Gallant Conduct at the Battle of Fair Oaks."

3:4. Charles Stewart (19th OH), "The Picture of Beatty's Brigade." [Stones' River]

3:4. George H. Cary (1st IA Cav), "Prairie Grove."

3:4. John Leary (7th MO), "Champion Hills Once More."

3_5-6. Picket Shots: last fight.

4:7. Obit.

September 22

1:1-6. Rife, Part 2.

3:1. Virgil True (10th ME), "The Valley Campaign."

3:2. O. H. P. Howard (2nd RI), "Williamsburg."

3:2. James Armstrong, "The 14th Indiana. Experiences of Some Hoosier Soldiers Before They had Cut Their Eye-teeth."

3:2. L. J. Dyke (111th PA), "Lookout Mountain."

3:3. T. G. Capps (122nd IL), "Fort Blakely."

3:3. R. C. Rankin (7th OH Cav), "The 2nd and 7th Ohio Cav. How They had so Few Men in the Fight at Buffington Island."

3:3. William Revill, "Losses of the 48th New York."

3:3. William H. Haley (73rd NY), "Wounding of Stonewall Jackson."

3:4-6. Picket Shots: Moving on Richmond, Atlanta, Vicksburg, Mobile.

4:5. Obit.

8:1. "Ohio at Gettysburg. Nineteen Regimental Monuments Dedicated on the Battlefield."

September 29

1:1-6. James D. Gay (25th PA), "At the Outbreak. A Pennsylvanian in Washington Early in 1861."

3:1. Michael Duncan (103rd OH), "Dallas."

3:1. John H. Johnson, "Purnell's Legion."

3:1. Thomas Montgomery, "The Flag of the 48th Ohio." [Tyler, TX, Camp Ford]

3:2. W. Bristow (24th KY), "Bleeding and Dying. A Comrade's Tussell with Kentucky Greenbriars."

3:2. J. P. Allum (1st WV Cav), "The Fight at Hanover."

3:2. (MI), "He Ran Well. The First to Get Back Over Long Bridge after Bull Run."

3:3. James M. Rogers (10th CT), "Gettysburg. Was It a Decisive Battle?"

3:3. E. R. Reed (2nd WI), "Who was He? A Mysterious Prisoner in the Hands of the Rebels." [Hiram Brown, 30th NY]

3:3. George A. Clarke (4th MN), "Give Credit Where It Belongs." [Jackson]

3:4-6. Picket Shots: Red River, Mobile, Harper's Ferry, Chattanooga, last fight.

4:7. Sumner A. Smith (49th NY), "Spottsylvania."

4:7. Obit.

5:3. A. J. Cropsey (124th IL), "R. E. Lee. Was He a Great General?"

5:4. Obit: James B. Ricketts.

8:1. "New York at Gettysburg. Regulations and Preparations for the Monument to be Erected."

October 6

1:2-3. Biog: John P. Rea (1st OH, 1st OH Cav).

1:6. Biog: Nelson Cole (1st MO).

3:1-2. T. W. Porter, "The 14th Maine. Its Colonel Resents Imputations on Its Conduct at Baton Rouge."

3:2. C. L. Overley, "The 16th Kentucky. Something About Its Organization in the Dark Days of 1861."

3:2. E. T. Hibbard (26th OH), "Wagner's Brigade. How It Climbed Missionary Ridge Along with the Rest of the Boys."

3:3. N. G. Price (12th IA), "The Sixteenth Corps. Complete Roster of Its Organization at Mobile."

3:3. H. A. Tripp (10th ME), "That 'Official List.' The Comrades Should Open Fire on the War Department."

3:4. John H. Stover, "Justice to the 106th Pennsylvania."

3:4. A. B. Hodge (Bty I, 2nd IL), "At Ringgold."

3:4. T. W. Harris, "A 'Wicked Fire.' An Ex-Confederate Officer Speaks His Mind." [*Cincinnati Times-Star*, about Missionary Ridge]

3:5-6. Picket Shots: Atlanta.

4:6. Obit.

8:2. J. W. Hinkley (3rd WI), "He Had Nerve. The Daring Exploit of a 5th Ohio Cavalryman." [4/62 Fayetteville, TN]

October 13

1:1-4. A. G. Brackett (9th IL Cav), "Waddell Farm. A Spirited Cavalry Argument in Arkansas." [6/12/62]

1:5-7, 2:1. S. P. Zehring (35th OH), "Chickamauga."

3:1. Robert B. Lincoln (USN), "In Mobile Bay."

3:1. David H. Porter (2nd IL Cav, 142nd IL), "Tribute to Lieut. Col. 'Tom' Smith, 48th Illinois." [Fort Donelson]

3:2. Thomas Montgomery, "A Flag in Prison. The Adventures of the 48th Ohio Flag at Camp Ford, Texas."

3:2. W. M. Gray, "Heroic Women. An Incident of the Relief of Knoxville."

3:3. Lyman U. Humphrey (76th OH), "Atlanta."

3:3. W. H. Scroggs, "The 111th U.S. Colored."

3:4-6. Picket Shots: Vicksburg, Atlanta, Gettysburg, prisons, Mobile, last fight.

3:6. "The 109th Illinois. A Regiment that Misbehaved in the Face of the Enemy." [editorial]

3:6. Charles P. Nettleton (1st CT Hvy Art), "A Sharp Stick for Mosby." [Warrenton Jct, 10/26/63]

4:3. Editorial: "Was Gettysburg a Decisive Battle?"

4:5. Obit.

5:2. "A Woman Veteran. The Astounding Revelation Made at the Dayton Soldiers Home." [James Fisher, 6th OH]

5:3. "Averill's Raid. Gen. B. F. Kelley Replies to Certain Statements of Gen. Averill."

8:2. Lorenzo D. Immell (Bty F, 2nd US), "Camp Jackson. A Soldier in a Regular Battery Tells How It was Captured."

8:3-4. H. D. Loftis, "Hunted Down. The Experience of a Southern Loyalist in 1861." [Knoxville]

October 20

1:1-5. J. C. Hall, "In the Wild West. Arizona at the Outbreak of the Rebellion."

3:1-2. John E. McPeck (126th OH), "Spotsylvania."

3:2. G. H. Holden (179th NY), "Fort Mahone."

3:2. O. S. Barrett, "The 4th Michigan. When and Where It First Crossed the Chickahominy."

3:2. R. C. Rankin (7th OH Cav), "They were Not 'Surprised'." [Morristown, TN, 12/12/63]

3:3. S. P. Conner (ADC to Gen. Casement), "Franklin."

3:3. Patrick Ballard (10th MO Cav), "Winslow's Brigade."

3:4-6. Picket Shots: Mobile, Harper's Ferry, Gettysburg, Carolinas, losses, Vicksburg.

4:4. Biog: Howard Henderson (Cahawba Commandant).

4:7. Obit.

5:3. "Gridley's Flour Sack. How $275,000 was Raised in 1864 for the Benefit of the Soldiers."

6:7. George W. Hones (98th OH), "The Fourteenth Corps."

October 27

1:1-5, 2:3-5. "A Boy Spy in Dixie. Service Under the Shadow of the Hangman's Noose." [Montgomery, Fort Pickens]

1:6-7, 2:1-2. William Small (10th OH Cav), "Judson Kilpatrick."

3:1. Harvey Reid (22nd WI), "A Case of Murder. An Episode of Gen. Sherman's Campaign Through the Carolinas."

3:2. Z. T. Griffith (122nd NY), "Johnson's Island."

3:2. J. C. Harris (83rd PA), "The Fighting They Did. About the Official Reports of the Battles and the 83rd Pa."

3:2. W. A. Clark (1st VT Cav), "At Cold Harbor."

3:3. Oliver W. Case, "The 65th Illinois."

3:3. Scott Sherman (2nd OH Cav), "Fighting Quantrill. A Brush with the Famous Bushwhacker at Independence, Mo." [2/18/62]

3:4-5. Picket Shots: Moving on Richmond.

4:6-7. Obit.

4:7. Biog: James W. Scully (Bty K, 1st US; 10th TN).

5:3-4. "Bull Run. A Visit to that Historic Twice Fought Field."

8:1-2. "Gen. Meade's Statue. Unvailed [sic] Last Week in Fairmount Park, Phila."

8:3. "The 14th Brooklyn at Gettysburg." [monument]

November 3

1:1-7, 2:1. Boy Spy, Part 2. [Fort Pickens, David D. Porter]

2:2-5. Small, Part 2.

3:1-2. Winslow H. Barger (1st WI Cav), "Picket and Prison."

3:2. F. M. Riddle (3rd IN Bty), "Up the Red River."

3:2. W. B. Roby (33rd OH), "Peach Tree Creek."

3:3. Robert Allich, "The 119th Pa. at the Battle of Rappahannock Station."

3:3. H. C. Olds (66th, 145th OH), "Corporal Pike. His Daring Exploits as Scout and Spy."

3:4-5. Picket Shots: Chattanooga, Shenandoah Valley, Red River, Moving on Richmond, Franklin, Helena, Prairie Grove, prisons, Vicksburg.

4:7. Obit.

5:3. Biog: Florence Donohue (94th NY).

8:3. Biog: Daniel Fish (45th IL), Wheelock G. Veazey (3rd, 16th VT).

8:4. "Captured a Locomotive. The Body of John Andrews Rescued from an Obscure Grave and Tenderly Interred at Missionary Ridge."

November 10

1:1-6. Boy Spy, Part 3.

1:7, 2:1-2. J. A. Bigelow (5th MI Cav), "Flashing Sabers. Chasing Lee's Columns after Gettysburg."

3:1. S. C. George (7th KS Cav), "A Charleston Episode. A Cheeky Prison Escape that Failed after All."

3:1. High Private (15th-16th IA), "Murphy's Chickens. How a Fight Got a Private Out of a Bad Scrape." {pat Murphy of an IA regiment]

3:1-2. D. L. Dean (8th IL Cav), "Troopers in Charge. Capt. Farnsworth's Way of Dealing with a Disloyal Preacher." [Alexandria, VA, early 1862]

3:2. Nicholas J. DeGraff (115th NY), "Harper's Ferry."

3:2. M. B. Bull (32nd WI), "The Salkahatchie Fight."

3:2. J. B. Harrod (9th IN Cav), "The Surrender of Athens, Ala."

3:3. W. H. Newlin (73rd IN), "A Mix of Taylors."

3:3. C. R. Glazier (MI Bg Band), "At Brandy Station." [10/63]

4:5-6. Mrs. John A. Logan, "War Memories of Cairo, Belmont, Henry and Donelson."

4:7. Obit.

5:4. Biog: William P. Black (11th IN, 37th IL).

November 17

1:1-6. Boy Spy, Part 4.

1:7, 2:1-2. Mrs. Ralph M. Parker, "At New Orleans. The Story of a Rebel Girl Who Joined the Union."

3:1. W. W. Cook (9th MI Cav), "Kilpatrick versus Wheeler. The Cavalry Fight at Waynesboro, Ga."

3:2. Julius D. Rhodes (5th NY Cav), "The Shenandoah Valley. With Banks and Milroy in 1862."

3:3. Louis C. Fisher (51st PA), "A Brave Man Rescues a Dare-Devil." [11/30/64]

3:3. Wiley Miller (6th MO SM Cav), "No Foraging Allowed—A Turkey Story."

3:3. C. F. Engle (82nd OH), "Gen. Milroy as a Fighter."

3:4-5. Picket Shots: Atlanta.

4:7. Obit.

5:3. Obit: Joshua T. Owen.

5:3. "Another Sixth Corps Monument." [Monocacy]

November 24

1:1-6, 2:4-5. Boy Spy, Part 5.

1:7, 2:1-3. Morton C. Hunter (82nd IN), "At Chickamauga."

3:1-2. D. C. Anderson (11th IN), "The Nineteenth Corps. An Amended Story of Gen. Emory's Command in the Valley Campaign."

3:2. John W. Call (7th ME, 6th VRC), "At Johnson's Island."

3:3. W. R. Carter (1st TN Cav), "Col. Jim Brownlow's Way. How Gen. Wheeler Failed to Scoop the 1st Tenn. (Union) Cavalry." [Spr 1862 near College Grove, TN]

3:3. H. W. Dickman (4th OH Cav), "Snap Generalship. Another Nervy Trick of Corp. Pike."

3:3. William Houghton (14th IN), "That Goose Story."

3:4-5. Picket Shots: Last fight, Mobile, Spotsylvania, Vicksburg, Chattanooga.

4:7. Obit.

December 1

1:1-6, 2:4-6. Boy Spy, Part 6.

1:7, 2:1-2. Frank Y. Commagere, "The Regulars. Staunch Loyalty of the Rank and File in 1861."

3:1-2. Samuel R. Strattan, "The 11th Pa. Cavalry. A Terse Sketch of One of the Best Regiments in the Eastern Army.

3:2. Henry W. Dickman (4th OH Cav), Corp. Pike's Comrade.

3:2. L. E. Pond, "The 7th Wisconsin. Its Service and Losses."

3:3. R. B. Wime (40th MO), "Mobile Bay. The Question of Who Fought There Settled by Maps."

3:3. J. J. Weiler (17th IN), "Col. Washington's Death." [John A. Washington of the Topographical Engineers, near Elkwater, WV]

3:3. D. N. Sharp (15th KY), "A Terse Story. A Big Brigade at Peach Tree Creek."

3_4-6. Picket Shots: Peach Tree Creek, prisons.

4:7. Obit.

5:3. Obit: Randolph B. Marcy (Inspector General).

8:1-3. William L. Welch (23rd MA), "Roanoke Island. A Review of the Article by Col. Hawkins, 9th N.Y."

December 8

1:1-6, 2:3-5. Boy Spy, Part 7.

1:6, 2:1-2. A. E. Matthews (1st MI Cav), "In a Tight Place. Gen. 'Jeb' Stuart's Close Call Near Verdiersville." [8/62]

3:1. Cromwell Marsh (2nd OH Cav), "At Independence."

3:2. H. W. Dickman (4th OH Cav), "Gen. Eli Long."

3:2. A. K. Miller (9th MI Cav), "Driving Wheeler. A Leaf from a Sergeant's Diary at Waynesboro."

3:3. R. M. Carson (128th OH), "Johnson's Island."

3:3. D. Carlos Sherman (8th US Cav), "Corp. Pike's Last Days."

3:3. C. E. Ringler (5th WV Cav), "'Mudwall' Jackson. The Bad Effect of Twitting Milroy's Old Mountaineers."

4:7. Obit.

5:3. Obit: William H. Emory.

8:3. J. B. Ridenour (55th IL), "Logan in Line. At Ezra Chapel, July 28, 1864."

8:3. "Another Monument at Gettysburg." [plans for 10th PA Res]

December 15

1:1-6, 2:4-5. Boy Spy, Part 8.

1:7, 2:1-2. William H. Ball (5th WI Bty), "At Perryville."

3:1-2. Joseph A. Moore (147th PA), "Lookout Mountain."

3:2. O. H. Ross (20th IL), "The Army Mails."

3:3. S. P. Zehring (35th OH), "Chickamauga."

3:3. James E. Sowders, "The 30th Indiana. From Fort Wayne to Jonesboro."

3:3. Samuel P. Combs (29th IA), "A Soldier's Story. How He Saw Things at Spanish Fort and Fort Blakely."

3:4-6. Picket Shots: Moving on Richmond, Mobile, Atlanta.

4:7. Obit.

5:3. Biog: William Vandever (9th IA).

8:1. "Blue and Gray. To Meet at Gettysburg Next July."

8:2. "Gettysburg Monuments. Meeting of the New York Commission—Monuments Accepted."

8:2. Biog: William H. Emory; Lewis M. Peck (173rd NY).

8:3. William F. Denmurf (USS *Santeo*, Antona), "A Dane's Story."

December 22

1:1-5. Thomas J. Wood, "Pickett's Mill."

1:6-7, 2:1-2. Boy Spy, Part 9.

3:1. N. P. Banks (Bty M, 1st IL, "Chickamauga Again."

3:1. E. A. Yontz (92nd IL), "At Waynesboro."

3:2. "The 44th N.Y. Plans for a Grand Memorial Building on the Battlefield of Gettysburg."

3:2. N. N. Davis (2nd VT), "Cedar Creek."

3:2. H. M. Brandle (3rd MO), "At Ezra Church."

3:3. George H. Palmer, "A Gallant Record. What the 20th Conn. Did in the Atlanta Campaign."

3:3. John A. Murphy, "An Explanation. The 89th N.Y. at Suffolk and Fredericksburg."

4:7. Obit.

3:3. "At Chattanooga. An Incident of the President's Visit to that City."

8:3. W. P. Wolf (175th OH), "At Franklin."

December 29

1:1-5. A. B. Sampson (1st CO Cav), "New Mexico. How One-third of the Union's Area was Saved."

1:6-7, 2:1-3. Boy Spy, Part 10.

2:6. Obit: William R. Murphy (10th NJ).

3:1. George W. Toms (5th NY Cav), "Light Cavalry. Custer's Division at Cedar Creek."

3:2-3. E. H. Low (55th USCT), "At Guntown."

3:3. David W. Smith (120th IN), "'Hovey's Babies.' The Twenty-third Corps at Kinston, N.C."

3:4. H. E. Mathews, "The 6th Maine. It was There, Although the Record Omits Its Say."

3:4. D. B. Devendorf (19th WI), "Richmond Again."

3:4. Noble D. Preston (10th NY Cav), "Another War Story. Was Comrade Griffin, 10th N.Y. Cav., the Youngest?"

8:2-4. G. W. Barber (112th NY), "Stealing a 12-Pounder. An Exploit on the Lines in Front of Petersburg."

1888

January 5

1:1-6. Noble D. Preston (10th NY Cav), "Trevilian Station."

1:6. "Gen. G. K. Warren. A Monument to be Erected to His Memory at Gettysburg."

1:7, 2:1-4. Boy Spy, Part 11.

3:1-2. James Wilson (9th IA), "Atlanta Again. Facts and Figures from the Official Redords."

3:2. James H. Orr (81st IL), "Guntown Again."

3:2. George W. Richards (14th IL Cav), "A Lucky Escape. How Two Prisoners Escaped the Rebels by Going to Church." [captured 12/13/63]

3:3. Lafayette Faris (48th OH), "Fort Blakely."

3:3. W. J. Shelton (70th OH), "Ezra Chapel."

3:4. John H. McGrail (USS *Saratoga*, *Shawmut*), "A Sailor's Story. How the Rebels Got the Sumter Privateer."

3:4. J. L. Coppoc (47th USCT), "The Colored Troops. They Did Not Kill Surrendered Rebels at Fort Blakely."

3:4. James Wilson (9th IA), "Gen. F. J. Herron."

4:7. Obit.

5:5. Obit: Samuel S. Blackford (19th, 86th OH).

8:1-3. F. L. Clarke (99th NY), "On Special Duty. An Incident of a Provost-Marshal's Life." [Winter 1862-63]

January 12

1:1-6. Carleton, Part 90. [Sumter and Alabama]

1:7, 2:1-4. Boy Spy, Part 12.

3:1-2. Thomas Gardner (122nd NY), "The Sixth Corps. Winchester and Cedar Creek Retold."

3:2. G. M. Dougherty (120th IN), "Old Battlefields. A Union Veteran Visits Nashville and Franklin."

3:2. William F. Smith (4th IA Cav), "A Brave Deed. A Daring Rescue by the Gallant Gen. Eli Long." [Alabama River at Selma]

3:3. Albert N. Swift (1st NY Dragoons), "Cedar Creek."

3:3. J. T. Roseberry (15th WV), "The Eighth Corps. A West Virginia Soldier Talks of Cedar Creek."

4:7. Obit.

8:2. "Volunteer Service. Capt. [Thomas A.] Pollok Claims the Longest Continuous Tour." [20th OH, 13th MO, 22nd OH, 57th USCT]

8:3. Lewis W. Moore (49th IL), "An Army Wedding."

8:3. J. H. Greene (8th WI), "'Old Abe.' The War Eagle the 8th Wisc. Carried Through the War."

8:5. William Watson (USS *Dragon*), "In Hampton Roads. A Pertinent Inquiry from a Participant in the *Monitor-Merrimac* Fight."

January 19

1:1-6, 2:4. Carleton, Part 91. [Kearsarge-Alabama, Galveston]

1:7, 2:1-3. Boy Spy, Part 13.

3:1. H. Choate (6th KY), "Nelson's Division. Something About the March to Shiloh."

3:1-2. L. B. Smith, "Minty's Cavalry. The Story of the 4th Michigan."

3:2. J. L. Richard (111th OH), "Andersonville. The Mortality There, and Why Exchange was Delayed."

3:2-3. James C. G. Smith (40th IN), "Wagner's Brigade. A Little Story of Franklin."

3:3. T. V. Brown, "Averill's Raid. A Hospital Steward's Story." [12/63]

4:7. Obit.

January 26

1:1-5. Albert G. Brackett (3rd US Cav), "The Cavalry Bureau. The Methods of Its Work. In the Western Armies. Scarcity of Horses. Recruiting Kilpatrick at Thomas's Expense. Troopers at Nashville. How Well the Dismounted Regiments Served."

1:6-7, 2:1-3. Boy Spy, Part 14.

3:1. S. P. Conner (ADC to General Casement), "Some Corrections." [Franklin]

3:2. Z. T. Griffin (122nd NY), "In the Wilderness."

3:2. Hiram Bowling (37th IN), "At Shelbyville. How Mitchell's Division Made an Easy Capture." [Summer 1862]

3:3-4. Kate M. Scott, "The Wild Cats. Some Random Sketches of the 105th Pa." [Fair Oaks and Gettysburg]

4:7. Obit.

5:3-4. Martin V. Hargrove (23rd NJ), "Mosby's Mistake. A Wagonmaster's Story of an Attempt to Capture His Camp." [Fall 1864]

February 2

1:1-6. Thomas Rafferty (71st NY), "Gettysburg. The Third Corps' Great Battle on July 2."

1:7, 2:1-5. Boy Spy, Part 15.

2:6. Hiram Berdan, "Berdan Sharpshooters. The Monument that is to Go Up at Gettysburg."

3:1-2. J. B. Ridenour (55th IL), "Jonesboro."

3:2. John T. Frederick (10th OH Cav), "An Exciting Squirrel Hunt."

3:2. James H. Orr (81st IL), "Mobile Again."

3:3. R. W. Bannatyne (52nd PA), "Entering Charleston."

3:3. William L. Hart (7th IN), "Hanged at Frederick City."

3:4. A. H. Boles, "The 4th Michigan. A Word from the Veracious Statistician of that Regiment."

3:4. J. H. Greene (8th WI), "Up the Yazoo."

3:4. Willis Dennis (57th OH), "Ezra Chapel."

4:7. Obit.

February 9

1:1-5. Mrs. J. A. Logan, "Cairo in 1861 . . . Battle of Belmont."

1:6-7, 2:1-5. Boy Spy, Part 16.

2:5. "A Gettysburg Bullet." [Charles Reese, wounded July 2 in nose]

3:1-2. William Cox (2nd CO Cav), "Apache Canyon."

3:2. W. B. Roby, "The 15th Kentucky at Peach Tree Creek."

3:2. Alfred Howes (8th CT), "The Battery at Suffolk."

3:3. William McCarter (116th PA), "A Sad Incident. How the Innocent Sometimes Suffer with the Guilty." [10/14/62 Charlestown, WV]

3:3. S. Pettet (104th OH), "Franklin."

3:3. D. W. Balmer, "The 11th Pennsylvania Cavalry."

3:4. A. H. Hutchinson, "Calling Things by Their Right Names."

3:4. A. A. Jones (11th IN Cav), "The Transport Mercury."

3:4. H. B. Scott (2nd IL Cav), "Smith's Guerrillas at Fort Blakely."

3:5. M. N. Cook (8th NY Hvy Art), "Cold Harbor."

3:5. Joseph S. Bray (Btys B&L, 2nd US), "Trevilian Station."

3:5. John Kelly (2nd US Cav), "The Spy at Frederick."

3:5. G. W. Lyman (12th OH Cav), "Stoneman's Night Hawks."

3:6. S. A. McNeil, "The 31st Ohio at Chickamauga."

3:6. L. A. Labadie, "The Flag of the 19th Michigan." [captured 3/4/63]

3:6. John Mitchell, "The 21st Missouri at Fort Blakely."

4:1-3. F. C. George (7th KS Cav), "Fort Pillow."

4:3. James M. Deems (1st MD Cav), "Gen. Milroy. A Staff Officer's Reminiscences." [Second Manassas]

4:3. L. O. Weeks (6th VT), "The Company Cook."

5:1-6. Rafferty, Part 2.

6:7. Obit.

7:6. H. E. Mathews, "The 6th Maine at Rappahannock Station."

7:6. William C. Rhoads (30th IL), "Who was Killed. Col. Rhoads Decries Gen. Leggett's Mule Story."

7:6. George A. Manning (2nd MA Cav), "He Corrects Comrades Newlin and Logsdon."

7:6. W. B. Curtis, "The Eagle of the 12th West Virginia."

9:2. M. V. B. Davis (2nd VT), "Cedar Creek."

9:2. E. Kenworthy (36th IA), "Execution of a Youthful Spy." [Little Rock, 1/64]

9:3. George Gibbons (4th IL Cav), "The Happy Family. They Lived on the Fat of the Land."

9:3. Henry Wakeford (29th IL), "Pittsburgh Landing."

9:3. E. F. Hopkins, "The 149th N.Y. at Lookout Mountain."

February 16

1:1-5. Carleton, Part 92. [James River, Apr 1864]

1:6-7, 2:1-4. Boy Spy, Part 17.

3:1-2. George A. Welton (6th MI), "Baton Rouge."

3:2. Julius D. Rhodes (5th NY Cav), "Cedar Creek."

3:2. J. L. Millikan, "The Charge at Monterey."

3:3. L. D. Immell (Bty H, 1st IL), "The 12th Wisconsin Battery at Corinth."

3:3. W. S. Wheeler (10th WV), "Rocky Gap and Droop Mountain."

3:3. Milton F. Murphy (10th MO Cav), "Vicksburg to Meridian."

3:3. G. W. Shrum (11th IL), "Atlanta and Ezra Chapel."

3:6. Zeno Whiting (4th MA Cav), "The First Flag on the Rebel Capital."

4:7. Obit.

February 23

1:1-5. Carleton, Part 93. [Bermuda Hundred]

1:6-7, 2:1-2. Boy Spy, Part 18.

2:6. David P. Muzzey, "Port Hudson. A Bill to Grant Medals to the Survivors of the Forlorn Hope."

3:1-2. J. A. Soliday (12th OH Cav), "The Saltville Raid."

3:2. S. A. Clark (1st VT Cav), "Hanover, Pa."

3:2. John Pennock (72nd IL), "Spanish Fort and Blakely."

3:2. James A. Williams (9th MI Cav), "Waynesboro Again."

3:3. T. L. Stewart (11th OH), "'Curly.' History of a Dog Which Deserved a Pension."

3:3. Henry C. Clark (83rd PA), "An Incident of Florence."

3:4. S. Longfellow (20th MA), "Fredericksburg."

3:5. R. R. Bratton (27th IN), "A Race for Life. How a Hand-Car Outran Rebel Cavalry."

3:5. James N. McMaster (9th OH Cav), "How They Surprised a Rebel Camp." [near Aiken, SC]

3:6. A. H. Reed (2nd MN), "Vandevere's Brigade." [Chickamauga]

3:6. John Alexander (18th IN), "Who was Responsible?" [Fall 1861, Glasgow, MO]

4:1-2. T. F. Ortrander (58th PA), "They Bought the Hog, But were Responsible for the Alleged Theft."

4:2-3. Isaac Ax (24th OH), "Columbia and Franklin, Tenn."

4:3. W. B. Hibbs (17th IA), "Andersonville. Closing Scenes in that Fatal Prison."

6:7. Obit.

9:1-3. A. L. Soule (10th MI Cav), "A Mounted Ghost. A Soldier's Experience in the Tennesse Mountains."

11:4. Martin Beem (9th IL), "The Mule in the War." [*Chicago Journal*]

March 1

1:1-5. Carleton, Part 94. [Grant and Petersburg]

1:6-7, 2:1-2. Boy Spy, Part 19.

3:1-2. C. H. Fish (signal corps), "The Signal Corps." [Allatoona]

3:2. Caspar Weissenfluh (1st US Dragoons), "Valverde."

3:2. A. F. Deniston (175th OH), "The Battle of Franklin."

3:2. J. P. Reed (46th IL), "Fort Blakely."

3:3. C. T. Hartley (64th IL), "On the Salkahatchie."

3:3. S. J. Burnett (33rd MO), "Southern Loyalists."

3:3. William Edmonds (4th WV), "The Smallpox Hospital at Milliken's Bend."

3:3-4. W. W. Calhoun (Bty I, 1st OH), "How He Got the Pork." [Chattanooga siege]

3:4. Jacob Smith (107th OH), "Who was He?" [Gettysburg—wounded comrade]

3:4. Theodore H. Mack (75th IL), "At Stones' River."

3:4. C. A. Tompkins (137th NY), "He Endorses Lt. Hopkins." [Lookout Mountain]

3:4. Henry Stokes, "The 5th Illinois Cavalry." [Mechanicsville, MS]

4:6-7. Obit.

March 8

1:1-5. Boy Spy, Part 20.

3:1. H. B. Turrill (72nd OH), "Guntown. The Hideous Butchery of the Colored Troops in the Disastrous Retreat."

3:1. John C. Patterson (14th NJ), "A Close Call. How the Lives of Two Deserters were Saved."

3:2. Perry Lewis (27th OH), "The 27th and 39th Ohio at the Battle of Parker's Crossroads."

3:2. J. K. Lowden, "Comrade Millikan Criticized in Turn." [Monterey Gap]

3:2. David C. Winder (14th PA Cav), "A Goat in the Soup Kettle."

3:2. J. B. Ridenour (55th IL), "The 116th Ill. and 30th Ohio at Ezra Chapel."

3:2. James McKee (11th IL Cav), "Vicksburg to Meridian."

3:3. D. Bates, "Negro Troops in the Rebellion."

3:3. E. L. Negus, "Monterey. The 1st Michigan [Cavalry] Claims the Midnight Charge."

3:3. E. J. Davis (Bty K, 4th US), "Seeley's Battery at Gettysburg."

4:6-7. Obit.

5:4-5. Biog: N. M. Curtis (16th, 142nd NY).

5:5. "The Boy Spy. Corroborations of His Statements."

March 15

1:1-5. Carleton, Part 95. [Petersburg]

1:6-7, 2:1-3. Boy Spy, Part 21.

2:4-6. James K. Magie (78th IL), "Mrs. Susan Sutton; Or, The Yankee Soldier's Wife." [Shelbyville, TN, 8/63]

3:1. John Ensfield (128th IN), "At Franklin."

3:1. W. W. Boney (78th PA), "The Transport Hastings."

3:2. George W. Dixon (81st OH), "DeGress's Battery."

3:2. H. E. Mathews, "The 6th Maine. The Gallant Work at Rappahannock Station."

3:2. S. W. Taylor (52nd PA), "The Swamp Angel Battery."

3:3. Will D. Butler, "The 9th Indiana Battery." [Mobile]

3:3. John H. Crawford (101st OH), "An Attempted Escape from Florence."

3:3. J. B. King (27th IA), "He has a Mounted Ghost, Too."

3:3. Leroy C. Starbuck (5th IL Cav), "Up the Yazoo."

3:3. Peter H. Kent (102nd NY), "Lookout Mountain."

3:4. Daniel B. Lincoln (Minnesota), "The Naval Expedition Up the Nansemond." [April 1863]

3:4. H. B. Griffing (1st WI), "Comrade Griffing's Account of Jonesboro."

3:4. R. B. Winn (40th MO), "He Explains to Comrade Pennock." [Mobile]

4:5-6. Obit.

4:6. Biog: Frank J. Magee (76th PA).

8:4. Francis M. Huff (19th IN), "Gen. Warren at Spottsylvania."

March 22

1:1-6. Thomas J. Cafer (9th IN Cav), "Chasing Hood."

1:7, 2:1-4. Boy Spy, Part 22.

2:4. John W. Risch (8th NY Hvy Art), "The Frederick Spy Again."

3:1. Noble D. Preston (10th NY Cav), "On to Richmond." [Trevilian Station]

3:2. J. F. Crawford (123rd IN), "Chicken Thieves."

3:2. Henry Vogt (4th OH Cav), "The Capture of Huntsville."

3:3. O. G. Atherton (40th KY), "The Saltville Raid."

3:3. George H. McKinney (AAQM, 4th Div, 13th Corps), "How the Wagon Train was Saved at Sabine Crossroads."

3:4. D. W. Griffis (151st NY), "He Saved His Stripes." [Fisher's Hill]

3:4. J. Reed (92nd IL), "The Nickojack Massacre." [4/24/64 near Ringgold, GA]

3:4. Campbell Walker (2nd PA Cav), "At Gettysburg."

3:4. J. M. Paul (3rd IA), "Alice Ferguson's Portrait." [9/17/61, Liberty, MO]

3:4-5. A. Woody (14th PA Cav), "Five Brothers in the Service."

4:6-7. Obit.

5:2. W. F. Lane, "A Joyous Trip of Paroled Prisoners on the R. E. Lee." [11/64 from Andersonville]

5:2-3. James Clark (Bty H, 1st IL), "He Knows Who Recaptured DeGress's Battery."

5:3. L. D. Immell (Bty H, 1st IL), "The 12th Wisconsin Battery, and the Part It Took at Iuka."

5:3. Louis Gable (35th NJ), "A Reminiscence of the Salkahatchie."

5:4-5. Thomas H. McKee (1st WV), "War Songs."

8:1-2. Cecil Clay (58th PA), "Fort Harrison."

8:2. A. H. Hunt (12th OH Cav), "He Corrects Col. Brackett." [Waddell Farm, AR]

8:2. W. A. McCallister (12th PA Res), "A Singular Fatality." [Second Manassas]

March 29

1:7, 2:1-4. Boy Spy, Part 23.

3:1-2. O. F. Dell (1st NE Cav), "The Andersons."

3:2. Isaac K. Young (89th IL), "Chickamauga."

3:3. I. S. Bangs, "A Youthful Soldier."

3:4. "The Colonel's Calf, and How It Got the Best of Him." [TN 1863]

3:4. Thomas A. Pierce (22nd IN), "The Paw-Paw Fight."

3:4. J. T. Cochran, "The 80th Indiana Heard From." [Franklin]

4:7. Obit.

5:4. D. R. Amadon (32nd WI), "In the Salkahatchie."

8:3. Biog: Samuel B. Horne (2nd, 11th CT).

April 5

1:1-6. "Orchard Knob."

1:7, 2:1-4. Boy Spy, Part 24.

3:1. John Ensfield (128th IN), "That Aching Void. A Foraging Expedition Which Ended Well After All." [NC 3/65]

3:2. J. W. Lacock (93rd IN), "A Strange Premonition."

3:2. J. D. Marquis (45th IL), "Catching a Tartar. How the Captors Became Captive." [near Marietta, GA, 1864]

3:3. William N. Brown (65th IL), "The 104th Ohio." [Franklin]

3:3. Charles F. Mansfield (Bty L, 1st US), "Fort Pickens."

3:4. (5th IA Cav), "Johnny Stole a Ham."

3:4. W. R. Batten (88th IL), "Franklin."

3:4. M. A. Cleveland (7th MA Bty), "Fort Blakely."

4:5. Obit.

5:4. "Gettysburg Monuments." [28th & 147th PA, Knap's Battery]

6:6. Obit: Commander Abner Read (USS *Wyandotte*, *New London*, *Monongahela*).

8:1-3. George B. Crawford (1st WV), "Belle Isle."

April 12

1:1-3. A. G. Brackett, "St. Louis in 1861-65."

1:4-7, 2:1. Boy Spy, Part 25.

3:1. Ira C. McClenthen, "The Baron DeKalb. How the Boys' Prize Money was Stolen and How the Thieves were Caught."

3:1. E. L. Lybarger (43rd OH), "The Salkahatchie."

3:2. George W. Cope (24h KY), "Nose's Creek."

3:2. G. W. McKinney (9th IN Bty), "Shelby Cole. Capture and Execution of a Missouri Bushwhacker."

3:2. James Coulter (37th IN), "Shelbyville to Huntsville."

3:3. John T. Hunt, "The 40th Illinois."

3:3. C. W. Chapman (19th IA), "Fourt's Battery Dog."

3:3. I. B. Dodge (30th IN), "At Shiloh."

3:4. Henry Austry (122nd IL), "At Parker's Crossroads."

3:4. J. H. Henderson (86th IL), "Peach Tree Creek."

3:4. A. K. Miller (9th MI Cav), "Death of Three Comrades on the Railroad." [Brown's Station, Dayton, OH, movement of 11th and 12th Corps]

3:4. "The 6th Maine at Rappahannock."

4:6. Biog: George Crook.

4:6. Obit: Quincy A. Gillmore.

4:7. Obit.

5:3. P. S. Moore (40th IN), "At Franklin."

5:3-4. A. V. Kendrick (33rd IA), "Forts Spanish and Blakely."

5:4. Biog: Myron P. Walker (10th MA).

5:4-5. H. H. Lyman (147th NY), "Old Prisons. A Visit to the Rebel Pens at Macon and Andersonville."

8:1-3. A. E. Glanville (10th MN), "Mobile."

8:3. "The Boy Spy. Acknowledgement of Letters Corroborating the Statements Made by Him."

8:3. W. J. Church (7th MI), "The Crossing at Fredericksburg."

April 19

1:1-4. Wiley Britton (6th KS Cav), "Fighting the Indians."

1:5-7, 2:1-3. Boy Spy, Part 26.

3:1-2. C. N. Hunt (11th MI Cav), "The Saltville Raid."

3:2. G. W. Kennedy (10th NY Cav), "Trevilian Station."

3:2. James Wilson (9th IA), "The DeGress Battery Again."

3:3. E. A. Yontz (92nd IL), "Waynesboro." [12/4/64]

3:3. S. A. Justice (125th IL), "Rocky Face and Buzzard's Roost."

3:3. A. A. Gildersleeve, "The Capture of Huntsville, Ala."

3:4. Daniel Coffman (70th OH), R. D. Parsons (7th IL Cav), "Shiloh."

3:4. R. D. Parsons (7th IL Cav), "He Also Differs With the Lieutenant." [Shiloh]

3:4. S. R. Evril (13th PA Cav), "The Spy at Frederick City."

4:7. Obit.

6:6. A. McVey (USN), "Gen. Ripley. A Tribute to the Memory of an Honest Rebel." [6/64 Charleston]

6:6. W. M. Sampson, "The 26th Illinois." [Atlanta]

6:7. "Gettysburg Monuments." [Vermont and New Jersey units]

April 26

1:1-3. Mrs. J. A. Logan, "Organizing Victory. Grant at Cairo in the Winter of 1861-'62."

1:4-7, 2:1-2. Boy Spy, Part 27.

3:1. T. J. Hadley (5th KS Cav), "Quantrall's Raid."

3:2. D. D. Proper (19th IA), "Morganza. Why the 19th Iowa and the 26th Indiana were Captured." [9/29/63]

3:2. James Colledge (146th NY), "A New Distinction. Claiming the Honor of Being in the Guardhouse."

3:3. Thomas Groody, "The 89th N.Y. The Crossing at Fredericksburg and the Capture of the Battery at Suffolk."

3:3. John S. Williams, "The 13th Kansas at Prairie Grove."

3:4. A. B. Crummel (30th OH), "Ezra Chapel."

3:4. Rober B. Valentine (13th PA Res), "The Picket's Last Watch." [song]

3:4. C. H. Peltz (NY Eng), "The Crossing at Fredericksburg."

5:5. "Stuart's Wagon Train. Gen. Alger's Night Attack At Monterey the Evening After Gettysburg." [from F. A. Burr's Rough Riders of the Rebellion]

5:5. "10th N.Y. Cavalry. Its Monument at Gettysburg."

6:7. Obit.

10:3. "Gettysburg Monuments Dedication Excursion." [Wisconsin]

12:1-4. Frank A. Myers (51st IN), "In Rebel Prisons. The Experiences of One of Streight's Raiders."

May 3

1:1-5. August V. Kautz, "The Fall of Richmond."

1:6-7, 2:1-4. Boy Spy, Part 28.

3:1-2. Z. T. Griffin (122nd NY), "Cedar Creek."

3:2. James G. Bennett, "The 5th Ill. Cavalry Heard From." [Meridian]

3:3-4. J. H. Whitney (9th NY), "The Hawkins Zouaves. The First Bayonet Charge of the War." [Roanoke Island]

3:4. Noble D. Preston (10th NY Cav), "Trevilian Station."

3:5. Walter H. Parcels (50th NY Eng), "Pick and Shovel. Splendid Service Performed by the Engineer Corps in Front of Petersburg."

3:6. Adam Hogle, "The 97th Ohio. An Incident of Kennesaw Mountain."

3:6. H. V. Boynton, "Chickamauga. Gen. Boynton Replies to Col. M. C. Hunter."

6:7. Obit.

11:5-7, 12:1-5. Wilbur H. Webber (6th MI), "Deadly Port Hudson."

May 10

1:1-6. Kautz, Part 2.

1:7, 2:1-3. Boy Spy, Part 28.

4:1-2. Frederick Rumble (58th IL), (14th IA), F. M. Riddle (3rd IN Bty), "Shelby Cole. Various Incidents of the Death of the Notorious Ruffian."

4:2. John Algoe, "Durant's Mill. Gallant and Successful Attempt of the 10th Michigan to Capture that Building." [Peach Tree Creek]

4:2. Hiram Martin , "The 3rd Ohio Cavalry,"

4:2. (14th IA), "From the Diary of Co. F." [Shelby Cole]

4:2. E. J. Davis (Bty K, 4th US), "The Crossing at Fredericksburg."

4:2. B. J. Davis (7th MI), "The Crossing at Fredericksburg."

4:3. O. S. Sisson (2nd WI Cav), "Helena to Clarendon. Story of a Midwinter March in the Snow and Sleet." [Winter 1862/63]

4:3-4. Joshua A. Stark (29th WI), "Sabine Crossroads."

4:4. James G. Bennett (5th IL Cav), "Poor Bunny. How It Happened that the Mess had a Rabbit for Dinner."

4:5. John E. Wildman, "The 105th Ohio at Chickamauga."

4:5. L. E. Ware, "A Novel Expedient. What Regiment Officiated as Telegraph Poles at Potomac Creek Bridge?" [June 1862]

5:1. Gus Hargesheimer (24th IL), "Huntsville to Tuscumbia."

5:1. W. F. Tait (89th IL), "Shiloh."

5:1. J. P. Platt (44th MO), "He Says Comrade Pennock is Badly Mixed." [Mobile]

5:2. J. R. Tisdale (29th MO), "Ezra Chapel."

5:2. Samuel C. Berstler (28th IA), "Another Family of Soldiers."

5:2. A. B. Sampson (1st CO Cav), "Valverde."

5:2. James Harman (22nd IN), "Peach Tree Creek."

5:3. J. F. Crawford (123rd IN), "A Pig This Time. More Efforts to Fill that Aching Void."

9:3-4. "The Boy Spy. His Visit to Virginia, and What He Saw There."

10:5. Gardner M. Dean (17th MA), "The Battle of Wise's Forks."

10:6. O. H. Ross (20th IL), The First Mail Carrier. The Army of the Tennessee Received Mail, Whether in Camp or Not."

12:1-4. R. C. Rankin (7th OH Cav), "Wilson's Raid."

12:5. Wiley Britton (6th KS Cav), "Gen. Ben. McCullough. The Rebel Leader was Killed by an Illinois Sharpshooter."

May 17

1:1-6. John Pope, "Siege of Corinth."

1:7, 2:1-3. Boy Spy, Part 29.

4:1. James M. Whallon (11th MI), "Chickamauga."

4:2-3. Lorenzo Forbes (1st WI Cav), "Andersonville."

4:3. Philip Roach (2nd US Cav), "Captain Rodenbaugh. Comrade Roach Corrects the Boy Spy."

4:3. (Bty E, 1st MO) "A Canine Forager." [Prairie Grove]

4:4. G. W. Gillis (6th OH), "Treatment of Rebel Prisoners at Camp Chase."

4:4. M. H. Van Buskirk (27th IN), "The Colors of the 38th Alabama." [Resaca]

4:4. George A. Smith (7th OH Cav), "An Escape Through the Bottom of the Car." [Feb 1863 from Richmond]

4:4. Matt F. Kippax (17th US), "Into a 15-inch Gun."

4:4-5. William R. Gabbard (47th KY), "Drunken Bill Brinegar."

4:5. C. W. Bryce (28th NY), "The Execution at Frederick."

4:5. H. A. Smith (48th IA), "He Defends the Mounted Ghost Story."

4:5. H. W. Carpenter (117th NY), "The 89th New York." [Suffolk]

4:6. Charles E. Stubbs (2nd ME Bty), "That Piano."

4:6. George Simmons (11th IN), "Champion's Hill."

5:3. E. M. Cafferty (89th NY), "The Crossing at Fredericksburg."

5:4. James Knight (12th NY Cav), "He Stopped the Rooster's Crowing."

5:4. E. H. Gregg (10th KS), "Fort Blakely."

6:7. Obit.

8:3. Biog: John W. Burst (15th, 105th IL).

9:1-3. "Boy Spy's Visit to Virginia," Part 2.

May 24

1:1-4. Pope, Part 2.

1:5-7, 2:1-3. Boy Spy, Part 30.

3:5-6. "Boy Spy's Visit to Virginia," Part 3.

4:1. "Union vs. Rebel Armies. The Superiority of the Former Proved on Many Bloody Fields."

4:2. W. E. Webster, "Cowan's 1st N.Y. Battery at Cedar Creek."

4:2. David Sigley (85th IL), "Peach Tree Creek."

4:2. D. F. DuBois (50th NY Eng), "Fredericksburg."

4:3. W. P. Wolf (175th OH), "Franklin."

4:4. E. B. Lufkin (13th ME), "Cedar Creek."

4:4. James N. McCurdy (49th OH), "Spears in the Rebel Army."

4:5. Cecil Clay (58th PA), "Fort Harrison."

4:5. George Grindley (56th OH), "Hovey's Division at Champion Hills."

4:5. Austin Curtin (45th PA), "A Chinese Pensioner." [Thomas Sylvanus, 81st PA]

4:5. L. R. Johnson (58th IL), "Last Review of the Sixteenth Corps."

4:6. F. Fenner (89th NY), "Crossing at Fredericksburg and the Capture of the Battery at Suffolk."

4:6. U. B. Pearsall (4th WI Cav), "What Col. Pearsall Thinks of Adam Badeau." [T. W. Sherman at Port Hudson."

4:7. Obit.

4:6. H. L. Potter (71st NY), "Seeley's Battery at Gettysburg."

5:1. D. C. Krone (41st IL), "Salkahatchie."

5:1. J. M. London (10th MO), "Corinth."

5:1. W. S. Wheeler (10th WV), "First Blood." [6/3/61]

5:2. "Shelby Cole. Another Account of the Missouri Outlaw's Execution."

5:2. J. B. Potter (83rd PA), "Rappahannock Station."

5:2. John W. Mack (138th PA), "The Death of Gen. A. P. Hill."

5:2. S. Pettit (104th OH), "Franklin Again."

5:3. H. C. Denny (18th IN), "The Paw-Paw Fight."

5:3. R. Crandall (5th IA Cav), "Stoop a Little."

5:3. J. A. Ankle (3rd US Cav), "Old Squeezer." [horse at Carlisle Barracks]

9:5. J. Pinnock (32nd OH), "Champion Hills."

11:1. Hiram Berdan, "The Sharpshooters. The Proposed Monument at Gettysburg to the Berdan Riflemen."

May 31

1:1-5. Mrs. J. A. Logan, "News from Donelson . . . Waiting at Cairo."

1:6-7, 2:1-2. Boy Spy, Part 31.

3:1-2. John W. Tucker (3rd IL Cav), "Cowardly Capt. Hunt. How He Murdered and Robbed Union Prisoners Committed to His Charge." [Captain William Hunt, 2nd MS]

3:2. William F. Denmure (naval bty), "Port Hudson."

3:3. James S. Robbins (95th IL), "Forts Spanish and Blakely."

3:3-4. Ira B. Goodrich (21st MA), "Roanoke Island."

3:4. Albert Ellis (12th KS), "The Grave at Little Rock."

3:4. Morton C. Hunter (82nd IN), "Chickamauga. Col. Hunter Admits His Error in Regard to Van Derveer's Brigade."

4:7. "Reunion at Gettysburg."

4:7. Obit.

June 7

1:1-3. W. H. Michael (USN), "Mississippi Flotilla."

1:4-6. Boy Spy, Part 32.

2:2-4. "Reminiscences." [Sheridan]

2:4. "Reunion at Gettysburg."

3:1-2. George A. Welton (7th MI Cav), "Cedar Creek."

3:2. L. B. Cutler (66th IL), "The Army Mule."

3:2. J. B. Ridenour (55th IL), "Jonesboro."

3:3. Arnold McMahon (21st OH), "Chickamauga Again."

3:3. "The Swenger Family in Service." [Elliottsburg, PA]

3:3. W. W. Sale (72nd IN), "Wilson's Raid."

3:3. L. W. Wilson (7th OH), "A Fraud Exposed." [false John Scott of the Andrews Raid]

3:4. J. B. King (27th IA), "Shelby Cole's Attempted Escape."

3:4. James N. McMaster (9th OH Cav), "A Rebel Spy Hanged at Knoxville." [fall 1863]

3:4. S. A. McNeil (31st OH), "Answer to Col. Hunter." [Stones' River]

4:7. Obit.

June 14

1:1-4. Michael, Part 2. [Shiloh, Island #10, Memphis]

1:5-7, 2:1-2. Boy Spy, Part 33.

3:1. J. H. C. Brewer (6th MD), "The Wilderness."

3:1-2. P. G. Jordan (79th IN), "First on Missionary Ridge."

3:2. J. M. Russell (1st IA Cav), "Guerrilla Warfare. Massacre at Centralia, Mo."

3:2. R. N. Maker, "The 6th Maine at Rappahannock Station."

3:2-3. J. B. Dunn (5th WI Bty), "Peach Tree Creek."

3:3. E. R. Reed, "21st Mass. at Roanoke Island."

3:3. Cyrus Pennock, "Valverde Once More."

3:4. George B. Fenn, "The 103rd Ohio." [Franklin]

3:4. O. B. Ormsby (18th IL), "Shiloh."

3:4. H. A. Camp (21st CT), "Fort Harrison."

3:4. "A Forlorn Hope. The Gallant Band at Port Hudson." [about Medals of Honor]

3:6. Perry Lewis (27th OH), "They Broke Up the Ball." [Memphis 1863]

4:3. "The Gettysburg Celebration."

4:6-7. "Gettysburg Reunion."

4:7. Obit.

6:5-6. "Boy Spy's Visit to Virginia," Part 4.

June 21

1:1-5. Michael, Part 3. [Vicksburg, Arkansas Post]

1:6-7, 2:1-2. Boy Spy, Part 34.

3:1-2. David Oglevie (88th OH), "Camp Chase. The Difference Between Rebel and Union Prisons."

3:2. William D. Robinson (4th NY Hvy Art), "Before Petersburg. Battery No. 20."

3:2. George W. Mead (9th MN), "Spanish Fort."

3:3. S. A. Clark (1st VT Cav), "Second Bull Run."

3:3. Celso Piermei (USN), "Expedition to Pascaquale." [from Ship Island]

3:4. John W. Crosby (46th PA), "Cedar Mountain."

3:4. W. R. Carter (1st TN Cav), "The Steamer Sultana."

3:4. S. J. Hinds (188th PA), "Fort Harrison Again."

3:4. William Godfrey (47th IL), "Plummer's Brigade Before Corinth."

4:7. Obit.

5:5. "Gettysburg Reunion." [Shaler's brigade]

8:1-2. "Frederick Town." [Frederick, MD]

8:2. F. M. McKeehan (208th PA), "Death of Gen. Hill."

June 28

1:1-4. Michael, Part 4. [Port Hudson]

1:5-7, 2:1. Boy Spy, Part 35.

2:3. "A Strange War Duel." [*Georgia Union*, regarding 6/12/63 event in Greene County, TN]

3:1-2. C. C. Clay (3rd OH Cav), "Wilson's Raid Again."

3:2. James G. Bennett (5th IL Cav), "A Lucky Dog. [Helena, Winter 1862-63]

3:3. Brewer Smith (65th OH), "Franklin."

3:3. A. C. Ranged (22nd IN), "The Paw-Paw Blunder."

3:4. Henry Beard (91st IL), "A Reminiscence of the War." [12/27/62, Elizabethtown, KY]

3:4. William E. Tiemann (159th NY), "Port Hudson."

3:4. I. H. Birdsley (50th NY Eng), "The Crossing at Fredericksburg."

4:7. Biog: Benjamin Harrison, Levi P. Morton.

5:5. Obit.

8:1-2. John T. Booth (36th OH), "Lewisburg, W.V."

8:5-6. "Gettysburg. Preparations for the Great Quarter Centennial."

July 5

1:1-3. Michael, Part 5. [Vicksburg, Helena]

1:4-7, 2:1. Boy Spy, Part 36.

3:1. Edwin W. Smith (54th OH), "Battle of Ezra Church."

3:2. S. H. Samuels (1st IN Hvy Art), "Port Hudson Again."

3:3. (15th IA), "A Reminiscence of the War."

3:3. James G. Bennett (5th IL Cav), "Fighting Them Over."

3:4. P. O. Avery (4th IL Cav), "A Pig Tale."

3:4. John O. Wagoner (11th IL Cav), "Parker's Crossroads."

3:4. L. Mitchelson (124th IL), "A Faithful Dog."

3:4. Daniel Weston (113th IL), "The Force of a Shell." [Arkansas Post]

4:6. Moses McLain (70th IN), "Gen. Harrison at Resaca."

4:7. Obit.

5:4-5. "Boy Spy's Visit to Virginia," Part 5.

6:7. Biog: Nathan Kimball.

8:1-2. (81st OH), "DeGress's Battery."

8:3-4. "Gettysburg. Preparations for the Great Quarter Centennial."

July 12

1:1-2. Michael, Part 6. [Red River]

1:6-7, 2:1. Boy Spy, Part 37.

3:1. Rush C. Hawkins (9th NY), "Hawkins's Zouaves. The Colonel Defends His Regiment Against Its Detractors." [Roanoke Island]

3:2. A. C. Learned, "The 18th Ohio."

3:2. M. G. Yarnell (36th IL), "Killing of Gen. McCullough." [Pea Ridge]

3:3-4. S. J. Bailey (9th IL Cav), "Guntown."

3:4. R. S. Sproux, "The 40th Illinois at Shiloh."

3:4. Charles Pumpelly (16th KY), "The Battle of Franklin."

3:6. Charles E. Stubbs (2nd ME Bty), "An Eccentric Character."

4:2. "The Gettysburg Celebration." [editorial]

4:2. "Berdan's Reconnaissance."

4:3. "The Gettysburg Orator." [Gen. William Curtis]

4:3. "The Fighting at Gettysburg." [editorial]

4:7. Obit: Washington L. Elliott.

4:7. Obit.

8:1-7. "25 Years After. Friend and Foe Tenting on the Old Camp Ground." [Gettysburg]

July 19

1:1-6. John W. DePeyster, "An Ideal Soldier. A Tribute to Major-General Daniel E. Sickles."

1:7, 2:1-3. Boy Spy, Part 38.

3:1. H. E. Mathews, "6th Maine Reminiscences." [Fredericksburg 1863; July 13, 1863]

3:1. Joseph M. Waldorf (24th, 177th OH), "Rebel Prisoners."

3:1. W. P. Wolf (175th OH), "The 104th Ohio at Franklin."

3:2. Pierre Gentieu (13th CT), "Molineux's Brigade at Cedar Creek."

3:2. Russell O. Frost (3rd NY Bty), "The Blunder at White Oak Swamp."

3:2. C. P. Nash (13th VT), "One of the Locomotive Captors." [Robert Buffum, postwar]

3:3. R. B. McCully (81st NY), "The Providential Spring."

3:3. David Oglevie (88th OH), "Camp Chase and the Rebel Prisons."

4:6-7. Obit.

6:7. John More, "The 79th N.Y."

8:2. "Meagher's Men. The Famous Irish Brigade at the Gettysburg Reunion."

8:3-5. John T. Booth (36th OH), "Turchin's Charge. How the Brilliant Dash was Made at Chickamauga Sunday Afternoon."

8:5. "Mrs. Sinnott's Way." [Shiloh nurse]

8:6. Robert Johnson (84th PA), "An Artistic Soldier." [Joseph C. Love, 1st Maine Heavy Artillery]

July 26

1:1-6. DePeyster, Part 2.

1:7, 2:1-2. Boy Spy, Part 39.

2:2. U. S. Graham, "Gen. Meade. The Actual Hero of Gettysburg."

2:3-4. W. H. Michael (USS *Tyler*), "The Sultana Explosion."

2:4. "Gettysburg Prices." [*New York Sun*]

3:1-2. D. H. Hutchins (27th IA), "Death of Shelby Cole."

3:2. Henry Jimmerson (28th CT), "Medals of Honor for Port Hudson."

3:2. A. B. Smith (97th OH), "How They Got Pumpkins at Chattanooga."

3:3. James L. Dunn (109th PA), "Rebel Gush. The Speech of Hooker, of Mississippi, at Gettysburg."

3:3. J. N. McMaster (9th OH Cav), "Kilpatrick's Cavalry at Aiken, S.C."

3:3. J. H. McKinnon, "The 110th Ohio at Monocacy."

3:4. A. B. Hodge (Bty I, 2nd IL), "Booneville and Blacklands."

3:4. William H. Blair (58th PA), "Fort Harrison Again."

3:4. T. L. Willey (50th NY Eng), "Who Laid the Pontoons at Fredericksburg?"

4:5-6. "DeGress's Battery." [editorial]

4:7. Obit.

5:4. "Bull Run. The 71st N.Y. Upon the Historic Field."

6:6. A. H. W. Sullivan (9th MO SM Cav), "Quantrall's Death."

August 2

1:1-4. John Pope, "Army of Virginia. Campaign in Front of Washington in 1862."

1:5-7, 2:1-3. J. B. Turchin (19th IL), "First Steps in War. Organizing a New Regiment and Taking It to the Field."

3:1-2. M. V. Ashby (16th IL), "'Rain' of Whiskey. The Only Occurrance on Record." [Sept 1861, New Market, MO]

3:2. A. M. Gurnsey (124th IL), "Spanish Fort and Fort Blakely Again."

3:2. John T. Booth (36th OH), "Gen. Heth's Cannon." [Lewisburg, WV, letter from J. M. Kurtz, 44th OH]

3:3. Erastus L. Harris (44th NY), "Little Round Top."

3:3. A. F. Brown (2nd CO Cav), "Valverde Again."

3:3. Horace Prescott (9th MA Bty), "Whiskey Caused the Trouble."

3:3. Cornelius Yost (33rd MO Enr Mil), "The Guerrilla Bill Anderson."

3:4. E. H. Bourman (27th IL), "The Battle of Belmont, Mo."

3:4. J. W. Bryan (24th OH), "Buell's Army at Shiloh."

3:4. W. H. Webber (6th MI), "A Correction." [Port Hudson]

3:6. S. M. Layman (9th NJ), "Roanoke Island."

4:7. Obit.

5:5-6. "Stonewall Jackson. His Death and Monument Dedication." [by the Boy Spy]

6:3. "The Zouaves Will Fight." [72nd PA monument at Gettysburg]

8:2-3. "The Explosion of the Sultana." [illustration by J. R. Brockway]

8:4. Obit: James Stevenson (13th NY).

8:5. "Statue for Gen. Warren." [Gettysburg]

August 9

1:1-4. Pope, Part 2.

1:5-7, 2:1-3. Frank Swigart (46th IN), "The Vicksburg Campaign."

3:1-2. Isaac K. Young (89th IL), "Chickamauga."

3:3. B. W. Wilson (28th IA), "Cedar Creek."

3:3. John S. Martin (9th IA), "DeGress's Battery Again."

3:3. Reuben T. Rains, "The 12th Kentucky at Franklin."

3:3. W. H. H. Kennedy (PA Res), "The Providence Spring."

3:4. James Wharton (9th IN), "The Fight at Buffalo Mountain, W.V."

3:4. Clarence F. Bronner, "Defending the Train. The 1st Michigan Engineers at Stones' River."

4:7. Obit.

5:4-6. Obit: Philip H. Sheridan.

8:1-2. C. A. Kuhl (14th IL), "Illicit Trading. The Capture of an English Syndicate's Steamboat." [Vicksburg, March 1864]

8:2. "Monuments at Gettysburg." [61st PA, 2nd PA Cav plans]

8:2. "Monument of the 3rd Massachusetts Cavalry." [Winchester]

8:5. "The Scott Legion Monument." [68th PA, Gettysburg]

August 16

1:1-4. Pope, Part 3. [Cedar Mountain]

1:5-7, 2:1-6. Coverage of Sheridan's Funeral.

3:1. F. Bedford (12th IL Cav), "Burnside and Hooker. A Defense of Fighting Joe."

3:2. B. F. Gates, "The 26th Conn. at Port Hudson."

3:2. H. P. Boon (1st WV Cav), "The Charge at Monterey, July 4, 1863."

3:3. W. L. Birney (17th IN), "Col. Washington's Death." [Elkwater, WV]

3:3. Leros Shelley (8th VT), "The 19th Corps at Cedar Creek."

3:3. L. H. Craig (140th IN), "A Forager Comes to Grief."

3:4. Gilbert Thompson, "U. S. Engineer Battalion. Their Services at Fredericksburg, Va., 1862,'3."

3:4. N. K. Force (37th IN), "Shelbyville to Huntsville."

3:6. J. H. Campbell, "Another Young Soldier." [Fred Whitlock, 30th OH]

3:6. C. Allen Purdy, "The Charge of Fremont's Body Guard." [10/25/61]

4:7. Obit.

8:1-3. S. E. Chandler, "Petersburg. The 24th N.Y. Cavalry at the Mine Explosion."

8:3. Obit: Alvin P. Hovey.

August 23

1:1-3. Pope, Part 4. [Manassas Junction]

1:4-7, 2:1-3. John G. Weaver (2nd OH Cav), "Salisbury Prison." [includes Belle Isle and Libby]

3:1-2. E. J. Smith (1st IA Cav), "The Centralia Massacre."

3:3-4. J. L. Anderson, "Gen. Milroy. His Gallant Three Days' Fight at Winchester."

3:4. F. L. Clarke (99th NY), "Another Whiskey Story."

3:4. Charles A. Dean (2nd LA), "Storming Port Hudson."

3:6. Jerry Ryan (86th NY), N. S. Swett (2nd Co MA Ss), "Who Killed Stonewall Jackson?"

4:6. Biog: George E. Seney (101st OH).

4:7. Obit.

8:1-3. Albert Knowles (120th IN), "Love's Captain. A Gunboat Captain Caught by a Trap Set by a Woman." [W. E. H. Fentress, USS *Rattler*]

8:6. W. E. Whittinghill (4th KY), "The Providence Spring.

August 30

1:1-6, 2:6. Thomas W. Knox (1st IA), "The Lost Army. Scouting and Fighting Adventures of Two Boys in Missouri and Arkansas in 1861, '62."

1:7, 2:1-3. Pope, Part 5. [Second Manassas]

2:3. "Address of J. H. Stone, Historian First Corps, Gettysburg, July 1, 1888."

3:1. A. D. Stewart (25th OH), "Gettysburg. A Defense of Meade, Howard and the Eleventh Corps."

3:2. George Slusser, "11th Ohio Cavalry."

3:2. James H. McCurdy, "The Sultana Explosion."

3:3. John Reed (92nd IL), "The Action at Aiken, S.C."

3:3. Elliott V. Smith (27th IA), "Some Unwritten History." [8/18/64, Tallahatchie River, A. J. Smith's troops]

3:4. John R. Leavenworth (107th NY), John W. Taylor (124th NY), Edward Sorgen (4th OH), "Stonewall Jackson."

3:4. Joseph Hall (22nd MI), Benjamin Williams (5th IA Cav), John A. Miller (1st OH), "The Providential Spring."

3:6. M. Patton (92nd OH), "Turchin's Charge at Chickamauga."

4:5. Biog: Samuel S. Yoder (128th OH).

4:7. Obit.

5:4-6. Weaver, Part 2.

8:4-5. Biog: Edward A. Dubey (10th NY), James A. Sexton (72nd IL), Delevan Bates (121st NY).

September 6

1:1-6, 2:5-6. Knox, Part 2.

1:7, 2:1-3. Pope, Part 6. [Second Manassas]

3:1. S. D. Webster, "Fighting Joe Hooker. His Part in the Gettysburg Campaign."

3:1. Frederick Fitch (46th IN), "Looking for Guerrillas." [White River, AR, 6/62]

3:1. Frederick H. Parker (8th CT), "A Claim from Connecticut." [Fredericksburg pontoons]

3:2. Victor Landergren (USN), "A Soldier for a Day. The Capture of Fort Fisher, N.C."

3:2. Charles Stacey (55th OH), "The First Day at Gettysburg."

3:2. Dutee Johnson (5th RI), "The Charge of Hawkins's Zouaves." [Roanoke Island]

3:3. O. B. Ormsby (18th IL), "Shiloh Again."

3:3. Steven E. Payne, "Providential Spring."

3:3. A. C. Beck, "The 84th Illinois." [Nathan Kimball's farewell order]

3:4. W. S. Pierce (20th WI), "Going for a Henroost."

3:4. R. Kincaid (4th OH Bty), "First Division, Fifteenth Corps."

3:4. B. R. Ellis (1st WI Cav), "The Killing of Col. Washington."

3:4. James Love (86th NY), E. L. Saunders (72nd NY), "Stonewall Jackson."

4:7. Obit.

8:1-4. Weaver, Part 3.

September 13

1:1-5, 2:6. Knox, Part 3. [Carthage]

1:6-7, 2:1. J. W. Long (2nd IA), "Flanking Johnston. The Army of the Tennessee Moving at Snake Creek Gap. Laying Pontoons in a Hot Place. Turning Resaca. . . . ."

3:1. W. P. Wolf, "175th Ohio at Franklin."

3:1. Charles L. Marshall (47th PA), "The Battle of Cedar Creek."

3:1. Amos H. W. Sullivan (9th MO SM Cav), "The Centralia Massacre."

3:2-3. M. L. Olmstead, W. Prescott (1st MA), "Stonewall Jackson."

3:3. Sidney M. Davis (6th US Cav), "A Missing Comrade." [Howard S. Jones]

3:3. T. M. Mozingo (7th IN), "Providential Spring."

3:3. M. W. Nelson, "The Capture of the 1st Illinois Cavalry." [Lexington, MO]

3:3. James Robinson, "The 61st Pa. at Marye's Heights."

3:4. A. Hottinger (10th MO Cav), "Sinking of the Runian." [7/21/64, Mississippi River above Vicksburg]

3:4. E. W. Pettys (51st NY), "Roanoke Island."

3:6. J. N. McMaster (9th OH Cav), "A Correction." [Aiken, SC]

4:7. Obit.

6:7. "At Gettysburg. Three N.Y. Regiments Dedicate Handsome Monuments to Their Fallen Comrades." [104th, 108th, 123rd]

8:1-3. Weaver, Part 4.

8:4-5. Biog: John M. Schofield, Albert G. Brackett (9th IL Cav).

September 20

1:1-5. Knox, Part 4. [Wilson's Creek]

3:1-2. S. A. Clark (1st VT Cav), "Kilpatrick's Raid. The Second Trip to Richmond."

3:3. L. H. Coon, "The Ram Arkansas. Passing Through the Union Fleet in Safety."

3:3. Perry Lewis (27th OH), "Parker's Crossroads."

3:3. William Feaga (72nd OH), "Providential Spring."

3:4. Gilbert Thompson US Eng Btn), "Stonewall Jackson. Who Killed the Rebel General?"

3:4. J. A. Wright (1st MN), "Give Unvarnished Accounts."

4:5-6. Biogs: William Warner (33rd, 44th WI), Moses H. Neil (1st OH Cav).

4:7. Obit.

5:5. "Monument of the 10th N.Y. Cavalry." [Gettysburg]

September 27

1:1-5, 2:5. Knox, Part 5. [Retreat to Springfield]

3:1-2. C. C. Cunningham (5th WI Bty), "A Cannoneer's Story." [Stones' River]

3:2. George Maltby (10th IN Bty), "Who Killed Gen. Polk?"

3:3-4. James M. Taylor (3rd MI), W. C. Beck (62nd PA), W. H. Wilson (134th NY), James Love (86th NY), "Stonewall Jackson."

3:4. Edwin Hewes (20th IL), George A. Smith (7th OH Cav), Joseph N. Walsh (4th MA Cav), "Providential Spring."

3:4. C. Henry Chapman (41st USCT), "Col. Ralston's Death." [Petersburg Mine]

4:7. Obit.

8:1-4. Weaver, Part 5.

8:4. "The 107th N.Y. Their Gettysburg Monument Dedicated in a Downpour of Rain."

October 4

1:1-5, 2:6. Knox, Part 6.

1:6-7, 2:1. "How I Won My Wife."

2:1-2. Eben Pixley (8th WI), "A Badger's Story. A Thrilling Elopement."

2:2. R. G. Bawbell (10th OH Cav), "An Ohio Comrade. He Got His Wife Through a 'Lottery Correspondence'."

3:1-2. "Playing Parson. Why a Soldier was Dubbed Chaplain." [147th NY at Gettysburg]

3:2. D. W. Leath (7th TN), "Who Marked the Terrapin?"

3:2. L. H. Tilden (127th IL), "The DeGress Battery Again."

3:3. E. T. Lee (41st IL), "Buell at Shiloh. The Battle of Sunday, April 6."

3:3. Frederick M. Little (71st NY), Henry C. Terry (27th IN), Charles W. Hathaway (1st MA), "Stonewall Jackson."

3:4. Clinton T. Hull (11th IA), "Providential Spring."

4:6. Biog: George S. Evans (56th MA).

4:7. Biog: Joseph Yocum (116th PA), H. Craig (135th PA).

4:7. Obit.

8:1-2. Frank Y. Commagere, "Knowing Dogs. A Cavalryman's Reminiscences of His Canine Companions."

8:3. "Gen. Wadsworth's Monument."

8:3. "Farnsworth's Brigade at Gettysburg." [meeting]

8:3. "Monuments at Gettysburg." [Maryland]

8:3. "Dedication of Monument." [12th NH at Gettysburg]

October 11

1:1-5. Knox, Part 7. [Lexington]

1:6-7, 2:1. William Goodman (89th IL), L. A. Ross (86th IL), "How I Won My Wife."

2:1. (84th PA), "How a Pennsylvanian Managed to Get His Wife."

3:1-2. F. Vogl (US Eng Btn), "Who Laid the Pontoons?" [Fredericksburg]

3:2. S. L. French, "The 16th N.Y. Independent Battery."

3:2. L. W. Robinson (11th IN), "To What Regiment Did the Sergeant's Squad Belong?" [Shiloh]

3:2. Ira S. Reynolds (120th NY), "The Excelsior Brigade." [Chancellorsville]

3:3-4. B. C. Rice (125th OH), "The Battle of Franklin."

3:4. A. F. Vogelbach (27th PA), "Honor to Whom Honor is Due." [Gettysburg]

3:4. C. K. Baxter (19th IN), "Catlett's Station."

3:4. C. Morehead (15th OH), "Shiloh's Bloody Field."

3:4. H. W. Sullivan, "The Battle of Fayette and the Centralia Massacre."

5:4. Biog: Joseph Hadfield (USS *Varuna*, Lodona, Monticello), Eugene F. Weigel (4th MO, 82nd IL).

6:7. "Gettysburg. Regimental Monuments Erected on that Historic Field." [93rd, 119th PA, 107th, 125th, 126th NY]

8:1-2. C. A. Kuhl (14th IL), "Illicit Trading. A Planter and Family Caught Smuggling."

8:2. M. W. Peters (1st WI), "A Terrible Experience." [Danville, Libby, Belle Isle]

8:3. Joseph A. Stuart (USS *Metacomet*), "Fort Blakely."

8:3. C. L. Thompson (153rd OH), "Smithland, Ky."

October 18

1:1-5. Knox, Part 8. [Fremont's Advance]

1:5. Lewis Blundin (28th PA), "Grapeshot Used by Rebels." [New Hope Church]

1:6-7, 2:1-2. Jennie Porter Arnold, "At Antietam. A True and Graphic Story of the 16th Connecticut."

2:2. P. E. Johnson (36th IN), "How I Won a Wife."

3:1. John C. Widdle, "The 1st Ky. Cavalry."

3:1. P. M. Evans (US Eng Btn), "Fredericksburg. Who Laid the Pontoons?"

3:2. A. G. Jones (27th USCT), "Colored Troops. March from Fort Fisher to Wilmington."

3:2. W. H. McIntosh (22nd WI), "Entering Atlanta. The Gate City Surrenders to Gen. Coburn."

3:3. Albert Mills (58th IN), R. T. Boyd (7th TN Cav), Leonidas Potter (21st IL), "Providential Spring."

3:4. H. L. Potter (71st NY), J. E. Doak (4th MI), C. G. Cooper (63rd PA), "Stonewall Jackson."

3:4. E. D. Foskett (5th Co OH Ss), "A True Story." [Fall 1863, Loudon, TN, Grant & Thomas taking railroad from Chattanooga to Knoxville."

3:4. H. Benton (91st IN), "First Across the Chattahoochie River."

5:2. Biog: Charles E. Belknap.

5:4. Biog: William E. Simonds (25th CT), Edwin S. Osborne (8th, 149th PA).

8:3. "Gettysburg. Regimental Monuments Erected on that Historic Field." [4th, 17th ME, 45th, 59th NY, 10th NY Cav, 6th PA Cav]

October 25

1:1-3. John Pope, "The Man on Horseback. Some of the Legacies of Our Civil War. A Sovereign People. The Character of Our Private Soldier. McClellan's Admirers. No King Nor Ministers to Depose."

1:4-7, 2:1. Knox, Part 9. [Refugees]

2:4. W. B. Johnson (4th Division, 15th Corps), "A Soldier's Recollections. What We had to Learn Before We Became Veterans."

3:1. George F. Peaks (6th ME), "The Light Division. Their Charge on Marye's Heights."

3:1. I. A. Taylor (122nd IL), "Parker's Crossroads."

3:2. Joseph F. Carter, "Vindicated at Last. The 3rd Maryland at Chancellorsville."

3:2. Robert M. Hartley (NY), "Relics of the Wilderness."

3:2. David Garver (17th IN), "Death of Col. John A. Washington."

3:3. N. J. Nichols (2nd VT), "For Consideration. Let Comrades Tell Only What They Actually Saw."

3:4. Mary A. Hovey, "Providential Spring. A Recent Visit to Andersonville."

3:4. F. B. Williams (50th NY Eng), "Who Laid the Pontoons at Fredericksburg?"

5:5. Biog: Josiah Holbrook (12th OH).

8:1-3. E. B. Lufkin (13th ME), "Away Down in Texas. Campaign of the Thirteenth Corps in the Winter of 1863."

November 1

1:1-4. John Pope, "The Man on Horseback. The Union Soldier. Influence of the War on His Character and Subsequent Career."

1:5-7, 2:1. Knox, Part 10. [Springfield]

3:1. J. E. Walton, "Mission Ridge. The 30th Ohio's Gallantry in the Battle."

3:2. "A Rebel Spy. It Sometimes Pays to be a Mason." [10/62, KY, Steedman's brigade]

3:3. W. H. Conley (6th MI), "The Mississippi Flotilla: Fight at Baton Rouge, La."

3:3. M. M. Saylor (161st OH), "Who was George?" [Guarding wounded Rebels from Monocacy Junction to Baltimore]

3:3. J. A. Armstrong, "The 105th Pa. at Fair Oaks."

3:4. B. E. Parkhurst (147th NY), "At Gettysburg."

3:4. Andrew Moran (11th MA), "Stonewall Jackson."

3:4. L. D. Lyon (12th IA), "Fight at the Mouth of White River." [AR, 6/22/64]

5:1. Biog: Joseph C. Breckinridge (2nd US Art).

5:3. Biog: C. F. Manderson (19th OH).

6:7. "Gettysburg. Regimental Monuments Erected on that Historic Field." [136th NY, 26th PA, MD]

8:5. "Libby Prison to Go to Chicago."

November 8

1:1-4. T. W. Rathbone (153rd OH), "Among the Johnnies. How Prisoners Moved from Charleston to Columbia. A Leap for Freedom."

1:6-7, 2:1-2. Knox, Part 11. [Enlisting Indians]

3:1-2. H. Learning (40th IN), "The Battle of Franklin."

3:2 M. Frisney (73rd NY), "Stonewall Jackson."

3:2. W. McEvoy, "Mr. Knox's Inaccuracies." [Wilson's Creek]

3:3. C. E. Mink (Bty H, 1st NY), "A Correction. Honor to Whom Honor is Due." [Gettysburg]

3:3. E. V. Jackson (6th IN Cav), "Deaths at Andersonville."

3:3. J. C. Filson (48th IL), "A Sucker's Big Capture." [Jonesboro]

3:3. W. T. Eddy (89th NY), "Asleep on His Post."

3:4. Gilbert Thompson (US Eng Btn), "U.S. Engineers. Who Laid the Pontoons at Fredericksburg?"

3:4. "Gen. Doubleday Vindicates the 3rd Maryland." [Chancellorsville]

4:7. Obit.

November 15

1:1-4. Rathbone, Part 2.

1:5-7, 2:1-2. Knox, Part 12. [Pea Ridge]

3:1. J. D. Strand (45th PA), "Salisbury Prison."

3:1. J. M. Gardner (12th IL Cav), "Banks's Expedition. A Duel Between Enlisted Men."

3:1. Michael Brunner (59th OH), "An Ohio Soldier's Prison Experience." [captured 9/19/63—many places]

3:2. George Hass (102nd OH), "The Sultana."

3:3. John Growney (Bty C, 3rd RI), "Fort Harrison."

3:3. "Antietam Campaign. The Hanging of the Spy Richards."

3:4. Nathan Benson (Bty C, 3rd US), "Kilpatrick's Raid in March 1864."

3:4. N. J. Bail (3rd KY Cav), "A Kentucky Cavalryman's Experience."

4:7. Obit.

5:2. Biogs: Joseph Fifer (33rd IL), Charles Becker (12th MO), William Hunt (12th IL), Charles W. Pavey.

6:7. H. V. Pease (Bty M, 1st NY), "How I Won My Wife."

November 22

1:1-4. Rathbone, Part 3.

1:6-7, 2:1-2. Knox, Part 13.

3:1. Joseph Cue (65th IL), "Crossing Nose's Creek."

3:2. U. D. Wood (50th NY Eng), "Fredericksburg. Who Laid the Pontoons?"

3:2. N. A. Pinney (104th OH), "At the Cotton-Gin." [Franklin]

3:2. Joseph W. Sweeney (31st NY), "The Charge at Marye's Heights."

3:3. D. S. Hart (32nd WI), "The Band-Box Regiment. Scenes and Incidents on Sherman's March."

3:3. Frank S. Reader (5th WV Cav), "Gen. Hunter's Coolness Under Fire." [Piedmont]

3:4. M. C. Connett, "34th Indiana Infantry, or 8th Indiana Cavalry."

3:4. F. A. Conlee (96th IL), "Time to Call a Halt." [controversies in paper]

3:4. W. H. Wilson (134th NY), "Composition of the First and Second Brigades, Eleventh Corps."

3:4. E. W. Pettys (51st NY), "Roanoke Island."

4:7. Obit.

November 29

1:6-7, 2:1-2. Knox, Part 14. [Indians]

4:1. Boy Spy, "Hancock and Howard." [Gettysburg]

4:2. Lucius W. Hull (18th OH), "The Youngest Soldier."

4:2. Lindsay Steele (30th IL), "Champion Hills."

4:3. L. S. Tyler (15th IA), "Salkahatchie Swamp."

4:3. S. R. Evril (13th PA Cav), "Gen. Milroy at Winchester."

4:4. R. B. McCully (81st NY), "Burial Details. With All the Horrors of Bloody War."

4:4. Joseph E. Vantine (USS *Richmond*), "The Originator of Chain Armor for U.S. Ships." 4:4. Michael Regan (23rd IL), "The Prisoners Captured at Lexington, Mo."

4:4. J. W. H. McGuire, "The 14th Indiana Battery at Lexington, Tenn."

4:5. Jacob Buck (5th US Cav), "Stoneman's Raid. Capturing the Rebel Mail at Fisher's Hill."

4:5. O. L. Chapman (5th IN Cav), "Stoneman's Raid in Georgia."

4:5. S. A. McNeil (31st OH), "The First to Enter Fayetteville, N.C."

4:6. William H. Holmes (Bty M, 1st NY), "Chancellorsville."

5:1-2. W. S. Furay (war correspondent), "Chickamauga. Rebel Testimony that It was a Fatal Blow to the Confederacy."

5:2. Edwin R. Young (Bty H, 1st US), "Stonewall Jackson."

5:2. William T. Ball, "The 11th Illinois Cavalry."

5:3. E. A. Wilson (1st US Ss), "Ex-Rebels in the GAR. A Plea for Men Forced into the Rebel Army."

5:3. R. Kincaid (4th OH Bty), "The Atlanta Campaign. What the Fifteenth Corps did on July 22, 1864."

5:6. Andrew T. Connett (31st NJ), "Shooting a Deserter."

6:7. Obit.

12:4. Biog: A. T. Bliss (10th NY Cavalry).

December 6

1:6-7, 2:1-2. Knox, Part 15. [Experiences in Rebel hospitals]

4:1. E. W. Niles (49th OH), "Campaign in Texas. Willich's Brigade on the March."

4:1. H. C. Slusher (22nd PA Cav), "The Brandon Family. Seventeen Sons in the Late War."

4:2. W. Seifreid (118th OH), Matthew Campbell (20th MI), D. E. Butler (Bty E, 2nd US), "Cotton at Knoxville. Was It Used in the Construction of Breastworks?"

4:2. James H. Sawyer (18th CT), "The Horrors of a Soldier. Embalming Dead Soldiers for Shipment."

4:3. S. A. Clark (1st VT Cav), "Kilpatrick Raid."

4:3. W. L. Gardner (110th OH), "The Battle of Monocacy."

4:3. William St. Martz (37th IL), "Correcting Col. Knox."

4:3. Jonathan Hopkins (2nd MA Hvy Art), "Yellow Fever. The Military Execution of Six Bounty Jumpers at New Berne, N.C."

4:5. W. D. Hudelson, J. J. Weiler, "How the 17th Indiana were Armed." [4/1/65]

5:1-2. C. A. Crandall (23rd WI), "A Lively Scout. Guppey's Brigade at Jackson, La."

5:3. W. H. Leidigh (16th OH), "A Fighting Family. [Barthson Family, Pulaski County, IL]

5:3. Henry H. Brinkley (14th IL Cav), "Entering Atlanta."

5:3. John G. Jones (12th WV), "The Battle of Piedmont."

5:4. W. F. Poor (2nd NY Cav), "The Angel of Mercy. The Name the Soldiers Gave Mrs. [Alice C.] Risley."

7:1-2. Biogs: Samuel P. Carter (USN), Henry H. Lockwood, Thomas O. Selfridge (USN).

9:1-3. W. A. Croffut (NY Tribune), "First Bull Run."

9:5. Obit.

December 13

1:6-7, 2:1-2. Knox, Part 16. [secret missions]

3:1. A. M. Brinkerhoff (4th IA), "The Battle of Pea Ridge."

3:1. John C. Phillips (Bty M, 2nd IL), "Cotton at Knoxville."

3:1. James F. Walker (101st IL), "Who was First in Atlanta?"

3:2. W. H. Hardwick, "The Battle of Piedmont. An Account by a Johnny Reb."

3:2. Robert M. Rogers (AAG, 3rd Brig, 2nd Div, 14th Corps), "The First Across Peach Tree Creek."

3:2. James Kyger (86th IN), "A Hoosier's Prison Experience." [Andersonville]

3:2. O. R. McNary (103rd PA), "Weapons Used by the Rebels." [Fair Oaks, Arkansas Toothpicks by LA troops]

3:3. Charles W. Hathaway (1st MA), "Stonewall Jackson."

3:3. John Shafer (143rd PA), "Shooting a Deserter." [6/12/63]

3:3. E. C. Winters (34th IL), "McCook's Division at Shiloh."

3:4. Edward Kelly (37th IL), "Correcting Col. Knox. Mixing Gen. Black and Gen. Post."

4:7. Obit.

5:1. Obit: Romeyn B. Ayres, Edward Simpson (USN).

8:3. "Gettysburg Commission. They Say Complaints from Regimental Associations are Unjust."

December 20

1:6-7, 2:1-2. Knox, Part 17. [Quantrill]

3:1. James Holehouse (7th MA), "Marye's Heights."

3:2. James E. M. Bright (85th IN), "Thompson's Station."

3:2. Peter E. Palen (143rd NY), "It Beat the Sucker's Big Haul." [Averysboro]

3:3. J. W. Darrow, "The 12th Illinois Cavalry."

3:3. John W. Fox (102nd OH), "Scouting Experiences." [Summer 1864 near Decatur, AL]

3:3. Samuel A. Ambrose (4th Btn OH Cav), "Stonewall Jackson."

3:4. H. D. Yelvington (56th IL), "Left in the Lurch. Abandoned on the Enemy's Front." [11/23/64, Lineville, TN]

3:4. J. N. McMaster (9th OH Cav), "Hell's Half Acre. An Ohio Soldier's Experience in Georgia." [Savannah River Island]

3:4. C. A. Brasher (17th KY), "Killing a Noted Guerrilla." [3/63 Powder Spring Gap, Clinch Mt, TN]

4:7. Biog: Marion T. Anderson (51st IN).

5:1. Biog: Joseph J. Reynolds, H. V. Boynton (35th OH).

5:3. Biog: John M. Thurston (17th WI, 1st WI Cav).

December 27

1:6-7, 2:1-2. Knox, Part 18. [Quantrall skirmish]

3:1-2. Alfred W. Harris (5th KY), "Captured by the Enemy." [9/19/63]

3:2-3. Fred S. Snow (9th NY), "Roanoke Island."

3:3. D. P. Vancourt (34th NY), "Ball's Bluff."

3:4. Morris Edwards (71st NY), "Fair Oaks."

3:4. Fred W. Hart, "'Fort Fizzle.' A True Story of Northern Rebels During the War." [Gambier, OH]

4:6. Biog: Stephen A. Marine (13th IA), Albert Claypool (5th, 13th OH Cav).

4:6. Obit.

4:7. Biog: Felix Agnus (5th, 165th NY).

5:1. Biog: Albert Ordway (24th MA).

5:1-2. Biog: John L. Davis (USN).

6:6. "Gettysburg Monuments. Report of the New York Board of Commissioners."

1889

January 3

1:6-7, 2:1-2. Knox, Part 19.

3:1-2. (23rd KY), "The Sergeant. What has Become of All the Regimental Liars?"

3:2. Buford Gaddie (16th IL), "Buzzard's Roost."

3:3. "Gen. Rosecrans. A Soldier's Recollections of His Courtesy."

3:3. S. R. Evril (13th PA Cav), "The Boy Who Took the Flag from the Capitol at Raleigh."

3:4. Silas Crowell (93rd OH), "Knives and Pikes. Specimens in the Ohio Relic Room."

3:4. J. Lemuel Jones (Bty B, MD), "The Battle of Piedmont."

4:7. Obit.

6:7. Phineas D. Parks (4th IL Cav), "The Sultana Disaster."

6:7. David H. Smith (20th PA Cav), "The 18th Connecticut at Piedmont, Va."

6:7. 22nd MA Association. "Who Captured the 6th Alabama's FLag."

8:1-3. Boy Spy, "Stonewall Jackson. Did the Great Chieftain Commit Suicide?"

January 10

1:6-7, 2:1-2. Knox, Part 20.

3:1. "The Youngest Soldier. The Little Drummer Boy of the Rappahannock."

3:1. Silas W. Crocker (6th PA Res), "Fredericksburg."

3:2-3. H. Ketzle (37th IL), "The Frontier Army. Experiences in the Battle of Pea Ridge."

3:3. L. E. Knowles (1st WI), "Gen. Rosecrans."

3:3. W. K. Spencer, "McLaughlin's Squadron."

3:4. L. D. Immell (12th WI Bty), "Battle of Corinth."

3:4. W. R. Carter (1st TN Cav), "Cotton at Knoxville."

5:3. Biog: Christopher R. P. Rodgers (USN).

5:4. "The Michigan Brigade's Fine Monument." [Gettysburg]

January 17

1:6-7. Knox, Part 21.

3:1-2. Silas W. Crowell (93rd OH), "Ohio's Flag Room."

3:2. H. H. Reed (35th IL), "Pea Ridge."

3:3. John V. Reeble (2nd MI), H. D. Loftis (2nd NC Mtd Inf), "Cotton at Knoxville."

3:3. R. C. Miller (81st IN), "Prisoners of War."

3:3. James V. Wood (1st ME Cav), "Shooting a Deserter." [6/12/63, 16th IN]

3:4. W. L. Gardner (110th OH), "Fighting Them Over. Keep It Up, Boys, Regardless of Croakers."

3:4. W. D. Hardwick (45th VA), "An Ex-Rebel. A Johnny's Experience at Cloyd's Farm."

4:6. Obit.

4:7. "Chaplains."

5:1. Biog: F. W. Paige (5th MA, 6th VRC).

January 24

1:6-7, 2:1-2. Knox, Part 22. [Battle near Des Ark, AR]

3:1. J. M. Gardner (12th IL Cav), "Harper's Ferry."

3:1. Isaac Sansbury (2nd WV Cav), "The Lynchburg Raid."

3:2. John A. Murphy (89th NY), "Fair Oaks." [12/64]

3:2. John W. Seay (14th IL Cav), "Stoneman's Raid."

3:2. W. R. Davis (101st OH), "Gen. Rosecrans."

3:3. "1st Alabama Cavalry. What Has Become of All the Old Boys?"

3:3. H. McNamee (150th NY), "Battle of Resaca."

4:6-7. Obit.

5:1. Biog: William H. Partridge (67th NY), William Fletcher (11th US).

8:1-3. Frank Y. Commagere, "Rifle and Carbine. Gradual Progress in the Use of These Weapons."

January 31

1:5-6. Knox, Part 23.

1:7, 2:1-2. "Cedar Creek. The History of an Eventful October Day." [H. G. Wright's official report, mainly]

3:1. Adolph Carby (1st TX Cav), "A Lively Scout. The 1st Texas Cavalry Wore Union Uniforms."

3:1. John S. Mather (9th IA), "Siege of Vicksburg. Obedience from Bad Discipline."

3:1. Thomas J. Alverson (17th KY), "Killing a Guerrilla."

3:2. E. M. Watson (9th MI Cav), "A Wrestling Match. One Time Where the Darky Showed Superiority."

3:2. George W. Dixon (81st OH), "Crossing the Oostanaula."

3:2. Edward C. Russell (65th IL), "The Battle of Franklin Again."

3:3. E. M. Watson (9th MI Cav), "A Contraband. A Shell Hunting for a Darky Cook."

3:3. R. W. Calland (orderly, 1st Bg, 3rd Div, 14th Corps), "The First in Fayetteville."

3:3. William H. Lawrence (1st NC), "Union Southrons. Hardships Endured by the Loyal Men of the South."

3:4. A. H. C. Jewett (4th NH), "A Nigger Sharpshooter." [Charleston siege]

3:4. (8th MO Cav), "How Capt. R— and Lieut. G— Lost the Day."

4:7. Obit.

4:7. Biog: James O. Beirne (37th NY).

5:1. Biog: Horatio G. Wright.

8:2. F. M. May (27th MO), "A Big Capture. A Missouri Man Takes in a Lot of Rebels." [Atlanta, 8/14/64]

February 7

1:6-7, 2:1-2. Knox, Part 24. [Helena, USS Mou*nd* Cit*y*]

3:1-2. Silas Crowell (93rd OH), "Ohio's Relic Room. Relics of the Rebellion and Other Wars."

3:3. John M. Ewing (15th OH), "Hugh Thompson. His Wounds Deprive Him of Memory for Years."

3:3. August Kissel (94th NY), "Who Got the Boots?"

4:6. Obit: J. M. Brown (77th IL), A. H. Biggs (9th MI Cav).

6:4. Biog: William S. Odell (7th IN).

February 14

1:1-3. A. G. Brackett (3rd US Cav), "Invading Virginia. The Rebels Fail to Fortify Alexandria."

3:1. Jeremiah S. Thompson (120th NY), "Stonewall Jackson."

3:1. William I. Hyde (18th CT), "The Battle of Piedmont, Va."

3:2. James Shanklin (41st OH), "Another Young Soldier."

3:2. E. T. Lee (41st IL), "McCook's Division at Shiloh."

3:3. A. C. Brown (2nd OH), "Andersonville, Ga. The Celebrated Prison and Cemetery Revisited."

3:3. W. M. Gray (60th IL), "Buzzard's Roost."

4:5-6. Obit: Henry J. Hunt.

4:6. Obit.

February 21

1:1-3. John Bresnahan (27th IN), "Battle of Antietam."

2:5. H. C. Potter (71st NY), "Army Chaplains."

3:1-2. Silas Crowell (93rd OH), "Ohio's Relic Room. Mementos from the Battlefields and of the Olden Time."

3:2. Charles W. Parker (16th CT), "Who were the Criminals?" [execution in 8th or 15th CT]

3:2. Samuel F. Ware (44th MO), "The Battle of Franklin."

3:3. Daniel White (19th, 20th IN), "War Relics. Battlefields Revisited by an Indiana Man."

3:3. M. Churchill (OH), "During War Times. What Loyal Women did for the Soldiers."

3:3. George C. Jenkins, "Report of Co. M, 1st Alabama Cavalry."

3:3. James N. McMaster (9th OH Cav), "The Brandon Family Again."

4:7. Obit.

5:1. Biog: Joseph C. Breckinridge (2nd US Art).

6:2. Biog: George L. Goodale (43rd MA).

6:4. Biog: Thomas J. Stewart (139th PA).

February 28

1:1-4. Frank Y. Commagere, "The Sixth Corps. Personal Reminicences of General Wright."

3:1-2. F. M. Posegate (175th OH), "Battle of Franklin."

3:2. Charles Elerick (15th IA), "That Big Capture." [Atlanta]

3:2. L. E. Clark, "Cotton at Knoxville."

3:3. H. C. Lambert, "The 25th Michigan, and Their Great Battle at Tebbs's Bend, Ky."

4:6-7. Obit.

March 7

3:1. L. D. Immell (12th WI Bty), "A Forlorn Hope. Heroism Shown at the Battle of Franklin."

3:1. J. G. Essington (75th IN), "The First in Fayetteville, N.C."

3:2. W. H. Hardwick (1st KY Cav), "Perryville, Ky. The Battle from a Rebel Standpoint."

3:2. Orville Thatcher, "The 1st Minnesota. Who Will Write the History of the Regiment?"

3:3. Charles Porter (11th VT), "Cold Harbor."

3:3. I. A. Taylor (122nd IL), "Parker's Crossroads."

4:7. Obit.

5:2. Biog: Ralph Chandler (USN).

6:3. Biog: James F. Grimes (17th US).

7:4. (23rd MA), "He Knew Beans."

8:2. J. W. Scott, "The Colors of the 83rd Ohio."

8:4. John Null (120th OH), "Gen. Morgan's Letter of Great Service." [Red River]

March 14

1:5-7, 2:1-2. Henry Capehart, "Shenandoah Valley. Operations in Virginia During the Year 1862." [Kernstown]

3:1-2. Silas Crowell (93rd OH), "Ohio's Relic Room. Rebel Flags and Other Curiousities."

3:2. Jabe Powell (1st MO Eng), "A Sweet Corpse. What was Unearthed on Sherman's March."

3:3. W. McEvoy (3rd IL Cav), "'The Lost Army.' Correcting Col. Knox Again." [Pea Ridge]

3:3. G. Sheifley (116th OH), "Battle of Piedmont."

3:5. R. H. Mead (8th IA Cav), "An Iowa Cavalryman's Experience with the Surgeon."

4:7. Obit.

7:6. (4th OH Bty), "An Artillery Duel." [Kennesaw Mountain]

8:1-2. S. H. Maunder (USS *Huron*), "Fort Fisher."

8:4. Obit: John Ericcson.

March 21

1:5-7, 2:1-2. Capehart, Part 2. [Shields and Jackson]

2:6. "Marching Through Georgia." [song of this title]

3:1. Tyler Dye (1st KY Cav), "Stoneman's Raid."

3:1. C. A. Brasher (17th KY), "The Stampede of Beatty's Brigade, Van Cleve's Division." [Summer 1863 between McMinnville and Pikeville, TN]

3:1. R. H. Maxwell, "Services Performed by the 15th Indiana."

3:2. Jonathan Harlan (34th OH), "Cedar Creek Again."

3:3. Charles Crouse (2nd Btn, MO SM Cav), "Wilson's Creek. The National Cemetery Near Springfield, Mo."

3:3. Charles F. Kimmel (66th IL), "Crossing the Oostanaula River."

4:6-7. Obit.

5:1-2. Biog: Stephen C. Rowan (USN), George C. Tichenor (10th, 39th IA).

6:4. Biog: Alonzo Williams (3rd RI Hvy Art).

8:1-3. B. F. Whitzel, "Ball's Bluff."

March 28

1:6-7, 2:1-3. Capehart, Part 3. [Jackson's retreat from Shields]

2:3. Biog: Geza Mihalozy (24th IL).

3:1-2. Thomas J. Orr (12th WV), George W. Toms (5th NY Cav), A. S. Otis (2nd NY Cav), Charles A. Dain, "Cedar Creek. Discussing Gen. Wright's Report."

3:2. Edward Armstrong (139th PA), "Spy or Deserter? Who was the Man Hung at Poolesville, Md.?" [1864]

3:3. L. A. Peirce (3rd VT), "Col. Proctor's Record. A Bread Riot at St. Johnsbury, Vt."

4:5. Biog: James Tanner (80th NY).

4:6-7. Obit.

5:4. Obit: Stanley Matthews (23rd, 51st OH).

6:3. Biog: Harrison Clark (125th NY).

8:1-2. Whitzel, Part 2.

April 4

1:6-7, 2:1-2. Capehart, Part 4. [McDowell]

3:1. H. Warren Phelps (95th OH), "Battle of Richmond, Ky."

3:2. Thomas J. Oar (12th WV), "Assaulting Petersburg. What Gibbon's Troops Did."

3:2. William H. Standish (153rd OH), "Second Bull Run. How Longstreet Got Through Thoroughfare Gap."

3:2. J. E. Bowers (7th TN), "Parker's Crossroads."

3:3. A. B. Platt (89th IL), "Downed by a Rebel Girl." [foraging during the Atlanta Campaign, near Allatoona]

3:3. J. E. Wharton (2nd IA Cav), "A Good Chaplain." [C. G. Truesdale]

3:3. (3rd MO Cav), "The Sequel. Capt. R's Wild Ride."

4:7. Obit.

6:1. Biog: Charles M. Travis (12th IL).

April 11

1:6-7, 2:1-2. Capehart, Part 5. [Banks-Winchester]

4:1. R. J. Monroe (8th OH), "Shenandoah Valley. Criticizing Gen. Capehart's Article on that Campaign." [Mt. Jackson, Edenburg]

4:1. James M. Russell (1st IA Cav), "Baxter's Springs."

4:1. D. J. Vasbinder (105th PA), "Fair Oaks."

4:2. C. E. McKay (1st ME Cav), "Dismounted Cavalry. How They Acted in the Shenandoah Valley."

4:2. C. A. Guider (11th OH Cav), "On the Plains. Scouting, Indian Fighting and Hunting."

4:2. (15th IA), "The Bummer at Holly Springs."

4:3. L. C. Stanley (16th IA), "What was the Purpose? A Mysterious Expedition into La." [8/63 to Monroe from Vicksburg]

4:3. Buford Gaddie (16th IL), "A Night March. An Expedition to Save a Bridge." [5/23/64 near Rome, GA]

4:4. (5th IA Cav), "Wilson's Raid. What Became of the Plunder Taken from the Men?"

4:4. Peter E. Palen (143rd NY), "Battle of Resaca. What Troops Saved the 5th Indiana Battery?"

4:5. Frederick C. Olney, "After 25 Years. Return of a Soldier's Diary from the Far South." [Thomas F. Holland, 2nd RI]

4:5. William M. Davis (4th MN), "Logan at the Battle of Champion Hills."

6:6. Biog: J. S. Weaver (11th PA Cav).

6:7. Obit.

8:3. Biog: John E. Phelps (3rd US Cav, 2nd AR Cav).

12:1. George C. Schmelz (USS *Ouichita*), "Expedition Up the Black and Ouichita Rivers."

April 18

1:7, 2:1-5. Capehart, Part 6. [Shields, Fremont, McDowell]

4:1. William S. Young (7th IN), "Shenandoah Valley." [Kernstown]

4:1. John S. Perrine (65th IL), "Franklin."

4:2. Joel B. Swett (8th NY Cav), "A Cavalryman's Story. A Tight Place and a Timely Leap." [picket duty 2/63]

4:2-3. H. J. Ambrose (12th IL), "Bushwhackers. How a Detail from the 12th Ill. Broke Up a Gang." [Richland Station, TN, winter 1863, gang of Samuel Moore]

4:3. Washington Marsh (1st NY Cav), "Piedmont Again."

4:3. E. T. Lee (41st IL), "Illinois's Death Record."

4:4. S. H. Rodenbaugh, "Sultana Disaster."

4:4. P. S. Duganne (77th PA), "Battle of Resaca."

5:5. "Who Wounded General Hancock?"

6:7. Obit.

7:1-2. Biog: Stewart Van Vliet (3rd US Art).

7:2. Obit: Edward P. Hatch.

12:2. Biog: George B. Squires (5th CT).

April 25

1:6-7, 2:1-3. Capehart, Part 7. [Ashby]

4:1. (89th NY), "Reminiscences. The Funny Side of Army Life."

4:1-2. Joseph Hall (22nd MI), "Pemberton Prison."

4:2. S. B. Jenkins (12th WV), "Piedmont and Fort Gregg."

4:3. H. T. Bird (8th IA Cav), "McCook's Raid."

4:3. Theodore Wheaton (92nd OH), "Who was First in Fayetteville, N.C.?"

4:4. A. W. Saint (36th IN), "Shiloh Again."

4:4. Michael W. Gray (50th IN), "Parker's Crossroads."

4:5. J. W. Hervey (5th RI Hvy Art), "Military Execution. The One at Fort Totten was More Like a Murder." [Newbern, NC]

4:6. "An Unrecorded Battle. Fisticuffs on the Picket Line." [7/64 in front of 10th Corps]

6:7. Obit.

7:2. "Major L. J. Sacriste. He is Given a Medal of Honor for Gallantry." [116th PA, Chancellorsville and Auburn]

7:4. Biog: Cushman K. Davis (28th WI).

May 2

1:7, 2:1-3. Capehart, Part 8. [Port Republic]

4:1. Cecil Clay (58th PA), "Fort Harrison."

4:1. William Hooker (23rd MO), "A Plea for Prentiss's Division." [Shiloh]

4:2. E. R. Graham, "King's Division. A Comrade of the Second Brigade Eulogizes Gen. Pope."

4:2. John L. Mathews (47th USCT), "Recollections of Miss Kline." [smuggling at Vicksburg]

4:3. F. M. Thomas (60th OH), "Reminiscences. Harper's Ferry and Knoxville."

4:3. George S. McKee (1/1/4th), "An Historic Brigade. It Furnished Grant, Carlin, Cruft, Sedgwick and Kirby."

4:4. Lew Ginger, "The 75th Indiana. It Does the Last Fighting in Which Infantry is Engaged in Sherman's Army." [near Goldsboro, NC]

4:4. James P. Foster (5th NY Cav), "Criticizing Capehart." [Banks's train saved]

5:3. S. H. Hendrix, "Union Southrons. What Loyalty Cost Natives of the Seceding States."

5:5. J. W. Conrad, "A Soldier's Neglected Grave." [near Bull Run RR bridge]

6:6-7. Obit.

7:1. Biogs: F. W. Benteen (10th MO Cav), William M. Stone (3rd, 22nd IA).

May 9

1:6-7, 2:1-3. Capehart, Part 9. [Jackson joins Lee]

3:1-2. James H. Simpson (14th IN), "Criticizing Capehart. Who Took the Stonewall at Kernstown?"

3:2. C. A. Brasher (17th KY), "Chickamauga."

3:2. Charles W. Sager (1st VT Hvy Art), "'A Soft Snap!'"

3:3. L. E. Knowles (1st WI), "Battle of Perryville."

3:4. George R. Shaw (75th IL), "Battle of Resaca. What Troops Saved the 5th Indiana Battery."

3:4. James N. McMaster (9th OH Cav), "How I Lost My Bacon." [SC 1865]

4:7. Obit.

8:3. "A Monument for the Pea Ridge Battlefield."

8:4. "Pennsylvania Monuments." [Gettysburg]

May 16

1:6-7, 2:1. D. Powell (1st WV), "Shenandoah Valley. Milroy's Defense of Winchester in June 1863."

3:1. John W. Merwin (161st NY), "Sabine Pass. The Reasons Why that Medal was Given Miss Dowling."

3:2. Thomas C. Fowler (84th PA), "Criticizing Capehart. The Troops that Captured the Stonewall at Kernstown."

3:3. E. M. Supplee (29th OH), "Shenandoah Valley."

3:3. M. D. Rodocker (185th OH), "A Queer Company. Ohio Boys Who Followed Washington's Example." [Danville, KY, 1865]

3:4. H. A. Johnson (3rd ME), "Gettysburg. What Regiment Supported Berdan's Sharpshooters?"

4:7. Obit.

5:2. H. O. Dudley (11th NH), "Gen. Roger A. Pryor's Capture."

5:3-4. J. K. L. Duncan (USN), "Admiral Porter. Some of the Work Done by the Mississippi Squadron."

6:1. Biog: Thomas M. Fisher (2nd PA Res, 190th PA), J. H. Mills (11th KS), E. B. McElroy (1st WV).

May 23

3:1. L. R. Hawthorne, "Loyal Southrons. What Part They Took in the Rebellion."

3:2. Edward Bennett (44th NY), "Round Top. What Corps Saved that Strategic Point?"

3:2-3. Solomon Rousculp (126th OH), "George D. Wilson. The Widow of the Hero Found at Last."

3:3. McCrager Lakey (13th IL Cav), "Breaking Up a Dance. Incidents of a Trip Through the Bogs and Brakes of Arkansas." [fall 1864]

3:4. H. B. Turrill (72nd OH), "Two of a Kind. How Two Mabrys Met in Andersonville Prison."

4:7. Obit.

6:1. Biog: A. B. Sampson (1st IA).

6:7. "Penna. Reserves. Each Regiment to Build Its Own Monument. [Gettysburg]

8:4. "A Sailor Captain of Infantry." [*Lewiston Journal*, regarding Captain Whitmore, 19th ME, at Gettysburg]

8:4. E. H. Maxwell (110th OH), "A Brotherly Company."

8:4. D. W. Lewis, "Where General Lyon is Buried."

8:5. George C. Schmelz (USS *Ouichita*), "Captain Byron Wilson. His Work on the Mississippi River."

May 30

1:7, 2:1-2. Henry Romeyn (14th USCT), "Hood's Campaign. Sherman Pursues Hood Northward."

3:1. A. H. C. Jewett (4th NH), "The Colored Troops. Testimony of a New Hampshireman to Their Gallantry." [Petersburg]

3:2. F. C. Robinson (1st WV Cav), "Capehart Criticized. The Doctor Finds a Friendly Critic."

3:2. William Houghton (14th IN), "In the Valley. The Fighting Done by Shields's Division."

3:3. J. R. Palmer (32nd IL), "Bloody Shiloh."

3:3. N. E. Powell (41st IL), "Shiloh Again."

3:3. E. M. Watson (9th MI Cav), "A Warm Bed."

3:4. Hiram Berdan (1st US Ss), "Gettysburg. What Regiment Supported Berdan's Sharpshooters?"

3:4. "A Fighting Family. A Father and Five Sons in the Army." [Homer B. Barnum family, RI]

4:7. Obit.

5:3. "Butler vs. Porter. The Administrator of the Navy States His Case."

5:5. E. M. Watson (9th MI Cav), "Up a Tree."

6:1. Biog: Eugene F. Weigel (4th MO, 83rd IL).

6:4. Biog: S. H. Hurst (73rd OH).

8:5. "Sherman's Farewell. Gen. W. T. Sherman's Last Order to His Army."

June 6

1:5-7, 2:1. Romeyn, Part 2. [advance to the Tennessee]

3:1. Samuel G. Brown (5th IA Cav), "McCook's Raid."

3:1-2. S. L. Ward, "Recollections of an 8th Indiana Cavalryman." [McCook's Raid]

3:2. Herman Dersh (3rd US), "Criticizing Capehart."

3:2. Henry Garver (5th PA Res), "The First Paper." [1st PA Res in 1861]

3:2. P. S. Reeves (23rd KY), "A Good Chaplain." [W. H. Black]

3:3. T. N. Russell (72nd OH), "Who Stole the Hams?"

3:3. B. H. Tripp (7th WI), "On the Peninsula. A Fly-blown Irishman of the Engineers." [1st Corps in 1863]

3:4. "Hero of Winchester. Another Defense of Gen. Milroy."

3:4. J. M. Gardner (12th IL Cav), "A Night Raid. How Liberty, Miss., was Captured." [11/18/64]

4:7. Obit.

6:6. W. H. Michael (US Rattler), "A Correction." [8/23/88 article]

6:6. Lawrence Wilson (7th OH), "Kernstown."

June 13

1:6. T. H. White (10th VT), "Sheridan and Custer. How They Met After the Battle of Winchester."

1:7, 2:1-2. Romeyn, Part 3. [Franklin]

3:1-2. Joel B. Swett (8th NY Cav), "Premonitions."

3:2. John S. Strain (15th IA), "Atlanta. Carrying Ammunition Under Unfavorable Circumstances."

3:2. William Houghton (14th IN), "Criticizing Capehart." [Kernstown]

3:3. R. D. Sanborn (6th VT), "The Vermont Brigade."

3:3. James M. Miller (11th PA Res), "Music by the Band." [5/64 on march to Spotsylvania]

3:4. A. L. Syphers (7th ME), "In the Wilderness."

4:6-7. Obit.

5:2. Biog: J. C.Kelton.

5:6. Biog: William Taylor (14th WI).

6:3. Biog: Stowell S. Hazen (12th OH, 1st OH Hvy Art).

8:1-2. (USS *Ocmulgee*), "Alabama's First Prize."

8:2. William B. Thompson, "The Tecumseh."

8:5. "Memorial Day at Andersonville."

June 20

1:6-7, 2:1-2. Romeyn, Part 4. [in front of Nashville]

3:1. Benjamin A. Spear (57th MA), "In Front of Petersburg. An Account of the Explosion of the Mine."

3:2. James W. Beller (2nd PA Prov. Hvy Art), "The Mine Explosion."

3:2-3. John T. Booth (36th OH), "The Eighth Corps. A Misnomer When Applied to the Army of West Virginia."

3:3. Elias H. Hoover (1st WI), "Battle of Perryville."

3:3. W. R. Smith (19th KS Cav), "A Night Burial. An Incident Away Out on the Plains."

3:4. James Thompson (Bty C, PA Art), "Cedar Mountain."

3:4. J. M. Gardner (12th IL Cav), "A Wasp Bite."

4:7. Obit.

8:1-2. W. H. Pascoe (USS *Lackawanna*), "Blockade Runner. A Long Chase and a Double Capture." [6/13/63]

8:2. "Michigan Monuments at Gettysburg."

June 27

1:7, 2:1-3. Romeyn, Part 5. [Nashville]

3:1. H. A. Johnson (3rd ME), "Gettysburg. What Regiment Supported Berdan's Sharpshooters?"

3:1. E. T. Lee (41st IL), "The Heavy Loss at Jackson, Miss." [7/12/63]

3:2. Silas Crowell (93rd OH), "The Carved Headboard. J. W. Johnston's Remains Moved to Florence, S.C."

3:2. W. M. Clark (2nd TN), "A Sad Affair. Thirty-three N.J. Soldiers Drowned." [Stegall's Ferry, Somerset, KY, 27th NJ, 1863]

3:3. Rollin L. Jones (29th OH), "The Battery Horses. They were Not Ridden Away, But were Killed." [Port Republic]

3:3. ENN, (Bty M, 1st IL), "Batteries to the Front."

3:3. G. H. Blakeslee (129th IL), "At Gallatin, Tenn. A Complimentary Order by Gen. Tweet." [8/21/63]

3:4. Guernsey W. Davis (13th IL Cav), "Breaking Up a Dance. A Sequel to Wounding Capt. Arnold and Capt. Dr. S."

3:4. G. W. Walker (USS *Black Hawk*), "Porter versus Butler."

4:6-7. Obit.

5:3. "Butler versus Porter." [New Orleans]

5:4. "Monument to Berdan's 1st U.S. Sharpshooters." [Gettysburg]

July 4

1:7, 2:1-4. Hyland C. Kirk (4th NY Hvy Art), "New York Draft Riots."

3:1. John H. Williams (44th MO), "Battle of Franklin."

3:2. H. C. Davidson, "War Reminiscences. Scouting in Southeast Missouri." [5/63]3:2. R. C. Rice (125th OH), "Franklin. Opdycke's Brigade in that Action."

3:3. S. A. Clark (1st VT Cav), "Lacy Springs, Va. A Ruse Played on the Rebels." [12/64]

3:4. Charles Porter (11th VT), "In the Valley. Reconnoissance of the Second Division, Sixth Corps." [9/13/64]

3:4. Silas Crowell (93rd OH), "Missionary Ridge. How 'Dutchy' Captured a Rebel Flag."

3:4. D. L. Way (ADC, 2/3/18), "The Colored Troops. Their Conduct at the Explosion of the Mine."

4:5-7. Biog: Cyrus Bussey (3rd IA Cav), William M. Meredith (70th IN).

4:7. Obit.

5:5. Obit: Simon Cameron.

July 11

1:7, 2:1-2. William Simmons (USS *Brooklyn*), "New Orleans."

3:1. E. S. Goodrich (ADC), "At Port Republic."

3:1. J. B. Cook (1st KS Bty), "Hood's Campaign. The Garrison at Johnsonville Did Not Stampede."

3:2. H. L. Ambrose (3rd KY Cav), "New Mexico. What the Loyal People Suffered During the War."

3:2. Samuel C. Kerr (126th OH), "The Widerness."

3:3. (7th IN Cav), "Traveling Haversack."

3:3. Isaac B. Rickey (33rd WI), "Strawberries."

3:3. W. W. Sprague (13th MA), "Belle Isle. Something About the Dog Slayer and a Female Soldier."

3:4. E. M. Watson (9th MI Cav), "Dock. A Faithful Colored Servant." [about May Johnson, 11th KY Cav]

3:4. J. E. Wharton (MD), "A Good God. The Death-bed of a Wisconsin Soldier."

4:7. Biog: Isaac B. Thatcher (15th IA).

4:7. Obit.

6:5. "The 61st N.Y. Monument at Gettysburg."

6:5. "Gettysburg Monument of the 120th N.Y."

8:2. "The 59th N.Y. Monument at Gettysburg."

July 18

1:7, 2:1-4. Henry A. Castle (73rd IL), "The Army Mule."

3:1. E. C. Wheeler (117th NY), "Petersburg. Baldy Smith's Corps in the Works at that Place."

3:1. Adam Hogle (97th OH), "Who Stole the Hams? Why, I Did."

3:2. J. Hinson (33rd OH), "Kennesaw Mountain."

3:2. Isaac A. Taylor (13th TN Cav), "Four Lives Saved. The Sign of an Entered Apprentice." [5/24/65]

3:2-3. Lewis Blundin (28th PA), "Battle of Resaca."

3:3. C. W. Bennett (13th USCT), "Johnsonville. Did the Garrison at that Place Stampede?"

3:4. J. Payne (151st NY), "The Wilderness."

4:6. Biog: Hiram Smith (11th VT).

4:7. Obit.

5:5. "The 6th N.Y. Cavalry Monument at Gettysburg."

6:7. "Gettysburg Monuments. The Supreme Court of Pa. Decides in Favor of the 72nd Pa."

6:7. "The 4th N.Y. Cavalry Monument." [Gettysburg]

8:1-2. J. D. Chandler (23rd PA), "Hettie Fletcher. A Smart Rebel Heroine of N.C." [8/64 Shenandoah Valley]

July 25

1:6-7, 2:1-3. "National Cemeteries . . . ." [Arlington]

3:1-2. C. W. Button (116th NY), "Cedar Creek."

3:2. Joseph Harris (75th OH), "On the Rapidan. The Great Battle of Cedar Mountain."

3:2. J. B. Wharton, "Pork in the Guardhouse."

3:3. August Horstmann (45th NY), "Battle of Resaca."

3:3. William Campbell (101st IL), "Battle of Resaca."

3:4. Nathaniel K. Bray (27th NJ), "That Sad Affair."

3:4. R. B. Scott (67th IN), "A Hard Time. An Incident of Prison Life in the Southwest."

4:7. Obit.

August 1

1:7, 2:1-2. Hyland C. Kirk, "Artillery Practice." [from his Chapter 5 of regimental history of the 4th NY Hvy Art]

3:1-2. Henry Capehart, "Capehart's Rejoinder. Gen. Shields and the Bridge at Port Republic."

3:2. George W. New (7th IN), "Criticizing Goodrich."

3:3. Abner Flint (85th NY), "Plymouth, N.C."

3:4. William H. Ambrose (15th KS), "Gen. Bussey. How He Treated Sergt. Todd, of the 1st Ark. Cavalry."

3:4. J. S. Thompson (11th VT), "Turning the Right Flank, May 6, 1864."

4:6-7. Obit.

6:6. "Pennsylvania Day. [Gettysburg Monuments of 28th, 147th, Battery E]

6:6. "Gettysburg Monument." [3rd PA Cav]

6:6. "Cavalry Monument at Aldie, Va."

6:6. "Monument to General Reno." [South Mountain]

August 8

1:6-7, 2:1. Harrison Millard (19th US), "Battle of Perryville."

3:1. H. T. Bird (8th IA Cav), "Behind the Scenes by a Captive of the McCook Raid."

3:1. E. M. Watson (9th MI Cav), "The Cold New Year's." [1864]

3:2. L. D. Phelps (8th PA Cav), "Prisoner of War." [Raleigh, NC]

3:2. J. M. Patrick (3rd IA), "He Meant Ambush."

3:2. L. H. Griffin (1st MI Cav), "Who Stole the Hams?"

3:3-4. William Reblin (USS *Cumberland*), "First Naval Expedition. Bombardment and Capture of Forts Hatteras and Clark."

3:4. "A Boy's Bravery. How the USS *Lehigh* was Rescued from a Perilous Position." [11/16/63 Charleston]

3:4. Convers Howe (15th CT), "New Berne, N.C. Military Execution and Yellow Fever at that Place."

3:4. George F. Stewart (19th MI), "Who Captured that Battery at Resaca?"

4:7. Obit.

August 15

1:6-7, 2:1-2. J. W. Chamberlin (123rd OH), "Libby Prison."

3:1-2. Z. T. Griffin (122nd NY), "The Wilderness. The Turning of the Right Flank, May 6, 1864."

3:2. B. F. Ward (8th KY), "Lookout Mountain."

3:2. E. M. Watson (9th MI Cav), "Who Stole the Ham?"

3:3. John W. Williams (36th OH), "Opequan. What Soldier Cut the Dam Before the Battle?"

3:3-4. (1st NY Eng), "False Alarm." [3/62 event]

3:4. F. M. Kelly (23rd OH), "Cedar Creek."

4:6. Obit.

5:6. Obit: Thomas Wallsh (74th NY).

6:1-2. Biog: F. G. Sheppard (1st MI Cav).

August 22

1:7, 2:1-3. Chamberlin, Part 2.

3:1-2. G. H. Slaybaugh (101st PA), "Battle of Plymouth."

3:2. D. C. Cameron (17th US), "A Game of Draw."

3:2. O. J. Lyon (45th IA), "A Premonition."

3:3-4. A. P. Merrill (USS *Port Royal*), "Mobile Bay."

3:4. John Stainsby (129th IL), "Who Captured the Battery at Resaca?"

3:4. Lewis Blundin (28th PA), "Who Captured the Battery at Resaca?"

4:7. Obit.

August 29

3:1-2. G. M. Ziegler, "Rebel Documents. Papers Captured from the Johnnies in Mississippi." [Meridian 5/64]

3:3. O. A. Coburn, "Commissary Department."

3:4. R. N. Trumbull (22nd NY Cav), "Rebs After Custer. The Johnnies Try to Capture the General at Lacy Springs." [12/21/64]

3:4. A. S. Folger, "A Remarkable School." [Carthage Public School, IN]

4:6. "Through Georgia. 'Old Tecumseh' Tells an Editor at Augusta Why He Slighted that City."

4:6. Obit: James Laird (MI).

4:7. Obit.

5:3. "The Indiana Monument. President Harrison Attends the Laying of the Cornerstone." [Indianapolis]

5:5. Obit: George R. Maxwell (1st MI Cav).

6:4. "Pennsylvania Day. Dedication of the 83rd Pa. Monument." [Gettysburg]

6:7. Biog: James A. Tyler (7th, 18th MI).

7:4-5. Winslow H. Barger (1st WI Cav), "Jeff Davis's Capture."

September 5

3:1-2. J. F. Huntington (Bty H, 1st OH), "In the Valley. The Campaign in the Spring of 1862."

3:2-3. N. T. Moore, "Winchester. Reminiscences of the Valley of the Shenandoah."

3:3. Warren C. Hursh (1st NJ Cav), "Criticizing Capehart."

3:4. (7th IN Cav), "Saves the Train. An Iowa Man Mounts the Engine and Lets Her Go." [Fall 1864, 20 miles from Little Rock]

3:4. George W. Nickum (12th NJ), "Little Jersey at Belle Isle."

4:4-6. Biog: Russell A. Alger (5th MI Cav), A. G. Weissert (8th WI).

4:7. Obit.

September 12

1:7, 2:1-2. Hyland C. Kirk (4th NY Hvy Art), "In the Wilderness." [from regimental history]

3:1-2. Frank Swigart (46th IN), "St. Charles. An Expedition Which Has Been Little Mentioned." [6/62]

3:2. Z. T. Griffin (122nd NY), "With Sheridan. Foraging in the Shenandoah Valley."

3:2. G. H. Blakeslee (129th IL), "That Four-Gun Battery Again." [Resaca]

3:3. D. D. McCallum (27th IA), "Red River Campaign. First Experience of an Iowa Boy Under Fire." [Fort DeRussy]

3:3. George H. Uhler (93rd PA), "Army Hardships. That Cold First of January, 1864."

3:4. William Zay (99th OH), "Lookout Mountain. Who Planted the First Flag on the Fort?"

3:4. P. C. Branch (13th IA), "A Hard Trip. The Mysterious Expedition into La. Again." [Monroe, LA]

4:7. Obit.

8:3. "Gettysburg Monuments." [90th PA, 10th NY, 4th NY Cav]

September 19

1:1-5. Kirk, Part 2.

1:6-7, 2:1-3. William E. Doyle (17th IN), "Between Two Fires. An Old Virginian's Experiences During the War." [Stevensburg]

3:1. Alonzo D. Mohn, "11th Illinois Cavalry."

3:1-2. W. T. Chaoman (103rd OH), "A Rough Campaign. A Cowardly Retreat from Dandridge, Tenn." [1/64]

3:2. Lewis Blundin (28th PA), "Criticizing Ward." [Resaca]

3:2. W. L. Welch (23rd MA), "The Commissary Department."

3:3. Isaac Sofield, "A Boy's Bravery. Another Account of the Grounding of the Lehigh."

3:3. George O. Brown (2nd MA Hvy Art), "Plymouth Again."

3:4. W. H. Yeo (40th OH), "Lookout Mountain."

3:4. C. A. Stockton (4th MI), "A Michigan Soldier at Fort Pendleton."

3:4. Samuel Kutz (91st IL), "A Blow-Up at Mobile, Ala." [5/65]

4:7. Obit.

5:5. "Gettysburg. Thousands of Soldiers Reune and Unvail [sic] Monuments on the Battlefield."

6:3. M. A. Hargre, "Chaplain of the 56th Pennsylvania."

September 26

1:1-5. G. J. Trenaman (USS *Chickasaw*), "Cahaba Prison."

1:6-7, 2:1-2. Doyle, Part 2.

3:1-2. James K. Magie (78th IL), "Death by the Rope. How Two Daring Rebel Spies Expiated Their Crime." [Franklin, TN, 6/9/63]

3:2. W. H. Langston (USS *Elfin*), "At Johnsonville."

3:3. Calvin Shaffer (15th NY Hvy Art), "The Draft Riots. Who Commanded the Tribune Building During Those Troublesome Times?"

3:4. John B. Ridenour (55th IL), "At Jackson, Miss." [7/11/63]

3:4. C. A. Brasher (17th KY), "Guarding Prisoners. Taking a Load of Johnnies to Camp Douglas." [12/64]

4:7. Obit.

5:3. Biog: George H. Hopkins (17th MI).

6:2. Biog: W. H. Childers (14th, 23rd KY).

October 3

1:1-6. Thomas F. Winthrop, "Ball's Bluff."

1:7, 2:1-3. Doyle, Part 3.

3:1. Jacob D. Brown (101st PA), "Plymouth, N.C."

3:1. Samuel Grimshaw, "The 52nd Ohio."

3:2. J. G. Burchfield (13th TN Cav), "Bull's Gap." [11/64]

3:3. William J. Haverly (65th NY), "The Wilderness. Turning of the Right Flank, May 6, 1864."

3:3. C. E. Garlinger (110th OH), "Another Account."

3:3. A. H. Kane (59th IN), "A Terrible Disaster. Burning of the Robert Campbell on the Mississippi." [9/63]

3:4. "Guerrillas in Kentucky. How Davison's Band Terrorized Citizens of Hawesville."

3:4. L. B. Crooker (55th IL), "Capt. Groce and the Forlorn Hope." [5/22/63 Vicksburg]

4:7. Obit.

5:3-4. Biog: J. N. Patterson (2nd NH).

6:2. Frank A. Hubbell (67th PA), "The New Libby Prison."

October 10

1:1-5. Augustus A. Buell (Bty B, 4th US), "The Story of a Cannoneer."

4:1-3. W. M. Morris (3rd WV Cav), "The Hunter Raid. A Night's Experience in the Allegheny Mountains."

4:3. Joseph Griffith (4th TN Cav), "The McCook Raid."

4:3. James H. Stover (101st OH), "Battle of Resaca. Who Supported the 5th Indiana Battery?"

4:4. J. R. Palmer (32nd IL), "McClellan and Pope. A Criticism of Little Mack's Methods."

4:4. Byron Phillips (3th IL Cav), "Lookout Mountain. The Troops Who Actually Planted the Flag."

4:4. Edwin Crockett (65th NY), "Turning the Right Flank, May 6, 1864."

6:7. Obit.

7:2-3. Obit: Asa P. Blunt (6th, 12th VT).

7:3. "Maine Veterans at Gettysburg."

10:4. Newton Krow (87th PA), "Providence Spring."

12:1-4. Doyle, Part 4.

October 17

1:1-6, 2:3-6. Buell, Part 2.

4:1-2. J. Hinson (33rd OH), "A Tough Night. The Skirmish-Lines of the Fourteenth Corps." [Atlanta Campaign]

4:2. Thomas S. Berry (110th OH), "In the Wilderness."

4:2. James H. Sawyer (18th CT), "A Sad Death. A Discharged Soldier Killed Near Baltimore."

4:3. McCrager Lakey (13th IL Cav), "A Keg of Brandy, and Other Incidents of a Trip Through the Enemy's Country." [Arkansas]

4:4. H. T. Bird (8th IA Cav), Off for Home, Or a Trip to God's Country." [POW exchange at Charleston, 1864]

4:4. H. M. Jones, "Gen. McClellan. A Fifth Corps Man's Estimate of 'Little Mac'."

6:7. Obit.

8:4. George E. Dolton (Bty M, 1st IL), "Chickamauga."

12:1-4. Doyle, Part 5.

October 24

1:1-6, 2:4-5. Buell, Part 3.

3:4-5. Obit: John F. Hartranft.

4:2. Watson G. Drinkwater, "The USS *Lehigh*. Another Account of Her Grounding in Charleston Harbor."

4:2. Samuel A. Ambrose (4th Co. OH Cav), "Who was the First Man Killed?"

5:1-3. Jesse H. Jones (60th NY), "Lookout Mountain."

5:3. (6th WV), "A Rebel Raid. The Disaster at New Creek, W.Va." [11/27/64]

5:3. H. A. Munger (154th NY), "That Four-Gun Battery." [Resaca]

5:4. Matthew F. Kippax (17th US), "In Portland Harbor. The Capture of the Revenue Cutter Caleb Cushing."

5:4. "A Gallant Doctor. The Varied Services of a Union Surgeon During the War." [E. Donnelly, 1st, 5th PA Res, 196th PA, 2nd PA Cav]

6:7. Obit.

7:4. "Gettysburg Monuments." [66th NY, VT]

7:4. "The 77th N.Y. Gettysburg Monument."

October 31

1:1-6, 2:4-5. Buell Part 4.

5:1-3. J. A. Brown (23rd OH), "Captured by Mosby."

5:3. Philip C. Helder (42nd IN), "Lookout Mountain."

5:4. Ira C. McCleuthen (USS *Baron de Kalb*), "Mississippi Flotilla. How the Soldier-Sailors were Treated in 1863."

5:4. O. R. McNary (103rd PA), "Jeff Davis's Capture. Did the Arch Traitor Wear Female Apparel?"

5:4. U. M. Greene (64th OH), "Pittsburgh Landing. An Ohio Comrade Visits the Battleground."

6:7. Obit.

7:3. Biog: Francis M. Ramsay (USN).

9:2. Catharine Chase (62nd NY), "A Female Veteran. Death of a N.J. Army Nurse."

10:5. "Connecticut Veterans Dedicate Monuments at Gettysburg." [17th, 27th CT]

November 7

1:1-6, 2:5-6. Buell, Part 5.

2:3. "An Old War Horse." [of Col. Samuel Fowler, 15th NJ]

3:1-3. Henry Capehart, "Capehart's Rejoinder. He Goes for Capt. Huntington and Comrade Hursh."

3:3. "Army and Navy. The Career of a Veteran Who is Now in the Patent Office." [William Hunt, USS *Ranger*]

3:3. H. J. Hawkins (6th MD), "That Right Wing. A Maryland Boy Knows All About It." [Wilderness]

3:3. William Clearwater, "An Assured Fact." [what the common soldier actually sees in battle]

3:4. John J. Scholl (51st PA), "Battle of Camden, N.C."

4:7. Obit.

6:4. "Connecticut Monuments." [Gettysburg, 17th, 27th]

6:4. "The 4th N.Y. Cavalry Monument." [at Gettysburg]

November 14

1:1-6, 2:4-5. Buell, Part 6.

3:1-2. Patrick Moroney (7th PA Cav), "Bushwhacking. How Tom Williams's Gang was Broken Up in Tenn." [1862]

3:3. E. K. Parker (Bty D, 1st RI), "In the Wilderness. The Turning of the Right Flank, May 6, 1864."

3:4. George A. Allen (76th NY), "After Antietam. Scenes in the Hospitals at Keedysville."

4:7. Obit.

5:3. Obit: William B. Hart (51st PA).

November 21

1:1-6, 2:4-5. Buell, Part 7.

1:7, 2:1-3. A. Comstock (13th CT), "Port Hudson."

3:1-2. Thomas H. Craig (84th PA), "Shields's Division. A Delayed Report of the 84th Pa. at Kernstown."

3:2. C. H. Kirk, "Arthur P. Lyon. Death of the Bravest Soldier in the 15th Pa. Cavalry."

3:2. Charles W. Wheaton (Bty K, 3rd NY), "Criticizing the Cannoneer."

3:3. W. H. Yoe (40th OH), "Chickamauga."

3:4. Z. T. Griffin (122nd NY), "In Front of Fort Fisher. The Assault of the Sixth Corps on the 25th of March, 1865."

4:7. Obit.

November 28

1:1-6, 2:4-5. Buell, Part 8.

1:7, 2:1-3. Charles E. Hovey (33rd IL), "Gen. Curtis's Army. The March Through Arkansas from Batesville to Helena."

2:4. William Houghton (14th IN), "Carroll's Brigade at Gettysburg."

3:1-2. (31st-32nd ME), "A Break for Liberty. What Happened at Salisbury Prison Nov. 25, 1864."

3:2. Joseph Bishop (14th CT), "Revisiting Gettysburg."

3:2. Charles W. Dey (126th NY), "The Burning of Kelly's Store."

3:2. W. L. Welch (23rd MA), "Capt. Hunt Criticized."

3:3. A. M. Brinkerhoff (4th IA), "Lookout Mountain."

3:4. M. A. Cleveland (7th MA Bty), "The Mobile Explosion."

3:4. (2nd WV Cav), "An Account of Gen. Powell's Services."

4:7. Obit.

December 5

1:1-5. Buell, Part 9.

1:5. Rufus R. Dawes, "Gen. Dawes and the Cannoneer."

1:6-7, 2:1-2. Hovey, Part 2.

3:1-2. J. F. Huntington, "Port Republic."

3:2. B. F. Wade (8th KY), "The First Flag." [Lookout Mt]

3:3. H. C. Whitaker (2nd NY Cav), "Gen. McClellan."

3:3. "Several Veterans of the Whole War Still Living."

3:4. F. B. Gillette (9th NJ), "Gettysburg. Why Did Not Meade Make a Countercharge?"

3:4. Isaac K. Young (89th IL), "That Church at New Market, Tenn."

3:4. J. R. McClure (14th IN), "'Old Bricktop'." [S. S. Carroll]

4:7. Obit.

December 12

1:1-5. Buell, Part 10

1:6-7, 2:1. Hovey, Part 3.

3:1. Charles Porter (11th VT), "The Great Explosion. The Terrible Disaster at City Point in 1864."

3:1. Bates Alexander (7th PA Res), "One of the Constituents. What a Pa. Man Thinks of Our Paper."

3:2. Eli Mundorf (11th IL Cav), "Catching Fresh Meat."

3:2. C. M. Rose (19th MI), "Who Captured that Battery at Resaca?"

3:3-4. Louis Fisher (74th PA), "At Gettysburg."

3:4. A. W. Peck (17th CT), "Gettysburg."

4:6. Obit.

6:4. "Gettysburg Monuments. Reunion of the 121st N.Y. and Dedication of Their Monument."

December 19

1:1-5, 2:6. Buell, Part 11.

1:6-7, 2:1-3. Joseph J. Bartlett, "Crampton's Pass."

3:1-2. William F. Fox (107th NY), "Michigan in the War."

3:2. William E. Doyle (17th IN), "Wilder's Brigade."

3:2. James T. Stewart (49th PA), "An Incident of the Battle of Antietam."

3:3. Samuel W. Cass, "Valley Campaign. A Comrade Sides with Capt. Huntington."

3:3. C. A. Brasher (17th KY), "What Battery was It?" [1864, Pulaski to Nashville march]

3:4. Louis N. Beaudry (5th NY Cav), "A Unique Celebration. How the 4th of July, 1863, was Spent in Libby Prison."

3:5-6. Picket Shots: Peter Birk (15th OH Bty), Ezra Church.

4:7. Obit.

December 26

1:1-6, 2:5-6. Buell, Part 12.

1:7, 2:1-3. Doyle, Part 6.

3:1. Alexander Eckel (4th TN Cav), "The Atlanta Raids."

3:2. Oliver W. Case (65th IL), "Battle of Franklin. How the 104th Ohio Got the Rebel Flags."

3:2-3. John W. Morgan (109th NY), "Trials of a Soldier. How a 109th N.Y. Man Joined the Army."

3:3. W. E. Webster (1st NY Bty), "Gettysburg."

3:3. Lewis Blundin (28th PA), "The First Flag." [Lookout Mt]

3:4. J. A. Bering (48th OH), "In Very Hard Luck. Col. Leake's Command in Camp Ford Prison, Texas." [20th IA captured 9/26/63]

4:7. Obit.

1890

January 2

1:1-6, 2:5-6. Buell, Part 13.

1:7, 2:1-4. Doyle, Part 7.

3:1-2. W. P. Haines (12th NJ), "Spottsylvania."

3:2-3. H. C. Whitaker (2nd NY Cav), "Second Bull Run."

3:3. J. E. Taylor (40th OH), "Lookout Mountain."

3:4. Edward J. Davis, "Record of the 146th New York."

3:4. J. F. Breakenridge (16th NY), "Crampton's Pass."

4:5. Biog: John C. Tarsney (4th MI).

4:7. Obit.

January 9

1:1-6, 2:5-6. Buell, Part 14.

1:7, 2:1-4. Doyle, Part 8.

3:1-2. James M. Russell (1st IA Cav), "Little Rock Campaign."

3:2-4. D. M. Haverly (8th IA), "Shiloh and Prison."

3:4. Elijah Bish (11th PA Res), "Which Division was Broken?" [Wilderness]

3:4. T. H. Leach (10th MO Cav), J. B. Bennett (5th IL Cav), William Bahr (1st IN Cav), "Curtis's Army."

4:7. Obit.

January 16

1:1-6, 2:5-6. Buell, Part 15.

1:7, 2:1-4. Doyle, Part 9.

3:1-2. Henry M. Reed (4th KY Mtd Inf), "The McCook Raid."

3:2. Briscoe Goodheart (Loudon Rangers), "Execution of Capt. Webster." [3/63 in Libby Prison]

3:2-3. J. V. Hunt (2nd KY), "Father Against Son."

3:3-4. James Bryson (27th IA), "Yellow Bayou. Shaw's Brigade in the Last Battle of the Red River Campaign."

3:5-6. Picket Shots: J. W. Forsyth, Loudoun Rangers.

4:7. Obit.

January 23

1:1-6, 2:5-6. Buell, Part 16.

1:7, 2:1-4. Doyle, Part 10.

3:1. (67th OH), "Gen. Commagere's Horse."

3:1. F. O. Talbot (1st ME Hvy Art), "The Heavy Artillery. What a Maine Soldier Has to Say About Their Service."

3:2-3. (2nd WV Cav), "A Close Call. A Reminiscence of the Shenandoah Valley." [10/64]

3:3. G. H. Dutton (147th NY), "Weldon Railroad."

3:3. W. H. Baker (3rd IA Cav), "Strange Episode of the War." [Samuel R. Curtis's army]

3:4. T. H. White (10th VT), "Unlucky David. A Vermont Soldier Who Always Got Ill."

4:6. Biog: Oscar S. Gifford (IL Elgin Bty]).

4:7. Obit.

January 30

1:1-6, 2:5. Buell, Part 17.

1:7, 2:1-4. John E. Shellenberger, "Nashville Campaign."

3:1. C. F. Farman (64th NY), "Stewart's Battery. What a Veteran Has to Say About the Charge at Bethesda Church."

3:1. Edward P. Brooks (6th WI), "As Seen by the Iron Brigade." [Bethesda Church]

3:2. H. W. George (44th NY), "They All Saw It On Bartlett's Line." [Wilderness]

3:2. L. E. Northrup (4th PA Cav), "They Looked Grim and Forbidding." [Bethesda Church]

3:2. H. L. James (140th NY), "'Yelling Like a Comanche!'." [Bethesda Church]

3:2. George W. Pyne (29th MA), "Phillips's Battery was There." [Bethesda Church]

3:2-3. Frank E. Bunnell (3rd IN Cav), "How Stewart Looks Nowadays."

3:3. L. A. Norcross (20th ME), "'Took Them All In'." [6/2/64]

3:3. J. J. Bartlett, "They Had to Fight." [6/2/64]

3:3-4. J. H. Kauffman, "Loss of the 151st Pa. at Gettysburg."

3:4. George W. Rowan (7th IA Cav), "Fighting the Sioux. Correcting the Statement of an 11th Ohio Cavalryman."

3:4. Peter Steinbach (4th US Cav), "Criticizing Whitaker. The Action of Minty's Brigade in June, 1863."

3:5. Picket Shots: J. C. Farnum (1st VT Cav), Farnsworth at Gettysburg; O. B. Seamans (104th OH), Franklin.

4:7. Obit.

February 6

1:1-6. Buell, Part 18.

1:7, 2:1-5. Shellenberger, Part 2.

3:1-2. Rufus R. Dawes (6th WI), "Chancellorsville. Across the Rappahannock in Pontoon Boats." [4/63]

3:2-3. Charles Lester (20th ME), F. C. Austin (5th Corps HQ), Augustus Edes (20th ME), "Stewart's Battery. What the Veterans Have to Say About the Charge at Bethesda Church."

3:3. E. M. Robinson (5th ME), "Rappahannock Station."

3:4-5. G. W. Spahr (3rd MO Cav), "Little Rock Outfit." [7/63]

3:5. George P. Hawkes (21st MA), "An Outrage. How Some of the Ninth Corps were Killed at Columbus."

4:6. Obit: John M. Brown (45th KY).

4:7. Obit.

February 13

1:1-6, 2:5-6. Buell, Part 19.

1:7, 2:1-2. Shellenberger, Part 3.

3:1-2. Henry Capehart, "Shenandoah Campaign. Gen. Capehart Again Pays His Compliments to Huntington, of Boston."

3:2-3. Solomon R. Smith, "Malvern Hill. Was the Army to be Surrendered After the Battle."

3:3. George E. Dolton (Bty M, 1st IL), "Chickamauga."

3:3. James Holehouse, "Testimony from a 7th Mass. Man." [Marye's Heights]

3:4. Abner Doubleday, William Glenning (6th NY Hvy Art), "Cannoneer Comments."

3:4. James M. Rogers, "Battle in a Swamp. The 10th Conn. at Kinston, N.C."

3:5. Picket Shots: Samuel F. French (st VT Cav), Gettysburg.

4:6-7. Obit.

8:4. Frank G. Carpenter, "John Wilkes Booth. End of the Assassin—Disposition of His Body—Recovered by His Family and Reinterred in Baltimore."

February 20

1:1-6, 2:5. Buell, Part 20.

1:7, 2:1-3. James L. Sherman, "Bay State Minutemen. As in '76, So in '61, First to Respond to the Call . . . ."

3:1-2. Charles A. Hobbs (99th IL), "Battery at Port Gibson."

3:3-4. Gilbert Thompson (US Eng Btn), Bemus Buckley (146th NY), J. H. Bush (45th PA), "Cannoneer Comments." [June 1864 & Spotsylvania]

3:5-6. Picket Shots: H. C. Whitaker (2nd NY Cav), versus Steinebach; John G. Faris (86th IL), Lookout Mountain; V. W. Krise (133rd PA), Chancellorsville.

4:7. Obit.

6:3. Biog: J. F. Denniston (70th NY).

February 27

1:1-6, 2:5-6. Buell, Part 21.

3:1. J. R. Palmer (32nd IL), "Defense of Grant."

3:2. John T. Davidson (50th NY Eng), "Cannoneer Comments." [Petersburg]

3:3. Edwin C. Gray, "Major [S. A.] Defoe. How He Foiled the La. Tigers."

3:3. G. E. Dolton (Bty M, 1st IL), "Snodgrass Ridge, Chickamauga."

3:4. E. H. Stuart (1st WI Cav), "Capturing Old Jeff. The Fight Between the Wisconsin and Michigan Troops."

3:4. O. S. Barrett (4th MI), "Kick of a Potomac Rat."

4:7. Obit.

6:3. Biog: M. E. Urell (2nd NY).

March 6

1:1-6. Buell, Part 22.

3:1. George W. Smith (7th PA Cav), "The Captured Gun. Minty's Brigade at the Duck River Crossing."

3:1-2. Michael Dunke (103rd OH), "Spring Hill."

3:2. P. S. Troutman, "A Man for the Emergency." [H. S. Ross, 87th IN, at Gallatin, TN, 1-2/63]

3:2. G. W. Ford (11th CT), "Failed to Capture the Johnny." [5/16/64]

3:2. "Capt. Huntington's Final Contribution."

3:3. Andrew Gongwer (25th MI), "Scoring Schofield. Another Account of the Franklin Campaign."

3:3. Carle A. Woodruff (Bty M, 2nd US), "Woodruff's Battery M." [6/11/64]

3:4. Edson C. Brace, "Battle of Philippi."

3:5. Picket Shots: C. Davis (56th OH), Port Gibson.

4:6-7. Obit.

March 13

1:1-6, 2:5-6. Buell, Part 23.

3:1-2. Thomas F. McCoy (107th PA), "At the Weldon Road."

3:2. A. R. Scholes (11th KS Cav), "Army of the Frontier. How They Drove Old Price Out of Missouri."

3:3. H. P. Mercereau (14th OH), "Malvern Hill. A Plan to Build a Monument on the Historic Ground."

3:4. James Beale (12th MA), "Gettysburg. Some Facts for the Eleventh Corps to Digest."

3:4. D. Henson, "Ohio Troops in the Eleventh Corps." [Gettysburg]

3:4. Paul Fay (3rd NY Art), "Battle of Kinston, N.C."

3:5. Picket Shots: S. J. Murphy (Bty I, 2nd IL), John Will (115th IL), Chickamauga.

4:6-7. Obit.

March 20

1:1-6, 2:5. Buell, Part 24.

3:1. Charles E. Thompson (5th VT), "'Aunt Liddy's' Brigade. An Old Vermonter Tells About Cedar Creek."

3:1. Nathaniel K. Bray (33rd NJ), "That Resaca Battery."

3:2. Fred I. Chitty (AIG, 1st Div, 19th Corps), "Cedar Creek."

3:2. J. N. Stephens, "Off Without Orders. How Co. L, 2nd Michigan Cavalry, Chased the Rebs." [11/63, Sparta, TN]

3:3. Jerome Smedley (122nd OH), "Cannoneer Comments. An Ohio Man's Opinion of the Sixth Corps."

3:3-4. William Hutchinson (116th NY), "A Nineteenth Corps Man Speaks Up." [Cedar Creek]

3:4. Jacob D. Brown (101st PA), "Battle of Kinston."

4:7. Obit.

March 27

1:1-6. Buell, Part 25.

1:7, 2:1-3. Doyle, Part 11.

2:3. William M. Doherty, "The Flag of the 6th Massachusetts."

2:4. W. S. B. Randall, "Libby Prison. The Experience of One of the Successful Tunnelers."

3:1. SWL (MI), "Chickamauga."

3:1-2. W. D. Johnston (3rd OH Cav), "Andersonville. The Keeper of the Cemetery Can Distinguish Ex-Prisoners from Other Visitors."

3:2. George Scott (16th US), "A Gallant Charge. Incidents of Lookout Mountain and Jonesboro."

3:2. William Ludgate (59th NY), "A New York Man Would Like to Get His Watch." [captured 4/7/65]

3:3. S. C. Kersey (79th OH), "Battle of Resaca. An Ohio Man Tells Who Captured the Battery."

3:4. H. M. Kenderdine (17th IA), "Charge at Jackson. How the 16th Wisconsin Battery Charged a Potomac Army Brigade."

3:4. Henry A. Bricker (10th VA), "Stonewall Jackson. A Confederate Version of His Killing."

3:4. Amos A. Shell (85th IN), "Hanging of the Spies Horton and Peter." [6/2/63, Franklin, TN]

3:4. O. G. Daniels (8th OH), "Carroll's Brigade at Spotsylvania."

3:5. Picket Shots: W. S. Coon (USS *Osceola*), Skipworth Landing, MS River).

4:7. Obit: George Crook, Robert C. Schenck.

April 3

1:1-6, 3:1-4. Buell, Part 26.

4:1. Frank Sourbeer (203rd PA), "Fort Fisher."

4:1-2. John Moore (52nd OH), "Kennesaw Mountain."

4:2. J. G. Beatty (Bty F, PA Art), "Second Bull Run."

4:3. Louis Fisher (74th PA), "Cannoneer Comments." [Chancellorsville]

4:3. Clinton Beckwith (121st NY), "Cannoneer Comments." [9/30/64]

4:4-5. Byron Phelps (3rd IL Cav), "The Cavalry. The Improvement Made in This Service During the War."

5:1-2. Rollin L. Jones (29th OH), "Bits of Gossip. Interesting Reminiscences of an Ohio Captain."

5:3. Picket Shots: G. W. Kuhns (34th IN), Port Gibson; Benjamin B. Chilicott (46th IN), Bruinsburg; A. B. Straw (9th PA Cav), Shelbyville; E. L. Woods (14th WV), Cedar Creek.

6:7. Obit.

13:6. Biog: Andrew Davidson (121st NY, 30th USCT).

April 10

1:1-6, 2:5. Augustus A. Buell, "The French in Mexico. Operations on the Rio Grande After the War."

3:1-2. "Iowa in the House." [Biogs of David B. Henderson (12th IA), Joseph H. Sweeney (27th IA), John P. Lacey (33rd IA), James P. Flick (4th IA).

3:3-4. Biog: Nelson A. Miles, Benjamin H. Grierson.

4:2. John A. Nourse, "The Captured Gun. The Chicago Board of Trade Battery Never Had a Gun Captured." [Duck River Crossing]

4:2. John S. Strain (15th IA), "Salkahatchie Swamp."

4:3. William N. Brown (65th IL), "Nashville Campaign. A Defense of Schofield and the Twenty-third Corps."

4:3. JPF, "Berdan Range-Finder."

4:4-5. Judson Knight (chief scout, Army of the Potomac), "A Scouting Experience. Virginia Revisited After 25 Years." [May 1864]

5:1-2. "The Cannoneer. Comrades Mingle Praise and Criticism of the Gunner." Letters from John G. Lee (AAG, 1st Division, 19th Corps) re Cedar Creek; C. E. Stevens (77th NY) re 5/11/64; John Wagner (16th MI) re Wilderness; A. W. Peck (17th CT) re Gettysburg; O. B. Ford (24th IA) re Cedar Creek; J. E. Otis (35th NY) re Antietam.

5:3. George W. New (7th IN), "The First Battle." [Philippi]

5:3. (10th CT), "Battle of Kinston."

5:4. Picket Shots: John L. Harper (49th PA), Golding's Farm; Charles Stacey (55th OH), Chancellorsville.

6:7. Obit.

9:5. John W. January (14th IL Cav), "A Survivor of Stoneman's Raid."

April 17

1:1-6. Buell, Part 2.

4:1-2. W. J. Wray (23rd PA), "Malvern Hill."

4:2. T. J. Hughes (5th MO Cav), "The Frontier Army. A Missouri Man's Experience on the Price Raid."

4:2. Edward F. Spofford (6th MA), "The Flag of the 6th Mass."

4:3. James M. Whallon (11th MI), "Chickamauga."

4:4. F. O. Talbot (1st ME Hvy Art), "A Genuine Heroine. Gentle Annie Etheridge of the 5th Michigan."

4:4. E. M. Suppler (6th OH Cav), "Appomattox. Gregg's Cavalry Division at the Last Ditch."

4:5. J. H. Collier (4th MI Cav), "Capture of Old Jeff."

5:1-2. "The Cannoneer. Praise and Criticism." Letters from S. E. Chandler (24th NY Cav) and W. J. Crosley (34th OH) re Winchester; Robert A. Shearer (11th PA) re Gettysburg; Charles J. Longly re Cedar Creek; Peter Colby (3rd MA Cav), O. B. Hayes (2nd Division, 6th Corps), re Cedar Creek; H. R. Schell (Bty H, 1st NY) re

Spotsylvania and Sedgwick; Joseph B. Potter (83rd PA) re 5/8/64; Spencer D. Hunt (50th NY Eng) re Jericho Mills.

5:5. R. W. Allen (16th NH), "A Race for Life. Crossing a Bridge in the Face of the Enemy." [Red River Campaign]

6:7. Obit.

April 24

1:1-6, 2:1-3. Frank E. Moran (73rd NY), "Release of Prisoners. Terrible Scenes of Suffering During the Last Days."

4:1-3. Samuel A. Ambrose (4th Btn OH Cav), "An Injustice Corrected. What Troops Opened Powell Valley?" [Cumberland Gap]

4:3. J. W. Sheaffer (75th IL), "Battle of Perryville."

4:4. A. W. Clyde (27th IA), "Nashville."

4:4-5. James Davis (23rd MI), "Battle of Franklin."

4:5. Charles H. Myerhoff (14th IN), "At Gettysburg."

5:1-2. "The Cannoneer." Letters from H. G. Klinefelter (7th WI & Bty B, 4th US); H. M. Jones (Bartlett's brig) re 5/8/64; George Hugunin (147th NY) re Wilderness; F. L. Phillips; S. W. Miller (4th IA Cav).

5:3-5. Picket Shots: Richard Youngs (94th NY), Cedar Mountain; B. A. Spring (34th IN), Port Gibson.

6:7. Obit.

May 1

2:5. "The Cannoneer." Letters from James Stewart (Bty B, 4th US); G. W. Shiefley (116th OH) and George W. Gageby (54th PA) re Cedar Creek.

3:1-2. Frank H. Foote (48th MS), "Front of Petersburg. The Confederate Defense of Fort Gregg, April 2, 1865."

3:3. George W. Nelson (11th OH Cav), "Out on the Plains. The Mud Springs and Rush Creek Affairs."

3:4. George E. Dolton (Bty M, 1st IL), "Chickamauga."

3:5. Picket Shots: George R. Brown (38th OH), David Hull (1st WI), Jonesboro.

4:6. Obit.

5:1. Reburial of Col. Edgar O'Connor, 2nd Wisconsin, to Arlington."

May 8

1:7, 2:1-4. F. H. Buffum, "Cedar Creek."

3:1-2. Robert H. G. Minty, "At Shelbyville, Tenn."

3:2. C. C. Hassler (21st PA Cav), "The Flat-Footed Cavalry."

3:2. H. G. Klinefelter (Bty B, 4th US), "Battery B at Antietam."

3:3. James K. Robson (8th NY Cav), "Holding Mosby, and a Race for Life with the Guerrilla Cavalry." [9/19/64]

3:4. Pleasant Bates (1st TN Cav), "At Duck River." [6/27/63]

3:5-6. Picket Shots: G. A. Harman (85th IN), Resaca.

4:6-7. Obit.

May 15

1:7, 2:1-3. Augustus Buell, "Appomattox."

2:4. "Battery Monument. Barnes' New York Battery Erects a Handsome Shaft at Gettysburg."

3:1-2. B. Owen (11th NJ), "Chancellorsville."

3:2. "Shipmates Ahoy! Experiences of the Sloop-of-War *Seminole*."

3:3. Henry Dillinberger (4th MO Cav), "The Big Raid. An Account of How the Rebs were Driven Out of Missouri."

3:3. M. Byrne, "Captain Webster. A Comrade Says He was a Murderer and a Robber."

3:4. "The Flag that Tripped Up Booth."

3:4. John N. Beach (40th OH), "Chickamauga."

3:5-6. Picket Shots: A. F. Brown (2nd CO Cav), R. B. Kelley (13th MO Cav), Edward

Probasco (1st MO SM Cav), Peter Riley (6th KS Cav), Daniel W. Carpenter (Bty L, 2nd MO), Price's Raid.

4:7. Obit.

May 22

1:5-7, 2:1-3. Buell, Part 2.

3:1-2. William Taylor (99th OH), "Nashville Campaign. The Last Troops to Enter the City Before the Battle."

3:2. Frank W. Mix (4th MI Cav), "Battle of Shelbyville."

3:3. Patrick Mooney (7th PA Cav), "Gen. Nelson. The Opinion He had of the Services of the Cavalry."

3:3. George I. Robinson (Chicago Board of Trade Bty), "The Captured Gun."

3:4. WHT, "Sherman's Bummers. How Co. E, 66th Ohio, Lost Their Mule and Cart."

3:4. Evelyn Kelsey (9th CT), "On Ship Island."

3:5-6. Picket Shots: G. W. McGraw (78th PA), Chickamauga; Ralph L. Barcroft (32nd OH), Harper's Ferry.

4:7. Obit.

May 29

1:7, 2:1-4. Frank W. Hess, "Volunteer Cavalry. The First Cavalry Battle at Kelly's Ford."

3:1-2. Robert I. Patterson (19th IN), "Behind the Reb Scenes. What a Member of the Iron Brigade Saw at the Battle of Gettysburg."

3:3-4. George W. Carpenter (8th MN), "Malvern Hill."

3:4. Charles A. Hausman (30th NY Bty), "Finding a Battery. An Incident of the Retreat from Winchester, Va., in July 1864."

3:5-6. Picket Shots: L. W. Mason (43rd OH), Salkehatchie River; J. H. Lapius (115th NY), Harper's Ferry; W. J. Shafer (65th OH), Franklin.

4:7. Obit.

6:6. Biog: P. H. Dowling (111th OH).

June 5

1:7, 2:1-4. Hess, Part 2.

2:6. "Andersonville Prison Purchased."

3:1-2. R. H. Martin (46th IN), "A Battery at Port Gibson. What Hovey's Division did to Help Benton's Brigade."

3:2. H. L. Chapman (124th OH), "Fun in a Small-Pox Hospital." [Camp Dennison]

3:3-4. William Reblin (USS *Cumberland*), "A Glorious Action. The Battle Between the Cumberland, Congress and Merrimac."

3:5-6. Picket Shots: J. E. Harding (12th WV), J. D. Baker (100th NY), Fort Gregg; John D. Myers (74th IN), Jonesboro; C. H. Porter (26th IN Bty), Harper's Ferry.

4:7. Obit.

5:4. Obit: Robert H. Milroy.

8:1-4. John Fredd, "USS *San Jacinto*. Her Cruise After Blockade-Runners and Her Final Wreck."

June 12

1:6. George W. Axtell, "Gentle Annie. The Services Rendered by Mrs. Annie Etheridge, 5th Michigan."

1:7, 2:1-3. Augustus Buell, "Gettysburg. Complete Analysis of the Official Records."

3:1-2. William M. Davis (6th OH Cav), "St. Mary's Church, Va."

3:3. E. D. Dawes (53rd OH), "Do Figures Lie? The Strength of Lee's Army in Its Last Campaign."

3:4. J. M. Rogers (10th CT), "Battle of Kinston."

3:4. H. C. Whitaker (2nd NY Cav), "The Lone Gunner. A Soldier Resolved to Take a Few Devils With Him." [Second Manassas]

3:5-6. Picket Shots: A. G. Jacobs (6th OH Cav), Appomattox; Milton Giles (13th IL), Vicksburg surrender; W. Jones (7th KS Cav), Independence, MO; Stephen Feather (4th US Cav), Shelbyville; Edward Clark (111th PA), R. Scanland (74th IN), Resaca; Z. N. Thomas (85th IN), 6/27/64.

4:7. Obit.

June 19

1:4. W. J. Wray (23rd PA), "Fitz-John Porter."

1:5-7, 2:1-2. Buell, Part 2.

3:1-2. "The Porters. Review of Commodore [W. D.] Porter's Military and Naval Achievements."

3:2. George E. Dolton (Bty M, 1st IL), "Dolton Once More." [Chickamauga]

3:3. J. W. Forsyth, "Loudoun Rangers. How They were Surrounded and Captured at Waterford."

3:3. Lewis H. Miller, "The Hanging of Captain Webster."

3:3-4. H. E. Eaton (2nd NY Cav), "A Climbing Horse." [Spotsylvania]

3:4. John T. Davidson (50th NY Eng), "Chancellorsville. Laying the Pontoons Before the Disastrous Battle."

3:5-6. Picket Shots: I. A. Packward (32nd IA), Pleasant Hill.

4:7. Obit.

6:5. "Trouble Over a Gettysburg Monument Site." [111th NY versus 12th NJ]

6:6. "Pennsylvania Reserves. A Little Difficulty Over Their Gettysburg Monuments."

June 26

1:7, 2:1-4, 8:4-5. Thomas F. McCoy (107th PA), "Five Forks."

3:1. Augustus Buell (Bty B, 4th US), "How It Happened. Why the Cannoneer Did Not Mention Crawford's Division Particularly." [Five Forks]

3:2. H. M. Kenderdine (17th IA), "The Charging Brigade. How the Second Brigade, 17th Corps, Got the Name."

3:2-3. J. P. Ross (78th OH), "A Sergeant's Strategy. How He Stole Whiskey from the Commissary."

3:3. W. S. Pierce (20th WI), "Prairie Grove."

3:3. P. B. Sylvis (87th OH), "Capture of a Rebel Officer's Horse." [Harper's Ferry 1862]

3:4. D. R. Sanborn (6th VT), "A Story of the War. How Gen. Sedgwick's Death was Avenged."

3:4. Walden Kelly, "Losses of the 26th Ohio at Chickamauga."

3:5-6. Picket Shots: Benjamin Petree (10th MO), Salkehatchie River; Joseph L. Carson (26th KY), Nashville.

4:7. Obit.

July 3

1:1-6. Wiley Britton, "Rock Creek Affair. The Place the Mormons Consider Their Holy Land. War in Missouri."

2:4-5. Biog: James W. Forsyth (18th US, 64th OH, ADC to McClellan).

3:1-2. E. M. Tuton (10th NY Cav), "St. Mary's Church."

3:2. A. B. Lynch (57th IL), "Pittsburgh Landing."

3:3. Gam Pease (69th OH), "Chickamauga."

3:4. R. M. Aikin (33rd IL), "At Prentiss, Miss. How Three Picket-Guards were Left Behind." [Summer 1862]

3:4. Sheridan McBratney (17th NY), "More About Jonesboro."

3:4. H. A. Smith (55th IL), "How Rebel Prisoners Fared at Johnson's Island."

3:5-6. Picket Shots: Henry Caryell (34th IL), Kennesaw Mountain; I. H. Stenbord (US Regs), Aylesbury Gregory (60th IL), Jonesboro.

4:7. Obit.

5:1. Biog: Richard N. Batchelder (1st NH, QM Dept).

July 10

1:1-4. R. H. G. Minty, "Kilpatrick's Raid. The Attack and Capture of Jonesboro . . . ."

3:1. William J. Church (7th MI), "Fredericksburg. What Regiment Crossed in the Pontoon Boats December 11, 1862?"

3:2. George W. Carpenter, "Fitz-John Porter."

3:2. S. J. Creese (Bty F, PA Art), "That Abandoned Battery Again." [Winchester 7/64]

3:3. W. H. Strayer (118th IN), "Walker's Ford." [12/2/63 Clinch River]

3:4. John M. Ewing (15th OH), "Blaine's Crossroads. A Night with the Girls in East Tennessee."

3:4. John M. Kemper (10th NY Cav), "A Cavalry Charge." [6/19/63]

3:5-6. Picket Shots: W. Welch (23rd MA), Kinston; J. A. Smith (16th US), Jonesboro; H. W. Phelps (95th OH), Nashville.

4:7. Obit.

July 17

1:1-5. E. Z. C. Judson, "Joiner's Ford. Exciting Memories of the Blackwater. . . ." [Suffolk 1863]

3:1-3. J. W. Landegon (2nd NY Cav), "Scouting Experiences. Sheridan's Chief of Scouts Wounded, But Escapes Capture."

3:3. Charles W. Hattaway (1st MA), "Chancellorsville."

3:4. AGJ, "Fort Fisher. The Part Taken by the 27th U.S.C.T."

3:4. James H. Beatty (Loudoun Rangers), "Webster and the Rebel Recruiting Officer."

3:5-6. Picket Shots: George Wetmore (26th NY), Fredericksburg crossing; John W. Herring (45th IL), Champion's Hill; Ted W. Kraftt (128th NY), Cedar Creek; H. Cordes (18th US), Jonesboro; James H. Cassidy (104th OH), Isaac Ax (106th OH), Franklin.

4:7. Obit.

8:4. Obit: John C. Fremont.

8:5. Biog: Alexander M. McCook.

July 24

1:1-6. James Bryson (27th IA), "Red River Campaign."

3:1-3. J. W. Hand (136th NY), "Gettysburg."

3:3. George W. Rowan (7th IA Cav), "Out on the Plains."

3:3. G, "The Fate of 'Captain Webster'."

3:4. George E. Dolton (Bty M, 1st IL), "Chickamauga. Dolton Reunes with the U.C.V. on the Field."

3:5-6. Picket Shots: R. O. Knowles (116th OH), Fort Gregg; G. L. Camp (92nd OH), Charles A. Robertson (16th IL), Thomas McClure (18th US), Jonesboro.

4:7. Obit.

July 31

1:1-3. Wiley Britton, "Bill Anderson."

1:4-6. William E. Doyle (17th IN), "Western Anecdotes. The Sergeant Who Resembled General Nelson. . . ."

2:5-6. Biogs: L. P. Williams (73rd IN), John M. Kline (49th PA), Oliver R. McNary (103rd PA), E. H. Williams (13th IN), John S. Ferguson (28th IA).

3:1. Joseph M. Alexander (2nd PA Hvy Art), "Army of the James. Fighting and Suffering Around Bermuda Hundred."

3:2. George H. McKinney (19th KY), "Battle of Tazewell."

3:2-3. Burritt Ingalls, "Andersonville."

3:3. Charles M. Castle (102nd IL), "Battle of Resaca. Who Captured the Four-Gun Battery?"

3:3-4. "The Morning of February 22, 1861." [Lincoln in Philadelphia]

3:5-6. Picket Shots: William E. Hatfield (17th NY), Jonesboro; Charles Graham (89th NY), Fredericksburg; W. D. Benedict (15th NY Cav), snowball fight.

4:7. Obit.

August 7

1:1-6, 8:5. H. C. Parsons (1st VT Cav), "Gettysburg. The Campaign was a Chapter of Incidents. . . ."

3:1. Lee H. Rudisill (38th OH), "Atlanta Campaign. What One Brigade did at Jonesboro, Ga."

3:2. J. L. Pray (signal corps), "The Signal Corps. How a Party Stood the Severe Shelling at the Avery House." [Petersburg 3/65]

3:2. J. A. Basom (128th OH), "Johnson's Island."

3:3. G. Irwin, "Downed the General. The Colonel Got the Best of the Division Commander." [Gordon Granger]

3:3. GAS, "Five Forks. A Fifth Corps Man on Warren's Removal."

3:4. J. W. Thompson (141st PA), "Fredericksburg."

3:4. J. M. Rogers (10th CT), "Roanoke Island."

3:5-6. Picket Shots: R. P. Stowe (IL), Prentiss, MS; C. P. Mears (17th PA Cav), Sheridan's Ride.

4:7. Obit.

August 14

3:1-2. ECD, "The Wilderness. Forces and Losses of the Army in that Campaign."

3:2-3. E. B. Lufkin (13th ME), "Red River Campaign."

3:3-4. George W. Dennis (13th WI), "The Action at Dover."

3:4. D. D. McCallum (27th IA), "Smith's Guerrillas. A 27th Iowa Man's Account of Pleasant Hill."

3:5-6. Picket Shots: F. W. Joslin (116th NY), Pleasant Hill; E. Ackerman (32nd IA), E. A. Thompson (10th KY), Jonesboro; E. M. Tinkham (148th NY), Fort Gregg; William Ramage (178th NY), M. V. Nevins (122nd IL), Nashville.

4:7. Obit.

August 21

3:1. M. Wetzel (39th IL), "Fort Gregg."

3:1-2. Frank S. Reader (5th WV Cav), "Stonewall Jackson's Sister."

3:2. J. E. Cutter (29th ME), "Up the Red River."

3:3. W. A. Flint (4th NY Hvy Art), "Before Richmond. A Picket-Line Episode of Deep Bottom, August 1864."

3:3. Lloyd G. Thompson, "Andersonville Horrors."

3:4. Briscoe Goodheart (Loudoun Rangers), "Captain Webster Again. His Execution, and Who He Really Was."

3:5-6. Picket Shots: Mark W. Knoop (8th OH Cav), Sheridan's Ride; S. Dickerman (33rd IL), Prentiss, MS; H. H. Hill (14th KY), Tazewell.

4:6-7. Obit.

4:7. Biog: W. G. Veazey (3rd, 16th VT), Richard F. Tobin (USS *Pinola*), George B. Creamer (10th MD).

August 28

1:1-4. J. B. Ridenour (55th IL), "Arkansas Post."

3:2. J. P. Ross (78th OH), "Capturing a Town, and a Subsequent Retreat in Good Order." [Montezuma, TN, 6/62]

3:3. G. H. Blakeslee (129th IL), "Resaca. Who Captured the Four-Gun Battery?"

3:3-4. J. M. Gardner (12th IL Cav), "A War of Races. How a Virginia Darky Did Up an Illinois Cavalryman."

3:4. John W. Scott, "Up the Red River."

3:5-6. Picket Shots: E. W. Pike (9th MN), G. W. Andruss (12th MO Cav), Nashville; W. F. Hoskins (87th IL), Jasper Guill (87th IL), Red River; W. N. Paine (83rd IL), J. H. Cook (83rd IL), Dover, TN; JWH, Lincoln in Phila, 1861; H. H. Fellows (14th MI), Jonesboro; Charles F. Damon (3rd RI Hvy Art), Charleston 3/65.

4:6-7. Obit.

September 4

1:1-6. William Simmons, "Semmes the Pirate."

2:6. "A Family of Fighters." [Brandon family, St. Clairsville, WV]

3:1-2. B. F. Nourse, "Board of Trade Battery."

3:2. Joseph F. Carter (3rd MD), "Lincoln vs. McClellan. A Comrade's Opinion of the 'Little Nap'."

3:3. E. R. Graham (56th PA), "Rice's Brigade. Their Gallant Charge in the Wilderness."

3:3. J. W. Forsyth, "Loudoun Rangers. Bullets More Effective Than the Word of God."

3:4. John Glynn (2nd PA Cav), "In the Wilderness. Which Corps Opened the Big Battle?"

3:4. Frank N. Scott, "The Forlorn Hope." [Port Hudson]

3:5-6. Picket Shots: D. C. Davis (1st VT Cav), George W. Toms (5th NY Cav), Hanover; Cyrus Bute (83rd IL), Dover; J. D. Forbes (175th NY), Cedar Creek.

4:7. Obit.

8:2. Biog: B. F. Stevenson (23rd, 22nd KY).

September 11

1:1-5. W. E. Doyle (17th IN), "Early War Days. Gen. R. E. Lee's First Defeat in West Virginia."

1:5. Biog: Joseph H. Goulding (6th USCT).

3:1-3. E. B. Lufkin (13th ME), "Away Down in Texas. The Campaign of the Thirteenth Corps in the Winter of '63."

3:3-4. William Houghton (14th IN), "The Wilderness. A Staff Officer's Recollections of the Salient Angle." [5/12/64]

3:4. J. V. Stewart (192nd OH), "Hanging Guerrillas. An Ohio Man's Story of the Reed Hill Affair." [6/27/65]

3:5-6. Picket Shots: James Bryson (27th IA), Fort DeRussy; M. Lingham (1st TX Cav CSA), C. B. Maxwell (2nd MA Bty), Red River; F. T. Graham (3rd MO), Arkansas Post.

4:7. Obit.

September 18

1:5. Marcus J. Wright, "General U. S. Grant."

1:6-7, 2:1-2. J. E. Cutter (29th ME), "Sabine Crossroads."

3:1-2. J. R. Thornbury (Btys A, F, 1st IL), "Atlanta Campaign. What was Done by the Fourth Division, Fifteenth Corps."

3:3. G. E. Dolton (Bty M, 1st IL), "The Dover Fight."

3:4. W. D. Taylor (125th NY), "Morton's Ford."

3:4. John W. Sheaffer (75th IL), "Stones' River."

4:7. Obit.

September 25

1:1-6, 2:5-6. John E. Farnsworth (1st WI Cav), "A Scout's Adventures. Making Preparations for the Famous McCook Raid."

1:7, 2:1-3. John T. Booth (36th OH), "Chickamauga."

2:3. Biog: Leland J. Webb (16th, 30th WI, Bty E, 1st IL).

3:1-2. QM (83rd IL), "Battle of Dover."

3:2. Joseph F. Carter (3rd MD), "Leasure's Brigade. Another Account of the Fight at the Salient Angle."

3:3. Charles B. Carey (10th NY Hvy Art), "Revisiting Battlefields. A N.Y. Comrade Goes to Bermuda Hundred."

3:3. Andrew McNamar, "The Bloody 106th Illinois."

3:4. Henry Cordes (18th US), "At Jonesboro."

3:4. "The Sixth Corps. What Gen. Meade Thought of Their Mettle."

3:5-6. Picket Shots: George W. Fowler (54th PA), Fort Gregg; G. W. Scovill (103rd IL), Griswold, GA.

4:7. Obit.

5:4. Biog: W. H. Enochs (1st WV).

October 2

1:1-6, 2:5-6. Farnsworth, Part 2.

1:7, 2:1-4. Booth, Part 2.

3:1-2. James H. Harold (1st NY Eng), "Pocotaligo Expedition."

3:2. J. H. Rogers (10th CT), "The Two Armies. What was Their Relative Strength in 1862?"

3:3. George E. Sloat (14th OH), "Jonesboro, Ga."

3:3. William J. Markham (9th NY Cav), "Shenandoah Campaign."

3:4. J. W. Everett (signal corps), "The Last Campaign."

3:5-6. Picket Shots: E. Sullivan (42nd NY), Fredericksburg crossing; William B. Stark (34th MA), Fort Gregg.

4:7. Obit.

6:2. Biog: E. J. SanSouci (SUV).

October 9

1:1-5. Farnsworth, Part 3.

1:6-7, 2:1-3. Booth, Part 3.

2:3. Biog: Smith A. Whitfield (2nd NH).

3:1. H. A. Magrath (11th CT), "Drewry's Bluff."

3:2. R. C. Rice (125th OH), "Kennesaw Mountain."

3:2-3. F. C. Jones (64th NY), "The Second Corps. Their Gallant Charge at the 'Bloody Angle'."

3:3. Thomas S. Nutter (10th WV), "Who was This Pa. Sergeant?"

[11th PA Res, 7/24/64]

3:4. James Fitzpatrick (USS *Lexington*), "Mississippi Flotilla. How They Assisted in Repelling the Attack on Fort Donelson."

3:4. B. F. Slaughter (55th KY), "Another Capt. Webster."

3:5-6. Picket Shots: John A. Mizon (83rd PA), Wilderness; Orlando B. Smith (126th NY), Morton's Ford; H. Lund (16th UIL), Milo Smith (14th OH), Jonesboro.

4:7. Obit.

October 16

1:1-6. Farnsworth, Part 4.

1:7, 2:1-3. Booth, Part 4.

3:4. Obit: W. W. Belknap (15th IA).

4:1-3. J. H. Sawyer (18th CT), "Battle of Winchester, As Seen by a Conn. Soldier from the Hospital."

4:3. P. D. Whitzel (61st IL), "The Bloody 106th Again."

6:7. Obit.

October 23

1:7, 2:1-2. Booth, Part 5.

2:4. Biog: John G. Dunbar (79th IN).

4:1. Charles H. Myerhoff (14th IN), "The Wilderness. The Charge of Carroll's Celebrated Brigade."

4:1-2. Jacob Buch (5th US Cav), "Lincoln at City Point. How the President was Escorted to Petersburg."

4:2. J. J. Clark, "That 'Outrage.' The 115th Ohio's Side of the Affair at Columbus." [OH]

4:3. George Scott (16th US), "Jonesboro."

4:3. S. P. Zehring (25th OH), "Chickamauga."

4:4. William Lochren, "1st Minnesota at Gettysburg." [from book]

4:5-6. Picket Shots: Theodore Humphteyville (52nd OH), Jonesboro; George W. Fowler (54th PA), Fort Gregg; W. J. Clark (1st VT Cav), Wilderness; Charles Slemmer (125th NY), Morton's Ford.

6:7. Obit.

October 30

1:1-5. Frank E. Moran (73rd NY), "A Fire Zouave."

3:5. Biog: James E. White (3rd IA).

4:1-3. William T. McMaken (14th IA), "Banks's Expedition. Shaw's Brigade at Pleasant Hill, La."

4:3-4. A. S. Smith (23rd MI), "Battle of Franklin."

4:4. Lee Frazier (13th IN), "At Winchester." [1862]

4:5-6. Picket Shots: Ferdinand Zimmerman (9th OH), Chickamauga; W. F. Clendenen (69th OH), Jonesboro.

6:7. Obit.

November 6

1:1-5. Moran, Part 2.

4:1-2. A. M. Potter (74th IL), "Kennesaw Mountain."

4:2. W. D. Ford (8th MI), "The Ninth Corps. What They Accomplished in South Carolina."

4:2. George Huginin (147th NY), "A N.Y. Soldier's View of the Fight at the Bloody Angle."

4:3. James H. Harold (1st NY Eng), "In the Far South. The Capture of St. John's Bluff, Fla."

4:5. Joseph F. Carter (3rd MD), "The Wilderness. The Controversy Between the Brigades of Rice and Carroll."

4:4-5. Picket Shots: William B. Stark (34th MA), Fort Gregg.

6:7. Obit.

November 13

3:1-5. Moran, Part 3.

4:1. John T. Booth (36th OH), "Chickamauga. Comrade Booth Replies to His Critics."

4:1-2. D. B. Floyd (75th IN), "Turchin's Brigade Cut Its Way Through the Rebs."

4:2-3. G. E. Dolton (Bty M, 1st IL), "To Booth's Rescue."

4:3. W. O. Johnston (3rd OH Cav), "Capturing a Locomotive. A Comrade's Recollections of the Late John William." [Andrews Raid]

4:4. Walden Kelly (26th OH), "Kennesaw Mountain."

4:4. Thomas Fay (42nd IL), "Who Spiked the Guns at Island No. Ten?"

6:7. Obit.

November 20

1:6-7, 2:1-4. Samuel M. Arnell, "Parson Brownlow."

4:1-2. D. W. Smith (120th IN), "Hood's Last Campaign. Experience with the Wagon Train from Columbia to Franklin."

4:2. MUB, "Mosby's Guerrillas. How the Loudoun County Rangers Got Away with a Pair of Them."

4:3. John H. Connell (7th VA Cav), "Summers and Koontz."

4:3. C. A. Brown (92nd OH), "Chickamauga."

4:3. Lizzie Beller, "A Rebel's Estimate of Lee's Forces at Gettysburg." [Gettysburg civilian]

4:4. W. L. Raymond, "The Regular Army. A Plea for Those Treasonable Regulars and Little Mac."

4:5-6. Picket Shots: William H. H. Davis (11th OH), Chickamauga; C. F. Greening (11th, 23rd WI), Red River.

6:7. Obit.

7:3. Obit: Charles Steedman (USN).

12:3. Obit: John C. Starkweather.

November 27

1:1-4. William E. Doyle (17th IN), "Race After Wheeler." [10/63]

3:5. "Gen. Warren. A Statue to be Erected by the G.A.R. in His Honor." [Gettysburg]

4:1-3. Will A. McTeer (3rd TN Cav), "Smith's Raid." [12/63]

4:3-4. Victor Gebhardt, "A Memorable Scout. Hardships Endured by the 4th MO. and 15th Ky. Cavalry." [6/24/63]

4:4. Jacob McAfee, "A Blast from a Member of the 106th Ill."

6:7. Obit.

7:6. Biog: N. M. Brooks (3rd, 12th NJ).

12:3-4. Obits: Richard F. Tobin (USN), Oliver S. Glisson (USS *Mt. Vernon*).

December 4

1:1-6. William E. Doyle (17th IN), "Contraband's Story. A Negro's Experience During the Fighting Around the Rapidan. . . ."

4:1. "A Summer's Horse Trade. How an Ohio Man Saved His Scalp in S.C."

4:1-2. John T. Booth (36th OH), "Mrs. Turchin and the Ammunition Train."

4:2. Silas Crowell, "The Dutch Oven. Experiences of the 93rd Ohio in East Tennessee." [11/63]

4:3. O. G. Daniels (8th OH), "At the Crossroads. The Charge Made by Carroll's Brigade." [Wilderness]

4:3. Earl M. Rogers (Wadsworth ADC), "The Wilderness."

4:3-4. T. J. Ashley (24th NY Cav), "Col. William C. Raulston. An Account of His Capture and Subsequent Death."

4:4. F. M. Herrick (10th NY Hvy Art), "In Virginia." [Bermuda Hundred]

4:4. James M. Irland (9th PA Cav), "The Little Napoleon."

4:5-6. Picket Shots: Patrick Hart (15th NY Bty), Bethesda Church; S. H. Toles (19th IN Bty), Chickamauga; E. M. Rogers (6th WI), Chancellorsville.

4:6. Robert Kincaid (4th OH Bty), "Near Atlanta."

6:7. Obit.

December 11

1:1-5, 2:6. John Pope, "War Reminiscences."

4:1. J. L. Shellenberger (IA), "Kennesaw Mountain."

4:2. A. Vosburgh (119th IL), "Red River Campaign."

4:2. George H. Stowits (100th NY), "Fort Gregg."

4:3. C. Woodruff (64th OH), "Chickamauga. A Comparison of Losses in Different Ohio Regiments."

4:3-4. Ira C. McClenthien (USS *Baron deKalb*), "Who Did Spike the Guns at Island No. Ten?"

4:4. D. Shaughnessy (124th OH), "The Fires that Comrade Booth Saw." [Chickamauga]

4:4. C. E. McCracken (54th PA), "Another Claim for the Capture of Fort Gregg."

4:5. Picket Shots: G. W. Raworth (64th IL), Kennesaw Mountain; W. C. King (125th IL), Jonesboro.

6:7. Obit.

7:3 Obits: Jedediah H. Baxter (12th MA), Cadmus M. Wilcox.

December 18

1:1-3. Pope, Part 2.

4:1-2. J. E. Cutter (29th ME), "Red River Campaign. The Formation of the Line at Pleasant Hill."

4:2. FW (1st CT Cav), "Prisoner of War. Confederate Testimony as to How They Treated Their Prisoners."

4:2-3. William H. Mayo (1st DC Cav), "Salisbury Prison."

4:3. J. J. Walley (152nd NY), "In the Wilderness. Another Account of the Fight at the Angle."

4:3. A. H. Boyle (USS *St. Louis*), "Soldiers and Seamen; Or, Who Actually Did Spike the Guns at Island No. Ten?"

4:5-6. Picket Shots: A. H. Smith (50th NY Eng), Fredericksburg; James R. Gilbert (124th IL), explosion on USS *James Watson*, 2/65; Robert J. Martin (84th IL), Stones River; Charles B. Randall (16th WI), Jonesboro.

4:7. William H. Lute (2nd OH Cav), "The Raiders in Andersonville."

6:7. Obit.

10:3. Biog: Stephen R. Whitney (7th NY Hvy Art).

December 25

1:1-3. Pope, Part 3.

4:1. T. D. Neighbor (52nd OH), "Kennesaw Mountain."

4:2. "Regulars and Little Mac. A Volunteer's View of the Peninsular Campaign."

4:2-3. W. L. Park (USS *Pittsburgh*), "Who Spiked the Guns at Island No. Ten?"

4:3. "Prairie Grove, Ark. Narrow Escape of Two Iowa Soldiers."

4:3. W. DeSano (USS *New Ironsides*), "Cheering the Admiral." [DuPont after first Charleston attack]

4:4. J. W. Landegon (2nd NY Cav), "Where the Rebs Were. A Scout's Trip from Raleigh Through Secessia Northward."

4:5-7. Picket Shots: I. W. P. Townsend (130th IL), Sabine Crossroads.

4:6-7. W. C. Willmore (89th IL), "Premonition." [Chickamauga]

4:7. Mary R. Isenhower, "The Fifteenth Corps at Jonesboro."

5:1-5. William E. Curtis, "Scared to Death? Opinions of Prominent Surgeons and Army Officers as to Whether Death May Result from Fright."

6:7. Obit.

10:7. Obit: Alfred H. Terry.

1891

January 1

1:1-3. Pope, Part 4.

1:4-7, 2:1. William E. Doyle (17th IN), "The Wilson Raid."

4:1-2. J. F. Carter (3rd MD), "In the Wilderness. The Controversy Between Carroll's and Leasure's Brigades."

4:2. C.T.&F. (84th IL), "In Richmond. The Great Sugar Raid by Union Prisoners."

4:2-3. "Rescued. A Pathetic Incident of the Late War." [Charles Coleman, 10th WI, at Perryville]

4:3. John Gayeth (2nd PA Hvy Art), "Col. William C. Raulston. An Account of His Death by an Eyewitness."

4:3. Thomas Tilton (97th OH), "In Hard Luck. Carrying Pork All Night for Another Fellow."

4:4. W. W. Allen (26th IL), "Battle of Iuka."

4:4. Christian Ehrisman (5th KY), "An Incident of the Battle of Chickamauga."

4:5. (56th PA), "The Fight in the Wilderness."

4:5. Thomas Fay (42nd IL), "Who Spiked the Guns at Island No. Ten."

4:6-7. Picket Shots: P. H. Barnes (100th NY), Fort Gregg; W. J. Hilliard (MS Marine Brigade), Columbia, MS.

6:7. Obit.

January 8

1:1-5. Pope, Part 5.

1:6-7, 2:1-3. Doyle, Part 2.

4:1. Ellis H. Timm (Bty B, NJ Art), "Clark's New Jersey Battery. They Fought in the Peach Orchard at Gettysburg."

4:2. John Clark (Bty I, 2nd IL), "Barnett's Battery. What They Performed on the Atlanta Campaign."

4:2. Austin H. Hall (3rd VT), "The Sixth Corps. The Part It Took in the Action of April 2, 1865."

4:2-3. James H. Harold (1st NY Eng), "Away Down South. Action at Port Royal Ferry, S.C., January 1, 1862."

4:3. John Glynn (2nd PA Cav), "The Wilderness. What Troops Brought on the Big Battle?"

4:4. Nathan P. Eckles (14th OH), "The Best Regiment. The Only Successful Charge During Sherman's Campaign." [Jonesboro]

4:4. William W. Perry (82nd PA), "At Petersburg." [4/2/65]

4:5-6. Picket Shots: R. C. Rankin (4th OH Cav), McPherson's horse; John Shissler (3rd MD), D. W. Brest (57th PA), Wilderness.

4:6. William E. Chick (85th PA), "Fort Gregg Again."

6:7. Obit.

9:4. Obit: F. E. Spinner (US Treasurer, 1861-75).

January 15

1:1-4. Pope, Part 6.

1:5-7, 2:1-2. Doyle, Part 3.

4:1. Joseph M. Sudsburg (3rd MD), "In the Wilderness."

4:1-2. James N. McMaster (9th OH Cav), "He Got Frightened. What Old Bill Saw on Picket in S.C."

4:2. James H. Harold (1st NY Eng), "The Stone Fleet. How the Rebel 'Rat-Holes' on the Southern Coasts were Stopped."

4:2. Charles H. Osgood (1st NY Eng), "A Sutler's Clerk. A Man Who Attended to the Wants of the Soldiers."

4:3-4. W. G. Putney (Bty I, 2nd IL), "Chickamauga."

4:4. S. Bullock (24th NY Cav), "Col. W. C. Raulston. An Account of His Death by the Regimental Quartermaster Sergeant."

4:4. Albert G. Leach (12th WV), "Fort Gregg."

4:5-6. Picket Shots: C. E. Smith (42nd IL), Island #10.

6:7. Obit.

7:2. J. J. Reynolds, "How Wilder's Brigade was Mounted."

12:4. Obit: Charles Devens.

January 22

1:7, 2:1-2. Pope, Part 7.

3:1. Joseph Griffith (4th TN Cav), "The Mississippi Raid." [W. S. Smith]

3:1. C. C. Cherrington (18th OH), "To Huntsville." [1862]

3:2-3. Thomas Ranson (1st NY Mtd Rifles), "A Bad Horse."

3:3. D. P. Kimbell (27th MI), "At Petersburg." [4/2/65]

3:3-4. G. B. Godfrey (4th VT), "In the Wilderness."

3:4. Silas Crowell (93rd OH), "Foraging. Capturing Pork Down in East Tennessee."

3:5. Picket Shots: Perry Rowe (Bty B, 4th US), Gettysburg.

3:6. Rollin L. Jones (29th OH), "Capture of Gen. Rhett." [3/65]

4:7. Obit.

January 29

1:7, 2:1-3. Pope, Part 8.

3:1. C. P. Bragg, "Admiral Farragut."

3:1. J. M. Rogers (10th CT), "Who Led the Assault on Fort Gregg?"

3:2. Wilbur F. Haughawut (3rd WI), "Through Georgia."

3:3. E. L. Hobart (28th IL), "Why Did They Go?" [Grand Junction, Spring 1863]

3:4-5. Charles Hulin (Btys F&K, 3rd US), "Gettysburg. Batteries that did Fight in the Peach Orchard."

3:5. F. E. Doak (4th ME), "In the Wilderness."

3:5. C. W. Sherwood (17th IN), "Wilson's Raid. From the Comrade Who Sabered Gen. Forrest."

3:6-7. Picket Shots: James K. Wilson (98th IL), Wilson's Raid); Christian Ehrisman (5th KY), Wilson after Nashville; C. H. Bothwell (98th IL), Plantersville; Charles Ward (60th IN), Sabine Crossroads; James M. Hendricks (64th IL), 6/27/64.

4:7. Obit.

February 5

1:7, 2:1-3. Pope, Part 9.

3:1-2. William J. May (13th KS), "Prairie Grove, Ark."

3:2. S. J. Creese (Bty F, PA Art), "Gettysburg. Positions of the Batteries in or Near the Peach Orchard."

3:3. N. Sessions (1st US Ss), "In the Wilderness."

3:3-4. J. C. Patterson (98th OH), "Jonesboro."

3:4. G. W. Shears; S. Bronson, "The 12th Illinois Cavalry. Its Part in the Gettysburg Campaign."

3:5-6. Picket Shots: Andrew J. Miller (Bty K, 4th US), Gettysburg.

4:7. Obit.

February 12

1:7, 2:1-2. Pope, Part 10.

3:1. John T. Frederick (10th OH Cav), "Battle of Waynesboro."

3:2. George H. Stowits (100th NY), "Fort Gregg."

3:2. J. B. Ridenour (55th IL), "The Fifteenth Corps at Jonesboro Again."

3:2-3. H. M. Parker, "The Commanding Officers of the 11th Illinois."

3:3. C. S. Sheldon (1st MO Art), "Gettysburg. A Comrade Locates the Batteries in and About the Peach Orchard."

3:3. Frank S. Smith (89th NY), "A N.Y. Man Thinks His Brigade was There." [Fort Gregg]

3:3. William Kunth (57th IL), "What Became of the Cow?"

3:4. J. H. Madden (11th IL), "Trying to Enlist. An Experience at Camp Yates with Gen. Pope."

3:5-6. Picket Shots: John Banks (87th PA), D. B. Friedline (61st PA0, 4/2/65; Charles Smith (3rd IN Cav), Wilderness; Neal C. Spring (67th OH), Fort Gregg.

4:7. Obit.

February 19

1:7, 2:1-2. Pope, Part 11.

3:1. Charles W. Ware (39th IL), "Fort Gregg Again!"

3:1. P. K. Faulk (11th PA), "A Fighting Regiment. The Part Taken by the 11th Pa. on the Plains of Manassas."

3:2. Alfred S. Burger (2nd IA Cav), "Sooy Smith's Raid."

3:3. Mrs. Frances A. Tuttle, "Gen. J. B. McPherson. Something About His Family and His Horses."

3:3. John P. Brook (35th OH), "That Sugar Raid. A Chickamauga Prisoner Gives His Experience."

3:4. George M. Buck (20th MI), "Petersburg. The Second Brigade, First Division, Ninth Corps First in the City."

3:5-6. Picket Shots: M. Hanifen (2nd NJ Bty), Gettysburg; George Philipot (3rd IA), J. P. Barron (32nd IL), Henry Palmer (53rd IL), Grand Junction.

4:7. Obit.

5:3-4. Obit: David D. Porter.

8:1-2. Obit: William T. Sherman.

February 26

1:6-7, 2:1. Pope, Part 12.

3:1-2. R. H. G. Minty, "Kilpatrick's Raid."

3:2. Lyman Root (125th OH), "Kennesaw Mountain."

3:3. J. Shaw (95th PA), "Battle of Gaines's Mill."

3:3-4. J. R. Boyce (33rd OH), "The Sugar and Salt Raid."

3:4. P. D. Swick (Bty H, 1st IL), "Those Batteries on Little Kennesaw."

3:5-6. Picket Shots: William Tailby (89th NY), N. Hooper (11th ME), Fort Gregg; R. R. George (5th VT), 4/2/65.

4:7. Obit.

March 5

1:6-7, 2:1. Pope, Part 13.

3:1. D. D. Rose (11th MI), "Capturing a Battery. How the 11th Michigan Took the Copperheads' Cannon." [9/24/64, Sidney, OH]

3:1-2. C. C. Daniels, (Bty B, 4th US), "From a New Regular. One of Steuart's [sic] Battery Gives an Account of 'Old Betsey's' Performances."

3:3. DWD (61st PA), "Marye's Heights, Va."

3:4. J. R. Tisdale (29th MO), "Siege of Vicksburg."

3:4. G. F. Baker (20th PA Cav), "It Was Only a Stampede." [Bath, VA, Sunday duty]

3:5-6. Picket Shots: A. H. Taylor (5th IA Cav), A. M. V. Shockley (10th MO Cav), Wilson's Raid; G. L. Camp (92nd OH), Waynesboro.

4:7. Obit.

March 12

1:4-7. Pope, Part 14.

1:7. John S. Kountz (37th OH), "Anecdote of General Sherman." [Chattanooga]

3:1. C. W. McKay (154th NY), "How They Fought. Bushbeck's Brigade at Chancellorsville."

3:2. Charles Banks (1st OH), "East Tennessee. Stealing Hams and Getting Sick on Bad Flour."

3:2. D. J. Dickson (J. W. Hofmann's aide), "In the Wilderness."

3:3. H. M. Kenderdine (17th IA), "Advance on Corinth. An Iowa Major's Opinion of Gen. Halleck."

3:3. John L. Wells (111th PA), "Found on a Battlefield. Two Photographs Taken from the Knapsack of a Dead Soldier." [from O. S. Kinnear, 83rd PA, Boydton Plank Road, 3/65]

3:4. John M. Geissler (4th MN), "The Old Army. Gen. Bragg One of the Best Officers in the Service."

4:7. Obit.

March 19

1:3. John M. Mahr (7th IL Cav), "The Old Battlefields. How They Look and How the People About Them Talk." [Colliersville, Germantown, Lafayette, Lagrange, Moscow, Grand Jct, Corinth, Saulsbury, Pocahontas]

1:4-7, 2:1. Pope, Part 15.

3:1. Will A. McTeer (3rd TN Cav), "Battle of Decatur. At Least One Instance Where Colored Troops Fought Nobly." [AL, 10/25/64]

3:1-2. David H. Porter (2nd IL Cav), "Retreat on Bolivar."

3:2. John B. Bachelder, "The Regulars. For a Monument to the 6th U. S. Cavalry at Fairfield, Pa."

3:3. Thomas Fay (42nd IL), "Evacuation of Corinth. The First Troops to Enter the Invested Town."

3:3-4. Julius Waldschmidt (19th, 152nd IN), "A German Comrade."

3:4. J. M. Gardner (12th IL Cav), "A Nice Little Raid. When the 12th Illinois and 2nd N.Y. Cavalry Got Within Sight of Richmond." [1863]

3:5-6. Picket Shots: Charles C. Calahan (4th OH), Gettysburg; J. P. Barron (32nd IL), James Boston (33rd IL), Grand Junction; James Van Houtin (9th IL Cav), Smith's Raid.

4:7. Obit.

8:4. Biog: John M. Palmer.

March 26

1:6-7, 2:1-2. William J. Landram, "Red River Campaign."

4:1-2. Wyman W. Holden (2nd NH), "Gettysburg. An Infantryman Confirms Capt. Hart's Story."

4:2-3. MWH (IL), "Kilpatrick's Raid."

4:3-4. Orlando Dunning (5th ME), "Gaines's Mill."

4:5. Picket Shots: Samuel Hayes (64th OH), Spring Hill; Francis J. Canaty (10th NY), Gaines' Mill; John C. Robbins (89th NY), Fort Gregg.

5:4. "A War-Time Letter. Brief Summary of Part of the Vicksburg Campaign." [O. H. Ross, 20th IL, to Jesse R. Grant, 6/63]

6:7. Obit.

7:2. Obit: Joseph E. Johnston.

10:3. Biog: Charles H. Freeman (141st NY).

April 2

1:1-6. E. T. Lee (41st IL), "The Battle of Shiloh."

1:6-7, 2:1-4. W. H. Sanderson (2nd US), "Sykes's Regulars. The Part They Took in the Gettysburg Campaign."

3:1-2. M. W. Walden (8th IA Cav), "The McCook Raid."

3:2. James Beale (12th MA), "Gettysburg. The Part of the Line Occupied by Carroll's Brigade."

3:2-3. G. L. Cruikshank (11th PA Cav), "Swift Retribution. A Severe Lesson Taught Rebel Bushwhackers." [Suffolk, 6/63]

3:3-4. S. M. Howard (28th IA), "'Why Did They Go?' and the Gallant Battle on the Hatchie River."

3:4. John V. Ruehle, Jr. (2nd MI), "Origin of the Badge Idea."

3:5. Picket Shots: F. Sholley (209th PA), Fort Stedman; Levi Mott (18th MO), Resaca.

6:7. Obit.

7:3. "Veterans in the City." [flag returned from SC to 97th Ohio]

7:4. Obit: Hannibal Day (6th US), James A. Ekin (12th PA, AQM).

10:2. Biog: E. B. Huse (15th NH).

April 9

1:1-7, 2:1-3. Leslie J. Perry (2nd WI), "A Study of Bull Run. The First Great Battle of the War of the Rebellion."

3:1-3. Judson Knight (chief scout, Army of the Potomac), "A Scout's Adventures. A Criticism of the Book 'Heroic Deeds by Blue and Gray'."

3:4. E. J. Wentz (9th OH Cav), "Battle of Waynesboro."

3:4. John O. Donald (14th IN), "The Wilderness. To What Battery Did the Two Guns belong?"

6:7. Obit.

10:1. Biog: Samuel L. Miller (20th ME), C. D. Parker (113th OH).

12:2. Obit: Albert Pike.

April 16

1:1-7, 2:1-2. Aquila Wiley (41st OH), "Sherman's Inaction. A Discussion of the Movements About Mission Ridge."

4:1. Giles H. Hamlin (1st MO Cav), "Prairie Grove, Ark."

4:1-2. James Delaney (96th PA), "At Petersburg. The Work Done by the Sixth Corps For Its Capture."

4:2. Clinton Beckwith (121st NY), "Capture of Petersburg."

4:2-3. Adam Herzinger (39th NJ), "Fort Mahone." [4/2/65]

4:3. E. L. Hobart (28th IL), "Mysterious Movement. [9/62]

4:4. W. E. Webster (1st NY Bty), "Cowan's Battery. Sergeant Webster at Cedar Creek, and the Guidon of McKnight's Battery."

4:4. Theodore Kluge (16th IL Cav), "Saving Porter's Fleet. A 16th Illinois Cavalryman Carries a Message to the Admiral from Sherman."

6:7. Obit.

April 23

1:1-6. M. W. Walden (8th IA Cav), "The Lost Brigade. Experiences of Croxton's Command in Northern Alabama." [3/65]

1:7, 2:1-3. Briscoe Goodheart (Loudoun Rangers), "Early's Invasion."

3:1. E. R. Graham (56th PA), "The Wilderness."

3:2. Theodore F. Northrop, "Gen. Rhett's Capture, As Told by the Man Who Took Him to Sherman." [Chief of Scouts to Kilpatrick]

3:2. J. P. Ross (78th OH), "Only Little Things, But the Impressions Made by Them Still Linger with Us." [F. P. Blair]

3:3. Silas Crowell (93rd OH), "East Tennessee. More Sick Wheat Bread Mixed with Honey."

3:3. William W. Watkins (5th IA Cav), "Correcting Gen. Minty." [Kilpatrick's Raid]

3:4. James A. McQuown (11th PA), "Gallant Boys. A Mess of the 11th Pa. that was Nearly Wiped Out."

3:4. B. Durant, "The Fugitive Slave Tom Sims." [Gen. Devens's obit]

3:5-6. Picket Shots: Trueman Proper (37th IL), Chalk Bluff, MO; Isaac Scofield (USN), Fort Sumter boat attack.

4:7. Obit.

5:1. Obit.

5:2. Obit.

April 30

1:1-5. James H. Harold (1st NY Eng), "Reducing Fort Sumter."

3:1. James Colledge (146th NY), "The Wilderness."

3:1-2. John H. Connell (7th VA Cav), "A Cavalry Fight. A Confederate Tells of the Collision Between the 7th Va. and 6th U. S. Cavalry." [Fairfield, PA]

3:2. W. H. Quay (68th PA), "Still in Error." [Gettysburg article by Capt. Hart]

3:2-3. John A. Murphy (89th NY), "Who Went with Burnside's Spy to His Home in North Carolina?"

3:3. (10th NY Hvy Art), "Between the Lines. A Terrible Experience of a N.Y. Comrade Before Richmond." [Petersburg siege]

3:4. Ira B. Goodrich (21st MA), "Helped Save the Day. [Wilderness]

3:5-6. Picket Shots: C. L. Riddle (Bty G, 1st OH), Spring Hill.

4:7. Obit.

May 7

1:1-5. Jesse H. Jones (60th NY), "Lookout Mountain."

3:1-2. William R. Lebert (1st IA Bty), "Gen. McPherson's Death."

3:2-3. W. S. Parr (33rd WI), "Fort DeRussy."

3:3. Louis C. Fisher (51st PA), "Traded Muskets."

3:3-4. (11th WI), "Fort Blakely."

3:4. W. S. Wickham (55th OH), "Gettysburg."

3:4. G. W. Rich (105th PA), "A Comrade of the Wildcat Regiment Places the Troops in the [Peach] Orchard."

3:5-6. Picket Shots: M. J. Riddle (3rd IA), N. E. Powell (41st IL), Grand Junction; C. P. Post (57th PA), Wilderness.

4:7. Obit.

May 14

1:1-5. Augustus Buell (Bty B, 4th US), "The Battle Month. The 'Bloody May' of Eighteen and Sixty-four."

3:1-2. "In the Valley. Charge of the 8th N.Y. Cavalry at Waynesboro." [conversation between Gen. Wharton and Major H. B. Compson]

3:2. J. N. McMaster (9th OH Cav), "Battle of Jonesboro, As Seen by a Orderly at Gen. Howard's Headquarters."

3:2. G. R. Leonard (29th OH), "A Balky Mule."

3:2-3. P. P. Wilson [5th CT], "'Hooker's Ironclads.' How the First Division, Twentieth Corps, Got that Name."

3:3. W. D. Ford (8th MI), "Fort Sanders."

3:3-4. R. H. G. Minty (4th MI Cav), "Kilpatrick's Raid."

3:4. Charles H. Myerhoff (14th IN), "Sprigg Carroll. Humorous Traits in 'Old Bricktop's' Character."

3:5-6. Picket Shots: G. N. Chaffee (50th PA), Wilderness.

4:7. Obit.

6:6. Biog: William B. Russell (8th NH).

May 21

1:1-6, 2:5-6. Buell, Part 2.

3:1-2. Frank W. Mix (4th MI Cav), "Kilpatrick's Raid."

3:2. H. C. Lines, "A Critic Criticized. Comrade H. C. Lines Replies to Comrade W. L. Gardner."

3:3. George H. Uhler (93rd PA), "The Wilderness."

3:3-4. J. J. Fitzgerald, "The California Boys. How They Marched and Sang Going to Canby's Relief." [Fort Craig]

3:4. JEW (3rd WV), "Was He In Fault? Gen. Miles's Surrender at Harper's Ferry, Va."

3:5-6. Picket Shots: William Simmons (USS *Brooklyn*), chain armor.

4:7. Obit.

5:4. Obit: Wells W. Leggett (78th OH).

8:3. Obit: Lewis M. Dayton (AAG on Sherman's staff).

May 28

1:1-6, 2:3. Buell, Part 3.

3:1. Charles M. Castle (102nd OH), "In North Carolina. How Harrison's Brigade Put Rhett's Artillery to Flight."

3:1-2. N. B. Easton (20th IN), "The Wilderness."

3:2. George W. Cooper (6th US Cav), "That Cavalry Fight." [Fairfield]

3:2. Isaac K. Young (89th IL), "Stones' River. A Vindication of Gen. R. W. Johnson in that Battle."

3:3. J. D. McGarraugh (14th IA), "The Battle of Shiloh."

3:3. H. W. Phelps (95th OH), "Fort Blakely."

3:3-4. D. D. Finch (3rd IA), "An Iowa Man Disagrees with Comrade Hobart." [9/62 movement]

3:4. Will A. McTeer (3rd TN Cav), "Smith's Raid."

3:5. Picket Shots: J. E. Conn (4th US Cav), Kilpatrick's Raid; Jacob Smith (6th IN), Garnett's death; F. W. Goodyear (7th CT), Andersonville Raiders; Charles Smith (16th US), Jonesboro.

4:7. Obit.

June 4

1:1-6, 2:5. Buell, Part 4.

3:1-3. J. William Hofmann (56th PA), "The Wlderness."

3:3. A. L. Soule (10th MI Cav), "John Morgan's Death."

3:4. James H. Harold (1st NY Eng), "In the Far South. The Post Bakery at Hilton Head, S.C."

3:4. GWF (68th IN), "Out on a Lark." [7/4/64]

3:5-6. Picket Shots: E. A. Gilbert (102nd IL), Resaca; Henry H. Perry (14th US), Gaines' Mill; W. L. Gardner (110th OH), Monocacy; James Orr (20th WI), Prairie Grove.

4:7. Obit.

6:1. Biog: Henry N. Fanton (23rd CT).

June 11

1:1-6. Buell, Part 5.

3:1-2. John Wilson (8th KY), "Lookout Mountain."

3:2. E. S. Norvell (6th MD), "Petersburg." [4/2/65]

3:2-3. George W. Thorne (11th PA), "A Fighting Regiment. A Pa. Comrade has an Interview with Belle Boyd."

3:3. C. S. Sargeant, "Sherman's Inaction." [Missionary Ridge]

3:4. C. T. Trowbridge (33rd USCT), "Way Down South. Foraging from a Dago in S.C."

3:4. George H. Warner (134th NY), "Chancellorsville."

3:5-6. Picket Shots: Andrew Henderson (5th IA), Iuka.

4:7. Obit.

6:1. Biog: S. G. Hillis (4th KY).

June 18

1:1-6, 2:6. Buell, Part 6.

3:1-2. Solomon Rousculp (126th OH), "Petersburg." [4/2/65]

3:2. J. H. Russell (IA), "Black River Bridge."

3:2-3. B. H. Tripp (7th WI), "The Iron Brigade. They Opened the Battle of Gettysburg."

3:3. James J. Lowden (6th US Cav), "Fight at Fairfield."

3:3. E. A. Pendleton, "The 9th Ohio Battery at Mill Springs, Ky."

3:4. M. M. Rogerson (3rd IA Cav), "Wilson's Raid. The Charge Made by Co. F, 3rd Iowa Cav., at Plantersville, Ala."

3:4. (69th NY), "Gen. George B. McClellan. An Opinion of the Little Napoleon by an Irish Veteran."

3:5. George E. Dolton (Bty M, 1st IL), "Battle of Adairsville."

3:5. James Cosgriff (USMC), "Fort Sumter."

3:6-7. Picket Shots: R. B. Wallace (1st CO Cav), A. F. Brown (2nd CO Cav), Pidgeon Range.

3:7. "The 'Lady Slocumb.' [Spanish Fort]

4:7. Obit.

5:4. Obit: Robert S. Widdicomb (29th MO).

8:2. "Andrews Raiders. Ohio's Tribute to the Gallant Band Unveiled at Chattanooga."

8:3. Obit: John McNeil; William B. Barton (4th NY).

June 25

1:1-3. William J. Landram, "Recollections of Gen. William T. Sherman."

3:1-2. Jesse H. Jones (60th NY), "Lookout Mountain." [letters received from Lewis Blundin (28th PA), James M. Carr (69th OH), H. W. Brandle (3rd MO, Osterhaus's orderly).

3:2-3. George E. Dolton (Bty M, 1st IL), "Chickamauga."

3:3. William H. Nichols (7th Sqdn RI Cav), "Harper's Ferry."

3:3. W. A. Pratt (48th OH), "Battle of Shiloh."

3:4. P. Playford (12th NY Bty), "The Grand Patrol. An Experience on the Sacred Soil of Virginia."

3:5-6. Picket Shots: George W. Bandy (12th IL Cav), Red River; Samuel Keenan (124th OH), Chattanooga; E. J. Wentz (9th OH Cav), Averysboro.

3:7. Joseph H. Vantine (USS *Richmond*), "On Deck, There. From the Man Who Originated the Chain-cable Idea."

4:6. Obit: Edward Whelahan (1st CT Cav).

4:7. Obit.

6:2. Biog: A. M. Warner (37th MA).

6:3. Biog: Donald G. Lovell (3rd MI, 6th MI Cav).

July 2

1:1-6, 2:6-7. I. B. Webster (10th KY), "Chickamauga."

3:1-2. L. B. Smith (4th MI Cav), "Kilpatrick's Raid."

3:2. Briscoe Goodheart (Loudoun Rangers), "Not Justifiable. Gen. Miles's Surrender at Harper's Ferry."

3:2. M. J. Stearns (106th NY), "Monocacy."

3:3. Samuel J. Henderson (4th IN Bty), "Confederate Forces. Where the 'Lost Cause' Got the Men to Fight Their Battles."

3:3. H. N. Minnigh (1st PA Res), "Gettysburg. What Troops Fought in the Peach Orchard."

3:4. Augustus Buell, "Who is Right? The Cannoneer Asks Col. Whitaker to Make Further Investigation."

3:4. B. F. Johns (49th PA), "Brown's House." [Spotsylvania]

3:5. John N. Beach (40th OH), "Lookout Mountain."

3:6-7. Picket Shots: E. W. Dayton (36th WI), Cold Harbor; J. C. Davis (85th PA), Fort Gregg; William R. Price (39th NJ), Petersburg; D. H. Chase (17th US), Gettysburg; W. C. McD. (7th MN), Resaca.

4:7. Obit.

5:4. Obit: George Thom (Halleck's topographical engineer).

5:5. Biog: F. G. Butterfield (6th VT).

July 9

1:1-5, 2:3-6. Robert McCully (81st NY), "Prison Experiences. What a Drummer Boy Suffered in Andersonville and Florence."

3:1-3. J. K. McChesney (23rd IL), "Siege of Lexington."

3:3-4. Thomas Ransom (1st NY Mtd Rifles), "In Old Virginia."

3:4. Jesse Tobias, "A Nervy Fellow. The Way a Youngster Marched Three Johnny Rebs Into Camp." [about A. A. Bartow, 145th OH]

3:4. Louis Abend (5th US Cav), "At Gaines's Mills."

3:5-7. Picket Shots: C. A. Story (3rd VT Bty), Fort Gregg.

4:7. Obit.

5:5. Obit: Hannibal Hamlin.

6:1. Biog: George W. Martin (25th OH).

6:3. Biog: William R. Smedberg (14th US).

July 16

1:6-7, 2:1-2. Theodore F. Lang (3rd WV), "Loyal Mountaineers. Intense Patriotism of the West Virginians."

3:1. A. W. Peck, "From the 17th Conn. as to the Position of the 4th Ohio—A Reply to Comrade Raines." [Gettysburg]

3:1. W. M. Jones (12th IL), "A Sixteenth Corps Kick." [Atlanta]

3:1. George W. Ferree (59th OH), "T. J. Wood's Division." [Chattanooga]

3:2. W. W. DeHaven (16th WI), "Battle of Atlanta."

3:2. James Stewart (Bty B, 4th US), "'The Old Man' Sustains the Cannoneer Regarding the Todd's Tavern Fight."

3:2-3. O. S. Barrett (4th MI), "A Miracle. St. Patrick Down on the Rappahannock."

3:3. Michael Dunn (199th PA), "Fort Gregg Again."

3:3-4. William M. Robbins (4th AL), "Battle of Antietam. What Became of Lieut. Petrikin's Watch?"

3:4. Joseph F. Carter (3rd MD), "'Little Napoleon.' A Maryland Yank's View of the Great Organizer."

3:5-6. Picket Shots: Charles Winters (USN), chain cable armor.

3:7. Max Vache (6th MO), "Badly Scared. How Two Rebel Soldiers were Frightened by a Cow."

3:7. (88th PA), "An Unfortunate Name." [Jacob Hell]

4:7. Obit.

6:2. Biog: A. J. Cahagan (1st TN Cav).

July 23

1:6-7, 2:1. Lang, Part 2.

3:1-2. J. K. McChesney (23rd IL), "Mosby's Guerrillas. A Scouting Adventure Attended by a Narrow Escape."

3:2. P. Winsor (29th MA), "Gen. John E. Wool."

3:3. W. S. Ayres (78th OH), "The Position Held by the Seventeenth Corps July 22."

3:3. W. A. Pratt (48th OH), "Battle of Shiloh."

3:4. W. H. Booth (4th IA), "Haynes' Bluff."

3:4. G. E. Dolton (Bty M, 1st IL), "Weather Observations. What Happened After Certain Big Battles."

3:4. John W. Parker (28th NC), "Battle of Cold Harbor."

3:5-6. Picket Shots: George S. Daughanbaugh (14th US), Gaines' Mill; John J. Thorp (6th US Cav), Fairfield; John S. Pierce (20th WI), Prairie Grove.

4:7. Obit.

5:2. Obit: Benjamin F. Kelley.

6:1-2. Biog: I. H. Duval (1st, 9th WV), S. H. Hurst (73rd OH), Albert J. Fountain (1st CA).

8:5. Obit: Thomas M. Browne (7th IN Cav).

July 30

1:7, 2:1-4. Lang, Part 3. [McDowell]

3:1. Alexander Thompson (61st PA), "Marye's Heights."

3:1-2. Hugh T. Carlisle (81st OH), "W. H. L. Wallace's Division at Shiloh."

3:2. Augustus Wentz (14th NY Hvy Art), "The Wilderness."

3:2. Thomas M. Scaggs (2nd IA Cav), "The Smith Raid."

3:3. "McPherson's Death."

3:4. Thomas N. Murphy (60th NY), "Lookout Mountain."

3:4. John T. Williams (32nd OH), "Harper's Ferry."

3:5-6. Picket Shots: E. L. Morris (5th NY Cav), L. F. Packard (5th NY Cav), Isaac N. Holland (99th PA), William P. Haines (12th NJ), Wilderness; L. P. Butler (Bty K, 2nd IL), Decatur.

4:7. Obit.

5:4. Obit: Madison M. Walden (6th IA, 8th IA Cav).

August 6

3:1-2. E. H. Vaughan (6th VA Cav), "Battle of Fairfield, Pa."

3:2. Wilbert Jones, "Fort Gregg Again." [father was in 12th WV]

3:3. B. M. Barnes (7th WI), "The Wilderness. Another Account of What Took Place on the Plank Road."

3:3. L. S. Tyler (15th IA), "Crocker's Iowa Brigade. An Opinion of Their Fighting Qualities by Cleburne's Adjutant-General."

3:3. B. F. Rogers (chaplain), "The Pious 15th Illinois."

3:4. Edward W. Whitaker (1st CT Cav), "Who is Right? Gen. Whitaker Places But Little Confidence in Rebel Official Records."

3:4. William Crane (1st MA Hvy Art), "The Heavy Artillery. A Mass. Comrade Thinks the Cannoneer Mistaken Regarding His Regiment."

3:4. Stephen M. Gaston (9th IN Cav), "Prison Life. An Indiana Comrade Shows Difference of Treatment North and South."

3:5-6. Picket Shots: Warren Goodrich (5th NY Cav), 5/21/64; G. S. Clements (25th OH),

Gettysburg; John W. Fought (199th PA), Fort Gregg.

4:7. Obit.

5:5. "The History of a Flag." [IA regiment]

8:3-4. Andrew McNamar (106th IL), "John A. Hurt. The Gallant Major of the 106th Ill., and the Fighting Chaplain."

8:5. John W. Burnett (4th PA Res), "Battle of Antietam. Who Got the Little Testiment Near the Forks of the Antietam Creek?"

August 13

3:1. H. F. Swick (18th US), "A Critic Criticized. [Chattanooga, versus Jesse Jones]

3:1-2. George E. Dolton (Bty M, 1st IL), "The Youngest Soldier. Dolton Makes Claim for Major Clem, The Drummer Boy of Chickamauga."

3:2. Allan McFee (2nd NY Cav), "Prison Hospitals."

3:2-3. J. A. Fitchpatrick (3rd IA), "Battle of Atlanta."

3:3. A. B. Balch (54th IL), "The York Association. An Illinois Soldier Tells How His Surgeon was Murdered."

3:3. FJA, "Fort Blakely."

3:3-4. Alexander Adams (100th PA), "Fort Sanders."

3:4. N. J. Marble (38th WI), "Another Account. A Wisconsin Comrade Tells How the 27th Michigan Captured Fort Mahone."

3:4. Mark Esgar (88th IL), "Adairsville, Ga."

3:5-7. Picket Shot s: Samuel Miller (1st CT Cav), Spotsylvania; George W. Toms (5th NY Cav), Wilderness.

4:5. Biog: John Palmer (91st NY).

4:6. untitled article by J. N. McCurdy (49th OH), regarding Philippi and wounding of Col. Kelley, 1st WV.

4:7. Obit.

4:7. Biog: Henry M. Duffield (9th MI).

August 20

1:7, 2:1-2. Lang, Part 4. [Second Bull Run]

3:1-2. A. M. Matthewson (137th NY), "Lookout Mountain."

3:2. Thomas B. Hildebrand (49th PA), "At the Bloody Angle."

3:2-3. L. W. Baker (9th MA Bty), "Held as Hostages. How Union Officers were Confined in Confederate Dungeons." [11/61]

3:3. "Old Salisbury. The Spot Described by a Comrade as It Now Looks."

3:4. W. W. Perry (82nd PA), "At Petersburg." [4/2/65]

3:4. J. B. Evans (102nd PA), "Wheaton's Brigade was in the Lead at the Wilderness."

3:5-6. Picket Shots: John Towle (1st US Vet Vols), Hancock's Corps; William J. Spencer (39th IL), Fort Gregg.

4:7. Obit.

6:5. Biog: T. S. Clarkson (Bty A, 1st IL; 13th IL Cav; 3rd AR Cav).

August 27

1:7, 2:1-2. Lang, Part 5. [Front Royal]

3:1-3. (11th IA), "Battle of Atlanta."

3:3. JEW, "Miles's Surrender."

3:3. Thomas Prothero (142nd PA), "One of the Youngest." [John Hendeshott of Co. G]

3:4. R. M. Fulton (25th OH), "Chancellorsville."

3:5-6. Picket Shots: Morgan Hughes (8th IL Cav), Gettysburg; W. D. Eldred (11th PA), regimental story.

3:7. William M. Robbins (4th AL), "Lieut. Petrikin Again. His Watch Recovered, But What Became of His Sword?"

4:7. Obit.

6:1. Biog: Judson Spofford (10th VT), M. W. Mann (Bty E, 2nd IL).

September 3

1:7, 2:1-4. Lang, Part 6. [Blenker and Bayard]

3:1-2. James H. Harold (1st NY Eng), "In the Far South. Bombardment of the Rebel Batteries at Pensacola, Fla."

3:3. H. Chumley (2nd TN), "East Tennessee. Why Do Historians Pass that Campaign By With But Brief Notice?"

3:3. Thomas Ranson (1st NY Mtd Rifles), "Murdered on Picket."

3:4. C. M. Welch, "Rescued by the 11th Indiana. How Sick and Wounded Soldiers were Removed from an Ice-Bound Ship." [2/65, Martha Washington, near Baltimore]

3:4. Edward Vernon (78th OH), "Dodging Bullets. A Close Call for an Ohio Comrade at Atlanta." [8/64]

3:4. Howard Barwis (119th PA), "Spotsylvania."

3:5-6. Picket Shots: W. W. Sawtelle (6th ME Bty), Wilderness; G. W. Miller (31st OH), Chattanooga; T. J. Jennings (4th IA Cav), Wilson's Raid; Wilson Grey (7th PA Cav), Kilpatrick's Raid.

3:7. C. W. Bennett (9th MI), "Robert Henry Hendershott is All Right." [youngest]

3:7. John F. Chavileer, "What About that Flag?" [70th NY]

4:6. Biog: Donald Gillies (2nd NY, 10th NY Bty).

4:7. Obit.

4:7. Biog: Frederick Phisterer (18th US).

September 10

1:7, 2:1-2. Lang, Part 7. [Cross Keys]

3:1-2. William L. Stork (29th PA), "Gettysburg. Why was Not the Twelfth Corps in the First Day's Fight?"

3:2. Augustus Buell (Bty B, 4th US), "'The Cannoneer' Replies to Critics of Gen. Alexander, C.S.A." [*Detroit Journal* of 8/3]

3:2. EHF, "Did Gen. Farnsworth Kill Himself?"

3:3. Samuel Keenan (124th OH), "Chickamauga."

3:4. G. R. Ames (8th WI), "Spanish Fort."

3:5-6. Picket Shots: Henry M. Day (39th IL), Fort Gregg; C. W. Felter (16th IA), Atlanta.

3:6. Augustus Buell, "Spotsylvania."

4:7. Obit.

6:1. Biog: Horace S. Clark (73rd OH), Timothy McCarthy (3rd US).

September 17

1:7, 2:1-2. William Simmons (USS *Brooklyn*), "Confederate Rams. Their Con- struction, Operations, and Final Disposition." [CSS *Webb*, *Stonewall*, *Atlanta*).

3:1-2. George H. Stowits (100th NY), "Fort Gregg."

3:2-3. Lewis Blundin (28th PA), "Lookout Mountain."

3:3. M. T. Pate (16th IL), "'General Pope's Pets.' A Regiment of Sunday School Teachers."

3:3-4. Manning F. Force, "Battle of Atlanta."

3:4. John H. Connell (7th VA Cav), "Fairfield Again."

3:4. "The Cannoneer. He is Profoundly Grateful for the Thanks of the 4th Ohio."

3:5-6. Picket Shots: H. I. Rhodes (100th PA), Wilderness; Rollin L. Jones (27th OH), Chickamauga, capture of General Adams.

3:6. Augustus Buell, "Gettysburg. The Troops that led the Advance of the First Corps to the Battlefield."

3:6. S. C. Wright (29th MA), "Fort Sanders."

4:7. Obit.

6:1-2. Biog: W. H. H. Clayton (124th PA), C. L. Eaton (67th, 74th IL, 23rd NY Bty), George W. Cook (50th, 140th IN).

September 24

1:6-7, 2:1-2. Simmons, Part 2. [CSS *Arkansas, Palmetto State, Tennessee, Merrimac, Albemarle, Louisiana, Manassas*]

3:1-2. E. Barnum (13th PA Res), "Shenandoah Valley."

3:2. J. A. Reep (19th OH), "Lookout Mountain."

3:2. H. O. Dodge (8th IL Cav), "Opening the Battle. Lieut. Jones, the 8th Ill. Cavalryman, Fired the First Shot at Gettysburg."

3:3. J. T. Williams (32nd OH), "Was Miles a Traitor?"

3:3. William H. Quayle (90th PA), "Rescued from Prison. The Man Who Helped John McGowan Out of Libby." [9/9/62]

3:4. Henry A. Ford, "Drummer Hendershott. Capt. Ford Insists that After Much Research He is a Fraud."

3:4. John H. Anderson (2nd WI), "Rebel Prisons. One of the First to be Confined as a Hostage."

3:5-6. Picket Shots: John O. Donald (14th IN), Wilderness; G. F. Meyer (12th IN), Chattanooga.

3:6. JEW (IN), "Gen. Grant. A Comrade Defends the Military and Private Life of the Great Commander."

3:7. Frank Doyle (1st VT Cav), "Did Not Commit Suicide." [Farnsworth]

3:7. Obit: Isaac F. Quinby.

4:7. Obit.

6:1. Biog: John W. Welsh (USN), ALbert E. Sholes (1st RI), Arthur A. Smith (52nd MA), George G. Boyer (69th PA).

6:7. Biog: S. M. Long (72nd PA).

October 1

1:1-6, 2:5. William E. Keyes, "The River Flotilla. Experiences on Board the Indianola and the Chillicothe."

1:7, 2:1-2. R. H. G. Minty, "Capture of Selma."

3:1-2. James H. Harold (1st NY Eng), "Wilson's Zouaves. Their Warm Reception to Gen. Anderson on Santa Rosa Island."

3:2. J. Shaw (95th PA), "Crampton's Gap."

3:2. O. F. Lyon (85th PA), "Another Premonition." [H. T. Reynolds, Co. A, 6/17/64]

3:3. Isaac K. Young (89th IL), "Mission Ridge."

3:4. W. H. Martin (93rd OH), "Death of Col. Richmond. He was Killed by a Member of the 93rd Ohio." [Col. M. B. Richmond, Gen. Polk's Chief of Staff, at Chickamauga]

3:4. Bruce Robinson, (124th IN), "An Indiana Comrade Who is Another 'Youngest Soldier'."

3:4. John N. Colsher (1st KY CSA), "Wilson's Raid. The Statement of a Confederate Officer in Regard to It."

3:4. H. O. Crosby, "The 5th U.S. Cavalry. Its Losses are Unknown, as Its Records were Destroyed."

3:5-6. Picket Shots: Louis C. Fisher (51st PA), Peebles' Farm.

3:6. O. F. Chase (8th WI), "A Touching Incident of the Heroism and Sacrifices Displayed During the War by Noble Women." [Corinth]

4:7. Obit.

6:1. Biog: Seymour Bullock (24th NY Cav), Charles H. Freeman (141st NY).

October 8

1:1-5. J. N. Terrill (14th NJ), "Shenandoah Valley. The Movement from Petersburg to Baltimore. Battle of Monocacy."

1:6-7, 2:1-2. William L. Welch, "Yellow Fever. The Great Epidemic at New Berne in 1864."

3:1-3. Judson Knight, "Gen. Phil Kearny."

3:3. Thomas Holt, Ransom Gaylord, John N. Coyne, "Flag of Co. C, 70th N.Y."

3:3. H. M. Jones (18th MA), "The Wilderness. What Troops Opened the Fight in the Brush?"

3:3. W. H. Walters (188th PA), "Last Call Man."

3:4. C. H. Osgood (4th USCT), "A Sutler's Clerk."

3:5-6. Picket Shots: R. E. Adams (2nd VT), Gettysburg.

3:6-7. B. F. Magee, "Around Atlanta. How the Second Cavalry Division Came Up from the Rear."

3:7. James E. Chaffee, "Craven House Guns." [Lookout Mountain]

4:7. Obit.

5:4. Obit: William McKee (67th, 83rd IN).

6:1. Biog: A. J. Woodman (2nd ME Cav), C. L. Davidson (27th IA).

8:6. Obit: W. B. Curtis (12th WV).

October 15

1:1-6, 2:6. Terrill, Part 2. [Winchester, Fisher's Hill]

1:7, 2:1-2. Rudolph S. Sommers (USN), "Exciting Adventures. Reconnaissances in North Carolina Waters. Capture of Plymouth."

3:1. H. W. Clarke (185th NY), "Who was He? An Unknown Cavalryman Killed at Appomattox as the White Flag Appeared."

3:1. H. H. Quiggle (14th OH), "Chickamauga."

3:1. Delos Robinson (129th IL), "A Flank Movement at Averysboro."

3:2. Charles Stacey (55th OH), "[John] Umbaugh the Guerrilla."

3:2. R. Baldwin, "The 8th N.Y. Heavy Artillery."

3:3. J. B. Kennedy (100th PA), "Fort Sanders."

3:3. M. C. Connett (7th IN), "Death of Gen. Garnett. The First Rebel General Killed in the Late War."

3:3-4. George T. Hoyt (140th NY), "A War-Time Letter. A Description of the Battle of Chancellorsville by a Soldier on the Field."

3:4. W. L. Greenleaf (1st VT Cav), "Spotsylvania."

3:5-6. Picket Shots: Morgan Hughes (8th IL Cav), Farnsworth at Gettysburg; P. Himrod (105th OH), capture of General Adams at Chickamauga.

3:6-7. Garner Stimsen (3rd OH Cav), "Kilpatrick's Raid."

4:7. Obit.

5:2. Obit: Greene Durbin (13th IN).

October 22

1:1-6, 2:5-6. E. R. Monfort (75th OH), "Chancellorsville. A Defense of the First Division, Eleventh Corps."

1:7, 2:1-3. Sommers, Part 2. [Cushing]

4:1-2. John H. Dye (115th NY), "Was Miles a Traitor?"

4:2. E. J. Hartshorn (17th VT), "Last Call Troops."

4:3. J. E. Williams, "Gettysburg. The Results that Led to This Great Fight."

4:3. J. H. Johnson (50th IN), "Parker's Cross Roads."

4:3. James G. Boardman (19th IL), "Missionary Ridge."

4:4. W. E. McCreary (81st OH), "Battle of Atlanta."

4:4. - - Beach (2nd NY Vet Cav), "Last Battle of the War." [Talladega, AL, 7/65]

4:4. WSP (20th WI), "Another Fighting Chaplain."

4:5-6. Picket Shots: James Flynn (69th NY), Cold Harbor; W. J. Britton (32nd MO), March to the Sea; William Telfor (USS *Canandaigua*), concerning USS *Mercedita*; Milton Laird 5th PA Res), Lt. Petrikin.

6:7. Obit.

7:3. Obit: Charles G. McCawley (USMC).

7:5. Obit: W. H. F. Lee, Duncan N. Ingraham (CSN).

October 29

1:1-6, 2:4-5, 3:4-5. Abner Doubleday, "Anecdotes."

1:7, 2:1-3. S. H. M. Byers (5th IA), "Letters from Libby."

4:1-2. Aquila Wiley (41st OH), "Battle Statistics. Comparison of Losses at Chickamauga and Gettysburg."

4:2. George E. Bryant (1st CT Cav), "Gen. Whitaker Right."

4:3. William L. Norton (10th CT), "Fort Gregg Again."

4:3. David H. Smith (20th PA Cav), "One of the Rescued." [ice-bound Martha Washington]

4:4. J. B. Potter (83rd PA), "Gettysburg. A Comrade Who Helped Drag Artillery Up Round Top."

4:4. W. H. Wiley (1st WV), "Gen. Kelley's Wound." [Philippi]

4:5. George W. Toms (5th NY Cav), "Visiting Old Scenes. A N.Y. Cavalryman Goes Over the Virginia Battlefields."

4:6-7. Picket Shots: R. J. Vermillion (12th WV), Fort Gregg; George L. Woolsey (179th NY), Fort Mahone.

6:7. Obit.

10:1. Biog: James R. Milliken (35th IN), William A. Bentley (9th IA), David L. Morgan (1st MN).

November 5

1:1-6. John Pope, "Secretary Seward."

4:1-2. S. Hendrick (Bty C, 1st OH), "Chickamauga."

4:2. Joseph A. Moore (4th NY cav), "Shenandoah Valley. The Troops that Attacked Jackson's Rear on the Night of June 1, 1862."

4:2-3. S. A. McNeil (31st OH), "Were They Demoralized? A Claim that the Army of the Cumberland had Lots of Fight Left." [Chickamauga]

4:3. (11th WI), "Black River Bridge."

4:3. J. B. Kirk (101st PA), "Treatment of Prisoners."

4:4. J. T. Marlan (40th OH), "Another Claim. [flag on Lookout Mountain]

4:4. Henry J. Hunt, "Meade's Intentions." [Gettysburg, letter to Alexander S. Webb]

4:5-6. Picket Shots: Samuel Books (49th IN), Big Black River; Robert C. Porter (105th OH), capture of General Adams at Chickamauga; B. Cunningham (19th IN), Gettysburg; Elisha B. Seaman (60th OH), Chattanooga.

6:7. Obit.

10:1. Biog: C. O. Parker (113th OH).

November 12

1:1-4. James H. Harold (1st NY Eng), "The Swamp Angel."

1:6-7, 2:1-3. Frank E. Moran (73rd NY), "About Gettysburg."

4:1. E. T. Lee (41st IL), "The Charge at Jackson."

4:2. P. K. Faulk (11th PA), "Hartsuff's Brigade."

4:2-3. A. Lammey, "The 88th Illinois. Another Regiment Claims to have Planted Its Flag First on Missionary Ridge."

4:3. William Edmonds (4th WV), "Snicker's Ford, W. Va." [7/18/64]

4:3. J. S. Lerch (39th OH), "Parker's Cross Roads."

4:4. Harry Hunterson (88th PA), "As to Gen. McDowell. A Comrade Thinks He Either a Traitor or a Poor General."

6:7. Obit.

10:2. Biog: W. H. Upham (2nd WI).

November 19

1:1-6. Jonathan Roberts, "The Quaker Scout. Life in the Old Dominion Before and During the War."

1:7, 2:1-4. Alexander C. Byerly, "The Mississippi Marine Brigade."

4:1-2. E. C. Winters (34th IL), "Buzzard's Roost Gap."

4:2. H. N. Minnigh (1st PA Res), "Who Occupied It? A Discussion of the Movements About the Round Tops."

4:2-3. William T. Cook (1st CT Cav), "Spotsylvania."

4:3. J. E. Williams (VRC), "Fair Criticisms. Tampering with Military Reputations Should be Done Carefully."

4:3. L. W. Baker (9th MA Bty), "The Hostages. Their Last Days in Prison, and How They were Exchanged." [Libby]

4:4. SMT (5th NH), "Cold Harbor."

4:4. D. J. Dickson, "The 56th Pa. Capt. Dickson's Claim for Them of Opening the Battle of Gettysburg.

4:5-6. Picket Shots: L. Blundin (28th PA), Ringgold; W. E. Lines (Bty C, 5th US), Gettysburg.

4:6. M. W. Lindsley (1st NY Dragoons), "In the Wilderness."

5:5. E. R. Beebe, "The First Interment at Arlington."

6:7. Obit.

12:4. Obit: John Hossack (underground RR in IL).

November 26

1:1-6, 2:5-6. Roberts, Part 2.

3:5. Eli Davis (40th OH), "Lookout Mountain."

3:5. B. C. Shaw (7th IN), "Wounding of Gen. B. F. Kelley."

4:1-2. Henry E. Clark (29th OH), "Peach Tree Creek."

4:2. Joseph A. Moore (147th PA), "After the Battle. Removing the Wounded from Ringgold to Chattanooga."

4:2-3. John R. King, "Convincing Testimony. The 6th Md. Wants a Share of the Glory of Capturing Petersburg."

4:3. James Holehouse (7th ME), "Marye's Heights."

4:3. Edward Armstrong (139th PA), "In the Wilderness. Another Account of the Affair at the Brock and Plank Roads."

4:4. Frank E. Hills (100th IL), "Chickamauga."

4:4. L. D. Immell (Bty F, 2nd US), "A Record of Which to be Proud."

4:5-6. Picket Shots: Christian Ehrisman (5th KY), 6/27/64; William E> Sill (3rd US Cav), Fort Craig; Charles L. Moeller (12th MO Cav), Nashville.

6:7. Obit.

7:5. Obit: Allen W. Prather (6th, 120th IN).

12:6. Obit: A. P. Hovey.

December 3

1:1-5. Roberts, Part 3.

3:4. Biog: Joseph E. Palmer, Jr. (158th NY).

4:1-2. S. A. Clark (1st VT Cav), "Farnsworth's Death."

4:2. W. George (139th PA), "Chancellorsville. Placing the Responsibility of the Disaster Where It Belongs."

4:2-3. Coleman H. Watts (7th PA Cav), "Lovejoy Station."

4:3-4. C. H. Myerhoff (14th IN), "In the Wilderness."

4:4. (NH hospital steward), "In the Far South. Ship Island at the Time Gen. Butler's Army Garrisoned that Place."

4:5-6. Picket Shots: James B. Tredwell (85th PA), Fair Oaks; E. T. Sexton (5th NY Hvy Art), Snicker's Gap.

4:6. C. Woodruff (64th OH), "Chickamauga."

December 10

1:7, 2:1-2. A. L. Soule (10th MI Cav), "Scouting in East Tennessee."

2:3-5. Frank G. Carpenter, "Lincoln's Death. New Stories of the Tragedy Which Happened 26 Years Ago."

2:6. "At Gettysburg. Where Soldiers Received Absolution Before Engaging the Enemy." [artist Paul Wood's painting of Father Corby]

4:1-2. John T. Nagle, "Battle of Snicker's Ford."

4:2. T. A. McMorris (86th IL), "Wanted to Get Even. An Officer Who was Willing to Die to have His Superior Punished."

4:2-3. L. W. Bartlett, "The 1st Mass. Cavalry."

4:3. S. Tinker (93rd IN), "The Sixteenth Corps. Some of the Things Smith's Guerrillas Did and Did Not Accomplish."

4:3-4. ECC (Bty D, 5th US), "Gettysburg."

4:4. J. E. Williams (VRC), "Gen. Miles's Character. Several Reasons Why He was Not Guilty of the Crime of Treason."

4:4. Edwin Nicar (15th IN), "Gen. W. H. F. Lee. A Reminiscence of Scouting in the Elkwater Valley."

4:6. Frank Tallman (9th NY Hvy Art), "Union Prisoners." [Danville, VA]

6:7. Obit.

10:5. E. A. LaBay (USMC), "Commodore Ingraham. The Fight of the Rebel ironclads with the Blockading Fleet at Charleston."

December 17

1:1-6, 2:6. Charles A. Hobbs (99th IL), "Vanquishing Vicksburg."

1:7, 2:1-2. James H. Harold (1st NY Eng), "Down in Florida. Restoring the Stars and Stripes to the Land of Flowers. A Bloodless Victory. The Rebels Abandon Fort Clinch and Fernandina."

3:4. (24th IL), "Saving the Country. A Sucker Soldier Found the Best Way to Do It." [hardtack problems]

3:4-5. "In the Old Trenches. How the Vicinity of Petersburg Appears Today—Armstrong's Mill."

3:5-6. John N. Beach (40th OH), "Lookout Mountain."

4:1. (NH hospital steward), Part 2.

4:1-2. James H. Stoutnour (55th PA), "Criticizing the Cannoneer." [Cold Harbor]

4:2. Enoch Barnum (13th PA Res), "In the Valley." [Harrisonburg]

4:4. J. A. Chalaron (Washington Artillery), "Vicksburg Campaign. What a Confederate Soldier Says of the Charge Made by Pugh's Brigade at Jackson, Miss."

4:4. Samuel A. Boyles (18th IN), "A Gallant Officer. Not Afraid of Shot and Shell, But Drew the Line on Minie Balls." [Martin Klaus, 1st IN Bty]

6:7. Obit.

December 24

1:1-6, 2:6. Hobbs, Part 2.

3:1-5. "Their War Histories. Veterans and Non-Veterans in the Present Congress."

4:1-2. Samuel J. Murphey (Bty I, 2nd IL), "Another Good Battery."

4:3. Thomas Hobart (60th NY), "Lookout Mountain."

4:4. William H. Nichols (7th Sqdn RI Cav), "Was Miles a Traitor?"

4:5-6. Picket Shots: J. S. Peckham (7th VT), Spanish Fort; W. G. Hahn (69th OH), James Mott (40th OH), Chattanooga; Edgar C. Petty (9th NY Hvy Art), Danville Prison.

6:7. Obit.

12:2. Obit: William E. Merrill (US Eng), Thomas Patterson (USN).

12:3-4. Obit: Preston B. Plumb (11th KS).

December 31

1:1-6. Hobbs, Part 3.

3:5. "Old Trenches," Part 2.

4:1-2. (NH hospital steward), Part 3.

4:2. J. M. Ray (140th PA), "Cold Harbor."

4:3-4. George E. Dolton (Bty M, 1st IL), "Chickamauga. An Explanation of How the 21st Ohio Came to Be Captured."

4:4. Charles E. Washburn (7th Sqdn RI Cav), "Was Miles a Traitor?"

4:4. E. T. Lee (41st IL), Samuel Pasco (3rd FL), "An Incident of the War. How Two Soldiers

Became Acquainted on the Battlefield During a Flag of Truce." [7/12/63]

4:6. Benton Kelley (8th IL Cav), "Gettysburg. An Account of Who Opened the Battle by One Who was There."

6:7. Obit.

7:4-5. Obit: V. A. J. Crewswell (MD AAG).

7:5. Obit: Edward Allsworth (38th MA, 119th USCT), Albert M. Evans (Bty F, PA).

1892

January 7

1:1-6. Hobbs, Part 4.

2:5-6. Judson Knight (2nd NJ), "The Quaker Scout. Sergt. Knight Goes for the Fighting Friend About the Annandale Map."

3:5. W. H. Smyth (98th OH), "Chickamauga. Articles Taken from a Dead Soldier Returned to Friends After 26 Years."

3:5-6. S. Hendrick (Bty C, 1st OH), "Mill Springs."

4:1. I. K. Young (89th IL), "East Tennessee. What Wood's Division, Fourteenth Corps, did After Missionary Ridge."

4:2-3. Theomuldo B. Vanvado (118th OH), "Hero of the 118th Ohio."

4:3-4. E. M. Watson (9th MI Cav), "A Reconnaissance. How Garrard's Cavalry Ran Into Jenkins's Whole Division." [Spring 1864, Bean Station]

4:5-6. Picket Shots: Henry Boley (191st PA), Danville Prison.

4:6. Fletcher Meredith, "The 7th Indiana Again. A Member of the Regiment Corrects Augustus C. Buell's Account of Its Service."

5:5. Biog: William P. Carlin.

6:5. Biog: R. W. Perkins (83rd IL, 16th USCT).

6:7. Obit.

7:6. Obit: Montgomery C. Meigs

12:1-3. F. G. Carpenter, "With 'Old Rosey.' The Old General Speaks of the War, and Tells New Stories of Its Heroes."

January 14

1:1-6, 2:5-6. Hobbs, Part 5.

1:7, 2:1-2. William L. Welch (23rd MA), "Yellow Fever." [Newbern, NC]

3:3. Obit: Christopher R. P. Rodgers (USN).

4:1-2. JFS (7th MI Cav), "At Brandy Station." [10/11/63]

4:2. J. H. Collier (4th MI Cav), "Kilpatrick's Raid."

4:3. F. S. Dickinson (5th NY Cav), "Death of Sergt. Sortore."

4:3-4. Andrew J. Wadlie (3rd NH), "The Swamp Angel."

6:7. Obit.

7:4. Obit: J. Irvin Gregg."

9:3. Biog: James S. Brisbin (6th US Cav).

January 21

1:1-6. Hobbs, Part 6.

2:4. "Old Trenches," Part 3.

4:1. Sanford W. Lyon (21st MI), "Bentonville, N.C."

4:2-3. Mark Howe (34th OH), "Shenandoah Valley. All the Fighting Not Done by the Sixth Corps, Nor All the Running by the Eighth Corps."

4:3. N. E. Miller (20th IN), "In the Wilderness."

4:3. H. B. York, "9th Ohio Battery." [Mill Springs]

4:5-6. Picket Shots: John W. Osburn (170th OH), Snicker's Ferry; J. H. Russell (23rd IA), Big Black River.

6:7. Obit.

7:6. Obit: James S. Robinson (82nd OH), James S. Brisbin.

9:3-5. "Lee and Longstreet. Their Classmates in West Point, and What Became of Them."

January 28

1:1-6, 2:4-5. Hobbs, Part 7.

4:1-2. J. J. Galbraith (2nd PA Cav), "Gen. John Irvin Gregg."

4:2. John Kelly (2nd US Cav), "Percentage of Losses. Another Estimate of the Forces at Gettysburg and Chickamauga."

4:3. George W. Owen, "The Old 4th Michigan."

4:5-7. Picket Shots: Charles V. Mesler (105th NYH), 2nd Manassas; John Waddell (Bty I, 1st OH), Cross Keys; Alden Brown (2nd IL Cav), Farnsworth at Gettysburg.

5:3. E. Y. Goldsborough, "Barbara Fritchie."

6:7. Obit.

10:5. C. Woodruff (64th OH), "Wide of the Mark. A New Version of the Death of the Rebel Gen. Gregg." [Chickamauga]

10:6-7. A. E. Zeitler (109th PA), "Peach Tree Creek, Ga."

February 4

1:1-6, 2:5-6. Hobbs, Part 8.

1:7, 2:1-4. William Simmons, "The USS *Brooklyn*."

4:1-2. W (PA), "Was He at Fault? Regarding Gen. Miles's Surrender at Harper's Ferry in September, 1862."

4:2. John W. Osburn, "The 170th Ohio."

4:3. T. Benton Kelley (8th IL Cav), "Seven Prisoners. How They were All Captured by One Illinois Cavalryman near Boonsboro, Md." [9/62]

4:3-4. H. C. Wilkins, "A Disgraceful Affair." [Sabine Pass]

4:4. A. Thompson, "The 1st Ohio Cavalry. What They Accomplished During the Battle of Lookout Mountain."

4:5-6. Picket Shots: N. E. Miller (20th IN), Wilderness.

6:7. Obit.

12:3. Obit: Henry A. Barnum (149th NY).

February 11

1:1-6, 2:6. Hobbs, Part 9.

1:7, 2:1-4. Simmons, Part 2.

4:1-2. H. E. Mathews (6th ME), "Marye's Heights."

4:2. J. D. Ferguson (158th NY), "Fort Gregg."

4:3. George Prets (69th OH), "That Battery Again. [Chattanooga]

4:3. H. A. A. Usburn, "The 2nd Tennessee Cavalry. How One of Their Officers Prevented a Stampede at Franklin, Tenn. [1863]

4:4. F. S. Dickinson (5th NY Cav), "Brandy Station, Va." [10/63]

6:7. Obit.

February 18

1:1-6, 2:6. Hobbs, Part 10.

1:7, 2:1-4. Simmons, Part 3.

2:5. William J. Turpin (Bty C, PA), "Comments on McDowell's Conduct at Cedar Mountain."

4:1-2. A. C. McShane (USS *Mississippi*), "Quelling a Mutiny. Admirable Conduct of Army Officers on Board a Transport." [2/65]

4:2. D. S. Baker (20th ME), "At Shepherdstown."

4:2. Thomas Moloney (8th MI), "A War Relic. A Michigan Comrade has a Muster-Roll of the Black-Horse Cavalry."

4:3-4. Burton C. Richardson (17th VT), "Salisbury Prison."

4:4. George E. Dolton (Bty M, 1st IL), "The 89th and 98th Ohio at Chickamauga."

4:5-6. Picket Shots: D. S. Breggs (11th WI), Big Black River; L. L. Scott (18th OH), Chattanooga; (126th PA), Chancellorsville.

6:7. Obit.

7:6. Obit: Peter H. Allabach (131st PA), Alfred M. Scales.

7:7. Biog: Samuel D. Paine (2nd ME Bty).

February 25

1:1-6. Hobbs, Part 11.

1:7, 2:1-3. R. H. G. Minty, "Minty's Saber Brigade. The Part They Took in the Chattanooga Campaign." [Chickamauga also]

4:1. J. B. Potter (83rd PA), "Gettysburg."

4:1-2. George E. Dolton (Bty M, 1st IL), "Chickamauga. Comrade Dolton Still Maintains that It was a Bigger Fight Than Gettysburg."

4:2. B. H. Stillman (Bty B, 4th US), "Captain James Stewart."

4:3-4. Frank Holsinger (8th PA Res), "Christians in War. A Pa. Comrade Who was a Loyal and Religious Soldier." [About Corporal J. B. Linn, 8th PA Res]

4:4. B. S. Bogarolus, "Snicker's Gap."

4:5-7. Picket Shots: William D. Eldred (11th PA), Gettysburg; I. N. Fordyce (1st WV), Kelley's wounding.

6:7. Obit.

9:6-7. I. K. Young (89th IL), "Army of the Cumberland. Oh! No! They were Not Demoralized Nor Starved at Chattanooga."

9:7. R. Flaiz (118th OH), "East Tennessee. How the Army Ate Green Corn, Apples and Sick Wheat."

March 3

1:1-6. Hobbs, Part 12.

1:7, 2:1-3. Minty, Part 2.

2:6. Biog: Thomas Majors (1st NE).

3:1-4. "Almira," "Grant at Home. What the Hero's Life was at Galena, Ill."

4:1-2. F. H. Patton (12th WV), "Fort Gregg Again."

4:2. C. Wood (11th NH), "Fredericksburg. A Confederate Diagram of the Battle Which Has a History."

4:3. William H. Rochelle (2nd NJ Cav), "On the Picket-Post. An Incident that Occurred with Forrest's Cavalry Near Memphis." [9/64]

4:3. P, McEnany (2nd US Dragoons), "Death of Sergt. Sortore."

4:4. W. H. Newlin (73rd IL), "Planting the First Flag on Missionary Ridge."

4:4. Sigmund Elble (16th WV), "Gen. Dixon S. Miles."

4:5-6. Picket Shots: E. D. Patterson (52nd OH), Peach Tree Creek.

6:7. Obit.

March 10

1:1-5. Hobbs, Part 13.

1:6-7, 2:1-3. Israel B. Webster (10th KY), "Missionary Ridge. The Battle Above the Clouds as Seen from Below."

2:3. "An Ironclad Destroyer. Gen. Berdan Invents a Semi Submersible Boat for Harbor Defense."

4:1-2. James Holehouse (7th MA), "Marye's Heights."

4:2-3. John T. Booth (36th OH), "Army of West Virginia. It was Never Connected with the Eighth Corps After June 1863."

4:3-4. RGG (48th PA), "The Mine Explosion."

4:4. George W. Toms (5th NY Cav), "Gen. J. H. Wilson."

4:5-6. Picket Shots: R. Borgnis (1st OH), relief of Knoxville.

6:7. Obit.

March 17

1:1-6, 2:6. Hobbs, Part 14.

1:7, 2:1-4. Frank E. Moran (73rd NY), "War Romance. Rebel Powder Mine at Libby, and the Tunnel Escape."

3:3-4. Biog: John A. Rawlins.

4:1. John Kelly (2nd US Cav), "Another Comparison. Comrade Kelly After Comrade Dolton Regarding Chickamauga and Gettysburg."

4:2-3. I. K. Young (89th IL), "East Tennessee. Movements of Wood's Division from Marysville to Rocky Face Ridge."

4:3. H. M. Kenderdine (17th IA), "A Gallant Charge. Conduct of Holmes's Brigade at the First Capture of Jackson, Miss."

4:4. Jerry Patten, "The 6th Minnesota."

5:3-4. Lizzie J. Beller, "Gettysburg. As the Historic Town Appeared Before and After the Battle."

6:7. Obit.

10:5. "Corps Badges. Gen. Butterfield Explains How He Came to Invent Them."

March 24

1:1-6, 2:5-6. Hobbs, Part 15.

1:7, 2:1-3. Moran, Part 2.

4:1-2. Morgan Hughes (8th IL Cav), "People of Gettysburg. How They Inspired the Cavalry to Do Their Effective Work."

4:2. S. A. McNeil (31st OH), "Army of the Cumberland. How that Gallant Aggregation of Men Always Came Out on Top."

4:2. J. E. Harding (12th WV), "Hell on Earth." [Andersonville]

4:3-4. John T. Nagle, "Snicker's Ford."

4:4. Monroe Daggett (11th ME), "Quelling a Mutiny."

4:4. "Battle of Antietam. Gen. Doubleday Tells What Troops Held the Cornfield."

4:5-7. Picket Shots: J. D. Whitham (12th WV), Fort Gregg; J. C. Morton (184th PA), 6/21/64; William T. Walker (4th DE), Five Forks.

6:7. Obit.

10:2. Biog: Isaac Dyer (15th ME), James K. Churchill (5th MA).

March 31

1:1-6, 2:6. Hobbs, Part 16.

1:7, 2:1-3. D. M. Perry (76th NY), "From the Rapidan to Groveton."

4:1-2. P. C. Smith (119th IL), "A. J. Smith's Guerrillas. Some of the Work They Performed on the Red River Expedition."

4:2. S. M. Gaston (9th IN Cav), "Treatment of Prisoners."

4:2. H. M. Parker (48th USCT), "Marine Brigade. They Evidently Didn't Do All the Fighting at Coleman's Plantation." [7/4/64]

4:3. "The 26th New York."

4:3. E. Crockett (65th NY), "The Sixth Corps."

4:4. James W. Taylor, "The 62nd Illinois."

4:4. R. S. Littlefield (1st MA Hvy Art), "The Charge at Jackson."

4:5-6. Picket Shots: W. W. Tyson (48th PA), Charles Tuttle (48th PA), Levi G. Foss (31st ME), Crater; J. F. Early (3rd MN), first volunteers; Moritz Tschoepe (24th WI), Peach Tree Creek.

6:7. Obit.

April 7

1:1-6, 2:5. Hobbs, Part 17.

1:7, 2:1-2. Edson Brace, "Gen. B. F. Kelley."

4:1-2. R. S. Littlefield, "Col. William B. Greene. Anecdotes of the Commanding Officer of the 1st Mass. Heavy Artillery."

4:2. B. F. Young (125th OH), "The Charge at Franklin."

4:3. Joseph F. Carter (3rd MD), "In the Wilderness."

4:4. J. C. Harris (83rd PA), "'Dr. Crawford' Case. The Officer Who Fought at Sumter and Appomattox Not the Person Who was Drunk." [Hatcher's Run, 2/65]

4:4. (21st IA), "Up the Red River. Where Two Guns of a Famous Battery were Found at the End of the War." [2nd MA Bty]

4:5-6. Picket Shots: William Godfrey (47th IL), Vicksburg; N. F. Endsley (2nd NY Cav), Cedar Creek.

6:7. Obit.

April 14

1:1-6, 2:5. Hobbs, Part 18.

1:7, 2:1-4. Mark Howe (34th OH), "The Lynchburg Raid."

3:3. "The Youngest Colonel." [Col. William Hobson, 13th KY]

4:1. Augustus B. Buell (Bty B, 4th US), "The 'Kids' of Battery B."

4:1. George E. Dolton (Bty M, 1st IL), "The First Flag on Lookout Mountain."

4:2. James R. Mathewson (7th MA), "Marye's Heights."

4:2-3. J. P. Ross (78th OH), "July 22, 1864."

4:3. C. E. Marvin (2nd NY Cav), "Gen. Irvin McDowell."

4:4. A. W. Clyde (27th IA), "The Sixteenth Corps."

4:4. A. W. Clyde (27th IA), "Confederate Backbone. An Outsider Thinks It was Not Broken at Either Chickamauga or Gettysburg."

4:5-6. Picket Shots: James Davis (112th NY), Fort Fisher; James H. Lewis (24th IA), Cedar Creek.

6:7. Obit.

10:1. Biog: Daniel Hall (Howard's staff).

April 21

1:1-6. Hobbs, Part 19.

1:6. "Remains of Gen. Mower Moved to Arlington."

1:7, 2:1-4. F. S. Dickinson (5th NY Cav), "The Wilson Raid."

3:3. Obit: Joseph Daniels (1st MN Cav).

4:1-2. John N. Coyne, "The 70th New York."

4:2. E. T. Lee (41st IL), "The Charge at Jackson."

4:3-4. I. B. Webster (10th KY), "Gen. Zollicoffer's Death."

4:5-6. Picket Shots: J. White (54th OH), Libby Prison; John W. Fought (199th PA), Fort Gregg; Robert A. Shearer (11th PA), 2nd Manassas.

4:6. Jonathan Roberts, "The Quaker Scout."

6:7. Obit.

9:1-2. "An Ex-Rebel's War Recollections." [West Tennessee]

12:4. Obit: Thomas W. Sweeny.

April 28

1:1-6, 2:3-4. (10th OH Cav), "Campaigning Through the Carolinas."

1:7, 2:1. William Simmons, "Confederate Torpedoes."

2:2. Ex-Rebel, Part 2.

4:1-2. W. George (139th PA), "In the Wilderness."

4:2. Charles F. Kimmel (66th IL), "Strength of the Rebel Army."

4:3-4. (1st IA Cav), "Gen. George A. Custer."

4:4. L. J. Cutter (77th OH), "Camp Ford Stockade."

4:4. Thomas Taylor (155th PA), "Little Round Top Saved by the 155th Pa."

4:4. Seth B. Mereness (102nd NY), "The First Troops in Savannah, Ga."

6:7. Obit.

12:5. Obit: William W. Burns.

May 5

1:1-6, 2:5-6. Carolinas, Part 2.

1:7, 2:1-2. James H. Harold (1st NY Eng), "Port Royal, S.C."

3:5. "Medal of Honor. [George D. Sidman, 16th MI]

4:1. F. M. Lee (13th NY Bty), "Peach Tree Creek."

4:2. Alonzo Johnson (82nd PA), "Marye's Heights."

4:3. Jesse M. Pirkle (3rd TN Cav), "Loyal Tennesseans."

4:3-4. S. D. Webster (13th MA), "Gen. Irvin McDowell."

4:4. William Simmons, "Taking Fort Fisher."

5:2-3. J. R. Keyes (5th OH Cav), "The Southern Side, or, Andersonville Prison."

6:7. Obit.

9:1-2. Ex-Rebel, Part 3. [conscription]

May 12

1:1-6, 2:5-6. Carolinas, Part 3.

1:7, 2:1-2. Harold, Part 2.

2:3-4. Ex-Rebel, Part 4.

4:1. James Stewart (Bty B, 4th US), "'The Old Man' Talks About the 'Kids' of His Famous Battery B, 4th U. S. Artillery."

4:2. Charles Banks (1st OH), "Missionary Ridge."

4:2-3. J. N. Gilley (9th NY Cav), "At Brandy Station." [10/63]

4:3-4. B. C. Shaw (7th IN), "Battle of Philippi. An Account of the Wounding of Gen. B. F. Kelley by an Eye-Witness."

4:4. J. Knight (2nd NJ), "That Map Again. Sergeant Knight Replies to the Quaker Scout's Critics."

4:5-6. Picket Shots: G. W. Toms (5th NY Cav), Farnsworth at Gettysburg; T. T. Cooney (Bty K, 1st US), Antietam.

5:3-4. Leslie J. Perry, "Gen. William H. Lytle."

6:7. Obit.

7:6-7. Biog: Calvin Brice (86th, 180th OH).

May 19

1:1-6. M. A. Sweetman (114th OH), "Capture of Blakely."

1:7, 2:1-3. Harold, Part 3.

3:3-4. Ex-Rebel, Part 5.

4:1. A. W. Peck (17th CT), "Gettysburg."

4:1-2. M. F. Ames (7th MA), "Marye's Heights."

4:2. George E. Dolton (Bty M, 1st IL), "That Backbone."

4:3. John Dwyer (63rd NY), "Crampton's Pass."

4:3-4. Charles B. Thomas (5th NY Cav), "Second Bull Run. Another Comrade Thinks McDowell's Actions in that Battle Unaccountable."

4:4. Matt F. Kippax (17th US), "Knew Major Dowling."

4:4. Matt L. Harbison (139th PA), "The Eighth Corps. A Sixth Corps Comrade Testifies to Their Gallantry at Fisher's Hill."

4:5-6. Picket Shots: W. C. Weygant (111th PA), Savannah; P. J. Knapp (5th IA), Vicksburg.

4:6. Carl A. Bancroft, "Gen. Garnett's Body." [WV]

6:7. Obit.

May 26

1:1-6, 2:4-6. Moses Wiley (1st TN Cav), "Life in Rebel Prison. A Tennessean's Experience at Macon, Charleston, and Columbia."

1:7, 2:1-3. John O'Dea (8th MO), "Vicksburg Again. Charge of the Storming Party May 22, 1863."

4:1-2. "McDowell and Porter. Gen. Capehart has Something to Say Regarding the Records of Both Commanders."

4:2-3. Fred W. Fout (7th IN), "At Philippi."

4:3. George E. Dolton, "Death of Gen. Gregg. [Chickamauga]

4:3-4. (68th PA), "The Red Diamond. A Comrade Who Helped Bury Many Men While a Prisoner at Chancellorsville."

4:4. Edmund Rutter (18th US), "The Regular Brigade. What Became of the Monumental Fund for the Stone River Killed?"

4:4. W. A. Headrick (1st TN Cav), "Prisoner of War." [captured 11/30/63]

4:5-6. Picket Shots: Robert A. Shearer (11th PA), Antietam.

6:7. Obit.

7:5. Obit: Oliver W. Longan (13th PA Cav), Andrew Patterson (51st NY), Charles E. Connor (4th NY Cav).

June 2

1:7, 2:1-4. F. A. Myers (32nd OH), "A Conflict of Death. Incidents Which Happened in the Battle of Atlanta."

4:1-2. Daniel Webster (1st WI Bty), "Arkansas Post."

4:2-3. D. W. Edmiston (ADC, 2nd Div, 23rd Corps), "Fort Sanders."

4:3-4. C. M. Welch (11th IN), "Between the Lines. Perilous Position of an Indiana Soldier in the Shenandoah Valley." [Fisher's Hill]

4:4. H. H. Bowles (6th ME), "Marye's Heights."

4:5-6. Picket Shots: Lorenzo Cady, 10/27/64; T. L. Steward (11th OH), Chattanooga; John C. Lewis (1st NY Cav), Piedmont.

4:6. N. W. Hayes (34th OH), "Libby Prison."

6:7. Obit.

9:3-4. Ex-Rebel, Part 6.

June 9

1:7, 2:1-2. William Simmons, "Our Naval Squadrons. Biographical Sketches of the U. S. Navy in the Late War." [Potomac Flotilla]

2:5-6. Ex-Rebel, Part 7.

4:1-2. L. H. Bleakley (6th NY Hvy Art), "Cedar Creek."

4:3. R. A. Gamer, "A Wake in Camp. A Joke Played by Co. D, 79th Pa. on One of the Boys."

4:3. J. R. Palmer (32nd IL), "Capture of Columbia."

4:4. Pat Breen (2nd US), "Gen. McDowell Again."

4:4. R. C. Rice (125th OH), "Battle of Franklin."

4:5-6. Picket Shots: A. E. Teall (21st NY Bty), Red River; C. H. Barnes, Rich Mountain; C. M. Woolsley (2nd NY Cav), capture of Kelley and Crook; Isaac K. Young, correcting his earlier article about East TN.

9:6. "High Water Mark. Dedication of the Monument at the Farthest Point of Pickett's Charge."

June 16

1:7, 2:1-4. Simmons, Part 2. [North Atlantic]

2:5-6. Ex-Rebel, Part 8.

4:1-2. William H. Githens (78th IL), "Unnecessary Cruelty. A Week of Tribulation and a Night in Zollicoffer Barracks." [Nashville]

4:2. Melvin J. Stearns (106th NY), "Brandy Station."

4:3. J. C. Vorhoes (Bty A, 1st MI), "Chickamauga."

4:3-4. William S. Parr (33rd WI), "Hayne's Bluff."

4:4. Edward M. Watson (1st MI Cav), "'Ain't I Glad to Get Out of the Wilderness'." [8/62]

4:5-6. Picket Shots: Fred Kapler (9th PA Cav), Elwood Mason (18th OH), R. H. Barger (6th TN Mtd Inf), Edward Beck (6th KY Cav), youngest; James Henderson (11th MI), Big Black River; W. W. Leathum (4th OH), Rich Mountain; John W. Herring (45th IL), Vicksburg.

4:6. Charles G. Kauffman (158th NY), "Fort Gregg."

6:7. Obit.

June 23

1:7, 2:1-2. Simmons, Part 3. [South Atlantic]

3:4-5. Ex-Rebel, Part 9.

4:1. "The First Corps. Remarks of Col. W. G. Veazey in Regard to a Call to Speak at the Dedication of the High Water Mark Monument at Gettysburg."

4:1-2. R. Britton (32nd OH), "'Fort Fizzle.' One of the Defenses in Ohio Intended to Resist the Draft."

4:2. John R. Rankin (27th IN), "Battle of Gettysburg."

4:3. Joseph F. Carter (3rd MD), "Libby Prison. Capt. Carter Thinks He Paved the Way for the Successful Tunnel from Rat Hell."

4:4. H. T. Bird (8th IA Cav), "Unwritten History. An Iowa Cavalryman's Experience in Escaping from the Enemy." [Atlanta]

4:4. R. S. Littlefield, "Charge at Jackson."

4:5-6. Picket Shots: Charles Mills (4th MI), Shepherdstown; J. B. Evans (102nd PA), Wilderness; J. D. Lytle (8th IN), Rich Mountain.

6:7. Obit.

7:6. Obit: Eli T. Stackhouse (CSA).

10:1. Biog: John P. Taylor (1st PA Cav).

June 30

1:7, 2:1-2. Simmons, Part 4. [East and West Gulf]

3:4-5. Edward M. Watson (1st MI Cav), "With Pope's Army."

3:5. L. Hendrick (Bty C, 1st OH), "Bentonville."

3:6. Owen Wright (14th IN), "At Gettysburg."

4:1-2. James Colledge (146th NY), "Little Round Top."

4:2. "Battle of Corinth. A Hot Fight in More Ways Than One-Iowa Losses in the Action."

4:2-3. James Holehouse (7th MA), "Marye's Heights."

4:3. S. A. Jonas, "Death of Gen. Gregg." [Chickamauga]

4:4. John Kelly (2nd US Cav), "Another Comparison. [Gettysburg-Chickamauga]

4:4. E. A. H. Beyland (9th OH), "Battle of Mill Springs."

4:5-6. Picket Shots: Thomas J. Bond (2nd OH), Chattanooga; N. P. Calkin (42nd IN), Lookout Mountain.

5:6. C. D. Brigham, "Gen. W. S. Hancock."

6:5-6. Obit.

10:1-2. Biog: C. B. Welton (103rd OH).

July 7

1:7, 2:1-2. Simmons, Part 5. [Western Flotilla]

4:1-2. J. H. Tourjee (2nd RI), "The Light Brigade. The Part Taken by Them in the Celebrated Peninsula Campaign."

4:2-3. W. F. Wieland (Btys L&M, 3rd US), "Fort Sanders."

4:3. J. R. Dobson (1st PA Res), "Gettysburg. Troops Engaged in the Celebrated Charge of Pickett."

4:3-4. J. W. Hinkley (3rd WI), "Battle of Antietam."

4:4. John W. Burnett (198th PA), "Hatcher's Run No. 2."

4:4. I. B. Webster (10th KY), "Missionary Ridge."

4:5-6. Picket Shots: H. B. Booth (27th IA), Shelby Cole; W. S. Tripp (33rd NY), youngest.

6:5-6. Obit.

7:6. Biog: John C. Foster (25th, 65th IN).

9:3. Biog: Robert Williams (1st MA Cav).

July 14

1:7, 2:1-6. "History of the Corps. How They were Formed and of What Troops Composed." [First]

4:1. J. A. Josselyn (4th MA Cav), "Around Petersburg."

4:1-2. Fergus Elliott (109th PA), "Peach Tree Creek."

4:2-3. Isaiah Mills (8th IN Cav), "Badly Scared. How a Sleepwalker Frightened an Indiana Cavalryman."

4:3. "Lamar and Yankee Bullets." [Q. C. Lamar and Petersburg 1864]

4:3-4. Walter Scott (47th IL), "Vanquishing Vicksburg."

4:4. C. G. Funke (49th NY), "In the Wilderness."

4:5-6. Picket Shots: C. M. Woolsey (2nd NY Cav), death of Colonel Hull; Mart Howe (9th WV), Cloyd's Mountain.

4:6. E. K. Parker (Bty D, 1st RI), "Second Bull Run."

6:7. Obit.

9:5-6. Biog: Abram W. Smith (19th US).

July 21

1:1-6. Corps History [Second]

1:7, 2:1-3. Judson Knight (2nd NJ), "Scouting Adventures. Opening Communications Between Meade's and Lee's Armies."

3:4. C. D. Brigham, "General A. E. Burnside."

4:1. J. B. Ridenour (55th IL), "Ridenour Speaks. Tells How His Brigade Executed a Dangerous and Important Service." [Chattanooga]

4:1-2. C. N. Barrett (46th PA), "How He Remembers It. A Pioneer Officer Differs Materially from the 10th Ohio Cavalry." [Carolinas]

4:2. Monroe Daggett (11th ME), "The Comrade Denies It."

4:2. Alexander Hunt (102nd NY), "Getting Into Savannah."

4:3. I. N. Durboraw, "On the Gettysburg Field."

4:3-4. B. A. Campbell (6th ME), "Marye's Heights."

4:4. R. S. Littlefield (14th MA, 1st MA Hvy Art), "Colonel Elie T. Lee. Capt. Littlefield Again After the Scalp of the Gallant Illinoisan."

4:4. J. W. Hinkley (3rd WI), "By an Eye-Witness. A Wisconsin Comrade Explains the Situation of the 27th Indiana and 2nd Massachusetts at Gettysburg."

4:5-6. Picket Shots: D. H. Smith (20th PA Cav), Piedmont; W. E. Brooks (75th NY), Thomas S. Timpson (165th NY), E. H. Wishon (Bty L, 1st OH), youngest; T. A. Cord, Philippi; Thomas D. Goundrey (141st NY), Bentonville.

6:7. Obit.

7:5. Obit: George A. Thurston (1st NV).

July 28

1:1-6, 3:6-7. Corps History [Second]

1:7, 2:1-3. Charles M. King (signal corps), "The Lynchburg Raid."

3:4-5. C. D. Brigham, "General R. B. Ayres."

4:1-2. J. R. Palmer (32nd IL), "Gen. McPherson's Death."

4:2. (30th OH), "The Forlorn Hope." [Vicksburg]

4:2. W. H. H. Barker (3rd IA Cav), "Winslow's Brigade. A Comrade Shows What Marvels They Performed in the Last Thirty Days of the War."

4:3. J. D. Richardson, "Rice was There." [Wilderness]

4:3. J. M. Rogers (10th CT), "The Importance of Gettysburg."

4:4. H. E. Mathews (6th ME), "Marye's Heights."

4:4. B. Spooner (13th MA), "Second Bull Run." [McDowell]

4:5-6. Picket Shots: Edwin French (19th VRC), Fort Stevens; James H. Luther (7th MA), Marye's Heights; Thomas Barker (2nd NY Cav), youngest.

6:7. Obit.

7:5. Biog: Eugene A. Carr.

7:5. Obit: Edward M. Hudson (4th US Art).

August 4

1:1-6, 3:5-6. Corps History. [Third]

1:7, 2:1-2. C. D. Brigham, "General Benjamin F. Butler."

2:5. (47th OH), "Louis Walker's Claim. He Captured Speaker Crisp and Saved Part of Sherman's Army."

3:3-4. "Capehart's Criticism. He Replies to Gen. Early on the Question of Stonewall Jackson at Antietam."

3:4. J. R. Palmer (32nd IL), "Battle of Franklin."

4:1-2. William Howard (80th OH), "A Foraging Expedition, In Which the Sublime and the Ridiculous are Badly Mixed." [Forest Hill, TN, Winter 1862-63]

4:3. John R. Rankin (27th IN), "Battle of Gettysburg."

4:3-4. S. D. Webster (13th MA), "Gen. McDowell Again."

4:4. James C. McCoughty (8th IL Cav), "Not Particularly Game. A Comrade Thinks It Mawkish Sentiment to Praise Rebel Bravery."

4:5. N. V. Hutchinson (7th MA), "Chancellorsville." [Marye's Heights]

4:6. Picket Shots: Burnham Cowdery (9th VT), capture of Richard B. Winder, Andersonville QM.

6:6. Biog: John H. Munroe (11th IA).

6:7. Obit.

7:6. Obit.

August 11

1:1-6, 3:4-7. Corps History. [Fourth]

1:7, 2:1-2. C. D. Brigham, "General William T. Sherman."

3:7. John Cook (Bty B, 4th US), "Battle of Antietam."

4:1-2. R. H. G. Minty (4th MI Cav), "The Saber Brigade."

4:2. L. R. Lackey (16th MI), "Second Bull Run."

4:3. W. H. Williams (129th PA), "At Chancellorsville."

4:3. R. H. Miller (63rd PA), "A Comrade Corrects the 'Little Sergeant' as to the Names of the Killed Officers." [Chancellorsville]

4:3-4. "Some Closing Remarks by Comrade E. T. Lee on the Charge at Jackson."

4:4. W. H. Booth (4th IA), "Kennesaw Mountain."

4:4. Joseph Yackey (4th, 12th IL Cav), "General George A. Custer."

4:5-6. Picket Shots: John L. Parker (11th MA), Hatcher's Run, 2/65; W. F. Gaul (4th NJ), youngest; C. A. Vredenburg (8th MI), Crater; George F. Thomas (2nd ME Bty), Cedar Mountain.

4:6. J. B. Work, "Fort Gregg Again."

6:6. Obit.

August 18

1:1-6, 3:5-6. Corps History. [Fifth]

1:7, 2:1. C. D. Brigham, "General William F. Smith."

2:2-3. "Ream's Station. Echoes from the Battlefield—Its Appearance To-Day—Wilson's Raiders—Five Forks as It Now Looks."

2:5. "Antietam Monument of the 4th New York."

4:1. P. W. Hughes (8th MI Cav), "Across the Mountains. The Rough Ride of Gen. Fry's Dispatch Bearer Into Knoxville."

4:2. Alfred Turner (5th NY Hvy Art), "In the Valley."

4:2-3. George W. Corey (34th MA), "At Cedar Creek."

4:3. Albert Roberts (29th WI), "A Good Battery." [1st WI Bty]

4:3-4. C. R. Thomas (28th KY), "Peach Tree Creek."

4:4. Melvin Mudge (11th MI), "The Regular Brigade."

4:5-6. Picket Shots: H. L. Chapman (124th OH), youngest.

4:6. S. A. Ranlett (36th MA), "Fort Sanders Again."

6:6. Obit.

August 25

1:1-6, 3:5-7. Corps History. [Fifth]

1:7, 2:1. C. D. Brigham, "General P. H. Sheridan."

4:1-2. J. M. Gould (10th ME), "At Antietam."

4:2. Samuel R. Hazen (140th NY), "At Gettysburg."

4:3. J. H. Hill (155th PA), "Armstrong's Mills."

4:3-4. J. W. Griswold (44th NY), "Who was Lost? A Comrade Takes Exception to Some of the School Histories." [Second Manassas]

4:4. Joseph Ray (41st IL), "Gen. McPherson's Death."

4:6. M. C. Connett (7th IN), "Death of Gen. Garnett."

6:7. Obit.

September 1

1:1-6, 3:6. Corps History. [Sixth]

1:7, 2:1-2. C. D. Brigham, "Admiral Goldsborough."

4:2. A. Turner (WV), "Prison Experience." [Salisbury]

4:2. Robert Hammond (15th OH), "Missionary Ridge."

4:2-3. R. L. Williamson (155th PA), "At Gettysburg."

4:3. J. C. Smith (75th NY), "That Disgraceful Affair." [Sabine Pass]

4:3-4. A. H. Huber, "Little Round Top."

4:4. R. N. Maker (6th ME), "Marye's Heights."

4:5-6. Picket Shots: Silas S. Holbrook (15th ME), fall 1863 operations in LA.

6:7. Obit.

September 8

1:1-6, 9:5-6. Corps History. [Sixth]

1:7, 2:1-2. William A. Olmsted (59th NY), "Saved the Bridge. It was Done by Col. Starbird and the Gallant 19th Maine. Fight at Sailor's Creek."

2:5. J. W. Anderson (10th IL), "The Grand Review."

3:3-4. C. D. Brigham, "General John E. Wool."

4:1. Pat Breen (2nd US), "General McDowell Again."

4:2. Jacob Reep (19th OH), "Cumberland Army."

4:2. Robert Collins (7th WV), "At Gettysburg."

4:2-3. Carl N. Bancroft, "Gen. Garnett's Body."

4:3. E. Tarrant (1st KY Cav), "Mill Springs."

4:3-4. D. E. Cronin (1st NY Mtd Rifles), "Run Against a Snag. A N.Y. Cavalryman Tells a New Story About Gen. Grant."

4:5-6. Picket Shots: David Shmid (20th IL), Vicksburg; Henry Cordes (18th US), siege of Chattanooga; Charles Banks (1st OH), Brown's Ferry; L. L. Burton (1st NY Light Art), E. A. True (8th ME), youngest.

6:5-6. Obit.

10:6-7. Biog: A. G. Weissert (8th WI), David S. Ray (1st RI Cav).

September 15

1:1-6, 3:5-6. Corps History. [Seventh]

1:7, 2:1-3. Briscoe Goodheart (Loudoun Rangers), "Ball's Bluff."

2:6. Austin Cannon, "John Brown's Tannery."

4:1-2. I. K. Young (89th IL), "Peach Tree Creek."

4:2. George W. Hilling (27th IA), "The Guerrilla Cole. What a Comrade Remembers of the Hanging of the Desperado."

4:2. R. A. Shearer (11th PA), "Hartsuff's Brigade." [Antietam]

4:3. Eli Holden (1st VT Cav), "Farnsworth's Death."

4:3-4. W. L. Welch (23rd MA), "For Simmons's Eye." [Burnside Expedition]

4:4. Henry D. O'Brien (1st MN), "At Gettysburg. Troops at the Stone Wall, The High Water Mark of the Rebellion."

4:4. Anson S. Taylor, "Should be Recognized. A Plea for the Men Who Hauled the Provisions and Ammunition."

4:5-6. Picket Shots: H. S. Sisk (5th TX Cav), Red River.

4:6. A. McNamar (106th IL), "Down in Arkansas." [8/63]

6:7. Obit.

10:1. Biog: Hugh Henry (16th VT).

10:6. C. D. Brigham, "General John A. Dix."

September 22

1:7, 2:1-2. Robert H. Woods, "The U.S.S. *Kearsarge*."

2:5. "Into the Wilderness. Barlow's Position at the Brock Road, and Hancock's and Longstreet's Positions on the Plank Road Revisited."

3:3-4. C. D. Brigham, "General W. S. Rosecrans."

4:1-2. R. H. G. Minty (4th MI Cav), "The Saber Brigade." [2/63]

4:2-3. Augustus Buell, "The Sixth Corps. The 'Cannoneer' Thinks More Should Have Been Said About the Valley Campaign."

4:3. B. H. Tripp (th WI), "At Gettysburg. Substantiating the Claim that the Iron Brigade Opened the Battle."

4:3. T. D. McGillicudy, "At Gettysburg. The Strength and Loss of Both Armies at the Big Battle."

4:4. John G. Langguth (17th MO), "At Vicksburg. A Comrade Gives the Date that Haynes' Bluff was Evacuated."

4:4. J. C. Millar (153rd PA), "At Gettysburg."

4:5-6. Picket Shots: R. Bargnis (1st OH), Brown's Ferry; R. M. Crawford (17th VT), Norris E. Bancroft (8th ME), A. D. R ose (11th IA), Hiram Richardson (MO), youngest; J. Buckmaster (3rd IA Cav), Bayou LaFourche, AR.

6:7. Obit.

7:6. Obit: John C. Howell (USN).

September 29

3:6. Obit: John Pope.

4:5. "A Monument at Antietam." [4th NY]

5:1-2. John W. Hill (1st CT Cav), "Salisbury Prison."

5:3-4. M. D. Gage, "Bragg in Kentucky. Battle of Munfordville, and Surrender of Wilder's Command."

5:4-5. Abner B. Stimpson (2nd MI Cav), "Battle of Booneville."

5:5. Aquila Wiley (41st OH), "Percentage of Losses. Col. Wiley Explains the Basis Upon Which He Estimated."

5:5. E. W. Sprague (15th ME), "Butler's Thieves. The General Did Not Get the Spoons—It was the 15th Maine."

5:6. Picket Shots: 9th MA Returning flag of Cleveland Guards, NC, captured 5/29/62.

6:7. Obit.

October 6

1:1-6, 3:3-6. Corps History. [Eighth]

1:7, 2:1-3. G. W. Houts (7th MO SM Cav), "War Recollections."

4:1-2. S. S. Rideout (1st ME Bty), "Then and Now. Old Battlefields Revisited by a Maine Batteryman." [Cedar Creek]

4:2. H. Churnley (2nd TN), "A Tennessean's Views. He Never Had a Doubt Regarding the Outcome of the War."

4:2-3. S. A. McNeil (31st OH), "Charged the Enemy. What was Done by Church's 4th Michigan Battery in Tennessee." [6/26/63]

4:3. Timothy W. Doyle (15th MI), "Gen. McPherson's Death."

4:3-4. John Carboy, "Capture of the Clifton."

4:4. William C. Webber (16th US), "The Regular Brigade. A Comrade Differs with Col. Mudge as to Its Formation."

4:5-6. Picket Shots: N. E. Bancroft (8th ME), John K. Fox (Bty I, 3rd NY), E. C. Storms (153rd IN), youngest.

4:6. H. C. Hackett (1st MI Cav), "Prison Experience." [Libby]

6:7. Obit.

9:5. 'Shenandoah Valley." [present day views]

10:1. Biog: Peter B. Ayars (99th PA).

October 13

1:1-6, 3:5-6. Corps History. [Ninth]

1:7, 2:1-4. Houts, Part 2.

3:1-2. C. D. Brigham, "Gen. Robert Anderson."

4:1-2. E. T. Lee (41st IL), "Battle of Shiloh."

4:2. J. P. Watkins (111th PA), "Peach Tree Creek."

4:2. J. H. Bowman (47th IL), "Spanish Fort, Ala."

4:2. E. L. Nicholl (Bty D, 1st RI), "A Little More Light Turned on the Subject of the Rebel General Garnett's Death."

4:3. "Battlefields Revisited. A 45th Pa. Comrade Goes Over the Places His Regiment Fought at South Mountain and Antietam."

4:3-4. H. H. Lyman (147th NY), "At Gettysburg. Cutler's Brigade Opened the Battle—Claim of the Iron Brigade Refuted."

4:4. Thomas S. Nutter (10th WV), "In the Valley. A Comrade Thinks Fighting Began at Harper's Ferry, July 4, 1864."

4:4. J. W. Hinkley (2nd MA), "At Gettysburg."

4:5-6. Picket Shots: S. A. Bendon (87th PA), Opequon, 8/64); W. H. Frost (4th IN Bty), Chickamauga; W. H. Thurston (Bty F, 1st PA), Gettysburg; John P. Fredd (USS *San Jacinto*), Sabine Pass; William R. Curtis (38th NJ), youngest.

10:3. Biog: Jesse B. Fuller (Bty D, 1st MI).

11:4. Obit.

October 20

2:1-5. S. H. Arnell, "Unwritten History. The Rout of Gen. Morgan's Forces at Greeneville, Tenn."

3:4-5. "In the Historic Shenandoah." [present day]

4:1-2. G. W. Ainsworth (11th VT), "A Thrilling Account. How the Pickets were Saved at the Battle of Cedar Creek."

4:2-3. "A Brave Soldier. The Recovery of the Body of a Soldier Killed at Cyprus Creek, Ark." [5/14/64, Lieut. William H. Ritter, 2nd MO Cav]

4:3-4. S. J. Bailey (9th IL Cav), "Who Can Tell? An Illinois Man Wants to Know Whom He Met Under Unfavorable Circumstances." [AR, 9/62]

4:4. J. G. Church (7th MA), "Marye's Heights Again."

4:5-6. Picket Shots: James H. Blackburn (4th TN Mtd Inf), capture of Champ Ferguson; Robert T. Thomas (28th IL), Jackson, MS.

7:4. Obit: O. H. Ross (20th IL).

7:6. Obit: Samuel L. Barr (5th US).

October 27

2:1-4. James H. Harold (1st NY Eng), "1st South Carolina."

4:1-3. George W. Kelly (57th NY), "On the Reserve. What Happened to the Second Corps in July and August 1864."

4:4. Frederick C. Waterman (2nd WI), "At Gettysburg. Another Comrade Thinks the Iron Brigade Opened the Battle."

4:4. A. D. Springer (7th IN), "Cut Down by Minies. What Happened to Quite a Large Tree in Front of the 7th Indiana." [Spotsylvania]

4:5-6. Picket Shots: Hugh Brady (84th IL), Lookout Mountain, 9/63; F. W. Ohlinger (13th WV), Lynchburg; Dabid Rainey (USS *Chip-*

pewa), Fort Fisher; Charles C. Calahan (4th OH), Gettysburg.

7:4. "Reburial." [Lovell H. Rosseau, Louis D. Watkins (6th KY Cav) to Arlington]

7:5. Obit: Thomas Stewart (USN).

10:7. Obit.

November 3

2:1-4. "Captain Daniel Ellis's Story. The Adventurous Career of a Loyal East Tennessean."

2:5. C. D. Brigham, "General John F. Hartranft."

4:1-2. C. T. Barr (148th PA), "The Second Corps. A Comrade Tells of Some of the Victories They Won After Hancock Left Them."

4:2. William A. Williams (Bty C, PA), "Gen. McDowell Again."

4:2. William R. Nash (25th IL), "Missionary Ridge."

4:3. Edward R. Dunigan (125th PA), "Battle of Antietam. A Pa. Comrade Says About the Death of Gen. Mansfield."

4:3. Solon R. Davis (1st VT Cav), "Brandy Station." [10/63]

4:4. Milan Brownson (8th IA), "Gen. John Pope."

4:4. Edmond W. Dayton (36th WI), "Hatcher's Run." [10/27/64]

4:4. Granville Fernald (25th PA), "Whose Flag was It? What Regiment from Maine Lost Their Colors at First Bull Run."

9:5. Obit: James M. Tuttle.

November 10

1:1-6. Corps History. [Ninth]

1:7, 2:1-4. Ellis, Part 2.

2:5-6. C. D. Brigham, "General Joseph Hooker."

4:1-2. J. R. Rankin (27th IN), "Battle of Gettysburg."

4:2. Augustus Buell, "First Gun at Gettysburg."

4:2-3. James Anthony (17th IN Bty), "At Cedar Creek."

4:3. I. N. Stanford (18th US), "Missionary Ridge."

4:3. G. A. Lyon (23rd MI), "Twenty-third Corps. A Comrade Mentions Some of Its Heroes Who have Gained Distinction in Civil Life."

4:4. Briscoe Goodheart (Loudoun Rangers), "Belle Isle Revisited."

4:5-6. Picket Shots: S. C. Miller (76th PA), Fort Wagner; W. V. Hutchinson (7th MA), Marye's Heights; Frank Pettis (1st WI Cav), youngest.

6:7. Obit.

10:7. Biog: William H. Tucker (14th WI), James Beggs (3rd KY Cav).

November 17

2:1-4. Ellis, Part 3.

4:1-2. "Battle of Antietam. Major Gould's Reply to Lt. Dunegan About the Death of Gen. Mansfield."

4:2. William Edmonds (4th WV), "At Vicksburg." [5/19/63]

4:3. "Chickamauga. What is Being Done to Mark the Positions of Ohio State Troops."

4:3. M. M. Campbell (20th MI), "Fort Sanders."

4:4. Martin V. Hargrave (27th NJ), "Marye's Heights."

4:4. William Simmons (USS *Brooklyn*), "Down in the Gulf. Capture of the Rebel Blockade Runner Magnolia."

4:5-6. Picket Shots: G. W. Miller (31st OH), Cage's Ford; Herman Perry (CSA), first flag of truce at Appomattox.

5:4. John D. Billings, "Reams's Station." [present day]

6:6. Obit.

7:5. Obit: F. Van Derveer.

10:1. Biog: Powell Clayton.

10:2. Biog: W. A. Bartlett (8th Ind Co NY Ss).

November 24

1:1-7, 2:1-3. Ellis, Part 4.

2:4-6, 3:5. Corps History. [Ninth]

3:1-2. Robert H. Woods, "The Stonewall."

4:1. Andrew Geddes (8th IA), "Spanish Fort."

4:2. A. W. Peck (17th CT), "At Gettysburg. Lieut. Peck Tells What Carroll's Brigade Did in the Battle."

4:2. R. C. Rice (125th OH), "With Sherman. Another Chapter of the Peach Tree Creek Battle."

4:3. R. C. Rice (125th OH), "Premonitions." [Kennesaw Mt]

4:3. A. W. Rogers (81st IL), "Spanish Fort."

4:3. "The 83rd Pa. Comrade Hutchinson Corrects Comrade Potter."

4:3-4. "Gibbon at Antietam. Capt. Stewart Tells How He Handled a Gun at that Battle." [Bty B, 4th US]

4:4. V. O. Gordon (22nd NY), "The Iron Brigade. How Certain Troops of the First Corps Came to Be Thus Designated."

4:4. C. W. Cook (76th NY), "Who Opened Gettysburg."

4:5-6. Picket Shots: Peter E. Palen (143rd NY), Peach Tree Creek; D. W. Richardson (110th OH), Winchester 1864; Charles H. Mason (17th US), youngest; Dan Burket (84th IN), Thompson's Station; John L. Parker (22nd MA), Gettysburg.

6:7. Obit.

10:1. Biog: E. B. Gray (4th, 28th WI).

December 1

1:1-6, 3:5. Corps History. [Tenth]

1:7, 2:1-3. Ellis, Part 5.

3:1-3. C. D. Brigham, "Unpublished History. The Grounds Upon Which Gen. Grant Took the Command of the Army."

4:1. Rudolph Kost (6th CT), "Fort Wagner."

4:2. Frank E. Willett (8th NY Cav), "Another Gettysburg. A Comrade Says the 8th N.Y. Cav. Opened the Great Battle."

4:2-3. A. H. Hutchinson (10th ME), "Gen. Mansfield's Death."

4:3. W. H. Bushfield (15th OH), "Gen. Morgan's Death. Gen. Basil W. Duke Tells a Comrade What He Knows About the Matter."

4:3-4. D. M. Perry (76th NY), "Gen. McDowell's Hat. Its Appearance on the Field was a Signal for Disaster."

4:4. Augustus Buell, "Archer's Brigade." [Gettysburg]

4:5-6. Picket Shots: youngest soldiers; Christian Smith (8th IA), Spanish Fort.

6:7. Obit.

December 8

1:1-6, 9:4-6. Corps History. [Tenth]

1:7, 2:1-4. Ellis, Part 6.

2:5-6. C. D. Brigham, "Unwritten History. President Lincoln Places McClellan in Command Against the Advice of His Cabinet."

4:1-2. I. N. Durboraw (1st PA Res), "The Big Battle. A Comrade Sends Reminiscences of a Citizen of Gettysburg." [D. H. Klingle]

4:2. J. L. Herbert (2nd IA Cav), "Sheridan at Booneville."

4:2. S. H. Wright (75th NY), "Capture of the Clifton."

4:3. A. H. Huber, "At Gettysburg. Cutler's Brigade First and the Iron Brigade Next on the Field."

4:4. Willis H. Booth (4th IA), "Battle of Atlanta."

4:4. M. H. Deem (8th IA), "Spanish Fort Again."

4:5-6. Picket Shots: J. Fishbeck (26th NY Bty), Spanish Fort; Lewis F. Fahrion (Bty B, 1st

OH), Philippi; William J. Brown (155th PA), Gettysburg.

6:7. Obit.

12:5. Obit: Henry M. Hoyt (52nd PA).

December 15

1:1-6, 9:4-7. A. C. Hamlin, "Chancellorsville. Actions at Hazel Grove, on Saturday, 7:30 p.m., May 2, 1863."

1:7, 2:1. Ellis, Part 7.

4:1. R. H. G. Minty (4th MI Cav), "The Saber Brigade." [3/4/63]

4:2. Isaac Sollers (4th US Cav), "Kilpatrick's Raid."

4:2. Thomas Murphy (45th IL), "At Vicksburg." [5/22/63]

4:2. James H. Bowman (47th IL), "First in Spanish Fort."

4:3. D. M. Ray, "The 2nd Tennessee Cavalry."

4:3. W. S. Brown (18th OH), "Atlanta Campaign. An Incident Which Happened at Sand Mountain, Ga."

4:4. William Drew (USN), "At Sabine Pass."

4:4. William Soden (23rd WI), "A Land Lubber Gives an Account of the Capture of the Gunboats." [Sabine Pass]

4:5-6. Picket Shots: E. T. Lee (41st IL), Shiloh; J. P. Waters (111th PA), Peach Tree Creek.

6:7. Obit.

December 22

1:1-6, 2:5-7. Corps History. [Tenth]

1:7, 2:1-4. Ellis, Part 8.

4:1-2. Minty, Part 2.

4:2. J. W. Evarts (4th US Col Cav), "Last Episode of the War. An Expedition that Brought New Orleans and Washington in Communication After Lee's Surrender."

4:3. Frank Tallman (8th NY Hvy Art), "A Mistake. A Comrade Tells Who Commanded His Regiment in 1864."

4:3. A. Vosburgh (119th IL), "Shelby Cole Again."

4:3-4. John S. Brayfield (65th IN), "He Struck a Knot. Foraging Experience of an Indiana Mounted Infantryman."

4:4. S. L. Barber (11th WV), "Fort Gregg Again."

4:5-6. Picket Shots: C. S. Fisk (11th VT), Fort Stevens; W. F. Henry (108th IL), Spanish Fort; Henry Thomas (colored CSA cook), Cedar Creek.

6:7. Obit.

7:6. Biog: Charles L. Cole (17th ME).

7:6. Obit: R. L. Gibson (CSA).

10:1-2. Biog: D. R. Lowell (121st NY).

December 29

1:1-6, 2:5-6. John M. Schofield, "The Armies of Tennessee.

1:7, 2:1-3. Ellis, Part 9.

4:1-2. Charles M. King (signal corps), "Shenandoah Valley."

4:2. J. R. Williamson (105th IL), "Medal of Honor? Who is Entitled to the Credit of Capturing the Cannon?" [Averysboro]

4:3-4. A. S. Jones (3rd WI), "Battle of Gettysburg."

4:4. S. A. Bendon (87th PA), "Opequon Again."

4:5-6. Picket Shots: Michael Hayes (Bty A, 2nd US), Gettysburg; D. S. Enverard (50th OH), Atlanta Campaign.

6:7. Obit.

9:5. C. D. Brigham, "General S. W. Crawford."

10:2. Biog: Theodore L. Poole (122nd NY).

1893

January 5

1:1-6, 3:4-5. Corps History. [Eleventh]

1:7, 2:1-3. Ellis, Part 10.

4:1-2. King, Part 2.

4:2. Samuel Creelman (101st PA), "Seven Pines."

4:3. William H. Carney (54th MA), "Fort Wagner, S.C."

4:3-4. S. C. Miller (76th PA), "Lieut. Kost Criticized."

4:4. Jacob G. Frick (129th PA), "Chancellorsville."

4:4. Jonathan B. Bowers (13th TN Cav), "Gen. Morgan's Death."

4:5-6. Picket Shots: Frank Walton (12th WI Bty), last gun.

6:7. Obit.

7:5. "Helped Hang Mrs. Surratt." [Officer Lloyd obit]

7:5. Obit: John G. B. Baxter (3rd WI).

7:7. John D. Billings, "Harper's Ferry." [present]

9:4-6. John M. Coyne (73rd NY), "The 4th Excelsior."

January 12

1:1-6, 3:4-6. Corps History. [Eleventh]

1:7, 2:1-3. Ellis, Part 11.

4:1-3. Judson Knight (2nd NJ), "With the Scouts. Sergeant Knight's Adventures in the Swamps of the Pamunkey." [post Spotsylvania]

4:3. J. W. Hinkley, "At Gettysburg."

4:4. George H. McKinney (77th IL), "At Vicksburg." [5/22/63]

4:4. Stephen Tripp (11th PA Cav), "The 11th Pa. Cavalry."

4:5. A. W. Rogers (81st IL), "Spanish Fort Again."

4:6. Picket Shots: W. H. Jack (23rd IA), Spanish Fort.

6:7. Obit.

10:1. Biog: J. J. Steadman (OH).

10:2-3. Biog: J. S. Brown (ME).

January 19

1:1-6, 3:5-6. Corps History (Twelfth]

1:7, 2:1-3. Ellis, Part 12.

4:1-2. Knight, Part 2.

4:2. Emory Sibley (USS *South Carolina*), "The Magnolia."

4:3. George W. Brower (USS *Tallapoosa*), "The Stonewall. The Reason the *Tallapoosa's* Sailors Did Not Get the Prize Money."

4:3-4. John P. Ames (6th NY Cav), "Carroll's Brigade. The Color-Bearer Gives Some Recollections of the Gettysburg Fight."

4:4. John R. Rankin (27th IN), "At Gettysburg."

4:5-6. Picket Shots: M. D. Grimshaw (73rd OH), Aberysboro; William Chastam (24th MO), brothers in regiment; W. E. Forbes (14th OH Bty), Resaca.

6:7. Obit.

10:1. Biog: Charles W. Whitehead (124th NY).

10:7. Biog: B. S. Osborn (USN).

January 26

1:1-6, 3:3-4. Corps History. [Twelfth]

1:7, 2:1-3. Ellis, Part 13.

3:5-6. Obit: Joseph J. Bartlett.

4:1-2. R. H. G. Minty (4th MI Cav), "The Saber Brigade." [3/20/63]

4:2. H. D. Johnston, "All Hands on Deck, For the Eye of the Crew of the Itasca, 1864-5."

4:3-4. Knight, Part 3.

4:4. W. H. Swail (10th VT), "The Bloody Angle. What a Comrade Remembers About the Tree Cut by Minies."

4:4. George L. Van Ness (21st NJ), "Marye's Heights."

4:5-6. Picket Shots: H. W. Phelps (95th OH), Spanish Fort; A. P. Benner (6th ME), Marye's Heights; O. B. Lawdrey (22nd IA), Vicksburg assault 5/22/63.

6:7. Obit.

12:4-5. Obit: Rutherford B. Hayes.

February 2

1:1-6, 3:7. Corps History. [Twelfth]

1:7, 2:1-4. Ellis, Part 14.

3:1-3. C. D. Brigham, "General B. F. Butler."

4:1-2. James R. Pilkington (34th MA), "The Hunter Raid."

4:2. "Truly a Hero. A Living Comrade Whose Grave is Kept Green by the Government." [John F. Wilson, 77th IL]

4:3. Harrison White (6th NY Cav), "Criticizing Hamlin." [Chancellorsville]

4:4. S. K. Crawford (50th OH), "Battle of Perryville."

4:4. Charles E. Newman (117th IL), "General J. A. Mower."

4:4. Walden Kelly (26th OH), "Missionary Ridge."

4:5-6. Picket Shots: G. A. Harman, Peach Tree Creek; William Simmons, Magnolia affair; Peter Dricken (27th WI), Spanish Fort.

5:7. D. Eldredge (3rd NH), "The Gilmore Medal."

6:7. Obit.

12:6-7. Obit: Abner Doubleday.

February 9

1:1-6, 3:4-6. Corps History. [Thirteenth]

1:7, 2:1-3. Ellis, Part 15.

4:1-2. E. Tarrant (1st KY Cav), "Brave Women. Incidents of Pegram's Raid in Central Kentucky." [3/63]

4:3. Thomas T. Cooney (Bty K, 1st US), "Sykes's Regulars." [Second Manassas]

4:3-4. Thomas Murphy (45th IL), "At Vicksburg." [Fort Hill, 6/26/63]

4:4. E. A. La Bay (USS *Keystone State*), "Running the Blockade. Account of the Capture of the Rebel Schooner Sarah." [6/19/62]

4:6. William Shultz (3rd NJ Bty), "Ream's Station." [8/25/64]

6:7. Obit.

February 16

1:1-6, 2:3-5. Corps History. [Thirteenth]

1:7, 2:1-5. Ellis, Part 16.

4:1. Miletus Garner, "The 48th Ohio's Flag. How It was Worshipped by Prisoners at Tyler, Texas."

4:1. A. C. Hamlin, "At Chancellorsville."

4:2. B. Hobart (125th PA), "Battle of Antietam. Comrade Hobart Says Gen. Mansfield Fell in Front of the 125th Pa."

4:2. C. E. Gallinger (110th OH), "At Opequon."

4:2. Joseph Ray (41st IL), "First to Land. A Comrade Tells What Troops First Occupied Pittsburgh Landing."

4:3. Free S. Bowley (30th USCT), "At the Crater."

4:3. J. W. Barney (1st DE), "The Second Corps."

4:4. E. T. Lee (41st IL), "Personal Recollections. [Jackson, 7/63]

4:4. J. R. Palmer, "The 32nd Illinois at Shiloh."

4:5-6. Picket Shots: M. S. Lake (14th WI), Spanish Fort; youngest.

4:6. Charles H. Eager (15th MA), "Ball's Bluff."

5:4. Obit: Samuel S. Carroll.

6:7. Obit.

February 23

1:1-6, 3:4-7. Corps History. [Thirteenth]

1:7, 2:1-3. Ellis, Part 17.

4:1-2. A. L. Soule (10th MI Cav), "Death of Gen. Morgan."

4:2. Charles S. Kimmel, "The 66th Illinois."

4:3. J. R. Rankin (27th IN), "At Gettysburg."

4:4. Henry C. King (100th IL), "Peach Tree Creek."

4:5-6. Picket Shots: George W. Malcolm (34th MA), Fort Gregg; youngest; Edwin Crockett (65th NY), Spotsylvania.

6:7. Obit.

March 2

1:1-6, 3:2-5. Corps History. [Fourteenth]

1:7, 2:1-2. R. H. G. Minty (4th MI Cav), "The Saber Brigade. [4/63]

2:3-6. Ellis, Part 18.

4:1-2. C. E. Belknap (21st MI), "For the Country. Some of the Service Performed by Michigan Soldiers."

4:2. EEJ, "The Bloody 20th Mass."

4:2-3. H. McEwen (18th CT), "Danville Prison."

4:3-4. Judson Knight (2nd NJ), "How Scouts Worked."

4:4. Charles A. Rolfe (11th ME), "Fort Gregg Again."

4:5-6. Picket Shots: Evelyn Kelsey (9th CT), Magnolia affair.

6:7. Obit.

March 9

1:1-5. Corps History. [Fourteenth]

1:6-7, 2:1-3. Charles E. Belknap (21st MI), "My Recollections of Stone River."

3:5. Biog: Samuel S. Carroll.

4:1-2. Knight, Part 2.

4:2-3. E. T. Lee (41st IL), "Fort Donelson."

4:3-4. "'Hell Roaring' Collins. The Trials of a Union Man in Texas During the War." [Stacy Collins, Hardin County]

4:4. James Holehouse (7th MA), "Marye's Heights."

4:4. J. L. Harnden (19th US), "Battle of Stones' River."

4:5-6. Picket Shots: T. J. Cannon (6th KY), Chattanooga; G. Rawlings (13th MD), Monocacy; Albert M. Routson (110th OH), Wilderness.

6:6-7. Obit.

9:3. Ellis, Part 19.

10:2. Biog: Thomas F. Gleason (25th NY).

March 16

1:1-6, 3:3-6. Arthur Linn (10th NY), "The *Monitor* and *Merrimac*."

1:7, 2:1-3. Corps History. [Fourteenth]

3:1-2. Ellis, Part 20.

4:1-2. C. W. McKay (154th NY), "The Eleventh Corps. What is the Real Animus of the Attacks Upon that Organization." [Chancellorsville]

4:2. H. C. Wilkins (21st IN), "After Thirty Years. Baton Rouge Battle-ground Visited by a Comrade."

4:3. R. S. Littlefield (1st MA Hvy Art), "Battle Losses. Unparalleled Casualties in the Faded End of Mott's Division."

4:3. S. H. Colborne (4th PA Cav), "With the Cavalry. The Last Campaign from Sailor's Creek to Appomattox."

4:3. George E. Dolton (Bty M, 1st IL), "Peach Tree Creek."

4:4. Joseph H. Bell (27th IA), "Smith's Guerrillas. Some of the Work Done by Them in the Red River Campaign."

4:4. H. F. Andrews (16th ME), "Lots of Powder Wasted. A Maine Comrade Tells of a Battle Between Union Troops." [Warrenton area, Fall 1863, vs. 1st NJ Cav]

4:5-6. Picket Shots: J. H. Bowman (47th IL), Spanish Fort; T. C. Jones (22nd IA), Vicksburg assault, 5/22; A. P. Carr (34th IN), 5/13/65; J. H. Hermance (67th OH), Fort Wagner; A. L. Fitch (14th OH Bty), Shiloh; Fred Barrett (5th NH), Fredericksburg; Theodore McAllister (Cole's MD Cav), Harper's Ferry.

6:7. Obit.

March 23

1:1-5. A. C. Hamlin, "Chancellorsville. The Midnight Charge of Sickles at Hazel Grove, and the Wounding of Stonewall Jackson, May 2, 1863."

1:6-7, 2:1-3. Corps History. [Fourteenth]

4:1-2. Knight, Part 3.

4:2. C. A. Hobbs (99th IL), "The Thirteenth Corps."

4:3. William L. Welch (23rd MA), "The First Troops. A Comrade Claims that Mass. Got There as Usual."

4:4. "Gen. William R. Terrill."

4:4. Jerome Bell (1st NY Cav), "Another Instance. A Maryland Regiment's Flag Spent Several Months in Captivity." [about Ben Swearer, 6th or 9th MD]

4:4. James Light (10th MI Cav), "Death of Gen. Morgan."

4:5-6. Picket Shots: H. D. Johnson, correcting earlier article; Clarence Wilson (2nd PA Hvy Art), Danville Prison.

4:6. M Quad, "He Hit a Shell and It Saved Him from Being Just a Common Nigger." [Chancellorsville]

5:4-6. Ellis, Part 21.

6:7. Obit.

10:2. Biog: Wilbur F. Rogers (4th NY, 35th NJ).

12:4. "The First Confederate Killed During the War." [Henry L. Wyatt, 1st NC]

March 30

1:1-6, 3:4. Hamlin, Part 2.

1:7, 2:1-6. Corps History. [Fourteenth]

3:1-2. Ellis, Part 22.

4:1-2. Knight, Part 4.

4:2. Augustus Buell (Bty B, 4th US), "At Gettysburg. The Cannoneer Explains His Allusions to the Eleventh Corps."

4:3-4. R. D. Barber, "Battle of Fair Oaks. A Comrade Says Casey's Division was Not Surprised."

4:4. Samuel R. Russell (96th PA), "The First Troops. Another Comrade Claims Pa. Sent Them to Washington."

4:4. Albert N. Shumard (48th OH), John A. Markley (8th IN), "Unfair Treatment." [Vicksburg]

4:5-6. Picket Shots: M. H. Sanders, Pulaski, 5/1/62; George H. Stowitz (100th NY), Fort Gregg; Abram Smith (91st NY), Farmville, General Smyth.

4:6. George W. F. Vernon (Cole's MD Cav), "Harper's Ferry."

6:7. Obit.

April 6

1:1-6, 3:4-6. C. E. Belknap (21st MI), "Chickamauga."

1:7, 2:1-6. Corps History. [Fifteenth]

3:1-2. Anna S. Reynolds, "The Tomb of Lincoln."

4:1. (41st IL), "Our Last Battle. Address of Col. E. T. Lee on the Anniversary of the Fight at Bentonville."

4:1. J. J. Lyon (AIG, 16th Corps), "Spanish Fort."

4:2. Knight, Part 5.

4:3. "Billy Barlow. One of the First Confederate Prisoners Captured in the War."

4:3. R. S. Mowry (1st MN), "He Quotes for the Book. A Minn. Comrade Makes a Decided Statement About the First Three Years Troops."

4:4. William T. Dart (4th OH), "Carroll's Brigade." [Gettysburg]

4:4. W. Revill (48th NY), "Fort Wagner Again."

4:5-6. Picket Shots: G. H. Blakeslee (9th OH), Chickamauga; W. E. Forbes (14th OH Bty), Dallas; E. J. Hendricks (67th NY), Wilderness; F. H. Knight (125th OH), Peach Tree Creek; D. M. Goodacre (9th MD), flag of regiment; M. H. Myrick (137th IL), Forrest's Memphis Raid.

5:3. R. H. Martin (46th IN), "The Thirteenth Corps." [Champion's Hill]

6:7. Obit.

7:4. Obit: Hiram Berdan (1st US Ss).

9:4-5. Ellis, Part 23.

10:2. Biog: Joseph P. Cleary (13th NY, 14th NY Hvy Art).

12:2. Obit: E. Kirby Smith (CSA), Frank Vallee (82nd PA).

April 13

1:1-6, 3:5-6. E. Y. Goldsborough (ADC to Gen. Tyler), "Early's Great Raid."

1:7, 2:1-5. Corps History. [Fifteenth]

3:1-2. Ellis, Part 24.

4:1-2. Augustus Buell (Bty B, 4th US), "Courage in Battle."

4:2. H. L. Miller (8th NY Cav), "Battle of Cedar Creek."

4:2. H. C. Hackett, "How Another Flag Went Through." [1st MI Cav captured at Gettysburg]

4:3. "Shiloh Then and Now. Address of Col. Lee at the Anniversary Exercises, April 6, 1893."

4:3. William H. Wood (2nd NY Cav), "Second Bull Run."

4:4. John J. Douglass (10th TN), "Correcting History. Maj. Douglass Shows Capt. Soule that He is Wrong." [Morgan's death]

4:4. Jacob Buch (5th US Cav), "Gen. Mansfield's Death."

4:4. S. A. McNeil (31st OH), "The Record is Wrong. A Comrade Shows that His Regiment was Not Properly Reported."

4:5-6. Picket Shots: Alfred Turner (5th NY Hvy Art), Salisbury prison; E. A. Crandall, Sabine Crossroads; J. Q. A. Young (12st PA Cav), Appomattox; J. O. Clark (74th IL), Spanish Fort; Frank Tallman (9th NY Hvy Art), Monocacy.

6:7. Obit.

7:6. Obit: Temple Clark (5th WI).

9:4-5. "The G.A.R. A Brief History of One of the Greatest Patriotic Orders in the World."

10:2. Biog: George T. Cranston (3rd RI Hvy Art; Bty B, 1st US).

April 20

1:1-5, 3:2-5. M. A. Sweetman (114th OH), "Chickasaw Bluffs."

1:7, 2:1-4. Corps History. [Fifteenth]

3:1. Ellis, Part 25.

4:1-2. Knight, Part 6.

4:2. G. L. Cruikshank (11th PA Cav), "The Contraband."

4:3. D. W. Smead (1st US Col Hvy Art), "Sam McQueen's Capture."

4:3-4. John E. Birney (3rd US Cav), "In New Mexico."

4:5-6. Picket Shots: John Haley (17th ME), William Liverman (3rd ME), William E. Cole (5th NJ), Chancellorsville; C. W. McKay (154th NY), march to Gettysburg; W. M. Neece (6th MO Cav), Sabine Crossroads; J. C. Hatrum (77th IL), Vicksburg assault, 5/22; J. B. Simpson, Snicker's Ford.

5:4. Nathan Longfellow (2nd MA), "At Gettysburg."

6:7. Obit.

9:1-2. Henry A. Castle (73rd IL), "The Sutler."

April 27

1:7, 2:1-4. Corps History. [Fifteenth]

2:5-6. Ellis, Part 26.

4:1-2. Knight, Part 7.

4:2-3. H. M. Jones (18th MA), "Fitz-john Porter. A Comrade Thinks He and McDowell were Responsible for McDowell's Defeat."

4:3-4. Richard W. Tuffs (4th MI), "Malvern Hill."

4:4. Alfred Davenport (5th NY), "Sykes's Regulars." [Second Manassas]

4:5-6. Picket Shots: J. W. Boyuce (28th NY), Chancellorsville; D. H. Hale (8th Wi), Spanish Fort; J. B. Waldermuth (73rd IL), his regiment called "The Preacher Regiment."

6:7. Obit.

7:5. Obit: Charles J. Murphy (144th IL), Mrs. Almira R. Hancock.

May 4

1:1-6, 3:4-6. Corps History. [Sixteenth]

4:1-2. Knight, Part 8.

4:2. Thomas C. Mathews (77th IL), "At Vicksburg." [5/22/63]

4:3. Ira B. Goodrich (21st MA), "Second Bull Run."

4:3-4. A. J. Hawkins (USMC), "The Naval Battle." [Hampton Roads]

4:4. D. M. Hollister (81st OH), "Smoke-House Fight." [1/63 near Cleveland, TN]

4:5-6. Picket Shots: L. J. Merchant (14th CT), G. W. S. Conant (1st MA), Chancellorsville; F. S. Morgan (1st PA Cav), Harrisonburg; James McQuade (16th MA), Hampton Roads; Levi B. Smith (122nd IL), C. F. Neighbors (122nd IL), Parker's Croasroads; J. Fordyce (7th WV), Gettysburg.

7:5. Obit: George O. Brown (19th MA, 2nd MA Hvy Art), Edward F. Brooks (6th WI), James P. Smith (4th NY Bty).

7:6. Biog: Henry C. Bell (29th IN).

7:6. Obit: John M. Corse.

May 11

1:1-5, 3:5. Corps History. [Sixteenth]

1:6-7, 2:1-3. Isabell Worrell, "The Soldiers' Homes."

4:1-2. Knight, Part 9.

4:2. R. C. Rankin (7th OH Cav), "The Sanders Raid." [6/63]

4:3. R. H. Fuller (77th NY), "Marye's Heights."

4:3. G. D. Bertholf (7th OH), "The Twelfth Corps. The Part They Took in the Big Battle of Gettysburg."

4:4. W. J. Landram, "Gen. George H. Thomas."

4:5-6. Picket Shots: John Clark (Bty I, 2nd IL), Chattanooga; Edwin A. Jones (3rd PA Hvy Art), Jeff Davis at Fort Monroe; H. C. Clowes (155th PA), Appomattox tree; Joseph Y. Funkhauser (36th IA), Camp Ford; J. D. Masters (125th OH), Peach Tree Creek.

6:6-7. Obit.

10:2. Biog: William Simmons (USN).

May 18

1:1-5. Corps History. [Seventeenth]

2:3-4. Ellis, Part 27.

3:1-2. Knight, Part 10.

3:2. C. M. Castle (102nd IL), "Peach Tree Creek."

3:3-4. H. Calkins (12th IL Cav), "Brandy Station." [10/63]

3:4. A. B. Sampson (1st CO Cav), "Apache Canyon."

3:5-6. Picket Shots: C. P. Maxwell (43rd OH), Kennesaw Mountain; P. C. Mills (33rd MA), Chancellorwsville.

4:7. Obit.

May 25

1:1-5. Corps History. [Seventeenth]

3:1. Knight, Part 11.

3:2-3. Charles W. Hathaway (1st MA), "Chancellorsville."

3:3. Lee H. Rudisille (36th OH), "The Fourteenth Corps."

3:3-4. Dwight Warren (189th NY), "Hatcher's Run."

3:4. E. M. Payne (34th IL), "At Kennesaw Mountain."

3:5-6. Picket Shots: youngest; Jacob Reep (19th OH), Chickamauga.

3:6. "Truly Brave. A Tribute to the Memory of Col. Kibbe, 6th N.Y. Heavy Artillery."

4:5. Biog: William Lochren (1st MN).

4:7. Obit.

8:1. Mary S. Gist, "A Faithful Negro. An Incident of the Surrender of the City of Vicksburg."

8:3. Biog: William P. Carlin.

8:3. "No Place for a Trolley. An Electric Road to be Built to Run Through the Gettysburg Battlefield."

8:4. Ellis, Part 28.

June 1

1:1-5. Corps History. [Seventeenth]

1:6-7, 2:1-4. Henry A. Harman (12th NY Cav), "A Year in Six Rebel Prisons."

3:1-2. (77th NY), "Antietam. Where Gen. McClellan Received Reports During the Battle."

3:2. Knight, Part 12.

3:3. "Fitz-John Porter."

3:3. E. Cook (8th NY Hvy Art), "Not Raw Troops."

3:4. Henry P. Ayres, "The 77th Ill. Its Behavior at the Assault on Vicksburg, May 22, 1863."

3:4. J. W. Hinkley (3rd WI), "At Gettysburg."

3:5-6. Picket Shots: C. S. Yawger (9th MD), Belle Isle; A. J. Ferguson (62nd PA), Appomattox tree; youngest; N. W. Elmendorf (6th PA Res), 2nd Manassas; William Evans (23rd IA), Big Black River; G. L. Cruikshank (11th PA Cav), Hampton R oads.

4:7. Obit.

8:4. "Gettysburg Battlefield. What the Government May Do to Stop Its Defacement by the Railroad."

June 8

1:1-4. Corps History. [Seventeenth]

1:5-7. Harman, Part 2.

3:1. Charles Rapp (11th NJ), "Chancellorsville."

3:1. "Col. Hamlin Interposes." [Chancellorsville]

3:1-2. Knight, Part 13.

3:2-3. J. F. Carter (3rd MD), "At the Crossroads." [Wilderness]

3:3. S. K. Crawford (50th OH), "Rear of Perryville."

3:4-5. Picket Shots: Horace Baker (8th WI), POW march from Iuka to Tupelo; Judge S. Klinefelter (28th PA), Gettysburg; youngest.

4:7. Obit.

5:4. Biog: G. M. Sternberg (surgeon general).

June 15

1:1-5. Corps History. [Seventeenth]

1:6-7, 2:1-3. Harman, Part 3.

3:1-2. John H. Connell (7th VA Cav), "Sacking the Valley. A Plea for the People Who Suffered from This Visitation."

3:2. Mary S. Gist, "Grant's Heart. One of the Occasions When He Showed His Humanity." [Vicksburg]

3:2-3. John Haley (17th ME), "Chancellorsville."

3:3. S. C. Jones (22nd IA), "Jones Makes Answer. He Scores a Critic Who Wrote About Vicksburg."

3:3. S. C. Frey (Bty D, 1st OH), "The Saunders Raid."

3:4-5. Picket Shots: Noah T. Frederick (22nd IA), John Sewell (77th IL), Vicksburg; A. C. Hamlin, Chancellorsville.

4:6-7. Obit.

June 22

1:1-6. A. C. Hamlin, "Chancellorsville. The Attack of Jackson and the Resistance of the Eleventh Corps."

1:7, 2:1-4. Harman, Part 4.

3:1-2. J. A. Vaughan, "Zollicoffer's Death."

3:2. Daniel Matson (4th US Col Art), "Supports Comrade Moss. Notwithstanding the Incomplete Testimony of the Rebellion Records."

3:2-3. E. M. Watson (9th MI Cav), "'Where's Dat Darky?' "

3:3. Samuel S. Kelso (Bty D, 1st OH), "The Saunders Raid."

3:4-5. Picket Shots: William Joden (23rd WI), Camp Tyler; S. C. Bradley (111th NY), Gettysburg.

4:7. Obit.

8:3. "Gettysburg Battlefield. The Vandals Pursuing Their Work Regardless of the Numerous Objections Raised."

June 29

1:1-4. Hamlin, Part 2.

3:1-2. Joseph F. Carter (3rd MD), "Hooker's Errors."

3:2. J. H. C. Brewer (6th MD), "Recollections."

3:2. PPW, "Into Atlanta, and What the 5th Conn. Did on the Way There."

3:3. A. J. Merrifield (122nd NY), "At Cedar Creek."

3:4-5. Picket Shots: August E. Zeitler (109th PA), Gettysburg; T. D. McGillicuddy, Stroupp family of Venango County, PA.

4:6. Obit.s

8:4. "Another Monument. A Description of the Statue Erected by New York at Gettysburg in Honor of Her Soldiers."

July 6

1:1-5. Hamlin, Part 3.

3:1-2. R. H. G. Minty (4th MI Cav), "Picketing and Scouting." [6/63]

3:2. C. R. Warfield (121st OH), "Benton's Crossroads."

3:2. J. E. De Forest (116th NY), "In the Valley." [9/64]

3:3. Charles W. Hathaway (1st MA), "In Time of Danger. A Belief Expressed that No Man is Absolutely Fearless."

3:3. John Brogan (67th NY), "Front of Petersburg." [4/2/65]

3:4-5. Picket Shots: A. P. Connolly (6th MN), Zollicoffer's sword; W. H. Haines (22nd IA), Thomas C. Mathews (77th IL), Vicksburg.

4:5. "The Farragut Statue." [Boston]

4:6. Biog: Lyman M. Ward (14th WI).

4:6. Obit.

July 13

1:1-6. Hamlin, Part 4.

3:1-2. Minty, Part 2.

3:2. C. Woodruff (64th OH), "Gen. Zollicoffer's Death."

3:2-3. Martin Schacht (Bty G, 2nd US), "First Bull Run."

3:3. George W. Butterfield (22nd MI), "A Trying Situation. Signaling the Presence of Forrest in the Face of Almost Certain Death." [Franklin, TN, 6/4/63]

3:6. Picket Shots: J. B. McDonald (1st Btn NY Ss), death of Colonel Raulston, 24th NY Cav.

4:7. Obit.

5:5. Biog: William Newby (40th IL).

6:2. Biog: L. H. Williams (4th OH Cav).

8:1-3. "Gettysburg Vandalism. How the Sacred Soil is Being Used by a Corporation."

8:3. "At Gettysburg. Annual Meeting of the Battlefield Memorial Association."

8:4. "New York Day. The Dedication of the Shaft in Honor of the Dead Heroes of the State." [Gettysburg]

July 20

1:1-6. Hamlin, Part 5.

1:7, 2:1-2. S. M. Howard (28th IL), "A Ride of Horror. The Peabody Encounters a Fierce Storm in the Gulf of Mexico." [2/65]

3:1. G. L. Camp (92nd OH), "Sherman's Bummers. A Trip to Kingston, N.C., for Rations and the Capture of Horses and Hams."

3:1-2. Eugene Sullivan (42nd NY), "Ball's Bluff."

3:2-3. G. A. Harman, "Peach Tree Creek."

3:3. Edward Webster, "The 2nd Tenn. Heavy Artillery."

3:4-5. Picket Shots: Youngest; Alfred Turner (5th NY Hvy Art), Cedar Creek; C. F. Hull (11th IA), Atlanta; Cyrus Fanning (101st IL), first in Atlanta.

3:5. George T. Fonda (7th MO), "The Cannoneer. A Comrade Praises Both Him and Johnny Cook."

4:6. Obit.

4:7. "Col. Edward E. Cross."

5:3. Obit: William H. Enochs (1st WV), John C. Kelton.

5:4. "Gen. Baird at Jonesboro."

6:1-2. Biog: Thomas G. Sample (127th PA).

July 27

1:1-5. Hamlin, Part 6.

1:6-7, 2:1-2. R. F. Whitzel (61st IL), "War Time Tales."

3:1-2. S. C. Miles (8th WI), "Capture of Jackson."

3:2. William Simmons, "The Congress. Comrade Simmons Tells of Her Last European Cruise."

3:3. C. F. Barnes (5th WI), "Petersburg." [4/2/65]

3:3. J. J. Stevens (18th NY), "Pet of the Regiment."

3:5. E. M. Watson (1st MI Cav), "Shaking a Brigadier. Why Leaving One's Jacket Open Became a Serious Offense." [S. W. Crawford]

3:4-5. Picket Shots: Youngest.

3:5. E. C. Wilcox (19th MI), "First Into Atlanta."

4:7. Obit.

5:3. "The Trolley at Gettysburg."

August 3

1:1-5. Hamlin, Part 7.

1:6-7, 2:1-3. Whitzel, Part 2.

3:1-2. Miles, Part 2.

3:2-3. R. C. Rankin (7th OH Cav), "The Saunders Raid."

3:3. "The 55th Indiana."

3:4-5. Picket Shots: R. R. Risley (10th IN), death of Zollicoffer.

3:5. R. H. G. Minty (4th MI Cav), "The Saber Brigade. Gen. Minty Tells of Its Part in the Shelbyville Battle."

4:7. Obit.

5:6. "Reunions of Battery C, 1st N.Y." [includes Gettysburg monument]

8:4. Obit: George W. Morgan.

August 10

1:1-5. Hamlin, Part 8.

2:4. Biog: John E. Craig (6th OH, 5th OH Cav).

3:1. Rankin, Part 2.

3:2. R. A. Moss (4th US Col Art), "Colored Troops."

3:2. Arthur Linn (10th NY), "*Merrimac* and *Monitor*."

3:3. Carl Hartmann, "Hard Times. How Battery M, 5th U. S. Artillery, Went to Dry Tortugas."

3:4-5. Picket Shots: Youngest.

3:5. "Chancellorsville. A Veteran Defends Gen. Pleasonton Against Col. Hamlin's Charge."

4:7. Obit.

6:6-7. Biog: Charles H. Shute (2nd NH), J. C. Bigger (92nd IL).

August 17

1:1-5, 2:6. R. F. Whitzel (61st IL, editor), "'Kaintuck'. Experiences of Residents in a Border State in 1861."

3:1. Charles Rapp (11th NJ), "Chancellorsville."

3:2. Clarence Wilson (4th PA Hvy Art), "At Cold Harbor."

3:3. John Wessels (3rd MO Cav), "'Don't Burn Us!' A Hitherto Untold Exploit of a Squad of Missouri Cavalrymen." [winter 1861]

3:4-5. Picket Shots: Levi Curkins (7th IA), Belmont; youngest.

3:5. "At Gettysburg. Dedication of N.Y.'s Monument and Reunion of Greene's Brigade."

4:7. Obit.

5:4. Obit: Thornton A. Jenkins (USN).

August 24

1:1-4. Charles F. Benjamin (40th NY), "Third Corps Line at Gettysburg. A Presentment of the Meade-Sickles Controversy."

1:5-7, 2:1-4. P. S. Michie, "A Regular at Fort Wagner."

3:1-2. E. M. Watson (1st MI Cav), "Gen. Crawford's Escort. Comrade Watson Tells About the Taking of Orange Court House."

3:2. Samuel Dunham (63rd PA), "Chancellorsville."

3:2-3. "A Pure Romance. No Sunday Bells—All Stopped by Shelling."

3:3. N. V. Hutchinson (7th MA), "Eleventh Corps. A Discussion of Its Behavior at Chancellorsville."

3:3. Patrick Fitzgerald (57th IL), "'Corp' Sweeny, and His Predecessors and Successors in Command of a Division."

3:4-5. Picket Shots: A. B. Wells (8th PA Cav), Chancellorsville.

4:6. Biog: Hubert Dilger (Bty I, 1st OH).

4:7. Obit.

6:5-6. Biog: S. H. Hurst (OH), William James (100th PA).

August 31

1:1-5, 2:6. Charles A. Clough, "A Little Boy's War Experience. A Narrative of Hospital Service in Alabama."

1:6-7, 2:1-2. John P. Bard (13th PA Res), "The Affair at Harrisonburg, Va."

3:1-2. R. H. G. Minty (4th MI Cav), "Picketing and Scouting." [post Chattanooga]

3:2-3. Alonzo B. Searing (11th NJ), "Chancellorsville."

3:3. G. T. Dennis (85th NY), "Wise's Forks."

3:4-5. Picket Shots: C . W. Murdock, Gen. J. J. Bartlett, 9/3/63.

3:5. G. L. Cruikshank (11th PA Cav), "*Merrimac* and *Monitor*."

4:7. Obit.

September 7

3:1-2. Minty, Part 2.

3:2. E. M. Watson (1st MI Cav), "Crawford's Escort. A Forgotten Message and a Fighting Brigadier."

3:3. William A. Millen (78th PA), "Feasts of Ham." [1/64]

3:3. "The Body of Col. Fletcher Webster."

3:4-5. Picket Shots: George W. Toms (5th NY Cav), Orange Courthouse, 8/2/62; A. L. Jones (17th KY), Corinth; Ira M. Carpenter (2nd VT), Wilderness; S. A. Evans, Cooper Shop Volunteer Saloon.

4:7. Obit.

September 14

2:6-7. F. S. Dickinson, "In Old Virginia. The 5th N.Y. Cavalry—Gen. John Pope's Campaign."

3:1-2. A. D. Cutler, "His First Week."

3:2-3. A. Roberts (29th WI), "A Great Feat. The Part Taken by the 29th Wisconsin in the Building of the Dam Across the Red River."

4:4-5. Biog: John G. B. Adams (19th MA), Louis Wagner (88th PA).

5:6. Obit.

September 21

1:6-7, 2:1-3. Dickinson, Part 2.

3:1-2. Cutler, Part 2.

3:2-3. George E. Dolton (Bty M, 1st IL), "A Desperate Field." [Chickamauga]

3:3-4. Edwin F. Spotford, "A Good Record. Some of the Experiences of Co. M, 'Lander Guards," 14th Mass. Heavy Artillery."

4:7. Obit.

8:2. Biog: John W. Parks (23rd, 28th, 147th PA).

September 28

1:1-5. W. H. Sanderson (9th VT), "Harper's Ferry and Its Surrender."

1:6-7, 2:1-2. R. H. G. Minty (4th MI Cav), "The Saber Brigade." [10 11/63]

3:1-2. S. C. Miles (8th WI), "Live Eagle Brigade. One of Mower's 'Guerrillas' Tells of Some Doin's by 'We-uns'."

3:2-3. H. B. Turrill (72nd OH), "Jackson, Miss. The Part Played by the 95th Ohio, and the First Flag on the Capitol."

3:3. "At Chancellorsville. Reynolds and Meade Wanted to Attack Jackson." [A. S. Webb letter to J. H. Stine]

3:4-5. Picket Shots: H. A. Dudley (5th VT), brothers in Company E; youngest.

3:5. J. B. Work (52nd OH), "At Chickamauga."

4:7. Obit.

8:3. Biog: Charles G. Davis (1st MA Cav).

October 5

1:1-5, 2:6. Sanderson, Part 2.

1:6-7, 2:1-3. W. H. Brearley (17th MI), "Siege of Knoxville."

3:1-2. "The Bloody Lane." [Antietam]

3:3-4. James Larson (4th US Cav), "Within the Rebel Lines." [9/20/63]

3:5. Picket Shots: A. A. Cvantrell (12th IL Cav), Alexandria, LA, shooting by General Custer.

4:7. Obit.

October 12

1:1-5. George S. Wilson (12th US), "Wilder's Brigade. The Mounted Infantry in the Tullahoma-Chickamauga Campaigns."

1:6-7, 2:1-4. Brearley, Part 2.

3:1-3. "Men on Horseback. The Cavalry, and Its Behavior and Importance in the Civil War."

3:3. W. W. Whitmarsh (29th ME), "Building the Dam." [Red River]

3:3. H. W. Phelps (95th OH), "At Jackson, Miss."

3:4-5. Picket Shots: W. E. Dann (3rd NY Light Art), Wise's Forks; ZM. W. Nelson (40th IA), brothers; M. G. Ries, death of Zollicoffer.

4:7. Obit.

October 19

1:1-5. Wilson, Part 2.

1:6-7, 2:1. N. H. Karns (18th OH), "The Loss of the Sultana."

2:2-3. "To 'Little Mac'." [Philadelphia statue]

3:1-3. Thomas Murphy (45th IL), "Shiloh."

3:3. George W. Reed (55th IN), "The Old 55th."

3:3. M. M. Horton (77th PA), "Rabbit Hunting."

3:4-5. Picket Shots: J. L. Joseph (8th WI), Jackson, MS; J. H. Bloom (Bty F, 1st OH), brothers; youngest.

3:5. "At Cane River. Sad Scenes that Came to a Veteran's Notice There." [4/64]

4:7. Obit.

October 26

1:1-6. Wilson, Part 3.

1:7, 2:1-2. Karns, Part 2.

3:1-2. "As an Orator. A Pen Picture. Gen. Howard, by Pvt. Dalzell."

3:2-3. S. C. Miles (8th WI), "A Surrejoinder." [Jackson, MS]

3:3. R. H. G. Minty (4th MI Cav), "Minty and Crook. The Cavalry Commander Objects to Some of Comrade Doyle's Statements."

3:4-5. Picket Shots: L. L. Lancaster (2nd WI Cav), shooting in Alexandria, LA.

3:5. Thomas J. Williams (56th OH), "In a Norther." [12/65]

4:7. Obit.

8:5. Obit: Henry Rush (6th PA Cav).

November 2

1:1-5. Karns, Part 3.

3:1-3. R. S. Littlefield (14th MA Hvy Art), "'The Heavies.' Service Around Washington During Pope's Campaign."

3:3. W. E. Doyle (17th IN), "Wilder's Brigade, and a Few Comparative Statements With Reference to Knoxville."

3:4-5. Picket Shots: E. T. Lee (41st IL), Shiloh; youngest; Jacob Kling (7th PA Cav), first in Atlanta; R. R. Risley (4th KY), death of Zollicoffer; brothers.

3:5. H. W. Phelps (95th OH), "Jackson, Miss."

4:7. Obit.

November 9

1:1-5. George E. Dolton (Bty M, 1st IL), "Chickamauga. Some Disputed Points as to the Fighting on Sunday."

1:6-7, 2:1-2. R. C. Rankin (7th OH Cav), "The Story of a Fighting Regiment."

3:1-2. Elliott Winscott (7th IN), "Knoxville Revisited."

3:2. Jacob Fink (55th IL), "Shiloh. How a Comrade Always Understood the Matter of Gen. Johnston's Death."

3:3. R. H. G. Minty (4th MI Cav), "Minty Speaks, Apropos the Story of Being Left on a Skirmish." [Chickamauga]

3:3. R. M. Walsh (CSA), "The Eagle Brigade. Indorsement of a Johnny Reb of a Comrade's Graphic Article." [3/21/64]

3:4-5. Picket Shots: W. S. Wade (5th IL Cav), shooting in Alexandria, LA.

3:5. John Barnard (137th NY), "Lookout Mountain."

4:6. Obit.

November 16

1:1-3. R. H. G. Minty (4th MI Cav), "The Saber Brigade." [Atlanta]

1:4-7, 2:1-2. Rankin, Part 2.

3:1. John H. Keatley (125th PA), "Ill-Timed Bravery. How One Competent General Lost His Life Through Carelessness." [Mansfield]

3:1-2. H. B. Turrill (72nd OH), "Jackson and the 95th Ohio."

3:2. W. C. Yard (4th PA Cav), "Almost Taken In. Two Narrow Escapes of a Cavalry Company in One Day." [9/62]

3:3. George W. Smith (7th PA Cav), "More About Johnston."

3:3. "A Computation. Comparison Between the Work Done by a Soldier and a Coalheaver."

3:4-5. Picket Shots: P. P. Wilson (5th CT), first in Atlanta; nrothers; Marion Cox (87th OH), Harper's Ferry.

4:7. Obit.

5:3. Biog: George D. Ruggles (AAG).

November 23

1:1-5. Rankin, Part 3.

1:6-7. William Simmons, "First Naval Movement. An Early Union Expedition on the Coast of North Carolina." [Hatteras]

3:1-2. JRP (32nd IL), "On the Hatchie."

3:2. (81st OH), "'Veteran Thieves.' A Counter Claim to the Honor of Being First Hands at Stealing from the Enemy."

3:2-3. S. C. Miles (8th WI), "Still at It."

3:3. G. J. Hastings (2nd KY Cav), "'Speaking Up.' A Kentucky Cavalryman Puts in a Word for Another Fighting Regiment."

3:4-5. Picket Shots: James Holehouse (7th MA), Marye's Heights; Alfred Durand (9th IL), Orange Courthouse; brothers; Edmond W. Dayton (36th WI), High Bridge.

4:7. Obit.

November 30

1:1-4. "From Culpeper to Spottsylvania." [Second Division, Fifth Corps.]

1:5-7, 2:1. John A. Joyce (24th KY), "Sheridan. Personal Reminiscences of the Great Cavalryman."

3:1-2. M. C. Huyette (125th PA), "On a Bloody Field." [Antietam]

3:2. Joseph Swan (52nd OH), "At Chickamauga."

3:3. S. C. Miles (8th WI), "Sad to Relate. How the Fair Fame of a Brave Company was Forever Tarnished."

3:3. James E. Robinson, "The 72nd Indiana."

3:4-5. Picket Shots: F. A. Ashby (17th KY), P. A. Bryant (17th KY), Corinth; John F. Wentz (Bty C, 1st PA), Williamsburg deserters.

4:7. Obit.

5:3. "At Appomattox." [historical tablets]

8:5. Obit: Jeremiah M. Rusk (25th WI).

December 7

1:1-4. Edward F. Chever (89th IL), "Just Before the Battle. Thrilling Midnight March of Sherman's Rear-Guard. . . ." [Spring Hill]

1:5-7. Henry D. O'Brien, "The 1st Minnesota at Gettysburg."

3:1-2. B. F. Boring (30th IL), "Belmont."

3:2. N. N. Ogden (25th MI), "A Musician's Story."

3:3. W. L. Welch (23rd MA), "The Army Discredited. Will L. Welch Corrects Some Statements About the First Naval Expedition."

3:3. James Larson (4th US Cav), "Left on Picket."

3:4-5. Picket Shots: C. G. Post (2nd KY Cav), Wheeler's Raid.

3:6. E. A. LaBay (USMC), "Fort Fisher."

4:7. Obit.

5:5-6. "Again on Once Gory Fields. [NY Commission at Chattanooga]

December 14

1:1-4. J. P. Ross (78th OH), "On Veteran Furlough. The Surrender of an Ohio Regiment Without a Shot Being Fired." [10/11/63]

1:5-7, 2:1-3. William Simmons, "The Great Blockade."

3:1-2. W. C. Yard (4th PA Cav), "The Escape. Daring and Suffering in the Rebel Country by Two 4th Pa. Cavalrymen."

3:2-3. E. H. Fuller (77th NY), "Marye's Heights."

3:3. William Schwartz (1st OH Cav), "Claims Too Much. A Question as to Who Formed the Advance of Sherman's Relieving Force at Knoxville."

3:4-5. Picket Shots: J. Balsley (27th IN), Gordon (5th CT), Atlanta; Ezra Peters (95th OH), Nashville; J. N. Stephens (2nd MI Cav), Corinth.

4:7. Obit.

December 21

1:1-5, 2:5-6. S. C. Miles (8th WI), "Fighting at Tupelo."

1:6-7, 2:1. R. H. G. Minty (4th MI Cav), "The Saber Brigade."

3:1-2. J. B. Work (52nd OH), "Perryville."

3:2-3. Boring, Part 2.

3:4-6. Picket Shots: William Simmons (USN), Hatteras Inlet; D. J. Vasbinder (105th PA), Fair Oaks; B. F. Boring (30th IL), Jackson, MS.

4:7. Obit.

December 28

1:1-3. J. W. Cotes (12th IA), "The Iowa Brigade on Shiloh's Field."

1:4-7. William Simmons, "Naval Sketches. Some of the Most Effective Federal Vessels in the Civil War." [New Ironsides]

3:1. J. H. Prather (91st OH), "Cedar Creek."

3:1-2. R. H. G. Minty (4th MI Cav), "No Injustice. The Part Taken by Minty's Brigade in the Pursuit of Wheeler."

3:2-3. James Larson (4th US Cav), "Wilson's Body-Guard did Not Support the 4th U.S. Artillery—A Cavalry Stampede—A Fruitless Charge."

3:3. George E. Dolton (Bty M, 1st IL), "Dolton Speaks. Tells What He Knows About the Notice of Relief to Knoxville."

3:4-5. Picket Shots: P. P. Wilson (5th CT), Frank P. Delany (I7th WI), Atlanta; Thomas J. Bond (2nd OH), Roswell Gap; Edward W. Rogers (43rd MA), Hatteras Inlet; William Dewalt (101st OH), Nashville; George H. Uhler (93rd PA), Marye's Heights; brothers; J. W. Polk (39th OH), Corinth.

4:7. Obit.

1894

January 4

1:1-4. Simmons, Part 2. [Mississippi, Susquehanna, Powhatan]

1:5-7, 2:1-2. T. H. Wheeler (1st MI Cav), "In the Army. Reminiscences of a Quartermaster-Sergeant."

3:1-2. A. G. Hatry (183rd OH), "A Lost Opportunity." [Spring Hill]

3:2-3. H. M. Coburn, "One of Carney's Stories. The Close Call a Scout Experienced in the Hands of Bloodless Secessionists."

3:4-6. Picket Shots: James R. Clerihan (6th IL Cav), M. L. Price (12th MO Cav), Zenas J. Wright (130th IN), Nashville; E. T. Parr (17th IN), relief of Knoxville; John Hillis (16th KY), Wilmington; W. Siegfried (118th OH), Knoxville; Edgar E. Adams, Spring Hill.

4:7. Obit.

January 11

1:1-6, 2:6. W. H. Sanderson (2nd US), "Sykes's Regulars." [Chancellorsville]

1:7, 2:1-2. W. L. Welch, "'Baldy' Smith's Vindication. A Review of the Situation of the Federal Army from Chattanooga to Petersburg."

3:1. W. M. Clark (2nd TN, "At Rogersville." [11/6/63]

3:2. G. W. Ford (11th CT), "An Errand of Charity. The Kindheartedness of Two Conn. Yanks Whose Chicken Dinner was Spoiled."

3:2. John P. Woodward (12th CT), "'Horse and Man.' A Nineteenth Corps Comrade Tells How Sheridan Came Down to the Front of the Front."

3:3. W. L. Welch (23rd MA), "Welch Hits Back." [Hatteras Inlet]

3:3. George E. Dolton (Bty M, 1st IL), "Saving the Guns." [Roswell Gap]

3:4-6. Picket Shots: G. B. Sherman (121st OH), Perryville; M. M. Webb (8th KY), Lookout Mountain; A. M. Taylor (5th IA Cav), Pulaski, 12/64; William H. Kuhn, USS *Conn*; William K. Johnson (12th MO), Jackson, MS; brothers; youngest.

4:7. Obit.

January 18

1:1-4. Welch, Part 2.

1:5-7, 2:1. Simmons, Part 3. [Harriet Lane, San Jacinto]

3:1. C. W. keifer (14th IL), "On the Hatchie."

3:1-2. J. Hinson (33rd OH), "Entering Corinth."

3:2. Francis O'Leary (130th IN), "At Nashville."

3:2-3. J. K. Wallace (98th IL), "A Little 'Scrap.' Incidentally, a Word About Long's Brigade on the March to Knoxville."

3:3. P. K. Faulk (11th PA), "Cavalry Losses."

3:3. R. H. G. Minty (4th MI Cav), "Casts No Discredit. Gen. Minty Raises But One Question with Comrade Larson."

3:4-5. Picket Shots: Heaviest losses.

3:6. Robert Henderson (6th KS Cav), "A Knight Errant. Some Recollections of Col. William A. Phillips."

4:7. Obit.

January 25

1:1-4. Welch, Part 3.

1:5-7. Simmons, Part 4. [monitors]

3:1. T. W. Holman (21st MO), "Tupelo."

3:2. Carl Hartmann (Bty M, 5th US), "Cedar Creek."

3:2-3. C. E. Faulkner (5th PA Res), "In Pemberton. The Trick that was Worked on Prisoners When Moving to Belle Isle."

3:3. Charles Winters (USS *Monticello*), "Welch Criticized." [Hatteras Inlet]

3:3. C. G. Post (4th OH Cav), "He Specifies." [Minty, 10/63]

3:4. H. T. Carlisle (81st OH), "Death of Bread. A Yankee Device for Securing Decent Rations."

3:4. Dan Ashton (39th IL), "Found Out. Volunteers Who Sought to Know if Sumter was Evacuated." [11/63]

3:5-6. Picket Shots: H. N. Minnigh (1st PA Res), Glendale.

3:6. J. M. Thomas (7th OH Cav), "Add Their Testimony. Corroborating Letters About the Story of a Fighting Regiment."

4:7. Obit.

5:3. "Bravery Recognized." [Medals of Honor for Moses Veale & E. A. Carr]

February 1

1:1-6. Welch, Part 4.

1:7, 2:1-3. John K. Shellenburger (64th OH), "More About Spring Hill."

3:1-2. E. Tarrant (1st KY Cav), "Knoxville. How Gen. Burnside Learned of the Approach of Gen. Sherman."

3:2. T. A. Smith (32nd IL), "On the Hatchie."

3:2. "Brothers."

3:3. W. E. Webster (1st NY Bty), "Takes Issue. Some Comparative Statements as Presented by a Sixth Corps Man." [Cedar Creek]

3:4. H. C. Connelly (14th IL Cav), "A Hot Time. The 14th Ill. Cav. in a Fight with the Cherokee Indians of N.C."

3:5-6. Picket Shots: R. D. Whitaker (28th IL), Hatchie River; Joseph G. Ogden (1st NJ), heaviest loss; L. W. Cogswell (11th NH), Knoxville.

4:7. Obit.

February 8

1:1-6, 2:6. David S. Stanley, "Corinth."

1:7, 2:1-2. William Simmons, "Up the Red River."

3:1-2. Joseph W. Grant (14th ME), "Davis in Custody."

3:3-4. Eben Gordon (2nd RI), "On Bull Run's Field."

3:4. S. C. Miles (8th WI), "Under Arrest. One of Smith's 'Guerrillas' Jollies Gen. Mower with Satisfactory Results."

3:5-6. Picket Shots: Dennis L. Dunham (15th OH Bty), Hatchie River.

3:6. M. S. Harman (53rd IL), "On the Hatchie."

4:7. Obit.

5:4. "Deserved Honors; Medal to Lyman Wheaton." [8th IL, Fort Blakely]

February 15

1:1-5. A. Brandley (23rd KY), "A Kentucky Regiment at Chickamauga."

1:6-7, 2:1. B. F. Boring (30th IL), "The Fight at Britton's Lane."

3:1. Gordon, Part 2.

3:1-2. Thomas Fay (42nd IL), "First Into Corinth."

3:2. L. S. Fallis (8th IN Cav), "Tunnel Hill." [2/64]

3:3. W. H. H. Benefiel (17th IN), "Wilder's Men. More About the Wheeler Raid, and the Trip from Chattanooga to Knoxville."

3:3. R. H. G. Minty (4th MI Cav), "Michigan's Cavalry." [losses]

3:4-5. Picket Shots: Brothers; longest service; D. W. Rank (7th PA Cav), J. F. Galtry (37th IN), Chickamauga; Charles H. Eastman (2nd NH), Drewry's Bluff.

4:7. Obit.

February 22

1:1-5, 2:5-6. G. V. Loud (73rd IL), "From Pulaski to Nashville."

1:6-7. H. O. Crosby (5th US Cav), "Soldiers of the Saddle."

3:1-2. A. G. Hatry. "The 18th Kentucky. How It Behaved at Chickamauga—Some Personal Experiences."

3:2. A. H. Boies (4th MI), "A Time of Trial. The Kind of Service that Made Men of Striplings."

3:3. B. H. Tripp (7th WI), "Brains and Brawn. The Engineers of the First Corps Headquarters, Their Work and Endurance."

3:3. H. C. Connelly (14th IL Cav), "A Hot Time." [Cherokees in NC]

3:4. Benefiel, Part 2.

3:5-6. Picket Shots: S. C. Miles (8th WI), Tupelo; Henry C. Kern (3rd PA Hvy Art), sutlers; longest service.

3:6. M. W. Lindsley (1st NY Cav), "Worthy of Custer." [8/26/64]

3:6. H. A. Cooper (3rd MO), "An Artillery Charge." [Vicksburg]

4:7. Obit.

March 1

1:1-4. R. Hannaford (2nd OH Cav), "A Cavalryman at Cedar Creek."

1:5-7, 2:1-2. R. H. G. Minty (4th MI Cav), "The Saber Brigade." [McAfee's Crossroads, Big Shanty]

3:1-2. W. C. Yard (4th PA Cav), "Unable to Help. Men Obliged to Set Their Horses in Silence at Fredericksburg."

3:2-3. C. L. Holbrook (92nd IL), "Raiding Around Atlanta."

3:3. James McMahon (41st OH), "Rear-Guard Duty." [Chickamauga]

3:4. W. L. Welch (23rd MA), "Will Not Retreat. Comrade Welch Makes His Position Plain to the Naval Veterans."

3:4. D. Redfield, "Gen. Bailey." [Red River]

3:4. J. H. Campbell (50th PA), "At Knoxville."

3:5-6. Picket Shots: G. J. Hastings, concerning Miller R. McCulloch, 2nd KY Cav; longest service; Truman Proper (37th IL), Pea Ridge; J. H. Van Eman (39th OH), Corinth; Norman C. Daman (12th WV), Appomattox tree.

3:6. John W. Ratcliff (5th KY Cav), "Under a Dog-Tent."

4:7. Obit.

8:1-3. "Old Forts. Those that are Decaying Around Washington."

March 8

1:1-5. W. A. Donaldson (Sickles's Brigade), "Fighting Before Richmond." [Seven Pines]

1:6-7, 2:1. Hannaford, Part 2.

3:1-2. David Nation (69th IN), "Unwritten History. Some Incidents of the Fight at Richmond, Ky."

3:2. B. F. Boring (30th IL), "Some Reasons Why the Cavalry and Infantry Did Not Fraternize."

3:3. J. R. Martin (1st IA Cav), "Got the Ham." [Red River]

3:3. R. H. G. Minty (4th MI Cav), "Rossville Gap."

3:4. W. H. Sanderson (2nd US), "From a Regular. He Shows Forth the Acts and Merits of His Fellows."

3:5-6. Picket Shots: J. M. Paulk (39th OH), Corinth; longest service; T. B. Hambledon (79th PA), Chattanooga; heaviest loss.

4:6-7. Obit.

March 15

1:1-6, 2:5-6. B. F. Boring (30th IL), "From Cairo to Donelson."

1:7, 2:1-2. Charles H. Eager (15th MA), "Ball's Bluff."

3:1-2. "Famous for Charging. More About Old Town Creek and the Battle of Nashville."

3:2. EAW (4th MN), "Saving a Sutler."

3:3. P. Playford (12th NY Bty), "'Goin' Through Im.' A Comrade Tells of an Incident of Sutler Raiding."

3:3-4. (11th MO), "Corinth." [battle]

3:4. C. J. Hermann (4th MA), "A Terrible Night." [picket duty among the dead]

3:5-6. Picket Shots: J. H. Coffman (27th IA), Red River.

3:6. R. H. G. Minty (4th MI Cav), "Columbus, Ga."

4:7. Obit.

5:4. "Longstreet on Early."

March 22

1:1-6, 2:6. W. W. Porter (7th IL Cav), "Always at the Front."

1:7, 2:1-2. RT (Bty D, 5th US), "On the Second Day." [Gettysburg]

3:1. J. H. Prather (91st OH), "Cedar Creek."

3:2. A. P. Cutting (82nd OH), "This Is How It Was." [Spring Hill]

3:3. William Wallis (117th IL), "A Night Attack." [Tupelo]

3:3. Joseph F. Carter (3rd MD), "Poplar Spring Church."

3:3-4. (45th PA), "One Night in the Pits. A Period of Danger and Suffering at Knoxville."

3:4. A. V. Bailey (2nd US Cav), "Boots and Saddles." [Cedar Creek]

3:5-6. Picket Shots: Brothers; longest service; J. R. Sherwood (9th IN), Corinth; C. D. Cooper (72nd IL), Nashville.

4:6. Obit.

6:1. Biog: S. G. Blakeman (17th CT).

7:6. Biog: W. C. Beck (7th NY Cav, 19th NY Bty).

March 29

1:1-5. Porter, Part 2.

1:5. Camilla B. White, "The Battle of Gettysburg." [poem]

1:6-7, 2:1-2. Patrick Breen (2nd US), "Regulars to the Van. Their Untarnished Record and Brilliant Service."

3:1. A. B. Carney (5th US Cav), "In Tight Places. Adventures of One of Our Scouts on the Kilpatrick Raid."

3:2. James M. Whallon (11th MI), "Another Claim. The 11th Michigan and the 18th Ohio at Rossville Gap."

3:2-3. Launcelot L. Scott (18th OH), "At Chickamauga."

3:3. W. S. Brown (18th OH), "Davis's Crossroads." [9/11/63]

3:4-5. Picket Shots: N. A. Pinney (104th PA), Pulaski to Nashville; George H. Lusk (122nd NY), Cedar Creek; George W. Toms (5th NY Cav), 10/9/64; longest service.

3:5. J. W. Holcomb, "The 5th Connecticut. [Cedar Mountain]

3:5. J. R. Palmer (32nd IL), "On the Hatchie."

4:7. Obit.

6:2. Biog: William Emsley (116th PA).

8:1-4. "The Union Soldier. Mr. Pickler's Grand Speech in the House Recently."

April 5

1:1-5. Thomas H. Peabody (4th MI Cav), "A Daring Dash." [Wilson's Raid]

1:6-7, 2:1-2. Porter, Part 3.

3:1. Carney, Part 2.

3:2. Richard W. Tuffs (4th MI), "Constant Fighting. Something of the Terrible Struggles Along the Chickahominy in '62."

3:2-3. John Wessels (3rd MO Cav), "A Lively Scrimmage. Fighting Under Prentiss in Missouri in 1861." [12/61]

3:3. B. F. Boring (30th IL), "Champion's Hill."

3:4-5. Picket Shots: M. Waters (13th MI), sutler; W. E. Webster (1st NY Bty), Cedar Creek; William Friend (38th IN), Chattanooga; Peter Shipp (97th NY), Appomattox tree; S. Hathaway (3rd IA Cav), Guntown.

4:7. Obit.

6:1. Biog: W. P. Campbell (16th KY Cav).

April 12

1:1-4. Porter, Part 4.

1:5-7, 2:1-2. William H. Nichols (7th Sqdn RI Cav), "A Cavalry Escape. The Successful Elusive Movement at Harper's Ferry."

3:1-2. S. A. McDonald (122nd NY), "The Fort Stevens Affair."

3:2. Isaac Cates (52nd OH), "When and Where." [Rossville Gap]

3:3. J. R. Pilkington (2nd CT), "In the Early Days."

3:4-5. Picket Shots: Longest service; S. Hathaway (3rd IA Cav), Old Town Creek; Charles Banks (1st OH), Rossville; H. B. F. Keller (1st KS Bty), Colonel Moonlight; C. C. Clay (3rd OH), Knoxville; W. P. Baker (7th OH Cav), Pea Ridge; William Davis, USS *Susquehanna*; G. W. Scoville (103rd IL), Atlanta.

4:7. Obit.

6:1-2. Biog: J. W. Gilman (20th ME), Thomas G. Lawler (19th IL), David R. Pierce (7th ME Bty).

April 19

1:1-6. George J. Mosher (53rd IL), "A Regiment of Gallant Men."

1:7, 2:1-2. Porter, Part 5.

3:1-2. McDonald, Part 2.

3:2. R. C. Rankin (7th OH Cav), "First Company. Capt. Jacob Ammen's Little Band Signed to Go to War on April 13."

3:2-3. H. W. Phelps (95th OH), "Fighting Kirby Smith." [Richmond, KY]

3:3. A. J. Merrifield (122nd NY), "How They Did It. [Rappahannock Station]

3:4-5. Picket Shots: Thomas Moore (13th WV), Libertyy, 6/64; Thomas K. Baird (5th CT), Cedar Mountain.

3:5. "Blaine's Crossroads. Kind Providence, in the Gise of a Lady, Relieved the Suffering of One Comrade."

4:7. Obit.

April 26

1:1-4. Porter, Part 6.

1:5-7, 2:1-4. Mosher, Part 2.

3:1. Johnson Taylor (3rd OH Cav), "Carrying the News." [Knoxville]

3:1-2. S. L. Wilson (5th US Cav), "A Crow Story." [Shenandoah Valley 1864]

3:2-3. "Grant and Butler. A Discussion of the Comparative Excellence of the Two Generals."

3:3. TBJ (14th IN Bty), "What the Whistle Told. Extraordinary Circumstance Relating to the Evacuation of Corinth."

3:3. R. L. Howard (124th IL), "Straightening Him Out. Lieut. Howard Reads Comrade Boring a Lesson in Geography." [Champion's Hill]

3:4. "Nelson and Corinth. A Defense of the Daughty Chieftain Whose Prime Fault was His Temper."

3:5. Picket Shots: W. W. Hull (123rd OH), Appomattox tree; W. J. Boon (125th IL), Rossville.

4:7. Obit.

May 3

1:1-5. Porter, Part 7.

1:6-7, 2:1-2. William Simmons, "Engines of Destruction. Career and Fate of Some Confederate War Vessels." [Florida, Shenandoah]

3:1. James Tarbell (16th VT), "Lincoln to Sickles. There was Glory Enough at Gettysburg to Go Around."

3:1-2. Grant and Butler, Part 2.

3:2. "'Scooped.' And Now One of the Unfortunates Wants to Find the Captor." [12/1/64, Stony Creek Station]

3:2-3. H. C. Connelly (14th IL Cav), "Gallant and True. Some Interesting Recollections of Gen. Jacob Ammen."

3:3. Charles Winters (USS *Monticello*), "Did See Rebels. It was on Oct. 5, and Yet the Day of the Shelling." [Chickamacomico]

3:4-5. Picket Shots: J. I. McGinnis (2nd TX), Corinth; Gustavus C. Kothi (58th IL), Fort DeRussy; H. B. Booth (27th IA), Tupelo.

3:5. Taylor, Part 2.

4:7. Obit.

May 10

1:1-4. Porter, Part 8.

1:4. B. F. Clarkson, "The Flag of Cemetery Hill." [poem]

1:5-7, 2:1-3. Alfred Davenport (5th NY), "On the Second Bull Run Field."

3:1-2. T. M. Robertson (6th IN Cav), "Richmond, Ky."

3:2. Charles Banks (1st OH), "Rossville Gap."

3:2. "Strawberry Plains."

3:3. J. H. Bradford (30th IL), "Does Not Agree." [Fort Donelson]

3:4. M. L. Moore (2nd IL Cav), "Holly Springs."

3:5. Picket Shots: B. R. Grimstead (3rd IA Cav), capture of Jeff Davis; Benjamin Beha (3rd MO), Vicksburg; L. O. Colburn (51st IL), Pulaski to Nashville.

4:7. Obit.

6:1. Biog: Ivan N. Walker (73rd IN).

May 17

1:1-4. Porter, Part 9.

1:5-7, 2:1-3. Davenport, Part 2.

3:1. Bradford, Part 2.

3:2. J. H. Brewster (5th CT), "'Pope's Whole Army.' What Three Regiments Did at Cedar Mountain."

3:2. "Up Bald Hill. That was a Great Charge at Nashville, and No Mistake."

3:3. (111th NY), "Who Cheered Jackson? Disbelief in the Statement that Yankee Prisoners did at Harper's Ferry."

3:3. John Clark (1st WI Cav), "Had a Hand In It. The 1st Wisconsin Cavalry Aided in Jeff Davis's Capture."

3:4-5. Picket Shots: C. K. Baxter (1st WI Bty), Arkansas Post; T. T. Daniels (2nd IL Cav), Holly Springs; J. H. Bradford (30th IL), Jackson, MS.

3:5. "Disagrees with Grant. A 30th Illinois Man Refers to a Champion's Hill Incident."

4:7. Obit.

5:4. "For Bravery." [Medals of Honor to Edwin Goodrich, Ernest Torgler, Edward Welsh, Hiram W. Purcell, Alphonso M. Lunt]

6:3. Biog: Samuel F. Street (33rd IA).

6:5-6. "Union and Confederate. List of the Members of the House of Representatives and Their Military Service."

8:1-2. "Where Heroes Rest. National Cemeteries Containing Nearly Half a Million Honored Dead."

May 24

1:1-4. J. B. Van Eman, "Making a Brave Stand. The 39th Ohio at the Second Corinth Fight."

1:5-7, 2:1-3. Porter, Part 10.

3:1. J. W. Ratliff (5th KY Cav), "Fired the Last Shot."

3:1. A. A. Gardner (93rd NY), "Bear and Forbear. A Plea for the Presentation of Kindly Sentiment."

3:2. R. C. Rankin (7th OH Cav), "Meant What He Said." [Columbus, GA, 4/16/65]

3:2. R. H. G. Minty (4th MI Cav), "Gen. Minty Protests. Proves that He Casts No Aspersions on the Ohio Brigade."

3:3. W. H. Collingwood (4th PA Cav), "Who the Captor Was." [12/1/64 incident]

3:4. L. S. Fallis (8th IN Cav), "The McCook Raid. To What the Capture of Gen. Stoneman was Due."

3:5. Picket Shots: John R. King (4th CA), human interest story; C. W. Keifer (14th IL), Hatchie River.

4:7. Obit.

May 31

1:1-5. Elliott Winscott, "Fighting Jackson. The 7th Indiana in the Shenandoah Valley in 1862."

1:6-7, 2:1-3. R. H. G. Minty (4th MI Cav), "Picketing and Scouting." [Kennesaw, Roswell, Macon . . .]

3:1-2. J. W. Landerson, "He was There, and Proceeds to Tell How Richmond was Not Entered." [Kilpatrick Raid]

3:2. Reuben S. Little (18th US), "Another Claim." [Rossville Gap]

3:3. Fallis, Part 2.

3:4. J. W. Griswold (44th NY), "Second Bull Run."

3:4. (87th OH), "Denies the Allegation. No 'Lusty Shouts' or 'Cheering Like Mad' When Jackson Passed." [Harper's Ferry]

3:4. (NY), "More Testimony." [Harper's Ferry]

3:5. Picket Shots: I. W. Shideler (93rd OH), Spring Hill; W. H. Phipps (8th NY Cav), Rappahannock Station; A. Davenport (5th NY), corrections to his articles; A. M. Beach (8th WI), L. W. Lacy (8th WI), Holly Springs.

4:7. Obit.

June 7

1:1-4. H. C. Connelly (14th IL Cav), "A Long Chase. Morgan's Raid Through Kentucky, Indiana, and Ohio in 1863."

1:5-7, 2:1-3. E. Cotton, "The Men Who Made the Music. How the 24th Michigan Band Went Through the War."

3:1. B. F. Boring (30th IL), "Cairo to Donelson. Comrade Boring Upholds His Recent Statements.

3:2. EHM (159th OH), "Again in Vicksburg. A Northern Comrade Goes South and Wanders Over the Old Ground."

3:2-3. R. I. Cowden (49th NY), "Fort Stevens."

3:3. John B. Mendenhall (99th NY), "A Night Attack. Confederates Succeed in the Destruction of the Underwriter."

3:3. M. S. Berry (8th NY Bty), D. C. O'Neal (16th NY Hvy Art), "Shot on His Coffin." [3/7/64]

3:4. R. H. G. Minty (4th MI Cav), "The Chief Johnny. Gen. Minty Does Not Coincide with Lieut. Grant's Story of the Capture."

4:7. Obit.

June 14

1:1-4. William Simmons, "Formidable Craft. Two Rebel Rams that Caused Consternation in the North." [Stonewall, Arkansas]

1:5-7, 2:1-2. S. C. Miles (8th WI), "With Smith's Guerrillas." [8-9/64]

3:1-2. S. J. McCullough (3rd PA Cav), "A Tight Squeeze." [9/63]

3:2-3. Elliott Winscott, "In the Old Dominion. Something About the Varied Service of the 7th Indiana in 1862."

3:3. William Clingman (6th KY), "Defense of the General." [William B. Nelson]

3:4-5. Picket Shots: Heaviest loss; M. W. Lindsley (NY), Cedar Creek; G. E. Dolton (Bty M, 1st IL), G. W. Butt (10th MO Cav), last cannon.

4:7. Obit.

June 21

1:1-4. J. R. Palmer (32nd IL), "No Surprise at Shiloh."

1:5-7, 2:1-2. A. G. Hatry (18th KY), "After Chickamauga."

3:1-2. Francis Cordrey (126th OH), "The Wilderness."

3:2-3. Thomas H. Mokee (1st WV), "Correcting Col. Oates. [Port Republic]

3:3. F. W. Metcalf (1st US Chasseurs), "The Chasseurs. Lively Doings in the Valley and on the Peninsula." [65th NY]

3:4-5. Picket Shots: Longest service; W. H. Sanderson (9th VT), Harper's Ferry; Francis O'Leary (130th IN), 7/19/64.

3:5. D. H. Hall (8th WI), "Too Close for Comfort. Running a Train Under Difficulties in Dixie Land."

3:5. Alfred Davenport (5th NY), "Retracts Nothing. Davenport Advises His Critics to Read More Carefully." [Second Manassas]

4:7. Obit.

6:1. Biog: John C. Shotts (12th NY).

6:7. "Where Heroes Rest," Part 2.

June 28

1:1-4. Palmer, Part 2.

1:5-7, 2:1. William Simmons, "The Trent Affair."

3:1. James M. Whallon (11th MI), "Thought It Settled. " [Rossville Gap]

3:1-2. "A Queer Case, Which Shows the Way of the Transgressor is Hard." [9th Corps deserter]

3:2. George W. Henry, "The 11th Missouri at Corinth."

3:2. George S. Orr (77th NY), "Death of Col. Visscher. A Gallant Soldier of the 43rd N.Y. Hit by a Random Shot." [Fort Stevens]

3:3. J. L. McGinnis (2nd TX), "Corinth to Vicksburg."

3:5. J. L. Hummel (8th IN), "Hummel Interposes. Wishes to Help Comrade Bradford Out in His Statements."

3:5. George I. Mosher (53rd IL), "Cavalry at the Hatchie."

3:5. F. M. Way, "No Cowardice There. The Ivy Farm Fight, and What the Battery Support Did." [Okolona]

4:7. Obit.

5:1. Medals of Honor to Adelbert Ames and Edward McGinn.

5:3. Obit: Bishop W. Perkins (83rd IL).

6:1. Biog: S. R. Van Sant (9th IL Cav).

July 5

1:1-3. George R. Sherman, "To Do Or To Die. Intrepid Charge on Fort Gilmer by a Detachment of the 7th U.S.C.T."

1:4-7. H. O. Crosby (5th US Cav), "On the Move. Cavalry Doings in Virginia During the Last Days of the Rebellion."

3:1-2. William E. Loring, "On the Second Day. The 141st Pa. in the Gettysburg Battle—A Loss of Over 75 Per Cent."

3:2. A. B. Carney (5th US Cav), "Carney Protests. Thinks Comrade Landegon Not Warrented in His Reflections."

3:2. James C. Agnew (USN), "Nothing to Laugh At. The Ram Arkansas and Her Dash Through the Fleet at Vicksburg."

3:3. Joseph Hall (20th Btn, OH Nat Gd), "Gunning for Morgan."

3:4-5. Picket Shots: James Williams (1st IA), Wilson's Creek; S. K. Eicher (155th PA), Gettysburg and the wounded; youngest.

3:5. W. L. De Munbrun (11th KY), "Morgan and His Men."

3:5. "Criticism. Comrade Boring Thinks Gen. Sherman Showed Bad Generalship When Fighting Hood."

4:7. Obit.

5:3. Obit: William G. Temple (USN).

6:2. Biog: Charles H. Baker (USN).

July 12

1:1-3. Crosby, Part 2.

1:4-7, 2:1-3. Alfred Davenport (5th NY), "One of the Seven Days. What the Duryea Zouaves Experienced at Gaines's Mill."

3:1-2. S. D. Pond (45th OH), "In the Dead of Night. Whitaker's Brigade in the Passage from Duck River to Franklin."

3:2. R. C. Rankin (7th OH Cav), "Straightens Them Out. Capt. Rankin Tells How the Charge at Columbus, Ga. was Arranged."

3:2. C. Chandler (6th IA), "A Bold Yankee Trick. Taking a Rebel Officer from Under the Very Noses of His Men." [3/21/65]

3:3. William E. Doyle (17th IN), "Raiding in Georgia. Gen. Long's Timely Aid to Kilpatrick When the Latter was in a Tight Place."

3:3-4. C. A. Howe (139th OH), "Poor Fellows. They Fared Better in a Union Prison Than in the Ranks of Their Own Army."

3:4. James Hill (12th MI), "A Comparison and Difference Between the Defense of Middleburg and that at Holly Springs."

3:5. Picket Shots: T. W. Smith (11th NY Cav), last fight.

4:7. Obit.

6:5. Biog: George A. Neuman (6th NY Cav), George W. Carpenter (21st, 116th NY).

July 19

1:1-4. S. C. Miles (8th WI), "Smith's Guerrillas at Nashville."

1:5-7, 2:1-2. Davenport, Part 2.

3:1-2. Elliott Winscott (7th IN), "A Military Tramp. Experiences During an Involuntary Absence from the Regiment."

3:2. L. H. Stanley (18th IN), "Defends the Eighth. [Cedar Creek]

3:2. J. H Springer (1st IA Cav), "Silver Creek."

3:3. M. N. Cook (8th NY Hvy Art), "A Johnny Began It. Firing During a Truce Precipitates a Day's Cannonading." [10/64]

3:3. Gus Snyder (34th OH), "His First Fight." [Fayetteville, WV, 9/10/62]

3:4-5. Picket Shots: R. H. Sheldon (3rd OH Cav), Corinth; H. H. Collins (9th MI Cav), Morgan; W. P. Clingsten (USN), Arkansas Post.

3:5. M. N. Chamberlin (23rd OH), "Our Last Beans." [Spring 1864]

3:7. S. R. Evril (13th PA Cav), "Stony Creek."

4:7. Obit.

5:4. Obit: James B. Fry, Daniel McCauley (11th IN).

July 26

1:1-5. Miles, Part 2.

1:6-7, 2:1-3. Davenport, Part 3.

3:1. Carl Hartmann (Bty M, 5th US), "A Case of 'Scooped.' Involuntary Desertion that was Scratched Off the Books."

3:2. C. W. Belknap (125th NY), "At Harper's Ferry."

3:2. B. H. Tripp (7th WI), "Shared With Them. Bound to Relieve Necessity, If It Did Not Help the Rebellion." [foraging 8/62]

3:3. Cook, Part 2.

3:3. T. G. Wakefield (4th OH Cav), "Lovejoy Station."

3:4. Picket Shots: Addison Tanquary (86th IL), Rossville.

3:4-5. James Larson (4th US Cav), "He was There Too." [Rossville Gap]

3:5. Perry C. Hagerty (73rd IN), "A Hard Campaign. No Fun Fighting Johnnies During the Terrible Winter of 1862-'63."

3:5. Joseph H. Bell (27th IA), "'It was Just This Way'." [Fort DeRussy]

4:7. Obit.

August 2

1:1-5. Davenport, Part 4.

1:6-7, 2:1-4. Thomas Scott (Bty D, 5th US), "On Little Round Top."

3:1. William F. Annis (2nd KY Cav), "Wheeler 'Lit Out'."

3:1-2. Admiral R. Castle (17th IN), "'A Daring Dash.' Some Sharp Work in the Vicinity of Macon."

3:2. Chamberlin, Part 2.

3:3. L. O. Colburn (51st IL), "A Lead Furlough." [Chickamauga]

3:3. H. C. Holter (45th PA), "Did No Running. Denies that the Ninth Corps Broke at Poplar Spring Church."

3:4-5. Picket Shots: W. I. Martin (94th OH), Fayetteville, 9/11/62.

3:5. Peter Fagan (22nd MA), "Imagination's Work. The Queer Experience of a Veteran at Gaines's Mill."

3:5. Isaac R. Sherwood (111th OH), "A Hero of Franklin. Something About the Death of Col. Merrin R. Clark." [83rd OH]

3:7. B. F. Hearford (20th IL), "Baker's Creek." [Champion's Hill]

4:7. Obit.

August 9

1:1-4. John N. Coyne (70th NY), "'Excelsior!' The Five Regiments that Composed an Ideal Brigade. The First Fight. . . ."

1:5-7, 2:1-3. B. F. Boring (30th IL), "Fighting for Vicksburg."

3:1-2. R. C. Rankin (7th OH Cav), "Tells All About It." [Rogersville]

3:2-3. James Larson (4th US Cav), "Last to Cross the Bridge. What was Revealed by a Little Foraging at Noonday Creek."

3:3. Carl Hartmann (Bty M, 5th US), "Music Hath Charms. 'Yankee Doodle' Worried the Rebs in the Wilderness and Broke Up a Yankee Breakfast." [5/6/62]

3:3. Daniel P. Donnell (2nd IA), "At Fort Donelson."

3:5. "Some Figures. Comrade Davenport Replies to Griswold and Stoutenburg." [Second Manassas]

3:6-7. Joseph G. Winger (155th PA), "At Gettysburg."

4:7. Obit.

August 16

1:1-5. Boring, Part 2.

1:6-7, 2:1-3. Coyne, Part 2.

3:1. "Stirred Him Up. Comrade Scott's 'On Little Round Top' Moves the 'Cannoneer' to Reminisce."

3:1-2. D. Conger (8th WI), "Explains It. An Eagle Regiment Man Supplements Lieut. Moore's Statements."

3:2. William E. Webster (1st NY Bty), "The Old Sixth." [Cedar Creek]

3:2. James Marer (Bty B, 4th US), "Justly Entitled." [US Regulars]

3:3. R. F. Little (18th US), "Not Yet Settled." [Rossville Gap]

3:3. A. F. Posey, "Thanks to an Adversary. A Few Words More About Gen. Maxcy Gregg and the Palmetto Regiment."

3:4-5. Picket Shots: J. N. Rickey (8th IA Cav), Burnt Hickory; E. D. Cloyd (55th OH), Peach Tree Creek; John Logan (5th OH Cav), Hatchie River.

3:5. "Columbus, Ga. About the Bridge Taken There, and What the 4th Iowa Cavalry Did."

3:5. W. J. Landram, "Vicksburg. Gen. Landram Tells of the Events Leading Up to the Surrender."

4:7. Obit.

6:1. Biog: Charles H. Shute (2nd NH).

8:4-5. "Where Thomas Stayed the Flood. Monuments that Mark the Historic Battlefield of Chickamauga."

August 23

1:1-3. William Simmons, "USS *Hartford*."

1:4-7, 2:1-2. Boring, Part 3.

3:1-2. William E. Doyle (17th IN), "17th Indiana Did It. Wilder's Mounted Infantrymen Fought the Last Fight East of the Mississippi." [4/20/65]

3:2. S. R. Smith (8th OH Bty), "Yost's Captured Battery." [Champion's Hill]

3:3. W. H. Collingwood (4th PA Cav), "How It was Done. 'Capt.' is Informed Who Took Him In and Why." [Stony Creek Station]

3:3. H. W. Phelps (95th OH), "Two Terrible Days." [Nashville]

3:4-5. Picket Shots: Fred Smith (Bty I, 1st NY), accident in Louisville, 10/4/63; D. H. Drummond, Vicksburg; P. D. Thomas (18th MS), Vicksburg.

3:5. S. C. Miles (8th WI), "A Critical Moment. An Incident in Which a Lieut. Figures Heroically." [Nashville]

3:5. Daniel A. Johnson (89th IN), "'Shell 'Em All Around.' A Small Correction of Comrade Holman's Disposition of a Brigade at Tupelo."

3:7. Patrick Breen (2nd US), "A Friendly Shot. Never Saw Anything Like Brutality in Warren's Actions." [Gaines' Mill]

3:7. John Otto (11th IN Bty), "A Few Points in Error. As to Sheridan's Division and the 11th Indiana Battery." [Chickamauga]

4:7. Obit.

8:4. "Battleflag Day in Iowa."

August 30

1:1-5. W. S. Neely (51st OH), "In the Hands of the Philistines." [captured 9/19/63]

1:6-7, 2:1-3. (13th VT), "Three Days' Fighting." [Gettysburg]

3:1. William N. Brown (65th IL), "That Night March." [Spring Hill]

3:2. Augustus Buell, "For Valor. How Johnny Cook, as Private Citizen, Helped Battery B, 4th U.S. Artillery, at Bethesda Church."

3:2-3. F. M. Metcalf (1st US Chasseurs), "A Poor Case of Melting. [Wilderness, 65th NY]

3:3. (29th MA), "The Guest of Honor. How a Private Dined in a Rebel Family to the Disgust of His Superiors."

3:4-5. Picket Shots: W. L. Munbrun (11th KY), Morgan's Raid.

3:5. George Kelly (57th NY), "Hard Marching. Toilsome Traveling from the Monocacy to Uniontown." [Gettysburg]

3:5. J. E. Merrifield (15th WV), "Defends the Eighth Corps." [Cedar Creek]

3:7. M. Anderson (19th OH), "Still on Nelson."

4:6. Obit.

September 6

1:1-5. Neely, Part 2.

1:6-7, 2:1-2. William Simmons, "Reducing Roanoke. Early Operations in the Sounds of North Carolina."

3:1-2. C. R. Warfield (121st OH), "Charging Kennesaw."

3:2. Edward B. Heaton (30th IA), "The End of It. What a Comrade Saw the Day Vicksburg was Surrendered."

3:3. "With a Big B. Sergt. Davenport Holds to His Statements as to Tyranny in His Regiment, But Did Not Mention Col. Warren as Concerned."

3:4-5. Picket Shots: H. B. Turrill (72nd OH), Vicksburg; M. D. Price (12th MO Cav), Nashville.

3:5. John C. Lea (70th NY), "Serenading Sibleys. A Melodious Quartet, And How It Won Favor with Gen. Meade."

3:6-7. Nelson L. Lane (15th PA Cav), "Nashville."

4:7. Obit.

4:7. R. N. Spohr (183rd OH), "There was No Shirking, And Col. Mervin Clark Did Not Die as Col. Sherwood Relates." [Franklin]

5:4. Obit: Nathaniel P. Banks.

8:4-5. "What Might Have Been. How McClellan's Authority was in Danger of Being Disregarded at Antietam." [George W. Smalley in Harper's]

September 13

3:1-2. William S. Bedford (8th IN), "Defends His Corps." [Vicksburg Campaign]

3:2. W. H. Powell, "Powell Puts In. Has Something to Say About the Cedar Creek Controversy."

3:3. Samuel R. Hazen (140th NY), "Fighting the Good Fight." [Gettysburg]

3:4-5. Picket Shots: D. Flower (59th OH), Chickamauga; Jacob Reynerson (16th IA), foraging, 2/65; W. H. Phipps (8th NY Cav), Gettysburg.

3:5. W. N. Gillett (94th OH), "Still Leaving the Gap." [Rossville]

3:5. M. Parshall, "2nd Iowa at Fort Donelson."

3:6-7. F. O. Talbot (1st ME Hvy Art), "With One Hand. The 1st Maine Heavy had a Small Man Who was a Fighter, Too."]

4:7. "Typical of Freedom. First Federal Soldier Monument Erected in a Foreign Country." [Edinburgh, Scotland]

8:5-6. Obit: George Stoneman.

September 20

3:1-2. Ignatz Hartmann (3rd MA Cav), "An Orderly's Story. Interesting Haphazard Reminiscences of New Orleans and the Red River Expedition."

3:2. A. H. Taylor (5th IA Cav), "Taking the Bridge." [Columbus, GA]

3:3-4. James M. Whallon (11th MI), "Knows He is Right." [Rossville Gap]

3:4. S. H. Wright (75th NY), "Cedar Creek."

3:4. John Chalfant (20th IL), "Not the Right Bower. The 30th Illinois Played that Card to the 20th's Joker." [Vicksburg]

3:5. Picket Shots: John S. Van Arsdel (65th IL), Pulaski to Franklin.

3:6-7. Alfred Turner (5th NY Hvy Art), "A Screw Loose. But It was Not the Fault of the 8th Corps, Who Did the Best They Could." [Cedar Creek]

4:5-6. Biog: Thomas G. Lawler (19th IL), Charles H. Shute (2nd NH), Albert P. Burchfield (123rd, 194th PA).

4:6-7. Obit.

September 27

1:1-6. H. C. Connelly (14th IL Cav), "Campaigning with Burnside. Personal Experiences in East Tennessee in 1863."

1:7, 2:1-4. R. C. Rankin (7th OH Cav), "A Brave Band. Services of the 4th Independent Ohio Cavalry."

3:1. Augustus Buell (Bty B, 4th US), "No Cruelty That! 10 to 1 the Act was Necessary to Preserve Espirit du Corps." [5th NY]

3:1-2. W. E. Webster (1st NY Bty), "Sixth Corps to the Front! A Comparison Between It and the Eighth Not Complimentary to the Latter." [Cedar Creek]

3:2-3. I. Sofield (USS *Nahant*), "A Monitor at Sea." [1/63]

3:3. W. L. De Munbrun (11th KY), "Stories of Nelson."

3:3. S. E. Chandler (24th NY Cav), "Bayou Boeuf, La. The Narrative of a Colored Citizen of N.Y. State, Who was Kidnapped, and For Years Held a Slave." [Solomon Northrop]

3:4. Picket Shots: R. B. Valentine (13th PA Res), regimental story; D. N. Robinson (8th IN), Big Black River.

3:5. B. F. Boring (30th IL), "Answers His Critics."

4:7. Obit.

8:2. H. Calkins (12th IL Cav), "A Day in Petersburg. How the 12th Ill. Cav. was Surprised and Taken Prisoner There."

October 4

1:1-5. Connelly, Part 2.

1:6. C. L. Shultz (19th OH), "Regiment with a Library."

1:7, 2:1-3. S. C. Miles (8th WI), "The Affair at Farmington."

3:1-2. Matthew F. Kippax (17th US), "Sykes's Regulars. Something About Their Terrible Fight at Gettysburg on July 2."

3:3. C. M. Parker (46th IN), "McClernand's Inaction. One of Hovey's Men Presents the Question from His Point of View."

3:4-5. Picket Shots: B. F. Young (20th KY), Morgan's Raid; N. D. Sanford (95th IL), J. H. Rhoads (36th IL), Vicksburg.

3:5. Frank L. Merrill (31st ME), "Poplar Spring Church."

3:5. Augustus Buell (Bty B, 4th US), "Tell Good Stories, Instead of Criticizing Unimportant Mistakes."

October 11

1:1-4. H. Clay Neville, "A Unique Battleground. Operations in Southwest Missouri in the Early Part of the War."

1:5-7. John S. Bosworth (15th IA), "An Ill-Advised Expedition. Terrible March of Crocker's Iowa Brigade Through Louisiana's Swamp." [Monroe]

3:1-2. I. R. Sherwood (111th OH), "Sherwood Rejoins." [Death of Col. Clarke, Franklin]

3:3. W. E. Webster (1st NY Bty), "Cedar Creek."

3:4. D. Eldredge (3rd NH), "'No Quorum.' Gen. Banks had Orders to Prevent Maryland Seceding."

3:4. "A Slave 12 Years. One of the Characters of a Remarkable Piece of Fiction Still Alive."

3:4. Patrick Breen (2nd US), "Remarks to the Point." [Gaines' Mill]

3:5. Picket Shots: B. F. Boring (30th IL), General McClernand; Henry Coryell (34th IL), Kennesaw Mountain.

4:7. Obit.

8:2. Biog: Elwood T. Carr (11th PA Cav).

8:4. Biog: Thomas J. Majors (1st NE).

8:4-5. "Chickamauga Field. Progress of the Work of the National Commission."

8:5. Obit: Andrew G. Curtin.

October 18

1:1-3. Neville, Part 2.

1:4-7, 2:1. T. J. Vinyard (33rd IA), "A Plan of Co-operation. Gen. Steele's Expedition Through Arkansas."

3:1. John Shearer (12th WI Bty), "Hand-to-Hand. [Allatoona]

3:2-3. E. T. Best (10th WI), "Stood Up to It. A Narrative of the Defense of Paint Rock Bridge, Ala."

3:3. William E. Doyle (17th IN), "Perryville."

3:3-4. John Hurley (USS *New London*), "Captured the Cutter. An Adventure of a Federal Crew in the Bayous of Louisiana." [5/64]

3:4. James O'Connor (27th MO), "Fell Into the Trap. How the Fifteenth Corps was Thrown Into Confusion at Cheraw."

3:5. Picket Shots: Madison Craigo (8th WV), Cedar Creek; A. C. Deboe (20th KY), Morgan's Raid; William H. Hartwell (9th NH), Company I story.

4:7. Biog: Michael R. Morgan (commissary dept), Michael Griffin (12th WI).

4:7. Obit.

October 25

1:1-7. O. O. Howard, "Atlanta Campaign."

3:1. Edward C. Garrigan (2nd NY Cav), "One of the 500. Col. Ulric Dahlgren's Command, And What Became of It."

3:1-2. S. D. Pond (45th OH), "Under Burnside. Story of the Loss of Law's Guns at Philadelphia, Tenn." [10/20/63]

3:2. William E. Doyle (17th IN), "Confederate Losses."

3:2. Augustus Wentz (14th NY Hvy Art), "Poplar Spring Church."

3:3. E. R. P. Shurly (26th NY), "Built a Ferry." [Shenandoah Valley 1862]

3:4. "Has More to Say. Gen. Powell Does Not See Why Comrade Webster Should Continue to Insinuate Cowardice."

3:4. "Fighting for Vicksburg. Comrade Boring Takes Up Some of the Criticism of His Articles."

3:5. Picket Shots: Samuel Houston (2nd KS), Wilson's Creek; R. C. Rankin (7th OH Cav), Columbus, GA.

4:7. Obit.

6:1-2. Biog: T. H. Hagerty (93rd IL), Louis Grund (4th MO Cav), A. O. Marsh (15th, 46th OH, 49th USCT).

6:2. "Allen County Boys. Dedication of a Beautiful Monument at the Reunion of the 88th Indiana."

November 1

1:1-5, 2:6. Howard, Part 2.

1:6-7, 2:1-3. "Struggling for Supremacy. Some Operations in East Tennessee in 1863."

3:1. William E. Doyle (17th IN), "Franklin."

3:2. E. T. Lee (41st IL), "Face to Face Again. A Meeting at New Orleans Which Recalled Stirring Scenes." [Jackson, MS]

3:2. W. C. Yard (4th PA Cav), "Antietam."

3:3. J. P. De Beck, "Considers Him Abused. A 2nd Kentucky Man Knew the Charges Against Gen. Nelson."

3:3. J. I. McGinnis (2nd TX), "Rodgers's Death." [Corinth]

3:4-5. Picket Shots: James J. Dow, 2nd Manassas; W. S. Bedford (8th IN), General McClernand.

3:5. Augustus Buell (Bty B, 4th US), "Cedar Creek."

4:7. Obit.

6:1-2. Biog: David L. Way (79th OH), C. T. Watson (3rd ME), John W. Burst (15th, 105th IL).

6:7. "The 11th Connecticut Monument Located in the Famous Cornfield at Antietam."

November 8

1:1-6. Howard, Part 3. [Resaca]

1:7, 2:1-3. R. H. G. Minty (4th MI Cav), "Fighting, Scouting and Picketing." [Atlanta Campaign]

2:3. James B. Fiske (5th NY), "Desecration at Gettysburg."

3:1-2. Franklin Cox (61st IL), "Plenty to Do."

3:2. Joseph F. Carter (3rd MD), "Not a Fighting Regiment, But Nevertheless the 3rd Maryland Found Much Work Cut Out for It."

3:3. E. H. Wheeler (20th KY), "How They were Taken In. Morgan's Attack on Lebanon."

3:3. W. F. Denmure (USS *Santee*), "In the Dark. A Bold Night Expedition in Which Rear-Admiral [James E.] Jouett was a Leader." [11/7/61, Galveston, TX]

3:4. John P. Reinhardt (USS *Perry*), "A Sailor's Yarn. Some Unenviable Experiences in Rebel Prisons." [captured 12/5/63]

3:4. L. H. Stanley (18th IN), "Cedar Creek."

3:5. Picket Shots: D. M. Allen (45th IL), Vicksburg; Cyrus Walters (1st IA), Wilson's Creek.

4:7. Obit.

November 15

1:1-5. Howard, Part 4. [Adairsville]

1:6-7, 2:1-2. F. S. Dickinson (5th NY Cav), "Men on Horseback at Cedar Creek."

3:1-2. Edward B. Heaton (30th IA), "Desperate Men. Quantrall and His Band of Guerrillas in the Southwest."

3:2-3. I. M. Gray (52nd OH), "Kennesaw."

3:3. J. L. Younker (12th US), "Had Two Days' Start. Clever Ruse of an Indiana Boy to Get Out of Andersonville."

3:3. H. W. Phelps (95th OH), "A Brave Man. Gen. Nelson Shows His Efficiency in the Face of Defeat." [Richmond]

3:4. H. G. Fish (89th IL), "The Railroad Regiment."

3:4. Picket Shots: W. E. Webster (1st NY Bty), Cedar Creek; Joseph W. Grant (14th ME), capture of Jeff Davis.

4:7. Obit.

6:1. Biog: J. M. Walling (8th IA, 61st USCT), N. Rollins (2nd WI).

November 22

1:1-7. Howard, Part 5. [Cassville]

2:5. "Governor Curtin. A Sketch of His Magnificent Service for the Union."

3:1. J. K. Shellenberger (64th OH), "Never Retaken. Union Ground at Franklin, West of the Columbia Pike."

3:2. W. Siefried (118th OH), "Again it is Knoxville."

3:3. James A. Allen (12th MA), "Led Like Lambs. A Score of Johnnies Who Did Not Know They had a Prisoner." [Antietam]

3:4. W. C. Yard (4th PA Cav), "Rescued His Body. Devotion to Their Colonel Led to Noble Sacrifices by the 4th Pa. Cavalry." [St. Mary's Church]

3:4. Joshua Chetwood (7th IN Cav), "Let the Cat Out. Consternation Visited Upon a Loyalty in Professing Southern Hostess." [Hickman, KY]

3:5. Picket Shots: M. Gerwig (36th VA Cav), Cedar Creek.

3:7. M. L. Fratler (3rd IN Cav), "Unpleasant Experience. Did One of Hooker's Orderlies Meet Payne the Conspirator?"

4:7. Biog: William Dye (4th US).

4:7. Obit.

November 29

1:1-7. Howard, Part 6. [Kingston]

3:1. M. O. Perkins (36th OH), "Sheridan and Crook. Some Incidents of Cedar Creek Not Before Related."

3:2. (81st OH), "Atlanta Campaign. Part Taken by the 81st Ohio at Resaca and Lay's Ferry."

3:2-3. S. A. Clark (1st WV Cav), "One of the 5th N.Y. Cavalry. How They Halted a 4-Footed Host in the Darkness." [8/62]

3:3. R. G. Guide (48th PA), "A Fatal Gap." [Poplar Spring Church]

3:4. C. B. Gammon (9th IL), "Brought the Flag."

3:4. S. A. McNeil (31st OH), "Missed the Honor. The 31st Ohio had a Little Experience with Gen. Morgan." [11/62, Cage's Ford, Cumberland River]

3:5. Picket Shots: L. H. Thurman (15th NY Hvy Art), Cedar Creek; RAC 9148th PA), Barksdale at Gettysburg.

4:7. Obit.

6:1-2. Biog: Charles W. Buckley (47th USCT).

December 6

1:1-6. Howard, Part 7. [New Hope Church]

3:1-2. R. N. Spohr, "The 183rd Ohio. Corpl. Spohr Returns to the Charge Upon Col. I. R. Sherwood." [Franklin]

3:2-3. R. C. Rice (125th OH), "Explains the Break." [Franklin]

3:3. Theodosius Botkin (8th OH Cav), "Exoneration Useless. The 8th Ohio Cavalry as Usual Stands by the 14th Pa. Cavalry." [Cedar Creek]

3:3. G. Hubner (50th PA), "A Timely Arrival. While Looking for a Pair of Shoes, George Hubner Saves a Comrade's Life." [Petersburg 1864]

3:4. S. A. McDonald (122nd NY), "Clearing the Mystery. [Cedar Creek]

3:5. Picket Shots: H. P. Sherwin, Barksdale at Gettysburg.

8:3. "The Hancock Statue." [Gettysburg]

8:5. Obit: Stephen G. Burbridge.

December 13

1:1-6. Howard, Part 8. [Pickett's Mill]

3:1. Augustus C. Buell (Bty B, 4th US), "The Vermont Brigade. The Cannoneer Explains Why They were 'The Old Guard of the Potomac Army'."

3:2. Joseph F. Carter (3rd MD), "Made It Very Clear. About that Fatal Gap at Poplar Spring Church."

3:2. E. H. Wishon (Bty L, 1st OH), "Whose Flag?" [Cedar Creek]

3:3. J. F. Emert (50th OH), "Lost by an Error. [Franklin]

3:3. Willard Musson (107th IL), "A Worthless Trophy, and a Story of a Game Bird that Couldn't Fight." [East Tennessee 1863]

3:4. Richard Butler [20th IL], "A War Romance."

3:4. John T. Wiesman (Bty D, 1st IL), "Useless Sacrifice. Folly of the Fighting in the Crater at Vicksburg."

3:5. Picket Shots: TPM (114th PA), Barksdale at Gettysburg.

4:7. Obit.

6:1. Biog: Daniel O'Riley (3rd KY Cav).

8:4. Obit: James B. Coit (14th CT), E. P. Scammon (23rd OH).

December 20

1:1-6. Howard, Part 9. [Dallas]

1:7, 2:1-3. "General Robert S. Foster."

3:1-2. A. E. Evans (9th MI Cav), "Burning of the Mill." [East Tennessee]

3:2-3. William H. McIntosh [22nd WI], "Memorable Voyage. Gordon Granger's Corps Moves from Danville to Nashville in 1863."

3:3-4. W. F. Wieland (Btys L&M, 3rd US), "Did Not Lose Them." [Gaines' Mill]

3:4. G. Heebner (50th PA), "Captured an Outpost." [Wilderness]

3:5. S. A. Clark (1st VT Cav), "1st Vermont Cavalry on a Raid. Mosby Scooped the Pickets from Under Their Very Noses."

3:5. Picket Shots: (3rd WV Cav), Thomas W. Alderson (17th PA Cav, C. A. McNeil (OH), Cedar Creek.

4:7. Obit.

8:4. Obit: Josiah Porter.

December 27

1:1-7. Howard, Part 10. [Pine Top, Muddy Creek]

3:1-2. Thomas Scott (Bty D, 5th US), "Daring and Desperate. The Action of Battery D, 5th U.S. Artillery, at Spotsylvania."

3:2. (14th PA Cav), "From the Ranks. Here's a Comrade Who Won't Whitewash Col. Blakely."

3:3. William N. Brown (65th IL), "Franklin."

3:3. W. E. Webster (1st NY Bty), "Not in the 'Race.' Comrade Webster Replies to Some of His Critics." [Cedar Creek]

3:4-5. Picket Shots: David H. Herrell (8th IL), Mobile; Thomas Garner (51st MO), Franklin; S. F. Mayes (2nd GA), Andersonville.

4:7. Obit.

1895

January 3

1:1-6. Howard, Part 11. [Kolb's Farm]

1:7, 2:1-2. Henry Capehart, "Fighting His Way. The Night Passage of Kilpatrick Through Monterey Pass."

2:5-6. George S. Myers (101st OH), "Costly Errors. Gen. Davis's Division and the Army of the Cumberland at Stones' River."

3:1-3. Isaac R. Sherwood, "Sad to Relate. Gen. Sherwood Gives the Death Roll of the 111th Ohio at Franklin."

3:3. Alfred Davenport (5th NY), "Davenport Replies." [Gaines' Mill]

3:4-5. Picket Shots: C. S. Yaroger (4th MI), Gaines' Mill; J. Shipley (6th PA Res), death of Col. Raulston at Danville prison; Dan Sackrider (121st OH), Buzzard Roost.

3:5. John K. Pattison (12th WV), "Patriots' Sons. There was No Cowardice or Disloyalty About the 12th West Virginia." [Cedar Creek]

4:7. Obit.

January 10

1:1-6. Howard, Part 12. [Kennesaw]

1:7, 2:1-2. "Miraculous Escape." [Florence, Fall 1864]

3:1-2. N. Egbert (10th NY Cav), "A Live Ghost. A N.Y. Cavalryman's Adventures in an Old Southern Mansion."

3:2-3. William C. Fraser, "Terrible Fort Hill."

3:3-4. W. H. Powell, "Powell Speaks Again." [Cedar Creek]

3:4. W. B. Fry (8th TN), "The Franklin Controversy."

3:4. W. M. Clark (2nd TN Mtd Inf), "Burning the Mill." [Cumberland Gap]

3:5. Picket Shots: Hiram Place (6th US Cav), John M. Gould (29th ME) Cedar Creek.

4:3-4. Obit: P. S. Post (59th IL), John Taylor (12th PA).

4:7. Obit.

8:4. Obit: Edward M. Hoyt (3rd PA Cav).

January 17

1:1-6, 2:6-7. Howard, Part 13. [Kennesaw]

1:7, 2:1-2. Escape, Part 2.

3:1-3. Frank Miller (6th KY), "Unwritten History. Pen Pictures of Service in the South in 1864."

3:3. Solomon R. Smith (12th OH), "South Mountain."

3:4. A. M. Sumner (66th IL), "Atlanta Campaign." [Resaca, Lay's Ferry]

3:4. T. M. Mozingo (7th IN), "Kernstown."

3:5. Picket Shots: W. E. Webster (1st NY Bty), versus 12th WV; L. H. Brooks (63rd IN), Franklin.

4:7. Obit.

6:2-3. Biog: Henry H. Adams (125th OH).

8:4. Obit: Alfred W. Ellet (USN).

January 24

1:1-6, 2:6-7. Howard, Part 14. [Smyrna]

1:7, 2:1-2. William Simmons, "The Sounds of North Carolina."

3:1-2. T. S. Potter, "On Skirmish. Gallant Behavior of the 8th Ohio at Gettysburg."

3:2-3. "That Memorable Voyage. A Comrade Who Took It Adds Some Points of Interest."

3:3. Jack Crawford, "A Confession. How Capt. Jack Got the Credit of Being a Daring Defender of the Flag." [5/64]

3:3-4. S. A. Clark (1st VT Cav), "That March and Night. Another Story of Monterey Pass and Beyond."

3:4. "Sad Holidays. Stones' River and Christmas Week of 1862."

3:5. Picket Shots: RAC (148th PA), Barksdale at Gettysburg; George H. Lusk (122nd NY), Cedar Creek.

4:7. Obit.

January 31

1:1-5, 2:5-6. Howard, Part 15. [Chattahoochee River]

1:6-7, 2:1-3. Donald J. Adams, "The Fight in Doubtful Canon."

3:1-2. Potter, Part 2.

3:2. W. F. Wieland (Btys L&M, 3rd US), "No Yarn That. Enlisted Men of the Regulars Seldom Get Credit for Daring Deeds." [Gaines' Mill]

3:3-4. R. H. G. Minty (4th MI Cav), "Noonday Church."

3:4. H. T. Carlisle (129th OH), "Cumberland Gap. Its Final Capture in 1863—Troops on the North Side."

3:4. J. H. Coffman (27th IA), "First in Blakely."

3:5. Picket Shots: M. B. Duffie (19th MI), March to the Sea; W. J. Crosley (34th OH), Cedar Creek.

4:7. Obit.

6:1-2. Biog: W. M. Abbott (72nd NY).

February 7

1:1-4. Howard, Part 16. [Peach Tree Creek]

1:5-7, 2:1. D. W. Edmiston, "Fighting at Philadelphia. The Infantry in the East Tennessee Campaign of 1863."

3:1-2. William Simmons, "A Man of Distinction. Andrew H. Foote, Who Rose to be Admiral."

3:2-3. L. J. Cutler (77th OH), "Steele's Expedition."

3:3-4. (81st OH), "Crossing the Oostanaula. High Private has More to Say of the Movement at Snake Creek Gap."

3:5. Picket Shots: S. F. Moore (118th OH), Kolb's Farm; Myron H. Ranney (13th NY), 2nd Manassas; Post 9, MD GAR, Albemarle's flag.

4:7. Obit.

February 14

1:1-4. Howard, Part 17. [Peach Tree Creek]

1:5-7, 2:1. G. H. Blakeslee (129th IL), "Four-Gun Battery. Harrison's Brigade at the Battle of Resaca."

3:1-2. Peter Liberty (MA Hvy Art), "How They Got Out. The Keepers of Andersonville Not Above Bribery."

3:2. T. P. Ege, "Gettysburg Field. Remarkable Transformations on This Once Bloody Battleground."

3:3. M. B. Duffie (19th MI), "A Wild Night Ride." [winter 1863/64]

3:3-4. S. E. Chandler (24th NY Cav), "A Fatal Attempt. Death of Col. Raulston in Danville Prison While Trying to Escape."

3:4. D. M. Allen (45th IL), "Vicksburg Crater."

3:4. W. P. Wolf (175th OH), "Franklin. An Incident of the Battle."

3:5. Picket Shots: S. A. McNeil (31st OH), Chattahoocjie River crossing; M. N. Chapman (22nd WI), Resaca.

4:7. Obit.

February 21

1:1-4. Howard, Part 18. [Atlanta]

1:5-7, 2:1-2. Minty, Part 2. [end of Atlanta Campaign]

3:1-2. A. J. Swanger (120th OH), "'Way Down in Texas. A Visit to the Camp Ford Prison by One Who Suffered There Thirty Years Ago."

3:2-3. Thomas Moore (91st PA), "What Might Have Been. The Significant Closing Days of the Great Rebellion."

3:3. William E. Doyle (17th IN), "Brush Mountain."

3:4. S. C. Jones (22nd IA), "Black River Bridge."

3:4. C. Woodruff (64th OH), "She Dreamed It. How Col. Sherman was Forewarned of his Capture."

3:5. Thomas H. Means (12th WV), "Refutes the Charge. A 12th W.V. Man Says There was No Cowardice at New Market."

3:5. Picket Shots: Louis N. LaFantise (92nd NY), regimental library.

4:7. Obit.

February 28

1:1-4. Howard, Part 19. [Atlanta]

1:5-7, 2:1-3. J. W. Hinkley (3rd WI), "Cedar Mountain."

2:4-7. Blanche C. Petit, "The Twins of Company G." [76th PA]

3:1-2. J. R. Pilkington (34th MA), "They Killed Gen. Jones. Some Details of the Battle of Piedmont as Seen by a Comrade of the 34th Mass."

3:2. James Pusard (42nd IL), "Farmington."

3:2-3. John C. Lyon, "Had a Feast. Some of Custer's Men Lived High for One Day in the Johnnies' Country." [8/65 in LA]

3:3. J. H. Bradford (130th IL), "These Facts. Comrade Boring Made Some Mistakes in Correcting Comrade Bradford." [Fort Donelson]

3:3-4. F. L. Merrill (31st ME), "Poplar Spring Church."

3:4. S. D. Pond (45th OH), "'Got Up and Got.' Comrade Pond Tells More About the Philadelphia Fight."

4:4. Obit: Joseph B. Carr.

4:7. "Medal of Honor." [Carlos H. Rich, 4th VT]

4:7. Obit.

March 7

1:1-4. Howard Part 20. [Ezra Church]

1:5-7, 2:1-3. Jesse H. Jones (60th NY), "Saved the Day. Greene's Battery [sic] Behaves Nobly at Gettysburg."

2:7. E. W. Finch, "Seven Terrible Days for Prisoners on the Manassas Battlefield." [1862]

3:1-2. S. C. Miles (8th WI), "A Soaring Smokestack. How Yankee Ingenuity Put a Stop to the Assaults of a Persistent Foe." [Island Number Ten]

3:2-3. Joseph F. Carter (3rd MD), "Poplar Spring Church."

3:3. William H. Coon (45th OH), "Points Out Errors in Comrade Edmiston's Account of the Philadelphia Fight."

3:4. F. L. Braxton (48th IL), "'Hooa, Hooa, Hooa.' A Vivid Description of the Excitement Caused by a Supposed Night Attack by Cattle."

3:5. Picket Shots: Frank H. Irons (8th IL), Fort Blakely; J. B. Corning (11th WI), Big Black

River; E. G. Pierce (11th WI), Vicksburg; John Wingrove (1st WV), New Market.

4:7. Obit.

March 14

1:1-5. Howard, Part 21. [Ezra Church]

1:5. Marcus D. Elliott (Bty H, 1st MI), "Noonday Church."

1:5-6. L. C. Leeds (25th MI), "He Volunteered, Then Crossed the Chattahoochee in a Pontoon."

1:7, 2:1-2. William Simmons, "From Britain's Docks. Career of the Rebel Ram Atlanta."

3:1. R. H. G. Minty (4th MI Cav), "Minty Explains. Corrects Comrade Doyle in a Few Matters of Importance."

3:1-2. John J. Gray (Bty B, 1st PA), "New Market."

3:2. C. O. Ellis (4th PA Cav), "Drew Their Pay. Co. M., 4th Pa. was a Fine Troop, If It Did Balk Occasionally."

3:3. Thomas G. Jones (5th ME Bty), "An Exciting Time. [Chancellorsville]

3:3-4. S. A. McDonald (122nd NY), "Winding It Up." [Cedar Creek]

3:4. William E. Sell (3rd US Cav), "A Fishy Story. Incidents of the 'Doubtful Canyon' Fight Could Not Have Happened, Says a Regular."

3:4. Samuel Ivins (83rd OH), "Fort Blakely."

4:7. Obit.

8:1-2. Edward P. Doherty (16th NY Cav), "A Tragedy Retold. The Story of the Capture of John Wilkes Booth."

March 21

1:1-4. Howard, Part 22. [Jonesboro]

1:5-7, 2:1-2. Eugene Sullivan (42nd NY), "Ball's Bluff."

3:1-3. L. Phetteplace (19th MI), "No Glory There. The Four-Gun Battery at Resaca Not Worth Fighting For."

3:3. E. S. Hastings (5th MI Cav), "Monterey Pass."

3:4. John Felt (14th PA Cav), "Battle of Piedmont."

3:4. J. H. Bradford (30th IL), "Battle of Belmont."

3:4. N. Alland (124th IL), "A Protest." [Fort Hill]

3:5. L. S. Tyler (15th IA), "Thought of It. A Warm Bed Where Hot Coals had Lain Occupied by a 15th Iowa Man."

3:5. Picket Shots: A. B. Crummel (30th OH), Atlanta.

4:7. Obit.

March 28

1:1-4. Howard, Part 23. [Jonesboro]

1:5-7, 2:1-2. Sullivan, Part 2.

3:1-2. Birney McLean (2nd IA Cav), "Farmington."

3:2. James Larson (4th US Cav), "Noonday Creek."

3:2. James Lang (11th WI), "Black River Bridge."

3:3. Charlea F. Kimmel (66th IL), "The Atlanta Fight, and Something About the Recapture of DeGress's Battery."

3:3. H. H. Longwell (2nd IA Cav), "Tells How It Was. The Fight at Farmington and the Part of the 2nd Iowa Cav."

3:4. George H. Worden (16th NY Hvy Art), "The Army Galoot."

3:5. Picket Shots: Alex Johnson (111th PA), Resaca.

4:7. Obit.

April 4

1:1-4. Howard, Part 24. [Jonesboro]

1:4. "The Howard House. A Comrade Explains that It was the Frame Building Which was So Called." [Atlanta]

1:5-7. R. H. G. Minty (4th MI Cav), "Picketing and Scouting."

1:7. Michael Denterlein (47th OH), "The Howard House."

2:5. Joseph Rawlins (15th IN), "Was He Sergeant Long?" [Stones' River]

3:1-2. H. M. Kenderdine (17th IA), "Lively Times. Reminiscences of the Hood Raid in October, 1864."

3:3-4. E. H. Matthews (9th TN Cav), "Had Not Surrendered. Death of Gen. Morgan at Greenville, Tenn."

3:4. D. E. McGinley (16th WI), "Routing the Johnnies. Graphic Account of the Scenes at Noonday Church."

3:5. Picket Shots: Henry Capehart, Monterey Pass; R. C. Clawson (22nd WI), Resaca.

4:7. Biog: W. W. Greenland (125th PA), Sylvanus F. Osborn (62nd, 91st NY).

4:7. Obit.

April 11

1:1-3. Howard, Part 25. [Jonesboro]

1:4-7, 2:1. S. F. Chaw (Eng, Dept WV), "Averill's Mistake. McCausland's Raid and the Burning of Chambersburg."

3:1-2. R. H. G. Minty (4th MI Cav), "Noonday Church."

3:2. S. A. Clark (1st VT Cav), "Did Not Capture It. Buford and Kilpatrick Fought for Lee's Wagon Train at Hagerstown."

3:3. "Not at All 'Fishy.' D. J. Adams Replies Smartly to His Only Critic." [Doubtful Canyon]

3:3. E. B. Cook (9th IL Cav), "Saw the Insult. Gen. A. J. Smith Paid the Johnnies for Their Territory." [7/64]

3:3-4. (25th WI), "Four Coffee-Coolers. The Number 25 was a Magic One For These Veterans."

3:4. E. W. Pine, "Led by the Major. How the Stalwarts of the 95th Ohio Got Out of a Bad Scrape." [Richmond, KY]

3:4. Jerome Bell (1st NY Cav), "Never Did Run. The Lincoln Cavalry Always Stood Up to Their Enemies."

3:5. Picket Shots: D. J. Spencer (25th IA), Howard House.

4:6. Biog: O. P. Gooding (31st MA), William Moore (62nd NY).

4:6. Obit: Truxton Vanartsdalen (174th PA).

4:7. Obit.

8:2. Obit: A. J. Hamilton (12th KY Cav).

April 18

1:1-6. Howard, Part 26. [Jonesboro]

1:7, 2:1-2. Patrick Breen (2nd US), "Withheld His Troops. Why the Union Army did Not Win at Antietam."

3:1-3. S. C. Kersey (79th OH), "Those Four Guns. Who Captured Them, Who Brought Them Off, and Who Took Them to Resaca."

3:3. W. F. Wieland (Btys L&M, 3rd US), "The Cannon at Gaines' Mill."

3:4. John W. Eaton (12th KY Cav), "Whose Fault? It was 'Run or Andersonville' at Philadelphia, Tenn."

3:4. H. M. Kenderdine (17th IA), "A Sense of Terror. The Part of the 17th Iowa in Holding the Crater at Fort Hill."

3:4. M. M. Lacey (69th IN), "Fort Blakely."

3:5. Picket Shots: S. C. Williams (18th PA Cav), Cedar Creek; S. V. Porter (11th WI), Big Black River.

4:7. Obit.

April 25

1:1-4. Augustus Buell (Bty B, 4th US), "Mink's Battery. A Story of Doing and Daring During the Civil War." [Bty H, 1st NY]

1:5-7, 2:1-2. Thomas H. C. Kinkaid (22nd NY SM), "Thirty Days with the Militia." [Gettysburg Campaign]

3:1-2. J. C. Griggs (77th OH), "Brave Men These. But the Leaders Blundered and They Suffered." [Arkansas 1864]

3:2-3. S. C. Kersey (79th OH), "Those Four Guns." [Resaca]

3:3-4. Richard W. Johnson, "Twigg's Treachery."

3:5. John M. Follett (33rd IL), "Black River."

3:5. Picket Shots: C. A. Gibson (11th MO), Farmington.

4:7. Obit.

8:2. Obit: J. D. Williamson (4th CA).

May 2

1:1-4. Buell, Part 2.

1:5-7, 2:1-3. J. C. Julius Langbein (9th NY), "Back in Dixie. A Ten Days' Trip Through the Southland by Two Comrades."

3:1-2. William E. Doyle (17th IN), "General Eli Long."

3:2. James R. Beadles (27th MO), "The Howard House." [Atlanta]

3:3-4. W. H. Tucker (14th WI), "On Hard-Fought Fields. A Reminiscent Trip by Two Comrades of the 14th Wisconsin." [Shiloh, Corinth]

3:4. S. A. Clark (1st VT Cav), "A Little Fraces." [7/13/63]

4:6-7. Biog: E. T. Lee (41st IL), T. C. Tupper (6th US Cav).

4:7. Obit.

May 9,

1:1-4. Buell, Part 3.

1:5-7, 2:1-2. J. J. Galbraith (2nd PA Cav), "Brief But Brilliant. The Campaign from Petersburg to Appomattox."

3:1. Ezra F. Wetmore (26th NY), "What He Saw. Story of a N.Y. Boy at Fredericksburg."

3:2. J. K. Shellenberger (64th OH), "What Figures Show. A Comparison of Losses During the Atlanta Campaign."

3:2-3. Thomas Groody (89th NY), "A Danville Tragedy. Another Version of the Death of Col. W. C. Raulston."

3:3. Alfred Davenport (5th NY), "The Guns at Gaines' Mill."

3:4-5. Picket Shots: J. F. Kent (1st NY Cav), Winchester 1863; Levi W. Armstrong (10th IL), Vicksburg.

3:5. R. H. G. Minty (4th MI Cav), "Noonday Church."

4:7. Obit.

May 16

1:1-4. Buell, Part 4.

1:5-7, 2:1. V. Preuitt (1st MO Cav), "A Spring Campaign. Operations in Missouri Against Gen. Price." [1862]

3:1-2. James Larson (4th US Cav), "Spoiled a Breakfast."

3:2-3. William E. Doyle (17th IN), "Garrard's Cavalry. What the Wilder Brigade did in the Atlanta Campaign."

3:3-4. D. M. Allen (45th IL), "Vicksburg."

3:4. J. H. McCommon (102nd IL), "What He Saw. Some Things Not Told Before About that Four-Gun Battery." [Resaca]

3:5. Picket Shots: Jerome Bell (1st NY Cav), Winchester 1863; Jacob McAfee (27th USCT), Crater.

4:7. Obit.

May 23

1:1-3, 2:6. Buell, Part 5.

3:1-2. S. A. Clark (1st VT Cav), "Supped with Southrons. An Escapade Which Roused and Alarmed a Union Camp."

3:2. John Isonhart (28th IL), "Got No Potatoes."

3:2. H. B. Vanneman (84th IN), "Corse Sent the Message. How 'Hold the Fort' was Signalled from Rome, Ga."

3:3. George W. Loop (45th OH), "An Ohio Boy and His Pony. Adventures of an Orderly on a General's Staff."

3:3-4. Daniel Matson (24th IA), "They Got There. Amusing Experiences of Wounded Comrades in the Vicksburg Campaign."

3:4. A. J. Swanger (120th OH), "An Old Gate-Post, and the Memories It Calls Up Regarding Camp Ford."

3:5. Picket Shots: Thomas J. Spencer, Chickamauga; James N. Russell (IA), Big Black River; Cornelius Lasey (14th MI), Jonesboro.

4:7. Obit.

8:2. Obit: James A. Tait (1st DC).

8:5-6. C. G. Burnett (4th MO Cav), "Col. [George E.] Waring."

May 30

1:1-3. Buell, Part 6.

1:4-7. William Simmons, "A Rebel Terror. Depredations of the Cruiser Sumter During the War."

3:1-2. William E. Doyle (17th IN), "Garrard's Cavalry. Wilder's Lightning Brigade at Stone Mountain—In the Toils at Flat Rock."

3:2. S. A. Clark (1st VT Cav), "Fighting at Waynesboro."

3:3. John W. Ratliff (5th KY Cav), "'Little Invincible.' He was There, and Col. Long did Not Do It All at Lovejoy."

3:3. Will B. Smith (14th IL), "A Raw Recruit. His Experience Following Sherman on the Meridian Raid."

3:4. C. Woodruff (64th OH), "'Christian Soldiers.' One of Them Refutes the Cannoneer's Statement that They Prayed When They Ought to have Fought."

3:4. John M. Gould (10th ME), "Antietam Field."

3:5. James R. Wood (6th US Cav), "Who were They?" (Ely's Ford, 2/28/64]

3:5. Picket Shots: George P. Butler, reply to Doyle and Minty; C. A. Purdy (Fremont's bodyguard), 10/25/61.

3:7. R. E. McBride (190th PA), "At Appomattox."

3:7. S. M. Smith (24th IN), "First Man Ashore." [Bruinsburg]

4:7. Obit.

June 6

1:1-4. Buell, Part 7.

1:5-7, 2:1-3. Daniel E. Sickles, "An Ideal Leader. Reminiscences of 'Fighting Joe' Hooker."

3:1-3. Tilford Dagger (116th IN), " "Persimmon Knockers.' A Sketch of Wilcox's Division in the East Tennessee Campaign of 1863-'64."

3:3. S. R. Evril (13th PA Cav), "About that Running. Comrade Averill Returns to the Charge with the Lincoln Cavalry."

3:3. B. F. Jones (1st WV Cav), "No Terrors There. [Monterey Pass]

3:4. William Harvey (57th IL), "Grant versus McClernand."

3:4. Hirma Calkins (8th WI Bty), "At the Rear. Some Experiences at Home During the Fight for the Union."

3:5. Picket Shots: William Jones (42nd OH), Big Black River; Edward F. Fuller (12th MI), Jonesboro.

3:6-7. John S. Van Arsdel (22nd IN Bty), "The Howard House."

4:7. Obit.

6:2-3. Biog: J. K. P. Thompson (21st IA).

June 13

1:1-4. Buell, Part 8.

1:5-7, 2:1-3. Edwin Nicar (15th IN), "A Reminiscence of Stone River."

3:1-2. J. J. Lutz, "Men from the West. Interesting Figures as to Their Part at Gettysburg."

3:2-3. D. J. Martin (110th OH), "'Jolly Fellows,' These. A Veteran Refutes One of the Characteristic Lies About Good Treatment in Rebel Prisons." [Belle Isle]

3:3-4. L. B. Sampson (84th PA), "Reb versus Yank. Some Instances Where Several Rebs Could Not Whip Even One Yank." [Hancock, MD; Front Royal, VA]

3:4. C. F. Greening (11th WI), "A Parting Shot." [Black River]

3:5. "Substantiated Words. D. J. Adams Replies to the Criticisms of William C. Sell." [Doubtful Canyon]

3:5. Picket Shots: Grove H. Dutton (147th NY), Spotsylvania.

4:7. Obit.

June 20

1:1-5. Buell, Part 9.

1:6-7, 2:1. William Simmons, "On the High Seas. Capture of the Steamer Ariel by the Alabama." [12/7/62]

3:1-2. B. H. Tripp (7th WI), "A White-Haired Patriot. Reminiscences of Gen. J. S. Wadsworth by One Who Followed Him."

3:2-3. G. W. Daniel (7th KY), "The Richmond Fight."

3:4. T. S. Potter (8th OH), "Queer Cases. A Comrade Tells of Some Peculiar Wounds He Observed."

3:5. Picket Shots: Addison Tarquary, Jonesboro.

4:7. Obit.

5:4. Obit: Richard Oulahan (164th NY).

June 27

1:1-4. Buell, Part 10.

3:1-2. G. H. Blakeslee (129th IL), "Light of the Records. Comrade Blakeslee Sums Up the Four-Gun Battery Controversy." [Resaca]

3:2. R. P. Shurly (26th NY), "Got the Chicken."

3:3. Don C. Cameron (1st WI Bty), "How They 'Got There.' Graphic Description of Scenes at Black River Bridge."

3:3. W. Y. Power (39th IA), "Sherman was There." [Kennesaw]

3:4. Hosea Hudson (210th PA), "Saw Differently." [Gravelly Run]

3:4. W. E. Webster (1st NY Bty), "Lost the Most. A Claim for This Doleful Honor by the Vermont Brigade."

3:5. Picket Shots: John K. Patteson (12th WV), New Market; W. J. McMillan (1st WV Cav), responding to Evril, 6/6/ issue; George W. Hines (98th OH), Jonesboro.

4:7. Obit.

5:4. Obit: Edward A. Paul (NY Times correspondent]

July 4

1:1-4. Buell, Part 11.

1:5-7, 2:1. W. F. Goodhue (3rd WI), "Caught Them Napping. Arrest of the Secession Members of the Maryland Legislature."

3:1-3. R. H. G. Minty (4th MI Cav), "Minty Charges Again. The Veteran Cavalry Leader Replies at length to William E. Doyle."

3:3. Edwin Clark, "Providential Spring."

3:3. Delevan Bates (30th USCT), "The Mine Explosion."

3:4. Alfred Davenport (5th NY), "Warren's Regiment. A Thin Line of 100 Men All that were Left After Manassas."

3:4. Augustus C. Buell (Bty B, 4th US), "The Vermont Brigade."

3:5. Picket Shots: D. H. Smith (20th PA Cav), New Market; Jacob Hazlitt (3rd IL Cav), Big Black River.

4:7. Obit.

5:7. Obit: Edward A. Paul (NY Times correspondent).

8:1-3. James Larson (4th US Cav), "Thirty Years Ago. Scenes and Events of Active Camping Reviewed."

8:3. "The Buford Monument. Formal Dedication on the Battlefield of Gettysburg."

July 11

1:1-4, 2:6. H. C. Connelly (14th IL Cav), "To Nashville from the Tennessee. The Story of Hood's Advance in the Fall of 1864."

1:5-7, 2:1-3. R. Haggerstone, "Destroying a Ram. The Last Survivor of the Daring Crew that Went Out with Cushing Tells the Tale."

3:1-2. J. E. Williams, "Burnside's Mistake. A Review of the Fateful Fredericksburg Campaign."

3:2. J. S. Chandler (5th VT), "Comparisions are Odious, and Every Regiment Should Be Given Credit For Doing Its Duty."

3:3. J. K. P. Stephens (6th IN Cav), "Driving Forrest." [Pulaski, TN, 9/27/64]

3:3-4. R. E. McBride (190th PA), "White Oak Road."

3:4. David Allen (155th PA), "More About Mink. Action of the Battery at Poplar Spring Church."

3:4. W. G. Whitefield (35th AL), "What Battery was This? Its Friends the Enemy Want to Know About It." [Corinth]

3:4. C. A. Tompkins (137th NY), "It Is All Over Now." [4-gun battery at Resaca]

3:5. Picket Shots: A. P. McFarland (4th IA), Howard House.

4:7. Obit.

July 18

1:1-7, 2:1-4. "Chickamauga Park."

3:1-3. R. V. Mallory, "On an Outpost. The First Battle Into Which a Regiment of Missouri Youngsters was Thrown."

3:3. H. F. Olmstead (93rd IL), "Christian Soldiers."

3:4. J. P. J. De Beck (2nd KY), "Stories of Nelson."

3:5. Picket Shots: Don C. Cameron, Big Black River; Marion F. Finn (2nd KY Bty), Mill Springs; Theodore Westmoreland (CSA surgeon), 1865 NC incident.

3:6-7. Robert Armour (79th NY), "To His Commander. A Well-Deserved Eulogy of a Gallant Scotchman." [Col. David Morrison]

4:7. Obit.

8:2. "Col. Mix's Sword. War Memorials Presented to the 3rd N.Y. Cav. by Col. Turner."

July 25

1:1-4. Connelly, Part 2.

1:5-7, 2:1. Wiley Britton (6th KS Cav), "The Massacre at Centralia."

3:1-4. Edwin Nicar (15th IN), "The 'Cracker Line.' A Staff Officer's Recollections of Missionary Ridge."

3:4. W. E. Webster (1st NY Bty), "'Show Your Scars.' Comrade Webster Makes a Few Points at Issue with the 'Cannoneer'." [Vermont-Iron Brigade losses]

3:5. Picket Shots: J. A. Fitchpatrick (38th NJ), Robert P. McRae, Providence Spring; R. N. Gorsuch (16th OH), Big Black River.

4:7. Obit.

August 1

1:1-5. Connelly, Part 3.

1:6-7, 2:1-3. J. S. Gage (29th MO), "In the Front Line at Ezra Chapel."

3:1-2. Donald C. Cameron, "'Standing Up to It.' The 1st Wisconsin Battery had a Lively Time at Thompson's Hill." [Port Gibson]

3:2. "Minty is Wearied. Does Not See Why Comrade Doyle Persists in Attacking Him." [6/20/64]

3:3. Julius Waldschmidt (19th IN), "Proud of Their Losses."

3:3-4. George F. Davenport, "Historic Ground." [Petersburg]

3:4. William E. Doyle (17th IN), "The Louisiana Tigers. The Manner of Their Taking Off."

3:5. Picket Shots: P. D. Hall (1st AL Cav), snowball fight.

4:7. Obit.

5:3-4. "A Strange Story About One of the Men Who was Connected with Booth the Assassin." [from Col. McGonigle]

August 8

1:1-6, 2:3-6. W. M. Sweeny (editor), "Man of Resource. Active Service of Gen. T. W. Sweeny, as Told by His Letters."

1:7, 2:1-2. William Simmons, "A Game of See-Saw. Exciting Events in the Gulf During the War. Occupying Galveston. . . ."

2:2. "Once Captured Meade. Confederate General Shelby Tells a Story of the War." [capture of USS *Queen City* in 1863]

3:1-2. S. C. Miles (8th WI), "A Hot Skirmish-Line. Brave Stand of the Live Eagle Brigade at Lake Chicott."

3:3. Arnold Brandley (23rd KY), "Had a Fine Record." [mainly Missionary Ridge and New Hope Church]

3:3. J. G. Terrell (83rd PA), "Gaines'Mill."

3:4-5. Picket Shots: J. R. Martin (1st IA Cav), 1864 Arkansas; Thomas P. Allen I14th US), captured on 8/31/62.

4:7. Obit.

August 15

1:1-4. Sweeny, Part 2.

1:5-7, 2:1. Richard W. Johnson, "Men and Events. Recollections of Distinguished Generals of the Civil War."

3:1. B. F. Goodwin (14th WI), "In Atlanta's Front." [7/22/64]

3:1-2. Reuben L. Chase (7th VT), "Baton Rouge."

3:2. C. H. Adams (1st CA Cav), "The Union Overthrown. How Some Johnnies Celebrated on Receipt of Foolish News."

3:2. M. R. Stansbury, "Not Much Fighting. But the 107th Illinois did a Lot of Running After."

3:3. J. B. Round (121st NY), "Rappahannock Station."

3:3. Royal Lacobs (14th PA Cav), "His Memory Failed. Royal had the Password Sure, But They Stopped Him."

3:4-5. Picket Shots: R. F. Whitmeyer (106th PA), 6/22/64.

4:7. Obit.

August 22

1:1-5. Sweeny, Part 3. [Missouri 1861]

1:6-7, 2:1-2. M. A. Sweetman (114th OH), "From Milliken's Bend to Vicksburg."

3:1. JKMcC (57th IN), "'Surrounded' Eleven Rebs. Private Nash Got Desperate and Distinguished Himself." [Missionary Ridge]

3:1-2. W. S. Speer (78th OH), "Batle of Bald Hill."

3:2. William C. Reiff (91st PA), "His Worst Scare. Ghastly Adventure of a 91st Pa. Boy on the Antietam Field."

3:2. John T. Wiesman (Bty D, 1st IL), "Helped Save the Day." [Bald Hill]

3:4. A. A. Bowen (47th IN), "Hauling Heavy Guns. How a Large Detail Took Them from New Madrid to Point Pleasant."

3:4. Thomas F. McCoy (107th PA), "The Fifth Corps." [6/18/64]

3:4. S. A. Carter (27th IA), "Shaw's Brigade. The Dashing Charge It Made at Pleasant Hill."

3:5. Picket Shots: C. M. Seagraves (46th IN), Bruinsburg.

3:7. John W. Bentley, "Drummed Out. How Col. Powell Clayton Treated a Thief in the 5th Kentucky Cavalry."

4:7. Obit.

August 29

1:1-4. Sweeny, Part 4. [Missouri 1861]

1:5-7, 2:1. Sweetman, Part 2.

3:1-2. Nat. Mullin (10th IL), "A Sojourn in Dixie. What an Illinois Boy Experienced in Rebel Prisons."

3:2. Daniel McKinley (NY), "Grand Skedaddle. A Race on Bolivar Heights in Which the Johnnies did Not Catch Up." [7/64]

3:2. George W. Patten (73rd IL), "Memories of Sheridan."

3:3. G. H. Sutton, "Story of the Arizona. How She Carried Dispatches to Admiral Farragut."

3:3. A. Doering (9th IN), "Fought It Out. Hazen's Brigade did Noble Work at Chickamauga."

3:4-5. Picket Shots: C. W. Colby (97th IL), Grant in 4/63; N. N. Coons (16th IL), Buzzard's Roost.

3:5. Samuel Fetters (76th OH), "Calls Up Memories. The Ezra Chapel Story Reminds a Comrade of His Experience."

4:7. Obit.

September 5

1:1-5. Sweeny, Part 5. [Shiloh]

1:6-7, 2:1-2. Sweetman, Part 3.

3:1-2. George W. Morse (2nd MA), "Old Days in Camp. The 2nd Mass. and Its Experiences at Brook Farm."

3:2. Joseph A. Braddy (1st NE), "Left on the Field? Dispute as to Who Removed the Remains of A. S. Johnston."

3:3. W. L. Sanford (14th IL Cav), "Stoneman Raid."

3:4. (10th MO), "A Queer Accident. How a Freshly-Equipped Regiment Lost Its Guns." [Atlanta Campaign]

3:4. S. D. Blake (1st WI Bty), "Not Only the First. Other Battery Sections were in It at Thompson's Hill." [Port Gibson]

3:5. Picket Shots: R. A. Vance (72nd IN), capture of Jeff Davis; A. G. Jacobs (6th OH Cav), Monterey.

4:7. Obit.

September 12

3:1-3. William Simmons, "Famous War-ships. Vessels Which Played an Important Part in the War of the Rebellion."

3:3-4. Sanford, Part 2.

3:4. Edward H. Rogers, "Malvern Hill. Its Possibilities and Results, and a Defense of McClellan."

3:5. Picket Shots: Melton Gresham (86th IL), Kennesaw Mountain.

4:7. Obit.

8:4. Obit: August V. Kautz.

September 19

3:1-2. C. S. Wing (8th MI), "Woes of a Prisoner." [captured 7/31/64; at Macon, Andersonville, Florence]

3:2-3. I. W. Craig (2nd OH), "Rosseau and Sheridan. Discussion of Their Positions at the Battle of Perryville."

3:3. Sanford, Part 3.

3:4. George F. Morgan (155th PA), "A Cool Hand."

3:4. Picket Shots: S. C. Miles (8th WI), Lake Chicott; I. W. Craig (20th OH), Chickamauga monument to Lt. G. W. Landrum.

September 26

1:1-3, 2:5-6. Sweeny, Part 6.

1:4-6. James W. Abert, "Siege of Sumter. Quincy Adams Gilmore and His Brilliant Career. . . ."

1:7, 2:1-4. "On an Historic Field. Great Gathering of Veterans and Notables, Blue and Gray, at Chattanooga. Dedication of the Park.

3:1-2. Sanford, Part 5.

3:2-3. W. L. Munbrun (11th KY), "Hunting Bushwhackers." [4/65 in TN]

3:3-4. F. W. Sayre (15th KY Cav), "Unswerving Fealty. In the Face of an Awful Fate, Officers of the Colored Troops Did More Than Duty."

3:4. Duncan McArthur (Terry's TX Rangers), "Gen. A. S. Johnston's Body."

3:4. Frederick Smith (Bty I, 1st NY), "Company I Claims Heaviest Loss."

3:5. Picket Shots: Joseph H. Bell (27th IA), Shaw's Brigade; Henry Smith (24th WI), Nashville; Charles A. Lewis, Providence Spring.

4:7. Obit.

October 3

1:1-5. Sweeny, Part 7.

1:6-7, 2:1-2. Abert, Part 2.

3:1-2. W. S. Sanford (14th IL Cav), "In a Tight Place. Lively Times with the Johnnies at Duck River."

3:3. Samuel D. Irwin (12th KS), "Old Guerrilla Days. A Kansas Fighter Tells of Quantrall and His Fiends."

3:4. "Old Stalwart. Reminiscences of Gibbon and the Iron Brigade."

3:5. Francis Sweeny, "On the Mississippi. Indianola Blue Jacket Corrects Shipmate Sutton."

3:5. Picket Shots: A. B. Hodge (Bty I, 2nd IL), Perryville.

4:7. Obit.

October 10

1:1-4. Sweeny, Part 8.

1:5-7, 2:1-2. Donald J. Adams, "Lively for Aging. Maneuvering in a Section Infested by Harris and His Gang." [North GA Fall 1864]

3:1-2. W. J. Wray (23rd PA), "Three Grand Charges. What Couch's Division Resisted at Malvern Hill."

3:2. H. A. Tripp (10th ME), "Cedar Mountain."

3:3. H. C. Whitaker (2nd NY Cav), "'Last of the Tigers.' Some Good Stories of the Louisiana 'Terrors'."

3:3. S. E. Chandler (24th NY), "Perilous Undertaking. Comrade Tripp's Pluck Merited a Medal of Honor." [Rappahannock Station 1862]

3:4. D. H. Hall (8th WI), "He was 'in It.' An Eagle Regiment Boy Who Pulled Out One of 'Those Guns'."

3:4. James Wilson (2nd US), "How General Lyon Died."

3:5. Picket Shots: S. D. Pond (45th OH), Dutton's Hill.

4:2-5. "The Rebel Army. Its Strength Can Only Be Estimated, and Never Will Be Accurately Known."

4:7. Obit.

October 17

1:1-4. Sweeny, Part 9. [Atlanta]

1:5-7, 2:1-2. S. E. Chandler (24th NY), "In the Thick of It. What the Iron Brigade Experienced in the Old Dominion." [Spring Summer 1862] [Augur's brigade]

3:1. S. A. Clark (1st VT Cav), "Sheridan's Last Raid." [3/65]

3:2-3. Charles B. Maxwell (2nd MA Bty), "Ill-Starred Fate." [Sabine Crossroads]

3:3-4. W. C. Yard (4th PA Cav), "Raising a Company."

3:4. F. Hanson (4th MO Cav), "Saved Their Guns." [Brice's Crossroads]

3:5. Picket Shots: Frank Jones (184th PA), Reams' Station.

4:7. Obit.

8:3-4. Obit: E. D. Keyes, William H. Gibbon (15th IA).

October 24

1:1-3. Charles Cook (5th MN), "Behind Prison Walls." [Andersonville]

1:4-7, 2:1-3. Chandler, Part 2.

3:1-2. H. S. Hart (14th NY Hvy Art), "Helped Save the Flag. Sketch of the Active Service of the 14th N.Y. Heavy Artillery."

3:3. J. W. Angell (23rd WI), "Grand Gulf Fight."

3:3-4. E. E. Josef, "Way Clear to Richmond, But Sumner's Corps was Not Allowed to Advance."

3:4. H. E. Light (10th MI Cav), "Morgan's Last Raid. Some of the Incidents Relating to His Sudden Death at Greenville, Tenn."

3:5. William M. Sweeny, "The Death of General Lyon."

3:5. Picket Shots: T. D. Neighbor (52nd OH), Kennesaw Mountain; W. N. Gillett (94th OH), Resaca; A. G. Jacobs (6th OH Cav), Fort Stevens.

4:7. Obit.

October 31

1:1-3. Cook, Part 2.

1:4-7, 2:1-3. Wiley Britton (6th KS Cav), "A Noted Character. Capt. John R. Kelso, the Scourge of Southern Guerrillas."

3:1-3. L. H. Dickerson (4th IN Cav), "Raiding with McCook." [Atlanta]

3:3. J. K. Sturgeon (46th OH), "Their Christmas Goose."

3:3. Joseph A. Braddy (1st NE), "Albert S. Johnston Again."

3:4. "Laurel Hill. Presentiments of a Poor Comrade that Led to Death."

3:5. Picket Shots: O. B. Sawdey (22nd IA), Vicksburg.

4:7. Obit.

5:3. Obit: Charles H. Van Wyck (56th NY).

November 7

1:1-6. C. P. Bragg (USS *Signal*), "A Blue-Jacket in the Toils. Prison Life from a Naval Officer's Standpoint."

1:7, 2:1-2. John W. Lacock (93rd IN), "Battling with Hood. Smith's Guerrillas at the Siege of Nashville."

3:1-2. A. W. Stratton (16th ME), "Winning a Good Name." [Fredericksburg]

3:2-3. R. C. Rankin (7th OH Cav), "Made No Mistakes. Capt. Rankin Answers Some Recent Communications." [Stoneman's R Aid, Duck River]

3:3. C. W. Colby (47th IL), "Their March was Weary, But the Captured Fat Hams Made Up For It."

3:3. William L. Welch (23rd MA), "Not with Cushing. W. L. Welch Casts Doubt on the Story of the Albemarle's Destruction."

3:4. (79th NY), "A Tall Yarn. Narrow Escape of a N.Y. Soldier from a Swamp Monster."

3:5. Picket Shots: John C. Fario (86th IL), Peach Tree Creek; I. N. Wray (1st NE), A. S. Johnston.

4:7. Obit.

November 14

1:1-4. Lacock, Part 2.

1:5-7, 2:1. Bragg, Part 2. [Camp Ford]

3:1. C. E. Moon, "Midwinter Campaign. Pluck of Cavalry Makes Successful an Important Movement." [Hatcher's Run 2/65]

3:2-3. S. A. Clark (1st VT Cav), "Their Last Campaign."

3:3. John Moore (52nd OH), "A Rebel Spy. Cute Trick Played by a Mysterious Individual at Kennesaw."

3:4. R. B. Robbins (4th MI Cav), "At Reed's Bridge." [Chickamauga]

3:5. Picket Shots: William E. Cunningham (8th TN Cav), Morgan; Henry H. Cook (Bty H, 1st MO), 1864 battery history.

4:7. Obit.

5:3. Biog: H. D. Fisher (5th KS Cav).

5:4. Obit: Robert W. Shufeldt (USN).

November 21

1:1-4. Bragg, Part 3.

1:5-7. William A. Timbooker (11th KS Cav), "On Kanasas Soil. Exciting Times on the Price Raid Against St. Louis."

3:1-2. H. S. Keene (6th WI Bty), "Chattanooga."

3:3-4. Clark, Part 2.

3:4. S. D. Pond (45th OH), "Dutton's Hill."

3:5. Picket Shots: A. B. Hodge (Bty I, 2nd IL), battery history.

4:7. Obit.

November 28

1:6-7, 2:1. W. J. Wray (23rd PA), "The Left Wing at Fair Oaks."

3:1-4. JCK (MO), "Wood's Lake Landing. A New Regiment's First Time in the Enemy's Country." [AR, 10/62]

3:4. O. B. Curtis (24th MI), "No Reason for Dispute. 'Iron Brigade' Title Belongs to Two Organizations."

3:5. Picket Shots: Thomas F. Stevens (122nd IL), General Sweeny; Stevens (122nd IL), Fort Blakely.

4:7. Obit.

5:3-4. Biog: Henry Sherwood (4th MI Cav), Thomas H. McKee (1st WV).

8:2-3. Biog: Francis M. Drake (36th IA).

December 5

1:1-4, 2:6. Thomas H. Kinkaid (8th NY SM), "Rallying to the First Call. Story of a Three-Months Man's Experience."

1:5-7. William Simmons, "August Morning with Farragut. [Mobile Bay]

3:1-3. Keene, Part 2.

3:3. H. F. Andrews (16th ME), "Fought the Good Fight."

3:4. Robert Russell (64th IL), "Where McPherson Fell."

3:4. W. T. Brown (30th IL), "Gen. McPherson's Death."

3:4. H. Skinner (Bty I, 2nd IL), "At Kennesaw Mountain."

3:5. Picket Shots: T. F. McCoy (107th PA), Five Forks; Luther B. Hunt (45th IL), A. S. Johnston.

3:6-7. L. Whitney (82nd PA), "Sailor's Creek."

4:7. Obit.

8:4. Biog: Benjamin S. Calef (9th NY).

December 12

1:1-4. Oliver O. Howard, "Marching Through Georgia."

1:5-7, 2:1-4. Kinkaid, Part 2. [First Manassas]

3:1. "First to Enlist." [MN]

3:1-2. W. S. Parr (33rd WI), "Shooting His Head Off. An Incident of the Fight at Pleasant Hill Landing."

3:2. Oliver W. Case (65th IL), "Battling with Hood."

3:3. J. H. Steger (AAG, 3rd Bg, 1st Div, Arkansas), "A Surprised Lot. Lieut. [Wells S.] Blodgett's [37th IL] Daring Act in Capturing 8 Rebels."

3:3-4. William E. Doyle (17th IN), "Roanoke Island. Confederate Surgeon's Narrative of His Capture and the Death of Gen. Wise."

3:4. M. M. Horton, "Would Be No Conscript. How a Patriotic Horse Put to Flight a Band of Rebels." [Lisburn, PA, 1863]

3:5. Picket Shots: William B. Cary (5th NY Cav), Wilderness; C. C. Cary, John Brown.

4:7. Obit.

8:4. Obit: Charles G. Culver (8th, 105th IL).

December 19

1:1-5. Howard, Part 2.

1:6-7, 2:1-2. James W. Webb, "A Bold Rescue. Incident of the Mine Explosion at Petersburg." [told to author by Walter Jamieson, 139th NY).

3:1. R. W. Jacklinn, "The 16th Michigan. The Work It Helped to Do in Saving Little Round Top."

3:2. "Gen. A. S. Johnston. Senator Isham G. Harries Gives a Circumstantial Account of His Death and the Disposition of His Remains."

3:2-3. W. L. Sanford (14th IL Cav), "That Ex-Johnny. 'Beware, Capt. Rankin! He is Fooling Thee," Says Comrade Sanford." [Stoneman's Raid, Duck River]

3:3-4. Frank McCoy (81st PA), "'Steady There!'" [Five Forks]

3:4. Charles B. Maxwell (2nd MA Bty), "Port Hudson."

3:5. Picket Shots: Samuel R. Hazen (140th NY), Five Forks.

4:7. Obit.

December 26

1:1-4. Howard, Part 3. [Allatoona]

1:5-7, 2:1. J. Williams, "Campaign Criticisms. An Apt Comment Upon Topics of War Time."

3:1-2. William Simmons, "Cutting Down the Navy. Rearrangement and Consolidation of Forces at the End of the War."

3:2-3. W. J. Wray (23rd PA), "At Marye's Heights."

3:3-4. Austin P. Lowery (6th IA), "Scouting on Mule Back." [12/62]

3:4. Volney B. St. John (44th OH), "Helped Win Crook's Star." [Lewisburg, WV]

3:5. Picket Shots: W. C. Reiff (91st PA), Abraham Lincoln; Herman Bates (78th OH), General McPherson; Samuel H. Bolton (signal corps), Bentonville.

4:7. Obit.

1896

January 2

1:1-5. Howard, Part 4. [Allatoona]

1:6-7, 2:1. Hubert Vreeland, "A Young Marauder. Sketch of Sue Munday, the Kentucky Outlaw."

3:1-3. W. H. Mayo (1st DC Cav), "A Wild Ride. Raiding with Wilson in the Enemy's Country." [1/64]

3:3. Joseph Pontiers (15th PA Cav), "Sojourn in Dixie. Attempt to Conquer a Rebel Division Got a Yankee Regiment in Trouble." [Dandridge, TN, 12/24/63]

3:4. S. A. Clark (1st VT Cav), "That Lost Opportunity. Controversies Over Gen. Warren's Actions at Five Forks."

3:5. Picket Shots: H. W. Phelps (95th OH), Price's Raid; Phila vet, capture of Col. Barker, 37th NC, 5/12/64.

3:7. John McFall (6th NY Hvy Art), "A Night of Terror. Mysterious Sound that Threw a Brigade into Confusion." [Spotsylvania]

4:7. Obit.

5:3. Biog: Benjamin F. Russell (10th ME).

January 9

1:1-5. Howard, Part 5.

1:6-7, 2:1. J. E. Williams, "Campaign Criticisms." [First Manassas]

2:4-5. A. D. Frankenberry (signal corps), "Visiting War Scenes." [Nashville, Chattanooga, etc]

3:1-2. George Reynolds (15th IA), "He was an Eye-Witness." [McPherson's death]

3:2-4. S. L. Malcolm (9th NY), "The Raid of Company C. Hawkins's Zouaves Successfully Carry Out an Expedition." [NC 1862]

3:4. H. M. Kenderdine (17th IA), "Fired on Friends." [Iuka]

3:5. H. Skinner, "Setting a Comrade Right. Something About Those Six Rodman Guns in Battery I, 2nd Ill. Light Art."

3:5. W. E. Doyle (17th IN), Missionary Ridge.

5:3. Obit: William P. Lasselle (9th IN).

January 16

1:1-4. Howard, Part 6.

1:5-7, 2:1. Richard W. Johnson, "Contest of Skill. The Campaign and Battle of Stone River."

2:4-7. Frankenberry, Part 2. [Atlanta Campaign scenes]

3:1-2. W. B. Cary (5th NY Cav), "Wilson Raid."

3:2. J. W. Lacock (93rd IN), "In a Hot Box. Carload of Troops in Great Danger from Fire." [1864]

3:2. T. C. Yates (4th Co, OH Cav), "A Hero's Death. One of the Last to See Gen. McPherson in Life."

3:3. James C. Wheat (49th IN), "A Shake of the Hand. It Brought Up Events of 30 Years Ago." [Vicksburg]

3:3-4. Lunsford H. Stanley (18th IN), "Their First Fight." [Glasgow, MO]

3:4. John Wilkin (13th OH), "The Rebel Army. A Union Veteran Does Some Thinking and Figuring."

3:5. Picket Shots: John Moore (52nd OH), Peach Tree Creek.

4:7. Biog: William J. Shakspere (2nd MI).

4:7. Obit.

January 23

1:1-5. Howard, Part 7.

1:6-7, 2:1. Richard W. Johnson, "Chickamauga."

2:4-5. Frankenberry, Part 3. [Allatoona]

3:1-2. M. W. Chapman (22nd WI), "A Fatal Field. Facing Van Dorn and Forrest at Spring Hill."

3:4. Picket Shots: D. G. James (14th WI), Allatoona.

3:5-6. James McKenna, "Gen. McPherson's Death."

4:7. Obit.

January 30

1:1-5. Howard, Part 8.

1:6-7, 2:1. Richard W. Johnson, "Battle Above the Clouds."

2:4-6. Frankenberry, Part 4.

3:1-3. Frederick Mathew (7th NY Hvy Art), "Under Old Glory." [5-6/64]

3:3-4. Marcus S. Hopkins (7th OH), "Remarkable Experience. A Man Who Stopped a Cannon-Ball and Still Lives." [Diller B. Groff, 104th PA at Seven Pines]

3:5. Picket Shots: J. W. Blake (12th ME), captured after Port Hudson.

4:7. Obit.

February 6

1:1-4. Howard, Part 9.

1:5-7, 2:1. Madeleine V. Dahlgren, "Colonel Ulric Dahlgren. A Boy Hero Who Rendered Most Important Service. . . . Service at Gettysburg. Did It Change Gen. Meade's Plan of Battle?"

3:1-2. Dwight Warren (189th NY), "At Five Forks. A Fifth Corps Man Talks About Injustice of Sheridan."

3:2. William Shigley (48th IN), "A Joke that Didn't Go. An Objection to Major Kenderdine's Story of a Tight Place."

3:3. Sol Yewell (2nd NY Cav), "Who Took the Horses. Mystery of the Battle of Lacey's Springs Cleared."

3:4. C. H. Fish, "'Uncle Billy's' Praise. Signal Corps Invaluable in Many Ways on Sherman's Raid."

3:5. Picket Shots: George E. Plumley, longest march; J. C. Clay (107th OH), General Barlow; William Creutzman (Bty D, 1st MO), Corinth.

3:6-7. C. Chandler (6th IA), "Man With a Big Mule."

4:7. Obit.

February 13

1:1-4. Howard, Part 10.

1:5-7, 2:1. A. H. Boies (4th MI), "Malvern Hill."

3:1. F. C. Tarr (9th ME), "Swamp Angel."

3:1. W. W. H. Davis (104th PA), "The Man Who Stopped a Cannon-Ball."

3:2. M. M. Hooton (86th IL), "Alleged Misstatements. Dan McCook's Brigade Surgeon Criticizes Gen. R. W. Johnson."

3:2-3. "A Critical Moment. First Clash that Threatened Spilling Blood on Kentucky Ground."

3:3. James M. Page (6th MI Cav), "A Christmas Dinner."

3:4. R. E. McBride (190th PA), "Sheridan was Slow." [Five Forks]

3:6. Picket Shots: George A. Thuman (9th PA Cav), Lovejoy Station, 11/16/64.

3:6-7. A. W. Holden (2nd NH), "First Battle of Bull Run."

4:7. Obit.

February 20

1:1-4. Howard, Part 11.

1:5-7, 2:1. (52nd OH), "Army of Kentucky. Story of Kirby Smith's Second Invasion."

3:1-2. Henry H. Cook (Bty H, 1st MO), "The 'Cracker Line'. A Missouri Batteryman Tells of the Capture of Fort McAllister."

3:3. E. L. Barnes (95th NY), "The Blue and the Gray. Some Consideration of the Relative Strength of the Two Armies."

3:4. "Romance of a Sword. Cut a Way Through the Confederacy to Its Old Owner in God's Country." [P. H. White, Chicago Mercantile Bty, Sabine Crossroads]

3:4. S. F. Moore (118th OH), "'Howard House' Again."

3:5. H. W. Phelps (95th OH), "Down the Mississippi. Dangers to Federals from Ambushes on Shore."

4:7. Obit.

February 27

1:1-4. Howard, Part 12.

1:5-7, 2:1. Army of Kentucky, Part 2.

3:1-3. F. W. Preston, "Before Port Hudson. Survivors of the Forlorn Hope Ask for Their Medals of Honor."

3:3. E. J. Wentz (9th OH Cav), "Run Out of Camp. Col. [William] Stough's Presence of Mind Saved Kilpatrick's Men from Defeat." [3/10/65]

3:4. Fred Cook (2nd MI), "Covering a Retreat." [Manassas]

3:4. Henry N. Rothery (Bty D, 5th US), "D of the 5th U.S. Artillery, and Not B." [Malvern Hill]

3:5. Picket Shots: Lawrence Gates, Chickamauga; C. L. Bartlett (6th OH Cav), Colonel Dahlgren.

4:7. Obit.

March 5

1:1-4. Howard, Part 13.

1:5-7, 2:1-3. M. V. Dahlgren, "Admiral Dahlgren Off Charleston."

2:5. Obit: Lewis Merrill (2nd MO Cav).

3:1-2. Gilbert Thompson US Eng), "Topographer's Tale. The Warren-Sheridan Episode as Viewed by Gilbert Thompson."

3:2. J. W. Ratliff (5th KY Cav), "One of Wheeler's Men. A Chase that Ended in the Capture of Three Johnnies." [Atlanta 1864]

3:3. C. P. Bragg, "What the Osage Did."

3:4. LHD (1st IA), "'Making Tracks'." [MO 1861]

3:5. Picket Shots: L. W. Blum (5th IN Bty), Iuka; Dwight Warren (189th NY), march to Appomattox; A. G. Hills (165th NY), Port Hudson.

4:6-7. Obit.

6:1. Biog: Thaddeus S. Clarkson (Bty A, 1st IL; 13th IL Cav; Bty K, 2nd MO; 3rd AR Cav).

8:4. Obit: Charles C. Coffin.

March 12

1:1-5. Howard, Part 14.

1:6-7, 2:1-2. R. H. G. Minty (4th MI Cav), "A Noble Band. Sterling Work Performed by the 4th Michigan Cavalry."

3:1-3. R. E. McBride (190th PA), "White Oak Road. Gen. Warren's Conduct was All that Could be Desired."

3:3. Isaac P. Gregg (1st MA), "Covering a Retreat." [Manassas]

3:4. Samuel St. Clair (18th PA Cav), "Colonel Dahlgren's Wound. Desperate Fighting in the Streets of Hagerstown."

3:5. Scott Sherman (2nd OH Cav), "Who Stole the Ham?"

3:5. Picket Shots: W. H. Bettes (6th OH Cav), 11/62; W. H. H. Barker (3rd IA Cav), march to Pea Ridge.

4:7. Obit.

7:1-2. W. M. Perry (96th IL), "Fifer-Boy of Chickamauga."

8:3. Obit: Henry Walke (USN).

March 19

1:1-5, 2:6-7. Howard, Part 15.

1:6-7, 2:1. Delevan Bates (30th USCT), "Battle of the Mine."

3:1-2. A. H. Boies (4th MI), "Brave Old Woodbury. Recollections of the Battle of Gaines' Mill."

3:3. F. M. Houghton, "The 'Swamp Angel'."

3:3. A. J. McPeak (31st IA), "First into Columbia."

3:4. David B. Todd (6th MO Cav), "Capture of Fort Smith."

3:4. "The Youngest General." [George C. Rogers, 15th IL]

3:5. Picket Shots: J. W. Parsons, youngest; oldest.

4:7. Obit.

March 26

1:1-5, 2:6. Howard, Part 16.

1:6-7, 2:1-2. "A Lost History. Experiences of Co. A, 2nd California Cavalry, Not Recorded Officially."

3:1-2. James W. Kesler (USS *Katahdin*), "The Harriet Lane. Exciting Chase in the Gulf on a Bright May Morning." [1864]

3:2. J. Hinson (33rd OH), "Kicked with Artillery. Some Incidents of Chickamauga Told by an Ohio Veteran."

3:3. M. M. McDonald (111th NY), "March and Battle. Story of the 111th N.Y. from Culpeper to the Wilderness."

3:4. "Nashville in '65. Reminiscences of the Waiting Period Before the Muster-Out."

3:5. Picket Shots: Thomas F. Fitzgeralds (11th OH Bty), J. W. Homer (69th OH), Chickamauga; Henry Gebhardt (41st NY), 2nd Manassas.

4:7. Obit.

8:3. Biog: Walter Evans (17th, 25th KY).

April 2

1:1-5. "Memoirs of General William T. Sherman." [1820-46]

1:6-7, 2:1-3. Lost History, Part 2.

3:1-2. Israel W. Stone (Bty M, 1st IL), "Fifer-Boy Criticized." [Chickamauga]

3:2. H. M. Kenderdine (17th IA), "Hurrahed for Logan. An Incident that Occurred at the Sacking of Columbia."

3:3-4. W. W. James (9th OH By), "Among the Guerrillas. [12/63 TN]

3:4. McDonald, Part 2.

3:4. S. A. Clark (1st VT Cav), "Lost No Horses." [Lacey Springs 12/20/63]

3:5. Picket Shots: W. S. Parr (33rd WI), Nashville; G. W. Huggins (32nd IL), Columbia; Thomas W. Baird (5th CT), marches; F. Richter (12st WI Cav), capture of Jeff Davis; youngest; J. P. Rpss (78th OH), Atlanta.

4:6-7. Obit.

5:4. Obit: Thomas L. Casey.

6:1-2. Youngest Soldiers. [Byron R. Russell (63rd IN), I. F. Mack (7th OH), Henry E. Taintor (CT).

April 9

1:1-5, 2:6. Sherman, Part 2.

1:6-7, 2:1-2. A. J. Bradford (2nd MI Cav), "Hood's Lines Broken. But Gen. Cox Could Not Have Ordered a Charge." [Nashville] [misidentified as 20th MI Cav in article]

3:1. RT (1st KS), "War in the West. Gallant Struggle at Wilson's Creek of 5,000 Federals Against Six Times Their Number."

3:2-3. William Simmons, "Taking the Chesapeake. Piratical Seizure by Supposed Passengers and Subsequent Recapture." [12/63]

3:3. James, Part 2.

3:4. J. C. Kennedy (13th IA), "Entering Columbia."

3:5-6. Picket Shots: Christian Kinkley (71st OH), guerrillas summer 1864; W. M. Moore (14th IL Cav), Nashville Campaign; W. K. DeBoyd (3rd KY), 6/63 march; E. W. Mather (17th IA), Iuka.

3:6. Benjamin F. Pierce (35th USCT), "That St. John's River Affair."

4:7. Obit.

8:2. Biog: A. T. Bliss (10th NY Cav).

April 16

1:1-5. Sherman, Part 3.

1:6-7, 2:1-2. Bradford, Part 2.

3:1-2. S. A. Chamberlain (16th ME), "Lively Times." [Spotsylvania]

3:2. Austin P. Lowery (6th IA), "The Battle of Shiloh."

3:3. L. H. Conn (USS *Conestoga*), "Western Gunboats. Experiences on the Mississippi in 1861."

3:4. T. J. Williams (56th OH), "A Little Extra Duty. Sunday at Gen. Lew Wallace's Headquarters."

3:5. Picket Shots: Charles Hulin (2nd MI), 2nd Manassas; R. Hannaford (2nd OH Cav), Lacy's Springs.

4:7. Obit.

6:1-2. Biog: Daniel R. Ballou (12th RI), Frederick J. Cotton (114th IL).

April 23

1:1-6. Sherman, Part 4.

1:7, 2:1-6. Bradford, Part 3.

3:1-2. J. R. Martin (1st IA Cav), "Tale of a Trooper. The "Wet Raid' in Arkansas Under Carr." [2/65]

3:3-4. Chamberlain, Part 2.

3:4. "Changing Base. Experiences of the Pickets at Cold Harbor."

4:7. Obit.

April 30

1:1-5, 2:5. Sherman, Part 5.

1:2. Joseph H. Bradley (5th NY), "Praise for the Old 5th."

3:3. "'Was I a Coward?' Dread Bugaboo of the Black Horse Cavalry that Scared a Comrade."

3:3-4. H. M. Kenderdine (17th IA), "The Major Protests. These Comrades Should Tell What Their Regiments Did and Forbear So Much Criticism."

3:4. Rudolph B. Schwickardi (39th NY), "Covering the Retreat." [Manassas]

3:5. David A. Garrett, "Carries the Flag. A 70th Ohio Man Who Won Honor at Fort McAllister." [Michael Murry]

3:5. Picket Shots: Cyrus A. B. Fox (86th IL), Chickamauga; Joseph Felix (73rd USCT), Port Hudson.

4:7. Obit.

May 7

1:1-5. Sherman, Part 6.

1:6-7, 2:1. Henry Mann (59th NY), "Salisbury Prison." [captured 11/25/64]

3:1-2. Bradley, Part 2.

3:2. J. Shaw (95th PA), "Salem Church."

3:3-4. H. G. Otis, "Tracing the Lines. Field of Antietam After Thirty Years of Peace." [Ewing's brigade]

3:4. A. B. Fox (86th IL), "Bentonville."

3:5. Picket Shots: Joseph Langdon (1st WI Cav), capture of Jeff Davis; Levi J. Groom (2nd NY Cav), Christmas 1864.

4:7. Obit.

May 14

1:1-6, 2:6. Sherman, Part 7.

1:7, 2:1-2. Clarence Wilson (2nd PA Hvy Art), "Exploding a Mine." [Crater]

3:1-2. George Garland (USS *Chicopee*), "Another Survivor. A Man Who Went With Cushing Against the Albemarle."

3:2. J. B. Shallenberger (22nd PA Cav), "A Close Squeeze. Seven Pa. Cavalrymen Charged a Swarming Host of Johnnies." [Newtown, VA, 6/19/64]

3:3. Henry Motz (15th IA), "Drummed Into Coumbia."

3:4. F. A. Bushey (Greencastle Echo-Pilot), "That Historic Dispatch. How It was Captured by Dahlgren and His Little Band." [Gettysburg Campaign]

3:5. Homer Peck (122nd NY), "Just Missed It. Sixth Corps Sharpshooters were Close at Ewell's Heels." [Saylor's Creek]

3:5. Picket Shots: H. H. Collins (9th MI Cav), Columbia.

4:7. Obit.

8:5-6. Biog: John B. Scace (49th, 61st MA).

May 21

1:1-4. Sherman, Part 8.

1:5-7, 2:1-2. Wilson, Part 2.

3:1. Robert Tracy (1st KS), "Some War Tales. A Little Joke on Grant and Tom Higgins's High Jinks."

3:2-3. Wilson B. Strong, "Held Them at Bay. Incidents in the Career of Gen. George C. Strong."

3:3-4. T. R. Devor (13th NJ), "A Notable Charge. Action of the 13th N.J., July 27, 1864, Most Important."

3:4. Frank Waldron (29th OH), "What Capt. Dickinson Did." [Capture of the Columbine]

3:5. Picket Shots: John Hinsman (2nd US), Wilson's Creek.

4:6. Obit.

5:3-4. Obit: Thomas H. Stevens (USN).

May 28

1:1-5, 2:5-7. Sherman, Part 9.

1:6-7, 2:1-2. J. M. Guinn, "Its Last Campaign. Shields's Division Raced With Stonewall Jackson."

3:1. H. F. Andrews (ME), "Band of Patriots. The Farrington Family—How They and Their Ancestors Served Uncle Sam."

3:1-2. Henry Dillenberger (4th MO Cav), "On a Retreat. Disaster at Guntown, and the Fate of a Brave Officer."

3:2. Y. G. Dalton (147th NY), "Warren Defended."

3:3. John T. Weisman (Bty D,1st IL), "Field of Atlanta. Disgrace of a Monument to Gen. J. B. McPherson." [present appearance]

3:3-4. A. Turner, "A Dread Bastille." [Salisbury]

3:4. JGC, "Missouri Romance." [John Jenkins, W. S. Riggs, scouts]

3:4. Edward W. Dayton (36th WI), "A Pen Picture. Snap Shots from the Battle of Reams' Station." [8/25/64]

3:5. Picket Shots: Z. Harlan (39th OH), Iuka; Dwight Warren (189th NY), Five Forks.

4:7. Biog: Charles C. McCabe (122nd OH), Earl Cranston (16th OH).

4:7. Obit.

8:3. Obit: Lucius Fairchild (2nd WI).

June 4

1:1-5, 2:6-7. Sherman, Part 10.

1:6-7, 2:1-3. Guinn, Part 2.

3:1-2. Stephen Tripp (11th PA Cav), "Fitzhugh Lee's Capture."

3:3-4. "Early Days in Missouri. Springfield Light Guards Rendered Substantial Service to the Union."

3:4. W. R. Mitchell, "A Marching Regiment. The 12th Wisconsin Covered 3,380 Miles in 12 States During the War."

3:5. Picket Shots: S. W. Storm (57th PA), 1892 trip to Fredericksburg; H. C. Wilkins (1st IN Hvy Art), Port Hudson; J. B. Neal (10th CT), Appomattox.

4:7. Obit.

June 11

1:1-5. Sherman, Part 11. [begins 1850-55 era]

1:6-7, 2:1. T. W. Parsons (14th KY Cav), "Loyal Kentuckians. Formation of Home Guards in the Eastern Part of the State."

3:1-3. William Simmons, "West India Squadron. Defeat of the Alabama and Loss of the Adirondack."

3:3. J. Shaw (95th PA), "Our Surprise Party." [Fredericksburg, 4/63]

3:3. Alexander B. Campbell (13th WI), "Trying to Escape." [Macon]

3:4. George W. Bowers (9th PA Cav), "Memories of a Retreat. The 9th Pa. Cav. was in Rear of the 52d Ohio in the Back Track to Louisville."

3:5. Picket Shots: J. W. Brewer (48th IN), Iuka.

4:7. Obit.

8:3. Obit: John G. Bourke (15th PA Cav).

8:5-6. "Pennsylvania Heroes. Equestrian Statues to Generals Meade and Hancock Unveiled at Gettysburg."

June 18

1:1-5, 2:6. Sherman, Part 12.

1:6-7, 2:1-3. Parsons, Part 2.

3:1-2. Henry Mann (59th NY), "After the 'Break.' Incidents of the Closing Days at Salisbury."

3:2. Robert I. Smith (32nd IL), "Hurlbut's Men." [Corinth]

3:3. H. D. Harter (112th NY), "Pulled Him Out. How a Comrade Got Into a Hole and was Rescued."

3:3. Robert Tracy (1st KS), "A War Tale."

3:4. T. F. Haines (127th NY), "Man in a Boat. Exciting Moments While Trying to Blow Up Sumter." [8/28/64]

3:5. Picket Shots: P. H. Walker (7th WI), B. F. Laughlin (1st PA Res), Gettysburg.

4:7. Obit.

June 25

1:1-5, 2:5-6. Sherman, Part 13.

1:6-7, 2:1. E. W. Whitaker (Custer's staff), "Appomattox. The Reception of the Flag of Truce. . . ."

3:1-3. Henry W. Barr (3rd TN Cav), "Old Buck Sanders."

3:3. Homer Mead (8th IA Cav), "The Lost Brigade, And the Story of a Mysterious Box, With a Sequel." [Wilson's Raid]

3:4. JC, "Story of a Spy." [Pauline Cushman]

3:5. Picket Shots: S. L. Wilson (16th OH), Philippi; E. B. Seaman (66th OH)(, C. Woodruff (123rd OH), marching.

4:7. Obit.

5:2. Obit: Benjamin H. Bristow (25th KY, 8th KY Cav).

6:1. Biog: R. J. Greene (26th CT), Israel Rickard (76th NY).

July 2

1:1-5, 2:5. Sherman, Part 14. [1855-57]

1:6-7, 2:1-2. C. T. Jeffers (27th MI), "What the Ninth Corps Did. Experiences from Knoxville to Spottsylvania."

3:1-2. I. D. Newell, "Columbia Bend. Short and Sharp Fight by a Vessel of the Marine Brigade." [6/64]

3:3-4. J. G. Sonderman (1st MN), "First Bull Run."

3:4. Henry Miller (8th IN), "Port Gibson."

3:4. Levi J. Groom (2nd NY Cav), "Prentiss Got Even. An Avaricious Hotel Keeper, and the Trick He Played."

3:5. Picket Shots: R. P. Miller (USS *Santee*), Galveston, 11/7/61.

4:7. Obit.

5:3. Obit: Albert G. Brackett (9th IL Cav).

July 9

1:1-5. Sherman, Part 15.

1:6-7, 2:1-2. Jeffers, Part 2.

3:1-3. Arnold Brandley (23rd KY), "Brown's Ferry."

3:3. A. W. Edwards (1st AL Cav), "Sherman Said Nothing, Although the Signal Officer on Vining Station Sent Several."

3:4. H. M. Ford (9th KY Cav), "That Famous Retreat." [KY 1862]

3:5. Picket Shots: Pat Breen (2nd US), Casey's Tactics.

5:4. Charles H. Walker (2nd NJ Cav), "A Ride with the Enemy. Marching Miles Under a Flag of Truce Side by Side." [1865]

6:1. "Four in the Army. Record of the Cole Family of Poweshick County, Iowa."

8:3. Obit: Harriet Beecher Stowe.

July 16

1:1-5, 2:7. Sherman, Part 16.

1:6-7, 2:1-3. J. E. Lowden, "A Gallant Record. Michigan's 5th Cavalry in the Latter Period of the War."

3:1-2. William Simmons, "East Gulf Squadron."

3:3. J. B. Work (52nd OH), "A Famous Retreat." [KY 1862]

3:4. Joseph F. Carter (3rd MD), "At the Crater."

3:5. Picket Shots: B. T. McCutchen, 8th IN story.

4:7. Obit.

6:2. Biog: John H. Cook (119th IL).

July 23

1:1-5, 2:7. Sherman, Part 17. [1857-59]

1:6-7, 2:1-2. Lowden, Part 2.

3:1-3. C. C. Hassler (21st PA Cav), "Romance of the Field. How a Brave Girl Saved a Federal Force from Guerrilla Surprise." [Petersburg]

3:4. Henry W. Blair (1st VT Cav), "Without a Blemish. Stirling Record of Captain Harris Blair Mitchell."

3:4. Joseph C. Rogers (52nd OH), "Not Their Chattles. Comrade Bowers Declared to be Wrong About Nelson's Retreat."

3:5. Picket Shots: J. W. Brown (signal corps), Allatoona; John H. Morse (105th OH), retreat in Kentucky; Robert Russell (64th IL), Bentonville.

4:7. Obit.

8:4. Obit: Joshua K. Siegfried (48th PA).

July 30

1:1-5, 2:6. Sherman, Part 18. [1859-61]

1:6-7, 2:1-2. Lowden, Part 3.

3:1-3. Frederick Cook (2nd MI), "Bull Run Defeat."

3:3-4. Calvin Shaffer (15th NY Hvy Art), "That Mysterious Sound." [Spotsylvania]

3:4. W. M. Moore (14th IL Cav), "Under Leaden Hail. With the 14th Ill. Cav. at Duck River and at Nashville."

3:5. Picket Shots: Edgar E. Adams (2nd VT), Manassas; D. F. Lawler (73rd IL), General Lytle's death at Chickamauga.

4:7. Obit.

August 6

1:1-5, 2:6-7. Sherman, Part 19.

1:6-7, 2:1-2. Frank Myers (6th IA Cav), "Facing the Reds. Indian Fighting Under Sully in the Northwest."

3:1-2. W. C. Reiff (91st PA), "Struggle for the Union. Trials of a Boy in the Gettysburg Campaign."

3:3-4. LSM (3rd NY Art), "Seized an Opening. Wilson Smith Rendered Appreciated Service at Little Washington." [9/6/62]

3:4. C. H. Fish (signal corps), "On Kennesaw's Top. Here is the Officer Who Censured 'Uncle Billy'."

4:6. Obit.

August 13

1:1-5, 2:7. Sherman, Part 20. [MO 1861]

1:6-7, 2:1-3. Myers, Part 2.

3:1-2. B. Mendenhall (78th IL), "Secessionism Ran Riot. What a Comrade Saw on a Trip Through the South in 1860."

3:2-3. Reiff, Part 2.

3:3. J. R. Palmer (32nd IL), "Illinois Flag Hoisted. It was on Columbia's City Hall, When the 13th Iowa's Flew from the State House."

3:3. V. P. Twombly (2nd IA), "Explosion at Cheraw"

3:3. J. H. Gardner (1st AL Cav), "Alabama's Sons Fought." [3/10/65]

3:4. John Fee (CSA), "Guibor's Battery. From Warsaw, Mo., to Greensboro, N.C., With Many a Hard Fight Between."

4:7. Obit.

August 20

1:1-5, 2:5-6. Sherman, Part 21. [Manassas, KY, MO]

1:6-7, 2:1. Myers, Part 3.

3:1-2. J. G. Sonderman (1st MN), "Fun in Camp."

3:2. J. E. Williams (OH), "No Insubordination. Records Fail to Show Refusal to Obey McCook." [Chickamauga]

3:3. J. H. Brewster (5th CT), "Bullet and Shell. How the 5th Conn. and 46th Pa. Stood Up at Winchester."

3:3. Edward Bristow (8th MO Cav), "Comrades Together."

3:4. E. J. Yeck (1st VA), "In the Hands of Guerrillas. [6/64 VA]

3:4. Arthur McDonald (176th NY), "In Durance Vile. A New Yorker Contributes His Story to Salisbury's History."

3:5. Picket Shots: John E. Stevens (6th IN Cav), capture of Charleston; J. H. Drips (6th IA Cav), reds.

4:7. Obit.

6:2. Obit: Jacob Roemer (Bty L, 2nd NY).

August 27

1:1-5, 2:6-7. Sherman, Part 22.

1:6-7, 2:1. Fletcher Pomeroy (7th KS Cav), "Led by Gen. Smith. Marching and Skirmishing in '64 . . . ." [8/64]

2:2-4. Myers, Part 4.

3:1-2. Edward C. Aultman (5th OH Cav), "Saw an Army, But Uncle Billy Sherman Would Not Believe the Rebels were There in Such Force." [Shiloh]

3:2. D. L. Marks (10th IA), "An Order that Failed." [5/22/63]

3:2. George E. Dolton (Bty M, 1st IL), "Where was Gen. Lytle Killed."

3:3-4. W. W. Jacobs, "Custer's Charge. Little Hagerstown the Scene of Bloody Strife in 1863."

3:4. John Freeman (Patterson's Ind Co Cav), "Let the Johnnies Go. But the Kentucky Horses were Invaluable to the Yanks." [9/62]

3:4. Ole C. Olson, "A Dash for Life. Two Sergeants of the 5th Michigan Cavalry Escape a General Slaughter." [8/19/64]

3:5. Picket Shots: Luke A. Delozier (143rd PA), Hart's Island prisoners.

4:7. Obit.

5:4. Biog: Charles G. Sawtelle (QM).

September 3

3:1-2. Michael Heiman (87th PA), "Relief from Bondage. Closing Days in the Notorious Andersonville Prison."

3:2-3. Charles Porter (11th VT), "A Tongue-Lashing. Sometimes the Private was Not Treated as He Should Have Been."

3:3. Frederick M. Hammer, "The Old Connecticut. Some Things She Did in the Service of the Union Under Brave Commanders."

3:4. H. S. Lowry (14th IL), "His Not to Reason Why. A Few of the Mysteries and Mistakes of Army Life." [5/63]

3:4. Youngest Soldier.

3:5. Picket Shots: S. S. Drum (6th OH), long march.

4:7. Obit.

September 10

3:1-2. Heiman, Part 2.

3:2-3. C. E. Bradley (32nd NY), "On Antietam Field."

3:3-4. George Hopkins, "Notes of a Surgeon. Recollections of Hospital Service in the Western Squadron."

3:4. A. S. Freeland (21st IL), "Sherman at Pine Top."

3:5. Picket Shots: W. E. Webst er (1st NY Bty), Winchester 1864.

September 17

1:1-5, 2:5-7. Sherman, Part 23.

3:1-3. R. F. Whitzel (61st IL), "An April Sunday." [Shiloh]

3:3. Richard King (Bty C, 1st OH), "Fighting at Bentonville."

3:3. Denis Kilhool (13th PA Cav), "Winchester Battle, And Something of the Last Days at Raleigh Under Sherman."

3:4. Picket Shots: George H. Clark (Getty's division), Cedar Creek; D. C. Stevenson (22nd WI), Spring Hill.

4:7. Biog: Albert Clarke (13th VT).

4:7. Obit.

September 24

1:1-5. Sherman, Part 24.

1:6-7, 2:1-3. Henry Stocks (9th WI), "Letters Historical. Story Told by the Correspondence Between Blunt and Hindman at Prairie Grove."

3:1-4. John Brogan, "A Memorable Cruise. Lively Times on Board the Niagara in 1863."

3:4. H. E. Brewster (Bty E, 1st IL), "A Matter of History. Battery A, 1st Ill. Light Art., Said to Have Fired the First Shot." [Cairo, IL, 4/29/61]

3:5. Picket Shot: Charles D. Field (IA), MO 9/63; Charles Porter (11th VT), Shenandoah Valley 1864.

4:7. Obit.

6:1-2. Biog: J. H. Mullen (12th CT), H. S. Dietrich (19th IL), Mark D. Taylor (93rd IL).

8:4. Biog: Edward Schfield (11th PA Res).

October 1

1:1-5. Sherman, Part 25. [Shiloh]

1:6-7, 2:1-4. George T. Dudley (50th NY Eng), "Lincoln in Richmond. True Version of the War President's Famous Visit."

3:1-3. Brog an, Part 2.

3:3-4. S. E. Chandler (24th NY Cav), "More Fun in Camp."

3:4. Kit Anderson, "A Rebel Reminiscence." [Olustee, from the Macon Telegraph of August 2]

3:5. Picket Shots: C. B. Warfield (121st OH), Bentonville.

4:6-7. Biog: John H. Brown (47th OH).

4:7. Obit.

October 8

1:1-5, 2:4-6. Sherman, Part 26.

1:6-7, 2:1-3. Birney McLean (2nd IA Cav), "Sabers to the Front. Story of Coon's Brigade, of Hatch's Cavalry Division." [Nashville]

3:1-3. "Unwritten History. Squad of the 17th Conn. First Learned of Lee's Retreat at Gettysburg."

3:3-4. William Simmons, "Ram Stonewall."

3:5. Alexander Exkel (4th TN Cav), "Among the Guerrillas. [12/24/63 incident]

3:5. Picket Shots: A. J. Merrifield (122nd NY), Cedar Creek.

4:7. Obit.

October 15

1:1-3, 2:4-6. Sherman, Part 27. [April-July 1862]

1:6-7, 2:1. McLean, Part 2.

3:1-2. John W. Thompson (48th NY), "Florida Expedition." [Olustee]

3:3. "Perilous Times. What a Loyal Man in Kentucky had to Undergo During the War." [James Oden, 7th KY Cav]

3:4. Otto Spahr, "Field of Franklin. An Ex-Johnny Tells of the Horrors of that Great Battle."

3:4. G. R. Bathe (3rd IA Cav), "Tried to Capture Price. But Comrade Cline Got Taken in by the General's Bodyguard." [9/10/63]

3:5. John Allen (15th MO Cav), "Routing Bushwhackers." [11/63]

3:5. Picket Shots: W. S. Canon (1st NY Eng), Swamp Angel.

4:7. Obit.

October 22

1:1-7, 2:1-2. Sherman, Part 28.

2:3-6. Wiley Britton (6th KS Cav), "Battle of Poison Spring."

3:1-3. W. C. Yard (4th PA Cav), "Uncle Sam's Defenders. Experiences of the 4th Pa. Cav. During Its First Year of Service."

3:3. Michael Dunke, "Rescue that Failed. The 103d Ohio Could Not Carry Out Their Brave Plan to Aid the 100th Ohio." [Limestone Station, 9/7-8/63]

3:4. J. G. Sonderman (1st MN), "Affair at Flint Hill." [9/62]

4:7. Obit.

8:3. "War Correspondents. A Beautiful and Expensive Monument Erected to Them on the Scene of the Battle of Crampton's Gap."

October 29

1:1-6, 2:3-5. Sherman, Part 29. [July 1862-January 1863]

1:7, 2:1-2. Britton, Part 2.

3:1-3. Julian W. Hinkley (3rd WI), "Marching to the Sea."

3:3-4. Charles Porter (1st VT Hvy Art), "Straightening It Out." [Cedar Creek]

3:5. S. J. Parker (82nd OH), "Warfield Forgot. There were Some Twentieth Corps Fellows at Bentonville."

4:7. Obit.

5:3. "19th Connecticut Monument at Arlington."

November 5

1:1-5. Sherman, Part 30.

3:1-3. Hinkley, Part 2.

3:3-4. Edwin O. Fowler (20th OH Bty), "Over the Breastworks." [Franklin]

3:4. W. W. Brown (21st OH), "Another Raider Gone. Death of One of Mitchel's Men Calls to Mind an Incident of the Escape."

3:4. S. L. McMahon (7th IL), "Recalling Dread Days." [Shiloh]

3:5. Picket Shots: E. Cook (8th NY Hvy Art), City Point explosion.

4:7. Obit.

November 12

1:1-5. Sherman, Part 31.

3:1-2. J. S. Williams (OH), "How It was Done. Discussion of the Valley Campaign of 1862."

3:3. John D. Vautier (88th PA), "Killing Off 'Tigers.' Comrade Vautier Corrects an Impression as to Fighting Louisianians."

3:4. Edmund Marsh (32nd MO), "5 to 1. So the Confederates Outnumbered Their Adversaries at Helena."

3:4. J. A. Blair (3rd OH), "In a Scrape. What an Ohio Boy Went Through in Trying to Reach His Regiment."

3:5. Aaron Fretz (15th US), "On Shiloh's Field. A Regular Found Sidney Johnston After the Conflict."

4:7. Obit.

November 19

1:1-5, 2:5-6. Sherman, Part 32.

1:6-7, 2:1-4. George W. Rue (9th KY Cav), "The Great Morgan Raid."

3:1-2. William Simmons, "Privateer Florida."

3:3. A. A. Velie (136th NY), "Charged in a Swamp. [Bentonville]

3:3. W. E. Webster (1st NY Bty), "At Cedar Creek."

3:3. Frederick Smith (Bty I, 1st NY), "Give Credit Where Due." [March to the Sea]

3:4. William T. Jobe (148th PA), "As to Mr. Williams."

4:7. Obit.

November 26

1:1-5, 2:6-7. Sherman, Part 33.

1:6-7, 2:1-3. Rue, Part 2.

3:1. Simmons, Part 2.

3:2. E. M. Dop, "A Regiment of Men. The 28th Wisconsin at Helena, Ark., and Several Other Places."

3:3. James H. Purdy (59th NY), "Heroism in Battle." [Wilderness]

3:4. H. Warren Phelps (95th OH), "Spy-Hunting in Memphis."

3:5. Picket Shots: Jacob Fink (55th IL), A. S. Johnston's body at Shiloh; Henry Mann (59th NY), City Point explosion.

4:7. Obit.

6:3. Daniel J. O'Brien (7th NY Hvy Art), "Colonel Lewis O. Morris."

December 3

1:1-5, 2:6. Sherman, Part 34.

1:6-7, 2:1. P. D. Whitzel (61st IL), "Through the Muscle Shoals. Thrilling Escape of Two Illinois Boys from Guerrillas."

3:1. Lewis J. Hough (9th NJ), "Bad Day at Cold Harbor."

3:2-3. Francis C. Young (war correspondent), "The Mine Run Fiasco."

3:3-4. William F. Dunnington (2nd CA Cav), "In the Mormon Country."

4:7. Obit.

8:1. Biog: H. Clay Evans (41st WI).

December 10

1:1-5, 2:6-7. Sherman, Part 35.

1:6-7, 2:1-2. A. B. Houlette (86th OH), "Bloodless Victory. Part Taken by Ohio Men at Cumberland Gap." [1863]

3:1-2. John Brogan (67th NY), "Memorable Day." [Cedar Creek]

3:2. David Sheldon (10th NY), "A Friend in Need. [Second Manassas]

3:3-4. Francis C. Long (NY Tribune), "Getting War News."

3:4. S. E. Chandler (24th NY Cav), "'Grab a Root'."

3:5. Picket Shots: Riley Jessup (33rd IA), Helena; J. R. Palmer (32nd IL), mistaken identity of Johnston's body.

4:7. Obit.

3:6. Biog: Wallace Foster (13th IN).

December 17

1:1-5, 2:6. Sherman, Part 36.

1:6-7, 2:1. James H. Harold (1st NY Eng), "The Fight at Olustee."

3:1-3. Arnold Brandley (23rd KY), "Only a Few Left. Lively Times for Co. C, 23d Ky., at New Hope Church."

3:3. W. E. Webster (1st NY Bty), "A Final Rejoinder." [Cedar Creek]

3:4. William H. Clark (8th MI Cav), "About Raider Morgan."

3:5. Picket Shots: John S. Van Arsdel (22nd IN Bty), Spring Hill; John D. Allen (15th MO Cav), 9/63, Montevallo, MO.

4:7. Biog: Henry F. Thomas (7th MI Cav).

4:7. Obit.

December 24

1:1-5, 2:5-7. Sherman, Part 37. [Chattanooga, Knoxville]

1:6-7, 2:1-2. James H. Harrold (1st NY Eng), "Siege and Capture of Fort Pulaski."

3:1. W. D. Wylie, "Deadly Bullet Stayed. How a Line of Graybacks Treated a Union Color-Bearer." [Vicksburg, 5/22/63, Thomas J. Higgins, 99th IL]

3:1-2. J. P. Gray (4th NJ Bty), "Pet of the Battery."

3:2-3. Nathan Collins (16th OH), "DeCourcey."

3:3. Joseph Morford (36th IA), "Who Fought at Helena."

3:4. Charles Porter (1st VT Hvy Art), "Brogan Answered." [Cedar Creek]

3:4. S. J. Capps, "Sport Afloat." [USS *Forest Rose*]

3:5. Picket Shots: William Wilcox (2nd OH Cav), Cedar Creek; E. M. DuPuy (28th WI), Helena.

4:2-3. Obit: George E. Lemon (National Tribune).

4:7. Biog: W. H. Smith (62nd PA).

4:7. Obit.

December 31

1:1-5, 2:6. Sherman, Part 38.

1:6-7, 2:1-2. Harrold, Part 2.

3:1-2. W. E. Loring (141st PA), "Going to the Front."

3:2. J. W. Cotes (12th IA), "Grab a Root."

3:2. Simeon Gillis (68th OH), "Grab a Root."

3:3. Silas Crowell (93rd OH), "The General Wept. [New Hope Church]

3:3-4. G. W. H. Kemper, "In the Tennessee Mountains. Poetic Mind of a Soldier Recalls Nature's Beauties After 33 Years."

3:4. W. A. Smith (47th NY), "Died with His Eyes Fixed on Old Glory."

3:5. Picket Shots: S. F. Adair (7th IA Cav), E. F. Trask (7th, 14th, 41st IA), stories; Martin Hetherston (7th MA), J. G. B. Adams' Medal of Honor.

4:7. Biog: Robert W. Leonard (162nd NY), Theodore L. Poole (122nd NY).

4:7. Obit.

7:4-5. Benjamin W. Thompson, "At Headquarters. Some Extracts from a Clerk's Diary for 1864." [Dept WV]

8:3. Biog: Anson S. Wood (138th NY—9th NY Hvy Art).

1897

January 7

1:1-5, 2:6. Sherman, Part 39.

1:6-7, 2:1-2. Harrold, Part 3.

3:1-2. Loring, Part 2.

3:3. G. R. Clift (8th KY Cav), "Chasing that Rebel Fox. A Kentucky Cavalryman's Story of John Morgan's Raid."

3:3-4. A. Z. Green (73rd IN), "Fighting at Athens. Fun with the Johnnies in Alabama at Close Quarters."

3:4. Jonathan Hunt (189th OH), "The War as an Educator."

3:4. Henry C. Baker (86th IL), "Captured by Morgan." [11/7/62]

3:5. "For Gallant Conduct." [Charles Stacey, 55th OH]

3:5. Picket Shots: J. P. Crayon, fikrst gun at Fort Sumter; Robert McRae (11th PA Cav), grab a root phrase.

4:7. Obit.

5:3. Obit: Joseph S. Skerrett (USN).

8:3. Obit: Peter J. Classen (9th, 132nd NY).

January 14

1:1-5, 2:5-6. Sherman, Part 40.

1:6-7, 2:1. James H. Harrold (1st NY Eng), "A Stronghold Hard Beset. Story of the Confederate Defense of Fort Wagner."

3:1-3. N. S. Boynton (8th MI Cav), "The Great Morgan Raid."

3:3. Jacob Kesler (33rd MO), "Fight at Helena."

3:4. (8th VT), "Won a Proud Record. Comrade S. C. Hill, of Vermont, Had an Unenviable Experience at Cedar Creek."

3:4. John Dunlap, "Had Noted Members. Some Famous Union Men were in the 2nd U. S. Cavalry, and Some Who Became Leaders in the Rebel Forces."

3:4. Frank R. Showalter (4th PA Cav), "Gun versus Snake."

3:5. Picket Shots: R. H. Bell (12th MI), grab a root phrase; Riley Jessup (33rd IA), Helena.

4:6-7. Obit.

January 21

1:1-5, 2:6-7. Sherman, Part 41. [Meridian]

1:6-7, 2:1-2. Harrold, Part 2.

3:1-2. A. K. Miller (9th MI Cav), "Dick Morgan Gave Up. One of the Interesting Incidents of the Affair at Buffington Island."

3:2. W. B. Porter (11th PA Cav), "Captured Fitz-Hugh Lee."

3:3. C. E. Stevens (77th NY), "Was in the Front Line." [Cedar Creek]

3:3-4. T. R. Dice (33rd MO), "The Charge at Helena."

3:4. Cyrus Crilley (IL), "More About 'Grab a Root'."

3:5. Picket Shots: A. A. Jones (8th TN), Atlanta; S. C. Ferguson (35th MO), Helena; J. Q. A. Campbell (5th IA), Champion's Hill; Asbury Welsh (15th OH), Chattanooga.

4:7. Obit.

January 28

1:1-4, 2:6-7. Sherman, Part 42. [March-May 1864]

1:5-7, 2:1-2. Lewis A. Grant, "In the Wilderness."

3:1-2. Louis H. Breker (MO), "Krekel's Dutch. Missouri Patriots Who Stemmed the Tide of Rebel Victory." [St. Charles, 1861]

3:2. "Bradley's Brave Deed." [Thomas W. Bradley, 124th NY, at Chancellorsville]

3:3. "Non-Combatant's Service. William Withers, Jr., Who was Stabbed by John Wilkes Booth, was a Favorite in the 62nd Penna." [62nd PA band, orchestra leader at Ford's Theater]3:3-4. William Simmons, "Navy in the Civil War. Recognition of Its Valuable Services by Congress."

3:5. Picket Shots: John D. Alten (15th MO Cav), Pineville, MO, 12/63; John W. Cates (9th TN Cav), J. H. Morgan; Peter C. Sleath (47th PA), Cedar Creek.

4:7. Obit.

5:6. Thomas H. Ashmore (25th IL), "With Grant at Chattanooga."

February 4

1:1-5, 8:4-5. Sherman, Part 43.

1:6-7, 3:1-3. Grant, Part 2.

3:1-2. J. L. Will (171st OH), "That Raid Morgan Made. The Story Told by the Newspapers of the Time."

3:3. Thomas B. Myers (33rd IA), "On the Helena Field."

3:3. O. D. Moorhead (48th OH), "Ohio Boys at Shiloh."

3:4. John W. Edwards (11th IN Cav), "Spurred Men Onward. How the 11th Ind. Cavalry Band Helped Capture the Fort." [Nashville]

3:4. A. J. Jacobs (22nd KY), "No Sandbank for Them." [Chickasaw Bluffs]

3:5. Picket Shots: R. Hannaford (2nd OH Cav), Cedar Creek; W. P. Lawrence (122nd OH), William Harpham (55th OH), grab a root phrase.

4:4. Obit: Andrew Jackson Smith.

4:7. Obit.

February 11

1:1-5, 2:6-7. Sherman, Part 44.

1:6-7, 2:1-5. R. B. Wilson, "The Kanawha Division: Its Campaigns."

3:1-2. Daniel B. Freeman (10th VT), "Danger and Hardship. Reminiscences of a Convalescent Soldier on His Way to the Front."

3:2. Judson Williams (18th IN), "Insolence Rebuked. The Story of One Five Minutes Before Vicksburg."

3:3-4. A. J. Gleason (15th OH), "Confusion as to Names. New Hope Church, Pickett's Mill, Dallas." [5/27/64]

3:4. Gustave Kothe (58th IL), Robert Bruce, "Corporal Pike." [Macon, GA, POW, Summer 1862]

3:5. Picket Shots: E. W. Menaugh (5th IN Cav), 1/65 incident.

4:7. Obit.

February 18

1:1-5, 2:5-7. Sherman, Part 45.

1:6-7, 2:1. Wilson, Part 2.

3:1-2. T. R. Lackie (16th MI), "Peace at Appomattox. Flag of Truce that was Presented in Front of Bartlett's Brigade."

3:2. R. C. Rankin (7th OH Cav), "The Morgan Raid."

3:3. "Boy's Recollections. Commader DeSteese Became a Warrior at a Very Early Age." [William DeSteese, 38th WI]

3:4. John Mallard (2nd USCT), "Assault on Fort Wagner. Denial of Alleged Reflection on the 54th Mass."

3:4. "A War-Time Athens. Patriotism and Bravery of the People of Wells Valley, Pa." [Fulton County]

3:5. Picket Shots: Harry A. Miller (76th PA), Company F story; P. M. Holloway (39th IL), Fort Wagner siege.

3:7. George Robertson, "A Comrade Preacher. Some Things He Did In and Out of War Times." [John Burgess, 30th IA]

4:7. Obit.

February 25

1:1-5, 2:5-7. Sherman, Part 46.

1:6-7, 2:1-2. Wilson, Part 3.

3:1-2. John Brogan (67th NY), "Pertinent Points." [Cedar Creek]

3:2. S. T. Carrico (61st IL), "Claims the Credit. 'Grab a Root' Said to Have Originated with the 61st Illinois."

3:3. Owen T. Wright (14th IN), "Liked Gen. Grant's Story." [Wilderness]

3:3. E. C. Kitchin (155th PA), "Appomattox Apple Tree."

3:4. G. M. Eichelberger (6th MD), "Lost Opportunities. A Facetous Comrade Tells of Ways He Might Have Become Famous."

3:4. Henderson Synnamon (3rd PA Res), "A Sharpshooter's Rifle. Comrade George Wells and the Historic Gun He Presented to Reserve Post." [George Wells, 3rd PA Res]

3:4. F. Pomeroy (7th KS Cav), "'De Coffee's Hot'."

3:5. Picket Shots: J. H. Beatty, Boonville, MS, 7/1/62; W. A. Baldwin (6th VA), Cedar Creek; Charles H. Manning (93rd OH), J. H. Morgan.

3:7. Patrick Sweeney (36th NY), "Holding the Enemy." [Fair Oaks]

4:4. "A New Thought on Gettysburg." [editorial about New Orleans Times-Democrat article that Lee was sick because of his cook]

4:7. Obit.

March 4

1:1-7. Sherman, Part 47. [Atlanta 7/64]

3:1. C. W. Backus, "A Feminine Patriot. Some Brave Things Done by the Widow Kneeland for the Sake of the Flag." [Mary B. Austin, wife of J. W. Kneeland of TN]

3:2. Jacob Fewloss (100th OH), "Overwhelmed." [Knoxville Campaign]

3:2-3. John C. Coyne, "Brig.-Gen. [Thomas] Holt. Sketch of a Gallant Member of Sickles's Excelsior Brigade." [70th NY]

3:3-4. "Message from the Past. Comrade Myton, of Winfield, Kansas, Receives a War-Time Letter." [from John B. Morrison, 125th PA]

3:4. G. W. Lyman (12th OH Cav), "Morgan at Cynthiana."

3:4. "To Recover the Flag." [7th MI Cav at Gettysburg]

3:5. Picket Shots: J. W. Homer (69th OH), grab a root phrase.

4:5-6. Stephen Tripp (11th PA Cav), "The Rebel Army. A Careful Study of Its Strength and Its Sources of Strength."

4:7. Obit.

5:7. Obit: John C. Robinson.

March 11

1:1-6. John McElroy, "Andersonville. A Story of Rebel Military Prisons."

1:7, 2:1-2. Sherman, Part 48.

3:1-2. Wilson, Part 4. [Shenandoah Valley 1864]

3:3-4. Henry F. Tower, "Nipped in the Bud. How the Knights of the Golden Circle were Broken Up in Iowa."

3:4. J. M. Watson, "As to Saving Washington. Comrade Watson Also Has Something to Say About Medals of Honor." [8/62]

3:4. R. Salisbury (1st NY Dragoons), "A Warm Time. A Dragoon Tells About a Fight Near White House Between Battery and Gunboat." [6/21/64]

3:5. Picket Shots: W. C. Yard (4th PA Cav), operations near Fredericksburg.

3:6. A. J. Jacobs (22nd KY), "DeCourcey's Brigade." [Chickasaw Bluffs]

4:7. Obit.

March 18

1:1-4. McElroy, Part 2.

1:5-7, 2:1-2. Sherman, Part 49.

3:1. Daniel B. Freeman (10th VT), "A Day's Skirmish." [Monocacy]

3:2-3. Samuel Kleffman (47th IL), "Breaking Them In."

3:3. J. H. Weatherbe (6th WI), "That Historic Tree." [Appomattox]

3:3. L. H. Coon (11th MO Cav), "A Band of Good Fighters."

3:3. John H. Keatley (125th PA), "Across the Occoquan. How Raider Stuart Dodged an Ambush and Laid Waste the Country." [1/63]

3:4. Picket Shots: A. J. Merrifield (122nd NY), Cedar Creek; A. E. Rice (15th WI), Resaca; H. A. Keve (7th IL), USCT flag presentation in Corinth, 1862.

4:5. Biog: H. Clay Evans (41st WI).

4:7. Obit.

6:2. Biog: Daniel Ross (CT).

March 25

1:1-5. McElroy, Part 3.

1:6-7, 2:1-3. Sherman, Part 50.

3:1-2. Wilson, Part 5.

3:3-5. "Cavalry Maneuvers. Gen. [Henry E.] Davies's Story of What His Brigade Did the Last Few Days of the War."

3:5-6. Picket Shots: W. C. Phipps (11th IN), grab a root phrase; V. E. Waffle (Bty A, 1st NY), Pat Sweeney (36th NY), Fair Oaks; T. B. Watkins (14th WI), Edward Armstrong (139th PA), Cedar Creek.

4:5. Biog: Thomas W. Collier (16th, 80th OH).

4:7. Obit.

8:3. Biog: Powell Clayton (1st KS, 5th KS Cav), J. K. Gowdy (5th IN Cav).

April 1

1:1-6. McElroy, Part 4.

1:7, 2:1-3. Sherman, Part 51.

3:1-2. William Simmons, "Plotting on the Potomac. Bold Seizure of the Schooner St. Nicholas in 1861."

3:3. O. D. Moorhead (48th OH), "Sabine Crossroads."

3:3. Samuel J. Church (Bty G, 2nd IL), "How He Won His Medal. Incident of Nashville Battle Recalled After Many Years."

3:4. Henry Nordhaus (5th NY), "How Col. Winslow Died." [Bethesda Church]

4:6. Obit.

April 8

1:1-4. McElroy, Part 5.

1:5, 2:1-5. Sherman, Part 52.

3:1-2. John C. Kensil (150th PA), "When They Went Out."

3:2. William Maher (1st TX Cav), "An Unusual Experience. Scouting in the Lower Mississippi Country."

3:2. W. H. Reagan (11th TN Cav), "Climbing a Mountain. Fierce Fighting at Wareman's Mills and Subsequent Pursuit."

3:3. H. G. Morton (1st MO Hvy Art), "Fighting for Old Glory."

4:7. Obit.

7:1. F. B. McGillicuddy (50th IL), "A Battle-Stained Flag."

April 15

1:1-5. McElroy, Part 6.

1:6-7, 2:1-3. Sherman, Part 53.

3:1-2. John Lynch (6th IL), "Ghost at Post 1."

3:2-3. W. A. Rodgers (18th PA Cav), "Cavalry's Bold Move. Story of the Dash Sheridan Made at Richmond." [5/64]

3:3. R. Salisbury (1st NY Dragoons), "Johnnies on the Flank. Co. G, 1st N.Y. Dragoons, Nearly Escaped Capture." [9/64]

3:4. Picket Shots: J. Y. Roe (12th WI), Atlanta.

4:7. Obit.

6:2. D. Homer Bates, "Lincoln's Yarns. Used to Tell Them While Waiting for Dispatches."

April 22

1:1-5. McElroy, Part 7.

1:6-7, 2:1-4. Sherman, Part 54. [Sept-Oct 1864]

3:1-2. A. W. Armstrong (1st CO), "Miners and Cowboys. With the Regulars, They Kept New Mexico for Uncle Sam."

3:3. J. R. Pilkington (2nd CT), "A Fight that Failed." [Manassas]

3:4. R. B. Wilson (12th OH), "Golden Opportunity. Jackson Let It Pass and Washington Put Out of Danger."

3:4. Owen T. Wright (14th IN), "No Braver Patriot. Sumner the Man, Who in His Last Words Called Down a Blessing on His Country."

3:5-7. Picket Shots: Edmund Marsh, grab a root phrase; Daniel B. Freeman (10th VT), Cedar Creek.

4:7. Obit.

April 29

1:1-5, 4:7. McElroy, Part 8.

1:6-7, 2:1-2. Sherman, Part 55.

3:1-2. H. Herring, "Crossing of the Rappahannock by the 7th Michigan." [12/11/62]

3:2. J. H. Helweg (35th IA), "Rogers's Bold Action. Arrested a Brigadier General on the Field of Battle." [Clayton E. Rogers, 6th WI, at Gettysburg, arresting T. A. Rowley]

3:3. J. E. Walton (30th OH), "Caused the Stars to Fall. Promotions were Frequent in the Old Kanawha Division."

3:3. S. G. Grubb (Bty C, 1st IL), "Imminent Danger Averted. Promptness of Two Boys in Blue Saved Sherman's Army." [after Resaca]

3:3. T. C. Penington (15th IL Cav), "Shared Sherman's Breakfast." [9/1/64]

3:4. Picket Shots: H. M. Lambert (1st AL Cav), General McPherson's death.

4:6. Obit.

5:4. Obit: Richard W. Johnson.

6:3. "Oldest Veteran." [Daniel I. Cline, 75th OH).

May 6

1:1-5. McElroy, Part 9.

1:6-7, 2:1-2. Sherman, Part 56.

3:1. Austin P. Lowery (6th IA), "Stampede at Shiloh."

3:1-2. S. C. Miles (8th WI), "Hot Work at Pleasant Hill."

3:2. William E. Doyle (17th IN), "Jackson's Inconsistency. Something About His Position on the Slavery Question."

3:3. W. A. Rodgers (18th PA Cav), "Cavalry's Bold Move. More About the Dash Sheridan Made at Richmond."

3:3. Edgar E. Adams, "What Gen. Judah Thought. Why the Union Troops were Apathetic as to Morgan's Progress."

3:4-5. Picket Shots: T. R. Lackie (16th MI), Appomattox tree; youngest.

4:3. Biog: J. H. Brigham (69th OH).

4:7. Obit.

6:6. Biog: James Minot (140th NY), Leroy T. Carleton (9th, 32nd ME).

8:6. Thomas E. Hughes (23rd WI), "Wanted a Share of the Honor." [Sabine Crossroads]

May 13

1:1-5. McElroy, Part 10.

1:6-7, 2:1-2. Sherman, Part 57.

3:1-2. Richard W. Johnson, "How Atlanta Fell."

3:2. Daniel B. Freeman (10th VT), "'Twas a Grand Charge." [Cedar Creek]

3:2. J. S. Jones (2nd NJ), "Jackson's Quick Move. How a New Jersey Brigade Narrowly Escaped Annihilation."

3:3. C. H. Osgood (4th USCT), "Tricks of the Colored Soldiers. A Sutler's Clerk Tells of His Experiences in the Army of the James."

3:3. J. B. Work (52nd OH), "That Famous 'Apple Tree'."

3:5-7. Picket Shots: L. W. Putnam (50th NY Eng), Fredericksburg; A. W. Brewster (1st IN Hvy Art), Port Hudson.

4:1-4. John H. Wilson, "The Adventures of Alf Wilson." [Andrews's Raiders]

4:7. Obit.

May 20

1:1-5. McElroy, Part 11.

1:6-7, 2:1-2. Sherman, Part 58.

3:1-3. Wilson, Part 2.

3:4-5. John W. Burnett (198th PA), "Closing War Days. A Fifth Corps Comrade's Reminiscences After the Fall of Petersburg."

3:5. Charles W. Adams (27th OH), "Captured by Bushwhackers." [MO 1861]

4:6. Obit: Thomas Raynor (119th NY).

4:6-7. Biog: O. Summers (3rd IL Cav), John Whitacre (98th OH), Halbert B. Case (7th, 84th OH).

4:6-7. Obit.

5:3. Biog: James W. Forsyth (18th US).

May 27

1:1-4. McElroy, Part 12.

1:4. Gilbert Thompson (US Eng Btn), "Fight at Guinea Bridge." [5/21/64]

1:5-7, 2:1. Sherman, Part 59.

3:1-3. Wilson, Part 3.

3:4. W. A. Rodgers (18th PA Cav), "'Mid Bullet and Shell." [Mine Run]

3:4. C. C. Stanley (25th IA), "A Night and a Day in a Rifle Pit. Incident of the Siege of Vicksburg Told by a Participant."

4:7. Obit.

6:3. Biog: I. F. Mack (7th OH).

June 3

1:1-4. Sherman, Part 60.

1:5-7, 2:1. McElroy, Part 13.

2:6. Biog: William H. Michael (11th IA).

3:5. W. George (139th PA), "How They Met 'Stonewall.' More About the New Jersey Brigade's Experience at Manassas Junction."

4:4-6. Wilson, Part 4.

4:7. Obit.

June 10

1:1-4. Sherman, Part 61.

1:5-7, 2:1-2. McElroy, part 14.

3:1-3. Wilson, Part 5.

3:4. F. M. Kimball (6th VT), "A Hero of the Vermont Brigade. Daring of Capt. R. A. Bird at the Wilderness."

3:4. G. W. Shelton (8th KY Cav), "Tireless Pursuit of Morgan."

3:5. T. C. Ralston (43rd OH), "Fuller's Brigade. A 43d Ohio Man Tells How It Captured Decatur, Ala." [3/9/64]

3:5. George Bradley (11th MO Cav), "'Way Down in Arkansas. A Missouri Veteran Tells of a Lively Morning on Picket."

4:7. Obit.

5:2-3. Obit: Samuel P. Lee (USN).

June 17

1:1-4. Sherman, Part 62.

1:5-7, 2:1. McElroy, Part 15.

3:1-3. Wilson, Part 6.

3:4-5. Richard W. Johnson, "Thomas Checks Hood's Invasion."

3:5. Thomas A. Burns (66th OH), "A Sanguinary Conflict." [New Hope Church]

3:6. A. G. Jones (27th USCT), "Reminiscences of Fort Fisher."

3:6. Charles Chandler (6th IA), "One of Sherman's 'Bummers.' Some of His Experiences at the Griswoldville Fight."

3:6. M. Bartley (31st WI), "Fighting at Bentonville."

4:7. Obit.

June 24

1:1-6. Sherman, Part 63.

1:7, 2:1-2. McElroy, Part 16.

3:1-4. Wilson, Part 7.

3:5. Joseph Blascheck (6th PA Cav), "The Story of Rush's Lancers."

3:6. Thomas Scott (Bty D, 5th US), "On the Quaker Road." [3/65]

3:6. "A Man of Pluck. Sergeant Mears, Who Won a Medal of Honor for Daring at Gettysburg." [6th PA Res]

6:1. Biog: Albert Schimpff (26th MO).

July 1

1:1-5. Sherman, Part 64.

1:6-7, 2:1-2. McElroy, Part 17.

3:1-3. Wilson, Part 8.

3:4. Frank W. McClure, "Where Tide of Battle Rolled. Field of Stones's River and the National Cemetery."

3:4-5. John W. Cates (9th TN Cav), "Defending Their Hearthstones. How East Tenn. Patriots Routed the Johnnies at Morristown." [11/28/64]

3:5. Daniel P. Donnell (2nd IA), "Gen. Grant's Little Joke. It was About an Arkansas Pie, and a Lieut. was the Butt."

3:7. Samuel Kleffman (47th IL), "Breaking Them In."

4:7. Obit.

6:6. Biog: Uriah S. Hollister (13th WI).

July 8

1:1-6. Sherman, Part 65.

1:7, 2:1-2. McElroy, Part 18.

3:1-3. Wilson, Part 9.

3:5. "Saved from Surprise. Queer Story of a Cipher Whose Reading Startled the Federal Army." [Vicksburg]

3:5. R. Salisbury (1st NY Dragoons), "A Cavalryman's Mishap. Reminiscences of Sheridan's Advance Up the Shenandoah."

3:6. C. W. Colby (97th IL), " "Doing Provost.' Experiences of an Ill. Man at New Orleans and on the Gulf."

3:7. P. W. Bishop (94th IL), "An Act of Daring." [Prairie Grove]

4:7. Obit.

6:1. Biog: I. F. Mack (7th OH).

July 15

1:1-6, 2:6-7. Sherman, Part 66.

1:7, 2:1-5. McElroy, Part 19.

3:1-3. Wilson, Part 10.

3:4-5. George W. Barber (112th NY), "Bombarding Rebel Strongholds." [Charleston]

3:5. J. B. Schneider (2nd MO), "Held Up Hood's Army." [Tunnel Hill, 10/15/64]

3:5-6. John G. Langguth (17th MO), "A Dangerous Undertaking. Carrying Dispatches from Grant's Army to Porter's Fleet." [Vicksburg]

3:6. Joseph H. Bell (27th IA), "The Nashville Battle."

3:7. Picket Shots: W. R. Sanford (14th IL Cav), Morgan, 7/19/63.

4:7. Obit.

6:1. Biog: J. P. S. Gobin (47th PA).

July 22

1:1-6, 2:5-7. Sherman, Part 67.

1:7, 2:1-4. McElroy, Part 20.

2:7. Ferd. Conner (31st OH), "Tried Men's Nerves. Picket Post Duty and Some of the Dangers Connected With It."

3:1-3. Wilson, Part 11.

3:4. Samuel Kleffman (47th IL), "Matched Against Two Wily Foes." [Farmington, 5/9/62, and Corinth]

3:4-5. G. E. McEndree (5th VA), "At Cedar Mountain. An Ex-Johnny Tells How He Captured Two Flags on the Field."

3:5. John R. Tate (24th, 154th IN), "Rebels Could Not Keep Him. Comrade Tells of His Persistent Efforts to Escape from His Captors." [Andersonville]

3:5. H. Warren Phelps (72nd, 95th OH), "They were Like a Huge Family."

3:6. John M. Phillips (5th TN Cav), "Had a Varied Experience. First Battle with the Measles and the Last with Fire and Water at the Sultana Disaster."

3:6-7. Picket Shots: M. L. Lockerby (37th WI), Lincoln story.

3:7. F. C. Bird (31st IA), "Entering Columbia."

4:7. Obit.

6:1. Biog: G. W. Carpenter (21st, 116th NY).

July 29

1:1-5, 3:1-2. Sherman, Part 68.

2:4-7. McElroy, Part 21.

3:1-3. Wilson, Part 12.

3:4-5. AWP, "Life on a Mississippi Gunboat. Paymaster's Varied Experience with the Benton."

3:5-6. William B. Smith (14th IL), "Bass Drum and Smoked Bacon."

August 5

1:1-5, 3:1-2. Sherman, Part 69.

2:1-3. Wilson, Part 13.

2:4. Samuel Kleffman (47th IL), "Hard Fighting for Uncle Sam. What the 47th Ill. Did for the Cause After the Fall of Vicksburg."

2:4-5. G. W. Travis, "'A Cup of Cold Water.' In the Face of Yankee Kindness Rebel Bullets were Stayed.' [Chickamauga]

2:5-6. "A Corporal Bold. An Amusing Hoax that Ended in a Soldier's Wedding." [TN]

2:6. S. C. Holden (17th ME), "Clairvoyance in Camp."

4:7. Obit.

August 12

1:7, 2:1-3. Sherman, Part 70.

2:4-7. McElroy, Part 22.

3:1-3. Wilson, Part 14.

3:4. Samuel Roberts (72nd PA), "All in a Dense Fog. Pa. Major Tells of an Incident After Chancellorsville."

3:4-5. Jonathan Hunt (164th OH), "A Valuable Service. Interesting Story of Events at Johnson's Island in 1864."

3:5. T. R. Lackie (16th MI), "On the Quaker Road." [3/65]

3:6. George W. Barber (112th NY), "Masonic Lodge in the Field."

3:6. Charles Doran, "Brother Against Brother. Why the Merrimac Stopped Just Before Encountering the Congress."

3:7. J. W. Routledge (23rd OH), "Captured by Mosby's Men."

4:7. Obit.

8:5. Biog: John C. Linehan (3rd NH).

August 19

1:7, 3:5-7. Sherman, Part 71.

2:1-3. Wilson, Part 15.

2:4-5. Edwin Southard (119th NY), "The 119th N.Y. at Gettysburg."

2:5. George H. Lusk (122nd NY), "At Rappahannock Station."

2:5-6. Joseph Atwood (39th IL), "A Home Run. The Fun a Soldier Boy had When He Took a Sudden Furlough."

2:6. Annie M. Keiler, "In the Days of War. Scenes that had Their Counterparts All Over the Union." [Portland, ME, returning veterans in 1865]

2:6. "Brave in Danger. How Comrade John C. Hunterson Won His Medal of Honor." [3rd PA Cav]

3:1-4. McElroy, Part 23.

4:7. Obit.

August 26

1:1-6, 3:1-2. McElroy, Part 24.

1:2-5. Biog: Isaac F. Mack (71st OH), J. P. S. Gobin (47th PA), Jhohn C. Linehan (3rd NH), George H. Innis (10th MA Bty), James A. Sexton (72nd IL).

1:7, 2:1-3. Sherman, Part 72.

2:4. Albert Wike (31st OH), "Chronicle of a Long March. Incidents of a Jaunt from Somerset to Louisville." [2/62]

2:5. H. C. Van Gilson, "Episode of the Blockade. Graphic Description of a Midnight Expedition by a Union Officer and Men." [6/64]

2:6. Picket Shots: Youngest.

3:3-6. Wilson, Part 16.

September 2

1:1-6, 3:5-7. McElroy, Part 25.

1:7, 2:1-3. Sherman, Part 73.

2:4. Charles H. Hover (128th NY), "A Salisbury Prisoner."

2:5. Edmund Marsh (32nd MO), "Halleck's Advance on Corinth."

2:5-6. H. Nachtigall (75th PA), "Brave German Veterans."

2:6. R. S. Westbrook (49th PA), "At Rappahannock Station."

2:7. Picket Shots: Joseph Kihn (6th US Cav), Belle Isle; S> H. Lane (30th MA), Baton Rouge.

3:1-4. Wilson, Part 17.

4:7. Obit.

11:1, 7. Biog: William H. Black (72nd IL), George Hoxworth (65th OH), A. H. Sockland (63rd IN), Norton P. Chipman (2nd IA), Uriah S. Hollister (13th WI), Gustavus D. Bates (7th RI), J. S. Bradley (6th DE), Charles M. Ellis (USN), James P. Averill (21st, 144th OH), Lindol Smith (73rd IN), A. L. Schimpff (26th MO), James S. Dodge (3rd OH Cav), R. M. J. Shriver (78th OH), A. H. Evans (9th NJ), Theodosius Botkin (8th OH Cav), Andrew J. Tharp (14th KY Cav, 4th KY), Charles W. Keeting (13th MA, 3rd US), Leroy T. Carleton (9th, 32nd ME), George W. Johnson (8th MD), John M. Deane (29th MA), Aaron T. Bliss (10th NY Cav), Elisha B. Wood (7th IN Cav).

12:1, 7. Biog: John P. Platt (44th MO), Thaddeus C. Davidson (133rd, 185th OH, 5th Btn OH Cav), John A. Ehrhardt (52nd IL), James Minot (140th NY), Emanuel Sands (NY), Francis Downs (1st WI Bty, 49th WI), Albert D. Shaw (35th NY), Edward C. Gearey (149th NY, 32nd USCT), Henry Kissinger (93rd OH), C. R. Young (6th IN Cav), Frank Reisner (13th IN), William D. Stauffer (10th PA Res, 195th PA), Thomas S. Hopkins (16th ME), Livingston Scott (10th RI, 3rd RI Cav), C. B. Clark (25th IA), Halbert B. Case (7th, 84th OH), Edward Ketchum (13th NY NG, 176th NY), Erastus W. Jewett (9th VT), John W. Stebbins (9th NY Cav), John F. McLean (5th MA), Thomas A. Maulsby (Bty F, 1st WV), E. B. Gray (4th WI Cav, 28th WI).

September 9

1:1-6, 3:1-4. McElroy, Part 26.

1:7, 2:1-3. Sherman, Part 74.

2:4-5. Isaac C. Dennis (14th IL Cav), "The Raid of Gen. Stoneman."

2:5-6. John Russell, "How Morgan Met His Fate. The Story of the Affair by One Who Guided the Union troops to Where He Was."

2:6. T. M. Robertson, "There were No Bloody Angles, But the 6th Indiana Cavalry Performed Conscientious and Effective Service."

3:5-7. Wilson, Part 18.

6:4. Biog: William L. Distin (17th IA).

6:6. Obit.

September 16

1:1-6, 3:1-3. McElroy, Part 27.

1:7, 2:1-3. Sherman, Part 75.

2:4-5. W. H. McEnally (72nd OH), "On the Guntown Raid."

2:5. "This Comrade had a Hard Time. Paid Dearly for His Medal of Honor Before He Got It." [Leonidas M. Godley, 2nd IA, for 5/22/63]

2:5-6. M. K. Lewis (150th NY), "Discouraged Southrons. An Ex-Confederate's Letter that Betrayed the Sentiment During Sherman's Advance." [9/16/64]

2:6-7. Picket Shots: W. B. Baugh (33rd MO), Helena.

3:4-7. Wilson, Part 19.

5:4-5. Obit.

6:3. Biog: Cyrus Leland, Jr. (4th, 10th KS).

8:6-7. William H. Doughty (11th ME), "Siege of Charleston."

September 23

1:1-6, 3:1-2. Sherman, Part 76.

1:7, 2:1-3. McElroy, Part 28.

2:4-5. Horace S. Lowry (14th IL), "Taken In at Big Shanty." [10/64]

2:5. John Laroba (4th MN), "Graced the Captain's Table. The Story of a Desperate Raid in Hostile Territory." [Atlanta Campaign]

2:5. M. J. Clerihan (10th IL), "He was Never Rash. Answers to Comrade Marsh as to Gen. Halleck."

2:5-6. J. J Osborne (7th US Cav), "Andersonville Raiders."

2:6. Joseph Tennant (106th NY), "Cedar Creek Experience."

2:6. D. L. Marks (10th IA), "Champion Hills."

3:3-7. Wilson, Part 20.

3:7. Obit.

4:5. "Monument Dedicated. N.Y.'s 73d Regiment of Vols. Complete an Enterprise." [Gettysburg]

6:6. Biog: Albion W. Tourgee (105th OH).

7:1-2. Francis C. Long (New York Tribune), "Getting War News. Anecdotes, Mostly Humorous, About Correspondents."

September 30

1:1-6, 3:4-5. McElroy, Part 29.

1:7, 2:1-4. Sherman, Part 77.

2:5-6. EVA, "How Two Spies Died. A Tragic Event at Franklin, Tenn., in June, 1863."

2:6. "A Plucky Sergeant. Won a Commission by Unswerving Attention to His Duty as a Soldier." [Orlando W. Easton, 11th IA]

2:6-7. J. W. Clemson (46th OH), "Surprised the Johnnies. A Yankee Trick Played at New Hope Church, From Which the Rebs Suffered."

2:7. C. W. Cook (53rd IL), "An Average Regiment Written About By One Who Thinks He was an Average Drummer."

2:7. Obit.

7:1-3. Wilson, Part 21.

October 7

1:1-6, 3:4-6. McElroy, Part 30.

1:7, 2:1-3. Sherman, Part 78.

2:4. "Marching and Fighting. What a Comrade Experienced at Swift Creek, Va., May 9th and 10th, 1864."

2:4-5. J. R. Lynn (29th OH), "At Gettysburg."

2:5. S. M. Reeves (13th MO Cav), "Defends Their Record. A Mo. Comrade Tells Why a Certain Class of Troops Should Not Be Ridiculed."

2:5-6. C. H. Townsend (129th OH), "Checking a Raider. Who Prevented the Escape of John Morgan and His Entire Command at Buffington Island."

2:6-7. Picket Shots: Asa W. Slayton (25th MI), Resaca.

3:6. Obit: Samuel Harriman (37th WI).

4:6-7. Obit: Neal Dow.

4:7. Biog: Thomas L. Clingman.

6:5. Obit.

6:5-6. Biog: Thomas J. Stewart (138th PA), Charles Burrows (1st MA Hvy Art).

7:1-2. J. P. Cannon (27th AL), "Inside Rebeldom. Life of a Private in the Confederate Army." [2-3/64]

7:5. S. C. Holden (17th ME), "A Bit of War Experience. Maine Man's Recollection of Garrison and Field Work."

October 14

1:1-6, 3:4-7. McElroy, Part 31.

1:7, 2:1-3. Sherman, Part 79.

2:4. A. D. Tyson (2nd IL Cav), "A Disastrous Day." [Sabine Crossroads]

2:4-5. E. W. Roberts (8th IN), "Whole Confederacy Chased Him. At Least, That's the Way It Seemed to a Comrade at Cedar Creek."

2:5. G. H. Blakeslee (129th IL), "Brave Men of His Regiment."

2:5-6. Jacob Bucher (45th IL), "At Champion Hills."

2:6-7. Picket Shots: D. P. Donnell (2nd IA), dog mascot; G. K. Carson (22nd IL), Stones River.

2:7. Edmund Marsh (32nd MO), "A Johnny Reb in Blue. He and His Insignificant Mule Raised a Serious Question." [2/64, MS]

4:5. Obit.

6:3. Obit: John W. Horn (6th MD).

7:1-3. Cannon, Part 2. [3/64]

October 21

1:1-6, 3:4-5. McElroy, Part 32.

1:7, 2:1-4. Sherman, Part 80.

2:4-5. Picket Shots: L. J. Groom (2nd NY Vet Cav), Claybourne, AL, 4/65; William Simmons, Alabama-Hatteras fight; O. B. Schofield (40th MA), Drewry's Bluff.

2:7. Charles H. Flournoy (2nd MA Cav), "Cavalry at Cedar Creek."

3:6-7. Edmund Marsh (32nd MO), "'Col. Mike's' Douche." [Michael K. Lawler]

4:7. Obit.

7:1-3. Cannon, Part 3. [4/64]

7:4. George Scott (123rd NY), "A Home-Going Cut Short. How a Comrade Found the Way from Atlanta to Andersonville." [10/64]

October 28

1:1-6, 3:4-5. McElroy, Part 33.

1:7, 2:1-3. Sherman, Part 81.

2:4. C. C. Lobingier (100th PA), "Without a Countersign."

2:4-5. S. L. Simonds (8th VT), "A Vermonter at Cedar Creek."

2:5-6. Gregory C. McDermott (23rd KY), "A Fierce Hour at New Hope."

2:6-7. Picket Shots: Youngest.

3:5. W. A. Rodgers (18th PA Cav), "Saved a Rash Soldier. Lincoln's Pardon of a Man Who Stole Away to See Wife and Child."

3:6-7. Lyman Bridges (Fourth Corps Chief of Art), "A Strategic Point. Operations Around Chattanooga—Fighting in the Clouds."

4:7. Obit.

6:2-3. Biog: Alonzo Williams (3rd RI Hvy Art).

7:1-3. Cannon, Part 4. [5/64]

November 4

1:1-6, 3:6-7. McElroy, Part 34.

1:7, 2:1-3. Sherman, Part 82.

2:4-5. John H. Ladd (6th KY), "A Regimental Reminiscence."

2:5-6. T. A. Newman (9th TN Cav), "First Day at the Front."

2:6. William Fergusson (51st MO EM), "Defends the Enrolled Militia."

3:4-5. Bridges, Part 2.

3:5. Robert P. McRae (11th PA Cav), "The Andersonville Raiders."

4:7. Obit.

6:2-3. Biog: Eli Torrance (9th PA Res, 193rd PA).

7:1-3. Cannon, Part 5. [5-6/64]

7:5-6. Jonathan Hunt (189th OH), "His Art Rescued Him. A Soldier Who Made Good Use of Ventriloquism."

November 11

1:1-6, 3:5-7. McElroy, Part 35.

1:7, 2:1-3. Sherman, Part 83.

2:3. Abiel Chandler (6th ME Bty), "A Batteryman at Cedar Mountain."

2:4-5. T. E. Blanchard (24th IA), "The Cedar Creek Controversy."

2:5-6. W. W. Doughtry (11th ME), "Friends or Foes? A Critical Moment When two Regiments Faced Each Other in Darkness." [3/31/65]

2:6-7. Picket Shots: Oldest; youngest.

3:1-4. Wiley Britton (6th KS Cav), "The Battle of Honey Springs."

4:7. Obit.

7:1-3. Cannon, Part 6. [6/64]

November 18

1:1-5. "The Fight for Chattanooga."

1:5-6. J. R. Palmer (32nd IL), "Missionary Ridge."

1:7, 2:1-3. Sherman, Part 84.

2:4-5. J. E. Walton (30th OH), "'Fighting Regiments.' Comrade Walton Contends that Some were More Ready Than Others."

2:5. Edmund Marsh (32nd MO), "An Honest Enemy." [7/4/63, 4/9/64]

2:5. R. W. Burt (76th OH), "Surely a Fighting Regiment."

2:5. Thomas P. Allen (14th US), "A Charge at Gaines's Mill."

3:4-5. McElroy, Part 36.

4:7. Obit.

7:1-3. Cannon, Part 7. [7/64]

7:3-4. Kate B. Sherwood, "At Chickamauga. Dedication of Pa. Monuments in the National Park."

November 25

1:1-6, 3:4-5. McElroy, Part 37.

1:7, 2:1-3. Sherman, Part 85.

2:4-5. Newton B. Spencer (179th NY), "The 179th's First Charge." [6/17/64]

2:5. R. Hannaford (2nd OH Cav), "Cedar Creek."

2:5-7. F. C. Plantz (51st NY), "He Carried the Flag." [Roanoke Island]

4:7. Obit.

7:1-2. Cannon, Part 8. [7/64]

December 2

1:1-4. "The Battle of Gettysburg."

1:5-6, 3:4-5. McElroy, Part 38.

1:7, 2:1-2. Sherman, Part 86.

2:3. "The 'Rooster Regiment.' Fighting Dick was the Pride of the Gallant 121st Ohio." [*Buffalo Express*]

2:4-5. Augustus C. Buell (Bty B, 4th US), "'Cannoneer Goes In.' Unlimbers a Few Guns in the Cedar Creek Controversy."

2:5. A. P. Watson (67th PA), "A Prison Quartet. [Belle Isle]

2:5. George H. Lusk (122nd NY), "They Got the Rails." [Gettysburg Campaign]

2:5-6. Picket Shots: M. H. McMullen (52nd IN), Fort Donelson.

4:7. Obit.

7:1-3. Cannon, Part 9. [8/64]

7:3. E. J. Wentz (9th OH Cav), "The Capture of Co. G. Dr. Cannon's Story May Result in Justice to a Brave Man." [4/12/64, Cheatham's Ferry, AL]

8:5-6. Edmund Marsh (32nd MO), "'Who Goes There?' A Query Which Caused Consternation on a Dark Night." [7/62]

December 9

1:1-6, 3:4-5. McElroy, Part 39.

1:7, 2:1-3. Sherman, Part 87.

2:4. M. Reed (14th US), "A Timely Sprint." [Gaines' Mill]

2:5. L. F. Gould (73rd IL), "In and Out of the Guardhouse."

2:5-7. Picket Shots: Gilbert T. Young (22nd IL), Stones River; James Blackford (14th OH), Jonesboro.

4:7. Obit.

7:1-3. Cannon, Part 10. [8-11/64]

8:6-7. H. W. Brandle, "Takes Issue With Comrades. Points of Historical Interest Disputed by a 38th Missouri Man."

December 16

1:1-6, 3:6. McElroy, Part 40.

1:7, 2:1-3. Sherman, Part 88.

2:4-5. T. H. Burns "With the 37th Kentucky."

2:5. William Spencer (8th KS), "How He Went In."

2:5-6. E. R. P. Shurley (26th NY), "At Rappahannock Station."

2:6. William Houghton (14th IN), "Charge at Marye's Heights."

3:5. William Simmons, "A Confederate Ram." [Albemarle]

4:7. Obit.

7:1-3. Cannon, Part 11. [11/64]

7:3. R. Cruikshank (123rd NY), "The Death of Gen. Polk."

December 23

1:1-6, 7:4-5. McElroy, Part 41.

1:7, 2:1-3. Sherman, Part 89.

2:4. William H. Doughty (11th ME), "Battling at Fair Oaks."

2:5. William U. Wadhams (2nd CT Hvy Art), "Cedar Creek."

2:5-6. Nelson Ames (Bty G, 1st NY), "Gallant Battery G." [Gettysburg, May 1864]

2:6. John H. Wolff (25th NY Cav), "Driving the Enemy." [White House, 6/21/64]

5:1. Obit.

7:1-3. Cannon, Part 12. [11-12/64]

December 30

1:1-6, 3:4-6. McElroy, Part 42.

1:7, 2:1-3. Sherman, Part 90.

2:4. John T. Wiley (130th PA), "Charge at Marye's Heights."

2:4-5. William E. Webster (1st NY Bty), "The Cedar Creek Battle."

2:5-6. Andrew Eitchman (Bty E, 2nd US), "Benjamin's Battery."

2:6. E. L. Hobart (28th IL), "The Belmont Movement."

2:6. Picket Shots: George P. Hawkes (21st MA), Roanoke Island.

4:5. Obit.

6:5-6. F. B. Leonard (6th IA Cav), "Fighting the Reds. Sully's Expedition as Told by a 6th Iowa Cavalryman."

7:1-2. Cannon, Part 13. [12/64]

1898

January 6

1:1-6, 3:4-7. McElroy, Part 43.

1:7, 2:1-3. Sherman, Part 91

2:3. J. E. Walton (30th OH), "Settling the Question." [Vicksburg, 5/22/63]

2:3. George Luber (47th OH), "Taking Fort McAllister."

2:4-5. Volney B. St. John (8th OH Cav), "At Cedar Creek."

2:5. P. H. Steele (3rd IA Cav), "Gallant Troopers. A 3rd Iowa Cavalry Veteran Tells of the Battle of the Osage."

2:5-6. Thomas Morgan (74th IN), "The Jonesboro Battle."

2:6. W. L. Hilyard (25th IL), "Sigel at Pea Ridge."

2:6. J. M. Lyford (16th ME), "How One May Be Mistaken. Comrade Tells of an Incident at Gettysburg to Illustrate the Point."

2:6-7. J. V. Pownall (29th IN), "Saved the Officer." [Stones' River]

2:7. Picket Shots: B. W. Powell (74th IN), Vicksburg.

3:7. Edgar A. Hamilton (1st NY Mtd Rifles), "Fighting the Merrimac."

5:7. Obit.

6:6. "A Blockade Runner. How She was Captured by a Transport." [CSS *Emma* taken by USS *Arago*, 8/24/63, off Wilmington]

7:1-3. Cannon, Part 14.

7:3-4. D. D. Holm (5th IN Bty), "How Gen. Polk Died."

8:5-7. Clarence Wilson (2nd Prov PA Hvy Art), "In the Trenches." [6/17-18/64]

January 13

1:1-6, 3:4-6. McElroy, Part 44.

1:7, 2:1-3. Sherman, Part 92.

2:4. Abraham Brown (139th PA), "As a 139th Pa. Man Saw It. First Brigade of Wheaton's Division at Cedar Creek."

2:4. Will C. Phipps (11th IN), "A Rather Trying Position. An Indiana Comrade's Reminiscence of Shiloh."

2:4-5. D. P. Randall (107th IL), "That 4-Gun Battery." [Resaca]

2:5. "'Drawing Rations.' How the 2nd Iowa Boys Secured a Regular Supply of a Delicacy."

2:6. Picket Shots: Henry B. Hardy (60th IL), Jonesboro; J. J. Pepper (16th IA), General Polk's death; Addison Tanquary (86th IL), loss of USS *General Lyon*; William H. Wallace (10th VT), Cedar Creek; H. P. Sherwin (14th VT), flag of USS *Cumberland*.

3:7. "Historic Battleflags." [Oneida County Historical Society, NY]

4:7. Obit.

6:1. P. M. Wagner (3rd IL Cav), "A Dash by Forrest."

7:1-3. Cannon, Part 15.

January 20

1:1-6, 3:4-7. McElroy, Part 45.

1:7, 2:1-3. Sherman, Part 93.

2:4-5. Judson Williams (18th IN), "His Last Battle. It was Cedar Creek, and a Bullet Stopped His Fighting."

2:5. William F. Mosier (6th TN Cav), "Chasing the Johnnies." [Bolivar, TN, Spring 1863]

2:5. Jacob Fink (55th IL), "A Vicksburg Assault." [5/22/63]

2:5-6. George C. Fales (100th NY), "The Chase of the Emma."

2:6-7. Picket Shots: George P. Stiles (6th NJ), C hancellorsville; D. H. Porter, loss of USS *General Lyon*; E. C. Kitchen (155th PA), casualties on 6/18/64; John H. Mansur (signal corps), Bt y E, 2nd US, at Knoxville; E. A. Thompson (10th KY), Jonesboro.

2:7. R. A. Smith (100th PA), "How Gen. [Thomas G.] Stevenson Died."

4:7. Obit.

6:6-7. N. W. Greenman (20th CT), "Lost in the Pines. An Episode of Gen. Sherman's March Through the Carolinas."

7:1-3. Cannon, Part 16.

7:3. H. M. Reed (4th KY Mtd Inf), "Hood's Invasion."

January 27

1:1-6, 3:4-5. McElroy, Part 46.

1:7, 2:1-3. Sherman, Part 94.

2:4. T. E. Blanchard (24th IA), "A Charge by Comrade Blanchard. Efforts to Rout 'The Cannoneer' from His Position as to Cedar Creek."

2:5. W. S. Franklin (49th OH), "Under a Terrible Fire." [5/27/64]

2:6. E. J. Smith (1st IA Cav), "Could Not Have Been True. Mo. Comrade Discounts a Recent Assertion About Gen. Curtis." [Pea Ridge]

2:6. John Dwyer (63rd NY), "In Front of the Stone Wall." [Fredericksburg]

2:6-7. Picket Shots: W. H. W. Cox (29th IA), Helena; Lewis Hart (14th PA Cav), Cedar Creek; W. J. Boon (125th IL), Jonesboro; Z. M. Partridge (4th WV), Vicksburg assault, 5/22.

3:7. John N. Morton (1st MO Eng), "Exterminating Canines. All Dogs were 'Bloodhounds' on Sherman's March to the Sea."

4:7. Obit.

6:3-4. N. B. Spencer (179th NY), "Racing the Rebels. The Move from Cold Harbor to Petersburg."

7:1-2. Cannon, Part 17.

7:2-3. O. A. Rea (82nd OH), "A Soldier's Letter. The Situation After Peach Tree Creek and Some Unionist Views."

7:3. Dan Sims (Bty E, PA), "Could Not Have Been. A Knap's Batteryman Explains About Peach Tree Creek."

7:3-4. D. B. Spencer (7th IL Cav), "At Franklin and Afterwards."

February 3

1:1-6, 3:4-5. McElroy, Part 47.

1:7, 2:1-3. Sherman, Part 95.

2:4. Hugh W. Brandle, "They Followed Osterhaus. One of His Orderlies Tells of Lively Campaigning." [Chattanooga]

2:4. W. H. Smith (13th MO Cav), "Right at the Front." [Osage]

2:5. A. P. Watson (67th PA), "Sixth Corps Man at Cedar Creek."

2:5-6. George W. Stoke (103rd PA), "Made His Escape. At the Second Attempt Lieut. Stoke Got Away from Camp Sorgum." [Columbia, SC]

2:6. G. W. Hudson (60th IL), "The Charge at Jonesboro."

2:6. M. E. Boysell (58th OH), "A Reminiscence of Shiloh."

2:7. Picket Shots: L. S. Graves (117th IL), Andersonville; A. B. Rehmel (30th OH), Fort McAllister; John R. Zercher (70th OH), Vicksburg assault, 5/22; Thomas G. Jones (5th ME Bty), Chancellorsville.

4:7. Obit.

6:3-4. C. P. Bragg (USS *Signal*), "A Chase by Night. Serio-Comic Adventure on the Mississippi." [4/64]

7:1-3. Sir Arthur J. L Fremantle, "Three Months in the Southern Confederacy."

8:3-7. J. S. Wilson (43rd WI), "A Provost's Story. Life in Southern Middle Tennessee During the Last Months of the War."

8:7. C. W. Bennett (13th US), "'Let Them Go Forward'." [Chattanooga]

February 10

1:1-6, 3:4-6. McElroy, Part 48.

1:7, 2:1-3. Sherman, Part 96.

2:3. H. Shannon, "Gen. Polk's Death."

2:4-5. Robert G. Smith (2nd DE), "Guns at Chancellorsville."

2:5. N. W. Greenman (20th CT), "That Cannon Charge." [Resaca]

2:5-6. J. J. Frazier (14th PA Cav), "What the 14th Pa. Cav. Did. [Cedar Creek]

2:6-7. Frank S. Wells (45th IL), "With the Old 45th Ill. Reminiscences of the Struggles at Champion Hills and Vicksburg."

2:7. Picket Shots: Hiram H. Ashmore (25th IL), Pea Ridge; A. W. Acheson, Chancellorsville.

3:6-7. Charles Grant (18th OH), "A Stirring Incident." [Stones' River]

4:7. Obit.

7:1-3. Fremantle, Part 2.

7:6. "Youngest Soldier."

February 17

1:1-6, 3:4-7. McElroy, Part 49.

1:7, 2:1-4. Sherman, Part 97.

2:5. E. H. Gurney (153rd NY), "A Battle Lost, Then Won. [Cedar Creek]

2:5-6. A. J. Jacobs (23rd KY), "At Chickasaw Bluffs."

2:6. H. N. Williams (2nd CT Hvy Art), "Conn. Man's Views. On Picket at the Time of the Attack at Cedar Creek."

2:6. William Ployd (119th PA), "On the Mud March."

2:7. P{icket Shots: John McLaughlin (35th MO), Helena.

4:4. Obit.

5:1-3. Henry Romeyn (105th IL), "A Scouting Experience." [Ward's brigade, 3/63, Gallatin, TN]

7:1-3. Fremantle, Part 3.

8:4-7. "Dr. Cannon's Story. R eminiscences Suggested by the Reading of 'Inside Rebeldom' ":

8:4-5. R. C. Rankin (7th OH Cav), "With the 7th Ohio Cavalry. Capt. Rankin Says He Confronted Dr. J. P. Cannon Several Times." [Nashville]

8:5-6. Thomas A. Burns (66th OH), "At Peach Tree Creek."

8:6-7. J. P. Jones (65th IL), "Battle of Franklin."

8:7. W. S. Franklin (49th OH), "The Pickett's Mill Affair."

February 24

1:1-6, 3:5. "Letters of Charles A. Dana." [9/63]

1:7, 2:1-4. Horace Greeley, "The American Conflict." [John Brown]

2:5-6. Phil M. Wagner (28th IL), "When at Spanish Fort."

2:6. F. J. M. Titus (7th IN Cav), "A Midnight Charge." [Lamar, MS]

2:6. L. O. B. Hubbard (20th CT), "Cannon at Resaca."

2:6-7. Picket Shots: William G. Phillips (129th IL), Resaca.

3:5. James L. Ferris, "With the Old Kanawha. Lively Experiences in Mobile Bay Battle."

4:7. Obit.

7:1-3. Fremantle, Part 4.

8:5-7. Sherman, Part 98.

10:3-4. McElroy, Part 50.

10:5-7. H. M. Hempstead (2nd MI Cav), "Indorses Cannon's Statements as to the Cavalry Fight on the Union Left, Nov. 30, 1864."

10:7. J. C. Noble (118th OH), "Spring Hill and Franklin."

March 3

1:1-6, 3:4-6. Dana, Part 2. [Chickamauga]

1:7, 2:1-4. Greeley, Part 2. [John Brown]

2:5. CW (34th OH), "On the Picket-Line. [Cedar Creek]

2:5-6. A. E. Goldsberry (127th IL), "Charging at Vicksburg." [5/22/63]

2:6-7. William Harpham (55th OH), "At Resaca."

2:7. Picket Shots: W. B. Pepper (24th NJ), Fredericksburg; William Denatt; General Polk's death.

3:7. George H. Lusk (122nd NY), "How Dennis Halsted Saved His Head."

4:7. Obit.

6:3. Joseph S. Atwood (39th IL), "Driving Jackson." [1862]

7:1-3. Fremantle, Part 5.

7:3. James L. Ferris (USS *Kanawha*), "The Harriet Lane."

8:4-7. McElroy, Part 51.

March 10

1:1-6, 3:5-6. Dana, Part 3.

1:7, 2:1-3. Greeley, Part 3. [John Brown]

2:4. D. T. Peterson (10th WV), "Cedar Creek."

2:4-5. W. H. Van Horn (18th US), "The Regular Brigade."

2:5. H. Weaver (3rd IA Bty), "The Pea Ridge Battle."

2:5-6. James S. Robbins (95th IL), "Comrade Robbins Objects. Nobody Ran Over Ransom's Brigade at Vicksburg."

2:6. H. W. Brandle (3rd MO), "A Trifle Warm at Vicksburg."

2:6-7. Picket Shots: Jacob Fink (55th IL), Vicksburg assault, 5/22; M. L. Thornton (53rd PA), Chancellorsville; Dennis Kilhool (Bty D, 2nd US), Cedar Creek; Z. C. Burdick (116th IL), Fort McAllister.

2:7. Charles Winters (USS *Monticello*), "Blockade Runners."

3:4. A. Huber (7th PA Cav), "A Resistless Progress." [Wilson's Raid]

3:4. W. W. Booton (7th IL Cav), "'Forward, Boys!'" [Franklin]

4:7. Obit.

5:1-3. J. D. Myers (74th IN), "A Night with Guerrillas. Capturing a Rascally Leader and Upsetting His Plans Against Sherman." [11/64, Capt. Hendricks]

6:3. P. M. Wagner (28th IL), "A Mexican Adventure. When the 28th Ill. Lay in Camp Opposite Bagdad."

7:1-3. Fremantle, Part 6.

7:3. J. P. Crayon (4th NJ Bty), "A Little Camp Experience."

7:5. George Scott (123rd NY), "A Visit to Blackshear." [Thomasville Prison, GA]

7:5. J. M. Dennis (26th MO), "The General's Bovine." [J. E. Smith, March to Chattanooga]

8:5. E. A. Gilbert (102nd IL), "Discomfited Johnnies. The Busy Bee Served the Foraging Union Men a Good Turn." [March to the Sea]

March 17

1:1-6, 3:4-7. Dana, Part 4. [Chattanooga]

1:7, 2:1-2. Greeley, Part 4. [John Brown]

2:2-3. Kate B. Sherwood, "The John Brown Song."

2:3. J. H. Nott (6th IA), "That Dog Jeff."

2:4. A. D. Limberger (3rd NY), "As Recruits and Veterans. The 3rd N.Y.'s Experience at Big Bethel and Drewry's Bluff."

2:5. B. H. Bledsoe (11th IA), "With the 11th Iowa."

2:5. A. J. Jacobs (22nd KY), "Chickasaw Bluffs."

2:6. "Chasing Marmaduke. A 2d Wisconsin Man's Story of the Fight at Lake Chicot."

2:7. Picket Shots: George W. Witherspoon (14th MI), I. H. Doughman (17th OH), Jonesboro; William H. Payne (37th IN), Stones River.

3:7. Obit: Leavenworth Home, Quincy, IL.

4:7. Obit.

6:3. D. W. Shideler (93rd OH), "A New Hope Experience."

7:1-3. Fremantle, Part 7.

March 24

1:1-5, 7:3-5. Greeley, Part 5. [Fort Sumter]

1:6-7, 2:1-4. John McElroy, "A File of Infantrymen."

2:4. Picket Shots: H. H. Bellows (14th MI), Jonesboro.

2:5-6. J. M. Fowler (60th IL), "Soon 'Smelled Powder.' Some Members of Co. E, 60th Ill., Who Went Out in '64."

2:6. T. D. Groversmith (1st DE), "Charge on Marye's Heights."

2:6-7. Naaman K. Ployd (119th PA), "Gettysburg. What was Recalled by a Tramp Over Part of the Field." [first day]

4:7. Obit.

7:1-2. Fremantle, Part 8.

8:3-4. Dana, Part 5.

March 31

2:5. H. C. Whitaker (2nd NY Cav), "Not Without Pain. How a Veteran Performed a Neat Dental Operation on a Johnny."

2:5-6. Warren W. Irish (10th NY Cav), "Before the Battle. A N.Y. Trooper Tells How He and His Comrades Went to Gettysburg." [1861]

2:6. M. S. Hartman (53rd IL), "Mid Grape and Canister. An Illinois Comrade Tells of a Brigade Charge Before Atlanta." [7/21/64]

2:6-7. T. H. Preston (30th OH), "Incidents at Vicksburg." [5/22/63]

4:7. Obit.

5:1-4. McElroy, Part 2.

5:5-7. Greeley, Part 6.

6:3-4. Henry Romeyn (105th IL), "Guerrilla Hunting." [TN]

7:1-2. Fremantle, Part 9.

8:4-7. Dana, Part 6.

April 7

2:5. Thomas Cox (USS *Yantic*), "A Sham Monitor. [Wilmington]

2:5-6. H. W. Brandle (3rd MO), "A Hard March. Vicissitudes of a Tramp from Pea Ridge to Helena by the 3d Mo."

2:6. C. W. Cook (76th NY), "A Day at Gettysburg."

2:7. Picket Shots: Z. C. Burdick (116th IL), Bentonville.

4:7. Obit.

5:1-4. McElroy, Part 3.

6:3. Theodore F. Allen (7th OH Cav), "A Dangerous Mission. [Fall 1863, Lieut. James F. Little]

6:5-6. Benjamin S. Harrower (21st IN), "Two War Reminiscences. Surprising a Videt [sic] and Capturing a Rebel Cavalryman."

7:1-2. Fremantle, Part 10.

7:3-5. Dana, Part 7.

8:1-4. Greeley, Part 7.

10:4-5. A. D. Marble (129th IL), "Charge at Resaca."

10:5. Thomas Dixon (70th IN), "Should Be No Controversy." [Resaca]

April 14

2:6. A. J. Jacobs (22nd KY), "The 22d Ky. Under Fire." [Cumberland Gap, Summer 1862]

2:6-7. S. S. Harris (13th MO Cav), "The Fight at Independence." [Price's Raid]

2:7. W. H. Laning (13th NY Hvy Art), "Foiling a Torpedo Plot." [USS *Parke*, 7/17/64]

5:1-4. McElroy, Part 4.

6:3-4. Edward B. Heaton (30th IA), "In Mississippi's Capital." [Vicksburg Campaign]

6:5. Obit.

6:7. N. K. Ployd (119th PA), "How the General Escaped." [Schimmelfennig at Gettysburg]

7:3-4. Henry Romeyn (105th IL), "Scouting Incidents. Brisk Stories of Bushwhacker Hunting in Tennessee."

8:1-5. Greeley, Part 8. [Baltimore]

8:5. John L. Williams (7th MO SM Cav), "Battle of the Osage." [Mine Creek]

10:4. John M. Turnbull (36th IL), "Chickamauga."

10:5-6. Dana, Part 8.

10:6. W. G. Balting (137th NY), "Has No Doubts About It." [Resaca]

10:7. Stephen H. Lane (30th MA), "At Cedar Creek."

10:7. F. C. Forbes (8th VT), "A Vermonter's Story." [Cedar Creek]

10:7. Thomas M. Lewis (6th MD), "Kiefer's Brigade." [Cedar Creek]

11:1-4. Fremantle, Part 11.

11:6-7. Arthur Walsh (US Mil Telegraph), "About Major Fitzgibbon." [14th MI]

11:7. Patrick Sheridan (63rd NY), "Guns at Chancellorsville."

April 21

2:4. John T. Wiley (130th PA), "Marye's Heights."

2:5. P. M. Holloway (39th IL), "The 39th Ill. at Drewry's Bluff."

2:5-6. A. M. Macumber (59th IL), "After 'Pap' Price." [2/62]

2:6-7. Charles H. Preston (30th OH), "Scouting and Foraging." [Statesville, GA, March to the Sea]

2:7. Picket Shots: William H. Mott (71st PA), regimental flags.

3:6-7. John M. Thayer, "At Fort Donelson."

5:1-5. McElroy, Part 5.

7:3. Obit.

7:6. William Simmons, "The Lost Frigate. How the Old Vermont Escaped Davy Jones's Locker." [2/24/62]

8:4-7. Greeley, Part 9. [Manassas]

10:4. D. S. Baker (USS *Clover*), "A Torpedo's Work." [Charleston 1865]

10:5-7. Fremantle, Part 12.

11:1-3. C. P. Bragg (USS *Volunteer*), "A War-Time Cruise."

11:4. H. C. Keeler (45th OH), "Charge at Resaca."

11:4-6. G. Allen (70th IN), "First Brigade Took Them, He Says." [Resaca]

11:6-7. William Harpham (55th OH), "Third Brigade's Part." [Resaca]

April 28

3:6-7. Romeyn, Part 2. [Ward's brigade at Gallatin, TN, 1862-63]

5:1-5. McElroy, Part 6.

6:3. J. C. Clay (107th OH), "A Daring Passage." [Dingle Mills, SC, 4/9/65]

6:7. Obit.

7:3. S. J. Arnold (40th OH), "How Gen. Polk was Killed."

7:5-6. Joseph F. Culver (129th IL), "That Cannon Charge." [Resaca]

8:3-7. Greeley, Part 10. [Manassas]

10:5-7. Fremantle, Part 13.

11:4. Joshua Graft (14th PA Cav), "Cedar Creek."

11:5-6. M. M. Stoddard (11th IA), "A Sample Experience. Hard Soldiering for Seventeenth Corps Men on the Way to Atlanta."

May 5

3:6. W. W. Adams (27th OH), "Battery Robinett."

3:6-7. J. A. Bradshaw (6th MO Cav), "The Taking of Jackson."

3:7. Charles Porter (11th VT), "Sheridan's Report." [Cedar Creek]

5:1-5. McElroy, Part 7.

6:5. Obit.

7:5. S. H. Draper (13th NY), "Marye's Heights."

8:1-5. Greeley, Part 11. [Manassas]

May 12

3:6-7. James L. Gamble (9th OH Cav), "Capture of the 9th Ohio Cavalry."

5:1-4. McElroy, Part 8.

6:6-7. Obit.

7:1-3. Henry Romeyn (105th IL), "Our Special Correspondent. An Interesting Trip Over the Battlefields Around Chattanooga."

8:1-5. Greeley, Part 12. [Hatteras Inlet, Wilson's Zouaves, etc.]

11:1-4. Fremantle, Part 14.

May 19

2:6-7. James W. Kesler, "Dewey the Gallant. His Behavior on the Night the Mississippi Went Down With Flying Colors."

3:6-7. J. R. Donaldson (2nd IA), "Sweeny's Fighters. Plenty of Work for Them on July 22, 1864, at Atlanta."

3:7. J. R. Balsley (142nd PA), "A Gettysburg Reminiscence."

3:7. Solomon Bobb (64th OH), "Missionary Ridge."

4:7. Obit.

5:1-5. McElroy, Part 9.

8:1-3. Greeley, Part 13. [Port Royal, Mason-Slidell]

10:6-7. Fremantle, Part 15.

May 26

2:5. J. K. Buttolph (2nd IA Bty), "A Bullet-Swept Field." [5/22/63]

3:5. Joseph R. Lynn (USS *Winnebago*), "On the Mississippi." [Fort Morgan]

3:5-6. A. J. Jacobs (22nd KY), "A Vicksburg Experience." [5/22/63]

3:6. L. F. Becker (104th OH), "The 104th Ohio in 1862."

3:6-7. Picket Shots: G. W. Sherman (20th CT), Resaca.

3:7. George W. Holmes (22nd OH), "At Battery Robinett."

5:1-4. McElroy, Part 10.

6:6. Obit.

8:1-3. Greeley, Part 14. [Pea Ridge]

8:4. G. R. Barder (11th NY Cav), "A Private Foraging Expedition in Which Mother Goose' and a Few Geese had a Part."

10:5-7. Fremantle, Part 16.

June 2

3:7. T. W. Blakeney (125th IL), "Taking a Battery. A Comrade of the 125th Ill. Tells How It Happened at Jonesboro."

5:1-3. McElroy, Part 11.

7:4-5. Fremantle, Part 17.

6:2. Obit.

8:1-4. Greeley, Part 15. [Pea Ridge]

June 9

10:6-7. Fremantle, Part 18.

June 16

2:5-6. A. A. Jones (8th TN), "Many Days of Fighting. Incidents of the Retreat from Columbia to Nashville."

2:6. Picket Shots: Greg Allen (70th IN), Resaca.

2:7. "Honor for an Army Nurse. The Likeness of Mrs. Elmira P. Spencer Will Be Cut in the Albany Capitol Staircase."

3:5. Naaman K. Ployd (119th PA), "On the Gettysburg Field. A Visit to Cemetery and Culp's Hills by a Pa. Comrade."

4:7. Obit.

5:1-4. McElroy, Part 13.

6:7. G. L. Camp (92nd OH), "In Turchin's Brigade." [Chickamauga]

6:7. Thomas H. Glassco (32nd OH), "The Burning of the General Lyon." [3/65]

7:5. Biog: William E. Simonds (25th CT).

8:4-7. Greeley, Part 17. [Henry-Donelson]

June 23

2:5. T. J. Pate (94th IL), "A Dangerous Venture. Three Men in a Boat Running a Gauntlet of Death." [siege of Mobile]

2:5. Franklin Frederici (48th PA), "Charging at Petersburg." [6/17/64]

5:1-5. McElroy, Part 14.

6:4. Obit.

8:1-2. Fremantle, Part 19.

8:3-4. Charles B. Maxwell (2nd MA Bty), "Nims's Battery."

June 30

2:4. M. F. Hammod (16th WI), "Charge at Atlanta." [7/21/64]

2:5. Richard A. Wohlforth (48th NY), "Battle of Olustee."

2:6-7. Picket Shots: J. C. Vorhes (Bty A, 1st MI), Chickamauga.

2:7. Frederick W. Baker, "Banks's Orderly Corps."

5:1-5. McElroy, Part 15.

7:4-5. Fremantle, Part 20.

8:1-3. Greeley, Part 18. [Shiloh]

July 7

2:6. Lewis Henning (10th OH Cav), "On a Picket-Post." [March to the Sea]

2:6-7. Newton Stanford, "At Jonesboro. A Defense of the Regulars' Part in that Conflict."

5:1-4. McElroy, Part 16.

6:6. Obit.

7:4-5. Fremantle, Part 21.

8:1-6. Greeley, Part 19. [Shiloh]

July 14

2:6. A. C. Shafer (92nd OH), "An Exploit of Turchin's Brigade." [Chickamauga]

2:6-7. Charles W. Sarchett (9th IA), "Carr's Division at Pea Ridge."

2:7. J. R. Prentice (19th US), "Defending 'Old Rosey'."

2:7. Charles Banks (1st OH), "Valiant Sons." [Shawnee County, KS, veterans in the Spanish-American War]

3:7. Picket Shots: William McCarty (70th OH), Fort McAllister.

5:1-4. McElroy, Part 17.

5:5. Frank S. Wells (45th IL), "A Story of Grant. Abused by a Private Who Did Not Realize What the General was About."

July 21

2:5. D. H. Robbins (5th NY Cav), "A Good Battalion." [Wilderness]

2:5. Edwin Crockett (65th NY), "Near Spottsylvania." [5/10/64]

2:5-6. David Corsair (52nd IL), "Fighting at Corinth."

8:1-5. Greeley, Part 20. [Burnside in NC]

July 28

2:4-5. J. W. Angell (23rd WI), "An Incident of Sabine Crossroads."

2:5. E. B. Wood (7th IN Cav), "A Pathetic Episode." [7/64 Memphis hospital visit]

2:5. Obit: William P. Chandler (35th IL).

2:6. Picket Shots: Christian Stuck (16th WI), Atlanta 7/22.

5:1-4. McElroy, Part 18.

5:6-7. Naaman K. Ployd (119th PA), "At Gettysburg. What was Recalled by a Tramp Over Part of the Battlefield." [second day]

5:7. John Reynard, "John Brown in Kansas."

6:3. Obit.

7:4-5. Fremantle, Part 22.

8:1-5. Greeley, Part 21. [New Orleans]

August 4

2:5. Clarence Wilson (2nd Prov PA Hvy Art), "In Front of Petersburg." [6/17/64]

2:5. James R. Lynn, "On the Winnebago. Service with the Staunch Old Vessel During the Latter Part of the War." [Mobile]

5:1-4. McElroy, Part 19.

8:1-6. Greeley, Part 22. [New Orleans]

August 11

2:5-6. L. F. Becker (104th OH), "With the 104th Ohio. Campaigning Under Burnside Not Pleasant Work."

2:6-7. William Burghart (54th NY), "At Chancellorsville."

2:7. Charles Miller (156th NY), "Some Foraging Stories."

5:1-4. McElroy, Part 20.

7:4. Obit.

August 18

2:1. Harvey Reid (22nd WI), "Shafter in the Civil War."

2:1. Obit: W. A. Kirkland (USN).

2:5. James De Daines (27th OH), "Desperate Fighting There." [Corinth]

2:5-6. Sylvester Schrantz, "An Ex- Prisoner's Reminiscences." [Florence]

2:6. Naaman K. Ployd (119th PA), "Where Gen. Bayard Fell. Scenes at 'Mansfield' During the Battle of Fredericksburg."

5:1-5. McElroy, Part 21.

8:2-5. John M. Valleau (109th PA), "On Sherman's March."

August 25

2:5. John G. Langguth (17th MO), "One of Osterhaus's Men. He Relates Some Incidents of the Taking of Lookout Mountain."

2:6. Presley E. Johnson (36th IN), "A Boy Soldier. Some of His Experiences Early in the War."

2:6. George Billhymer (51st IN, 8th IN Bty), "For the Union. An Indiana Comrade Writes of Much Artillery and Infantry Service."

2:7. Picket Shots: L. D. Immell (12th WI Bty), Corinth.

4:7. Obit.

5:1-5. McElroy, Part 22.

8:1-6. Greeley, Part 23. [Fair Oaks]

September 1

1:1-6, 2:2-4. Greeley, Part 24. [Seven Days]

2:4. Benjamin Wilson (38th OH), "A Foraging Story." [10/64]

2:7. John M. Valleau (109th PA), "Saved the Day. How Infantrymen Turned Artillerists at Peach Tree Creek."

2:7. William H. Doughty (11th ME), "Recollections of Deep Bottom." [8/13/64]

5:1-4. McElroy, Part 23.

8:1-7. Emma E. Edmonds, "Nurse and Spy."

September 8

1:1-6, 2:6. Greeley, Part 25. [South Mountain]

2:4. W. S. Franklin (49th OH), "At Pickett Mill."

2:4-5. C. A. Ramsdill (7th IL), "Davies's Division." [Fall 1862 prior to Corinth]

5:1-4. McElroy, Part 24.

6:5. Obit.

8:1-7. Edmonds, Part 2.

9:5-6. Naaman K. Ployd (119th PA), "At Gettysburg. What was Recalled by a Tramp Over Part of the Battlefield." [third day]

9:6-7. P. D. Hall (1st AL Cav), "From a Cahaba Prisoner."

9:7, 10:1. D. H. Robbins (5th NY Cav), "Captured Gen. Lee. [W. H. F. Lee, 8/62]

September 15

5:1-4. McElroy, Part 24.

7:1-3. Greeley, Part 26. [Antietam]

7:5. William L. Carpenter (32nd IA), "A Brave Record. What Senator Allen's Co. G, of the 32nd Iowa, Experienced."

7:5. S. B. Judkins (1st US Cav), "A Cavalry Encounter." [7/8/63, Boonsboro]

8:1-5. Edmonds, Part 3.

10:7, 11:1. J. E. Hott (3rd WV Cav), "Through the Valley. Events Recalled by a Trip Through Shenandoah."

September 22

1:1-6. Greeley, Part 27. [Antietam]

1:7, :1-3. "A Bold Venture. Story of a Secret Mission to the Ram Arkansas."

2:4. Franklin Frederici (48th PA), "Before Petersburg." [6/64]

2:5. John N. Prentice (57th IL), "Crossing at Bear Creek." [4/63]

2:5. (81st OH), "No Refusal to Cross." [Bear Creek]

2:5. O. E. Balting (137th NY), "The Resaca Controversy."

3:1-3. "Corporal Pike, Gen. Sherman's Great Scout."

3:7. "Battleflags Returned." [21st, 58th, 60th OH]

5:1-4. McElroy, Part 25.

7:3. Obit.

8:1-5. Edmonds, Part 4.

9:1-4. W. L. Sanford (14th IL Cav), "Fighting Forrest." [11/64]

September 29

1:1-6, 2:4. "Bold Venture," Part 2.

1:7, 2:1-3. Greeley, Part 28. [Iuka-Corinth]

2:5-6. John M. Valleau (109th PA), "Their Baptism of Fire. The Story of the 109th Pa. at Cedar Mountain Battle."

2:6-7. W. W. Porter (78th OH), "On Leggett's Hill."

2:7. John G. Langguth (17th MO), "The Vicksburg Charge." [5/22/63]

3:1-3. Pike, Part 2.

5:1-5. McElroy, Part 26.

7:1-4. Lin C. Jones (IL), "Among the Guerrillas." [March to the Sea]

7:4. Obit.

8:1-4. Edmonds, Part 5.

8:5-6. Biog: Robert St. George Dyrenforth (13th IL Cav).

9:1-3. John Newlove (1st OH Cav), "A Cavalry Dash." [7/64]

9:4. John R. King (4th CA), "A Regimental 'Character'."

October 6

1:1-6. John Obreiter (77th PA), "An Exodus from Danville Prison."

1:7, 2:1-2. Greeley, Part 29. [Corinth]

2:3. "Missionary Ridge. What Osterhaus's Division Experienced During that Battle."

2:4. A. C. Tuthill (13th IL), "In and Out of Cahaba."

2:4. Joseph E. Walton (30th OH), "At South Mountain."

3:1-4. Pike, Part 3.

5:1-4. McElroy, Part 27.

5:5-6. John M. Valleau (109th PA), "A Soldier's Presentiment. How It Bore Fruit at the Chancellorsville Battle."

7:1-4. L. F. Becker (104th OH), "On to Atlanta."

8:1-6. Edmonds, Part 6.

October 13

1:1-6, 7:4-5. Greeley, Part 30. [Stones' River]

1:7, 2:1-2. Theodore F. Allen (7th OH Cav), "Met in the Field. Personal Recollections of Some Union Officers." [Sturgis, Keough, Sanders, Wilson]

2:3. B. E. Parkhurst (147th NY), "An Exposed Position. How a Comrade Made It Possible For His Regiment to Build Breastworks." [Chancellorsville]

2:3-4. Joseph M. Morgan (50th IL), "On the Corinth Field."

3:1-3. Pike, Part 4.

4:7. Obit: M. C. Wilkinson (23rd, 107th NY), T. J. Sheehan (5th MN).

5:1-4. McElroy, Part 28.

6:3. Obit.

7:1-3. J. C. Stevenson (100th PA), "Battle Days of the Roundheads."

8:1-4. Edmonds, Part 7.

October 20

1:1-6, 2:3. Greeley, Part 31. [Port Hudson]

1:7, 2:1-2. James Fulton (143rd PA), "Gettysburg Reminiscences."

2:4-5. R. A. Marsh (4th US Art), "Early Service. Lively Times in Missouri at the Outbreak of the War."

2:5. Erastus Winters (50th OH), "In Dread Cahaba."

2:5-6. Picket Shots: S. Daighters (17th IA), Corinth.

3:1-4. Pike, Part 5.

5:1-4. McElroy, Part 29.

6:4. Obit.

7:4-5. J. R. Holibaugh (100th PA), "Battle Days of the Roundheads."

8:1-6. Edmonds, Part 8.

October 27

1:1-6, 2:7. Wiley Britton (6th KS Cav), "Shelby's Raid in Missouri." [9/62]

1:7, 2:1-2. J. C. Patterson (14th NJ), "The Battle of Monocacy."

2:4. Henry LeBeau (2nd MI Cav), "Croxton's Brigade Fought, Too." [Nashville]

3:1-3. Pike, Part 6.

5:1-4. McElroy, Part 30.

7:1-3. Holibaugh, Part 2.

7:5. W. L. Robinson (7th IL), "Crossing Bear Creek."

8:1-4. Edmonds, Part 9.

8:5-7. Theodore F. Allen (7th OH Cav), "Wilson's Cavalry Corps."

November 3

1:1-6. Britton, Part 2.

1:6. William H. Huffman (100th PA), "At South Mountain."

1:7, 2:1-2. "A Brilliant Feat of Arms. Gen. Sheridan's Battle of Booneville, Miss." [from his Memoirs]

2:5-6. R. W. Burt (76th OH), "Foraging for Sherman's Army."

2:6. B. B. Gurley (79th PA), "An Escape from Danville."

2:6-7. Picket Shots: A. A. Jones, Harper's Ferry.

3:1-3. Pike, Part 7.

4:7. Obit.

5:1-4. McElroy, Part 31.

7:5. "A Rousing Reunion. Gen. Gregg Attends that of the 13th Pa. Cavalry, Which was Exceptionally Interesting."

8:1-5. Edmonds, Part 10.

November 10

1:1-6, 2:3-4. R. E. McBride (190th PA), "Penna. Reserves. Career of These Veterans from Cold Harbor to Appomattox."

3:1-4. Pike, Part 8.

3:4. Picket Shots: W. H. Allen (17th IA), Corinth; Joseph E. Turner (31st MS), Stones River.

3:5. R. A. Smith (100th PA), "In Front of Petersburg."

3:5-6. D. B. Spencer (7th IL Cav), "These Men Fought Forrest." [11/64]

3:6-7. A. M. Looney (1st AL Cav), "Spoiled Forrest's Breakfast." [Jack Creek, TN, 12/24/63]

5:1-4. McElroy, Part 32.

5:5. Obit: Lafayette Bingham (92nd NY).

7:1-3. J. P. Cannon (27th AL), "Inside Rebeldom."

7:5. "Recovery of a Standard." [7th NY Hvy Art]

8:1-5. Edmonds, Part 11.

8:6-7. J. B. Callis (7th WI), "John Burns of Gettysburg."

November 17

1:6-7, 2:1-4. Cannon, Part 2. [1861]

2:4. "The Kearsarge's Stern-Post." ["Curious Things" series]

3:1. J. D. Ulyers (74th IN), "The Jonesboro Charge."

3:1-2. John S. Van Arsdel, "A 'Non-Com's' Story. Service in 1864 with the 22nd Indiana Battery, Hood's Invasion."

3:2-3. T. M. Smith (10th OH Cav), "Bushwhackers in a Trap." [Sandtown, GA]

3:4. Simpson Harris (192nd OH), "A Summary Execution."

3:4. "Origins of 'Taps.' Gen. Butterfield Composed It While on the Peninsula."

5:1-3. McElroy, Part 33.

6:3-4. Biog: Henry A. Castle (73rd, 137th IL).

7:4. "The Color Guards. Just Tributes Paid to Exceptionally Valiant Men."

7:4. Obit.

8:3-6. Edmonds, Part 12.

10:1-4. Pike, Part 9.

November 24

1:1-5, 3:6-7. Cannon, Part 3. [Fort Donelson]

2:4-5. Obit: Don Carlos Buell.

3:1-3. Pike, Part 10.

3:4. J. F. Stewart, "With Gen. Burbridge. Opposing Raider Morgan in Kentucky in 1864."

3:4-5. W. T. Eddy (89th NY), "A Color Company."

3:5. Daniel Knight (5th IA Cav), "A Rush for Liberty." [Nashville Campaign]

3:5. Picket Shots: R. Grove (79th IL), Colonel Harker's death at Kennesaw Mountain.

5:1-3. McElroy, Part 34.

6:3. Obit.

7:3. "A Few Words in Defense. "A Veteran Who Objects to Some of C. A. Dana's Criticisms."

7:5. C. W. Wilcox (9th NH), "In a South Carolina Prison. Extracts from a War-Time Letter Written from Camp Columbia." [12/7/64]

8:3-6. Edmonds, Part 13.

December 1

1:1-5. Cannon, Part 4.

3:1-3. Pike, Part 11.

3:4-5. M. B. Loop (68th OH), "Sounding the Alarm." [Atlanta]

3:5-6. Charles B. Maxwell (2nd MA Bty), "The Killing of Capt. [Howard] Dwight." [5/4/63]

5:1-4. McElroy, Part 35.

6:5. Obit.

7:4-5. William E. Doyle (17th IN), "The Tricks of Soldiers."

7:7. M. F. Hammond (16th WI), "Enough to Go Around." [foraging on March to the Sea]

8:4-6. Edmonds, Part 14.

December 8

1:6-7, 2:1. Cannon, Part 5. [Perryville]

3:1-3. Pike, Part 12.

3:4. Theodore F. Allen (7th OH Cav), "A Famous 'Critter Co.' Col. Wolford and His Original Method of Managing the 1st Ky. Cavalry."

3:5. George Collins (15th IN Bty), "A Hard Ride." [Frederick W. Fout in E TN]

4:7. Obit.

5:1-4. McElroy, Part 36.

6:3. Biog: Nelson F. Kimball (125th IL).

7:1-3. F. F. French (29th WI), "The Lost Detachment." [10/64]

7:3. Obit: Quincy, IL, Soldiers Home.

7:4-5. Edmonds, Part 15.

December 15

1:5-7, 2:1. Cannon, Part 6.

2:1. A. J. Williams (11th IN), "A Union Boy at Donelson."

3:1-3. Pike, Part 13.

3:4. S. A. McNeil (31st OH), "Skirmish-Line Reminiscences." [Big Shanty, GA, ca 6/17/64]

3:4. John Casner (12th PA Cav), "On the Scout." [9/15/62, 3/18/65]

3:4-5. John Hollis (13th PA Cav), "How He Lost His Liberty. Some Incidents of Meade's Retirement from Culpeper."

3:5. W. H. Nichols (7th RI Sqdn), "Escape of the Cavalry." [Harper's Ferry]

3:6. Peter Storch (14th OH), "Third Brigade at Jonesboro."

3:6. Charles H. Ranert (100th NY), "Stand of the Pickets." [Fair Oaks]

3:6. J. V. Pownall (29th IN), "Quaker Guns at Corinth."

5:1-3. McElroy, Part 37.

5:6. Obit.

7:1-4. French, Part 2.

8:3-6. Edmonds, Part 16.

December 22

1:1-4. Cannon, Part 7.

3:1-4. Pike Part 14.

3:4. James R. Fifield (60th NY), "Gallant Officers. A Veteran's Tributes to Gen. George S. Green[e] and His Son, Capt. Charles T. Green[e]."

3:4. George W. McCloud (Bty G, 1st WV), "A Batteryman's Reflections." [Droop Mountain]

3:5. "In Front of Hood. A Reply to Some of the Statements of Capt. Allen, 7th Ohio Cav."

3:5-7. Addison J. Parker (38th WI), "Two Days' Soldiering." [Petersburg]

3:7. Robert F. Locke (21st KY), "At Kennesaw Mountain."

5:1-3. McElroy, Part 38.

6:4. Obit.

7:1-3. French, Part 3.

7:5. Biog: Washington Gardner (65th OH).

December 29

1:1-5. Cannon, Part 8.

3:1-4. Pike, Part 15.

3:4. Picket Shots: N. K. Ployd (119th PA), General Sedgwick's death; C. B. Maxwell (2nd MA Bty), human interest story.

3:5. M. B. Loop (68th OH), "Champion Hills."

3:5. Jesse B. Ditty (9th PA Cav), "Entering Raleigh."

3:5-6. "At Carter's Farm." [Kernstown, 7/20/64]

3:6. D. L. Beckwith (90th NY), "A Foraging Story."

3:6-7. C. R. Warfield (121st OH), "On the Skirmish-Line." [Pine Mountain]

3:7. John M. Valleau (109th PA), "Keeping the Flag to the Front."

5:1-3. McElroy, Part 39.

6:3. Biog: J. W. Hammond (23rd IN).

6:5. Obit.

7:4-5. Edmonds, Part 17.

1899

January 5

1:5-7, 2:1. Cannon, Part 9. [Port Hudson]

3:1-3. Pike, Part 16.

3:4. James McNeal (11th MO), "Charge of the Texans." [Corinth]

3:4-5. C. W. McKay (154th NY), "Resaca."

3:6-7. Picket Shots: W. L. Kester (79th IL), Missionary Ridge; youngest.

5:1-4. McElroy, Part 40.

6:5. Obit.

7:4-5. Edmonds, Part 18.

January 12

1:5-7, 2:1. Cannon, Part 10.

3:1-3. Pike, Part 17.

3:5. JSC (60th IL), "Capturing a Rebel Brigade." [Jonesboro]

3:5. Edwin Crockett (65th NY), "Stopped a Bullet." [Cedar Creek]

3:5. Valentine D. Nichols (23rd IN Bty), "The Work of a Battery."

3:6. John N. Morton (1st MO Eng), "Another Mule Story."

3:6. T. F. Allen (7th OH Cav), "Capt. Allen Rejoins." [Nashville]

5:1-4. McElroy, Part 41.

6:5. Obit.

7:4-5. Edmonds, Part 19.

8:1-5. Theodore F. Allen (7th OH Cav), "600 Miles of Fried Chicken. A Lively Narrative of the Pursuit After Raider Morgan in 1863."

January 19

1:5-7, 2:1. Cannon, Part 11. [4-5/63]

3:1-3. Pike, Part 18.

3:4-5. R. C. Rankin (7th OH Cav), "At Duck River."

3:5-6. L. D. Hord (32nd OH), "An Atlanta Experience." [7/22]

5:1-3. McElroy, Part 42.

6:4-5. Obit.

7:4-5. Edmonds, Part 20.

8:1-5. Allen, Part 2.

10:1-2. Naaman K. Ployd (119th PA), "John Burns of Gettysburg."

January 26

1:6-7, 2:1. Cannon, Part 12. [Vicksburg]

3:1-4. Pike, Part 19.

3:5. E. L. Clark (2nd MO SM Cav), "Scouting in Missouri." [1862]

3:5-6. H. O'Neil (7th MO), "Running Batteries." [Vicksburg]

3:6. "Reminiscences of Gen. Greene." [Antietam]

5:1-3. McElroy, Part 43.

6:4. Biog: Frederick S. Snow (9th NY, 5th MD).

6:4-5. Obit.

8:5-6. R. A. Smith (100th PA), "On the Picket-Line. A Roundhead's Reminiscences of Rebel Deserters at Petersburg."

February 2

1:5-7, 2:1-2. Cannon, Part 13. [Champion's Hill]

3:1-3. Pike, Part 20.

3:4. Charles Chandler (6th IA), "Meeting Bob White. [scouting near Chattanooga]

3:4. Homer Mead (8th IA Cav), "No Chicken and Pie There. An Iowa Cavalryman Who was on the Courier Line at Duck River."

3:4-5. I. R. Blackwell, "Busy Years for the 117th Illinois."

5:1-3. McElroy, Part 44.

5:4. Biog: Thaddeus H. Stanton (19th IA).

6:3-4. Obit.

8:4-5. Thomas G. Day (3rd IN Cav), "Pleasonton's Cavalry." [10/62, Philomont, VA]

February 9

1:5-7, 2:1. Cannon, Part 14. [6-7/63]

3:1-3. Pike, Part 21.

3:4. D. W. Deweese (10th TN Cav), "More About Pike's Raid."

3:5. Patrick McEneany (scout), "Carrying Grant's Dispatches. Four Men Took the News of the Wilderness Battle to Washington."

3:5-6. "An Indiana Battery. A Member of the 22nd Replies to Comrade Collins, of the 15th."

3:6. George W. Dixon (81st OH), "At Lay's Ferry." [Resaca]

4:2-3. Obit: James A. Sexton (67th, 72nd IL).

5:1-3. McElroy, Part 45.

6:2-3. "Bloody Angle Oak Tree." ["Curious Things" series]

6:4. Obit.

7:4-5. F. T. Gilmore (63rd OH), "Defending the 63rd Ohio. What Various Regiments Did at Fort Robinett."

8:4-5. S. F. Shaw (10th WV), "Wig-Wagging in '64. Some of the Experiences Undergone by Signalmen."

February 16

1:5-7, 2:1. Cannon, Part 15. [Jackson, MS]

3:1-3. Pike, Part 22.

3:3. Samuel McCullough (63rd OH), "Only Went Back When Ordered." [Corinth]

3:3. William E. Doyle (17th IN), "Negroes as Spies." [for the CSA]

3:4. Leroy S. Fallis (8th IN Cav), "Entering Raleigh."

3:4. J. A. Gilberg (5th OH Cav), "Another View of It." [Raleigh]

3:5. M. B. Loop (68th OH), "Would Try It Anyhow. How Co. B, 68th Ohio, Lost the Honor of Capturing Fort Donelson."

3:5-6. Frederick W. Fout, "The 15th Indiana Battery." [Nashville Campaign]

5:1-3. McElroy, Part 46.

8:6. J. H. Wyman (9th IA Cav), "Fighting Against Odds." [Ashley's Station, AR]

February 23

1:5-7, 2:1. Cannon, Part 16. [7/31-8/15/63]

3:1-4. Pike, Part 23.

3:4. J. L. Bowden (12th TX), "Where is His Prisoner? A Johnny Tells About Capturing a Boy in Blue at Jonesboro." [from 23rd IN]

3:4. Horace Baker (8th WI), "A Prisoner in the South."

3:5. A. Brandley (23rd KY), "Those Two Cannon. Capture of the Lady Breckinridge and the Lady Buckner." [Chattanooga]

3:5-6. J. Caster (40th IN), "Raised a Company." [Stones' River]

3:6. Thomas J. Bradney (39th OH), "Saw the 63rd Fighting." [Corinth]

4:7. Obit: Post 23, Dayton, OH.

5:1-3. McElroy, Part 47.

6:4. Obit.

8:4-6. George D. Mosgrove (4th KY Cav CSA), "Morgan's Escape."

March 2

1:5-7, 2:1. Cannon, Part 17. [8/16-9/2/63]

2:3-4. Obit: John J. Reynolds.

3:1-3. Pike, Part 24.

3:3. J. T. Shuman (63rd OH), "The 63rd Ohio at Robinett."

3:4. "A Little Controversy. Comrade W. R. Hopkins Disects Capt. Rankin's Duck River Story."

3:4-5. H. F. W. Little (7th NH), "In Civil War Days."

3:5-6. Alexander Gravel (USS *Shamrock*), "Destroying the Ram Albemarle."

5:1-3. McElroy, Part 48.

7:5. Obit.

March 9

1:5-7, 2:1. Cannon, Part 18. [9/3-10/2/63]

3:1-3. Pike, Part 25.

3:4. George D. Carrington (11th IL), "His First Service."

3:4-5. F. G. Ferguson (Bty M, 1st IL), "Cold Weather in Dixie. Terrible Suffering in Armies During Winter of 1863-'64."

3:5. W. G. Bartholomew (27th MA), "Were Not Surprised." [Kinston, NC, 3/63]

3:6. Picket Shots: J. R. Keyes (5th OH Cav), capture of Raleigh, NC.

4:7. Obit: Levi Maish (130th PA).

5:1-2. McElroy, Part 49.

6:1-3. "Fort Moultrie Garrison Flag." ["Curious Things" series]

7:1-2. Henry Romeyn (105th IL), "Scouting in Tennessee. With Ward's Cavalrymen in Spring of 1863."

7:4-5. Obit.

March 16

1:5-7, 2:1-2. Cannon, Part 19. [10/3-11/8/63]

3:1-3. T. J. Capps (8th TN Cav), "The Lincolnite. Steadfast Loyalty of East Tennesseans Under Terrible Rebel Persecutions."

3:4. R. B. Wilson (40th IN), "Stones' River. And Something About Marching to Shiloh in 1862."

3:4-5. William Friend (38th IN), "Scribner's Brigade. Its Glorious Part in the Fighting Around Chattanooga."

3:5. John Barnes (23rd KY), "Credit Due to Hazen's Brigade." [Chattanooga]

3:6. Picket Shots: H. O. Neil (7th MO), Vicksburg assault, 5/22; A. B. Straw (9th PA Cav), Tompkinsville, KY, 7/9/62.

5:1-4. McElroy, Part 50.

6:4. Biog: William H. Nelson (5th TN Cav).

7:1-3. W. L. Sanford (14th IL Cav), "Holding Duck River."

7:4. Obit.

March 23

1:5-7, 2:1. Cannon, Part 20. [11/9-12/22/63]

3:1-3. Capps, Part 2.

3:4. Samuel E. Preston (64th NY), "Out of Rebel Prisons."

3:5. P. M. Reynolds (5th MI Cav), "Experiences of a Cavalryman." [Gettysburg]

3:5. NBG (6th IN Cav), "A Narrow Escape." [Kennesaw Mt]

3:6. Picket Shots: A. M. Watson (52nd IL), Lay's Gferry; Charles H. Hults (10th IN Bty), Stones River; W. S. Snow (11th MO), Corinth; Alfred Spence (3rd IA Cav), reminiscence.

5:1-3. McElroy, Part 51.

7:1-2. Henry Romeyn (14th USCT), "Scouting in Tennessee. Recollections of Services There Toward the Close of the War."

7:4. Obit.

March 30

1:5-7, 2:1. Cannon, Part 21. [12/23/63-1/26/64]

2:3. Obit: Henry C. Egbert (12th US).

3:1-4. Capps, Part 3.

3:4. Homer Mead (8th IA Cav), "Croxton's Cavalry." [Duck River]

3:5. A. J. Jacobs (22nd KY), "Early War Days in Kentucky."

3:5-6. Charles P. Wing (IL), "Seeking the Enemy. A Veteran's Graphic Description of Going Into Action."

3:6. M. M. Rice (40th IA), "Under a Flag of Truce." [Little Rock, Winter 1864/65]

5:1-3. McElroy, Part 52.

7:1-2. Romeyn, Part 2.

7:3. R. E. Rankin (7th OH Cav), "Capt. Rankin Speaks Again."

7:3. "On Chickamauga's Field. Meeting of Old Messmates on the Spot Where They Parted 35 Years Before." [WI]

7:4. F. J. Grant (12th WI), "A Hot Skirmish." [Vicksburg]

7:4. Edwin Crockett (65th NY), "The Riddled Tree at Spotsylvania."

7:5-6. Biog: Robert D. Dyrenforth (12th, 13th, 17th IL Cav), George F. Foote (14th MI), John McElroy (16th IL Cav), Frederick F. Bogia (2nd PA Res), S. S. Yoder (128th, 178th OH), John Middleton (Orton's DC Co), W. P. Pierce (11th, 12th KY Cav), William V. Allen (32nd IA).

9:5. Obit.

April 6

1:5-7, 2:1. Cannon, Part 22. [1/27-2/11/64]

2:1. John M. Folett (33rd IL), "Flag of the 33rd Illinois." [7/11/63, Jackson, MS]

2:1. Obit: Daniel W. Flagler.

2:3. Biog: John W. French (7th NY, 8th US).

3:1-3. William H. Lawrence (2nd MA Cav), "Prison-Pen and Swamp."

3:4. Joseph W. Fletcher (1st DC Cav), "1st District of Columbia Cavalry. Sailors Transformed Into Mounted Troops. The Wilson Raid."

3:4-5. S. T. Maxey (6th IL Cav), "On Stone River Field."

3:5. J. D. Lytle (57th IN), "Capturing Two Cannon." [Missionary Ridge]

3:5. Solomon Babb (64th OH), "At Missionary Ridge."

3:6. Picket Shots: George E. Dolton (Bty M, 1st IL), Missionary Ridge.

5:1-3. McElroy, Part 53.

6:1-2. Biog: Adolphus W. Greely (19th MA, 81st USCT).

6:3. Obit.

6:4. Biog: Frederick Robie (paymaster).

April 13

1:5-7, 2:1. Cannon, Part 23. [2/12-18/64] END

3:1-3. Lawrence, Part 2.

3:3. R. D. Sayre (151st PA), "A Day at Gettysburg."

3:3. P. H. Burns, "The 22nd Indiana Battery."

3:4. Henry C. Archibald, "The 1st U.S. Volunteer Infantry."

3:5. William H. Huffman (100th PA), "On the Fighting Line. A Roundhead Who was with Pope's Army at Chantilly."

3:5. Manlius Holbrook (2nd US Ss), "Berdan's Crack Shots."

3:6. Picket Shots: Joseph Schlund (16th IL), Jonesboro.

5:1-3. McElroy, Part 54.

6:4. Biog: Henry Masterman (28th IA).

7:3. Obit.

April 20

1:1-4, 2:4-5. Free S. Bowley (30th USCT), "A Boy Lieutenant in a Black Regiment."

3:1-4. Lawrence, Part 3.

3:5-6. D. T. Stathem (39th OH), "Battle of Corinth."

4:7. Obit: John W. Turner.

5:1-2. James M. Aubery, "An Army Newsboy. A 'Kid's' Reminiscences of the Fiery Front, With the Famous Old Iron Brigade."

5:3-5. Obit.

5:6-7. Thomas Spellman (CSN), "As the Cabin Boy Saw It. The Alabama-Kearsarge Duel." [*Galveston Daily News*]

6:1-2. Biog: W. C. Johnson (89th OH, 42nd USCT).

April 27

1:1-4, 2:5-6. Bowley, Part 2.

3:1-3. Lawrence, Part 4.

3:4-5. George W. Witherspoon (14th MI), "A Dash in the Dark. How Sergt. Charles Clark Spoiled a Rebel Plan for Capturing a Regiment." [Franklin, TN, 11/63]

3:5. A. J. Jacobs (22nd KY), "Holding the Enemy." [Tazewell, 1862]

3:5. J. R Palmer (32nd IL), "Battling at Jackson."

3:5. Wait Scott (2nd VT), "The Riddled Tree." [Spotsylvania]

3:6. Michael Moss (100th PA), "Bringing in Deserters." [Petersburg, 1/19/65]

5:1-3. Aubery, Part 2.

7:4. Obit.

May 4

1:1-4, 2:3. Bowley, Part 3.

3:1-3. Lawrence, Part 5.

3:3. Wesley McCallister (7th IL Cav), "A Military Execution."

3:4-5. W. W. Gardner (100th USCT), "Confronting Hood. The Nashville Battle, And Some Other Exciting Events."

3:5. I. A. Chalaron (Washington Art), "At Missionary Ridge. Confederate Commander Writes of Capture of Guns by Union Troops."

3:5. J. H. Hoback (57th IN), "Capturing a Battery." [Missionary Ridge]

3:6. Picket Shots: Harvey B. Wilder (25th NY Cav), episode at Staunton, VA; S. W. Crane (9th NJ), Roanoke Island; Edward Popplestone (15th IN), Misionary Ridge; William Gray (92nd NY), Salisbury prison.

5:1-2. Aubery, Part 3.

6:1-2. "Grant Monument. Unveiling of Equestrian Statue at Philadelphia."

6:4. Obit.

May 11

1:1-4, 2:5. Bowley, Part 4.

3:1-3. D. Eldredge, "The Third New Hampshire."

3:4. H. G. Reynolds, "A Nursery of Heroes. Famous Camp Yates, And Some of the Things that Happened There."

3:5. Samuel Reeves (53rd IL), "Hot Work in Georgia." [Lay's Ferry]

3:5. B. F. Morland (49th IN), "Cumberland Gap Campaign." [1862]

3:5. J. H. Bell (27th IA), "Took Part in the Fighting." [IN Bty controversy]

3:6. Picket Shot: George W. Sparks (101st OH), incident at Huntysville, AL; Moses C. Berry (33rd MA), Wauhatchie.

3:6-7. H. B. Miller (84th IL), "Immortal Thirteen Hundred."

5:1-2. Aubery, Part 4.

7:4. Obit.

May 18

1:1-4, 2:4-5. Bowley, Part 5.

1:5-7, 2:1-2. August V. Kautz, "The Siege of Petersburg. Two Failures to Capture the 'Cockade City'."

3:1-3. Eldredge, Part 2.

3:4. M. Harmas, "The Campaigns of the 20th Indiana."

3:4. Charles F. Roberts [30th IN], "Had Himself Interviewed. How a Soldier Maneuvered to Get Shoes and Stockings."

3:5. Picket Shots: W. F> Outland (62nd OH), Fort Wagner; L. S. Hillabrandt (44th NY), Malvern Hill.

3:6. J. M. Hawks, "Origin of Memorial Day. Graves of Union Soldiers at Charleston Decorated in May, 1865."

5:4. "In Honor of Collis's Zouaves." [114th PA monument at Chancellorsville]

7:4. Obit.

May 25

1:1-4, 2:5-6. Bowley, Part 6.

1:5-7, 2:1-2. Kautz, Part 2.

3:1-2. Eldredge, Part 3.

3:3-4. John M. Whitehead (15th IN), "Two Terrible Days." [Stones' River]

3:4. Frederick W. Fout (15th IN Bty), "A Woman Soldier."

3:5. George W. Case (22nd NY Cav), "A Band of Rough Riders. How They Bore an Important Dispatch, as Told by a Comrade Now Deceased." [6/64]

3:5-6. George D. Carrington (11th IL), "Long-Remembered Days. Early Service at Camp Hardin with the 11th Illinois."

3:6. Picket Shots: William H. Steward (47th MO), foraging; R obert F. Locke (21st KY), Chattanooga.

5:5-6. W. S. Franklin (49th OH), "Random Notes. Something About Early Service in the 49th Ohio."

6:4. Biog: Joseph W. Kay (10th, 16th NY).

7:4. Obit.

June 1

1:1-4, 2:4-7. Bowley, Part 7.

1:5-7, 2:1-2. August V. Kautz, "The Wilson Raid."

3:1-3. Eldredge, Part 4.

3:3-4. Isaac C. Dennis (14th IL Cav), "Beyond the Picket-Line. Adventures of Two Young Cavalryman in Rebel Territory Hunting for Their Regiment."

3:5-6. B. Ellis (1st WI Cav), "Suffered Heavy Loss." [Lovejoy Station]

3:6. R. E. McBride (190th PA), "Killed at Appomattox."

5:1-4. R. W. McClaughy, "'The Enlisted Man.' An Eloquent Tribute to the Men Whose Muskets Rescued the Nation."

7:4. Obit.

June 8

1:1-4, 2:4-5. Bowley, Part 8.

1:5-7, 2:1. Kautz, Part 2.

2:5. Obit.

3:1-2. Porter D. Learnard (23rd WI), "Battle of Grand Coteau." [Carrion Crow Bayou]

3:3. F. A. Robbins (27th MA), "A Bitter Struggle." [Drewry's Bluff]

3:3-4. A. M. Brinkerhoff (4th IA), "After the Johnnies. Sharp Action Around Jackson in July, 1863."

3:4. J. W. Garner (1st KY Cav), "A Civil War Romance. How Wolford's Cavalry Broke Up a Double Wedding and Carried Off the Grooms."

3:4-5. J. M. Lynn (2nd MO CSA), "The Johnny's Fight. A Well-Dispositioned 2nd Mo. Veteran Tells of Fighting Uncle Sam's Boys in Arkansas." [Ashley Station]

3:5. Jesse B. Ditty (9th PA Cav), "The Fight at Morris Ravine." [Morris' Ford, 7/2/63]

3:6. Picket Shots: B. F. Thomas (14th IA), Fort Donelson; Robert Simpson (74th IL), Missionary RIdge.

June 15

1:1-4, 2:4-5. Bowley, Part 9. [Crater]

1:5-7, 2:1. Kautz, Part 3.

2:3. Obit: John B. Wilson (5th MD).

3:1-2. "Mallet," "Firing on Fort Sumter. Experiences of a Northern Mechanic in Charleston."

3:3-4. Theodore F. Allen (7th OH Cav), "The Old Camp Ground."

3:5. William W. Aspinwall (47th IN), "Charge at Jackson, Miss."

3:6-7. Picket Shots: John Body (65th OH), Stones River; C. B. Cozens, Ringgold, 11/63; John A. Goddard (3rd US), Don Carlos Buell; Jesse E. Jones (19th IN), Wilderness-Spotsylvania.

3:7. W. R. Bunting (38th IL), "A Yankee Prisoner." [Stones' River]

4:4. S. P. Breighley (5th MN), "Some of Mower's Men." [Vicksburg]

4:4. J. E. Miller, "A Claim Regarding Famous Caves." [exploration of Luray Cavern during war by 1st WV]

5:4. Obit.

June 22

1:1-4, 2:4-5. Bowley, Part 10. [Crater]

1:5-7, 2:1-2. William E. Doyle (17th IN), "Recollections of Chattanooga."

3:1-3. Fort Sumter, Part 2.

3:4. William F. Denmure, "The Santee Expedition. A Night Attack on Rebel Vessels in Galveston Harbor in November, 1861."

3:5. J. P. Crayon (4th NJ Bty), "How Butler Captured New York. He Held It For Law and Order During Election Day in November, 1864."

3:6. Henry C. Jack (2nd IL Cav), "On the Move."

3:7. Picket Shots: Paul Grabill (74th OH), capture of Raleigh, NC; James E. Shellenberger (94th OH), Missionary Ridge.

5:5-7. Charles W. Wilson (18th US), "Army Life in the Rockies." [1864/65]

6:1-2. Biog: A. F. Dill (43rd MA, USN).

6:3. Obit.

June 29

1:1-4. Bowley, Part 11. [Crater]

1:4. G. W. Morris (81st IN), "The Story of the 81st Indiana."

1:5-7, 2:1. Doyle, Part 2.

3:1-2. Fort Sumter, Part 3.

3:2. George H. Laut (95th PA), "A Gettysburg Jaunt. A Veteran's Impressions of the Historic Battlefield as Gathered in a Recent Trip."

3:3-4. James Oates (9th IL), "The Hornets' Nest."

3:4-5. E. M. Day (38th OH), "A Day's Adventure. Foraging in Georgia During the Famous March of 1864." [alias Ben Wilson]

3:5. James McNeal (11th MO), "The 11th Mo.'s Part." [Corinth]

3:5. R. H. Gunn (50th IL), "A Military Execution." [Corinth, MS, Summer 1863]

3:6-7. Mrs. A. C. McPherson, "Entertaining an Enemy. How Raider Morgan Borrowed Gen. Hobson's Name and Feasted in Consequence." [7/63]

3:7. Picket Shots: Joshua Dewes (97th OH), Missionary Ridge; Neil Sutherland (33rd MA), Wauhatchie.

5:4-5. George H. Slusser (11th OH Cav), "Lost in the Black Hills." [Fall 1864]

7:4-5. Obit.

July 6

1:1-4, 2:5. Bowley, Part 12. [Crater]

1:5-7, 2:1-2. Doyle, Part 3.

3:1-2. Fort Sumter, Part 4.

3:2. W. M. Lomax (1st AL Cav), "At Monroe's Crossroads."

3:3. L. D. Hord (32nd OH), "Forcing a Hard Campaign. The Battle of July 28, 1864."

3:4. James L. Stratton (112th IL), "The Battle of Nashville."

3:4. D. L. Beckwith (90th NY), "A Surprise." [Newtown, VA, 12/25/64]

3:4-5. Patrick McEnany, "The Wilson Raid."

3:6. William E. Doyle (17th IN), "A Ride with Kautz. A N.C. Johnny Reb Recalls a Meeting with the General in 1864." [Co.G, 7th SC Cav]

3:7. Picket Shots: J. N. Hazzard (13th OH), 9/13/63; Matthew Park (2nd OH Cav), J. C. McCleery (53rd PA), last shot at Appomattox; Henry M. McFarland (78th IL), Jonesboro.

5:3. Obit.

7:4-6. W. R. England, "The 22nd Indiana. Roster of Survivors of a Gallant Command."

July 13

1:1-4, 2:5. Bowley, Part 13.

1:5-7, 2:1. John McElroy, "Gettysburg Thirty-six Years After. The Great Battlefield as It Looks Today—The Dedication of the Monument to Gen. Reynolds."

3:1-4. H. H. Mills (2nd MN), "The Second Minn. Reminiscences of Four Years' Service at the Front."

3:4. C. B. Mitchell (12th KY Cav), "A Brave Little Frenchman. The Example Afforded in the Career of Gabriel Netter, Col., 38th Ky. Cavalry."

3:5. Picket Shots: W. S. Anderson (15th IN), Missionary Ridge

3:6. "Faced Shot and Shell. N.Y.'s 118th Regiment Made a Gallant Record in the Civil War."

3:6. Phil M. Wagner (3rd IL Cav), "A Cavalry Episode. Brush with Texas Rangers that Ended Fortunately for Some of the 3d Ill. Cav." [AR 1862]

3:7. P. H. Burns (22nd IN Bty), "Intercepting Morgan." [1863]

7:4. Obit.

July 20

1:1-4, 2:5-7. Bowley, Part 14.

1:5-7, 2:1. Augustus C. Buell (Bty B, 4th US), "Losses at the Crater."

3:1-3. Mills, Part 2.

3:4. A. A. Tyler (6th MI Cav), "Wrestling with Butternuts. The Pea Ridge Battle as Told by a 6th Mich. Cavalryman—How the Fighting Began."

3:4-5. A. J. Jacobs, "The 22nd Kentucky's Service. Some Dealings with John Morgan that were Interesting If Vexatious."

3:5. Charles D. Chase (1st WV), "The First Gun at Philippi."

3:5-6. George L. Banks (15th IN), "Storming the Ridge." [Missionary Ridge]

3:6. Phil M. Wagner (3rd IL Cav), "A Nervy Non-Com." [5/22/63, Vicksburg]

3:6. E. E. Wilson (29th OH), "Fighting Jackson." [Port Republic]

3:7. Picket Shots: J. B. Carr(100th PA), Petersburg siege; J. U. Roberts (19th OH), 9/13/63; Leroy S. Fallis (8th IN Cav), capture of Ralreigh, NC.

7:4. Obit.

July 27

1:1-4, 2:6-7. Bowley, Part 15.

1:5-7, 2:1-2. "A Union Man in Richmond. Personal Recollections of the Great Rebellion, By a Man on the Inside."

3:1-3. Mills, Part 3.

3:4. John B. Williams (3rd KY Cav), "Captured at Lovejoy's Station."

3:4-5. P. C. Richards (5th IA Cav), "Foiling Wheeler, Forrest and Company." [Fort Donelson, 2/3/63]

3:5-6. James McMahon (41st OH), "Those Captured Cannon." [Missionary Ridge]

3:6. H. G. Reynolds, "Soldiers' Battle Reports. A Few Samples of Them, Grim Humorous, Tell an Interesting Story." [7th IL Cav]

3:6. S. W. Northrup (89th NY), "Crossing in Pontoons." [12/12/63]

3:7. Picket Shots: Frederick L. S. Webster (USS *Cayuga*), Galveston; Moses Bone (74th OH), Stones River.

6:4. Obit.

7:4-6. John C. Patterson, "The 14th New Jersey. Roster of Survivors of a Fighting Regiment."

8:3-4. Jorge Owens, "Liquor in the Army. From the Potomac to Chattanooga in Tunnels and Candlesticks."

August 3

1:1-4, 2:6. Bowley, Part 16.

1:5-7, 2:1-2. Richmond, Part 2. [secession, 1861]

3:1-3. P. Mitchell (16th OH Bty), "The Struggle at Champion's Hill."

3:3. Joseph S. Fleming (24th WI), "At Chickamauga."

3:4-5. W. S. Franklin (49th OH), "Buell's March to Shiloh."

3:5. F. J. Groat (12th WI), "Besieging Vicksburg."

3:6-7. Picket Shots: Frank Fisk (4th IL Cav), zPea Ridge, wounding of Forrest; James T. Skees (9th KY Cav), reminiscence; J. W. Homer (69th OH), Jonesboro.

6:3. Obit.

7:3-7. George F. Streahlin, "Seventh Penna. Cav. Roster of Survivors of the 'Saber Regiment of the Army of the Cumberland'."

August 10

1:1-4, 2:6. Bowley, Part 17.

1:5-7, 2:1-2. Richmond, Part 3. [John M. Botts, Manassas]

2:7. Obit: Rufus R. Dawes (6th WI).

3:1-3. Mitchell, Part 2.

3:4. H. W. Day (AAIG, Fifth Corps), "An Episode of Appomattox. Interesting Details of the Killing of Lieut. Hiram Clark." [185th NY]

3:4-5. Jacob Short (13th IN), "Up the Potomac. Incidents of a Trying Period—Run for Safety." [Green Spring Run]

3:6. J. W. Eggert (13th OH), "At Stone River."

3:6. Picket Shots: G. W. Jordan (33rd IL), Jackson, MS.

3:7. A. Brandley (23rd KY), "A Fair Foe. How a Southern Matron Entertained Two of Nelson's Men."

5:5. "DeGress's Battery. The Rebels Now Disputing Over the Honor of Its Capture." [Savannah News, 42nd GA reunion]

6:1-2. Biog: Thomas R. Shinn (OH).

6:3. Obit: R. C. Rankin (7th OH Cav).

6:4. Obit.

6:5. "Wilder's Brigade Monument." [Chickamauga]

7:1-4. Washington B. Pulis (58th IL), "Solomon Loney's Prediction. The Story of a Soldier Who Died a Prisoner."

7:4-7. Streahlin, Part 2.

7:7. "John Brown's Men. Their Bones Removed from Harper's Ferry to North Elba, N.Y."

August 17

1:1-4, 2:6. Bowley, Part 18.

1:5-7, 2:1-2. Richmond, Part 4.

4:7. Obit: Thomas F. McCoy (107th PA).

4:7. Biog: Gershom H. Swayze (14th MI), William E. Birkheimer (4th IA Cav).

6:1-3. Pulis, Part 2.

7:1-3. Mitchell, Part 3.

7:4-5. Patrick McEneany, "Some Scouting Experiences. With Guerrillas, Gunboats, and 100-Days Men on the James."

7:5-6. Robert Hammond (15th OH), "Charge of a Corps. Willich's Brigade Claims the Honor of Capturing the Lady Breckinridge and Lady Buckner." [Chattanooga]

August 24

1:1-4, 2:6. Bowley, Part 19.

1:5-7, 2:1-2. Richmond, Part 5.

2:6. A. J. Jacobs, "The 22nd Kentucky Under Fire." [Vicksburg]

3:1-3. Augustus C. Buell (Bty B, 4th US), "A Personal Reconnaissance. Quiet, Unostentatious Daring of One of Gen. Warren's Staff Officers." [Major Cope, 3/29/65]

3:4. Picket Shots: J. W. James (88th OH), Camp Chase, 7/3/64; L. C. Garman (158th PA), USS *Hunchback*; U. C. James (40th OH), 1863 skirmish.

3:5. H. Warren Phelps (95th OH), "Soldiering in Earnest. Campaigning in 1864 Against 'Pap' Price and Other Restless Rebel Leaders."

3:5-6. W. I. Watts (12th OH), "A Light-Weight Patriot."

6:5. Obit.

8:1-4. Pulis, Part 3.

8:4. Mrs. Joseph I. Foot (13th WI), "With the Contrabands. The Reminiscences of an Army Chaplain's Wife in Alabama."

August 31

1:1-4, 2:7. Bowley, part 20.

1:5-7, 2:1. Richmond, Part 6.

2:1. Obit.

2:4-6. J. M. Comstock, "The Gettysburg Battle. A Discussion of Its Importance and the Results of a Rebel Victory."

3:1-2. Will A. McTeer (3rd TN Cav), "Close Quarters with Forrest. Cutting Out at Athens and the Affair at Sulphur Trestle." [9/23, 25/64]

3:3. Arthur Dreifus (9th OH), "Their 'Dutch' was Up." [Chickamauga]

3:4. Henry Nordhaus (5th NY), "With the Army of the Potomac." [1864]

3:4-5. James H. Hatheway (43rd OH), "Fierce Fighting at Robinett."

3:6-7. "A Drummer-Boy and His Dog." [Joseph H. Munro, 6th IA]

6:2-3. Biog: Leo Rassieur (36th MO).

7:4-7. "The 24th Michigan." [survivors]

September 7

3:1-4. Frank Bruner (70th USCT), "Red River Campaign."

3:5. George W. Keckler (16th IA), "Some Recollections." [7/22/64, 2/17/65]

3:5. "Middle Fork Bridge." [VA 7/6/61]

3:5. William E. Doyle (17th IN), "Wounding Gen. Forrest."

3:6. Picket Shots: John T. Bell (7th IA), Shiloh; L. D. Hord (32nd OH), Champion's Hill.

4:5. Obit.

6:1-4. Biog: H. L. Worcester (USN), John E. Gilman (12th MA), O. H. Coulter (50th IL), Henry Harden (1st WI Cav).

7:1-4. Richmond, Part 7.

7:4-7. 24th Michigan, Part 2.

8:4-6. Bowley, Part 21.

September 14

3:1-3. T. W. Holman (21st MO), "The Story of Shiloh."

3:3. P. B. Conner (66th OH), "Marching with Sherman."

3:3. John L. Richardson (26th OH), "At Missionary Ridge."

3:4. William Dewalt (101st OH), "On the Jump. Trials of Some Green Troops with False Alarms and Sudden Skirmishes."

3:4-5. James E. Bates (4th MA Cav), "Real and Imagined Danger."

3:6. Picket Shots: W. F. Westfall (10th WV), Beverly, 9/63; Clinton Hull (11th IA), captured 7/22/64.

8:3-6. Richmond, Part 8.

September 21

1:1-4. Richmond, Part 9.

1:5-7. August V. Kautz, "The Cavalry Division of the Army of the James. Its Organization and First Experiences Around Peterburg."

3:1-3. J. W. Boyd, "Military Telegraphing."

3:3. George W. Stover (16th OH), "Going Into Philippi. An Ohio Boy's Story of the Release of Some Union Prisoners and How He Lost a Flag."

3:4. Stephen Tripp (11th PA Cav), "The Wilson Raid."

3:5. A. J. Jacobs (22nd KY), "A 22d Ky. Reminiscence. Stories of Sherman and Osterhaus and a Night on Picket."

3:5-6. A. C. Shafer (92nd OH), "Bragg's Army. His Overwhelming Force at the Battle of Chickamauga."

5:3. "Unveiling of the 123rd Ohio Monument." [Winchester]

7:6. "A Hero and His Hatchet. A Story of a Gallant Veteran's Exploit at Gettysburg." [Captain Stephen F. Brown, 13th VT]

7:6. "Other Survivors of the 7th Pa. Cav."

September 28

1:1-4, 2:6. Kautz, Part 2.

2:6. "The Wilder Monument. Dedication on the Anniversary of the Battle of Chickamauga."

3:1-3. Boyd, Part 2.

3:4-5. J. W. Lacock (93rd IN), "Took the 25th Georgia." [Jackson]

3:5. J. Bullard (27th MA), "Stretcher Corps." [7/63]

3:6. N. Mayrath (13th IL Cav), "Hardtack vs. Hardtack."

6:2. Jesse Coll (8th WI), "Smith's Guerrillas. One of Them Accounts for Their Queer Nickname with a Story."

6:2. "Another Comrade of the 24th Michigan."

6:2. "Another Comrade of the 7th Pa. Cav."

7:4-5. Obit.

8:1-3. Richmond, Part 10.

8:4. Clarence Wilson (2nd Prov PA Hvy Art), "The Crater Fight."

October 5

1:4. Jacob Fink (55th IL), "Shelling the Johnnies." [Shiloh]

1:5-7, 2:1. August V. Kautz, "Cavalry Division. Operations on the North Side of the James River—Winning a Brevet."

3:1-4. W. H. H. Monroe (42nd OH), "Battle in the Bayous." [Chickasaw Bluffs]

3:4. Picket Shots: I. N. Stanford (18th US), Chickamauga; W. G. Miller, New Creek Station, 8/64.

3:5. G. W. Daniel (7th KY), "A Fierce Little Fight." [Wild Cat, KY, 10/21/61]

3:5-6. T. C. Murphy (31st IL), "Entering Vicksburg."

3:6. Abel Comstock (21st OH), "Saving a Battle-Flag. How the 21st Ohio Boys Got Possession of the Banner of the 69th Ohio." [Jonesboro]

5:3. Obit.

7:1-4. William Seeger (Brackett's MN Cav Btn), "Sully's Sioux Campaign."

8:1-3. Richmond, Part 11.

October 12

1:1-4, 2:3. Kautz, Part 2.

2:4-5. W. D. Cook (21st IA), "A Quartermaster's Exploit. Singlehanded, He Captured Three Rebels." [James Hill at Champion's Hill]

3:1-3. Monroe, Part 2.

3:4. F. J. Groat (12th WI), "A Few Recollections. The Fate of a Blackberry Sauce and the Capture of Star Fort." [Harrisonburg, LA, 9/4/63]

3:4-5. C. C. Parke (5th KY Cav), "Locating the Johnnies." [Resaca]

3:5-6. Frank Fisk (4th IL Cav), "Wounding Forrest." [4/8/62]

3:6. H. W. Phelps (95th OH), "Helping Them Out." [Nashville Campaign]

4:7. Obit: Elias Fraunfelter (114th, 120th OH).

5:5. (1st OH Cav), "The Charge at Monterey."

6:2. Obit.

7:1-3. Seeger, Part 2.

8:4-5. J. T. Peet (3rd OH Res), "The Iron Grays. Sturdy Workers in Metal Who Proved Their Grit and Steadfastness in the Field of Strife."

October 19

1:5-7. Henry Romeyn (14th USCT), "Exciting Provost Duty. Stirring Times at Knoxville at the Close of the War."

3:1-2. Monroe, Part 3.

3:4-5. A. E. Stebbins (88th IL), "A Daring Movement." [Chickamauga]

3:5. James Oates (9th IL), "The 9th Illinois's Busy Day." [Shiloh]

7:1-3. Seeger, Part 3.

7:5. Obit.

October 26

1:1-4, 2:4-6. "The Great Copperhead Conspiracy. Gigantic Plot to Establish a Northwestern Confederacy and Recognize Southern Independence."

2:7. John A. Wyeth, "Gen. Forrest."

3:1-2. Monroe, Part 4.

3:3. Free S. Bowley (30th USCT), "Battle of the Crater."

3:3. Picket Shots: A. A. Jones (8th TN), Franklin.

3:4-5. H. B. York (9th OH Bty), "A Memorable March. Occupation of Cumberland Gap in 1862 and the Retreat to the Ohio River."

3:5-6. O. A. Bussard (Bty M, 1st MO), "A Batteryman's Recollections. [Red River]

5:5. Obit.

6:2. Obit: Quincy, IL, Soldiers Home.

7:1-3. Seeger, Part 4.

8:7. E. Z. Hays (32nd OH), "The Taking of a Battery." [Champion's Hill]

November 2

1:1-5, 2:6. Copperhead, Part 2.

3:1-4. Gustav Bischoff (39th NY), "A Private's Story."

3:5. S. E. Chandler (24th NY), "The Iron Brigade. An Interesting Statement About the Two Organizations that Bore the Name."

3:5. W. H. Surles (2nd OH), "More About Scribner's Brigade."

3:5-6. J. J. Purman (140th PA), "The American Golgotha. A Visit to Chancellorsville 36 Years After the Battle."

3:6-7. Robert N. Snodgrass (84th IN), "Steedman's Division." [Chickamauga]

6:2. Biog: Charles O. Ballou (11th RI), H. Crumbliss (1st TN).

6:2. Obit.

7:1-3. Seeger, Part 5.

7:4. "10th Mass. Battery. Roster of Survivors."

7:5. Obit.

November 9

1:5-7, 2:1-3. Copperhead, Part 3.

3:1-3, 7:4-6. W. H. Polhamus (2nd OH Cav), "The Way I Met John Morgan's Men." [7/63]

3:4. John H. Wolfe (25th NY Cav), "Defending the Capital." [7/64]

3:4-5. William C. Claxton (25th MO), "Opening the Fight." [Shiloh]

3:5. H. H. Ashmore (21st IL), "Around Chattanooga."

3:5. Isaac C. Dennis (14th IL Cav), "Reminiscences of Stoneman's Raid."

3:5. George H. Mellish (6th VT), "Foresaw His Death."

3:6. Picket Shots: Wesley McCallister, Tupelo; W. S. Parr (33rd WI), Forrest.

6:4. Obit.

7:1-3. Seeger, Part 6.

November 16

1:1-4. Copperhead, Part 4.

3:1-3. L. F. Becker (104th OH), "Campaigning with the Grand Army." [11/64 onward]

3:4. "A Trio of Anecdotes. War Experiences as Sketched by a Member of the 84th Ohio."

3:4-5. L. A. Boysel, "The Flag of the 69th Ohio." [Jonesboro]

3:5. E. S. Vernon (78th OH), "Charging Up Brush Mountain."

3:5. C. H. Godbold (3rd CA), "California Volunteers. The Bear River Expedition and Some of Its Unpleasant Features." [1/63]

3:6-7. Picket Shots: W. H. H. Wallace (15th IN), Andersonville; Henry Strong (93rd IL), John E. Ingham (93rd IL), Champion's Hill, Vicksburg, Jackson.

6:5. Obit.

7:1-3. Seeger, Part 7.

7:4-6. John P. Logan (1st KY Cav), "Gallant Wolford. His Men Not Always 'Drilled,' But They Knew How to Shoot."

November 23

1:1-5, 7:3-4. Francis F. Brown, "Every-Day Life of Abraham Lincoln."

1:6-7, 2:1-2. W. H. Younce (58th NC), "The Adventures of a Conscript."

3:1-5. Becker, Part 2.

3:5-6. J. R. Palmer (32nd IL), "Perils of Shiloh."

3:7. Obit.

5:5-6. B. H. Tripp (7th WI), "A Shot in Time." [Iron Brigade controversy]

6:1-3. Biog: C. R. Lavalley (18th ME, 1st ME Hvy Art), D. B. Searle (War Dept clerk), Edwin Kirby (160th NY).

6:4. "Return of Rebel Flags."

6:5. Obit.

7:1-2. Seeger, Part 8.

7:5. Patrick Dillon (8th PA Cav), "A Not Forgotten Episode. The Story of Keenan's Charge at Chancellorsville Told in Verse."

November 30

1:1-5, 7:3-5. Brown, Part 2.

1:6-7, 2:1-2. Younce, Part 2.

3:1-3. P. E. Johnson (36th IN), "Random Reminiscences." [Shiloh]

3:3. FTW (5th PA Res), "An Engineering Feat. A Piece of Rapid Bridge Building Which Saved a Union Division." [Fair Oaks, 6/62]

3:4-5. J. W. Fletcher (1st DC Cav), "Rushing Into Prison. Out of the Frying Pan Into the Fire on the Back of a Frisky Mule." [9/15/64]

3:5. John J. Hughes (11th MO Cav), "In Haypress Forts." [Ashly's Station, AR, 8/27/64]

3:5-7. Crawford Griswold (1st NY Mtd Rifles), "A Mounted Rifleman." [Johnson's Farm]

5:5-6. E. A. Stoneburner (114th OH), "The Siege of Blakely."

6:1-3, 5. Biog: William H. Moystin (72nd PA, 12th NJ), Alexander Mattison (25th OH), Maurice M. Kaign (1st PA Cav, 197th PA), Ralph Sheldon (7th NY Cav, 78th NY).

6:4. Obit.

7:1-2. Henry Romeyn (105th IL), "Scouting in Tennessee. Guerrilla, Smuggler, and Horse Hunting—How the Chaplain Got a Mount." [Gallatin, spring 1863]

8:3-5. N. J. Myers (10th KS), "Lively Prison Duty."

December 7

1:1-5, 7:3-5. Brown, Part 3.

1:6-7, 2:1. Younce, Part 3.

3:1-3. Johnson, Part 2.

3:3. John R. Easterday (3rd TN), "Brave Mountaineers." [Captain Vincent Meyers's Company in fall 1863]

3:4. C. W. McKay (154th NY), "Features of Chancellorsville. Wherein Hooker Neglected Opportunities. Jackson's Attack."

3:5. Walter H. Parcels (50th NY Eng), "A Boy Sentinel."

3:5. (84th OH), "Morgan's Capture. How the Citizens of New Lisbon Got Together to Repel the Invaders."

3:5-6. A. J. Jacobs (22nd KY), "Going Back at Chickasaw."

5:5. J. A. Moore (147th PA), "The Unknown Dead on Culp's Hill."

6:5. Obit.

7:1-2. Willard Glazier (2nd NY Cav), "Harris Light Cavalry."

December 14

1:1-4, 7:5. Brown, Part 4.

1:5-7. Younce, Part 4.

3:1-4. P. D. Hall (1st AL Cav), "A Loyal Southron."

3:5. Nathan R. Gardner, "Rhode Island Sons. Reminiscences of Gov. Sprague and Gov. Burnside, Soldiers and Statesmen."

3:5. A. J. Jacobs (22nd KY), "Fierce Fighting at Thompson Hill." [Port Gibson]

6:5. Obit.

7:1-2. Glazier, Part 2.

December 21

1:1-4, 7:5. Brown, Part 5.

1:5-7, 2:1. Free S. Bowley (30th USCT), "Corporal Bob's Christmas. A True Romance of 'Eastern Sho' Folks, White and Colored."

3:1-3. Mrs. NJB, "Life in Richmond."

3:4-5. William H. Ilsley (9th IL), "A Wounded Man at Shiloh."

3:5. W. H. Bricker (3rd PA Cav), "Pouring Forth Destruction. A Fierce Little Scrimmage Which Saved Two Union Guns." [Willis Church, VA, 6/29/62]

3:5-6. R. P. Cormack (89th NY), "Crossing at Fredericksburg."

3:6-7. Picket Shots: Horace Welch (12th OH), Missionary Ridge; W. M. Gifford (89th IN), Red River incident.

5:3. Obit.

6:1-3. Younce, Part 5.

December 28

1:1-4, 7:4-5. Brown, Part 6.

2:5. Obit: W. S. Williams (Bty B, 4th US).

2:6. F. J. Groat (12th WI), "At Baker's Creek." [Champion's Hill]

3:1-4. Younce, Part 6.

3:5. Frank Bruner (39th OH), "War-Time Christmases."

3:5-6. Theodore F. Allen (7th OH Cav), "More About Wolford's Men. Col. Allen Tells How They and the 7th Ohio Cav. Did Some Fighting Together.""

3:6. Thomas P. Conner (32nd OH), "A Rush on a Battery. [Champion's Hill]

4:7. LeRoy Park (82nd OH), "Early Service."

5:4. G. A. Randolph, "Capture of the 16th Illinois Cavalry. Reminiscences of the Fight at Jonesville, Va." [1/3/64]

6:5. Obit.

7:1-2. A. V. Kendrick (33rd IA), "The Camden Expedition."

8:7. James H. Webb (13th TN Cav), "Ann Pitman." [Fort Pillow, Copperhead Conspiracy]

1900

January 4

1:1-5, 2:4-6. Brown, Part 7.

2:3. Biog: Daniel Butterfield.

3:1-4. Younce, Part 7.

3:5. H. H. Hills (2nd MN), "Charging Without Orders." [Chickamauga]

3:5-6. John B. Hembree (24th MO), "Trampin' and Scrappin'. Some Incidents from the Service Under A. J. Smith, of the 24th Mo."

3:6-7. F. J. Groat (12th WI), "A Badger State Boy Tells of Some Things the Regiment Did and Saw in the South."

7:1-5. J. M. Branum, "Letters from the Field. Contemporaneous Accounts of Events in the History of the 98th Ohio." [10/26, 10/31/63]

7:5. Obit.

January 11

1:1-4, 4:7. Brown, Part 8.

2:6. Obit.

3:1-2. Younce, Part 8.

3:3. A. E. Stebbins (88th IL), "Holding 'Em Back. Timely Service of the 88th Ill. at a Critical Moment in the Franklin Battle."

3:3-4. (28th IL), "Another Boy Sentinel."

3:4-5. John McCoack (1st KS), "Flogging in the Army. The Last Occasion Upon Which It was Done in 1861 at Clinton, Mo."

3:5. R. A. Marsh (4th US Art), "Other Cases of Flogging."

3:5. Theodore F. Allen (7th OH Cav), "'Now Will You Be Good.' The Practical Joke Played by a Lieut. on the Capt. of His Company."

3:6. Picket Shots: Daniel Mangan (102nd PA), Fort Stevens.

5:4. Obit: Edwin S. Osborne (8th, 149th PA), Zenas R. Bliss (7th, 10th RI).

7:1-3. Branum, Part 2. [5/5, 5/8/64]

January 18

1:1-4, 7:4. Brown, Part 9.

3:1-3. John D. Martin (25th IN), "Campaigning with the Western Army." [Hatchie River, 10/62]

3:4-5. W. S. Franklin (49th OH), "More About Shiloh."

3:5. Samuel W. Bird (35th IL), "Willich's Brigade at the Ridge." [Missionary Ridge]

3:5-7. G. H. Turner (19th MI), "The Story of a Bugle."

4:7. Biog: W. T. Bennett (1st, 102nd USCT), Gilbert R. Stormont (58th IN).

4:7. Obit: George H. Sharpe (120th NY), Charles A. Hamilton (71st NY).

6:4-5. Obit.

7:1-3. Harmon W. Brown, "Gen. Grant's Spies."

January 25

1:1-4, 7:4-6. Brown, Part 10.

3:1-3. Martin, Part 2. [Atlanta Cmpn]

3:4. Samuel Blattner (7th IL Cav), "An Andersonville Prisoner."

3:5. Richard R. Foster (19th MA), "Crossing at Fredericksburg."

3:5-6. Mordecai Williams (89th NY), "Fredericksburg Recollections."

3:6. E. J. Wentz (84th OH), "Some People of the 84th Ohio."

3:6. R. I. Smith (32nd TN), "A War Mystery." [4/15/62, TN River]

3:7. H. Clay Marlow (17th KY), "A Bit of 17th Ky. Service."

7:1-2. Branum, Part 3. [5/13/64]

7:3. Obit.

February 1

1:1-4, 7:1-4. Brown, Part 11.

1:5-7, 2:1. Branum, Part 4. [5/16-30/64]

3:1-4. Martin, Part 3. [11/64 to end]

3:4. Jacob Fink (55th IL), "More About Shiloh."

3:5-6. Warren W. Irish (10th NY Cav), "Getting Back to the Army. [Wilson Raid, 6/64]

3:6. E. Tillotson (18th IA), "The Camden Expedition."

3:6. Charles W. Ricker (6th MA), "The 6th Mass. What Became of It After Its Baltimore Adventure."

6:3. Obit.

6:5. Biog: E. R. Monfort (6th, 75th OH).

February 8

1:1-4, 7:2-4. Brown, Part 12.

1:5-7, 2:1. Branum, Part 5. [6/1-7/64]

3:1-3. W. F. Jones (42nd OH), "Besieging a Stronghold." [Vicksburg]

3:4-6. Isaac C. Dennis (14th IL Cav), "Hand-to-Hand Encounter." [Sunshine Church]

3:7. J. M. Potts (12th IL Cav), "Flogging in the Army."

6:2. Biog: Delevan Bates (30th USCT).

6:3. Obit.

6:5. Erodocht F. Nella (7th OH Cav), "A Tin Soldier."

7:1. Christopher C. Parke (5th KY Cav), "His Early Service. Picket Duty that was Hazardous, Sometimes Amusing."

7:5. George D. Mosgrove (4th KY Cav CSA), "Old-Time Enemies."

8:1-7. Julius C. J. Langbein (9th NY), "The Dismal Swamp. The Famous Morass in War Time, and Some Experiences in Soldiering There."

February 15

1:1-4, 7:4. Brown, Part 13.

1:5-6, 2:6. Branum, Part 6. [6/8-16/64]

2:5. "Pennsylvania Monuments." [Fairmount Park, Phila]

3:1-3. Jones, Part 2.

3:4. W. L. Kester (79th IL), "Capturing Two Guns." [Missionary Ridge]

3:4-5. Allen Wilkins (49th OH), "Soldiering with a Vengeance." [Chickamauga]

3:5-6. J. R. Lupton (10th KS), "Battle of Prairie Grove."

3:6. C. W. Bennett (13th US), "'Above the Clouds'."

4:7. Picket Shots: D. Nichols (23rd IN Bty), Franklin; Benjamin V. Carye (24th OH), Sgt. Addington, 41st IL, at Shiloh; F. D. Smith (2nd WI Cav), flogging; M. S. Heskin (2nd IN Cav), New Haven, KY.

5:7. Obit.

February 22

1:1-4, 7:1-5. Brown, Part 14.

1:5-7, 2:1-2. Branum, Part 7. [6/21-28/64]

3:1-3. Jones, Part 3.

3:3. I. N. Stanford (18th US), "A Queer Mission." [Lafayette, GA, Spring 1864]

3:3. Rufus R. Lord (25th NY Cav), "Defense of the Capital."

3:4. S. J. Hazelbaker (8th IL), "1st Mississippi Battery. The Scrap for Some Guns at Champion's Hill."

3:4. L. E. Robinson (1st NY Mtd Rifles), "Checking the Enemy. [Darbytown Road, 10/7/64]

3:4-5. Henry C. Williams (32nd OH), "Right Up to the Guns. The Way the 1st Miss. Battery Found Itself Put Out of Action." [Champion's Hill]

3:5-6. D. T. Stathem (39th OH), "Trying to Get Home. The Tribulations of Two Privates in Seeking Our Rear After Muster Out."

3:6. Picket Shots: H. O'Neil (7th MO), John A. Boston (75th IL), flogging; J. Waidner (8th IL), I. L. Shreve (124th IL), Champion's Hill; A. Volkshausen (119th NY), Gettysburg.

4:7. Biog: Earl M. Rogers (6th WI).

5:5. Obit.

5:6-7. James A. Smith (124th IL), "Advised the General to Get Out." [Grant at Vicksburg]

7:5. Taylor Vaughan (35th MS), "A Johnny's View. Gives a Few Points About Blakely as He Saw Them."

March 1

1:1-4, 7:1-5. Brown, Part 15.

1:5-7, 6:4-5. Branum, Part 8. [6/29-7/16/64]

3:1-3. Theodore F. Allen (7th OH Cav), "Dutton Hill."

3:4-5. J. F. Murphey (20th MA), "Crossing at Fredericksburg."

3:5-6. N. P. Banks (Bty M, 1st IL), "Steedman's Division." [Chickamauga]

4:7. Biog: John W. Haley (17th ME), B. M. Hutchins (6th IN), E. A. Koerper (75th PA).

6:5. Obit.

8:1-6. William J. Dewes, "The 'Spooks' Causeway'." [WV Home Guards in Pendleton County]

March 8

1:1-4, 7:1-4. Brown, Part 16.

1:5-7, 2:1. Branum, Part 9. [7/20-24/64]

3:1-4. J. A. Wright (1st MN), "Old Peninsular Days." [Yorktown]

3:4. A. Washburn (5th IN Bty), "Men Behind the Guns."

3:5-7. Picket Shots: S. E. Chandler (24th NY Cav), Crater; B. F. Sweitzer (79th IL), Franklin.

6:4. Obit.

March 15

1:1-4, 7:1-5. Brown, Part 17.

1:5-7, 2:1. Branum, Part 10. [7/28-8/6/64]

3:1-4. Wright, Part 2. [through Fair Oaks]

3:4. J. W. Lacock (93rd IN), "Cold Cheers for Patriots. Hardships Borne Without Complaint by Men Supporting the Old Flag."

3:5. Charles A. Clark, "On an Old Battleground. Petersburg Guide Tells of Conditions in a Once Bloody Section."

3:5-7. Picket Shots: B. Rushton (17th IA), Champion's Hill.

6:5. Obit.

March 22

1:1-4, 7:4-5. Brown, Part 18.

1:5-7. Branum, Part 11. [8/10-25/64]

2:3. A. C. Wallin (3rd WI), "Interesting Casualty Records."

2:3-4. D. L. Glenn (82nd IN), "On the Old Battle-ground. Something About the 82nd Indiana's Doings at Chickamauga."

2:4. G. W. Wilson (13th NY), "Gen. Bayard's Death."

3:1-5. Wright, Part 3.

3:5-7. Picket Shots: J. W. Gee (111th IL), Fort McAllister; J. H. Springer (1st IA Cav), Frank N. Bailey (MA), flogging.

6:3. Frank Evans (3rd IA), "A Brave Colonel." [Col. M. M. Trumbull at Hatchie River]

6:3. Obit.

7:1-2. Patrick McEneany, "Gettysburg. Snapshot Impressions of a Great Battle as Told by the Chief of Orderlies."

7:2. A. J. Jacobs (22nd KY), "Raid on a Beef Transport."

7:3. S. E. Chandler (24th NY Cav), "Picket Incidents."

8:4. T. J. McCune (48th OH), "In a Tight Place. An Unpleasant Adventure with Guerrillas, Which Included a Tragedy."

8:5. Moses A. McCord, "The Charge of the 2nd Iowa at Fort Donelson." [poem]

8:6. Paton D. Dillon (29th IA), "A Chicken Story."

March 29

1:1-4, 7:3-4. Brown, Part 19.

1:5-7, 2:1-2. Branum, Part 12. [8/29-9/10/64]

2:2. Charles Graham (89th NY), "Crossing Under Fire." [Fredericksburg]

3:1-4. Wright, Part 4. [6/30-7/1/62]

3:5. Thomas Addington (84th IN), "The Story of Chickamauga."

3:5-6. R. Guyton (139th PA), "Facing Early." [7/12/64]

3:6-7. "'The Lay of the Land.' An Anecdote of Gen. O. O. Howard—An Incident of a Great Flanking Movement." [Atlanta, 8-9/64] [author either in 7th OH Cav or 9th MI Cav]

5:4-5. J. D. Myers (74th IN), "Battling with Bragg. The Story of the Work Done by the Second Brigade, Third Division, 14th Corps." [Chickamauga]

5:5-7. LeRoy Park (82nd OH), "Racing with Jackson." [1862 Shenandoah Valley]

7:1-2. Theodore F. Allen (7th OH Cav), "Prisoners for Life. Cupid's Bow and Arrow in the Civil War."

7:2. D. T. Stathem (39th OH), "A Song of Battle. Fuller's Brigade and the Way It Fought at Parker's Crossroads."

7:2. TFA, "Coals of Fire." [1/64—Strawberry Plains, TN]

7:4-5. Obit.

8:5. G. H. Dutton (147th NY), "Lincoln as a Guardian."

8:7. "A Lead on a Conscience. A Confederate Veteran Pays for Goods Taken Near Gettysburg."

April 5

1:1-4, 7:3-4. Brown, Part 20.

1:5-7, 2:1-2. Branum, Part 13. [9/29-10/7/64]

3:1-4. J. M. Waterman (1st WI Cav), "The Rosendale Squad."

3:5. H. O'Neil (7th MO), "'Wiping Out' a Battery. Some Fighting Done by the 8th Ill. and 7th Mo. at Champion's Hill."

3:5-7. George Goshorn (149th PA), "Two Days in the Wilderness."

6:3. Biog: Peter P. Laughlin (53rd, 133rd IL).

6:5. Obit.

7:1. Augustus Meier (112th IL), "Jimtown Raid." [NC]

7:1-2. J. N. Jones (8th IN Cav), "Cutting Their Way Out." [McCook's Raid]

7:4. G. W. Healey, "A Brief Chapter About Co. E, 5th Iowa Cavalry."

7:4. S. J. Weiler (2nd PA Cav), "Cavalry at Fort Stevens."

April 12

1:1-4, 7:4-5. Brown, Part 21.

1:5-7, 2:1. Branum, Part 14. [11/2/64]

3:1-4. Waterman, Part 2.

3:5. John P. Logan (1st KY Cav), "Wolford's Brave Boys."

3:5. N. Ferguson (66th IN), "Gathering Him In. Capturing a Rebel Recruiting Officer. The Affair at Richmond, Ky."

3:5-6. I. B. Webster (10th KY), "Battling Above the Clouds."

3:6-7. Lewis Blosser (151st OH), C. O. Welch (2nd MA Cav), "Defending the Capital."

8:5. Frank Evans (3rd IA), "A Negro and Some Bees. How They Caused a Rumpus on Picket Post One Night."

8:6-7. J. P. Budd (20th NY Cav), "A Run for Camp. How a Hardheaded Little Stallion Got Ahead of a Too-Confident Rider."

April 19

1:1-4, 7:4. Brown, Part 22.

1:5-7, 2:1. Branum, Part 15. [11/3-16/64]

3:1-4. Waterman, Part 3.

3:5. W. P. Wolf (175th OH), "In Stirring Moments. Incidents of the Day and Night Before Franklin."

3:5-6. Samuel Bird (35th IL), "Up the Ridge." [Missionary]

3:6. Harrison Lohr (142nd PA), "Preferred the Front to the Hospital."

5:6. Obit.

6:1. Frank Bruner (39th OH), "A Story of Five Generals." [Mower at Jackson, 5/63]

6:1-2. "Capt. Kelley Honored." [Medal of Honor to L. M. Kelley, 36th IL, for Missionary Ridge]

7:1-2. J. R. Hummel (54th PA), "The Record of a Live Regiment."

7:4-5. Will A. McTeer (3rd TN Cav), "Escaping from Forrest. How Union Men Again Reached Our Lines After the Surrender of Athens and Sulphur Trestle."

10:1-2. A. F. Weaver (117th IL), "Busy Days at Soldiering."

10:2. "With Grant at Lookout Mountain." [Congressman Freer (WV) in the April Success]

10:2. John C. Yadow (1st AR), "A Confederate Conscript. Deserted and Later Served Nearly Three Years in the Union Army."

April 26

1:1-4, 7:3-5. Brown, Part 23.

1:5-7, 2:1.. Branum, Part 16. [11/17-29/64]

3:1-4. Waterman, Part 4.

3:4. E. A. Stoneburner (114th OH), "At Blakely."

3:5. William Batterson (7th OH Cav), "Co. G's Repulse. Waiting for Morgan's men, Some of Them Met with the Wonderful Adventure."

3:5. W. W. H. Wax (29th IA), "Repulsing Shelby. [Camden]

3:5-6. J. Fred Loeble (98th PA), "No Doubt of Their Presence." [7/11/64]

3:6. A. J. Gleason (15th OH), "Potatoes a la Commissary."

4:7. Biog: Madison Davis (1st RI Cav, 1st NH Cav).

7:1. E. T. Hebb (1st IN Cav), "A Reconnaissance. A Lively Call with Dahlgren at Falmouth Station."

7:1. S. E. Chandler (24th NY), "Quick Bridge Building. How Details from McDowell's Corps Spanned a River in 1862." [5/8/62]

7:2. Obit.

May 3

1:1-4, 7:3-4. Brown, Part 24.

1:5-7, 2:1. Branum, Part 17. [12/8-15/64]

2:4. H. M. McFarland (78th IL), "A Battle with Wheeler." [3/3/65, Cape Fear River]

3:1-5. Waterman, Part 5.

3:5. William E. Doyle (17th IN), "Crossing the Rappahannock." [from Howson's history of Fredericksburg]

3:6. S. T. Carrico (61st IL), "A Story of Shiloh."

6:4-5. Obit.

7:1. S. M. Pingree, "4th Vermont."

May 10

1:1-4, 7:4. Brown, Part 25.

1:5-7, 2:1. Branum, Part 18. [12/18/64-2/8/65]

3:1-4. Waterman, Part 6.

3:4-5. F. J. Groat (12th WI), "Saw Service with Sherman. Kennesaw Mountain and Atlanta—Saving a General's Tents."

3:5. James E. Porter (PA), "A Moving Experience." [wounded 5/14/64]

3:6. Picket Shots: S. J. Hazelbaker (8th IL), Champion's Hill; A. S. Kinser (5th PA Cav), Lincoln story; F. M. Daugherty (104th IL), J. A. Rogers (13th OH), Missionary Ridge; Thomas Britton (57th NYH), Fredericksburg; George W. Hess (82nd OH), 2nd Manassas.

7:1-2. B. F. Johnston, "Sultana Disaster."

7:2. Lindsay Steele (30th IL), "The Belmont Fight. With a Glimpse at Champion's Hill—Facing the 30th Alabama."

7:2-3. Charles Banks (1st OH), "Between the Lines. How Two Hospital Convalescents Found Their Regiment After Interesting Experiences."

7:4-5. Thomas O'Conner (10th IL Cav), "The Old Pigeon Roost." [Brownsville, AR]

7:5. Obit.

May 17

1:1-4, 6:3-5. Brown, Part 26.

1:5-7, 2:1. Branum, Part 19. [2/9-29/65]

3:1-4. Waterman, Part 7.

3:5. James Kephart (13th US), "Regulars at Champion's Hill."

3:5-6. C. B. Mitchell (12th KY Cav), "A French Major."

5:5-7. Obit.

May 24

1:1-5, 7:3-5. Brown, Part 27.

1:6-7, 2:1. Branum, Part 20. [2/26-3/5/65]

2:5-7. "The Comrade's Offering. A Splendid Statue of Gen. Grant Set Up in the Rotunda of the Capitol."

3:1-5. Waterman, Part 8.

3:5. A. E. Teall (21st NY Bty), "An Accidental Feast."

6:2. "Butterfield's Brigade. Monument to This Famous Organization to be Erected at Marye's Heights."

6:2. Obit: Quincy, IL, Soldiers Home.

6:2-3. Biog: W. L. Curry (1st OH Cav).

7:5. "The Palmetto Regiment's Flag."

May 31

1:1-4, 7:3-5. Brown, Part 28.

1:5-7, 2:1. Branum, Part 21. [Bentonville ORs]

3:1-4. T. W. Williams (175th OH), "Checking a Pursuing Foe." [Franklin]

3:4. A. J. Williams (11th IN), "Some Army Mounts."

3:5. Rufus R. Lord (25th NY Cav), "Comrade Lord Rejoins." [Fort Stevens]

3:5. Thomas P. Connor (32nd OH), "The Champion's Hill Charge."

3:5. George Nester, "Want Their Flag. First Indiana Battery Survivors Looking for Their Captured Standard." [Sabine Crossroads]

3:6. Picket Shots: Lewis T. Stover (63rd IN), Franklin.

4:7. Biog: Lambert Nagaele (1st MN Bty).

5:3-4. "Fredericksburg Battlefield. Laying of Cornerstone of Fifth Corps Monument."

5:4. "Monument to Gen. Mansfield." [Antietam]

6:5. Obit.

June 7

1:1-5, 7:5. Brown, Part 29.

1:6-7, 2:1-2. Branum, Part 22. [Bentonville ORs]

3:1-5. (7th OH Cav), "The Last Raid of Morgan. The Union Victory at Cynthiana, Ky., June 12, 1864."

3:6-7. Picket Shots: E. J. Orr (6th WI Bty), Etowah River crossing; William E. Doyle (17th IN), Selma.

5:6-7. Obit: Nicholas R. Ruckle (11th IN).

6:2. "Battle-Scarred Banner. Flag of the 30th Indiana and the Record of the Regiment."

6:4. "Antietam Monument. President McKinley Greeted by Survivors of Both Armies."

6:5. A. F. Burns, "Battery A, 1st Pa. Light Art. Reunion Announced by Secretary Burns."

6:6. Obit.

7:4. E. L. Hobart (58th USCT), "Assassination of Lincoln. Ill-Fated Steamer Sultana First to Carry the News to Natchez, Miss."

June 14

1:1-5, 7:5. Brown, Part 30.

1:6-7, 2:1. Branum, Part 23. [3/13/65]

3:1-2. "Raid of Morgan," Part 2.

3:3. John R. Palmer (32nd IL), "The Situation at Shiloh."

3:4. F. J. Groat (12th WI), "Crippling the Enemy. A Reminiscence of the Meridian Raid—An Ex-Prisoner's Little Joke."

3:4. Phil M. Wagner (3rd IL Cav), "Three of Them Scared."

3:4. N. O. Robinson (6th WV Cav), "Fighting in the Saddle."

3:4. Hugh J. Creighton, "The Fighting 13th Ohio."

3:5. Z. C. Burdick (116th IL), "Taking Fort McAllister."

3:5. William Querry (23rd MO), "10 to 1. A Three Days' Fight Before Price Could Take Mulligan and His Men." [Lexington, MO]

3:5-6. D. B. Spencer (7th IL Cav), "A Brush in a Lane." [Covington, TN, 3/9/63]

6:5. Obit.

June 21

1:1-5. Brown, Part 31.

1:6-7, 2:1. Branum, Part 24. [3/17-4/6/65]

2:1. Obit: Belle Boyd.

3:1-5. John M. Valleau (109th PA), "Gallant Soldier Sons. Bright Record of the 109th Pa. in Armies East and West."

3:5. Orange Daniels (102nd IL), "The Averysboro Fight."

3:5. M. S. Hartman (53rd IL), "'Me Undt My Chum'. A Little Swedish-American Reminisce. Dot Yankee Thrick."

3:5. J. M. Vaughan (Bty L, 7th US Col Hvy Art), "The Fort Pillow Affair."

3:6. W. A. Hess (161st NY), "Sabine Crossroads."

3:6-7. Thomas A. Burns, "The Gallant 66th Ohio."

6:5-6. Obit.

7:5. D. N. McClintock (168th PA), "A Pa. Regiment."

June 28

1:1-4, 7:5. Brown, Part 32.

1:5-7, 2:1. Eugene Powell (66th OH), "'Rebellion's High Tide.' Dashed Against the Immovable Rocks of Gettysburg. The Splendid Work on Culp's Hill by the Twelfth Corps."

3:1-3. Valleau, Part 2.

3:3. Napoleon B. Williams (23rd IN Bty), "Fighting at Knoxville. A Dashing Poem About Rebel Boldness and Yankee Pluck."

3:4-5. Thomas J. Martin (7th IL), "Back to Our Lines. The Narrative of How a Comrade Missed Andersonville." [captured 5/2/63]

3:5-6. T. Haley (113th OH), "Three Months with Sherman. Steady Soldiering for the 113th Ohio in the Last Period of the War."

3:6. Asbury Welsh (15th OH), "Up the Ridge." [Missionary]

4:3-4. Biog: Timothy McCarthy (3rd US), John C. Lyon (1st IA Cav).

4:5. Obit.

8:7. "Another Antietam Monument." [15th MA]

July 5

1:1-4, 7:4-5. Brown, Part 33.

1:5-7, 2:1-2. Powell, Part 2.

3:1-3. J. W. Lacock (93rd IN), "Hurling Back Hood." [Nashville]

3:3. J. A. McCamon (104th OH), "On the Field at Franklin."

3:4. W. R. Carter (1st TN Cav), "How Brownlow Rode Out." [McCook raid]

3:4-5. George Nester (1st IN Bty), "An Indiana Battery."

3:5-6. Joseph F. Swan (103rd IL), "Doings in Columbia."

3:6. L. H. Bower (179th NY), "Gallant Empire State Command."

3:7. Picket Shots: H. C. Vaughn (24th KY), Buzzard's Roost; W. W. Hill (123rd OH), High Bridge.

6:5. Obit.

July 12

1:1-4, 7:3-5. Brown, Part 34.

3:1-3. Theodore V. Brown (10th US), "Gaines's Mill."

3:3. R. S. Mowry (1st MN), "The Highest Percentage of Loss." [12th MA, 9/17/62]

3:4-5. Jeremiah Lamberson (12th IL Cav), "First Saber Charge. Lt. Col. Davis's Brisk Fight Against a Superior Force in 1862." [9/62, Darkesville, MD]

3:5-6. I. B. Rickey (33rd WI), "Such was War. Recollections of the Meridian Raid."

3:6. J. A. Tivy (7th MI), "Crossing at Fredericksburg."

3:6-7. Picket Shots: William Buchanan, Fort Stevens; Gaddis Bayless (USN), Bell's Mills, TN, 12/64.

6:4. Obit.

7:1-3. J. W. Over (15th PA Cav), "Rough Riding with Palmer."

7:5. "A Military Quintet." [Johns family from Chambersburg, PA]

8:4-7. JWM, "Fall of Richmond. Evacuation of the Capital of the Confederacy as Seen by a Boy."

July 19

1:1-4, 7:5. Brown, Part 35.

3:1-3. Patrick Breen (2nd US), "Recollections of a Regular." [pre-war]

3:3. Bowman Harrison (7th PA Res), "Army Red Tape. How an Escaped Prisoner Got Tied Up in It Trying to Get Home."

3:4. G. A. Shepherd (16th IL Cav), "A Night Rush." [Nashville Campaign, 11/23/64]

3:4-5. J. G. Bridaham, "Held the Johnnies Until the Sixth Corps Arrived and Beat Back Early."

3:5. J. A. McGuire (10th IL), "'Getting a Move On.' A Comrade Who was in a Hurry, But Got Away Last, Tells About It." [Bentonville]

3:5-6. G. L. Camp (92nd OH), "Battle Above the Clouds."

3:6-7. Picket Shots: S. D. Owens (43rd OH), Savannah; George R. Lewis (61st PA), John C. Clevenger (1st NJ Cav), Fort Stevens.

6:5. Obit.

7:1-5. Over, Part 2.

July 26

1:1-4, 7:5. Brown, Part 36.

3:1-3. Breen, Part 2. [7/21/61-Seven Days]

3:3. Allen Buckner (79th IL), "Col. Buckner Wants His Sword." [lost on 5/9/64]

3:4-5. (73rd IN), "Battlefield and Prison Adventures of Capt. I. D. Phelps and Fellow Officers During the War."

3:5-6. A. B. Shaw (9th PA Cav), "Hot Chase on a Hot Day." [Tompkinsville, KY, 7/9/62]

3:6. R. M. Peck, “On the Border. Episodes of the Bitterness Between Men in Kansas and Missouri.”

3:6-7. H. C. Freeland (12th MI), “Alpha of Shiloh. A 12th Michigan Veteran Explains How His Regiment Went In.”

6:2-3. “A Notable Spring.” [Alexandria, VA]

6:3. Biog: J. S. Fairchild (117th NY).

6:5. Obit.

7:1-3. Jennie Chambers, “Saved by Pickets. A Brave Union Girl’s Daring in the Face of the Enemy.” [Harper’s Ferry, 10/61]

7:4. “Monuments at Shiloh. A Circular from the Ohio Commission.”

August 2

1:1-4. Brown, Part 37.

2:6. Biog: Charles F. Humphrey (Bty E, 5th US).

3:1-3. Breen, Part 3. [Second Manassas, Chancellorsville, Gettysburg]

3:4. Thomas M. Dickson (83rd OH), “Sabine Crossroads.”

3:4. (102nd PA), “At Fort Stevens.”

3:4. L. B. Griffith (62nd MO Enr Mil), “True-Blues of the Border.”

3:5. John C. Lyon (1st IA Cav), “Ordered by Custer. That Flogging Episode Not So Terrible as It Seemed.”

3:5. Joseph M. Waldorf (24th OH), “Going for Water.” [Shiloh]

3:5. W. C. Leonard (9th OH Cav), “A Surprise and a Rally.” [Monroe’s Crossroads]

3:6-7. Picket Shots: Jacob Burdene (6th POA Cav), capture of a train, 4/63; G. C. F. Meyer (12th IN), Richmond, KY.

6:6. Obit.

7:4. [15th NY Cav], “A Desperate Reconnaissance. How a Lieut. Baptized His Commission and Showed His Mettle.” [Moorefield, WV, Spr 1864]

August 9

1:1-4. Silas W. Crocker (191st PA), “Dread Days in Dixie.” [captured 8/19/64]

1:5-7, 2:1-2. Brown, Part 38.

3:1-3. Breen, Part 4.

3:3. Charles U. Brooks (18th CT), “Opposing Johnny Reb.” [Shenandoah Valley 1864]

3:4. James L. Ferns (USS *Kanawha*), “Cutting Out a Prize. An Adventure with [Capt. John C.] Febiger Under the Guns of Fort Morgan.” [CSS *Ann*, 6/62]

3:4-5. A. D. Sanders (13th KS), “Fighting at Prairie Grove.”

3:5. J. D. Martin (25th IN), “Taking Fort McAllister.”

3:5. Isaac Clark (45th OH), “Pursuing Morgan.”

3:6. A. F. Jackson (1st ME Cav), “Dismounted Cavalry. Fighting at Fort Stevens on July 11 and 12—Who Saved the Fort?”

3:6. O. M. York (25th WI), “Down the Yazoo. Some Incidents of a Hard March Under Kimball.”

3:6. Daniel Stuckey (129th OH), “At Cumberland Gap.”

6:3. Biog: David E. Breem (14th IN), Joel M. Longenecker (21st IL).

6:6. Obit.

7:1. Horatio G. Gibson, “Stories of the Regiments. 2nd Ohio Heavy Artillery.”

7:1-2. W. N. Pickerill, “The Prisoner and His Captive. Civil War Romance of a 3rd Indiana Cavalryman.”

August 16

1:1-4, 7:6. Crocker, Part 2.

1:5-7, 2:1-2. Brown, Part 39.

2:7. Biog: Peter D. Smith (14th MA—1st MA Hvy Art).

3:1-3. Breen, Part 5.

3:3. Lawrence Wilson (7th OH), "Modern Gettysburg Campaign. A Breezy Description of a Trip from Washington to the Battlefield."

3:4. Henry C. Smith (3rd AR Cav), "Tribulations of a Conscript."

3:4. S. M. Stafford, "Green Men at Fort." [Fort Reno, 7/64—father was Thomas Stafford, 7th NY Hvy Art]

3:5. J. H. Stevenson (100th PA), "One that was of High Rank. How the 'Roundheads' Attended a Military Funeral at Beaufort, S.C."

3:5. L. D. Barker, "Bill Lewis's Battery. The Confederate Flag Brought Down by the Joint of a Stovepipe." [*Omaha World-Herald*, Missouri River]

3:6. Picket Shots: Philip Kelly (7th KY), Vicksburg; J. M. Barnes (23rd KY), Shiloh; L. B. Marsh (41st IL), Fayetteville, NC.

6:5. Biog: D. E. Proctor (13th NH, 30th USCT).

6:6. Obit.

7:1-2. John H. Austin (20th IL), "Scouting at Dead of a Night." [Corinth, MS, area after city occupied by USA]

7:2. George M. Prior (40th IL), "Going After Chalmers. Davis's Mills and a Raid by Railway."

7:2. W. H. H. Shreckengaust (43rd OH), "At the Ogeeche Canal." [Savannah]

7:3. A. Dillon (59th IN), "Through Moon Lake. A Trying Expedition from Memphis to Helena and Elsewhere."

7:3. Joseph R. Hummel (54th PA), "The High Bridge Fight."

7:3-4. J. V. Pownall (29th IN), "Buell and Foragers. How Rebel Property was Protected Early in the War."

7:4-5. John J. Gray (Bty B, MD), "An Artillerist's Yarn. What Battery B, 1st Md. Light Art., did from Gaines's Mill to the Landing."

August 23

1:1-4, 7:5-6. Crocker, Part 3. [Salisbury]

1:5-7, 2:1. Ira M. Mallory (17th IL Cav), "Missouri Bush & Prairie."

3:1-4. Valleau, Part 3.

3:4. J. W. Lister, "The Queen of the West."

3:5-7. Picket Shots: W. L. Kester (79th IL), Stones River; L. W. Armstrong (10th IL), 12/63; H. C. Barker (8th IN Cav), mule story.

3:6-7. M. V. Traugh, "Visit to Andersonville."

5:1-2. Brown, Part 40.

6:3. Biog: Arnold Brandley (23rd KY).

6:6. Obit.

7:1-2. Jerome B. Quinn, "Rough-Riding Infantry. How the 123rd Ill. Helped Whip Morgan and to Hold Hoover's Gap." [Vaught's Hill, 3/20/63]

7:2. Thomas Clego (Coswell's IN Bty), "Some Good Service."

7:3. A. G. Jacobs (6th OH Cav), "Getting There in Time." [Fort Stevens]

7:3-4. J. A. Irvine (4th US Cav), "On Wilson's Raid."

7:4. John M. Hart (7th KY Cav), "One of Forrest's Brave Dashes. How 500 of His Men Descended on a Small Scouting Party."

7:4. John Shissler (3rd MD), "A Wartime Visit." [Harper's Ferry, 5/62]

7:4. S. E. Chandler (24th NY Cav), "Letters from the Field."

August 30

1:5-7, 2:1. Crocker, Part 4.

3:1-3. Valleau, Part 4.

3:4-5. A. F. Perkins (1st US Cav), "Cavalry Rushes. Fighting Days on the Peninsula with Sheridan, Gregg, Merritt and Custer." [1864]

3:5. J. H. Watson (24th OH), "No Cowardice in His Regiment." [Shiloh]

3:6. J. D. Hendershot (62nd OH), "A March Out of Ranks. A Well-Remembered Night with Friends in the Rebel Country."

3:7. E. J. Essex (28th, 140th IL), "Getting Out of Rebeldom." [leaving AR in 1861]

4:5. I. B. Webster (10th KY), "Steedman at Chickamauga."

4:5. Robert Bayles (16th KS Cav), "As to Col. Jennison."

5:1-3. George D. Carrington (11th IL), "A Drummer Boy at Donelson."

6:2. Biog: John R. McFie (30th IL).

6:4. Obit.

6:5-7. Thomas H. Goodwin (3rd IA Cav), "Fighting Forrest." [Brice's Crossroads]

7:1-4. Mallory, Part 2.

8:1-6. William J. Dewes, "A Spurious Clerk. Desperate Game of a Confederate Spy and Midnight Capture." [New Creek, WV, a Mr. Meerton]

September 6

1:5-7, 2:5. Crocker, Part 5.

3:1-3. Valleau, Part 5.

3:3. Frank Bruner (39th OH), "A Fruitless Search at Vicksburg. How a Stubborn Guard Prevented the Finding of a Dead Comrade."

3:4. A. D. Cutler (1st Brig, 1st Div, 5th Corps), "Defending Porter and the Fifth."

3:4-5. J. N. Jones (8th IN Cav), "Zagonyi's Charge."

3:5. George W. Craig, "One of Fremont's Body-Guard. He Tells Some of His Recollections of Zagonyi's Charge."

3:5. W. S. Parr (33rd WI), "About A. J. Smith's Command."

3:6. T. W. Reneau (5th KY Cav), "Montrose Crossroads." [Monroe's]

3:6-7. John H. Williams (44th MO), "They were All Patriots. A Defense of the Enrolled Mo. Militia of Early War Days."

4:5-7. M. Jay, "'Papa.' Unexpected Heroism Developed in Face of the Enemy." [OH, mid-1862]

8:1-5. Mallory, Part 3.

September 13

1:1-4, 7:5-6. Crocker, Part 6.

1:5-7, 2:1. Mallory, Part 4.

2:4. "Shiloh National Park. Splendid Progress Being Made in Making the Battlefield–Monuments Erected and Contemplated."

3:1-3. George D. Carrington (11th IL), "Against the Tide at Shiloh."

3:3. W. W. Stockton (11th MO Cav), "Interesting Incidents. Some Happenings of a Raid to Break Up Shelby's Operations." [Summer 1864]

3:4. S. W. Richardson (68th OH), "Some Meditations."

3:4. T. W. Hibbs (12th WV), "The Piedmont Fight."

3:4. E. N. Benson (44th OH), "At Franklin."

3:5-6. "Pistol and Saber. Stoneman Raid and the Cavalry Fight at Aldie." [from letters of Benjamin P. Knowles, 1st ME Cav, of 5/12/63 & 7/26/63]

3:6-7. Picket Shots: Elihu Willey (39th KY), 6/64 Morgan-Burbridge; John Body (65th OH), Stones River; Stephen Johnson (44th IL), Franklin.

5:7. Obit.

8:1-5. William J. Dewes, "Old Virginia Days." [Norfolk area]

September 20

1:1-4, 7:3-5. Crocker, Part 7.

1:5-7, 2:1-2. C. D. Westbrook, "On the Firing Line. The 120th N.Y.'s Firm Stand on the Second Day at Gettysburg."

3:1-3. John Rupp (29th OH), "With a Fighting Regiment."

3:3. John T. Standiford (46th IL), "Around Vicksburg." [Pearl River, 7/64]

3:4. L. B. March (41st IL), "A Color-Bearer's Story. Carrying a Field Flag at the Battle of Jackson." [7/63]

3:4-5. M. B. Aldrich (6th VRC), "Defense of the Capital."

3:5. H. W. Stubblefield (16th KS), "About Jennison and Others."

3:6. F. J. Groat (12th WI), "An Incident of Atlanta."

3:6-7. Fred Smith (Bty I, 1st NY), "It was Wiedrick's Battery." [Gettysburg]

6:5. Obit.

8:1-3. Dewes, Part 2.

September 27

1:5-7, 2:1. Hiram T. Peck (10th CT), "The Fall of Richmond."

2:4. D. H. Mangan (102nd PA), A. C. Fletcher (1st VT Hvy Art), "At Fort Stevens."

3:1-3. Rupp, Part 2.

3:4. James M. Jacks (9th MO Cav), "Beating Bushwhackers." [Fayette, MO, ca 9/23/64]

3:4-5. William H. Bolson (16th WI), "Opening the Battle." [Shiloh]

3:5. J. C. Shatton (9th OH Cav), "A Bit of Experience." [8/64]

3:5. H. J. Sloan (52nd IL), "An Act of Daring. Stealing the Rebel Colors Off Their Works at Lay's Ferry."

3:6-7. Picket Shots: W. C. Chatfield (2nd KS Cav), Colonel Jennison; Henry Oliver (13th US), reminiscence.

4:2-3. Obit: John A. McClernand.

5:4. William Fergusson (51st MO Enr Mil), "Injustice to Some Missouri Comrades."

6:5. (14th IL Cav), "Shot by Gen. Forrest." [11/23/64]

6:5-6. Obit.

7:1-4. M. B. Loop, "Campaigning with the Buckeyes. Ten Thousand Miles with the 68th Ohio."

7:4. Charles Porter (11th VT), "The Fort Stevens Fight."

8:1-4. Dewes, Part 3. [Suffolk operations]

8:6. Isaac A. Hawk (102nd PA), "Fort Stevens. Mrs. Lincoln was Present During the Fighting of July 11."

8:6-7. J. M. Valleau (109th PA), "The Doctor's Medicine Chest."

October 4

1:5-7, 2:1-2. Peck, Part 2.

3:1-4. Jerome B. Quinn (123rd IL), "Wilder's Lightning Brigade."

3:4. A. B. Shaw (9th PA Cav), "Kipatrick's Version." [Monroe's Crossroads]

3:4. William Querry (23rd MO), "Death of Bill Anderson."

3:5. Isaac Ax, "Defending the 104th Ohio." [Franklin]

3:5-6. Oscar Evans (7th KS Cav), "Col. Jennison Again."

3:6. Picket Shots: John W. Blume (66th IN), Lay's Ferry.

5:5. Obit.

7:1-3. Loop, Part 2.

8:1-3. Dewes, Part 4.

October 11

2:6-7. Obit.

3:1-3. Quinn, Part 2.

3:3. I. H. Eastburn (76th IL), "Out of Vicksburg." [Pearl River Expedition, 7/64]

3:4. Robert Blackburn (89th IN), "Marching and Fighting. Not Much Rest for the Lively Soldiers of A. J. Smith's Command."

3:4-5. J. F. Growe (93rd IL), "Holding the Fort." [Allatoona]

3:5. Samuel Gamble (25th MO), "How It All Happened." [Shiloh]

6:1-5. Dewes, Part 5.

7:1-2. Loop, Part 3.

October 18

1:5-6, 2:5. Henry A. Castle (73rd IL), "Sheridan with the Army of the Cumberland." [Perryville]

3:1-3. Quinn, Part 3.

3:3. E. J. Kilmer (14th US), "Another Regular Speaks." [Second Manassas]

3:4-5. T. H. Goodwin (3rd IA Cav), "When Forrest was Whipped." [Tupelo]

3:5. Thomas M. Dickson (83rd OH), "Yazoo River and Fort Hindman."

3:5-6. Austin D. Springer (7th IN), "Sergeant Fisk Got It. The 29th Ohio's Flag and How It was Recaptured—An Escape by Night." [Winchester]

3:6. I. P. Adams (23rd KY), "A Texas Voice. Personal Experience of More Value Than Attempts to Describe Battles."

3:6. R. M. Peck (1st US Cav), "'Acknowledges the Corn.' On One Point, But Says Other Statements Cannot Be Refuted." [regarding 15th KS Cav]

3:6. Z. T. Walker (15th IL Cav), "Where is the Flag?"

6:5. Obit.

7:1-4. Loop, Part 4.

October 25

2:7. Obit: Luther Bradford (16th ME).

3:1-3. Quinn, Part 4.

3:3. E. A. Proctor (2nd MO Cav), "Killing of Bill Anderson."

3:4-6. Picket Shots: Jonas Shackley (5th MA Bty), Gettysburg; L. B. March (53rd IL), regimental service; John H. Standiford (46th IL), 3/65; Mills W. Buck (50th PA), Petersburg, 4/2/65; John Trunk (2nd OH Hvy Art), reminiscence; W. A. Helt (140th PA), Gettysburg Campaign; L. S. Brun (29th OH), Savannah.

3:6. T. H. B. Baker (5th IN Cav), "A Plucky Chaplain." [James B. Hamilton, 31st IN]

3:6-7. J. A. Hodges (Bty A, 4th US), "A Bandsman's Experience."

5:5. Obit.

5:6. George C. Wilson (58th IL), "A Reminiscence of Shiloh."

7:3. Loop, Part 5. [11/62-1/63]

8:1-5. Castle, Part 2. [Stones River, Chickamauga]

November 1

3:1-5. Loop, Part 6. [Vicksburg]

3:5. Leroy S. Fallis (39th IN), "Chickamauga."

3:6-7. S. T. Carrier (61st IL), "Holding on at Shiloh."

4:7. Obit: Charles M. Rockefeller (7th, 8th NY SM, 178th NY).

6:4-5. George E. Smith, "The Iron Brigade. Addresses of Members Wanted by Secretary of Survivors' Association."

7:1-3. Castle, Part 3. [Chattanooga]

7:5. James Commons, "Led Him Out of Danger. How a 1st R.I. Cavalryman Assisted the President on the Night of July 12, 1864."

7:6-7. Obit.

November 8

1:1-4, 7:4-6. Allan Pinketon, "The Spy of the Rebellion."

2:3. Obit: D. M. Frost (MO brig gen), John G. Davis (81st IN), A. A. Jones (65th IL).

3:1-3. Loop, Part 7. [Vicksburg Campaign]

3:3. FJF (52nd PA), "One on the Colonel. How He was Convicted, by Overwhelming Circumstantial Evidence, of Foraging."

3:4. James McKay, "Prisoners at Fort Hatteras. Reminiscences of the Assistant Provost-Marshal."

3:4. Chesley Dolsberry (22nd IN), "Jeff C. Davis's Old Regiment."

3:5. Isaac C. Dennis (14th IL Cav), "Recollections of the Rebellion. Slim Pickings in East Tennessee in the Winter of '63."

3:6. Picket Shots: C. F. Laflin (5th VT), Fort Stevens.

4:7. Obit: John G. Brown (175th NY).

6:5-6. Obit.

8:1-5. J. M. Branum (98th OH), "Letters from the Field." [8/62]

November 15

1:1-4, 5:5. Pinkerton, Part 2.

2:6-7. Obit.

3:1-5. Loop, Part 8. [Vicksburg siege]

3:5. Patrick Cohlin (57th OH), "A 'Kid' Soldier."

3:5-6. Alfred Chill (7th KS Cav), "Col. Jennison's Regiments."

3:6. E. F. Tucker, "A Sketch of the 13th Kentucky."

3:6-7. C. R. Warfield, "Men and Doings of the 121st Ohio."

4:7. Obit.

8:1-7. Branum, Part 2. [9/62]

November 22

1:1-4, 2:3-5. Pinkerton, Part 3.

2:1. Obit: Andrew Filer (12th NY).

2:2. Obit.

3:1-3. Loop, Part 9. [Vicksburg-Jackson]

3:4. W. W. Booton (7th IL Cav), "In Front of a Battery." [Nashville]

3:4-5. George P. Wood (29th WI), "More About A. J. Smith."

3:5. J. R. Tisdale (29th MO), "Makes a Few Corrections. A Comrade Tells Some Things About Fort Hindman and Chickasaw Bayou."

3:5-6. John Watkins, "With the 18th Missouri."

3:6-7. H. J. Sloan (52nd IL), "At Lay's Ferry."

3:7. J. B. McGahan (32nd MO Enr Mil), "The Missouri Militia."

8:1-5. Branum, Part 3. [Perryville]

November 29

1:1-4, 7:5. Pinkerton, Part 4.

3:1-3. Loop, Part 10. [to 1/64]

3:3. J. W. Blundon (72nd OH), "No Surprise to Them." [Shiloh]

3:4. F. A. Rogers (1st WI Cav), "A Wisconsin Raider. With Wilson from Chick. Landing to Montgomery."

3:4-5. J. V. Pownall (29th OH), "On the Move."

3:5. David Corsair (52nd IL), "Men of Mettle."

4:7. Obit: David Shearer (3rd MD PHB).

5:6-7. Obit.

8:1-6. Branum, Part 4. [10/16/62-1/9/63]

December 6

1:1-4, 5:4-5. Pinkerton, Part 5.

1:5-6, 2:3-4. Henry A. Castle (73rd IL), "Supreme Soldiership. The Great Charge of Opdycke's Brigade at Franklin—Victory Snatched from the Jaws of Defeat."

3:1-4. John Pope, "Meade at Gettysburg."

3:5. L. J. Groom (2nd NY Vet Cav), "A Yankee Soldier at Law."

3:6-7. John D. Vautier (88th PA), "Tower-Hartsuff-Baxter Brigade."

4:3. Obit: James D. Brady (63rd NY), William F. Stewart (20th, 213th PA).

5:5. Obit.

7:5. I. B. Webster (10th KY), "Remembers It All. Comrade Webster Adds Some of His Own Experiences to 'Battling Bragg'." [Chickamauga]

8:1-4. Branum, Part 5. [1/23-2/19/63]

December 13

1:1-4, 7:5-6. Pinkerton, Part 6.

1:5-6, 5:4-5. John Pope, "Meade Under Grant."

3:1-3. Branum, Part 6. [2/20-7/10/63]

3:4-6. Loop, Part 11. [2-3/64]

3:6-7. L. W. Bissell (8th VT), "The Colonel's Bon Mot. His Views as Expressed in the Case of a Prisoner." [Col. Stephen Thomas]

4:4-7. Obit.

5:3. S. F. Shaw (10th WV), "A Rebel Raid. Averill, McCausland, and New Creek, as Viewed by a Chief Engineer."

6:5. Obit.

December 20

1:1-4, 5:5. Pinkerton, Part 7.

1:5-7, 2:5. Green B. Raum, "The Battle of Corinth."

3:1-3. Branum, Part 7. [8/1-9/11/63]

3:3. A. L. Spencer (15th IL), "Claims Buell was Not Needed." [Shiloh]

3:4-5. M. Reed (14th US), "Still Another Regular." [Second Manassas]

3:6-7. Picket Shots: B. Gum (65th IN), reminiscences; James A. Herrick (36th IL), Franklin; M. V. B. Davis (90th PA), Antietam.

4:2. Obit: John G. Parke.

4:3. Obit: A. C. Reinoehl (76th PA).

5:3. Biog: John Ford (141st PA).

5:5. Obit.

6:1-2. Harry M. Kieffer (150th PA), "Tale of a Turkey. How an Impertinent Drummer Boy Escaped Christmas in the Guard House."

December 27

1:1-4. Pinkerton, Part 8.

1:5-7, 2:6. Raum, Part 2.

2:5. Thomas Downs (2nd MN), "Wants Information. Comrade Downs Wants Comrade Castle to Clear Up Some Points About Sheridan."

3:1-3. Branum, Part 8. [9/4-23/63]

3:4-5. BLT, "With the Wagon Train. Reminiscences of the Chattanooga Campaign."

3:5. William M. Becktell (84th IN), "Written on the Field." [Tunnel Hill, 5/64]

4:7. Leroy S. Fallis (8th IN Cav), "Kilpatrick Surprised." [Monroe's Crossroads]

4:7. Lafayette M. Foster (123rd OH), "The Fight at High Bridge."

4:7. Obit: William Starling (3rd KY Cav, 9th KY).

5:3. R. A. Marsh (4th US Art), "Rebel Prisons. Distortions of Facts in Southern Histories."

6:5. Obit.

1901

January 3

1:1-4, 6:5. Pinkerton, Part 9.

3:1-3. Branum, Part 9. [9/27-10/25/63]

3:3. C. B. Cope (77th PA), "The Fighting Line." [Stones River]

3:4-5. Benjamin F. McMillan (92nd IL), "Taking Chattanooga."

3:5. A. A. Jones (65th IL), "One of the Fighting Kind."

3:5-6. Daniel Webster (1st WI Bty), "That Vicksburg Explosion." [USS *City of Madison*]

3:6. James Allen (16th NY), "The 14th U.S. at Gaines's Mills."

4:4. Biog: David Redfield (14th KS Cav), Henry W. Blair (15th NH), Amos J. Cummings (26th NJ).

4:7. Biog: David A. McKnight (9th PA Res).

6:3-4. Picket Shots: Allen Atkinson (9th IA Cav), 7/4/64 celebration at Devall's Bluff, AR.

6:4. Obit.

8:1-2. Frank H. Taylor, "Elmira Prison."

January 10

1:1-4, 5:4-5. Pinkerton, Part 10.

2:6. Fred G. Walters (7th IA), "At Lay's Ferry."

2:7. John Body (65th OH), "An Ohio Officer's Experience."

3:1-3. Branum, Part 10. [10/26-11/22/63]

3:4. Henry A. Castle (73rd IL), "Sheridan at Chickamauga."

3:4-5. Crawford Griswold (1st NY Mtd Rifles), "[John] Dolan's Doings."

3:5. Charles Banks (1st OH), "Fighting a Watery Enemy. It Would have Conquered Comrade Banks But for prompt Action by Comrades."

3:5-6. J. R. Palmer (32nd IL), "Losses at Shiloh."

3:6. Add H. Sanders, "Gen. Sanders's Sword. Surrendered at Atlanta When the 16th Iowa was Overwhelmed by Numbers, He Now Seeks to Recover It."

3:6-7. W. F. Hodge (86th IL), "Knows What 'Slim Pickings' Were." [Madisonville, East TN]

4:7. Obit: Richard N. Batchelder (1st NH, QM]

4:7. Biog: Victor Vifquin (97th IL).

6:5. Obit.

January 17

1:1-4, 5:5-6. Pinkerton, Part 11.

1:5-7, 2:5-6. Green B. Raum, "Gen. Hazen at Chattanooga."

2:3. R. H. Alderson, "The 23rd Missouri at Shiloh."

3:1-3. Branum, Part 11. [11/24/63]

3:3. G. W. Cramer (12th PA Cav), "A Few Recollections."

3:3. E. W. Dace (115th IL), "An Incident of Chickamauga."

3:4-5. J. G. Sonderman, "The 1st Minnesota's Daring." [Gettysburg, excerpting from Lochren]

3:5. S. A. McNeil (31st OH), "Not a Useless Appendage. Comrade McNeil Writes About the Value of Buell's Army at Shiloh."

3:5-6. John W. Dilley (84th IL), "On Franklin's Field."

3:6-7. Daniel W. Brown (2nd IA), "An Iowan at Donelson."

6:5. Obit.

January 24

1:1-4, 5:4-5. Pinkerton, Part 12.

1:5-7, 2:4-6. T. W. Holman (21st MO), "The Battle of Shiloh."

2:3. S. R. Averill (13th PA Cav), "He was Not the President." [Fort Stevens]

3:1-3. Branum, Part 12. [11/27-12/2/63]

3:3-4. Ansen L. Harman (10th OH Cav), "Woods Full of Johnnies." [Monroe Crossroads]

3:4. L. L. Langworthy (12th IL), "The Battle of Corinth."

3:4-5. M. J. Clarke (11th MS), "From an Ex-Johnny. Wants to Hear from a Union Lieut. and a Srgt. Whom He Captured." [Atlanta]

3:5. Wesley McCallister (7th IL Cav), "Franklin and Nashville., and a Visit to Memphis, the Scene of Former Experiences."

3:5. T. J. LeVake (10th IA), "Blowing Up the [City of] Madison."

5:6-7. Obit: Frank W. Paige (5th MA).

6:5. Obit.

7:5. F. E. Saunders (16th ME), "In Salisbury Prison."

January 31

1:1-4. Pinkerton, Part 13.

1:5-7, 2:4-6. Holman, Part 2.

3:1-3. Branum, Part 13. [12/3-9/63]

3:4-7. J. W. Lacock (93rd IN), "Under Rebel Guns. Incidents of Close Quarters at the Siege of Vicksburg."

6:4-5. Pickety Shots: L. D. Immell, J. C. Ralton (43rd OH), Corinth; J. R. Yoes (1st ARK Cav), reaching Union lines in 1862; Wesley A. Howard (72nd OH) Shiloh.

6:5-6. Obit.

8:1-6. Charles Franz (10th WI), "Paint Rock River Bridge. Gallant Defense of Gen. Mitchel's Line of Communications Along Memphis & Charleston Railroad by a Wisconsin Squad." [4/18/62]

February 7

1:1-4. Pinkerton, Part 14.

1:5-7, 2:4-5. Holman, Part 3.

3:1-4. Branum, Part 14. [12/11/63-4/27/64]

3:5-6. John K. Shellenberger (64th OH), "Sheridan at Chickamauga."

4:7. Biog: James M. Munn (7th IL).

6:4. Obit.

7:5. D. S. Brown (7th OH Cav), "Capture of Maysville." [Ohio]

8:1-5. Willard Glazier (2nd NY Cav), "Maj.-Gen. Kilpatrick."

February 14

1:3-4, 2:1-5. Pinkerton, Part 15.

2:6-7. Obit.

3:1-4. George D. Mosgrove (4th KY Cav, CSA), "Bugle Notes from Dixie. Personal Recollections of a Confederate Cavalryman." [through spring 1863]

3:5. S. E. Chandler (24th NY Cav), "This is the Way to Do It." [how to write letters]

3:5-7. E. J. Kilmer (14th US), "On the Bull Run Field." [Second Manassas]

4:7. Biog: Charles A. Orr (187th NY).

7:4-5. Henry Castle (73rd IL), "War's Brighter Side. An Unsuccessful Confidence Game Played by One of John Morgan's Spies." [10/62]

8:5. S. A. Parker (40th NY), "Good Work Under Fire. Who Saved the Flag of the 40th N.Y. at Spotsylvania, May 12, 1864?"

February 21

1:5-6, 2:4-6. Pinkerton, Part 16.

2:3. H. Denney (7th OH Cav), "Under the Mountains. Strawberry Plains and Other Events of Campaigning." [6/63]

3:1-3. Mosgrove, Part 2. [Blue Springs]

3:4. John McCormick (5th US Cav), "On the Peninsula."

3:4. George Burdick (13th NY), "Took Over 300." [Hanover Court House]

3:5. J. Frederick (80th OH), "That Dread Day at Franklin."

3:5-6. Theodore Facer (14th US), "Did Not Run Away." [Gaines's Mill]

3:6-7. Richard Scanland (70th IN), "A Deal in Hams."

4:7. Biog: William H. Boyle (5th NY Hvy Art), Ole P. H. Balling (145th NY), A. W. Smith (19th US), Gideon Wheeler (32nd IA).

5:4-5. John D. Vautier (88th PA), "That Much-Named Brigade." [Tower-Hartsuff]

6:5-6. Obit.

February 28

1:5-7, 2:3-5. Pinkerton, Part 17.

3:1-3. Mosgrove, Part 3. [Henderson's Mill, Pugh's Mill, Rheatown]

3:4-5. S. N. Munger (72nd IL), "The 72nd Ill. at Franklin."

3:5. William Snider (14th IL Cav), "Made It Hot for the Soldier."

3:5. Jacob Fink (55th IL), "Some 55th Illinois Losses."

3:6-7. Scott Lovelace (10th US Cav), "A Slave's Story."

6:4-5. W. L. Blackman (10th CT), "Visit to Historic Spots. A Conn. Vet. Finds that Old Landmarks in the South Have Disappeared." [Richmond, Newbern, Kinston]

6:6. Obit.

March 7

3:1-3. Mosgrove, Part 4. [Big Creek]

3:4. H. H. Hills (2nd MN), "Sheridan at Chickamauga."

3:4-5. Henry Milburn (48th IN), "A Round of Reminiscence. Boy Lieut. Writes of Corinth and Discusses Mooted Points."

3:5-6. W. L. Welch (23rd MA), "A Queer Wedding Party. W. L. Welch Tells of a Humorous Experience at Hatteras Inlet."

6:3. Obit.

7:1-4. Pinkerton, Part 18.

7:5. M. R. Collins (4th TN Cav, CSA), "Paint Rock River Bridge."

March 14

2:5-7. Biog: Nehemiah M. Dyer (USN), Theodore Schwan (10th US), Milton Garrigus (39th, 137th, 142nd IN).

2:5-7. Obit: Gilbert A. Pearce (9th IN), Robert Pollock (US Reg), Jesse J. Phillips (9th IL), John D. Probst (21st NJ).

3:1-3. Mosgrove, Part 5. [Knoxville]

3:3-5. T. R. Lackie (16th MI), "On the Right Flank. The Sharp Battle at Hanover Court House, It Opened the Way for McDowell."

3:5-7. A. N. Ellis (49th OH), "Buell at Shiloh."

6:4-5. C. F. Waldron (29th OH), "Southern Battlefields. An Ohio Comrade Visits Historic Places of Ga. and Tenn."

6:5-6. Obit.

7:1-5. Pinkerton, Part 19.

March 21

2:3. Frank McClure, "Stone River Battlefield. An Association Formed at Murfreesboro, Tenn., To Secure the Historic Grounds for a National Park."

2:3. Calvin Shaffer (15th NY Hvy Art), "Elias Howe." [17th CT]

2:4. Obit: Benjamin M. Prentiss.

2:6. B. F. Johns (49th PA), "A Young Rebel." [Saylor's Creek]

3:1-3. Mosgrove, Part 6.

3:3. S. T. Maxey (6th IL Cav), "A Corn Campaign. Recollections of What A. J. Smith's Command Experienced in the Winter of 1864-'65."

3:4-5. James B. Hitchcock (44th NY), "A Rebel Trap. How the 44th N.Y. Eluded It—Monkeyshines for Titled Foreigners." [Hanover Court House]

3:5. W. H. Hittle (8th IA), "The Division of Davies." [Corinth]

3:5-6. William T. Ivy (5th AL Btn), "The Battle of Gettysburg." [first man killed]

3:6. William E. Doyle (17th IN), "The Capture of the 100th Ohio." [Telford Station, TN]

4:2. Obit: Colly B. Holland (MO Mil Brig Gen]

5:4. Thomas C. Murphy (31st IL), "Scaling-Ladders at Vicksburg." [5/22/63]

5:5. B. Sumner (5th IN Cav), "Battle of Henderson's Mill."

5:5. "Fought the Silent Battle. Yellow-Jack's Campaign Against the 90th New York—A Good War Record."

6:4-5. Obit.

7:1-4. Pinkerton, Part 20.

7:4. John A. Brooks (4th US Cav), "Branding in the 4th U.S. Cavalry."

March 28

3:1-4. Mosgrove, Part 7. [Mount Sterling]

3:4. Theodore F. Allen (7th OH Cav), "Inhospitable Kentuckians. Col. T. F. Allen Writes of Treatment at Hands of 4th Ky. Cav. While a Prisoner."

3:5. G. H. Hayward (1st ME Hvy Art), "Fought Single-Handed."

3:5. M. H. Powers (25th NY), "Didn't Want that Prisoner." [5/27/62, Hanover Court House]

3:5-6. T. C. Murphy (31st IL), "How We Forget."

3:6-7. W. L. Gilman (15th MA), "Easy to Criticize."

4:3. "The Credit at Chattanooga." [editorial]

5:5. Mort Stiles (13th IN), "Carrying the Colors." [Cold Harbor]

5:6-7. Biog: George N. Stone (7th RI), Abraham K. Arnold (5th US Cav).

6:4-5. Obit.

6:6. George A. Smith (7th OH Cav), "The Rogersville Fight."

7:1-4. Pinkerton, Part 21.

8:6-7. S. J. Lindsay (58th IN), "Chickamauga." [poem]

8:7. Alonzo E. Land (VT), "Christmas in 1864."

April 4

2:6. Jesse Wells (Bty H, 1st WV), "Not Held by the Enemy." [11/28/64, New Creek, WV]

3:1-2. Mosgrove, Part 8.

3:3. C. H. Fish (52nd IL), "How It was Made Up. A Sturdy Old Band of Fighters Told of by Comrade Fish."

3:3. William Ball, "The Ranks of the 3rd Kentucky." [Chattanooga]

3:4-5. M. Reed (14th US), "Too Busy to Run." [Gaines's Mill]

3:5-6. Edwin P. Walker (89th IL), "A Captain's Recollections. Ways of Sutlers—Willich's Love For His Old Brigade."

3:6. R. P. Cormack (89th NY), "Capture of a Battery." [Suffolk]

3:6-7. Alexander Cameron (52nd IL), "Gen. Sweeny's Brigade." [Corinth]

6:5. Obit.

April 11

2:3. Joseph Jones (11th MO), "Almost a Riot." [incident at Helena]

2:3. Paul J. Ward (47th IL), "Into Spanish Fort."

2:4. Levi Carkins (7th IA), "Lay's Ferry."

2:4-5. Isaac C. Dennis (14th IL Cav), "A Reckless Ride." [12/1/63, Walker's Ferry, TN]

2:5-6. Frank Heinzmann (9th OH), "Mill Spring Battle."

2:6. Joshua Dewees (97th OH), "Taking Chattanooga."

2:6. J. P. Platt (44th MO), "Preferred to Fight." [Franklin]

2:6-7. William F. Finigan (USS *North Carolina*), "A Close Call. An Experience with the Alligator Sub-Marine Boat."

3:1-2. Mosgrove, Part 9. [Cynthiana, 3rd battle]

3:2. J. A. Isenberg (Bty A, 1st TN), "Battle of Rogersville."

3:3. W. L. Sanford (14th IL Cav), "Bugle Notes from Dixie. A Fair and Impartial Narrative."

3:4-7. Theodore F. Allen (7th OH Cav), "Rogersville."

5:5-6. John R. Palmer (32nd IL), "The Field of Donelson."

5:6-7. J. K. Merrifield (88th IL), "Into the Works." [Franklin]

6:4-5. Obit.

8:6-7. B. C. McWilliams (16th PA Cav), "An Old Prisoner."

April 18

2:5-6. Frank Bruner (70th USCT), "The Capture of Fort Pillow."

3:1-2. Mosgrove, Part 10. [Morgan's Raid]

3:3-4. James T. Flack (44th OH), "In Dreary Old Pemberton. An Ohio Man Tells of Fighting at Beverly and Subsequent Trip to Richmond."

3:4. W. F. Outland (62nd OH), "Shields's Division."

3:4. B. F. Johns (49th PA), "Pursuit of Lee. Events Following the Battle of Gettysburg."

3:5. Edwin Crockett (65th NY), "Fierce Frenzy of Battle." [Shenandoah Valley 1864]

3:6. Samuel Peabody (16th ME), "The 16th Maine at Gettysburg."

5:3-4. J. A. Pine (1st IN Cav), "Battle of Pine Bluff." [Fall 1863]

5:5-6. "The Logan Statue. The Magnificent Equestrian Memorial Unveiled at Washington."

6:6-7. Obit.

8:6-7. A. S. Whetsel (7th IN Cav), "True Son of the Union. One of Gen. [J. P. C.] Shanks's Old Troopers Tells of His Colonel."

April 25

2:3-4. J. A. Pine (1st IN Cav), "Winning a Brigadier General's Star. Two Decisive Battles that Brought a General's Commission to Powell Clayton, Minister to Mexico."

3:1-4. Mosgrove, Part 11. [Morgan]

3:4. Theodore F. Allen (7th OH Cav), "Blue Springs Battle."

3:5. H. M. Foster (24th NY Cav), "Dinwiddie Court House."

3:6. William Gordon, "Missionary Ridge. Credit for Capture of 'Lady Buckner' and 'Lady Breckinridge' is Claimed by the 41st Ohio."

3:6-7. George E. Stanley (129th IN), "Who Stole that Flour?"

5:1-4. John B. Foote (12th NY), "How Serg't. [C. F.] Rand Became a Private. A Tale of Self-Sacrifice and Heroism."

5:7. Biog: Cyrus S. Roberts (150th NY), John C. Gilmore (16th, 193rd NY).

5:7. Obit: Joseph S. Bryce (staff officer, NY).

6:3-4. David Criswell (105th PA), "Boydton Plank Road."

6:6. Obit.

May 2

2:3-5. Gilbert S. Prior, "The Rebel Ram Albemarle. Experiences of the Engineer Who Accompanied Lieut. Cushing."

3:1-2. Mosgrove, Part 12.

3:2. S. W. Stookey (89th OH), "Regiments Captured at the Snodgrass House." [Chickamauga]

3:3. John R. Hughes (12th US), "An Army Newsboy. Captured by Rebel Pickets Only to be Rescued and His Captors Made Prisoners." [Petersburg]

3:4. W. P. Wolf (175th OH), "Battle of Franklin."

3:4-5. J. W. Cotes (12th IA), "Hornets' Nest." [Shiloh]

3:5. Charles Graham (89th NY), "Capture of the 5-Gun Battery." [Nansemond, Spring 1863]

3:5. R. E. Fitch (14th IA), "The Battle of Shiloh."

3:5. James Allen (16th NY), "The Battle of Gaines's Mill."

3:6. W. H. Anderson (80th OH), "His Rebel Confidant. How Gen. Sherman Gave Away the Secret of His Destination."

3:6-7. T. D. Osborne (17th OH), "Capture of Brown's Ferry."

5:1-4. J. N. Jones (8th IN Cav), "Rosseau's Raid." [7/64]

6:7. Obit.

7:1-2. J. A. Pine (1st IN Cav), "A Midnight Alarm. Advance of Contrabands on the Union Camp Causes the Sound of the 'Long Roll'."

7:2. "One of the Youngest." [J. J. Hall, 27th KY, 53rd KY Mtd Inf]

7:5-6. W. W. Stockton (11th MO Cav), "Over the Plains in '63."

May 9

2:1-2. M. B. Loop, "Rounding Up the Confederacy. Veteran Campaigns of the Gallant 68th Ohio, Under Uncle Billy Sherman."

2:3. Isaac McDowell (1st NJ), "Visit to Battlefields."

2:4-5. "The Old-Time Navy. Vessels Which Did Good Service in the Rebellion Still on Duty."

2:5-6. "Battle of Peach Tree Creek. Gen. Coburn and Others Make Some Statements in Regard to It."

3:1-4. Mosgrove, Part 13. [Saltville]

3:5-6. John M. Valleau (109th PA), "Gettysburg."

3:6. Charles M. Maltby (125th OH), "Battle of Franklin."

3:6-7. J. A. Moore (12th OH Bty), "Campaigning in West Virginia." [McDowell]

3:7. R. A. Ferris (151st NY), "Patriotic Record of a N.Y. Town." [Wilson]

5:1-4. J. T. Woods (99th OH), "A Regimental Surgeon."

6:6. Obit.

7:4. Pizarro Cook (31st WI), "How the Rebels Captured a Battery." [Bentonville]

7:4. Theodore F. Allen (7th OH Cav), "Gen. Hobson's Surrender." [Kellan's Bridge]

7:5-6. Marion Anderson, "Abraham Lincoln. The Greatness and Tenderness of the Martyr President. An Address by Major Marion Anderson, Past Commander, Department of the Potomac, G.A.R., Before Lincoln Post, Washington, D.C."

May 16

3:1-4. Mosgrove, Part 14. [Shenandoah Valley 1864]

3:4. Picket Shots: Samuel Kleffman (47th IL)(, Spanish Fort G. I. Nash, Sheridan at Cedar Creek.

3:5. J. W. Nelson, "The 169th Pa."

3:6. John K. Shellenberger (64th OH), "On Missionary Ridge. The Capture of Lady Buckner and Lady Breckinridge of Cobb's Battery."

3:6-7. Ira S. Owens (74th OH), "The Grand Review."

3:7. J. K. Dean (14th WI), "The Battle of Corinth."

5:1-4. Woods, Part 2.

6:5. Obit.

6:6-7. W. L. Sanford (14th IL Cav), "Battle of Blue Springs."

7:1-3. Loop, Part 2. [Kennesaw Mt]

7:3-4. John S. Hall (15th IL), "A Story of Capture. Surprised by Texas Rangers and Carried to Andersonville." [Ackworth, GA, 10/64]

7:6. Silas Benham, "Death of Gen. Garnett." [Carrick's Ford]

8:1-2. "Veteran Missionary. Rev. Hong Neck Woo, A Soldier of the Civil War." [56th PA Mil]

8:2-3. Mrs. M. A. Robinson, "After the Battle. Two Girls on the Scout for Hospital Supplies." [Antietam]

May 23

1:5-7, 2:1-2. James P. Shaw (31st OH), "Recollections of a Forager."

2:6. John H. James (4th KY Cav), "One of Stoneman's Raiders. A Ky. Cavalryman's Experience in Action and at Andersonville. [captured at Lovejoy Station]

2:6. T. J. Wright (8th KY), "A Loyal Tennessean. Rebel Neighbors Burn House Over Heads of Union Refugees."

2:7. G. L. Roy (21st IN, 1st IN Hvy Art), "That Brazil Raid." [Brazil, IN]

3:1-3. Mosgrove, Part 15. [East TN]

3:3. Richard Dobson (7th MI Bty), "A Famous Michigan Battery."

3:4-6. W. H. H. Minturn (39th OH), "Battle of Corinth."

3:6. Isaac C. Dennis (14th IL Cav), "A Footrace. Excitement Attendant Upon the Capture of a Rebel Captain." [Rheatown-Pugh's Hill]

3:6-7. William S. Horton (5th MI Cav), "Last Days at Andersonville."

5:1-3. A. Ernest Marston, "A Perilous Role. Adventures of One of McClellan's Spies."

5:5. "Records of the Rebellion. The Great Work Completed at a Cost of Over $3,000,000."

6:1-3. Thomas L. Hanna (83rd NY), "A Day at Gettysburg."

6:6. Obit.

7:1-3. Loop, Part 3. [Peach Tree Creek, Atlanta]

7:3-4. Eugene Sullivan (42nd NY), "Grapevine Bridge."

May 30

1:5-7, 2:1-2. Shaw, Part 2.

2:3. Obit: Fitz-John Porter.

2:4. "Ohio Battleflags."

3:1-4. Mosgrove, Part 16.

3:4. Theodore F. Allen (7th OH Cav), "Battle of Blue Springs."

3:4. J. N. Hubbard (7th IN), "Death of Gen. Garnett."

3:5. John Bresnahan (27th IN), "A Famous Command. Splendid Record of Ruger's Brigade from 1861 to 1865."

3:6-7. John A. MacDonald (7th NJ), "The Grand Review."

3:7. B. F. Loring (8th TN), "Supports Col. Allen." [Blue Springs]

5:1-4. Marston, Part 2.

6:6-7. Obit.

7:1-3. Loop, Part 4.

7:3. Charles M. Brooks (18th CT), "Death of Gen. William E. Jones." [Piedmont]

7:3. L. G. Miller (31st OH), "The Capture of Brown's Ferry."

7:3. Calvin Shaffer (15th NY Hvy Art), "Elias Howe."

June 6

2:1-3. Shaw, Part 3.

2:4-5. Jesse H. Jones (60th NY), "A Pair of Breastplates. A Story of the Fierce Fighting on the Right at Gettysburg."

3:1-3. Mosgrove, Part 17. [Marion, Stoneman's 1865 Raid]

3:4-5. William E. Doyle (17th IN), "Chickamauga."

3:6. Robert F. Conover (7th IN), "Death of Gen. Garnett."

3:6-7. J. N. Waddell (12th WV), "The Battle of Piedmont."

3:7. J. R. McBride (33rd IN), "Records of the Rebellion."

5:1-5. Marston, Part 2.

6:6. Obit.

7:1-4. Loop, Part 5. [10-11/64]

June 13

2:1-2. A. E. Shearman (117th NY), "In Hostile Hands. A Plain Tale of Trial and Suffering in Salisbury Prison." [captured 9/29/64]

3:1-2. Mosgrove, Part 18.

3:2. M. A. Harbert, "Reminiscences of a 5th Indiana Cavalryman." [Henderson Mills]

3:3. Charles M. Castle (102nd IL), "A Night on Picket. Kirby Smith's Cavalry Turns Out to be 3 Escaping Slaves."

3:3. S. A. McNeil (31st OH), "Recollections of a Forager."

3:4. J. H. Prather (91st OH), "Sheridan's Ride. The Part Taken by the 91st Ohio at the Battle of Winchester."

3:4-5. W. J. Adams (44th NY), "Some Heavy Brigade Losses."

3:5. John C. Weddle (1st KY Cav), "Battle of Mill Springs."

3:5. Hiram K. Brooke, "With the 15th Ohio." [Garnett's death]

3:6. L. W. Armstrong (10th IL), "Nigger-Stealing."

3:6. Picket Shots: Robert Watson (7th IN), death of Gen. Garnett.

5:1-3. Shaw, Part 4.

5:6. Biog: George B. Davis (1st MA Cav), Abel F. Leavenworth (9th VT).

6:6-7. Obit.

7:1-3. Loop, Part 6.

7:4-5. S. D. Burger (6th NY Hvy Art), "Spotsylvania."

June 20

2:6-7. "At Andersonville. The Memorial Fountain Over Providence Spring Dedicated on Memorial Day."

3:1-3. Mosgrove, Part 18.

3:4. W. I. Sanford (14th IL Cav), "Battle of Blue Springs."

3:5. A. C. Simonton (118th IN), "Wilcox's Division." [Blue Springs]

3:6. S. H. Draper (21st NY Cav), "Death of Gen. Jones." [Piedmont]

3:6. Picket Shots: M. Boyer (13th IN), Fort Stribling, Suffolk.

4:7. Biog: Samuel R. Peters (73rd OH).

5:1-3. Shaw, Part 5.

5:6. Obit.

6:5-6. Obit.

7:1-3. Loop, Part 7. [1/65]

7:4-6. Eugene Powell (66th OH), "Lee's First Invasion."

June 27

2:1-4. Powell, Part 2.

3:1-2. Mosgrove, Part 19.

3:2. J. N. Liscomb (4th WI Cav), "Around Baton Rouge."

3:3. George P. Hayward (1st ME Hvy Art), "Why They Do Not Write. A Maine Comrade Believes that Fear of Contradiction Prevents Veterans from Telling Their Experiences."

3:3. T. D. Cornell, "The 78th New York."

3:4. Thomas P. Alexander (11th IN), "Gen. Sheridan's Charger." [Cedar Creek]

3:4. Albert N. Jennings (121st NY), "Pursuit of Lee's Army." [Gettysburg]

3:4. John A. Leonard (49th OH), "Who Stole the Turkey?"

3:4. E. G. Adams (6th MA), "Wounded in Baltimore."

3:5. Picket Shots: Silas Staples (47th IL), Corinth.

4:3. Biog: Eli Torrance (9th PA Res, 193rd, 97th PA).

5:1-4. Shaw, Part 6.

5:6. Biog: Milton Garrigus (142nd IN).

5:6. Obit: Robert Nugent (69th NY), Thomas S. Sloan (Bty E, PA), James E. Taylor (artist), Byron Laflin (34th NY).

7:1-3. Loop, Part 8.

7:6. Obit.

July 4

2:7. Theodore F. Allen (7th OH Cav), "The Blue Springs Controversy."

3:1-4. Mosgrove, Part 20.

3:5-6. Frederick W. Fout (7th IN), "Killed by Georgians. The Battle of Carrick's Ford and Death of Gen. Garnett, July 13, 1861."

3:6-7. J. N. Jones (39th IN), "Chickamauga."

3:7. Frank Waldron (29th OH), "A Prison Incident." [Florence]

5:1-3. Shaw, Part 7.

5:4. Biog: J. M. Weaver (27th OH), James Van Kleeck (17th MI).

6:6. Obit.

7:1-3. Loop, Part 9.

7:3. George L. Thayer (10th MA), "Administering the Oath. Soldiers Make a Midnight Raid on Maryland Slaveholders."

7:4-5. W. H. Ilsley (9th IL), "Against Heavy Odds. A Little Band of 30 Withstand an Attack of 500." [Moulton, AL, 3/21/64]

July 11

2:1-5. W. C. Tyler (141st PA), "Strategy and Tactics. Events Leading To and Constituting the Battle of Gettysburg."

2:6. "First Medal of Honor. Interesting Correspondence Between Comrade William Hunter Myers and the Record and Pension Office." [Andrews' Raid]

3:1-3. Mosgrove, Part 21.

3:4. H. C. Wilkins (21st IN), "Baton Rouge."

3:4. William T. Ivy (5th AL Btn), "At Gettysburg. Who was the Lone Cavalryman Killed Between the Lines?"

3:5-7. Gilbert Thompson (US Eng Btn), "Work of U.S. Engineers. Military Bridges of the Army of the Potomac on the Chickahominy, 1862."

5:1-3. Shaw, Part 8.

5:3. Obit: Julian Scott (3rd VT).

6:3-4. S. H. Draper (21st NY Cav), "Sheridan's Charger."

6:4. R. P. McCoy, "Service in Co. C, 122nd Ohio."

6:5. J. J. Smith, "The 7th Indiana and Its Gallant Commander."

6:5. H. A. Dickson (6th MA), "Not Wounded at Baltimore."

6:6. Obit.

7:1-4. Loop, Part 10.

July 18

2:5-6. (80th OH), "A Civil War Romance."

3:1-2. Mosgrove, Part 22.

3:2-3. Joseph B. Newbtry (79th OH), "Peach Tree Creek."

3:3. H. T. Drake, "The 54th Ohio at Cedar Creek."

3:4. George V. Marshall (Bty F, PA), "Hampton Battery."

3:5-6. Picket Shots: George Myers (9tn NJ), color-bearer; W. W. Hill (29th OH), death of Gen. Garnett; F. H. Rice (2nd MI Cav), Sheridan's horse; J. C. Seaward (13th IN), Cold Harbor.

3:6-7. James B. Taylor (16th OH), "A Gallant Buckeye Command."

4:2. Biog: James Kilbourne (95th OH).

5:1-4. M. H. MacNamara (9th MA), "Story of 1,000 Irishmen."

5:5. Obit: Edwin Dunn (25th NY Cav), Robert J. Coffey (4th VT).

5:5. Biog: James P. Worrell (40th, 86th IL).

6:2. Darius Vasbinder (105th PA), "Battle of Seven Pines."

6:2. A. C. Simonton (118th IN), "The Battle of Blue Springs."

6:3. Obit: Thomas S. Sloan (Bty E, PA). [corrects error in 1891 obit]

6:6. Obit.

7:1-3. Lyman D. Widney (34th IL), "From Louisville to the Sea. A Soldier's Diary of the Civil War." [to 9/20/61]

7:4. "Gen. George H. Thomas's Sword. Gift from Neighbors that His Implacable Sisters Retained." [*Richmond Times*]

July 25

2:4-5. Lawrence Wilson (7th OH), "Modern Shenandoah."

2:6-7. J. B. Kirk (101st PA), "Morgan's Invasion. Reminiscences of an Exciting Day in Salem, Ohio."

3:1-2. George D. Mosgrove (4th KY Cav CSA), "Stonewall Jackson. Firm Stand of the Virginians at Manassas Under This Intrepid Leader."

3:3. W. H. Rosser (52nd PA), "A Gallant Keystone Command."

3:3. Elmore Hurdman (1st WV Cav), "A Daring Feat." [Shenandoah Valley 1865]

3:3. John N. Corgan, "The City of Madison."

3:4-5. George S. Myers, "Guerrilla Chasing. Operations of the 101st Ohio Around Huntsville, Ala."

3:5. SC, Co. G (13th PA Cav), "With the Army of the Potomac." [1/65 Mosby]

3:6-7. Henry S. Wells (27th NY), "Forty Years Ago. Captured at Bull Run, July 21, 1861, Comrade Wells was for 318 Days a Prisoner of War."

4:1. Biog: Wager Swayne (43rd OH).

4:2. Obit: Daniel Butterfield.

4:7. "50th Illinois Colors."

5:1-4. MacNamara, Part 2.

5:6-7. W. H. Sanderson (2nd US), "U.S. R egulars. No Monuments to Mark the Historic Spots Where Their Gallant Soldiers Fought." [Gettysburg]

6:6. Obit.

7:1-4. Widney, Part 2. [9/25-10/18/61]

7:4. Frederick W. Fout (7th IN), "Col. Dumont."

7:4. W. J. Wray (23rd PA), "Rappahannock Station."

8:6-7. J. T. Parker (IA), "Within Prison Walls. Conferring Degrees at Columbia, S.C., During the War."

August 1

1:5-7, 6:3-6. George C. Eggleston, "A Bitter Indictment of Jeff Davis's Civil and Military Administration."

2:7. Theodore F. Allen (7th OH Cav), "Blue Springs."

3:1-6. James B. Hitchcock (44th NY), "War's Brighter Side."

3:6. Stanley Lathrop (1st WI Cav), "Bugle Notes from Dixie."

3:6. John D. Kemp (72nd IL), "Illinois Men Favored Lincoln." [1864 election]

3:6. J. N. Liscomb (4th WI Cav), "Baton Rouge."

3:7. S. W. Clark (9th NY Cav), "Killed Between the Lines. Corp'l. James. 9th N.Y. Cavalry, was the First Man to Lose His Life at Gettysburg."

4:7. Biog: C. E. Henry (42nd OH), Richard R. Eskridge (2nd IA, 14th MO Cav).

5:1-4. MacNamara, Part 3.

6:2. "Colors of the 50th Illinois. Historic Old Flag Returned to Hannibal, Mo., After 40 Years."

6:6. Obit.

7:1-4. Widney, Part 3. [10/19-11/20/61]

7:4-5. Charles P. Maguire, "Sheridan's Famous Ride."

7:5. Samuel Peabody (16th ME), "First Day at Gettysburg."

8:1-4. Theodore F. Allen (7th OH Cav), "The Wanderers. Confederate Flag and Grave on Navigator Islands."

8:4. F. F. Hubbell (5th NY Hvy Art), "Battle of Piedmont."

8:4. J. R. McBride (33rd IN), "Who Killed Lieut. Gen. Leonidas Polk?"

August 8

2:1-4. George C. Eggleston, "End of the War and the Beginning of Reconstruction."

2:5-6. C. E. Henry (42nd OH), "Garfield as a Soldier."

3:1-3. Eugene Powell (66th OH), "The Battle Above the Clouds."

3:4-5. R. H. Martin (46th IN), "Champion's Hill."

3:5-6. Hiram Peck, "The 34th Ohio. A Hard Campaign in Which the Regiment was Conspicuously Engaged." [July 1864]

3:7. Picket Shots: A. D. Cutler (6th MA), Baltimore.

3:6. Salathiel Prater (96th OH), "Blowing Up of the City of Madison."

6:6. Obit.

6:6. Biog: Thomas MacVey (150th PA).

7:1-5. Widney, Part 4. [11/25/61-1/16/62]

8:1-5. MacNamara, Part 4.

August 15

2:1-2. Wilson, Part 2.

2:4. William Pittinger, "The First Medal of Honor."

2:6-7. J. H. Powell (7th IL Cav), "A Pathetic Letter. The Story of a Loyal Tennessean Who as a Boy Defended Old Glory." [*Canton* (IL) *Gazette*]

3:1-4. S. B. Boynton (18th WI), "The Boy Who Saved Corinth."

3:4. W. H. H. Minturn, "Brave Acts Unrewarded. Two Members of the Ohio Brigade Who Deserve Medals of Honor." [Charles H. Smith (27th OH) and Frank T. Gillmore (63rd OH), for Corinth]

3:5-6. Simeon Gillis (68th OH), "The First Gun at Shiloh."

3:6. J. W. Banks (6th MI), "Outnumbered 3 to 1." [Baton Rouge]

3:6. D. M. Maxson, "Col. Payne, a 4th Wisconsin Cavalryman, Writes of Events at Baton Rouge."

3:7. A. J. Jacobs (22nd KY), "Occurrences Before the Siege of Vicksburg."

4:3. Obit: James S. Negley.

4:7. Obit: Henry C. Conde (18th US), William Smith (2nd WI).

6:4. "Two Board of Trade Battery Relics."

6:6. Obit.

7:1-4. Widney, Part 5. [1/17-2/21/62]

8:1-5. MacNamara, Part 5.

August 22

2:3-4. John A. Halderman, "Wilson's Creek."

2:4. J. W. A. Gillespie (78th OH), "Champion's Hill."

2:5-6. Wilson, Part 3.

2:6-7. T. H. McCorkle (72nd IN), "Bushwhacking of Bob McCook."

3:1-4. A. S. Whetsel, "Campaigning with the 7th Indiana Cavalry."

3:4. W. H. Webber (6th MI), "Checked by the Indiana Troops." [Baton Rouge]

3:4. Henry H. Thornton (1st KY Cav), "Capture of the 3rd Georgia [Cavalry]." [New Haven, KY]

3:4. E. C. Ayres, "Voting in the 72nd Illinois."

3:5. Henry S. Wells (27th NY), "Marching to the Front. Experience of a Convalescent Returning to the Front."

3:5-6. Valentine Moulder, "The 16th New York Heavy Artillery."

3:6. Daniel W. Shawe (12th VRC), "Incidents of the Battle of Fort Stevens."

3:6. Charles W. Wood (13th US), "Battle of Collierville." [10/11/63]

3:7. Edward L. Knight, "A Relic of Camp Chase."

3:7. Picket Shots: F. H. Huron (7th IN), Carrick's Ford.

5:4. John W. Blake, "The 4th Wisconsin at Baton Rouge."

6:6. Obit.

7:1-4. Widney, Part 6. [2/22-3/15/62]

7:4. H. M. Foster (24th NY Cav), "An Exciting Race. Why a Cavalryman No Longer Suffered With Cold."

7:5-6. Lawrence Wilson (7th OH), "Cedar Mountain. Blue and Gray Unite to Mark Positions on This Famous Battlefield."

7:6. G. W. Wallace (15th NY Cav), "Who Stole the Mare?"

8:1-5. MacNamara, Part 6.

August 29

2:1-4. Vernon F. Henderson (6th PA Res), "Diary of a Penna. Reserve." [8-9/62]

2:5-7. D. A. Grimsley (6th VA Cav), "Cedar Creek."

3:1-4. Whetsel, Part 2.

3:4. M. B. Loop (68th OH), "The First Gun at Shiloh."

3:4. R. H. Martin (46th IN), "Quimby's Division." [correction of 8/8/01] [Champion's Hill]

3:5-6. William E. Doyle (17th IN), "Wilder's Brigade. Superb Fighting Around the Widow Glenn House." [Chickamauga]

3:6. S. M. Douglass (6th MI), "Fight at Baton Rouge."

3:7. George W. Holmes (22nd OH), "Chickamauga. Blunder of a Staff Officer Caused Disaster to the Union Force."

4:3. Obit: Robert Williams (1st MA Cav).

6:6. Obit.

7:1-3. Widney, Part 7. [3/16-4/7/62]

7:6. J. S. Ritchey, "One of Pat Cleburne's Men." [primarily Franklin battle]

8:1-7. MacNamara, Part 7.

September 5

2:1-4. D. A. Grimsley (6th VA Cav), "Cedar Mountain." [*Culpeper Exponent*, 5/14/00]

3:1-5. B. M. Cobb (113th IL), "War Reminiscences."

3:5. G. M. Williams (2nd KY), "Bushwhacking of Bob McCook."

4:3. Obit: William Ludlow (chief eng, 20th Corps).

6:1. "The Heavy Loss of the 24th N.Y. Statement Read by Comrade Norman G. Cooper at Annual Reunion."

6:5. Obit: John P. Lyon (81st OH).

6:6. Obit.

7:1-4. Widney, Part 8. [4/8-5/7/62]

8:1-6. MacNamara, Part 8.

September 12

2:1-4. Thomas C. Kincaid (102nd NY), "Short-Term Organizations. Valuable Service Rendered the U.S. Government by One Hundred Days' Regiments."

3:1-3. J. K. Shellenberger (64th OH), "Schofield at Franklin. The Mistake that Sacrificed Wagner's Brigade."

3:3. John Gwin (USS *Springfield*), "An Ohio Boy's Enlistment into the Naval Service."

3:3. John Baker (9th NY Cav), "The First Man Killed at Gettysburg."

3:3. John Scott, "A 116th Illinois Man' at Fort McAllister."

3:4-5. T. D. McGillicuddy (50th IL), "Through Georgia." [letter written on 1/1/65]

3:5-6. S. B. Boynton, "The 18th Wisconsin at Shiloh."

3:6. John A. Brooks (8th PA Res), "A Lucky Guess. A Forager Gives the Countersign and the Picket Passes the Party with the Chickens."

3:7. S. T. Carrico (61st IL), "With the Western Armies."

6:6. Obit.

7:1-4. Widney, Part 9. [5/8-28/62]

8:1-7. MacNamara, Part 9.

September 19

4:7. Obit: A. S. Twitchell (7th ME Bty).

4:7. Biog: E. L. Schroeder (5th MD).

6:1-4. H. F. Christy (11th PA Res), "The 'Reserves' at Fredericksburg."

6:4. L. W. Armstrong (10th IL), "Capturing a Rebel Wagon-Master." [10/63]

6:4. Jacob Fink (55th IL), "Gunboats at Shiloh."

6:4. J. N. Liscomb (4th WI Cav), "A Letter, and What Became of It." [Mosgrove]

6:5. Fred W. Fout (15th IN Bty), "Miles at Harper's Ferry."

6:5-7. William Myce (2nd NY Cav), "A Prisoner in Libby."

7:1-4. Widney, Part 10. [thru 10/2/62]

8:1-7. MacNamara, Part 10.

September 26

1:1-4. Charles Brewster, "Captured by Mosby's Guerrillas." [11/64]

3:1-4. Samuel A. Ashe, "North Carolinians at Gettysburg. A Critical Review of the Famous Confederate Charge on July 3, 1864 [sic]."

3:4. John A. Brooks (8th PA Res), "Mosby's Guerrillas." [10/63]

3:5-6. John W. Dilley (84th IL), "Thomas at Chickamauga."

3:6. Harry Caldwell, "The 11th Indiana Battery at the Glenn House."

5:6. Mrs. J. B. Work, "A Girl's Recollections of a Great Cavalry Battle." [Brandy Station]

5:6. L. B. Dawson (36th IL), "Mississippi Losses at Franklin."

5:6. Warren S. Brown, "The Burial of Luther C. Ladd." [6th MA in Baltimore]

6:6. Obit.

7:1-4. Widney, Part 11. [10/3-11/3/62]

7:5-6. "A Civil War Heroine. The Story of Jennie Wade, Killed at Gettysburg."

8:1-7. MacNamara, Part 11.

8:7. G. W. McDonald, "Drummer Boy of the 65th Illinois."

October 3

1:1-5. Brewster, Part 2.

1:6-7, 2:1-4. Hiram T. Peck (10th CT, clerk for the Medical Director, 25th Corps), "The Last Campaign. A Veteran's Experience in Texas with Weitzel's 25th Corps."

3:1-4. Ashe, Part 2.

3:5. John H. Buss, "With the Engineer Corps." [Dept of the Rappahannock]

3:6. R. H. Martin (46th IN), "Champion's Hill."

3:6. Almeron Chapman (1st PA Cav), "The Battle of Cedar Mountain."

3:7. Theodore F. Allen (7th OH Cav), "Gen. Israel Garrard."

6:6. Obit.

7:1-4. Widney, Part 12. [11/4-12/21/62]

8:1-4. MacNamara, Part 12.

October 10

1:1-4, 7:5. W. R. Bond, "Pickett or Pettigrew?"

2:4. "Regimental Monument at 'Bloody Angle'." [49th NY at Spotsylvania]

2:5. Obit: Edward H. Hobson (13th KY).

3:1-2. W. G. Bartholomew (27th MA), "A Fighting Regiment's First Battle. A Colonel's Recollections of the Burnside Expedition and Capture of Roanoke Island."

3:2. S. W. Warren (4th TN), "A Civil War Relic. A Battle Flag Captured at Manassas, Va., in 1861."

3:3-4. C. E. Goldsborough, "The Hunterstown Fight." [PA]

3:4. George D. Mosgrove, "The Mule Wouldn't Surrender."

3:5. W. W. Booton (7th IL Cav), "Some Queer Characters."

3:5. J. B. Williams (2nd IN Cav), "Capture of the 3rd Ga. Cavalry." [New Haven, KY]

4:2. Obit: George W. Getty.

5:3. J. V. Pownall (29th IN), "How the Explosion Occurred." [4/10/62]

5:4. Biog: William M. Van Horne (2nd, 184th, 195th OH), Albert D. Shaw (4th DC Btn).

6:6. Obit.

7:1-4. Widney, Part 13. [12/22-31/62]

October 17

2:1-4. Bond, Part 2.

2:4. S. R. Nelson (2nd MO Cav), "A Hero in Gray." [4/65, Wofford's surrender]

2:5. W. L. Kester (79th IL), "At Missionary Ridge."

3:1-4. J. D. Bloodgood (141st PA), "Chancellorsville."

3:4-5. H. M. Foster (24th NY Cav), "Some Narrow Escapes."

3:5-6. H. C. Wheeler (7th IN), "Carrick's Ford." [Garnett's death]

3:6-7. T. W. Holman (21st MO), "First Guns at Shiloh."

3:7. C. A. Pelton, "Elias Howe's Service."

5:5. Biog: T. J. Kennedy (1st NY), A. E. Page (1st MO Cav).

6:6. Obit.

7:1-4. Widney, Part 14. [1/1-6/9/63]

October 24

2:1-5. Bond, Part 3.

3:1-3. Alexander Borthwick, "The Red River Campaign."

3:4. Horace Fountain, "Service with the 74th Indiana."

3:4. D. J. Southerland (9th MI), "Gen. Rosecrans's Cracker Line."

3:5. Cyrus Sears (11th OH Bty), "Winning a Medal." [Iuka]

4:7. Obit: Isaac Arnold (2nd US Art), James C. Michie (6th OH).

5:4. Obit: Francis M. Bunce (USN).

6:4. "The 48th Ohio at Shiloh. Survivors Notified at Annual Reunion of Marking of Regiment's Position."

6:4. "Reunion of the 70th Ohio." [flag]

6:5. "Flag of the 34th Ohio."

6:6. Obit.

7:1-3. Widney, Part 15. [6/23-7/1/63]

8:4-6. "The Grant Collection. Priceless Relics in the National Museum at Washington."

October 31

2:1-5. Bond, Part 4.

3:1-2. John H. Deane (USN), "Torpedo Boats of the Rebellion.' Attack on New Ironsides and Sinking of the *Housatonic*."

3:2-3. George D. Mosgrove, "Captain J. B. Kirk's Strategics. How He Kept 150 N.C. Home Guardians from Attacking His 15 Men in Blue." [101st PA, fall 1863]

3:3. H. S. Haskin (2nd IN Cav), "Capture of the 3rd Ga. Cavalry." [New Haven, KY]

3:4-6. J. N. Jones (39th IN), "The Widow Glenn's." [Chickamauga]

3:6-7. Fred W. Fout (7th IN and 15th IN Bty), "Two War Topics." [Carrick's Ford, Franklin]

4:3. Biog: H. C. Merriam (20th ME).

5:6. Isaac R. Reynolds (3rd AR Cav), "A Union Family in the South."

6:5. Picket Shots: M. H. McMullen (7th IN), death of Gen. Garnett; N. L. Cutts (10th CT), Morris Island; John J. Scribner (1st WI Cav), youngest.

6:6. Obit.

7:1-4. Widney, Part 16. [7/6-9/6/63]

November 7

2:6. "Gen. John B. Turchin. A Scout's Recollections of the Gen. and His Wife."

3:1-5. Eugene Powell (66th OH), "Sad Days at Chancellorsville."

3:5-6. George W. Pitner (77th OH), "With Weitzel in Texas."

3:6-7. B. Ellis (1st WI Cav), "An Act that Should Have Won a Medal." [Red Clay Station, GA]

4:3. T. C. Harbaugh, "At Gettysburg." [poem]

4:3. Obit: James Rochford (24th MA).

5:1-2. "Trophies of Valor. Project to Establish a War Museum in Washington."

5:4-5. R. K. Beecham (2nd WI), "Pettigrew's North Carolinians." [Gettysburg]

7:1-4. Widney, Part 17. [through 10/4/63]

7:5. William E. Chick (85th PA), "Bridges Over the Chickahominy."

7:5-6. Noble B. Easton (20th IN), "The Charge at Gettysburg."

November 14

2:1-4. William T. Rigby (24th IA), "The Vicksburg National Park."

2:4. James K. Powers (51st IN), "First Man Killed at Stone River."

3:1-4. Powell, Part 2.

3:4. C. W. Cook (18th IN), "Benton's Brigade at Vicksburg."

3:4. Theodore Jones (5th IA), "The 11th Ohio Battery." [Iuka]

3:4. J. B. Kirk (101st PA), "A Suggestion." [regarding the controversies]

3:5-6. R. S. Andrews (50th WI), "The 6th W.Va. Cavalry. The Arrest of the Regiment at Fort Leavenworth for Refusal to Go on the Plains."

3:6-7. Noble B. Easton, "The 20th Indiana at Chancellorsville."

4:3. Rufus W. Lewis (18th VRC), "The Guard of Honor at Lincoln's Funeral."

5:5. Biog: William H. Carney (54th MA).

6:5-6. C. P. Stone, "Defense of the Capital. Organization of the Militia of the District of Columbia."

7:1-4. Widney, Part 18. [11/15/63]

8:6-7. William Simmons, "The Rebel Privateer Savannah."

November 21

2:1-3. C. M. Parker (46th IN), "Down the Mississippi. A Revisit to Scenes of Camp and Battle—Changes Wrought by Time and the Great River." [Island #10, Memphis, Milliken's Bend, Champion's Hill]

3:1-2. William B. Threapleton (88th PA), "Globe Tavern."

3:3. Hiram T. Peck (10th CT), "With Weitzel in Texas."

3:4. S. S. Hammitt (36th OH), "Sheridan's Ride."

3:4-5. P. P. Demorest (10th US), "Recollections of the Orphan Company." [Company C, 10th US]

3:5. Will C. Phipps (11th IN), "A Night March. A Reminiscence of the Vicksburg Campaign." [to Grand Gulf]

3:6. W. B. Harrison, "Inaccuracy of Battle Losses." [Baton Rouge]

3:6-7. G. W. Mattoon (6th MI Cav), "Custer's Fight at Hunterstown."

6:5. C. W. Colby (97th IL), "An Incident Occurring at Fort Blakely."

7:1-3. Widney, Part 19. [Chattanooga]

November 28

1:1-4, 6:1-7. B. K. Benson, "Who Goes There? Story of a Spy in the Civil War."

1:5-7, 2:1-4. Green B. Raum, "With the Western Armies." [first Vicksburg campaign]

3:1-3. Widney, Part 20. [Chattanooga]

3:3. George W. White (106th PA), "Col. Baker's Californians."

3:4. G. H. Uhler (93rd PA), "The Sixth Corps at Chancellorsville."

3:4. W. G. Hubbard (24th NY Cav), "Recollections of a N.Y. Cavalryman."

3:4. E. G. Mansfield (27th CT), "Howard's Corps at Chancellorsville."

3:5. Wright Works (60th NY), "Hand-to-Hand Fighting." [Chancellorsville]

7:1-5. George D. Mosgrove, "The Crossing of the River." [6/63 Morgan Raid]

December 5

1:1-4, 6:2-6. Benson, Part 2.

2:1-5. Raum, Part 2. [Arkansas Post]

3:1-3. Widney, Part 21. [12/19/63-1/20/64]

3:4. G. W. Mattoon (6th MI Cav), "Sheridan at Cedar Creek."

3:4. "Died for His Contry. Timothy Webster, the Famous Union Spy, Buried at Onarga." [*Eastern Illinois Register*]

3:5. F. S. Miller (116th IN), "My Friend. A War Poem, and the Circumstances Under Which It was Written."

3:5-6. Obit.

3:6. Biog: Charles H. Blinn (1st VT Cav).

6:6. Obit.

7:1-6. Mosgrove, Part 2.

December 12

1:1-4, 6:1-6. Benson, Part 3.

2:1-4. Raum, Part 3. [bayou routes]

3:1-3. Widney, Part 22. [2/29-3/20/64]

3:6-7. Henry H. Thornton (1st KY Cav), "A Complete Surprise. Capture of the 3rd Georgia Cavalry by a Company of the 1st Kentucky Cavalry Under Captain Adams."

4:7. Obit: Albert W. Bishop (1st AR Cav), Abraham K. Arnold (US Reg).

4:7. Biog: Samuel S. Hager (49th OH).

7:1-4. Mosgrove, Part 3.

7:6. Obit.

8:1-3. Augustus C. Buell (Bty B, 4th US), "American Generals. A Brilliant Galaxy of Men Who have Risen by Meritorious Soldiership." [John R. Brooke, Nelson A. Miles, Elwell S. Otis (140th NY)]

December 19

1:1-3, 6:3-5. Benson, Part 4.

2:1-4. Raum, Part 4. [Vicksburg Campaign]

2:4. Biog: S. A. Moore (2nd IA).

3:1-3. Widney, Part 23. [3/21-5/7/64]

3:3. W. W. Boston (7th IL Cav), "Colored Troops at Tupelo."

3:4-5. R. K. Beecham (2nd WI), "Pettigrew's North Carolinians. Not to Them, But to Gallant Minnesotans Belongs the Honor of Greatest Loss at Gettysburg."

3:5. George E. Stanley (129th IN), "Franklin, and Other Topics."

3:6. William K. Johnson (36th OH), "Sheridan at Cedar Creek."

3:6. Horace Baker (8tH WI), "The Blame for Holly Springs."

3:6. W. H. Rosser (52nd PA), "Bottom's Bridge."

4:6. Obit: William A. Spencer (8th IL Cav).

6:7. Obit.

7:1-3. Mosgrove, Part 4.

7:4. W. H. Jack (23rd IA), "Benton's Brigade at Vicksburg."

8:1-4. Buell, Part 2. [S. B. M. Young (4th PA Cav), Adna R. Chaffee (6th US Cav), Arthur McArthur (24th WI), Lloyd Wheaton (8th IL]

8:4. William H. Crook, "Lincoln's Last Christmas. Recollections of One Who Spent the Day with Him."

8:5-7. Isabel W. Ball, "Mother Bickerdyke."

December 26

1:1-4, 7:5-6. Benson, Part 5.

1:5-7, 2:1-2. Raum, Part 5. [Vicksburg]

3:1-2. Widney, Part 24. [5/8-12/64]

3:2-3. S. M. Warren, "A Loyal Tennessean." [father was in 13th TN Cav]

3:3. P. L. Sanford (82nd OH), "Howard at Chancellorsville."

3:4. Charles Porter (11th VT), "The Old Sixth Corps." [Chancellorsville]

3:4-5. J. R. Conway (6th WV Cav), "Loyal West Virginians."

3:6-7. Abram Smith, "Gen. [George H.] Stuart's [sic] Bible is Returned to Him 36 Years After the Civil War." [captured at Saylor's Creek]

5:6. William H. Raymond (108th NY), "Charge of the 1st Minnesota." [poem]

5:6-7. C. E. Abbey (22nd NY), "The Iron Brigade."

6:2. W. W. Hicks (32nd NY), "Matheson's 1st California."

6:3. Diton Phelps (6th PA Res), "Capture of Gen. Stoughton."

6:3. James M. Jack (9th MO SM Cav), "The Centralia Massacre."

6:3. W. M. Lomax (1st AL Cav), "The Torpedoes at Savannah."

6:3. John Bogley (29th ME), "A Reminiscence of the Red River Expedition."

6:6. Andrew Joubert (30th NY), "The Iron Brigade."

7:1-3. Mosgrove, Part 5.

7:4. Theodore S. Vawler (24th IN), "An Incident Occurring at Fort Gaines."

8:1-5. "National War Souvenirs. Relics from the Fields of American Valor Preserved in the National Museum."

1902

January 2

1:1-4, 6:2-5. Benson, Part 6.

2:1-4. Raum, Part 6. [Champion's Hill]

3:1-3. Widney, Part 25. [5/13-19/64]

3:4-5. "A Wartime Event. Reception of the 17th Wisconsin at Madison, Wis., Upon Their Veteran Furlough in March, 1864." [from a contemporary newspaper]

3:5. George Bowers (66th NY), "A Fighting Regiment."

3:6. W. B. Lowry (62nd OH), "A Prisoner's Story." [Libby, Salisbury, Danville, captured 8/16/64]

3:7. George H. Hayward (1st ME Hvy Art), "A Veteran Quartermaster."

4:3. Obit: William J. Sewell (5th, 38th NJ).

6:6. Theodore F. Allen (7th OH Cav), "A Confidence Game. One of Morgan's Raiders Pays for Good Whiskey with Counterfeit Coin."

7:1-3. Mosgrove, Part 6.

7:4. John McAnally (63rd NY), "Between the Lines. Duel Between Yank and Reb at Petersburg."

7:5. "Mother Bickerdyke. Her Experiences at Donelson and Shiloh."

January 9

1:1-4, 6:4. Benson, Part 7.

2:1-3. Raum, Part 7. [Big Black River Bridge]

2:6-7. J. B. Kirk (101st PA), "From Bondage to Liberty. Scenes Incident to the Transition in N.C."

3:1-3. Widney, Part 26. [5/23-6/3/64]

3:4-6. Andrew Wykle (36th OH), "A Fighting Regiment."

3:6-7. Daniel Webster (1st WI Bty), "Gen. Albert W. Bishop."

5:1-4. Free S. Bowley, "In Battle Line." [fiction]

5:5. W. D. Munson (13th VT), "The Vermont Brigade. Capture of Gen. Stoughton, and Other Events Occurring at Fairfax Station."

6:6. Obit.

January 16

1:1-4, 6:4-7. Benson, Part 8.

2:1-4. Raum, Part 8. [Vicksburg]

3:1-3. Widney, Part 27. [6/3-19/64]

3:4-6. Samuel D. Tobey (8th MI Cav), "The Stoneman Raid. Extracts from a Long-Forgotten Diary."

3:6-7. Joseph Groves (8th IL), "Charge at Fort Blakely."

4:3. E. D. Bruner (2nd MA Cav), "Californians in the Civil War."

5:1-3. Bowley, Part 2.

7:6-7. Obit.

8:1-4. Theodore F. Allen (7th OH Cav), "$1,000,000 Picnic." [Mosgrove series]

January 23

1:1-4, 6:4-5. Benson, Part 9.

2:1-7. Raum, Part 9. [Vicksburg]

2:7. George H. Rowell (2nd MO Cav), "Michigan Battalion, Merrill's Horse."

3:1-3. Widney, Part 28. [6/19-28/64]

3:4. Lee Martz (34th IN), "With Weitzel in Texas."

3:4. Samuel D. Potts (30th NY), "The Iron Brigade."

3:6. W. J. Forsyth, "A Long Jump. A Feat that Landed One of Morgan's Men in Old Kentucky with Two Gallons of Whiskey."

5:1-2. Bowley, Part 3.

6:5. Samuel Kleffman (47th IL), "The 47th Ill. at Iuka."

7:5-6. T. W. Higginson (1st SC), "War-Time Caste. Col. Higginson Discusses Jews and Negroes in the Army."

7:6-7. Obit.

January 30

1:1-4, 6:3-6. Benson, Part 10.

2:1-3. Raum, Part 10. [Vicksburg]

2:3. Obit: Allen C. Fuller (Adjutant General of IL).

2:3-4. R. M. Aikin (33rd IL), "Charge at Black River Bridge."

2:6. Biog: John Ryan (28th, 61st MA), William H. Howard (8th NJ).

3:1-4. Widney, Part 29. [6/29-7/20/64]

3:4. Thomas E. Camburn (9th MI Cav), "With Kilpatrick's Cavalry Around Savannah."

3:5-6. L. O. Colburn (51st IL), "From Louisville to the Sea."

3:6-7. Zenus E. Hogue (36th IL), "A Skirmisher's Retreat." [7/22/64]

5:1-4. Bowley, Part 4.

7:1-4. George D. Mosgrove (4th KY Cav CSA), "Back to Old Kentucky. The Story of John Morgan's Imprisonment and Escape."

8:7. W. A. Johnson (2nd SC), "A Confederate's Views. Blames Hooker for Disaster at Chancellorsville and Sedgwick's Defeat."

February 6

1:1-4, 6:5. Benson, Part 11.

2:1-4. Raum, Part 11. [Vicksburg]

3:1-2. Widney, Part 30. [7/21-28/64]

3:3. S. F. Shaw (10th WV), "West Virginia Troops in the Army of the Potomac."

3:3. Samuel D. Tobey (8th MI Cav), "A Remarkable Circumstance." [Stoneman's Raid]

3:4. J. W. A. Gillespie, "Journeying Dixie-ward. Experiences of a 78th Ohio Officer En Route to Fort Donelson."

3:4-5. Z. T. Walker (15th IL Cav), "Benton's Brigade."

3:5. Ira S. Owens (74th OH), "Who was the Gray-Headed Veteran?"

3:5. J. Canfield (7th USCT), "Colored Troops at Tupelo."

5:6. Obit: Addison A. Hosmer (1st MA Hvy Art), Sanders D. Bruce (20th KY), Lewis A. Kimberley (USN).

6:2. Samuel Chalfant (52nd PA), "Bottom's Bridge."

7:1-2. Mosgrove, Part 2.

7:3. A. V. Johnson, "The Morgan Raid. Preparations for Defense Against the Wiley Raider."

7:4-5. "Early War-Time Days. Mrs. Grow's Recollections of President Lincoln." [from Collier's]

7:5-6. Obit.

8:7. J. B. Ferguson (206th PA), "Gen. R. E. Lee's Parting with His Staff."

February 13

1:1-4, 6:5-6. Benson, Part 12.

1:5-7, 2:1-2. Raum, Part 12. [post-siege operations]

2:6. A. B. Brown (23rd WI), "Pemberton's Flag of Truce."

3:1-3. Widney, Part 31. [7/29-8/23/64]

3:3. Hiram T. Peck (10th CT), "With Weitzel in Texas."

3:4-5. B. F. Johns (49th PA), "Closing Scenes. The Capture of Ewell's Command, and the Exhausting March to Burksville with the Prisoners."

3:5-7. Theodore F. Allen (7th OH Cav), "The Capture of a Battery as Told by One of the Colored Troops." [Nashville, Washington Grundy]

5:1-5. Prentiss Ingraham, "Port Hudson. The Forlorn Hope and the Siege Viewed from the Confederate Standpoint."

6:2. E. Cotton (24th MI), "The Iron Brigade."

7:1-4. Mosgrove, Part 3.

7:5. Obit.

7:6. Theodore F. Allen (7th OH Cav), "The Whiskey Not Forgotten."

February 20

1:1-4, 5:5-7. Benson, Part 13.

1:5-7, 2:1-2. Raum, Part 13. [north on leave]

3:1-3. Widney, Part 32. [8/25-9/26/64]

3:4. A. C. Menor (13th WI), "Horrors of Cahaba."

3:4-5. B. F. Loring (8th TN), "Maj. Bradford Only Wounded."

3:5. George P. Wood (29th WI), "Hovey's Division at Port Gibson."

3:5. J. L. Roler (116th OH), "West Virginia Troops."

5:1-3. C. F. Morse (2nd MA), "From Second Bull Run to Antietam."

7:1-2. Mosgrove, Part 4.

7:3. Obit.

7:4. Biog: A. O. Marsh (15th, 46th OH, 59th USCT).

7:5. Obit.

February 27

1:1-4, 6:3-6. Benson, Part 14.

2:1-4. Raum, Part 14. [home on leave]

3:1-3. Widney, Part 33. [9/28-10/64]

3:3-4. S. E. Chandler (24th NY Cav), "Incidents of the Morgan Raid."

3:4. D. D. Holm (5th IN Bty), "With Sherman's Army."

3:5-6. "First Medal of Honor. It was Given to Jacob Parrott, 33d Ohio, One of the 'Engine Thieves'."

5:4. Biog: Robert H. Atkinson (16th PA Cav).

7:1-4. George D. Mosgrove, "Morgan's Men Under Duke."

7:6. Obit.

8:1-3. J. G. Wilson, "Recollections of General Sherman." [*Criterion*]

March 6

1:1-4, 6:3-6. Benson, Part 15.

2:1-3. Raum, Part 15. [Chickamauga]

2:4-5. "The Iron Brigade. Letters from Gen. Bragg and Others Substantiate Claim Made by Western Regiments."

2:6. Obit: John F. Fisk (KY Gov).

2:6. J. Canfield (7th USCT), "Killing of Major [William F.] and Captain [Thomas F.] Bradford at Fort Pillow."

2:7. Obit.

3:1-3. Widney, Part 34. [10/18-11/15/64]

3:6-7. G. K. Campbell (116th OH), "Capture of Fort Gregg."

5:1-3. Theodore F. Allen (7th OH Cav), "The American Private Soldier."

6:2. B. F. Maull (3rd NJ), "A Musician's Story. Why Only One Shot was Required in the Attack on a Rebel Outpost."

7:1-3. Mosgrove, Part 2.

March 13

1:1-4, 6:3-5. Benson, Part 16.

2:1-4. Raum, Part 16. [relief of Chattanooga]

2:4. Obit: Edward I. Kidd (25th WI).

2:5. M. H. Van Scoten (54th PA), "Closing Scenes of the War." [High Bridge]

3:1-3. Widney, Part 35. [11/16-24/64]

3:4-6. Picket Shots: Daniel A. Wilbur (12th IL), Corinth.

3:6. W. T. Lewis (AAG), "Colored Troops in the Sixteenth Corps."

3:7. C. H. Murray (5th OH Cav), "A Woman's Heroism at Antietam." [Anna Etheredge]

4:7. J. N. Liscomb (4th WI Cav), "The Women at Home."

5:1-3. Allen, Part 2.

6:6. Obit.

7:1-4. Mosgrove, Part 3.

7:5. William T. Patterson (38th IA), "Under the Guns of Fort Morgan."

7:6. William E. Doyle (17th IN), "Two Commanders from One Regiment and Company."

8:7. D. B. Spencer (7th IL Cav), "Gen. Sherman Besieged." [Collierville, 10/13/62]

March 20

1:1-4, 6:3-5. Benson, Part 17.

2:1-4. Raum, Part 17. [colored troops]

2:5. "Vicksburg Battlefield. Ohio Commission's Efforts to Mark Positions of Troops from that State."

2:6-7. Picket Shots: D. A. Iverson (158th NYH), Fort Gregg.

3:1-5. Widney, Part 37. [11/27-end of march]

4:7. Elijah A. Gilbert (102nd IL), "Service in the West."

5:1-2. Mosgrove, Part 4.

6:6. Obit.

March 27

1:1-4, 6:5-6. Benson, Part 18.

2:1-3. Raum, Part 18. [Cracker Line]

3:1-4. James W. Coapman (Carlisle Barracks), "Capture and Escape." [captured 6/64 at Chambersburg]

3:5. John R. Tisdale (29th MO), "Vicksburg Campaign."

3:6. S. F. Hildebrand (139th PA), "Brothers in One Company."

5:3. Obit: A. P. Martin (3rd MA Bty), J. W. Hofmann (56th PA), Benjamin Brooke (124th, 203rd PA).

6:4. Asher S. Childers (11th KS Cav), "Hunting Mule-Footed Hogs."

7:1-4. Mosgrove, Part 5.

April 3

1:1-4, 6:4-6. Benson, Part 19.

1:5-7, 2:1-3. Raum, Part 19. [Sherman's march to Chattanooga]

2:4. W. W. Angel (5th IN Bty), "Stoneman's Surrender."

2:5. Biog: R. P. Scott (78th PA).

3:1-3. Coapman, Part 2.

3:3. S. F. Shaw (10th WV), "West Virginia Troops."

3:4-5. Picket Shots: George W. Miller (5th IN Cav), Morgan's capture; Wesley McAlister (7th IL Cav), Colliersville.

3:6-7. William E. Kennedy (34th IL), "Louisville to the Sea."

5:3. Biog: E. S. Otis (140th NY), Thomas Hinds (1st MD Cav), L. J. Cutter (77th OH).

5:3. Obit: Elisha B. Hamilton (118th IL).

6:6. Obit.

7:1-2. Mosgrove, Part 6.

7:3. "Grant and Lee at Appomattox. The Second Meeting." [from a paper by Gibbon in The Century]

7:6. "Lee's Refusal to Disperse." [E. P. Alexander in The Century]

April 10

1:1-4, 6:3-6. Benson, Part 20.

1:5-7, 2:1-2. Raum, Part 20. [Chattanooga]

3:1-4. Coapman, Part 3.

3:4. Thomas J. Harris (40th IL), "Capture of Big Shanty."

3:5-6. Picket Shots: John Reed, Kilpatrick's Raid; Charles W. Arrand (30th NY), Iron Brigade name; John hendricks (57th IL), Shiloh; M. J. Rupp (28th PA), General Polk's death; W. H. Barnes, City of Barnes.

5:5. Biog: David R. Hunt (25th OH).

5:6-7. Obit.

6:6. Obit.

7:6. Augustus C. Buell (Bty B, 4th US), "Opening the Battle." [Gettysburg]

April 17

1:1-4, 6:4-5. B. K. Benson, "A Friend with the Countersign. Story of a Spy in the Civil War."

2:1-4. Raum, Part 21. [Chattanooga]

3:1-3. W. A. Johnson (2nd SC), "Life in Fort Delaware."

3:4-6. Picket Shots: John M. Valleau (109th PA), Samuel W. Fraley (IN), John C. Lyon (1st IA Cav), youngest; S. L. Scofield (CT), Port Hudson; D. T. Peterson (10th WV), D. P. Hubbard (116th OH), David R. Bryan (54th PA), Fort Gregg; Abial W. Francis (28th IA), brothers in Company A; D. F. Fryer (80th OH), E. F. Keller (67th PA), Ambrose F. Craft (15th KS Cav), brothers.

6:2-3. Earl Edwards (3rd LA), "A Confederate Home. A Typical Institution Maintained by Maryland for Veterans Who Went South in 1861."

6:5. Obit.

7:1-5. James O. Churchill (11th IL), "Wounded at Fort Donelson."

7:5-6. H. C. King, "Fredericksburg National Park."

7:6. William C. Phipps (11th IN), "The Army Mule."

April 24

1:1-4, 6:5. Benson, Part 2.

2:1-5. Raum, Part 22. [Chattanooga]

3:1-3. Johnson, Part 2.

3:4. W. R. Carter (1st TN Cav), "Tullahoma Campaign."

3:4. Edwin R. Neal (10th IL Cav), "Death of Gen. Stein." [Prairie Grove]

3:5-7. Picket Shots: C. B. Barnes (7th WI), Iron Brigade name; W. B. Chandler (8th KY Cav), J. W. Isle (9th MO SM Cav), John Chestnut (38th IL), brothers; John Stockdale (67th OH), D. B. Henry (55th PA), Fort Gregg; Henry Harrington (18th IL), Shiloh; H. B. Prose (25th IL), death of General Polk.

5:1-4. James C. Sullivan (USS *Osage*), "Capturing a Smuggler. An Incident in the Gunboat Service on the Miss. River in 1863."

6:6. Obit.

7:1-2. A. B. Wilson, "Death of Morgan. Correction of Errors in Some Alleged Histories."

7:2-3. John Baker (9th NY Cav), "Opening the Battle of Gettysburg."

7:3. J. E. Walton (30th OH), "The Western Armies."

7:6-7. "John Wilkes Booth. Memories of Lincoln's Assassin Revived by the Interment of the Last of the Booth Family." [*Pittsburgh Gazette*]

May 1

1:1-4, 6:4-6. Benson, Part 3.

2:1-4. Raum, Part 23. [Chattanooga]

2:4-5. "How Gen. Meagher Came to His Death. Col. Sanders Tells the Story of the End of the Brilliant Irish-American."

2:5. Gilbert Thompson (US Eng Btn), "Who Can Complete the Story?" [Seven Days]

3:1-3. Johnson, Part 3.

3:4-5. R. C. Rice (125th OH), "Battle of Franklin. A Defense of the Conduct of Gen. Schofield."

3:5. "Monument to General Polk."

3:6-7. Picket Shots: H. Annis (96th IL), death of General Polk; Joseph F. Sollenberger (Bty F, 1st OH), George W. Buck (110th PA), Joseph Couch (62nd PA), brothers; N. H. Decke (8th NY Cav), Gettysburg; William F. White (11th WV), Fort Gregg.

4:7. Biog: Jacob H. Smith (2nd KY).

5:1. J. R. McBride (33rd IN), "Who Killed General Polk?"

5:1-4. Free S. Bowley (30th USCT), "The Little Chaplain." [77th NY]

5:6. Obit: Egbert L. Viele; Gustave Kaemmerling (9th OH).

6:6. Obit.

May 8

1:1-4, 6:4-6. Benson, Part 4.

2:1-5. Raum, Part 24. [Chattanooga]

2:6. Robert Tracy (1st KS), "Repeal of Ordinance of Secession. Georgia Legislature

Organized at Milledgeville by Sherman's Men and Its Interesting Session."

3:1-2. W. A. Johnson (2nd SC), "Closing Days with Johnston."

3:3. George W. Kennedy (Danville Art, CSA), "A Boy Soldier. Pathetic Incident of the Battlefield of Chancellorsville Told by an Ex-Confederate."

3:4-6. Picket Shots: Warren Blackburn (18th KY), youngest; Perrin B. Cole (96th IL), Lookout Mountain; O. Starkey (39th IL), Fort Gregg; E. P. Everitt (9th MI Cav), H. H. Collins (9th MI Cav), capture of General Morgan; E. D. Lloyd (55th OH), Chancellorsville; B. F. Gordon (36th IA), John M. Foulks (115th OH), Lot Abraham (4th IA Cav), Cyrus Criley (80th IL), J. V. Pownall (29th IN), brothers.

3:6-7. C. C. Haskell (16th VT), "Raiding a Sutler's Tent."

5:1-2. Augustus C. Buell (Bty B, 4th US), "Lone Cavalryman. Opening Shot of the Great Battle Fired by Alphonse Hodges at Heth's Advance."

6:6. Obit.

7:1-2. Moses S. Stuyvesant (USN), "Fate of the Cumberland."

7:2-3. Henry S. Wells (27th NY), "Chancellorsville."

8:5-7. "Saved William H. Seward's Life. Major George F. Robinson's Part in the Tragedy of April 9, 1865." [*Baltimore Sun*]

May 15

1:1-4, 6:6. Benson, Part 5.

2:1-3. Raum, Part 25. [post-Chattanooga]

3:1-3. Johnson, Part 2.

3:3. Daniel Vesper (Bty M, 1st OH), "Shultz's Ohio Battery."

3:4-5. Picket Shots: William H. Roberts (3rd OH Cav), Kilpatrick's Raid; James M. Baird (112th IL), death of General W. P. Sanders; P. H. Andrews (11th ME), G. K. Campbell (116th OH), Fort Gregg; J. C. Conkling (47th OH), running the Vicksburg batteries; W. L. Roney (8th MO SM Cav), W. S. Wood (78th IL), brothers.

3:6. George W. Kennedy (Rice's Bty CSA), "Defending Fort Gregg."

3:6. D. W. Kinne (6th WI), "The Iron Brigade."

4:1. Obit: W. T. Sampson (USN).

5:1-3. T. C. Harbaugh, "Battlefields of Virginia. Fredericksburg, Petersburg, Chancellorsville, and the Wilderness as They Appear To-day."

6:3. D. J. Vance (4th IA Cav), "Capture of Columbus."

6:5. Obit.

8:7. Augustus C. Buell (Bty B, 4th US), "The Opening of the Battle of Gettysburg."

May 22

1:1-4, 6:5. Benson, Part 6.

2:1-4. Raum, Part 26. [Chattanooga from CSA viewpoint]

2:5. S. H. Beckwith, "A Ransom Anecdote. Enlisting a Drummer Boy in the Old 11th Illinois."

3:1-2. Johnson, Part 3.

3:2-3. Joel C. Pector, "Captured by Wheeler." [5/24/64 near Cassville]

3:3. S. F. Shaw (10th WV), "Capture of Fort Gregg."

3:4-7. Picket Shots: H. T. Jones (25th IL), Stones River; Charles Horn (74th PA), Chancellorsville; W. H. H. Beckwith (89th NY), Fort Gregg; George A. Smith (7th OH Cav), Rogersville, 11/6/63; George W. Moore, MO militia; W. H. Raft (19th OH), Peter W. Anderson (86th IN), A. H. Rowe (102nd IL), brothers; W. G. Miller (11th WV), Petersburg; D. D. Holm (5th IN Bty), death of General Polk.

4:3. Biog: Edward S. Bragg.

4:7. Frank Rogers (9th VT), "Miles at Harper's Ferry."

6:2. George W. Norris (14th IL Cav), "Fighting for His Boots."

6:4. W. A. Johnson (2nd SC), "Life in Fort Delaware."

6:4. J. M. Witt (158th PA), "The Keystone Brigade. The Farewell Address of Gen. Spinola."

6:6. Obit.

7:1-4. John C. Parker, "A Night with Farragut." [Port Hudson, 3/14/63]

7:4. William Simmons, "The First Confederate Ram." [Manassas]

7:5. O. H. Ditzler (8th IL Cav), "The First Gun at Gettysburg."

May 29

1:1-4, 6:5. Benson, Part 7.

1:7. Biog: John T. Stauffer (100th IN).

2:1-4. Raum, Part 27. [post-Chattanooga]

3:1-3. Johnson, Part 4.

3:3. T. C. Murphy (31st IL), "Logan at Atlanta."

3:4-5. J. H. Van Eman (39th OH), "Battle of Iuka."

3:5. William E. Doyle (17th IN), "Fate of a Scout." [Culpeper 1862]

3:6. Picket Shots: S. A. McNeil (31st OH), Missionary Ridge; E. O. Fowler (20th OH Bty), Franklin; Peter H. Williams (34th OH), T. M. Robertson (6th IN Cav), brothers.

6:3. S. H. Beckwith (11th IL), "[T. E. G.] Ransom's Last Days. Visit to Gen. Grant at City Point, and His Death While Returning to Sherman's Army."

6:6. Obit.

7:1-3. Free S. Bowley (30th USCT), "A War-Time Breakfast."

June 5

1:1-4, 6:4-6. Benson, Part 8.

2:1-4. Raum, Part 28. [preparations for 1864]

3:1-3. Johnson, Part 5.

3:3-4. George H. Turner (9th MI Cav), "A Perilous Enterprise. The Reconnaissance of Cumberland Gap in the Face of the Enemy." [9/63]

3:4. W. W. Jones (42nd MO), "How News of Appomattox was Received in Tennessee."

3:4. G. W. Mattoon (6th MI Cav), "Opening of the Battle of Gettysburg."

3:5. C. D. McNeill (Fanning's GA Ss), "Death of Gen. McPherson."

3:6-7. Picket Shots: J. C. Weddle (1st KY Cav), Knoxville; J. W. Banks (6th MI), Port Hudson; E. M. Stakebake (69th IN); regimental flag; Almyer Neigh (51st PA), Ford's Theater relic.

5:6-7. Obit.

7:1-5. Asa B. Isham (7th MI Cav), "Through the Wilderness to Richmond."

June 12

1:1-4, 6:2-6. Benson, Part 9.

2:1-4. Raum, Part 29. [1864 start]

2:5. "Capture of Jeff Davis. A Joint Statement of Two Veterans Who were First in the Confederate Chieftain's Tent." [*Philadelphia Record*, concerning George Rinke and Casper Knobel]

3:1-3. Grenville M. Dodge, "Stories of Sherman."

3:3-4. William E. Chick (85th PA), "Capture of Fort Gregg."

3:4. W. D. Thompson (97th OH), "Battle of Franklin."

3:5. Augustus C. Buell (Bty B, 4th US), "The First Shot at Gettysburg."

3:5. J. W. Lacock (93rd IN), "Indiana Battle-Flags. Pathetic Incidents of the Farewell to the Old Regimental Colors."

3:5. A. A. Jones, "The 8th Tennessee at Atlanta."

3:6-7. Picket Shots: John D. Muir (21st OH), fathers-sons in service); John Curtis (78th IL), brothers; John W. Blume (66th IN), Lynch's Creek, SC, 2/65; Jacob Stambaugh (19th OH), Florence prison.

4:7. Biog: John C. Bates (11th US).

5:1-5. Eugene Powell (66th OH), "Shields in the Shenandoah."

7:6. Obit: Robert A. Brown (Chaplain, 100th PA).

June 19

1:1-4, 8:3-6. Benson, Part 10.

2:1-4. Raum, Part 30. [Rocky Face]

2:4. Joseph E. Parmelee (10th CT), "That Little Mix-Up at Fort Gregg."

2:4. Joel Wright (65th OH), "Operations Around Chattanooga."

2:7. R. M. Underwood, "With the 5th Indiana Cavalry. Operations Against Morgan, and Fighting Around Bristol, Tenn."

3:1-3. Joseph M. Beale (31st ME), "Home on Furlough."

3:3. William E. Doyle (17th IN), "Artillery at Mission Ridge. Effective Work of Howe's Battery, 4th U.S. Artillery."

3:3-4. William H. Handy (67th OH), "Fort Gregg."

3:4. J. W. A. Gillespie (78th OH), "Grant and Logan." [Belmont]

3:5-7. Picket Shots: W. P. Wolf (175th OH), Franklin; J. R. Worth (23rd MO), brothers; W. H. Hill (PA), Spotsylvania; J. O. Vanarsdel (4th IA Cav), capture of Columbus, GA; William H. Atkerson, spy executions at Pine Bluff, AR, William Hicks; H. T. Lucas (39th IL), Fort Gregg.

7:1-4. N. M. Baker (116th IL), "Besieging Vicksburg."

7:6. Charles Porter (11th VT), "Dunlap's Sharpshooters."

8:6. Obit.

9:1-5. Cornelius E. Hunt (CSS *Shenandoah*), "The Last Privateer."

9:6-7. William M. Davis (4th MN), "Battle of Iuka."

9:7. D. H. Wheaton (3rd NJ Cav), "The New Jersey Butterflies."

10:4-5. Loyd G. Harris (6th WI), "Army Music."

June 26

1:1-4, 8:2-6. Benson, Part 11.

2:1-4. Raum, Part 31.

3:1-5. Baker, Part 2.

3:5-6. "Candy's Brigade at Gettysburg. The First Union Troops to Occupy Little Round Top."

3:6-7. Picket Shots: W. H. Gilliard (11th MO), Iuka; H. A. Dudley (5th VT), brothers.

4:7. J. A. Brace (16th PA Cav), "The Last War Horse."

4:7. Biog: R. L. Boon (3rd IA Cav).

4:7. R. L. Boon (3rd IA Cav), "Brothers."

7:1-4. Richard N. Bowerman (4th MD), "Cutting Off Lee. Gallant Part Taken by the Maryland Brigade in the Terrific Fighting Along the Weldon Railroad." [8/64]

8:6. Obit.

9:1-5. Hunt, Part 2.

July 3

1:1-4, 6:4-6. Benson, Part 12.

1:5-7, 2:1-2. Raum, Part 32. [5/15-24/64]

3:1-5. B. F. Stevenson (22nd KY), "Cumberland Gap." [1862]

3:5-7. Picket Shots: William R. Keyser (17th CT), Elias Howe; E. H. Ditzler (8th IL Cav), Gettysburg; Samuel C. Burwell (122nd OH), captured 6/63; W. A. Douglas (47th OH), Chattanooga.

6:6. Obit.

7:1-4. Hunt, Part 3.

July 10

1:1-4, 6:5-6. Benson, Part 13.

2:1-5. Raum, Part 33. [New Hope Church snd Dallas]

3:1-2. A. B. Wilson, "Loyal East Tennesseans. Story of a 150-Mile March to Reach the Union Lines."

3:2-3. C. C. Reed (1st OH Art), "Death of McPherson."

3:3-4. Mrs. Minnie J. L. Smith, "A Yankee Lieutenant. Service Rendered a Confederate Family in La." [Lieut. John D. Hanning, 2nd RI Cav]

3:4. W. H. Barlow, "The 157th New York at Gettysburg."

3:5-7. Picket Shots: Asa W. Slayton (25th MI), grapeshot; sword of Lt. John Norris, 2nd PA HvY Art, captured at Crater; Joseph Scott (46th IN), brothers; R. I. Smith, Indian chiefs in DC in 1864.

6:3. John A. Brooks (8th PA Res), "Who was She?" [woman in uniform, 1863 picket duty]

6:3. Obit.

7:1-4. Hunt, Part 4.

July 17

1:1-4, 6:3-6. Benson, Part 14.

1:5-7, 2:1-3. Raum, Part 34.

3:1-5. William Day (2nd MA Bty), "Capture and Escape. Thrilling Adventures Inside the Confederate Lines at Salisbury. Drifting Down the Neuse River to Morehead City."

3:6. Picket Shots: Pomeroy Mitchell (16th OH Bty), brothers; D. Alverson (158th NY), W. H. H. Beckworth, David R. Bryan (54th PA), Fort Gregg

3:6-7. T. F. Stevens (122nd IL), "First Night on Picket."

4:7. George W. Kennedy (Danville Art, CSA), "Fort Gregg."

5:1-4. John C. Parker (USS *Anglo-American*), "A Daring Feat. Running the Port Hudson Batteries in a Frail, Defenseless Steamer."

7:1-4. Hunt, Part 5.

7:6. Obit.

July 24

1:1-4, 6:5. Benson, Part 15.

1:6-7. Biog: Charles Naylor (10th OH, 48th KY Mtd Inf), Josiah A. Brown (4th OH Cav), George W. Karns (133rd PA, 5th PA Hvy Art).

2:1-3. Raum, Part 35. [Guntown]

3:1-3. J. R. McBride (33rd IN), "Confederate Spies at Franklin."

3:3-4. N. M. Baker (116th IL), "Wounding of Gen. Giles A. Smith." [Chattanooga]

3:4-5. C. D. Rathbone (24th OH), "Three Years at the Front. Sketch of the Services of the 24th Ohio."

3:5. Gilbert Thompson (US Eng Btn), "A Friend with the Countersign. The Sequel to the Order Carried to Gen. Smith by Berwick." [5/28/64]

3:6-7. Picket Shots: A. J. Walling (48th NY), losses; B. Vandyke (14th IA), prison escape; Charles B. Palmer (1st WI Hvy Art), grapeshot; H. D. Beard (175th OH), Franklin; W. W. French (115th NY), Miles at Harper's Ferry.

4:3. Biog: Thomas J. Morgan (14th US), William A. McKellip (6th MD).

5:1-5. George A. Thayer (2nd MA), "On the Right at Gettysburg."

6:1. "Slocum Monument Dedication. Ceremonies to be Held at Gettysburg, September 19 and 20."

6:6. Obit.

7:1-7. Hunt, Part 6.

July 31

1:1-4, 6:3-6. Benson, Part 16.

2:1-3. Raum, Part 36. [Kennesaw]

3:1-3. R. W. Burt (76th OH), "Letters from the Trenches." [Vicksburg]

3:3-4. William Simmons, "Facing a New Orleans Mob. Reminiscences of the Raising of Old Glory Over the Custom House."

3:4. John L. Beveridge (8th IL Cav), "First Shot at Gettysburg."

3:4-5. John W. Burnett (4th PA Res), "Charles City Crossroads."

3:5. W. P. Kremer (NY), "New Hope Church."

3:6-7. Picket Shots: O. D. Johnson (15th IN Bty), Harper's Ferry; J. L. Wilson 32nd IA), Lynch's Creek; John C. West (USN), youngest; George O. Bridges (11th KS Cav), brothers.

6:6. Obit.

7:1-4. Hunt, Part 7.

8:6. Biog: Henry Stegkamper (37th OH).

August 7

1:1-4, 3:5. Benson, Part 17.

2:1-4. Raum, Part 37. [Morgan's Raid]

3:1-2. W. G. Bartholomew (27th MA), "Battling Against Heavy Odds." [Drewry's Bluff]

3:3-4. George M. Harrison (Landis'MO Bty, CSA), "A Truce at Vicksburg."

3:4-5. G. D. Harvey (8th WI), "'Old Abe'."

3:5-6. John A. Brooks (8th PA Res), "Inside the Confederate Lines. Perilous Picket Duty Performed by the Pa. Reserves at Gaines' Mill."

3:6-7. Picket Shots: J. T. Wiesmen (1st IL Lt Art), death of General McPherson; Daniel Sims (PA BtY E), death of General Polk; George S. Myers (101st OH), Jonesboro.

4:7. Obit: William H. Barnes (7th, 76th NY).

6:6. Obit.

7:1-6. Hunt, Part 8.

7:6. "Where Gen. William H. T. Walker Fell." [monument]

8:6-7. Biog: D. F. St. John (79th OH), W. J. Wambaugh (signal corps), A. S. Fair (27th MI), John T. Iden (7th IL), L. M. Sear (49th KY), D. L. Wise (1st MO Eng), John H. Williams (44th MO).

August 14

1:1-4, 6:5-6. Benson, Part 18.

2:1-3. Raum, Part 38. [Kennesaw]

3:1-5. R. K. Beecham (2nd WI), "Adventures of an Iron Brigade Man."

3:5. L. B. March (41st IL), "Hunting Torpedoes Near Savannah."

3:6-7. Picket Shots: Cyrus A. B. Fox (86th IL), Chattanooga; Stephen Tripp (11th PA Cav), Charles City Crossroads.

6:1-3. George D. Mosgrove (4th KY Cav CSA), "Longstreet at Chickamauga."

6:3. Obit.

8:5-7. Biog: Loa H. Collins (19th, 32nd ME), E. B. Helwig (51st OH), M. D. Watson (57th PA), Jacob Ferree (44th OH, 100th PA), Ziba M. Lane (195th OH).

August 21

1:1-4, 6:4-5. Benson, Part 19.

2:1-5. Raum, Part 39. [Kennesaw]

3:1-4. Beecham, Part 2.

3:4. "Ohioans at Antietam. Monument to McKinley and Markers to be Erected on the Battlefield."

3:5-6. Will A. McTeer (3rd TN Cav), "Ellejoy Knobs. Recollections of War Days in a Loyal Section of Tennessee." [Blount County]

3:6-7. F. S. White (146th NY), "White Oak Road."

5:6. "Queer Wounds. Remarkable Cases Recorded in the Army Medical Museum."

6:6. Obit.

8:5-6. Biog: John C. Hull (22nd NJ).

August 28

1:1-4, 6:3-6. Benson, Part 20.

2:1-4. Raum, Part 40.

2:5. "Justice Holmes as a Soldier. His Distinguished Father's Search for Him When Lying Wounded." [Antietam, 20th MA]

3:1-4. Beecham, Part 3. [Mud March]

3:5-6. J. G. Sonderman (1st MN), "Charles City Crossroads."

3:6-7. Picket Shots:

7:7. Obit.

8:6. Biog: Barney Carey (20th OH Bty).

September 4

2:1-4. Raum, Part 41.

2:4-5. Daniel Trine (145th PA), "Battle of Five Forks."

2:5. George S. Myers (101st OH), "Occupying Franklin."

2:6. Lindsay Steele (30th IL), "Gen. Logan at Belmont."

3:1-5. Beecham, Part 4. [winter-spring 1863]

3:6-7. Picket Shots: W. J. Frazier (78th OH), Corinth, 5/62; J. B. Schneider (2nd MO), Rebel spy at Dalton, GA.

6:1-2. W. W. Allen (Signal Officer, Army of the Tennessee), "Death of Gen. McPherson."

September 11

2:1-6. Raum, Part 42.

3:1-6. Beecham, Part 5. [Gettysburg Campaign]

3:7. "Winning a Medal of Honor." [David L. Smith, Bty M, 1st NY, for 4/6/62]

8:5. Biog: F. M. Cline (73rd, 174th, 181st OH, 4th OH Cav).

September 18

1:5-7, 2:1-4. Raum, Part 43. [7/21/64]

2:5. "Last Shot of the Rebellion. A Texan Claims to Have Fired It." [*Washington Post*, 5/13/65 claim by S. H. Barton]

3:1-5. Beecham, Part 6. [Gettysburg]

3:5. Charles Van Gorder (39th IA), "Snake Creek Gap."

3:5. H. C. Green (87th IN), "Sherman's Bummers."

3:6. Alexander Calhoun (84th IL), "The Charge at Kennesaw."

3:6. Henry Sheward (65th NY), "A Corn-Husking Match."

6:1-3. George Redway (103rd OH), "A Bloodless Victory." [Chattahoochie crossing]

6:6. Obit.

7:1-2. George D. Mosgrove (4th KY Cav), "Fort Donelson."

September 25

2:1-4. Raum, Part 44. [Atlanta]

2:6. Obit.

3:1-3. Beecham, Part 7. [Gettysburg]

3:3. J. D. Young (120th IL), "An Andersonville Prisoner."

3:4-5. J. W. A. Gillespie (78th OH), "A Letter from the Field. A Lieutenant's Observations at Fort Donelson and Dover."

3:5. Allen L. Fehnestock (86th IL), "Volunteers from McCook's Corps." [crossing of the Tennessee]

3:5. Redway, Part 2.

3:6-7. Picket Shots: G. W. Huddleston (Bty H, 2nd IL), brothers; John T. Wilson (42nd IN), youngest.

8:5-7. S. B. Evans, "Averill's Ride. 300 Miles Through the Enemy's Country to Warn Emory." [spring 1861]

October 2

3:1-5. Beecham, Part 8. [Gettysburg]

3:5. John A. Brooks (8th PA Res), "My First Sight of Richmond."

3:6-7. Lewis C. Killian (25th MI), "Death of Gen. Polk."

6:1-6. T. T. Munhall (11th IL), "Last Flag of Truce." [surrender of Gen. Newsom, 5/65]

6:6. Obit.

7:1-2. Raum, Part 45. [Rosseau's raid]

October 9

2:6. Biog: J. H. Edgerly (3rd NH), Leonard Dolph (118th NY), James B. Burbank (20th CT).

3:1-5. Beecham, Part 9. [Gettysburg]

3:5. W. L. Beckwith (140th NY), "White Oak Road."

3:5. E. L. Foster (11th VT), "Family Members in One Company."

3:6-7. "Dedication of Marker. First Brigade, Second Division, Twelfth Corps, Holds Exercises on the Battlefield of Gettysburg."

6:1-3. Raum, Part 46. [Stoneman's raid]

6:3. "The 28th N.Y. Monument at Cedar Mountain."

6:6. Obit.

October 16

1:1-4. H. Clay Trumbull (10th CT), "War Memories of a Chaplain."

3:1-5. Beecham, Part 10.

3:5. Picket Shots: I. Brinkworth (38th IN), brothers.

3:6. James E. Northrup (89th NY), "Fort Gregg."

4:3. Obit: James E. Jouett (USN).

9:1-3. Raum, Part 47. [Ezra Church]

10:5-7. Biog: W. F. Bright (12th, 124th IN), C. H. Mattingly (3rd KY Cav), H. L. Howard (49th KY), R. A. Martin (7th WV), Squire Toney (33rd WI).

October 23

1:1-4, 6:5. Trumbull, Part 2.

2:4. D. L. Wellman, "The 4th Minnesota. Led Sherman's Army in the Grand Review of 1865."

2:7. Obit.

3:1-4. Beecham, Part 11.

3:4. Augustus C. Buell (Bty B, 4th US), "The Assault on Cemetery Hill."

3:5-7. W. W. Jacobs, "Campaigning with Buell." [KY 1862]

4:7. Obit: Thomas O. Selfridge (USN).

5:6-7. Biog: David L. Way (79th, 127th OH, 5th USCT), David E. Godfrey (5th CT), Wilbur F. Dickerson (8th MI).

7:1-3. Raum, Part 48.

8:5-7. Biog: A. T. Somerby (6th ME), H. P. Cross (19th US, 2nd MD), A. L. O. Johnston (21st WI), Alfred Mosher (16th IL), S. L. Shaw (1st MI Ss), William H. Hartley (11th IN, 7th IN Bty), Isaac Massie (91st OH), Philip Sutton (17th IL Cav), Henry Darnall (2nd IL Cav).

October 30

1:1-4, 6:3-4. Trumbull, Part 3.

3:1-4. Beecham, Part 12.

3:4. T. E. Mathews (112th IL), "Capt. Carter of Gen. Cox's Staff." [retreat from Franklin]

3:5. Picket Shots: F. S. White (146th NY), White Oak Road; R. J. Buttolph (2nd IA Bty), brothers.

3:5-6. "Boy Soldier of the 34th Ohio." [John W. Packham]

3:6-7. David C. Eberhart (87th PA), "Chaplains Held as Prisoners."

4:7. Obit.

5:6-7. T. G. Day (1st IN Cav), "First Shot at Gettysburg."

7:1-3. Raum, Part 49. [Wheeler's raid]

8:5-7. Biog: W. R. Bartlett (13th NY Hvy Art), Julius W. Higley (123rd NY, 109th USCT), G. P. Wood (29th WI), F. C. Seitz (13th NY), William T. Brewer (49th IL).

November 6

1:1-4, 2:5-6. Trumbull, Part 4.

3:1-3. Beecham, Part 13.

3:4. William A. Gordon (30th IA), "Death of Gen. McPherson."

3:5. Kate M. Scott (105th PA), "Many Brothers in this Regiment."

3:5. William M. Patrick (37th IL), "Sharpshooting at Vicksburg."

6:1-3. Raum, Part 50. [Wheeler's raid]

6:5. Biog: William H. Olin (36th MA), J. Henry Holcomb (3rd PA Hvy Art, 188th PA).

8:5-7. Biog: John Ruch (19th OH), B. H. Huber (7th PA Cav), B. F. Adams (35th MA), Charles C. Stone (38th, 105th OH), C. E. Garlinger (110th OH), B. F. Longwell (145th OH).

November 13

1:1-4, 2:5-6. Trumbull, Part 5.

2:4. "The Maryland Monument. A Testimonial at Chattanooga to the Blue and Gray."

3:1-5. Beecham, Part 14. [23rd USCT]

3:5. Julian C. Manchester (1st CT Hvy Art), "The 'Petersburg Express.' The Real History of that Celebrated Gun."

8:1-5. Raum, Part 51. [Wheeler's raid]

8:5-6. Obit.

9:5-7. Biog: A. D. Gilbert (44th IN), J. T. Starr (42nd IL).

November 20

1:1-4. Trumbull, Part 6.

2:1-6. Raum, Part 52. [Macon Railroad operations]

3:1-5. Beecham, Part 15. [Crater]

3:6. Picket Shots: Ira Keplinger (12th IN), Grand Review; James Thompson (4th NY Hvy Art), youngest.

7:4. Obit: Andrew Davidson (121st NY, 13th USCT).

7:4. Biog: Benjamin C. Thorp (55th NC).

7:4. "The Ill-Fated City Belle." [Red River, 5/3/64]

8:6. Obit.

9:1-2. Thomas B. Rodgers (140th PA), "Paroles at Gettysburg."

November 27

1:1-4, 2:6. Trumbull, Part 7.

2:1-3. Raum, Part 53.

3:1-5. Beecham, Part 16. [Crater]

3:5. T. G. Day (3rd IN Cav), "His Name was There."

3:5. S. A. McNeil (31st OH), "A Pathetic Incident of the Atlanta Campaign." [8/12/64]

3:6. Picket Shots: E. H. Dodge (47th OH), youngest; William C. Hansell (51st PA), Petersburg Express.

4:7. Biog: Henry H. Preston (6th NY Cav).

6:6. Obit.

December 4

1:1-4, 10:1-6. B. K. Benson, "Bayard's Courier. A Story of Love and Adventure in the Cavalry Campaigns."

2:1-3. Raum, Part 54.

2:7. Obit.

3:1-4. Beecham, Part 17.

3:5-6. John C. Ladd (21st CT), "True 'Petersburg Express.' Parrott 32-pounders that Threw Iron Messages Into the Besieged City."

3:7. I. Peters (16th KY), "The Retreat to Franklin."

7:5-7. Biog: H. Jaques (2nd PA Hvy Art), William F. Haney (Bty E, 1st WV), P. J. McCullon (4th IA Cav).

11:1-5. Trumbull, Part 8.

December 11

1:1-4, 9:4. Benson, Part 2.

2:1-3. Raum, Part 55.

3:1-3. Beecham, Part 18.

3:4-7. Picket Shots: Lewis T. Stover (63rd IN), Spring Hill; W. E. Stevens (8th MO), G. A. Smith at Missionary Ridge; Jacob Rieder (18th

MO), death of General McPherson; D (6th KY Cav), brothers; Fillmore M. Brist (1st WI Cav), youngest.

5:1-5. John F. Marsh (6th WI), "Making Soldiers."

5:6-7. "Vicksburg National Park. Gen. William H. Raynor [56th OH] Tells of a Recent Visit to It."

9:1-2. Trumbull, Part 9.

December 18

1:1-4, 9:4. Benson, Part 3.

2:1-5. Raum, Part 56.

3:1-5. Beecham, Part 19.

3:5. E. H. Colcord, "The Western Army. An 11th Illinois Man Gives His Recollections of the Battle of August 6, 1864."

3:5. Brooks D. Stewart (11th ME), "The Petersburg Express."

3:6-7. Picket Shots: Roberts brothers (Samuel A., 52nd PA; William and Edward, 45th PA); J. C. Fulton (101st IN), Fayetteville, NC.

5:1-6. Trumbull, Part 10.

5:6-7. Frederick W. Fout (15th IN Bty), "Harper's Ferry."

December 25

1:1-4, 5:4-7. Benson, Part 4.

2:1-5. Raum, Part 57.

2:5. "Fredericksburg National Park. The Veterans of the Army of the Potomac Anxious for Something to be Done."

3:1-3. Henry A. Castle (73rd IL), "The Inferno in the Cedars." [Stones River]

3:3. EMW (21st IL), "With Grant in Missouri."

3:3. P. C. Smith (119th IL), "Record of an Illinois Company." [brothers]

3:4. Walter F. Sage (1st CT Hvy Art), "Before Petersburg. An Account of the Operations of the Artillery Contingent, by an Officer of the Siege Train."

3:4-5. J. F. Richards [129th IN], "What Company was It?" [Spring Hill-Franklin]

3:5. Walter F. Sage (1st CT Hvy Art), "The Siege Train at Petersburg."

3:5. "The 77th Illinois at Vicksburg." [monument site]

5:1-3. Trumbull, Part 11.

9:2. Obit.

1903

January 1

1:1-5, 2:6-7. Benson, Part 5.

1:6-7, 7:1-3. Trumbull, Part 12.

2:1-5. Raum, Part 58. [surrender of Atlanta]

2:5. Chester G. Higbee (12th WI), "Saving Logan's Right." [Ezra Church]

2:5. N. W. Elmendorf (191st PA), "An Ex-Prisoner of War." [Salisbury]

3:1-4. J. A. Bering (48th OH), "Uncle Tom's Cabin. Fierce Battle on Legree's Plantation in La." [Cane River Crossing]

3:4. George S. Van Meter (7th WV), "The Petersburg Express."

3:5-7. Robert Welch (165th NY), "Port Hudson."

4:4. Biog: F. V. Greene (60th NY).

4:4. Obit.

8:5-6. George D. Mosgrove (4th KY Cav), "A Brilliant Editor. George D. Prentice, Wit, Politician, Journalist, and Staunch Patriot." [Louisville Journal editor]

January 8

1:1-5. Benson, Part 6.

1:6-7, 2:4-6. Trumbull, Part 13.

2:1-2. Raum, Part 59.

2:3. L. H. Vokes (3rd US Cav), "The Fight in the Crater. Will Capt. Beecham or Lt. Bowley Explain?"

3:1-2. E. P. Alexander, "The First Signal Message." [Manassas]

3:5. William L. Riley (21st NY Cav), "Asylum Pen. Recollections of Gloomy Days in Southern Prisons."

3:5. D. C. Hagadorn, "On the Field of Gettysburg." [Willard]

3:6-7. Picket Shots: C. L. Maranville (2nd VT), youngest; David R. Bryan (54th PA), brothers; John Coffman (63rd IN), Franklin; Chandler family from IL.

3:7. A. I. Ellis (54th PA), "The First Colors on Fort Gregg."

3:7. O. F. Sweet (Bty F, 1st PA), "The Petersburg Express."

4:3. Obit: Eli Long (4th OH Cav).

4:7. Obit: J. L. Abernathy (8th KS), Mart Schuler (7th OH Cav).

8:6. Obit.

January 15

1:1-5, 2:5-7. Benson, Part 7.

1:6-7, 2:1-4. Raum, Part 60. [Tupelo]

3:1-5. Trumbull, Part 14.

3:5. J. B. Ferguson (206th PA), "Dealing with Bounty-Jumpers and Deserters."

3:5. W. T. Bass (Boyce's SC Bty), "A Confederate's Story." [post-Knoxville]

3:6. Charles Porter (11th VT), "Gilbert's Ford." [9/13/64]

3:6. M. A. Cleveland (7th MA Bty), "Banks's Red River Campaign."

3:7. Picket Shots: Browne family, Oswego, NY; Henry B. Allen (23rd IN), Fayetteville, NC.

7:4-5. George D. Mosgrove (4th KY Cav), "Two Mighty Armies Racing. Nashville or Louisville was Their Goal—Generals Buell and Bragg Maneuver Across the States of Tennessee and Kentucky."

8:6. Obit.

January 22

1:1-5, 2:6. Benson, Part 8.

2:1-4. Raum, Part 61. [Hood Moves North]

2:5. Obit.

3:1-6. Trumbull, Part 15.

3:6. J. B. Cole (1st MO Eng), "Marched with the Head of Sherman's Army."

3:7. James E. Catlin (45th PA), "Battle of the Crater."

6:2. William Bennett, "Co. E, 54th Penna. Reports." [brothers]

6:3-7. R. H. G. Minty (4th MI Cav), "Raiding Hood's Rear. Minty's Division in the Rush on Jonesboro."

7:6. Thomas W. Scott, "Jeff Davis's Pistols. Three Weapons Captured with the President, and What Became of Them."

8:5-7. Biog: James McDermott (4th KY), P. E. Weller (14th US), W. H. Newlin (73rd IL), Robert McKistry (70th NY), George E. McEndree (5th VA).

January 29

1:1-5, 2:6-7. Benson, Part 9.

3:1-3. Trumbull, Part 16.

3:4. John H. Kirby (123rd IN), "An Unsuccessful Charge." [8/6/64]

3:4. William Taylor (84th PA), "Youngest Veteran of the Civil War." [*Philadelphia Record*, regarding Daniel Williams of the 24th NJ, 23rd PA)]

3:5. William Ludgate (14th CT), "Horrors of Belle Isle."

3:6-7. Picket Shots: J. W. Demunbrum (13th KY), brothers.

6:4-6. Raum, Part 62.

8:1-7. Biog: G. W. Keckler (1st, 16th IA), J. C. Griggs (77th OH), L. B. March (41st IL), William Ripley (164th OH), C. H. Turner (Knapp's Bty PA Art, 1863 militia), George McAdams (99th OH), David Casey (22nd OH), R. D. McCarter (4th OH), R. A. Young (106th IL), Henry W. Webb (Bty D, 1st NY), J. B. Wilhelm (15th MI), H. B. Allen (16th CT, 23rd IN), J. Whister (39th IN, 8th IN Cav), Dennis W.

Vanwie (76th NY), E. C. Walten (54th IL), D. W. Thomas (96th OH).

10:6. Obit.

February 5

1:1-5, 2:7. Benson, Part 10.

2:1-6. Raum, Part 63. [post-Atlanta]

2:6. Silas Owen (USN), "Saw Booth After Death. Capt. Owen Ridicules the Story of the Oklahoma Suicide."

2:6. B. A. Dunn (9th IN), "Losses in the Atlanta Campaign."

3:1-4. George D. Mosgrove (4th KY Cav), "The Battle of Perryville."

3:4. Samuel R. W. Snyder (199th PA), "The Assault on Fort Gregg."

3:4. Henry Dormeyer (1st MO Art), "Missouri Light Artillery." [commenting on Phisterer]

3:5. D. L. Wellman (4th MN), "First to Enter Vicksburg."

3:6. P. C. Smith (119th IL), "Saved the Regimental Colors. Gallantry Before Atlanta Won a Medal of Honor." [Capt John Orr, 78th OH]

3:6. J. H. Barney (3rd MD PHB), "The Surrender of Harper's Ferry."

3:6. Charles H. Hughes (20th IN Bty), "The Hughes Family in the War."

3:7. Picket Shots: Thomas M. Shields (6th IL Cav), Spring Hill; I. B. Christ (138th PA), David Rose (16th PA Cav, 47th PA), youngest.

8:3-7. Biog: E. H. Burnham (39th MA), C. T. Blumenrather (6th, 68th NY), J. Ray (41st IL), A. P. Doolittle (55th IL), W. A. Street (NY), Christian Borner (193rd, 97th PA), R. Montgomery (51st IN), H. Kinney (1st IA Cav, USN), [William H.] Kiester (103rd PA), John Wagner (16th MI), E. C. Scarlett (1st NE), John Cope (98th OH).

9:1-5. Trumbull, Part 17.

9:6. Obit.

February 12

1:1-5, 2:5-6. Benson, Part 11.

2:1-4. Raum, Part 64.

2:6-7. J. N. Waddell (12th WV), "Hunter's Lynchburg Raid."

3:1-7. Trumbull, Part 18.

3:7. Picket Shots: Manson Wolfe (1st TN Cav), Franklin; H. F. W. Little (7th NH), 7/18/63; John M. Kline (142nd OH), brothers.

8:1-3. Biog: John Beacher (3rd PA Hvy Art), A. Farnsworth (11th OH), James kenrick (138th IN), Hiram Roop (1st MI Cav), Samuel Sheppard (52nd IN), Daniel Hoover (9th PA Cav), Benjamin D. Prichard (4th MI Cav), John T. Booth (18th, 36th OH).

8:4. Obit.

9:1-5. William J. Dewes, "The Bushwhacker's Daughter. A Story of the Civil War in Virginia."

9:5. George Petry (123rd IL), "In the Streets of Selma. Surrender of a Confederate Battalion to Two Dismounted Cavalrymen."

9:6. Obit.

February 19

1:1-5, 2:6-7. Benson, Part 12.

2:1-5. Raum, Part 65.

2:5. "Lee Monument at Gettysburg. Vigorous Opposition from the Allegheny County Grand Army Association."

3:1-3. Trumbull, Part 19.

3:4-5. J. Balsley (27th IN), "Famous Western Regiment."

3:5. L. D. Immel (Bty F, 2nd US), "With Lyon in Missouri. Capture of Camp Jackson and the Battle of Wilson's Creek."

3:5-6. "Echoes Re-Echoed. Humerous [sic] Incidents Related by Soldiers of the Civil War." [J. L. Kinney (USCT) about Mobile, John B. Scott (WI), Harry Wilbur, Pea Ridge]

6:7. Obit.

8:4-5. Biog: A. H. Miller (39th OH), O. N. McCurdy (30th IN), William A. Limbooker (11th KS), A. A. Tewkesbury (3rd MI), C. J. Lind (6th WI), E. C. Hollis (2nd OH), David Baldridge (211th PA).

9:1-3. Dewes, Part 2.

9:4. John W. Hartley (8th KS), "The Great War. Was It a Rebellion, or was It a 'War Between the States'?"

9:5. Obit.

February 26

1:1-5, 2:7. Benson, Part 13.

2:1-4. Raum, Part 66.

2:5. H. C. Saint-Pierre (7tth NY), "Appearance of the Devil., A Startling Apparition to Frighten the Andersonville Guards."

2:5-6. E. B. Houghton, "'Scrap' on the James in 1864. Michigander Maintains His Rights to Forage. Fist Fight with a Johnny." [*McKee's Rocks Gazette* (PA), Jun 1864]

3:1-7. Trumbull, Part 20.

3:7. Calvin Shaffer (15th NY Hvy Art), "Petersburg Express."

3:7. S. B. Dearborn (1st MA Hvy Art), "Reverend Leverett Bradley." [obit]

8:4-5. Biog: W. J. Norman (100th NY), William W. Henderson (28th NJ), L. C. Campbell (65th IL), George W. Scott (10th PA Res), Eustis Mellen (4th NY), C. D. Jones (4th, 66th OH), Joseph Wham (21st IL).

9:1-3. Wilhelmus B. Bryan, "Washington in War Time. The National Capital During the Great Struggle. Just Before the War."

9:3. J. H. Storey, "Last Fight of the War." [*New York Sun*, Palmetto Ranch]

9:4-5. Picket Shots: John Weisheimer (13th IN Bty), death of General Polk.

9:6. T. E. Camburn (9th MI Cav), L. B. Marsh (41st IL), "Marching Through North Carolina."

March 5

1:1-5. Benson, Part 14.

1:4-5, 9:4-6. Raum, Part 67. [Resaca]

3:1-2. John R. King (6th MD), "Border Loyalists."

3:3. Thomas M. Skaggs (2nd IA Cav), "General Sooy Smith's Raid." [Tupelo]

3:4-5. Wilbur F. Crummer (45th IL), "Entering Vicksburg."

3:5-6. J. E. Harding (12th WV), "Hunter's Raid."

3:6. C. A. Brasher (17th KY), "Destruction of the Montgomery Railroad."

3:6. F. A. Barrett (1st IA Cav), "Totten's Battery." [Wilson's Creek]

4:2. Obit: William F. Smith.

8:1-2. Biog: J. D. Maurer (94th OH), Samuel Gilson (121st PA), H. B. Stanhope (11th ME), T. C. Patterson (79th OH).

9:1-3. Bryan, Part 2.

10:1-6. Henry A. Castle (73rd IL), "A Perilous Trip Remembered. Col. [James F.] Jacques's [73rd IL] Mission to Jeff Davis—An Important Episode of the Civil War."

March 12

1:1-4, 9:6-7. Benson, Part 15.

3:1-6. Marrius Buchanan (118th IN), "The Persimmon Brigade. An Account of Service from the Diary of an Officer."

3:7. A. A. Seaverns (7th MA), "Bottom's Bridge. The 7th Mass. Claims the Honor of First Crossing."

3:7. J. B. Shumate (45th IL), "Entering Vicksburg."

3:7. Thomas Manuel, "Starving Prisoners at Camp Lamb." [Wilmington, NC]

4:7. Obit: William B. Franklin.

6:5-7. Raum, Part 68.

7:6. Obit: Frank D. Wicker (28th NY), Charles C. Doolittle (18th MI).

8:1-2. Biog: Ezekiel Cast (2nd OH Hvy Art), John Haussauer (27th NY Bty), W. F. Layton (14th N?), M. P. Phillips (73rd OH, 4th OH Cav), J. S. Miller (3rd IA Cav).

9:1-6. John G. Barnard, "Washington in War Time. The Defenses of Washington."

10:6. Obit.

March 19

2:1-3. Raum, Part 69.

2:3. J. D. Graham (50th IL), "Lieut.-Col. [William] Hanna at Allatoona."

2:6. Richard Wainwright, "The Bluejackets. The Part Taken by the Naval Forces in the Defense of Washington During the Civil War."

2:7. Obit.

3:5. John W. Waite (6th IA), "After Atlanta's Surrender. Sending Citizens Through Confederate Lines and the Exchange of Prisoners."

3:5. William E. Doyle (17th IN), "Battle of Perryville."

3:6-7. Picket Shots: J. G. Sonderman (1st MN), 1st Manassas; J. W. Hendrick (13th TN Cav), brothers; Lewis Butler (67th OH), death of Col. Putnam; A. A. Jones (8th TN), 8/6/64; T. E. Camburn (9th MI Cav), Fayetteville, NC; Philip Z. Hart, John Brown's pikes; E. C. Martin (6th KY Cav), Resaca, 10/64.

8:1-4. Biog: Daniel K. Knauss (176th PA), B. L. Griffith (37th IL), C. W. Armstrong (43rd OH), Garrett Albertson (89th IL), S. H. Beach (3rd WI).

9:1-5. Thomas M. Vincent, "Washington in War Time. Early's March to Washington."

March 26

2:1-4. Raum, Part 70.

3:1-5. David M. Strain (15th IA), "Afield with Crocker's Brigade." [Shiloh, Corinth]

3:5. Theodore F. Allen (7th OH Cav), "Valley Forge of the Civil War. East Tennessee Campaign of the Winter of 1863-'64."

3:6-7. Picket Shots: William W. Gillespie (63rd IL), youngest; W. A. Faulk (59th IN), first in Vicksburg; A. P. Carr (34th IN), Pine Mountain.

3:7. F. A. Parrott (2nd IA Cav), "Battle of Farmington."

4:3. Obit: Schuyler Hamilton.

6:7. "Lincoln's Last Official Act. He Pardoned a Young Man Who had been Condemned to Death as a Confederate Spy."

6:7. W. H. Rosser (52nd PA), "Bottom's Bridge."

7:5-6. Biog: Henry S. Cohn (5th WV, 106th OH), Robert S. Foster, Albert N. Burns (10th, 44th WI), J. M. Fisher (93rd IL), W. S. B. Randall (2nd OH).

7:6-7. Frederick S. White (146th NY), "Battle of Five Forks."

8:1-2. Biog: J. R. Deardorff (121st OH), J. F. Ross (1st MI Cav), S. H. Dean (134th IN), Jacob Ferree (44th OH, 100th PA), T. H. Kitterman (144th IN), W. H. H. Beckwith (89th NY), Charles Buchner (103rd NY).

9:1-4. William V. Cox, "Washington in War Time. The President in Battle."

9:7. E. J. Orr (6th WI Bty), "Re-Enforcing Allatoona."

10:5. Obit.

April 2

1:5-7, 2:1-4. Raum, Part 71. [March to the Sea starts]

2:4. J. W. A. Gillespie (78th OH), "Death of Gen. Polk."

2:6. James H. Wiswell (4th US Cav), "Totten's Battery." [Wilson's Creek]

2:6. H. C. Holter (45th PA), "The Battle of the Crater."

2:7. E. B. Reese (59th IN), "Forty Years After." [first in Vicksburg]

2:7. B. Fernow (4th MO Cav), "The 2nd N.J. Did Not Stampede." [Tupelo]

3:1-5. Strain, Part 2.

3:5. John R. Robertson (9th NY Cav), "Opening the Battle. How I Saw the First Shot Fired at Gettysburg."

3:5. J. O. Vanarsdal (4th IA Cav), "Battle of Tupelo."

3:6-7. Picket Shots: E. Codling (26th IA), first in Vicksburg; J. D. Fulton (97th OH), brothers.

3:7. George W. Healey (5th IA Cav), "Guarding Jeff Davis. A Contemporaneous Account in Letter Written by Comrade Healey."

8:1-2. Biog: John H. Stuntz (10th PA Res), J. S. Henniger (1st PA Cav), John Lowell (13th ME), Charles O. Wadsworth (16th ME).

9:1-3. Thomas M. Vincent, "Washington in War Time. The Death of President Lincoln."

10:1-2. John A. Spring, "The Dying Cavalryman. A Reminiscence of President Lincoln—Receipt of News of Assassins at City Point."

10:6. Obit.

April 9

2:1-5. Raum, Part 72.

2:6. D. Eldridge (3rd NH), "Gen. Foster at Bermuda Hundred." [6/16/64]

3:1-4. R. H. Martin (46th IN), "Sabine Crossroads."

3:4. C. D. McNeil (Fanning's Btn, GA Ss), "Recovery of McPherson's Body."

3:5. B. R. Barr (74th OH), "Organizing the 12th U.S.C.T."

3:5. JHS (17th OH Bty), "Thirteenth Corps in the Vicksburg Campaign."

3:5-6. George W. Bowers (129th OH), "The Persimmon Brigade."

3:6. T. G. Day (3rd IN Cav), "Barbee's Crossroads."

3:6. Harvey O. Williams (12th IN), "The Prisoner Exchange at Rough and Ready."

3:7. S. C. Evans (1st NY Bty), "Short-Term Men."

3:7. Pius J. Clark (114th OH), "The Mobile Explosion."

4:7. Picket Shots: E. M. DePuy (28th WI), Mobile explosion; M. D. Sanford (95th IL), first in Vicksburg; S. L. Bibbins (22nd WI), Fayetteville, NC; J. R. Rowley (96th OH), brothers.

7:3. Obit.

9:1-3. Brainard H. Warner, "Washington in War Time. Washington a Southern Village. Political and Social Conditions During the War."

10:5. Obit.

April 16

2:1-3. Raum, Part 73.

2:7. W. J. Spencer (39th IL), "Fort Gregg."

3:1-6. Thomas H. C. Kinkaid (192nd NY), "A Battle-Highway. The Shenandoah Valley, and the Armies Which Surged Along It in Victory and Defeat."

3:6. Abner Said (121st OH), "A Picnic on the Skirmish Line." [Kennesaw Mt]

3:6. Charles Lowary (137th IL), "Forrest Caught Them Napping, But They Woke Up." [Memphis]

3:6. Benjamin B. Priest (76th OH), "In Front of Vicksburg." [5/18/63]

3:7. F. S. Hemingway (29th WI), "The Mobile Explosion."

9:1-4. John W. Buckley (surgeon, Patent Office Hospital), "Washington in War Time. The War Hospitals."

10:5. Ira E. Gosby (1st WV), "Belle Isle."

10:5. Obit.

10:6. George W. Bonsman (5th US Cav), "With Sheridan in the Valley."

April 23

2:1-5. Raum, Part 74.

2:5. R. H. Cheadle (signal corps), "The Death of Gen. McPherson."

3:1-2. John A. MacDonald (7th NJ), "The Last Campaign. From Hatcher's Run to Appomattox with the White Diamonds."

3:2-3. M. A. Cleveland (7th MA Bty), "Contemporaneous Account of the Mobile Explosion from Soldier's Diary."

3:3. Jule Warren (12th WI), "One of Sherman's Bummers."

3:3. James A. Vinson (53rd IL), "The 5th Ohio Battery was There." [Jackson, 7/12/63]

3:3. J. P. Jones (45th IL), "The 45th Illinois's Entrance into Vicksburg."

3:4. A. S. Whetsel (7th IN Cav), "The Cavalry Stampede. An Incident of Gen. Sooy Smith's Raid" [2/22/64]

3:4. William H. Winchester (112th NY), "Before Petersburg."

3:5. L. L. Scott (18th OH), "Stone River."

3:5-6. C. W. Fulford (45th IL), "The First to Enter Vicksburg."

3:6. George D. Mosgrove (4th KY Cav), "The Killing of Gen. Polk."

3:6. H. E. Houghtaling (10th WI), "Two Scared Pickets Rout One Frightened Hog."

3:7. W. H. Anderson (80th OH), "'You Steal a Shicken, Hah!'"

3:7. Robert H. G. Minty (4th MI Cav), "Minty's Cavalry." [Jonesboro]

4:3. Obit: Charles W. Drew (75th NY, 76th USCT).

6:7. Andy Ray (1st IA), "The Iowa Grayhounds."

6:7. Obit.

9:1-5. William J. Rhees, "Washington in War Time. The Humanities of the War. Noble Work of the Christian and Philanthropic People of the Country."

9:6. Obit: Freeman S. Bowley (30th USCT).

9:7. Daniel Sims (Bty E, PA Art), "Killing of Gen. Polk."

April 30

2:1-4. Raum, Part 75.

3:1-3. John D. Vautier (88th PA), "Second Bull Run."

3:3. Hezekiah Moody (117th IN), "The Persimmon Brigade."

3:3. William H. Palmer (53rd IL), "The Western Armies." [March to the Sea]

3:4. A. Roberts (29th WI), "The Explosion at Mobile."

3:4. George W. Bowers (129th OH), "A Reminiscence." [9/9/63, Cumberland Gap]

3:4-5. Edwin W. Haynes (117th IN), "Persimmon Brigade—A Family of Soldiers."

3:5. William H. Shriver (3rd WV), "Libby and Belle Isle."

3:5. Cornelius Gandy (15th WV), "Cedar Creek."

3:5. J. Y. Patin [12th OH Cav], "Bridging a Tennessee Stream."

3:6. Walter C. Strickler (106th NY), "How a Lie Saved the Capital." [captured at Monocacy]

3:6. Reuben D. Quick (102nd NY), "Death of Gen. Polk—The 13th N.Y. Independent Battery."

3:6. Artemas Smith, "The Chicago Mercantile Battery in the Red River Campaign."

3:6. Ira S. Owens (74th OH), "Death of Gen. Polk."

3:7. Picket Shots: George W. Hines (98th OH), brothers.

6:1-3. Thomas M. Vincent, "Washington in War Time. The Military Power of the U.S. as Shown During the War of the Rebellion."

8:7. Obit.

May 7

2:1-3. Raum, Part 76.

2:6. Leroy S. Fallis (8th IN Cav), "Kilpatrick's Cavalry."

2:6-7. S. R. Nelson (2nd MO Cav), "The Passing of Fremont's Bodyguard."

3:1-3. L. E. Alden (12th MA), "Second Bull Run."

3:3. H. Green, "Totten's Battery and the Regulars." [Wilson's Creek]

3:4. J. W. Cotes (12th IA), "Gallant Band of Iowans. Surrender of the 8th, 12th and 14th Iowa at Shiloh Occurred Not in the Morning But in the Evening After an All-Day Battle."

3:4-5. James A. Bird (2nd IA Cav), "'Critter Companies.' An Iowa Cavalryman Tells that the Infantry are Claiming All the Glory."

3:5. C. W. Colby (97th IL), "Discomfort and Alarm on a Transport." [USS *Robert Campbell*, 1/63]

3:6. John Wadell (Bty I, 1st OH), "The Battle of Cross Keys."

3:6. William Quigley (67th OH), "Fort Gregg."

4:7. Biog: John F. Martin (73rd OH).

4:7. Obit.

5:6. J. M. Williams (8th WI), "Battle of Farmington, Miss."

6:1-4. Thomas M. Vincent, "Washington in War Time. The Greatest of Military Nations."

6:6. Obit.

7:1. E. A. Gilbert (102nd IL), "In South Carolina. Capture of the Camden Bank."

7:1. Picket Shots: S. S. Martin (12th IA), youngest.

8:5-6. M. A. Luce, "Custer's First Battle. The Story of the Defeat of the La. Tigers Told by a Participant." [5/22/62]

May 14

2:1-4. Raum, Part 77.

2:4. Frederick T. Cook (105th OH), "In Fayetteville."

3:1-3. George D. Mosgrove (4th KY Cav), "Battle of Murfreesboro."

3:3-4. W. H. Montgomery (13th OH Cav), "The Petersburg Express—Dismounted Cavalry Charge with the Bayonet—The Youngest Soldier."

3:4. L. D. Immell (Bty F, 2nd US), "Wilson's Creek."

3:5. Aaron Ossman (50th PA), "Getting Even with the Major."

3:5. Marshall M. Cashier (6th MA Cav), "Sabine Crossroads."

3:6. H. B. Hawes (20th PA Cav), "Hunter's Raid to Lynchburg."

3:6. O. C. Bissell (29th WI), "One Mother's Sacrifice for Her Country." [Mrs. John M. Wiley, Hartford, WI]

3:6. J. C. Blackwood (2nd NJ Cav), "Ivy Hill Farm Stampede."

3:7. S. H. Beach (3rd WI), "Arresting the Maryland Legislature."

6:1-5. Vincent, Part 2.

6:5-6. "A Daring Enterprise. A Union Spy by Impersonating a Confederate Secretary of War Secures Valuable Information." [*Dallas Herald* about the Petersburg Mine]

6:7. Obit.

May 21

1:6-7, 2:6-7. Raum, Part 78.

2:1-6. Henry A. Castle (73rd IL), "One of the War's Unrecognized Heroes. The Value of John A. Rawlins to Grant and the Country."

3:1-2. F. I. Barker (47th MA), "Chased by the Alabama? Incidents of a War-Time Voyage from New York to New Orleans on Transport Mississippi."

3:3. John R. McCrillis (5th NH), "Granite State Colors at Fredericksburg."

3:3. G. H. Blakeslee (129th IL), "Pine Mt. and the Death of Gen. Polk."

3:4-5. Edward Wiske (1st MO), "Wilson's Creek."

3:5. R. W. Underwood (5th IN Cav), "Valley Forge in East Tennessee."

3:6-7. M. C. Thompson (122nd IL), "Diary of the Tupelo Campaign."

3:7. H. C. Ferguson (23rd IN), "Entering Vicksburg."

3:7. Donald C. Cameron (1st WI Bty), "The Trip for Mules."

4:7. Obit: Luther M. Strong (49th OH), Dwight S. Chamberlain (9th NY Hvy Art).

5:7. Obit.

6:1-3. Isabel W. Ball,"Washington. Sacred Arlington."

May 28

1:5-7, 2:4. Raum, Part 79. [Savannah]

3:1-2. John McElroy, "Washington. The Grand Review."

3:2-3. A. Baker (44th VA), "A 'Johnny's' Tribute." [to black slaves] [1862 MD Campaign]

3:3. H. V. Ashbaugh (78th PA), "Captured by Wheeler in the Sequatchie Valley."

3:3. George Seely (84th IN), "Killing of Gen. Polk."

3:4. E. A. Crandall (23rd WI), "With Banks's Expedition." [Red River]

3:5-6. Picket Shots: W. S. Hammond (192nd PA), Shenandoah Valley; John A. Wilson (81st OH), J. W. Denumbrun (13th KY), brothers.

5:7. Obit.

June 4

1:5-7, 2:6-7. Raum, Part 80. [Savannah]

3:1-4. Asa W. Slayton (24th MI), "Kentucky Stategy. Munfordville an Important Point Several Times During the War."

3:4. E. J. Orr (6th WI Bty), "Allatoona and Other Matters."

3:4. James H. Wiswell (4th US Cav), "Battle of Farmington, Miss."

3:4. Daniel G. Urmston (14th NJ), "Fort Urmston." [Petersburg]

3:5. William H. Dryden (15th IN), "Brave and Faithful. How Chaplain [John M.] Whitehad, of the 15th Ind., Won the Congressional Medal of Honor." [Stones' River]

3:5-6. D. S. Way (ADC, 1/3/18), "The Battle of the Crater."

3:6-7. John Landram (19th KY), "Red River Expedition."

3:7. George E. Dolton (Bty M, 1st IL), "Death of Gen. Polk."

4:7. Obit: Oliver W. Woods (121st OH).

4:7. Biog: William G. Jewell (18th OH).

5:7. Obit.

8:5. Will C. Phpps (11th IN), "Forty-One Years After. Revisit to the Shiloh Battlefield to Dedicate Indiana Monuments."

June 11

1:5-7, 6:6. Raum, Part 81. [Savannah]

3:1-4. Jerome B. Quinn (123rd IL), "Wilder's Lightning Brigade. A Soldier's Diary of the Closing Days of the War."

3:4. Levi Nicholson (161st OH), "Who Saved Washington City?"

3:4. M. W. Buck (50th PA), "Last Man Killed of Army of Potomac." [George W. Boyer, 50th PA, 7/5/65]

3:5-6. D. C. Hagadorn (78th NY), "A Fighting New York Regiment."

3:6-7. R. H. Martin (46th IN), "Entering Vicksburg."

6:1-3. Biog: James M. Frazier (5th KS Cav, 8th KS), William S. Settle (3rd PA Hvy Art), George Miner (144th NY), John A. McGregor (42nd OH), Noah McCormack (36th IN), Charles S. Gay (2nd NY Cav).

8:4-5. "The First Negro Regiment. It was Raised in New Orleans for the Confederacy." [*New York Sun*]

8:6. Obit.

June 18

1:5-7. Raum, Part 82. [Savannah]

2:1-6. George W. Ballich, "The Twentieth Corps. A Splendid Body of Troops Which Swung Clear Around the Circle."

2:7. Obit.

3:1-2. Quinn, Part 2.

3:2-3. S. W. Hart (29th OH), "These 'Cowboys' Lost Some Cattle—An Extraordinary Time Down in Georgia."

3:4. Donald C. Cameron (1st WI Bty), "Bravest of 'Em All. The Artillery Driver, Who Encountered All the Danger, But Got Neither Glory Nor Promotion."

3:5. J. C. Lindsey (7th OH), "The Battle of Port Republic."

3:5. C. C. Mathews, "The 12th W. Va.'s Eagle." [Fort Gregg]

3:6-7. S. H. Beckwith (10th IL), "The Great War Secretary. Some Sidelights on E. M. Stanton's Personality."

4:2. Obit: Alexander M. McCook.

5:4. "Statue of General McClellan.' [Washington]

5:4. Ervin H. Matthews (9th TN Cav), "A Relic of the Battle Above the Clouds." [signal flag pole]

6:1-3. Biog: D. F. Drenner (1st MD PHB), James Karnes (5th OH Cav), W. W. Drummond (Bty F, 1st OH), T. G. Van Meter (37th IN), E. P. Brown (39th MO), William G. Kemp (1st WV), Phil Johnson (26th OH, 9th OH Cav).

6:4. J. F. Richards (2nd OH Cav), "A Nameless Mountain Heroine." [Sanders' Raid]

June 25

1:5-7. Raum, Part 83. [Johnsonville, TN]

2:4. M. Buchanan (118th IN), "The Persimmon Brigade 'Kids.' The East Tennessee Campaign—The Valley Forge of the Civil War."

2:5. D. L. Way (ADC, 2/3/18), "Horrors Following the Battle of the Crater."

2:5-6. L. R. Barnard (2nd NJ Cav), "Gen. Sooy Smith's Raid."

2:6. D. E. Hagadorn (78th NY), "Greene's Brigade at Gettysburg."

3:1-4. George W. Quimby, "Captured by Forrest. Peril and Suffering Encountered by Two Adventurous Infantrymen in Their Efforts to Reach the Union Lines."

3:5. J. Q. Adams (30th USCT), "Battle of the Crater."

3:6-7. Picket Shots: N. A. Bowser (55th PA), youngest.

4:3. Obit: Frank Wheaton.

5:5. Patrick Kennedy (40th IL), "On Shiloh's Bloody Field. A Comrade's Remarkable Wounds."

5:5-6. J. E. Walton (30th OH), "A Visit to Antietam and South Mountain."

5:6. Thomas C. Murphy (31st IL), "Vicksburg. In the Crater—Marching Into the City."

6:1-3. Biog: Rudolph Schultz (24th IL), R. C. Hill (7th TN Cav), C. Penn (2nd WV Cav), Henry C. Thompson (16th IN), Harrison Hays (24th MO), L. M. Wilkins (59th IN), J. H. Tourgee (2nd RI), John Kerdolph (27th OH), Charles A. Sargent (4th VT).

8:5. J. L. Eby (7th IL), "'Hold the Fort, For I Am Coming.' Accidental Meeting of Three Comrades."

8:5. B. F. Laughlin (11th PA Res), "An Incident of Second Bull Run. The Good Samaritan Who Ran Away with a Wounded Comrade's Canteen."

8:5. J. H. Bell (27th IA), "The Battle of Yellow Bayou."

8:6. W. P. Kremer (6th IA), "The Oldest Enlisted Man in the Army."

8:6. Obit.

8:7. Obit: William J. Carlton (48th NY).

July 2

1:5-7, 2:1-2. Raum, Part 84. [TN Campaign]

3:1-4. Quimby, Part 2.

3:5-6. H. W. Phelps (95th OH), "Vicksburg National Park. A Revisit to the Battlefield to Locate Positions."

3:6. A. J. Learned (18th OH), "Incidents of Stone River."

3:6-7. Joseph H. Livingston (1st PA Cav), "Battle of Draneville."

6:1-3. Biog: C. W. Armstrong (43rd OH), A. G. Harter (2nd NY Cav), William King (6th IL Cav), H. B. Hudson (1st, 9th MI Cav), R. A. Barnes (31st USCT), James W. Loomis (18th CT), J. C. McMillen (50th PA), Levi Craig (23rd IN Bty), D. Mann (2nd NY Hvy Art), Lewis Grim (20th OH).

6:4-5. "An Unparalleled Loss. A Whole N.C. Company Destroyed at Gettysburg." [Co. F, 26th NC] [*Richmond Dispatch*]

7:3. Obit.

July 9

1:5-7, 2:1-2. Raum, Part 85. [Hood vs Schofield]

2:3. Charles Veil (9th PA Res), "Death of Gen. Reynolds. He was Not Killed by A N.C. Sharpshooter, as Claimed."

3:1-3. Will A. McTeer (3rd TN Cav), "Going to the Union Army. A Tennessee Refugee's Perilous Journey to Kentucky—Guided by a Federal Spy."

3:4. N. W. Pulsifer (13th OH Cav), "Rounding Up Lee."

3:4-5. George T. Drulley (50th NY Eng), "Never Meant Anything." [March to the Sea]

3:5. Aresman Stepp (6th US Cav), "An Old Soldier." [Patrick Mack, 6th US Cav]

6:1-3. Biog: J. E. Harding (12th WV), "George M. Hood (89th IL), W. H. Bushnell (9th IL Cav), J. S. Gasper (184th NY), J. J. Flora (6th MD).

8:7. Obit.

July 16

1:5-7. Raum, Part 86. [Franklin]

3:1-2. Augustus B. Clement (Btys HM, 4th US), "The Artillery at Stone River."

3:3. C. C. Barton (18th OH Bty), "Bravest of Them All." [Chickamauga]

3:3. H. J. Sloan (52nd IL), "What Became of Gen. Dodge's Scout?" [Atlanta]

3:4-6. Otis Crawford (9th IA), "Color Guard of the 9th Iowa. The 'Pea Ridge Flag' at Vicksburg." [5/22/63]

3:7. George Kimball (12th MA), "The John Brown Song."

4:2. Obit: E. B. Gray (28th WI).

6:1-2. Biog: George W. Blake (18th CT), E. E. King (7th CT), J. R. West (16th WI), S. T. Wallace (15th OH), L. R. Titus (137th NY), Theodore Busterdes (25th NY Cav), O. J. Tomlinson (13th VT, 26th NY Cav).

6:6. "New Jersey at Antietam. Monuments and Markers Erected to the New Jerseymen on that Field."

6:6. W. J. Adams (44th NY), "A Corporal's Adventures."

8:7. Obit.

July 23

1:5-7, 2:1-3. Raum, Part 87. [Nashville]

2:4-7. Patrick Breen (2nd US), "Regulars in the Civil War."

2:7. T. A. Parrott (2nd IA Cav), "Smith-Grierson Raid."

3:1-4. George C. Round (Signal Corps), "The Last Signal Message. Flashing the Magic Word 'Peace' from the N.C. Statehouse to Sherman's Army."

3:5-6. R. H. Martin (46th IN), "Sabine Crossroads."

3:6-7. Frank Ellicott (Bty M, 1st NY), "How Fayetteville was Captured."

3:7. Gilbert Thompson (US Eng Btn), "Officers of Colored Troops."

4:7. Obit: John Q. Lane (97th OH).

6:1-2. Biog: T. H. Tryon (150th PA), John R. McElwain (154th OH), R. J. Puckett (71st IL), Peter J. Wekland (USN), Eben B. Stanwood (19th, 48th MA), G. N. Miller (2nd PA Hvy Art), David Hill (25th MA), J. L. Hall (52nd IL).

7:2-3. H. Morris, "The 1st N.J. Cavalry. Its First Charge at the Wilderness."

7:3. W. H. Rickman (4th IA Cav), "The Retreat from Guntown."

July 30

1:5-7, 2:1-2. Raum, Part 88. [Nashville]

3:1-2. Theodore V. Brown (hospital steward), "With Averill on His Raid to Salem in December 1863.

3:2-3. A. L. Stevens (1st MI Cav), "Sheridan's War Horse."

3:3. W. S. Shusler (90th OH), "Gen. Kimball's Farewell to the 90th Ohio."

3:4-6. Thomas G. Day (3rd IN Cav), "Opening the Battle." [Gettysburg]

4:7. Obit: J. H. H. Ward.

6:1-2. John Brogan (67th NY), "Gen. Frank Wheaton at Cedar Creek."

6:1-2. Biog: G. W. McKinley (34th OH), James Durham (11th US), George Wineland (18th US).

7:4. Obit.

August 6

1:5-7, 2:5-7. Raum, Part 89. [Nashville]

3:1-4. John W. Fry (96th OH), "The Red River Expedition."

3:4. Frederick W. Fout (15th IN Bty), "Death of Polk."

3:5. A. McKinney (20th NY Cav), "Richmond Under the Flag."

3:5-6. F. D. Quick (102nd NY), "Green's [sic] Brigade at Chancellorsville."

3:6. L. D. Immell (12th WI Bty), "Iuka and Corinth."

3:6. "Dan McCook's Brigade at Kennesaw." [association meeting]

3:7. Picket Shots: J. M. Lindley (1st KS), Wilson's Creek.

6:1-2. Biog: S. K. Sanders (3rd IL Cav), James Smith (7th MI Cav), A. Jones (89th NY), L. B. Newel (2nd US Ss), J. P. Cornes (22nd NY Cav).

7:3. Obit.

August 13

1:5-7, 2:1-2. Raum, Part 90. [Nashville]

2:5-6. S. W. Hart (29th OH), "From Battlefield to Prison. Recollections of the Battle of Port Republic, and of Prison Life at Lynchburg and Belle Isle."

2:7. Biog: John L. Greene (8th, 169th, 186th OH).

2:7. Obit.

3:1-3. Lyman D. Widney (34th IL), "From the Sea to the Grand Review."

3:4. W. T. Eldridge (10th PA Res), "Sportive Hospital Cadets. A Young Surgeon Their Victim."

3:4-5. T. J. Bull (5th IA Cav), "Wheeler's Raid Into Tennessee and Kentucky."

3:5. Samuel L. Hartman (79th PA), "Battle of Perryville."

3:5-6. Levi M. Poor (19th ME), "Andersonville."

3:6. John W. Harris (115th IN), "The Tribulations of a 'Persimmon Knocker'."

3:6. Edmund W. Dayton (36th WI), "Reams' Station."

3:7. L. D. Immell (Bty F, 2nd US), "Another Comrade Wrong." [Farmington]

5:6. J. A. Watrous (2nd WI), "Lincoln's Last Review."

5:7. Obit.

6:1-2. Biog: B. F. Johns (49th PA), Andrew Meaker (89th NY), Samuel Brooke (49th IN), C. F. Waldron (29th OH), A. A. Eberhart (16th PA Cav).

8:5. "Relic of Bull Run. A Valuable Souvenir of the 1st Minnesota's Share in the Battle." [tree]

8:6. W. I. McFarland, "Fighting with Forrest." [LaGrange, TN, etc]

August 20

1:5-7, 6:3-5. Raum, Part 91. [Nashville]

2:7. Biog: James A. Barker (8th WV, 7th WV Cav), Henry Pebler (Bty D, 1st WV).

2:7. Obit.

3:1-3. Widney, Part 2.

3:3-4. Oliver Edwards (37th MA), "President Lincoln at Fort Stevens."

3:4. R. B. Wadsworth (9th NY Cav), "Before Chancellorsville. The Confederates Capture a Dispatch-Bearer on the Rapidan."

3:5-6. J. A. Gilberg (5th OH Cav), "With the Cavalry. Kilpatrick Tilting with Wheeler Down in Georgia."

3:6. D. C. Wellman, "Flag on Court House. Entering Vicksburg—Honors Claimed by the 45th Illinois."

5:6. Biog: James Miller (50th MA, 4th MA Cav), Edmund Rice, A. H. Bowman (91st PA), James H. Page (Chic Board of Trade Bty).

5:7. James D. Thompson (8th IN), "First Brigade of Kilpatrick's Division on the March to the Sea."

6:1-2. Biog: Bartlett Early (19th OH), William R. Townsend (124th OH), Z. B. Beach (77th OH), Alfred Nye (1st CO Cav), John D. Laughlin (12th Corps).

7:2. Obit.

8:4. Alonzo D. Stoddard (77th IL), "The Red River Expedition. Recollections of the First Day at Sabine Crossroads."

August 27

1:4-7. Raum, Part 92. [Nashville]

2:7. Simon Clare (USS *Choctaw*), "Guarding the Mouth of the Red River. How the Blue Jackets Charged Rebel Cavalry."

2:7. Peter Price (124th OH), "Before Kennesaw Mountain."

3:1-3. Widney, Part 3.

3:3. Theodore F. Allen (7th OH Cav), "Gen. Thomas Justified. Delay in Attacking Hood Unavoidable."

3:4. C. R. Allen (2nd IL Cav), "Recollections of an Orderly. Marching into Vicksburg—Sabine Crossroads."

3:4. C. Webster (5th NY Hvy Art), "Cedar Creek."

3:4-5. W. R. Bunting (38th IL), "A Lieutenant's Heroism at Stone's River."

3:5-6. A. Newland (124th IL), "Surrender of Vicksburg."

3:6. J. M. Griffith (87th PA), "With Milroy in the Valley. A Wounded Federal Found Refuge in a Confederate Home."

3:7. Picket Shots: William K. Brown (91st PA), oldest; G. W. Hanes (25th IN), Fayetteville, NC.

4:7. Biog: Daniel D. Wheeler (ADC), Michael Sheridan (MO), S. B. M. Young (12th PA Cav).

6:1-2. Biog: J. B. Eames (70th IL, 3rd IL Cav), J. B. Brown (124th IL), Charles Bullard (16th IN), N. C. Adams (11th OH).

6:1-2. A. A. Barnes (2nd IA), "The First Day at Shiloh."

6:2. J. N. Handy (33rd MO), "Celebrating the 4th of July." [Helena, AR]

6:5. Marshall M. Cashier (31st MA), "On the Ocean Wave. Tribulations of Butler's troops En Route from Boston to New Orleans."

8:5. P. F. Hodge (55th PA), "A Lost Sword. The Proud Relic Returned to Its Owner After Many Years." 8:6. William J. Howe (20th IA), "Going the Grand Rounds. Discomfiture of the Officer of the Day."

8:6-7. George Petry (123rd IL), "Marched from Home to Battlefield." [Perryville]

8:7. Obit.

September 3

1:5-7, 6:6. Raum, Part 93. [Nashville]

2:5. John Clemens (1st NY Cav), "To Captivity Led. Results of a Daring Enterprise." [7/5/63]

3:1-4. Widney, Part 4.

3:5. H. E. Houghtaling (10th WI), "Down in Alabama. Capture of Huntsville. Sending an Amazonian Bushwhacker into Exile."

3:5. Stephen Tripp (11th PA Cav), "Death of Lieut.-Col. Kimball." [9th NY]

3:5-6. George Schultz (52nd NY), "From 'Coffee Hill' to Richmond. Libby and Belle Isle." [captured 10/14/63]

3:6. Charles D. McClure (72nd IN), "Another Richmond in the Field. More of the Smith-Grierson Raid."

3:6-7. R. W. Underwood (5th IN Cav), "Valley Forge in East Tennessee."

5:5. Obit: Benjamin Starr (2nd IN Cav), William H. Penrose.

6:1-2. Biog: J. T. Bloomfield (9th NY Cav), G. G. Keener (10th PA Res), George Matthews (76th OH), J. Y. Rose (129th IL).

6:3. John Wright (107th IL), "The Siege of Knoxville."

6:3. Peter R. Williams (2nd NY Mtd Rifles), "From Petersburg to Appomattox."

6:6. Obit.

September 10

1:5-7, 3:6-7. Raum, Part 94. [Nashville]

3:1-4. George D. Mosgrove (4th KY Cav), "Morgan and His Men."

3:4-5. Leroy S. Fallis (8th IN Cav), "Cavalry at Waynesboro."

4:7. Biog: John H. Austin (20th IL), L. L. Ward (8th IN Cav).

4:7. Obit: William A. Johnson (8th MO, 15th KS Cav), George F. Steahlin (11th PA Cav).

6:3. Biog: M. A. Douglas (47th OH), William R. Townsend (24th OH), H. C. Tipton (113th OH), Richard Hoff (USN), L. O. Colburn (51st IL), D. B. Henry (55th PA).

7:2. Obit.

8:5. Biog: C. M. Kinne (2nd MA Cav).

September 17

1:5-7, 3:6. Raum, Part 95. [Nashville]

3:1-4. Mosgrove, Part 2.

3:4-5. J. P. Jones, "The Flag of the 45th Illinois." [Vicksburg]

3:5. S. H. Wright (75th NY), "Fireworks at Port Hudson."

3:5. Samuel Grimshaw (52nd OH), "The Battle of Perryville as Seen by a Member of Sheridan's Division."

6:1-2. Biog: W. M. Mercer (2nd KS Cav, 83rd USCT), Isaac Armstrong (53rd OH), A. G. Gorvell (34th IN), J. C. Clowes (73rd IL), J. J. Yeakle, Elijah Gray (1st ME Cav).

6:5-7. Biog: William P. Lyon (13th WI), W. H. Whitelaw (19th US, 2nd US Art), Frank Baldwin (19th MI).

7:2. Obit.

September 24

1:5-7, 2:6-7. Raum, Part 96. [Nashville]

3:1-6. Mosgrove, Part 3.

3:6. James W. Jacobs (12th IN Bty), "Fort Negley was Silent. How the Commandant Faced an Angry General." [Gordon Granger and Vicksburg salute]

3:7. S. H. Almon (31st IL), "Fort Hill—The Tossing of Hand-Grenades."

5:5. Obit: Edward E. Bryant, George B. Wright (106th OH).

6:4-5. "A Ringing Patriotic Address. President Roosevelt Speaks at Dedication of New Jersey's Monument at Antietam."

6:5. A. R. Kibbe (12th WI Bty), "Iuka and Corinth."

6:5. Biog: S. B. M. Young (12th PA Cav) [corrections]

7:2. Obit.

October 1

2:3. Obit.

2:5. E. Starbuck (AQM), "Hold the Fort. Recollections of the Battle of Allatoona."

2:7. Obit.

3:1-5. Mosgrove, Part 4.

3:5. A. T. Sylvester (2nd MA Btn), "Origin of 'John Brown's Body'."

3:5. W. R. Moore (77th IL), "Reminiscences of Red River."

3:6. A. A. Jones (8th TN), "Battle of Franklin."

3:6. Martin I. Holston (16th IL Cav), "Raid Reminiscences."

3:7. John B. Williams (3rd KY Cav), "Major Estes' Raid."

8:5-6. Obit: Wilson S. Deam (22nd IN), C. V. Deland (1st MI Ss).

8:6. Biog: William Faulkner.

October 8

2:4-6. Biog: Theodore E. Sauls (6th KS Cav), James A. Fisher (40th, 51st OH).

2:6. Obit.

3:1-4. Mosgrove, Part 5.

3:4. Stephen H. Lane (30th MA), "Attack on Baton Rouge."

3:5. Squire D. Rhodes (14th NY Hvy Art), "Battle of the Crater."

3:5. William H. Gardner (25th NY Cav), "Executions at Front Royal."

3:6. Duane Mowry, "Gen. Joseph Bailey. The Construction of the Famous Red River Dam."

3:6. Sylvester Doss (USN), "'City of Madison' Explosion."

4:7. Obit: William P. Carlin.

7:1. Obit.

October 15

2:7. Biog: Basil B. Brashear (surgeon in 13th Corps).

3:1-4. Mosgrove, Part 6.

3:4. B. Van Dyke (14th IA), "Both Sides Defeated." [Pleasant Hill]

3:4. John Carroll (59th IN), "Gen. Grose's Brigade." [Lookout Mt]

3:4. Luke Phillips (Bty I, 1st MI), "A Tale of Two Batteries." [death of Polk]

3:4-5. William H. Huffman (100th PA), "From a Prisoner's Diary." [captured 8/21/64]

3:5. A. S. Bean (65th NY), "The 1st U.S. Chasseurs."

3:5. D. E. Stevens (13th WI), "Colonel William P. Lyon."

3:6-7. Picket Shots: Albion Thurlow (3rd WI), Scott's Tactics; P. W. Crawford (3rd IA), Vicksburg.

3:7. "The 150th Ohio at Fort Stevens."

3:7. T. P. Marshall (13th IA), "Haskin and Hoskin." [Cruft's provisional division, 12/64]

6:4. S. W. Hart (29th OH), "Meade at Gettysburg."

October 22

1:5-7, 5:5-7. "The Master-Strategist. Honoring One of the Greatest Captains of History. Unveiling of the Statue to Gen. W. T. Sherman . . . ."

2:5. Obit.

2:6. James E. Smith (CSA artillery), "Confederate Confession. Some Startling and Also Incredible Statements About Missionary Ridge."

3:1-4. Mosgrove, Part 7.

3:4-5. C. R. Van Tress (149th OH), "Saved the Day at Monocacy."

3:5. H. C. York (19th NY Bty), "Siege of Petersburg." [Fort Stedman]

3:5. J. P. Lloyd (161st NY), "How the Bullets Flew." [Port Hudson]

3:6. B. F. Johns (49th PA), "Gettysburg and Chambersburg. Bradley Johnson Prevented Nighttime Burning of the Latter."

3:6. S. S. Hammitt (36th OH), "Sheridan's Black Horse."

3:6. J. B. Coleman, "The 24th Ohio at Shiloh."

3:6-7. Phil L. Wagner (3rd IL Cav), "An Unhistoric Battle."

3:7. Walter F. Sage (1st CT Hvy Art), "How Jim Rode the Mule."

6:6. J. W. Edwards (4th US Vet Vol), "The Execution of the Lincoln Conspirators."

7:3. Obit.

8:4. "Ohio at Antietam."

October 29

1:6-7, 2:7. "Army of the Ohio. One of the Smallest Armies, Which had a Glorious History."

3:1-4. Mosgrove, Part 8.

3:4. F. X. Wagner, "The 9th Illinois at Shiloh."

3:4. J. W. B. Cole, "'Hold the Fort'."

3:4. J. F. Richards (129th IN), "The Mountain Heroine Again." [Sanders' Raid]

3:5-6. Josiah McKinnon (3rd MO SM Cav), "History of a Militia Regiment."

3:6-7. A. Eppenhault (37th OH), "Served and Suffered. Personal Reminiscences of Experiences in Field and Hospital."

3:7. S. E. Iams (2nd MN), "At the Mill Spring Spat."

4:4. Obit: D. F. Dewolff (55th OH), Orland Smith (73rd OH).

6:4-5. Joseph Harris (75th OH), "Captors Captured." [Chancellorsville]

6:5-6. Picket Shots: C. A. Pelton, Spotsylvania tree.

November 5

1:7, 5:5-6. "Generals. An Interesting List of Those of the Armies of the Tennessee, Cumberland, and Ohio."

3:1-4. Mosgrove, Part 9.

3:4. J. F. Richard, "The 2nd Ohio Cavalry."

3:5. Robert Tracy (1st KS), "The 10th Kansas."

3:5. George S. Brinkerhoff (47th IN), "The Red River."

3:6-7. A. B. Shaw (9th PA Cav), "Tullahoma Campaign."

November 12

1:5-7, 6:4-6. George L. Christian, "Virginia's Reply to North Carolina. A Masterly Analysis of the Old North State's Claim to Confederate Preeminence." [Gettysburg]

2:7. Obit.

3:1-4. Mosgrove, Part 10.

3:4. C. V. Donaldson (10th WI), "Battle of Perryville."

3:5. E. J. Peck (Bty K, 1st WV), "How Gen. Jones was Killed." [Piedmont]

3:5. E. H. Dierdorff (50th IL), "A Mistake of Gen. Raum." [Allatoona]

8:6. Biog: Harry G. Kessler (104th PA).

November 19

2:5-6. Johnny Catlin (5th NY Cav), "Johnny the Bugler."

3:1-4. Mosgrove, Part 11.

3:4. John A. Malone (22nd IL), "Farmington."

3:4-5. Martin Dashiell (3rd IN Cav), "Feast of Eggs."

3:5. W. H. Hall, "Regulars in the Civil War. The 4th U.S. Artillery, Battery G, and Some of Its Officers at Gettysburg."

3:5. Martin Dashiell (3rd IN Cav), "Prayer by a Southern Woman."

3:5-6. L. D. Immell (Bty F, 2nd US), "Close Call at Spring Hill."

3:6. James L. Clark, "Actors in Our Army."

3:6. William H. Huffman (100th PA), "Criticizes Powell's Chantilly."

6:6. Obit.

8:3-7. Obit.

November 26

2:4-5. David R. Bryans (54th PA), "Fort Gregg is Taken Again."

2:5. S. R. Nelson (2nd MO Cav), "Chasing Price. How 'Merrill's Horse' Helped Carry a St. Louis Election in 1864."

2:6. John A. Duncan (3rd OH), "Fighting in Pairs. Nine Pairs of Brothers in One Campany."

3:1-4. Mosgrove, Part 12.

3:4. G. I. Nash (Bty A, 1st MI), "Best Possible Authority. Sheridan Quoted About His Black Horse, the Famous Rienzi."

3:5-6. Leroy S. Fallis (8th IN Cav), "With the Cavalry. Fight at Buck Head Creek, Miller's Grove, and Reynolds Plantation."

3:6. James Harman, "Service of the 22nd Indiana."

3:6-7. George S. Scullen (Bty A, 1st NY), "Horrors of Fair Oaks."

8:1-4. H. A. Castle, "Historic Manassas. Singular Experience of a Minnesota Comrade on the Old Battlefield."

December 3

3:1-5. Mosgrove, Part 13,

3:5. Charles O. Welch (2nd MA Cav), "Retaliatory Executions. Those at Front Royal were for Murders by Mosby's Men."

3:5. M. S. Harris (2nd MN), "The 9th Ohio Marched There." [Mill Springs]

5:6. Obit.

8:1-4. Charles I. Adkins (27th OH), "Fuller's Ohio Brigade."

December 10

2:6-7. Obit: George R. Ray (18th CT).

2:6-7. Biog: Enoch Stahler (3rd NY Cav), John M. Brown (69th IN).

3:1-5. Mosgrove, Part 14.

3:5. Henry S. Wells (4th MI), "Col. Fox and the 20th Maine. Percentage of Losses—Correct Basis for Ascertaining Real Percentage for Comparisons."

8:1-4. Adkins, Part 2.

8:5. Gideon A. Lyon (23rd MI), "Battle of Franklin."

8:6. Obit.

December 17

3:1-4. Mosgrove, Part 15.

3:4. Alfred Stenson (17th IL), "An Unconscious Hero." [Fort Donelson]

3:5. O. F. Weeks (32nd OH), "Interrupted Forage Scout." [after McDowell engagement]

3:5. Daniel Sims (Bty E, PA), "Saw Polk Killed."

3:5-6. George P. Wood (29th WI), "That Campaign for Cotton." [Red River]

3:6. "Smallest Living Grand Army Man." [John Brown, 94th IL]

6:6. Z. M. McCleary (42nd IN), "Twins and Triplets."

8:1-3. Adkins, Part 3.

8:6. "Quantrill's Bones. Kansas Historical Society Exhibits the Legs of the Notorious Guerrilla."

8:6. Obit.

December 24

2:5. W. R. Carter (1st TN Cav), "Gen. Morgan and Rebel Morgan. Some Criticisms of Mosgrove's Statements About General Morgan's Retreat and Rebel Morgan's Feats." [Cumberland Gap retreat]

3:1-3. Mosgrove, Part 16. [Rolling Fork]

3:5. John Baker (9th NY Cav), "First Man Killed at Gettysburg."

3:5. James M. Jacks (9th MO SM Cav), "War Without Quarter."

3:5-6. G. Cilley (4th OH Cav), "Capture of Huntsville, Alabama."

3:6. T. H. B. Baker (5th IN Cav), "Cross Keys and Port Republic."

3:6. G. H. Purdy (11th WV), "Did Not Take Fort Gregg."

3:7. Charles F. M. Gurnsey (72nd OH), "Tardiness Saved Them." [City of Madison explosion]

3:7. T. C. Yates (4th Co OH Cav), "Always Close to Death." [City of Madison explosion]

5:7. A. J. Jacobs (22nd KY), "A Kicking Surgeon."

6:3. Biog: Winfield Scott (126th NY).

8:1-5. Adkins, Part 4.

December 31

2:5. John A. Matthews (55th PA), "Others Got the Prisoners. But a 55th Pa. Comrade Thinks His Regiment Should Have the Credit." [4/1/65]

2:6. John Pannock (72nd IL), "Franklin in the Night."

2:7. William K. Hampton (5th US Cav), "Executions at Front Royal."

3:1-5. Mosgrove, Part 17. [Cluke's 2/63 KY raid]

3:6-7. Picket Shots: Alfred Demorest (93rd OH), brothers.

5:6. J. S. Belknap (85th NY), "Who Joked the Colonel?" [Washington, NC]

5:7. Chauncey L. Knapp (2nd PA Prov Hvy Art), "Notable Regiments."

6:3. Martin Dashiell (3rd IN Cav), "The Sequatchie Guerrillas. Relentless Pursuit and Extinction of a Horde of Villains by the 3rd Indiana Cavalry." [fall 1863]

6:4. W. A. Fulk (59th IN), "Entitled to Honors." [Chattanooga]

6:4. R. D. Reefy, Thomas A. Brierly (Beatty's Brigade), "Error in Markers on Mission Ridge."

6:4-5. J. W. Starr (62nd OH), "Who Charged Fort Gregg?"

6:5. C. H. Bacheler (1st RI Cav), "Executions at Front Royal."

8:1-5. Adkins, Part 5.

Compiler's Biography

A native of Lewisburg, PA, Richard A. Sauers received his B.A. in History from Susquehanna University, and both his M.A. and Ph.D. in history from The Pennsylvania State University.

Dr. Sauers is the author of more than two dozen books, including *A Caspian Sea of Ink: The Meade-Sickles Controvers*y (1989), the highly acclaimed two-volume *Advance the Colors! Pennsylvania Civil War Battle Flags* (1987-1991), and his latest, *The Fishing Creek Confederacy: A Story of Civil War Draft Resistance* (2013). Dr. Sauers serves as the executive director of the Western Museum of Mining and Industry in Colorado Springs.